DICTIONARY OF
MARKETING

THIRD EDITION

DICTIONARY OF
MARKETING

THIRD EDITION

A. Ivanovic M.B.A.
P.H. Collin

BLOOMSBURY

A BLOOMSBURY REFERENCE BOOK

Originally published by Peter Collin Publishing

First edition published 1989
Second edition published 1996
Third edition published 2003
This edition published in the United States of America 2004

Bloomsbury Publishing Plc
38 Soho Square, London W1D 3HB

Bloomsbury Reference titles are distributed
in the United States of America by
Independent Publishers Group
814 N. Franklin St., Chicago, IL 60610
1-800-888-4741
www.ipgbook.com

ISBN 1 904970 04 4

All papers used by Bloomsbury Publishing are natural, recyclable products
made from wood grown in well-managed forests. The manufacturing
processes conform to the environmental regulations of the country of origin.

Text processing and computer typesetting by Bloomsbury
Printed in the United States of America by Quebecor World Fairfield

Preface to third edition

This third edition of the dictionary takes into account the many new terms that have come into marketing with the growth of e-commerce and the Internet. The supplements at the back of the book have also been comprehensively updated.

We are grateful to the following for their valuable comments on the text: Ian Linton, Georgia Hole, Dinah Jackson, and Sandra Anderson.

Preface to second edition

Business terminology changes rapidly, and this second edition includes a variety of new terms and expressions which have come into use since the first edition was published. We have also included new examples and quotations from recent magazines.

Also included is a pronunciation guide for the main entry words.

Preface to first edition

This dictionary provides the user with a comprehensive vocabulary of terms used in marketing. It covers such aspects of the subject as market research, advertising, promotional aids, and selling techniques.

The main words are explained in simple English, and, where appropriate, examples are given to show how the words are used in context. Quotations are also given from various magazines and journals, which give an idea of how the terms are used in real life.

The supplements at the back of the book give some further information which may be of use to the user.

We are particularly grateful to Margaret Jull Costa and Stephen Curtis for valuable comments which they made on the text.

Pronunciation

The following symbols have been used to show the pronunciation of the main words in the dictionary.

Stress is indicated by a main stress mark (') and a secondary stress mark (,). Note that these are only guides, as the stress of the word changes according to its position in the sentence.

Vowels		*Consonants*	
æ	back	b	buck
ɑ	harm	d	dead
aɪ	type	ð	other
aʊ	how	dʒ	jump
ɔ	course	f	fare
ɔɪ	annoy	g	gold
e	head	h	head
eɪ	make	j	yellow
eʊ	go	k	cab
ɜr	word	l	leave
i	keep	m	mix
ə	about	n	nil
ɪ	fit	ŋ	sing
u	pool	p	print
ʊ	book	r	rest
ʌ	shut	s	save
		ʃ	shop
		t	take
		tʃ	change
		θ	theft
		v	value
		w	work
		x	loch
		ʒ	measure
		z	zone

A

ABC method /ˌeɪ biː 'siː ˌmeθəd/ *noun* a sales method, where the customer's attention is attracted, the salesperson then shows the benefits of the product to the customer, and finally closes the deal. Full form **attention, benefit, close**

ABCs *abbreviation* Audit Bureau of Circulations

above-the-fold /əˌbʌv ðə 'fəʊld/ *noun* the part of a webpage which is seen first without having to scroll, and so is preferred for advertising

above the line /əˌbʌv ðə 'laɪn/ *adjective, adverb* **1.** used to describe entries in a company's profit and loss accounts that appear above the line separating entries showing the origin of the funds that have contributed to the profit or loss from those that relate to its distribution. Exceptional and extraordinary items appear above the line. ○ *Exceptional items are noted above the line in company accounts.* ◊ **below the line 2.** relating to revenue items in a government budget

above-the-line advertising /əˌbʌv ðə laɪn 'ædvətaɪzɪŋ/ *noun* advertising for which commission is paid to the advertising agency, e.g., an advertisement in a magazine or a stand at a trade fair. Compare **below-the-line advertising** (NOTE: as opposed to direct marketing)

absenteeism /ˌæbs(ə)n'tiːɪz(ə)m/ *noun* the practice of staying away from work for no good reason ○ *Low productivity is largely due to the high level of absenteeism.* ○ *Absenteeism is high in the week before Christmas.*

absolute /'æbsəlut/ *adjective* complete or total

absolute advantage /ˌæbsəlut əd 'væntɪdʒ/ *noun* an advantage enjoyed by an area of the world which can produce a product more cheaply than other areas ○ *For climatic reasons, tropical countries have an absolute advantage in that type of production.*

absolute cost /ˌæbsəlut 'kɒst/ *noun* the actual cost of placing an advertisement in a magazine or other advertising medium

absolute monopoly /ˌæbsəlut mə 'nɒpəli/ *noun* a situation where only one producer produces or only one supplier supplies something ○ *The company has an absolute monopoly of imports of French wine.* ○ *The supplier's absolute monopoly of the product meant that customers had to accept her terms.*

absorb /əb'sɔːb/ *verb* to take in a small item so that it forms part of a larger one □ **overheads have absorbed all our profits** all our profits have gone in paying overhead expenses □ **to absorb a loss by a subsidiary** to include a subsidiary company's loss in the group accounts □ **a business which has been absorbed by a competitor** a small business which has been made part of a larger one

absorption /əb'sɔːpʃən/ *noun* the process of making a smaller business part of a larger one, so that the smaller company in effect no longer exists

absorption costing /əb'sɔːpʃən ˌkɒstɪŋ/ *noun* a form of costing for a product that includes both the direct costs of production and the indirect overhead costs as well

accelerator /ək'seləreɪtər/ *noun* the theory that a change in demand for consumer goods will result in a greater change in demand for the capital goods used in their production

accept /ək'sept/ *verb* **1.** to take something which is being offered □ **to accept delivery of a shipment** to take goods into the warehouse officially when they are delivered **2.** to say "yes" or to agree to something ○ *She accepted the offer of a job in Australia.* ○ *He accepted $2,000 instead of one week's notice.* **3.** to agree formally to receive something or to be responsible for something

acceptable /ək'septəb(ə)l/ *adjective* easily accepted ○ *Both parties found the offer acceptable.* ○ *The terms of the contract of employment are not acceptable to the candidate.*

acceptance /ək'septəns/ *noun* □ **acceptance of an offer** the act of agreeing to an offer □ **to give an offer a conditional acceptance** to accept an offer provided that specific things happen or that specific terms apply □ **we have their letter of acceptance** we have received a letter from them accepting the offer

acceptance against documents /ək,septəns ə,genst 'dɑkjəmənts/ *noun* a transaction where the seller takes charge of the shipping documents for a consignment of goods when a buyer accepts a bill of exchange ○ *Acceptance against documents protects the seller when sending goods which are not yet paid for.*

acceptance sampling /ək'septəns ,sæmplɪŋ/ *noun* the process of testing a small sample of a batch to see if the whole batch is good enough to be accepted

accepted bill /ək,septɪd 'bɪl/ *noun* a bill of exchange which has been signed, and therefore accepted by the buyer

acceptor /ək'septər/ *noun* a person who accepts a bill of exchange by signing it, thus making a commitment to pay it by a specified date

access /'ækses/ *noun* □ **to have access to something** a way of obtaining or reaching something ○ *She has access to large amounts of venture capital.* ■ *verb* to call up data which is stored in a computer ○ *She accessed the address file on the computer.* ◇ **access to the market 1.** the legal right to sell in a particular market **2.** the ability to reach a market by promotion and distribution

accessibility /ək,sesɪ'bɪləti/ *noun* the ability of a market to be reached by promotion and distribution ○ *There is much demand in the market, but, because of the great distances involved, accessibility is a problem.* ○ *We must analyze the geographic aspects in assessing the market's accessibility.*

access time /'ækses ,taɪm/ *noun* the time taken by a computer to find data stored in it

accommodation bill /ə,kɑmə 'deɪʃ(ə)n ,bɪl/ *noun* a bill of exchange where the person signing (the "drawee") is helping another company (the "drawer") to raise a loan

account /ə'kaʊnt/ *noun* **1.** a record of financial transactions over a period of time, such as money paid, received, borrowed or owed ○ *Please send me your account* or *a detailed* or *an itemized account.* **2.** (*in a store*) an arrangement in which a customer acquires goods and pays for them at a later date, usually the end of the month ○ *to have an account* or *a charge account with Nordstroms* ○ *Put it on my account* or *charge it to my account.* □ **to open an account** (*of a customer*) to ask a store to supply goods which you will pay for at a later date □ **to open an account, to close an account** (*of a store*) to start or to stop supplying a customer on credit □ **to settle an account** to pay all the money owed on an account □ **to stop an account** to stop supplying a customer until payment has been made for goods supplied **3.** □ **on account** as part of a total bill □ **to pay money on account** to pay to settle part of a bill □ **advance on account** money paid as a part payment **4.** a customer who does a large amount of business with a firm and has an account with it ○ *Smith Brothers is one of our largest accounts.* ○ *Our sales people call on their best accounts twice a month.* **5.** □ **to keep the accounts** to write each sum of money in the account book ○ *The bookkeeper's job is to keep the accounts.* **6.** □ **overdrawn account** an account where you have taken out more money than you have put in, i.e. the bank is effectively lending you money □ **to open an account** to start an account by putting money in ○ *She opened an account with the Northeast Credit Union.* □ **to close an account** to take all money out of a bank account and stop the account ○ *We closed our account with U.S. Trust.* **7.** a period during which shares are traded for credit, and at the end of which the shares bought must be paid for **8.** a notice □ **to take account of inflation, to take inflation into account** to assume that there will be a specific percentage of inflation when making calculations **9.** an arrangement which a company has with an advertising agency, where the agency deals with all promotion for the company ○ *The company has moved its $3m account to another agency.* ○ *The small agency lost the account when the company decided it needed a different marketing approach.* ○ *Three agencies were asked to make presentations, as the company had decided to switch its account.* ■ *verb* □ **to account for** to explain and record a money transaction ○ *to account for a loss* or *a discrepancy* ○ *The reps have to account for all their expenses to the sales manager.*

accountancy /əˈkaʊntənsi/ *noun* the work of an accountant ○ *They are studying accountancy* or *They are accountancy students.*

accountant /əˈkaʊntənt/ *noun* **1.** a person who keeps a company's accounts or deals with an individual person's tax affairs ○ *The chief accountant of a manufacturing group.* **2.** a person who advises a company on its finances ○ *I send all my income tax questions to my accountant.* **3.** a person who examines accounts

account book /əˈkaʊnt bʊk/ *noun* a book with printed columns which is used to record sales and purchases

account director /əˈkaʊnt daɪˌrektər/ *noun* a person who works in an advertising agency and who oversees various account managers who are each responsible for specific clients

account executive /əˈkaʊnt ɪgˌzekjətɪv/ *noun* an employee who looks after customers or who is the link between customers and the company

account handler /əˈkaʊnt ˌhændlər/, **account manager** /əˈkaʊnt ˌmænɪdʒər/ *noun* a person who works in an advertising agency, and who is responsible for a particular client

accounting /əˈkaʊntɪŋ/ *noun* the work of recording money paid, received, borrowed, or owed ○ *accounting methods* ○ *accounting procedures* ○ *an accounting machine*

accounts department /əˈkaʊnts dɪˌpɑrtmənt/ *noun* a department in a company which deals with money paid, received, borrowed, or owed

accounts manager /əˈkaʊnts ˌmænɪdʒər/ *noun* the manager of an accounts department

accounts payable /əˌkaʊnts ˈpeɪəb(ə)l/ *noun* money owed by a company

accredited agent /əˌkredɪtɪd ˈeɪdʒənt/ *noun* an agent who is appointed by a company to act on its behalf

accurate /ˈækjərət/ *adjective* correct ○ *The sales department made an accurate forecast of sales.* ○ *The designers produced an accurate copy of the plan.*

accurate description /ˌækjərət dɪˈskrɪpʃən/ *noun* an honest and true description of a product or service in an advertisement or catalog ○ *As the advertisement was clearly not an accurate description of the product, the company had to pay a fine.* ○ *It is not an accurate description of the product to state that it gives out more light than the sun.*

accurately /ˈækjərətli/ *adverb* correctly ○ *The second quarter's drop in sales was accurately forecast by the computer.*

achiever /əˈtʃiːvər/ *noun* a person who is successful or who tends to achieve his or her objectives ○ *It was her reputation as a high achiever that made us think of headhunting her.* ◊ **VALS**

acknowledge /ək'nɑlɪdʒ/ *verb* to tell a sender that a letter, package, or shipment has arrived ○ *He has still not acknowledged my letter of the 24th.* ○ *We acknowledge receipt of your letter of June 14th.*

acknowledgement /ək'nɑlɪdʒmənt/ *noun* the act of acknowledging ○ *She sent an acknowledgement of receipt.* ○ *The company sent a letter of acknowledgement after I sent in my job application.*

ACORN /'eɪkɔrn/ *noun* a classification of residential areas into categories, based on the type of people who live in them, the type of houses, etc., much used in consumer research ○ *ACORN will help us plan where to concentrate our sales visits.* Full form **a classification of residential neighborhoods**

acquire /ə'kwaɪr/ *verb* to buy ○ *to acquire a company* ○ *We have acquired a new office building in the center of town.*

acquirer /ə'kwaɪrər/ *noun* a person or company which buys something

acquisition /ˌækwɪ'zɪʃ(ə)n/ *noun* **1.** something bought ○ *The chocolate factory is our latest acquisition.* **2.** the act of getting or buying something □ **data acquisition, acquisition of data** obtaining and classifying data **3.** the action of acquiring new customers, as opposed to retention, which is keeping the loyalty of existing customers

acquisition rate /ˌækwɪ'zɪʃ(ə)n reɪt/ *noun* a figure that indicates how much new business is being won by a company's marketing activities

acronym /'ækrənɪm/ *noun* a word which is made up from the initials of other words ○ *The name of the company was especially designed to provide a catchy acronym.* ○ *BASIC is an acronym for Beginner's All-purpose Symbolic Instruction Code.*

across-the-board /əˌkrɔs ðə 'bɔrd/ *adjective* (*of an advertisement*) running for five consecutive days from Monday through Friday

action shot /'ækʃən ˌʃɑt/ *noun* a scene with movement either in a movie or on TV

activity sampling /æk'tɪvəti ˌsæmplɪŋ/ *noun* an observation of tasks and their performances, carried out at random intervals ○ *Activity sampling was carried out to see how fast the machinists worked.*

ad /æd/ *noun* same as **advertisement** (*informal*) ○ *We put an ad in the paper.* ○ *She answered an ad in the paper.* ○ *He found his job through an ad in the paper.*

Ad-A-Card /'æd ə ˌkɑrd/ *noun* a type of perforated card bound into a magazine which a reader can tear off and return to the advertiser

adapt /ə'dæpt/ *verb* to change something a little to fit in with changing circumstances ○ *This product must be adapted in line with recent technological developments.* ○ *The device has been adapted for use on board aircraft.*

adaptation /ˌædæp'teɪʃ(ə)n/ *noun* **1.** a change which has been, or can be, made to something ○ *With a few minor adaptations, the machine will cut square holes as well as round ones.* **2.** the process of changing something, or of being changed, to fit new conditions ○ *adaptation to new surroundings*

adaptive control model /əˌdæptɪv kən'troul ˌmɑd(ə)l/ *noun* a model for planning advertising expenditure in line with changes in consumer responses to advertising

ad banner /'æd ˌbænər/ *noun* same as **banner**

ad click /'æd klɪk/ *noun* same as **click-through**

ad click rate /'æd klɪk ˌreɪt/ *noun* same as **click-through rate**

added value /ˌædɪd 'vælju/ *noun* an amount added to the value of a product or service, equal to the difference between its cost and the amount received when it is sold. Wages, taxes, etc. are deducted from the added value to give the profit. ◊ **VAT**

add-on sales /'æd ɑn ˌseɪlz/ *noun* the sale of items which complement items being bought, e.g., dishwashing detergent sold with a dishwasher

address label /ə'dres ˌleɪb(ə)l/ *noun* a label with an address on it

ad hoc /ˌæd 'hɑk/ *adjective* for this particular purpose ○ *They run ad hoc surveys to test customer reaction when products are launched.* ○ *Shipping by airfreight was an ad hoc arrangement initially.*

ad hoc research /ˌæd hɑk rɪ'sɜrtʃ/ *noun* research carried out for a particular client or in a particular market

ad impression /'æd ɪmˌpreʃ(ə)n/ *noun* same as **ad view**

adjacency /ə'dʒeɪs(ə)nsi/ *noun* a commercial which is run between two TV programs

adjust /ə'dʒʌst/ *verb* to change something to fit new conditions ○ *Prices are adjusted for inflation.*

adman /'ædmæn/ *noun* a man who works in advertising (*informal*) ○ *The admen are using balloons as promotional material.*

administer /əd'mɪnɪstər/ *verb* to organize, manage or direct the whole of an organization or part of one ○ *She administers a large pension fund.*

administered channel /əd ˌmɪnɪstərd 'tʃæn(ə)l/ *noun* a distribution channel in which there is cooperation between businesses

administered price /əd'mɪnɪstərd praɪs/ *noun* a price fixed by a manufacturer which cannot be varied by a retailer (NOTE: The U.K. term is **resale price maintenance**.)

administration /ədˌmɪnɪ'streɪʃ(ə)n/ *noun* the running of a company in receivership by an administrator appointed by the courts

administration costs /ədˌmɪnɪ 'streɪʃ(ə)n ˌkɔsts/, **administration expenses** /ədˌmɪnɪ'streɪʃ(ə)n ɪk ˌspensɪz/ *plural noun* the costs of management, not including production, marketing, or distribution costs

administrative /əd'mɪnɪstrətɪv/ *adjective* referring to administration ○ *administrative details* ○ *administrative expenses*

administrator /əd'mɪnɪstreɪtər/ *noun* **1.** a person who directs the work of other employees in a business ○ *After*

several years as a college teacher, she hopes to become an administrator. **2.** a person appointed by a court to manage the affairs of someone who dies without leaving a will

adopt /ə'dɑpt/ *verb* to agree to something or to accept something

adopter /ə'dɑptər/ *noun* a customer who adopts a particular product

adoption /ə'dɑpʃən/ *noun* the decision to buy or use a particular product ○ *More promotion was needed to speed up adoption of the product.* ○ *Widespread adoption of its new shampoo line has made the company the market leader.*

adoption curve /ə'dɑpʃən kɜrv/ *noun* a line on a graph showing how many consumers adopt or buy a new product at various time periods after the launch date ○ *The adoption curve shows that most people who buy the product do so at a fairly late stage.*

Adshel /'ædʃel/ *noun* a trademark for a poster site for advertisements in a bus shelter

adspend /'ædspend/ *noun* the amount of money spent on advertising

ad transfer /'æd ˌtrænsfɜr/ *noun* same as **click-through**

ad valorem duty /ˌæd və'lɔrəm ˌduti/ *noun* the duty calculated on the sales value of the goods

advance /əd'væns/ *noun* **1.** money paid as a loan or as a part of a payment to be made later ○ *She asked if she could have a cash advance.* ○ *We paid her an advance on account.* ○ *Can I have an advance of $100 against next month's salary?* **2.** an increase **3.** □ **in advance** early, before something happens ○ *freight payable in advance* ○ *prices fixed in advance* ■ *adjective* early, or taking place before something else happens ○ *advance payment* ○ *Advance vacation bookings are up on last year.* ○ *You must give seven days' advance notice of withdrawals from the account.* ■ *verb* **1.** to pay an amount of money to someone as a loan or as a part of a payment to be made later ○ *The bank advanced him $100,000 against the security of his house.* **2.** to increase ○ *Prices*

advance freight 6

generally advanced on the stock market.
3. to make something happen earlier ○ *The date of the shipping has been advanced to May 10th.* ○ *The meeting with the German distributors has been advanced from 11:00 to 9:30.*

advance freight /əd'væns freɪt/ *noun* freight which is payable in advance

advance man /əd'væns mæn/ *noun* a person who publicizes a performance and sells tickets for it before the performers arrive

advert /'ædvɜrt/ *noun U.K.* same as **advertisement** (*informal*)

advertise /'ædvərtaɪz/ *verb* to arrange and pay for publicity designed to help sell products or services or to find new employees ○ *to advertise a vacancy* ○ *to advertise for a secretary* ○ *to advertise a new product*

advertisement /əd'vɜrtɪsmənt/ *noun* **1.** a notice which shows that something is for sale, that a service is offered, that someone wants something, or that a job is vacant **2.** a short movie on television or a short announcement on the radio which tries to persuade people to use a product or service

advertisement manager /əd'vɜrtɪsmənt ˌmænɪdʒər/ *noun* the manager in charge of the advertisement section of a newspaper

advertisement panel /əd'vɜrtɪsmənt ˌpæn(ə)l/ *noun* a specially designed large advertising space in a newspaper

advertiser /'ædvərtaɪzər/ *noun* a person or company that advertises ○ *The catalog gives a list of advertisers.*

advertising /'ædvərtaɪzɪŋ/ *noun* the business of announcing that something is for sale or of trying to persuade customers to buy a product or service ○ *She works in advertising* or *She has a job in advertising.* ○ *Their new advertising campaign is being launched next week.* ○ *The company has asked an advertising agent to prepare a presentation.* □ **to take advertising space in a paper** to book space for an advertisement in a newspaper

advertising agency /'ædvərtaɪzɪŋ ˌeɪdʒənsi/ *noun* an office which plans, designs, and manages advertising for other companies

advertising appeal /'ædvərtaɪzɪŋ əˌpil/ *noun* the appeal of an advertisement to the intended audience

advertising appropriation /'ædvərtaɪzɪŋ əprouˌpriˌeɪʃ(ə)n/ *noun* money set aside by an organization for its advertising ○ *The marketing director and the chief accountant have yet to fix the advertising appropriation.* ○ *We cannot afford as large an advertising appropriation as last year.*

advertising billboard /'ædvərtaɪzɪŋ ˌbɪlbɔrd/ *noun* a billboard or wooden surface onto which advertising posters are stuck ○ *Advertising billboards have been taken down since the city council banned posters.* ○ *Giant billboards were placed in fields on either side of the road.*

advertising brief /'ædvərtaɪzɪŋ brif/ *noun* basic objectives and instructions concerning an advertising campaign, given by an advertiser to an advertising agency ○ *The brief stressed the importance of the market segment to be targeted.* ○ *The advertising brief was not detailed enough and did not show what sort of product image the advertiser wanted to create.*

advertising budget /'ædvərtaɪzɪŋ ˌbʌdʒət/ *noun* money planned for spending on advertising ○ *Our advertising budget has been increased.*

advertising campaign /'ædvərtaɪzɪŋ kæmˌpeɪn/ *noun* a coordinated publicity or advertising drive to sell a product

advertising control /'ædvərtaɪzɪŋ kənˌtroul/ *noun* legislative and other measures to prevent abuses in advertising ○ *If voluntary advertising control doesn't work, then the government will step in with legislation.*

advertising department /'ædvərtaɪzɪŋ dɪˌpɑrtmənt/ *noun* the department in a company that deals with the company's advertising

advertising expenditure
/ˈædvərtaɪzɪŋ ɪkˌspendɪtʃər/ *noun* the amount a company spends on its advertising

advertising jingle /ˈædvərtaɪzɪŋ ˌdʒɪŋg(ə)l/ *noun* a short and easily remembered tune or song to advertise a product on television, etc.

advertising manager
/ˈædvərtaɪzɪŋ ˌmænɪdʒər/ *noun* the manager in charge of advertising a company's products

advertising medium
/ˈædvərtaɪzɪŋ ˌmidiəm/ *noun* a type of advertisement, e.g., a TV commercial ○ *The product was advertised through the medium of the trade press.* (NOTE: The plural for this meaning is **media**.)

advertising message
/ˈædvərtaɪzɪŋ ˌmesɪdʒ/ *noun* whatever a company is trying to communicate in an advertisement ○ *Bad copywriting made the advertising message unclear.* ○ *The advertising message was aimed at the wrong target audience and therefore got little response.* ○ *The poster does not use words to get its advertising message across.*

advertising rates /ˈædvərtaɪzɪŋ reɪts/ *noun* the amount of money charged for advertising space in a newspaper or advertising time on TV

advertising space /ˈædvərtaɪzɪŋ speɪs/ *noun* a space in a newspaper set aside for advertisements

advertising specialties
/ˈædvərtaɪzɪŋ ˌspeʃəltiz/ *plural noun* special items given away as part of an advertising campaign, e.g., T-shirts, mugs, umbrellas, etc.

advertising time /ˈædvərtaɪzɪŋ taɪm/ *noun* the time on television or radio set aside for advertising ○ *Advertising time is cheapest in the afternoon.* ○ *They spent a month selling advertising time over the telephone.* ○ *How much advertising time does this program allow for?*

advertising weight /ˈædvərtaɪzɪŋ weɪt/ *noun* the amount of advertising given to a brand

advertorial /ˌædvərˈtɔriəl/ *noun* text in a magazine which is not written by the editorial staff but by an advertiser

advice /ədˈvaɪs/ *noun* a notification telling someone what has happened ◇ **as per advice** according to what is written on the advice note

advice note /ədˈvaɪs noʊt/ *noun* the written notice to a customer giving details of goods ordered and shipped but not yet delivered. Also called **letter of advice**

advice of dispatch /ədˌvaɪs əv dɪˈspætʃ/ *noun* communication from seller to buyer stating that goods have been sent, specifying time and place of arrival ○ *We have paid for the goods but as yet have received no advice of dispatch.* ○ *The advice of dispatch informed the buyer that the goods would arrive in Los Angeles on the morning of the 10th.*

ad view /ˈæd vju/ *noun* the number of times an advertisement is downloaded from a webpage and assumed to have been seen by a potential customer

advise /ədˈvaɪz/ *verb* to tell someone what has happened ○ *We have been advised that the shipment will arrive next week.*

advocacy advertising /ˈædvəkəsi ˌædvərtaɪzɪŋ/ *noun* advertising by a business that expresses a particular point of view on some issue ○ *Because of its prestige as a producer, the company's advocacy advertising had great influence.* ○ *The food company's advocacy advertising condemned unhealthy additives in canned produce.* ○ *Advocacy advertising has changed the public's attitude to smoking.*

aerial advertising /ˌeriəl ˈædvərtaɪzɪŋ/ *noun* advertising displayed in the air from balloons or planes or in smoke designs ○ *Aerial advertising proved to be an effective gimmick.* ○ *Aerial advertising was used to attract the attention of people on the beach.*

affiliate /əˈfɪlieɪt/ *noun* a local TV station which is part of a national network

affiliated /əˈfɪlieɪtɪd/ *adjective* connected with or owned by another company ○ *Smiths Inc. is one of our affiliated companies.*

affiliate directory /əˌfɪliət 'rektəri/ *noun* a directory that lists websites belonging to affiliate programs (NOTE: Affiliate directories provide information both to companies that want to subscribe to a program and to those who want to set up their own affiliate programs.)

affiliate marketing /əˈfɪliət ˌmɑrkətɪŋ/ *noun* marketing that uses affiliate programs

affiliate partner /əˈfɪliət ˌpɑrtnər/ *noun* a company which puts advertising onto its website for other companies, who pay for this service

affiliate program /əˈfɪliət ˌproʊɡræm/ *noun* a form of advertising on the web, in which a business persuades other businesses to put banners and buttons advertising its products or services on their websites and pays them a commission on any purchases made by their customers. Also called **associate program**

affinity card /əˈfɪnəti kɑrd/ *noun* a credit card where a percentage of each purchase made is given by the credit card company to a stated charity

affluence /ˈæfluəns/ *noun* wealth and a high standard of living

affluent /ˈæfluənt/ *adjective* rich ○ *Our more affluent clients prefer the luxury model.* □ **the affluent** rich people □ **the mass affluent** people with more than $100,000 in liquid assets

affluent society /ˌæfluənt səˈsaɪəti/ *noun* a type of society where most people are rich

affordable method /əˈfɔrdəb(ə)l ˌmeθəd/ *noun* a method of budgeting how much can be spent on marketing and promotion, which is based on what you can afford, rather than what you want to achieve ○ *Affordable method appeals to accountants, but won't help us achieve a high enough market share for the product.*

after-date /ˈæftər deɪt/ *noun* a reference on a bill of exchange to the length of time allowed for payment after a specific date ○ *The after-date allowed the buyer three months in which to pay.*

after-sales service /ˌæftər seɪlz 'sɜrvɪs/ *noun* a service of a machine carried out by the seller for some time after the machine has been bought

after-sight /ˈæftər saɪt/ *noun* a type of bill of exchange which is due to be paid on a specific day after acceptance

agate /ˈæɡət/ *noun* a measurement of advertising space in a newspaper, equal to one-fourteenth of an inch

age group /ˈeɪdʒ ɡrup/ *noun* a category including all people whose ages fall between two established points ○ *What age groups is this product meant to appeal to?* ○ *Research shows an increase in smoking among the 18–20 age group.*

age limit /ˈeɪdʒ ˌlɪmɪt/ *noun* the top age at which you are allowed to do a job ○ *There is an age limit of thirty-five for the position of buyer.*

agency /ˈeɪdʒənsi/ *noun* **1.** an office or job of representing another company in an area ○ *They signed an agency agreement* or *an agency contract.* **2.** an office or business which arranges things for other companies

agency commission /ˈeɪdʒənsi kəˌmɪʃ(ə)n/ *noun* the commission charged by an advertising agency

agency mark-up /ˌeɪdʒənsi 'mɑrk ʌp/ *noun* an amount added by an advertising agency to purchases, which forms parts of the agency's commission

agency roster /ˈeɪdʒənsi ˌrɑstər/ *noun* a group of different advertising agencies all working for a large company

agent /ˈeɪdʒənt/ *noun* **1.** a person who represents a company or another person in an area ○ *to be the agent for BMW cars* ○ *to be the agent for IBM* **2.** a person in charge of an agency ○ *an advertising agent* ○ *The real estate agent sent me a list of properties for sale.* ○ *Our trip was organized through our local travel agent.*

agent's commission /ˌeɪdʒənts kə'mɪʃ(ə)n/ *noun* money, often a percentage of sales, paid to an agent

aggregate /'ægrɪgət/ *adjective* total, with everything added together ○ *aggregate output*

aggregate demand /,ægrɪgət dɪ 'mænd/ *noun* the total demand for goods and services from all sectors of the economy including individuals, companies, and the government ○ *Economists are studying the recent fall in aggregate demand.* ○ *As incomes have risen, so has aggregate demand.*

aggregate supply /,ægrɪgət sə 'plaɪ/ *noun* all goods and services on the market ○ *Is aggregate supply meeting aggregate demand?*

aggregator /'ægrɪgeɪtər/ *noun* a website which collects news from other websites, allowing rapid syndication of information

AGM *abbreviation U.K.* Annual General Meeting

agora /'ægərə/ *noun* a marketplace on the Internet

agree /ə'griː/ *verb* **1.** □ **to agree on something** to come to a decision that is acceptable to everyone about something ○ *We all agreed on the need for action.* **2.** □ **to agree to something** to say that you accept something that is suggested ○ *After some discussion he agreed to our plan.* □ **to agree to do something** to say that you will do something ○ *She agreed to be chairman.* ○ *Will the finance director agree to resign?*

agree with *phrasal verb* **1.** to say that your opinions are the same as someone else's ○ *I agree with the chairman that the figures are lower than normal.* **2.** to be the same as ○ *The auditors' figures do not agree with those of the accounts department.*

agreed /ə'griːd/ *adjective* having been accepted by everyone ○ *We pay an agreed amount each month.* ○ *The agreed terms of employment are laid down in the contract.*

agreed price /ə,griːd 'praɪs/ *noun* a price which has been accepted by both the buyer and seller

agreement /ə'griːmənt/ *noun* a spoken or written contract between people or groups which explains how they will act ○ *a written agreement* ○ *an unwritten* or *verbal agreement* ○ *to draw up* or *to draft an agreement* ○ *to break an agreement* ○ *to sign an agreement* ○ *to reach an agreement* or *to come to an agreement on something* ○ *a collective wage agreement*

agreement of sale /ə,griːmənt əv 'seɪl/ *noun* a written contract that sets out in detail the terms agreed on by the buyer and the seller when a property is sold

AICPA *abbreviation* American Institute of Certified Public Accountants

aid /eɪd/ *noun* something which helps ■ *verb* to help

AIDA *noun* a model showing stages in the effects of advertising on consumers, i.e. you attract their Attention, keep their Interest, arouse a Desire, and provoke Action to purchase. Full form **attention, interest, desire, action**

aided recall /,eɪdɪd rɪ'kɔːl/ *noun* a test to see how well someone remembers an advertisement by giving the respondent some help such as a picture which he or she might associate with it ○ *Even aided recall brought no reaction from the respondent.* ○ *Aided recall has shown that we must make our advertising more striking.* (NOTE: also called **prompted recall**)

aid-to-trade /,eɪd tə 'treɪd/ *noun* a service which supports trade, e.g., banking and advertising ○ *The recession has affected aids-to-trade and the industries they support and supply.* ○ *At that time, advertising was the fastest expanding aid-to-trade.*

aim /eɪm/ *noun* something which you try to do ○ *One of our aims is to increase the quality of our products.* □ **the company has achieved all its aims** the company has done all the things it had hoped to do ■ *verb* to try to do something ○ *Each member of the sales team must aim to double their previous year's sales.* ○ *We aim to be No. 1 in the market within two years.*

air /eɪr/ *noun* a method of traveling or sending goods using aircraft ○ *to send a letter* or *a shipment by air*

air carrier /'er ˌkæriər/ *noun* a company which sends cargo or passengers by air

air forwarding /'er ˌfɔrwərdɪŋ/ *noun* the process of arranging for goods to be shipped by air

air freight /'er freɪt/ *noun* the transportation of goods in aircraft, or goods sent by air ○ *to send a shipment by air freight* ○ *Air freight tariffs are rising.*

airfreight /'erfreɪt/ *verb* to send goods by air ○ *to airfreight a consignment to Mexico* ○ *We airfreighted the shipment because our agent ran out of stock.*

airline /'erlaɪn/ *noun* a company which carries passengers or cargo by air

airmail /'ermeɪl/ *noun* a postal service which sends letters or parcels by air ○ *to send a package by airmail* ○ *Airmail charges have risen by 15%.* ■ *verb* to send letters or parcels by air ○ *We airmailed the document to New York.*

airmail envelope /'ermeɪl ˌenvəloup/ *noun* a very light envelope for sending airmail letters

airmail transfer /'ermeɪl ˌtrænsfɜr/ *noun* an act of sending money from one bank to another by airmail

airtight /'ertaɪt/ *adjective* which does not allow air to get in ○ *The goods are packed in airtight containers.*

air time /'er taɪm/, **airtime** *noun* the time set aside for advertising on television or radio ○ *How much air time do we need for this commercial?* ○ *We should look for air time on the new radio station.* ○ *All the air time in the world won't sell this product.*

aisle /aɪl/ *noun* a space or passageway between the shelves of products on display in a supermarket

à la carte /ˌa la 'kart/ *noun* a system whereby advertisers use the services of a whole range of businesses rather than relying on one agency over a long period

all-in rate /ˌɔl ɪn 'reɪt/ *noun* a price which covers all the costs connected with a purchase, such as delivery, tax and insurance, as well as the cost of the goods themselves

allowable expenses /əˌlauəb(ə)l ɪk 'spensɪz/ *plural noun* business expenses which can be claimed against tax

allowance /ə'lauəns/ *noun* money removed in the form of a discount ○ *an allowance for depreciation* ○ *an allowance for exchange loss*

alpha activity /'ælfə ækˌtɪvəti/ *noun* the measurement of a person's brain activity as a way of measuring their reaction to an advertisement

alternate /'ɔltərnət, ɔl'tɜrnət/ *adjective* different from what is actually used

alternate media /ˌɔltərnət 'midiə/ *adjective* forms of advertising which are not direct mailing, e.g., TV commercials, magazine inserts, etc.

alternative close /ɔl'tɜrnətɪv klouz/ *noun* an act of ending a sales negotiation by asking the customer to choose something such as a method of payment

ambient media /ˌæmbiənt 'midiə/ *noun* advertising media outdoors, e.g., posters, advertisements on the sides of buses, etc.

ambush marketing /'æmbʊʃ ˌmarkətɪŋ/ *noun* the linking of a promotion campaign to an event such as a sporting contest which is sponsored by another manufacturer without paying a fee

American Institute of Certified Public Accountants /əˌmerɪkən ˌɪnstɪtjut əv ˌsɜrtɪfaɪd ˌpʌblɪk ə'kauntənts/ *noun* the national association for certified public accountants. Abbreviation **AICPA**

analysis /ə'næləsɪs/ *noun* a detailed examination and report ○ *a job analysis* ○ *market analysis* ○ *Her job is to produce a regular sales analysis.* (NOTE: The plural is **analyses**.)

analyst /'ænəlɪst/ *noun* a person who analyzes ○ *a market analyst* ○ *a systems analyst*

analyze *verb* to examine someone or something in detail ○ *to analyze a statement of account* ○ *to analyze the market potential*

ancillary-to-trade /æn,sɪləri tə 'treɪd/ *noun* a service which supports trade, e.g., banking and advertising ○ *The recession has affected ancillaries-to-trade and the industries they support and supply.* ○ *Advertising was the fastest expanding ancillary-to-trade at that time.*

animatic /,ænɪ'mætɪk/ *noun* a rough outline version of a television commercial shown to the advertiser for approval ○ *The animatic was sent back to the agency with several criticisms.* ○ *The animatic impressed the advertiser because it put the message over stylishly.* ○ *If the animatic is approved, the creative team will begin work on the final product.*

animation /,ænɪ'meɪʃ(ə)n/ *noun* a cartoon movie, a movie made from drawings

annual /'ænjuəl/ *adjective* for one year ○ *an annual statement of income* ○ *They have six weeks' annual leave.* ○ *The company has an annual growth of 5%.*

annual accounts /,ænjuəl ə 'kaʊnts/ *plural noun* the accounts prepared at the end of a financial year ○ *The annual accounts have been sent to the shareholders.*

annual depreciation /,ænjuəl dɪ ,priʃi'eɪʃ(ə)n/ *noun* a reduction in the book value of an asset at a particular rate per year. ◊ **straight line depreciation**

Annual General Meeting /,ænjuəl ,dʒen(ə)rəl 'miːtɪŋ/ *noun U.K.* same as **annual meeting**

annual income /,ænjuəl 'ɪnkʌm/ *noun* money received during a calendar year

annual meeting /,ænjuəl ,dʒen(ə)rəl 'miːtɪŋ/ *noun* an annual meeting of all stockholders of a company, when the company's financial situation is presented by and discussed with the directors, when the accounts for the past year are approved and when dividends may be declared and audited. Also called **annual stockholders' meeting** (NOTE: The U.K. term is **Annual General Meeting.**)

Annual Percentage Rate /,ænjuəl pə'sentɪdʒ reɪt/ *noun* a rate of interest (such as on a hire-purchase agreement) shown on an annual compound basis, and including fees and charges. Abbreviation **APR**

annual report /,ænjuəl rɪ'pɔːt/ *noun* a report of a company's financial situation at the end of a year, sent to all the shareholders

annual stockholders' meeting /,ænjuəl ,dʒen(ə)rəl 'miːtɪŋ/ *noun* same as **annual meeting**

anonymous product /ə,nɒnɪməs 'prɒdʌkt/ *noun* a product with no apparent brand name, used in advertisements to highlight the product being promoted ○ *Brand X is the anonymous product which never gets your washing completely white.* ○ *No one watching the commercial would believe the anonymous product was as bad is it seemed.* ○ *What happens if the respondent chooses the anonymous product instead of ours?*

anti- /ænti/ *prefix* against

anti-dumping /,ænti 'dʌmpɪŋ/ *adjective* intended to stop surplus goods being sold in foreign markets at a price that is lower than their marginal cost

anti-inflationary measure /,ænti ɪn'fleɪʃ(ə)n(ə)ri ,meʒər/ *noun* a measure taken to reduce inflation

anti-site /'ænti saɪt/ *noun* a website devoted to attacking a particular company or organization. An anti-site often imitates the target organization's own site and is usually set up by a customer who has a complaint against the organization that he or she has been unable to express on the organization's own site. Also called **hate site**

anti-trust /,ænti 'trʌst/ *adjective* attacking monopolies and encouraging competition ○ *anti-trust measures*

any other business /,eni ,ʌðər 'bɪznɪs/ *noun* an item at the end of an agenda, where any matter can be raised. Abbreviation **AOB**

AOB *abbreviation* any other business

appeal /ə'piːl/ *noun* the fact of being attractive

apperception /ˌæpər'sepʃ(ə)n/ noun ♦ **thematic apperception test**

application form /ˌæplɪ'keɪʃ(ə)n ˌfɔrm/ noun a form to be filled in when applying for a new issue of shares or for a job

appointment book /ə'pɔɪntmənt bʊk/ noun a book in which you can write notes or appointments for each day of the week ○ *She checked her engagements in her appointment book.*

appraisal /ə'preɪz(ə)l/ noun a calculation of the value of someone or something

appro /'æproʊ/ noun same as **approval** (*informal*) □ **to buy something on appro** to buy something which you will only pay for if it is satisfactory

approach /ə'proʊtʃ/ noun an act of getting in touch with someone with a proposal ○ *The company made an approach to the supermarket chain.* ○ *The board turned down all approaches on the subject of mergers.* ○ *We have had an approach from a Japanese company to buy our car division.* ○ *She has had an approach from a firm of headhunters.* ■ verb to get in touch with someone with a proposal ○ *He approached the bank with a request for a loan.* ○ *The company was approached by an American publisher with the suggestion of a merger.* ○ *We have been approached several times but have turned down all offers.* ○ *She was approached by a headhunter with the offer of a job.*

appropriation /ə,proʊpri'eɪʃ(ə)n/ noun the act of putting money aside for a special purpose ○ *appropriation of funds to the reserve*

appropriation account /ə,proʊpri 'eɪʃ(ə)n ə,kaʊnt/ noun the part of a profit and loss account which shows how the profit has been dealt with, e.g., how much has been given to the shareholders as dividends and how much is being put into the reserves

approval /ə'pruv(ə)l/ noun 1. the act of saying or thinking that something is good ○ *to submit a budget for approval* 2. □ **on approval** in order to be able to use something for a period of time and check that it is satisfactory before paying for it ○ *to buy a photocopier on approval*

approve /ə'pruv/ verb 1. □ **to approve of something** to think something is good ○ *The chairman approves of the new company letterhead.* ○ *The sales staff do not approve of interference from the accounts division.* 2. to agree to something officially ○ *to approve the terms of a contract* ○ *The proposal was approved by the board.*

APR abbreviation Annual Percentage Rate

area /'eriə/ noun 1. a subject ○ *a problem area* or *an area for concern* 2. a part of a country, a division for commercial purposes ○ *Her sales area is the Northwest.* ○ *He finds it difficult to cover all his area in a week.* 3. a part of a room, factory, restaurant, etc. ○ *a no-smoking area*

area code /'eriə koʊd/ noun a special telephone number which is given to a particular area ○ *The area code for Boston is 617.*

area manager /ˌeriə 'mænɪdʒər/ noun a manager who is responsible for a company's work in a specific part of the country

arithmetic mean /ˌærɪθmetɪk 'min/ noun a simple average calculated by dividing the sum of two or more items by the number of items

armchair research /ˌɑrmtʃer rɪ 'sɜrtʃ/ noun looking for information that has already been compiled and published in reference books such as directories ○ *Most of our armchair research can be done in libraries.* ○ *If we cannot find all the data through armchair research, we shall have to do a market survey of our own.* (NOTE: also called **desk research**)

arrears /ə'rɪrz/ plural noun 1. money which is owed, but which has not been paid at the right time ○ *a salary with arrears effective from January 1st* ○ *We are pressing the company to pay arrears of interest.* ○ *You must not allow the mortgage payments to fall into arrears.* 2. □ **in arrears** owing money which should have been paid earlier ○ *The pay-*

ments are six months in arrears. ○ *He is six weeks in arrears with his rent.*

art director /'ɑrt daɪˌrektər/ *noun* a coordinator of creative work in advertising ○ *The art director briefed the copywriter and illustrator on the main points of the campaign.* ○ *After three years as an agency photographer, he was made art director.*

article /'ɑrtɪk(ə)l/ *noun* **1.** a product or thing for sale ○ *to launch a new article on the market* ○ *a black market in luxury articles* **2.** a section of a legal agreement such as a contract or treaty ○ *See article 8 of the contract.*

article numbering system /ˌɑrtɪk(ə)l 'nʌmbərɪŋ ˌsɪstəm/ *noun* a universal system of identifying articles for sale, using a series of digits which can be expressed as bar codes

artificial obsolescence /ˌɑrtɪfɪʃ(ə)l ˌɑbsə'les(ə)ns/ *noun* the practice of deliberately making old models seem out of date by bringing out new ones with changes and additional features which will attract the customer ○ *Artificial obsolescence is making our products seem cheap and disposable.* ○ *Artificial obsolescence means that no product can be fashionable for very long.*

artwork /'ɑrtwɜrk/ *noun* an original work to be used for an advertisement, e.g., drawings, layouts, photographs

asking price /'æskɪŋ ˌpraɪs/ *noun* a price which the seller is hoping will be paid for the item being sold ○ *the asking price is $24,000*

assay mark /'æseɪ mɑrk/ *noun* a mark put on gold or silver items to show that the metal is of the correct quality

assembly /ə'sembli/ *noun* **1.** the process of putting an item together from various parts ○ *There are no assembly instructions to show you how to put the computer together.* ○ *We can't put the machine together because the instructions for assembly are in Japanese.* **2.** an official meeting

assembly line /ə'sembli laɪn/ *noun* a production system where a product such as a car moves slowly through the factory with new sections added to it as it goes along ○ *She works on an assembly line* or *She is an assembly line worker.*

assessment /ə'sesmənt/ *noun* a calculation of value ○ *a property assessment* ○ *a tax assessment*

asset /'æset/ *noun* something which belongs to a company or person, and which has a value ○ *He has an excess of assets over liabilities.* ○ *Her assets are only $640 as against liabilities of $24,000.*

asset stripping /'æset ˌstrɪpɪŋ/ *noun* the practice of buying a company at a lower price than its asset value, and then selling its assets

asset value /ˌæset 'vælju/ *noun* the value of a company calculated by adding together all its assets

associate program /ə'soʊsiət ˌproʊgræm/ *noun* same as **affiliate program**

assortment /ə'sɔrtmənt/ *noun* a combination of goods sold together ○ *The box contains an assortment of chocolates with different centers.*

assumptive close /ə'sʌmptɪv ˌkloʊz/ *noun* an act of ending the sales negotiation by assuming that the customer has agreed to buy, and then asking further details of payments, delivery, etc.

asterisk law /'æstərɪsk lɔ/ *noun* a law which prevents telemarketing agencies from trying to sell to people who have indicated that they do not want to be approached by telephone salesmen by putting an asterisk against their names in the phone book

ATM *abbreviation* automated teller machine

atmosphere /'ætməsfɪr/ *noun* **1.** the general feeling in a store or shopping area **2.** the effect that the medium itself through which an advertisement is presented has on the audience

atmospherics /ˌætməs'ferɪks/ *noun* **1.** a way of encouraging customer interest by using the senses such as smell and sound **2.** creating an overall image of a company through the design of its premises and products

ATR *noun* a model showing stages in the effects of advertising on the consumer, where the customer becomes aware of the product, buys it once to try it, and then buys it again when he finds it is satisfactory. Full form **awareness, trial, repeat**

atrium /'eɪtriəm/ *noun* a very large open space in a building, usually with a glass roof, fountains, and plants, which acts as a central meeting point, linking shopping and office areas and restaurants

attention /ə'tenʃən/ *noun* careful thought or consideration

attitude /'ætɪtud/ *noun* the way in which a person behaves or thinks □ **a person's attitude towards an advertisement** a person's reaction to an advertisement

attitude measurement /'ætɪtud ˌmeʒərmənt/, **attitude testing** /'ætɪtud ˌtestɪŋ/ *noun* the act of ascertaining the way in which a person views something by assigning scores to various factors ○ *Attitude measurement has given us a good idea of how consumers view our product.* ○ *Will attitude testing lead to the redesigning of these heaters?*

attitude research /'ætɪtud rɪˌsɜrtʃ/, **attitude survey** /'ætɪtud ˌsɜrveɪ/ *noun* research that is intended to reveal what people think and feel about an organization, its products or services, and its activities (NOTE: Attitude research can be used to discover the opinions either of consumers and the general public or of an organization's own employees.)

attitude scale /'ætɪtud skeɪl/ *noun* a device which measures or tests attitudes by analyzing a subject's responses

attrition /ə'trɪʃ(ə)n/ *noun* a decrease in the loyalty of consumers to a product, due to factors such as boredom or desire for a change ○ *We must adapt our products if we are to avoid attrition.* ○ *Attrition showed the company that brand loyalty could not be taken for granted.*

auction /'ɔkʃən/ *noun* a method of selling goods where people who want to buy compete with each other by saying how much they will offer for something, and the item is sold to the person who makes the highest offer ○ *Their furniture will be sold in the auction rooms next week.* ○ *They announced a sale by auction of the fire-damaged stock.* ○ *The equipment was sold by auction or at auction.* □ **to put an item up for auction** to offer an item for sale at an auction ■ *verb* to sell something at an auction ○ *The factory was closed and the machinery was auctioned off.*

auctioneer /ˌɔkʃə'nɪr/ *noun* the person who conducts an auction

auction house /'ɔkʃən haʊs/ *noun* a company which specializes in holding auction sales, especially of items such as antiques or paintings

auction mart /'ɔkʃən mɑrt/ *noun* auction rooms

audience /'ɔdiəns/ *noun* **1.** the number of people who watch a TV program or listen to a radio program **2.** the number of people who are exposed to an advertisement

audience accumulation /ˌɔdiəns əˌkjumjə'leɪʃ(ə)n/ *noun* the building up of an audience by repeating advertisements over a period of time

audience composition /ˌɔdiəns ˌkɑmpə'zɪʃ(ə)n/ *noun* the way an audience is made up, i.e. the age range, sex, lifestyles, etc.

audience research /ˌɔdiəns rɪˈsɜrtʃ/ *noun* research into the attitudes of an audience to an advertising campaign

audimeter /'ɔdimitər/ *noun* an electronic device attached to a TV set, which records details of a viewer's viewing habits

audiovisual /ˌɔdioʊ'vɪʒuəl/ *noun* media that can be seen and heard, e.g., a TV commercial ○ *The exhibition was devoted to the latest in audiovisual equipment.*

audit /'ɔdɪt/ *noun* **1.** the examination of the books and accounts of a company ○ *to carry out the annual audit* **2.** a detailed examination of something in order to assess it ○ *A thorough job audit was needed for job evaluation.* ○ *A manpower audit showed up a desperate lack of talent.*

Audit Bureau of Circulations /ˌɔdɪt ˌbjʊrəʊ əv ˌsɜrkjʊˈleɪʃ(ə)nz/ *noun* an organization which verifies and publishes the circulation of magazines and newspapers. Abbreviation **ABCs**

augmented product /ɔgˌmentɪd ˈprɑdʌkt/ *noun* a product with added benefits such as warranties or installation service etc.

aural signature /ˌɔrəl ˈsɪgnətʃər/ *noun* musical sounds used as a signature to identify a product or service

automated teller machine /ˌɔtəmeɪtɪd ˈtelər məˌʃin/ *noun* a machine which gives out money when a special card is inserted and special instructions given. Abbreviation **ATM**

automatic /ˌɔtəˈmætɪk/ *adjective* working or taking place without any person making it happen ○ *There is an automatic increase in salaries on January 1st.*

automatic merchandising /ˌɔtəmætɪk ˈmɜrtʃəndaɪzɪŋ/, **automatic selling** /ˌɔtəmætɪk ˈselɪŋ/, **automatic vending** /ˌɔtəmætɪk ˈvendɪŋ/ *noun* selling through a machine ○ *Automatic selling is popular because of the low labor costs involved.*

automatic vending machine /ˌɔtəmætɪk ˈvendɪŋ məˌʃin/ *noun* a machine which provides drinks, cigarettes etc., when a coin is put in

automation /ˌɔtəˈmeɪʃ(ə)n/ *noun* the use of machines to do work with very little supervision by people

availability /əˌveɪləˈbɪləti/ *noun* **1.** the fact of being easy to obtain □ **offer subject to availability** the offer is valid only if the goods are available **2.** the time and number of advertising slots which are available to be used

average /ˈæv(ə)rɪdʒ/ *noun* **1.** a number calculated by adding several figures together and dividing by the number of figures added ○ *the average for the last three months* or *the last three months' average* ○ *sales average* or *average of sales* **2.** □ **on average, on an average** in general ○ *On average, $15 worth of goods are stolen every day.* ■ *adjective* **1.** equal to the average of a set of figures ○ *the average increase in salaries* ○ *The average cost per unit is too high.* ○ *The average sales per representative are rising.* **2.** not very good ○ *The company's performance has been only average.* ○ *He's only an average worker.*

   average out *phrasal verb* to come to a figure as an average ○ *It averages out at 10% per annum.* ○ *Sales increases have averaged out at 15%.*

average cost pricing /ˌæv(ə)rɪdʒ ˈkɔst ˌpraɪsɪŋ/ *noun* pricing based on the average cost of producing one unit of a product

average due date /ˌæv(ə)rɪdʒ ˈdu ˌdeɪt/ *noun* the average date when several different payments fall due

average frequency /ˌæv(ə)rɪdʒ ˈfrikwənsi/ *noun* the average number of times a consumer will see a particular advertisement ○ *We will have to buy a lot of advertising time to attain a high average frequency.* ○ *What average frequency do we need to get this advertisement across to the target audience?*

average quarter-hour figure /ˌæv(ə)rɪdʒ ˌkwɔrtər aʊr ˈfɪgər/ *adjective* the average number of people watching a TV program during a 15-minute period

awareness /əˈwernəs/ *noun* the state of being conscious of an advertisement's message or of a brand's existence and qualities ○ *The survey after the campaign showed advertising awareness had remained low.* ◊ **ATR, maximal awareness**

B

B2B /ˌbi tə ˈbi/ *adjective* referring to products or services that are aimed at other businesses rather than at consumers (NOTE: The word is most commonly used of business-to-business dealings conducted over the Internet.)

B2B auction /ˌbi tə bi ˈɔkʃən/ *noun* a web marketplace where supplier companies bid against one another to offer the lowest price for a particular product or service, while the buyer company waits until the sellers have reduced the price to one that it can afford (NOTE: Businesses have to register to take part in B2B auctions by providing their credit-card information and shipping preferences, and also have to agree to the site's code of conduct.)

B2B commerce /ˌbi tə bi ˈkɑmɜrs/ *noun* business done by companies with other companies, rather than with individual consumers

B2B exchange /ˌbi tə bi ɪks ˈtʃeɪndʒ/ *noun* same as **exchange**

B2B web exchange /ˌbi tə bi ˈweb ɪks ˌtʃeɪndʒ/ *noun* same as **exchange**

B2B website /ˌbi tə bi ˈwebsaɪt/ *noun* a website that is designed to help businesses trade with each other on the Internet

B2C /ˌbi tə ˈsi/ *adjective* referring to products or services that are aimed at consumers rather than at other businesses (NOTE: The word is most commonly used of business-to-consumer dealings conducted over the Internet.)

B2C website /ˌbi tə si ˈwebsaɪt/ *noun* an online store that sells products to consumers via its website

baby boomer /ˈbeɪbi ˌbumɜr/ *noun* a person born during the period from 1945 to 1965, when the populations of the USA and U.K. increased rapidly

back /bæk/ *noun* the opposite side to the front ○ *Write your address on the back of the envelope.* ○ *Please endorse the check on the back.* ■ *adjective* referring to the past ○ *a back payment* ■ *verb* **1.** to help someone, especially financially ○ *The bank is backing us to the tune of $10,000.* ○ *She is looking for someone to back her project.* **2.** □ **to back a bill** to sign a bill promising to pay it if the person it is addressed to is not able to do so

backbone /ˈbækboʊn/ *noun* a high-speed communications link for Internet communications across an organization or country or between countries

back cover /ˌbæk ˈkʌvər/ *noun* the back of a magazine cover, which can be used for advertising

backdate /bækˈdeɪt/ *verb* **1.** to put an earlier date on a document such as a check or an invoice ○ *Backdate your invoice to April 1st.* **2.** to make something effective from an earlier date than the current date ○ *The pay increase is backdated to January 1st.*

backdoor selling /ˌbækdɔr ˈselɪŋ/ *noun* the practice of bypassing an organization's bureaucracy and selling direct to the chief decision-maker in it ○ *If we did not resort to backdoor selling the right department might never hear of us.* ○ *The chairman was asked out for a meal by the sales director of the other company to try a little backdoor selling.*

backer /ˈbækər/ *noun* **1.** a person or company that backs someone ○ *One of the company's backers has withdrawn.* **2.** □ **the backer of a bill** the person who backs a bill **3.** a piece of publicity material placed at the back of a display or stand

background /'bækgraʊnd/ *noun* past work or experience ○ *My background is in the steel industry.* ○ *The company is looking for someone with a background of success in the electronics industry.* ○ *She has a publishing background.* ○ *What is his background?* ○ *Do you know anything about his background?*

background music /'bækgraʊnd ˌmjuːzɪk/ *noun* music played softly in a store, supermarket, atrium etc., as a means of pleasing or calming potential customers

backing /'bækɪŋ/ *noun* support, especially financial support ○ *She has the backing of an Australian bank.* ○ *The company will succeed only if it has sufficient backing.*

backload /'bækloʊd/ *verb* to make sure that most of the costs of a promotional campaign come in the later stages, so that they can be regulated according to the response received. The campaign can then be cut back if the response rate is inadequate. This is opposed to frontloading, where most of the costs are incurred in the early stages. Compare **frontload**

backlog /'bæklɔg/ *noun* an amount of work, or of items such as orders or letters, which should have been dealt with earlier but is still waiting to be done ○ *The warehouse is trying to cope with a backlog of orders.* ○ *We're finding it hard to cope with the backlog of paperwork.*

back of book /ˌbæk əv 'bʊk/ *noun* the last pages of a magazine containing advertisements

back-of-the-house   services /ˌbæk əv ðə haʊs 'sɜrvɪsɪz/ *plural noun* services which are in the back part of a store

back orders /'bæk ˌɔrdərz/ *plural noun* orders received and not yet fulfilled, usually because the item is out of stock ○ *It took the factory six weeks to clear all the accumulated back orders.*

back pay /'bæk peɪ/ *noun* a salary which has not been paid ○ *I am owed $500 in back pay.*

back payment /'bæk ˌpeɪmənt/ *noun* the act of paying money which is owed

backup /'bækʌp/ *adjective* supporting or helping ○ *We offer a free backup service to customers.* ○ *After a series of sales tours by representatives, the sales director sends backup letters to all the contacts.*

backup ad /'bækʌp æd/ *noun* an advertisement designed to accompany editorial material in a publication

backup copy /'bækʌp ˌkɑpi/ *noun* a copy of a computer disc to be kept in case the original disc is damaged

back wages /ˌbæk 'weɪdʒɪz/ *plural noun* same as **back pay**

backward integration /ˌbækwərd ˌɪntɪ'greɪʃ(ə)n/ *noun* a process of expansion in which a business which deals with the later stages in the production and sale of a product acquires a business that deals with an earlier stage in the same process, usually a supplier ○ *Buying up rubber plantations is part of the tire company's backward integration policy.* ○ *Backward integration will ensure cheap supplies but forward integration would bring us nearer to the market.* Also called **vertical integration**. Opposite **forward integration**

bad debt /ˌbæd 'det/ *noun* a debt which will not be paid, usually because the debtor has gone out of business, and which has to be written off in the accounts ○ *The company has written off $30,000 in bad debts.*

bait /beɪt/ *noun* an article which is sold at a loss to attract customers ○ *This is an attractive enough product to use as bait.* ○ *The store's best bargains were displayed in the window as bait.*

bait ad /'beɪt æd/ *noun* an advertisement for low-priced goods, used to attract customers into a store

bait and switch /ˌbeɪt ənd 'swɪtʃ/ *noun* a sales technique where the salesperson offers what looks like an attractive bargain and then says at the last minute that it is not available and replaces it with something inferior

balance of payments /ˌbæləns əv ˈpeɪmənts/ *noun* a comparison between total receipts and payments arising from a country's international trade in goods, services, and financial transactions. Abbreviation **BOP**

balance sheet /ˈbæləns ʃiːt/ *noun* a statement of the financial position of a company at a particular time, such as the end of the financial year or the end of a quarter, showing the company's assets and liabilities ○ *Our accountant has prepared the balance sheet for the first half-year.* ○ *The company balance sheet for the last financial year shows a worse position than for the previous year.*

COMMENT: The balance sheet shows the state of a company's finances at a certain date. The profit and loss account shows the movements which have taken place since the end of the previous accounting period. A balance sheet must balance, with the basic equation that assets (i.e. what the company owns, including money owed to the company) must equal liabilities (i.e. what the company owes to its creditors) plus capital (i.e. what it owes to its shareholders). A balance sheet can be drawn up either in the horizontal form, with liabilities and capital on the right-hand side of the page (in the U.K., they are on the left-hand side) or in the vertical form, with assets at the top of the page, followed by liabilities, and capital at the bottom. Most are usually drawn up in the vertical format, as opposed to the more old-fashioned horizontal style.

balloon /bəˈluːn/ *noun* a loan where the last repayment is larger than the others

balloon payment /bəˈluːn ˌpeɪmənt/ *noun* the last payment, usually much larger than the others, that is made when repaying a balloon loan

band /bænd/ *noun* a strip of paper or plastic or a rubber ring put round articles to attach them together

banded /ˈbændɪd/ *adjective* attached with a band

banded offer /ˌbændɪd ˈɒfər/ *noun* a type of sales promotion involving the offer of an additional item along with the main one ○ *The banded offer consisted of a full-sized bottle of shampoo along with a small bottle of hair conditioner.*

banded pack /ˌbændɪd ˈpæk/ *noun* a pack which includes two items attached to form a pack, or with an additional different item bound along with the main one ○ *These banded packs have been specially designed for our sales promotion drive.*

bandwidth /ˈbændwɪdθ/ *noun* a measurement of the capacity of a fiber-optic cable to carry information to and from the Internet (NOTE: The higher the bandwidth, the faster information passes through the cable.)

bangtail /ˈbæŋteɪl/ *noun* a type of folded mailer, with a pocket for an information card or reply coupon and a flap that tucks in

bankable paper /ˌbæŋkəb(ə)l ˈpeɪpər/ *noun* a document which a bank will accept as security for a loan

bank account /ˈbæŋk əˌkaʊnt/ *noun* an account which a customer has with a bank, where the customer can deposit and withdraw money ○ *to open a bank account* ○ *to close a bank account* ○ *How much money do you have in your bank account?* ○ *If you let the balance in your bank account fall below $1,000, you have to pay a fee.*

bank base rate /ˌbæŋk ˈbeɪs ˌreɪt/ *noun* a basic rate of interest, on which the actual rate a bank charges on loans to its customers is calculated. Also called **base rate**

bank bill /ˈbæŋk bɪl/ *noun* **1.** same as **banknote 2.** *U.K.* same as **banker's bill**

bank card /ˈbæŋk kɑːrd/ *noun* a credit card or debit card issued to a customer by a bank for use instead of cash when buying goods or services (NOTE: There are internationally recognized rules that govern the authorization of the use of bank cards and the clearing and settlement of transactions in which they are used.)

bank charge /ˈbæŋk tʃɑːrdʒ/ *noun* same as **service charge**

bank credit /'bæŋk ˌkredɪt/ *noun* loans or overdrafts from a bank to a customer

bank draft /'bæŋk dræft/ *noun* an order by one bank telling another bank, usually in another country, to pay money to someone

banker /'bæŋkər/ *noun* a person who is in an important position in a bank

banker's bill /'bæŋkərz bɪl/ *noun* an order by one bank telling another bank, usually in another country, to pay money to someone. Also called **bank bill**

bank giro /'bæŋk ˌdʒaɪrou/ *noun* a method used by clearing banks to transfer money rapidly from one account to another

banking account /'bæŋkɪŋ ə ˌkaunt/ *noun* an account which a customer has with a bank

bank manager /'bæŋk ˌmænɪdʒər/ *noun* the person in charge of a branch of a bank ○ *They asked their bank manager for a loan.*

banknote /'bæŋknout/ *noun U.K.* a piece of printed paper money (NOTE: The U.S. term is **bill**.)

bank transfer /'bæŋk ˌtrænsfɜr/ *noun* an act of moving money from a bank account to another account

banner /'bænər/ *noun* **1.** material stretched between two walls or buildings, carrying an advertising message ○ *There were banners across the street advertising the charity run.* **2.** an online interactive advertisement that appears on a webpage, usually at the top or bottom, and contains a link to the website of the business whose products or services are being advertised (NOTE: Banner ads often use graphics images and sound as well as text.)

banner advertising /'bænər ˌædvərtaɪzɪŋ/ *noun* a website advertising which runs across the top of a webpage, similar to newspaper headlines

banner exchange /'bænər ɪks ˌtʃeɪndʒ/ *noun* an agreement between two or more businesses, in which each allows the others' advertising banners to be displayed on its website

banner headline /ˌbænər 'hedlaɪn/ *noun* a headline set in very large black type, running across a page

bar chart /'bɑr tʃɑrt/ *noun* a chart where values or quantities are shown as columns of different heights set on a base line, the different lengths expressing the quantity of the item or unit. Also called **bar graph, histogram**

bar code /'bɑr koud/ *noun* a system of lines printed on a product which, when read by a computer, give a reference number or price

bar coding /'bɑr ˌkoudɪŋ/ *noun* the process of attaching an identifying label, written in machine-readable code and able to be read by a scanner, to a product or container (NOTE: Bar codes are useful for stock control and order picking and can be used to trace a product through every stage of a transaction from packaging to customer delivery.)

bargain /'bɑrgɪn/ *noun* **1.** an agreement on the price of something ○ *to strike a bargain* or *to make a bargain* □ **to drive a hard bargain** to be a difficult person to negotiate with **2.** something which is cheaper than usual ○ *That car is a (real) bargain at $500.* ■ *verb* to try to reach agreement about something, especially a price, usually with each person or group involved putting forward suggestions or offers which are discussed until a compromise is arrived at ○ *You will have to bargain with the dealer if you want a discount.* ○ *They spent two hours bargaining about* or *over the price.* (NOTE: You bargain **with** someone **over** or **about** or **for** something.)

bargain basement /ˌbɑrgɪn 'beɪsmənt/ *noun* a basement floor in a store where goods are sold cheaply □ **I'm selling this at a bargain basement price** I'm selling this very cheaply

bargain hunter /'bɑrgɪn ˌhʌntər/ *noun* a person who looks for cheap deals

bargaining /'bɑrgɪnɪŋ/ *noun* the act of trying to reach agreement about something, e.g., a price or a wage increase for workers

bargaining position /ˈbɑrgɪnɪŋ pə
ˌzɪʃ(ə)n/ *noun* the offers or demands
made by one group during negotiations

bargaining power /ˈbɑrgɪnɪŋ
ˌpaʊər/ *noun* the strength of one person
or group when discussing prices or
wage settlements

bar graph /ˈbɑr græf/ *noun* same as
bar chart

barrier /ˈbæriər/ *noun* anything which
makes it difficult for someone to do
something, especially to send goods
from one place to another □ **to impose
trade barriers on certain goods** to restrict the import of some goods by
charging high duty ○ *They considered
imposing trade barriers on some food
products.* □ **to lift trade barriers from
imports** to remove restrictions on imports ○ *The government has lifted trade
barriers on foreign cars.* □ **barrier to
entry into a market** something which
makes it difficult for a company to enter
a new market, e.g., start-up costs

barrier to entry /ˌbæriər tʊ ˈentri/
noun a factor that makes it impossible
or unprofitable for a company to try to
start selling its products in a particular
market (NOTE: Barriers to entry may be
created, for example, when companies
already in a market have patents that
prevent their goods from being copied,
when the cost of the advertising needed to gain a market share is too high,
or when an existing product commands very strong brand loyalty.)

barrier to exit /ˌbæriər tʊ ˈegzɪt/
noun a factor that makes it impossible
or unprofitable for a company to leave a
market where it is currently doing business (NOTE: Barriers to exit may be created, for example, when a company
has invested in specialist equipment
that is only suited to manufacturing
one product, when the costs of retraining its work force would be very high,
or when withdrawing one product
would have a bad effect on the sales of
other products in the range.)

barter /ˈbɑrtər/ *noun* **1.** a system in
which goods are exchanged for other
goods and not sold for money **2.** a system in which advertising space or time

is exchanged for goods from the advertiser ■ *verb* to exchange goods for other
goods and not for money ○ *They agreed
upon a deal to barter tractors for bar-
rels of wine.*

bartering /ˈbɑrtərɪŋ/ *noun* the act of
exchanging goods for other goods and
not for money

base /beɪs/ *noun* **1.** the lowest or first
position ○ *Turnover increased by 200%,
but started from a low base.* **2.** a place
where a company has its main office or
factory, or a place where a businessperson's office is located ○ *The company
has its base in London and branches in
all the European countries.* ○ *She has an
office in Madrid which he uses as a base
while traveling in Southern Europe.* ■
verb to set up a company or a person in
a place ○ *The European manager is
based in our London office.* ○ *Our overseas branch is based in the Bahamas.*

base line /ˈbeɪs laɪn/ *noun* the part of
promotional material that contains basic
information about the organization such
as its name and address

basement /ˈbeɪsmənt/ *noun* a section of a store which is underground

base rate /ˈbeɪs reɪt/ *noun* same as
bank base rate

base year /ˈbeɪs jɪr/ *noun* the first
year of an index, against which changes
occurring in later years are measured

basic /ˈbeɪsɪk/ *adjective* **1.** normal **2.**
most important **3.** simple, or from which
everything starts ○ *She has a basic
knowledge of the market.* ○ *To work at
the cash desk, you need a basic qualifi-
cation in math.*

basic commodities /ˌbeɪsɪk kə
ˈmɑdətiz/ *plural noun* ordinary farm
produce, produced in large quantities,
e.g., corn, rice or sugar

basic discount /ˌbeɪsɪk ˈdɪskaʊnt/
noun a normal discount without extra
percentages ○ *Our basic discount is
20%, but we offer 5% extra for rapid
settlement.*

basic industry /ˌbeɪsɪk ˈɪndəstri/
noun the most important industry of a
country, e.g., coal, steel or agriculture

basic necessities /ˌbeɪsɪk nə
'sesətiz/ *plural noun* the very least that
people need to live, e.g., food and clothing ○ *Being unemployed makes it difficult to afford even the basic necessities.*

basic price /ˌbeɪsɪk 'praɪs/, **basic
rate** /ˌbeɪsɪk 'reɪt/ *noun* the price of a
product or service that does not include
any extras ○ *This is a rather high basic
price.* ○ *Please make clear whether
$1,000 is the basic rate or whether it is
inclusive of spare parts.*

basic product /ˌbeɪsɪk 'prɒdʌkt/
noun the main product made from a raw
material

basics /'beɪsɪks/ *plural noun* simple
and important facts or principles ○ *She
has studied the basics of foreign exchange dealing.* □ **to get back to basics**
to consider the main facts or principles
again

basis /'beɪsɪs/ *noun* **1.** a point or number from which calculations are made ○
*We forecast the turnover on the basis of
a 6% price increase.* (NOTE: The plural
is **bases**.) **2.** the general terms of agreement or general principles on which
something is decided or done ○ *This
document should form the basis for an
agreement.* ○ *We have three people
working on a freelance basis.* (NOTE:
The plural is **bases**.) □ **on a short-
term**, **long-term basis** for a short or
long period ○ *He has been appointed on
a short-term basis.*

basket of currencies /ˌbæskət əv
'kʌrənsiz/ *noun* same as **currency
basket**

batch /bætʃ/ *noun* a group of items
which are made at one time ○ *This batch
of shoes has the serial number 25–02.* ■
verb to put items together in groups ○ *to
batch invoices* or *checks*

batch number /'bætʃ ˌnʌmbər/
noun a number attached to a batch ○
*When making a complaint always quote
the batch number on the packet.*

batch production /'bætʃ prə
ˌdʌkʃən/ *noun* production in batches

battle /'bæt(ə)l/ *noun* a fight □ **battle
of the brands** competition in the market
between existing product brands ○ *This*

*battle of the brands will lead to dramat-
ic price-cutting.*

Bayesian decision theory
/ˌbeɪziən dɪ'sɪʒ(ə)n ˌθɪəri/ *noun* a
method for helping decision-making,
often applied to new product development. The decision-maker is aware of
alternatives, can work out the probable
advantages or disadvantages of the alternatives, and makes up his or her mind
according to the value of the best alternative.

BDI *abbreviation* brand development
index

beginning inventory /bɪ'ɡɪnɪŋ
ˌɪnvənt(ə)ri/ *noun* on a balance sheet,
the closing stock at the end of one accounting period that is transferred forward and becomes the opening stock in
the one that follows (NOTE: The U.K.
term is **opening stock**.)

behavioral segmentation /bɪ
ˌheɪvjərəl ˌseɡmən'teɪʃ(ə)n/, **behav-
ioristic segmentation** *noun* the segmentation or division of the market according to customers' buying habits and
usage of a product ○ *Behavioral segmentation will mean there are several
distinct target audiences for our product.*

behind schedule /bɪˌhaɪnd
'skedʒəl/ *noun* late ○ *The agency is
way behind schedule with the promotional material.*

believer /bɪ'livər/ *noun* in the VALS
lifestyle classification, someone with
conventional values and strong principles who buy traditional, well-known
products

bells and whistles /ˌbelz ənd
'wɪs(ə)lz/ *plural noun* every possible
feature that has been included in an advertising campaign

below the line /bɪˌloʊ ðə 'laɪn/ *adjective, adverb* used to describe entries
in a company's profit and loss account
that show how the profit is distributed,
or where the funds to finance the loss
originate. ◊ **above the line 1**

below-the-line advertising /bɪˌloʊ
ðə laɪn 'ædvərtaɪzɪŋ/ *noun* advertising
which is not paid for and for which no

commission is paid to the advertising agency, e.g., work by staff who are manning an exhibition. Compare **above-the-line advertising**

below-the-line expenditure /bɪ ˌloʊ ðə laɪn ɪkˈspendɪtʃər/ *noun* **1.** payments which do not arise from a company's usual activities, e.g., severance payments **2.** extraordinary items which are shown in the profit and loss account below net profit after taxation, as opposed to exceptional items which are included in the figure for profit before taxation

benchmark /ˈbentʃmɑrk/ *noun* **1.** a standard used to measure performance (NOTE: a benchmark was originally a set of computer programs that was used to measure how well a particular computer performed in comparison with similar models) **2.** a point in an index which is important, and can be used to compare with other figures

benchmarking /ˈbentʃmɑrkɪŋ/ *noun* the testing of an audience's response using a benchmark

benchmark measure /ˈbentʃmɑrk ˌmeʒər/ *noun* the measure of a target audience's response at the beginning of an advertising campaign which are then compared to responses at the end of the campaign to test its efficiency

benefit /ˈbenəfɪt/ *noun* **1.** something of value given to an employee in addition to their salary **2.** the way in which a product or service will improve the quality of life of the purchaser, as opposed to "features" which highlight the particular important aspects of the product or service itself

benefit-cost analysis /ˈbenəfɪt kɑst/ *noun* same as **cost-benefit analysis**

benefit segmentation /ˌbenəfɪt ˌsegmənˈteɪʃ(ə)n/ *noun* the division of a market into segments according to the types of benefit obtained by the customer from a product such as ease of availability, light weight

berth /bɜrθ/ *noun* the place in a harbor where a ship can tie up ■ *verb* to tie up at a berth ○ *The ship will berth at Rotterdam on Wednesday.*

berth cargo /ˈbɜrθ ˌkɑrgoʊ/ *noun* cargo carried at especially low rates ○ *If we do not send the goods as berth cargo we will have to charge the buyer more.*

bespoke /bɪˈspoʊk/ *adjective* made to order or made to fit the requirements of the customer

bespoke tailoring /bɪˌspoʊk ˈteɪlərɪŋ/ *noun* the making of clothing for customers, to fit their individual measurements or requirements

best-before date /ˌbest bɪˈfɔr deɪt/ *noun* the date stamped on the label of a food product, which is the last date on which the product is guaranteed to be of good quality. ◊ **sell-by date, use-by date**

best-in-class /ˌbest ɪn ˈklæs/ *adjective* more effective and efficient, especially in acquiring and processing materials and in delivering products or services to customers, than any other organization in the same market or industrial sector

best practice /ˌbest ˈpræktɪs/ *noun* the most effective and efficient way to do something or to achieve a particular aim (NOTE: In business, best practice is often determined by benchmarking, that is by comparing the method one organization uses to carry out a task with the methods used by other similar organizations and determining which method is most efficient and effective.)

best-selling /ˌbest ˈselɪŋ/ *adjective* selling better than any other ○ *These computer disks are our best-selling line.*

Better Business Bureau /ˌbetər ˈbɪznɪs ˌbjʊroʊ/ an organization of local business executives that promotes better business practices in their town

bias /ˈbaɪəs/ *noun* the practice of favoring one group or person rather than another ○ *A postal survey will do away with bias.* ○ *The trainee interviewers were taught how to control bias and its effects.*

bid /bɪd/ *noun* **1.** an offer to buy something at a specific price. ◊ **takeover bid** □ **to make a bid for something** to offer to buy something ○ *We made a bid for the house.* ○ *The company made a bid* *for its rival.* □ **to make a cash bid** to offer to pay cash for something □ **to put in** *or* **enter a bid for something** to offer to buy something, usually in writing **2.** an offer to sell something or do a piece of work at a specific price ○ *She made the lowest bid for the job.* ■ *verb* to offer to buy □ **to bid for something** (*at an auction*) to offer to buy something □ **he bid $1,000 for the jewels** he offered to pay $1,000 for the jewels

bidder /'bɪdər/ *noun* a person who makes a bid, usually at an auction ○ *Several bidders made offers for the house.* □ **the property was sold to the highest bidder** to the person who had made the highest bid or who offered the most money □ **the tender will go to the lowest bidder** to the person who offers the best terms or the lowest price for services

bidding /'bɪdɪŋ/ *noun* the act of making offers to buy, usually at an auction □ **the bidding started at $1,000** the first and lowest bid was $1,000 □ **the bidding stopped at $250,000** the last bid, i.e. the successful bid, was for $250,000 □ **the auctioneer started the bidding at $100** the auctioneer suggested that the first bid should be $100

big box store /ˌbɪg bɑks 'stɔr/ *noun* a large retail superstore that sells a very wide range of merchandise from groceries to refrigerators or televisions

big business /ˌbɪg 'bɪznɪs/ *noun* very large commercial firms

big idea /ˌbɪg aɪ'diə/ *noun* the main new idea behind an advertising campaign, the aim of which is to attract potential customers

big picture /ˌbɪg 'pɪktʃər/ *noun* a broad view of a subject that takes into account all the factors that are relevant to it and considers the future consequences of action taken now (*informal*)

big-ticket /ˌbɪg 'tɪkət/ *adjective* costing a lot of money

big ticket item /ˌbɪg 'tɪkət ˌaɪtəm/ *noun* a large expensive item, e.g., a car, washing machine, etc.

bilateral /baɪ'læt(ə)rəl/ *adjective* between two parties or countries ○ *The*

minister signed a bilateral trade agreement.

bilateralism /baɪ'læt(ə)rəlɪz(ə)m/ *noun* a system whereby a country balances its trade with another ○ *With luck, bilateralism will put an end to the trade war.*

bill /bɪl/ *noun* **1.** a written list of charges to be paid ○ *The sales assistant wrote out the bill.* ○ *Does the bill include sales tax?* ○ *The bill is made out to Smith Inc.* ○ *The builder sent in his bill.* ○ *She left the country without paying her bills.* **2.** *U.K.* same as **check** ○ *Does the bill include service?* **3.** a written paper promising to pay money □ **bills payable (B** *or* **P)** bills, especially bills of exchange, which a company will have to pay to its creditors □ **bills receivable (B** *or* **R)** bills, especially bills of exchange, which are due to be paid by a company's debtors **4.** a piece of printed paper money ○ *a $5 bill* (NOTE: The U.K. term is **note** or **banknote.**) **5.** a draft of a new law which will be discussed in Congress **6.** a small poster □ **"stick no bills"** the unauthorized putting up of posters is prohibited ■ *verb* to present a bill to someone so that it can be paid ○ *The plumbers billed us for the repairs.*

billboard /'bɪlbɔrd/ *noun* **1.** a poster site of double crown size (30 x 20 inches) **2.** a large outdoor poster site (measuring 12 x 25 feet) ○ *The railroad track was lined with billboards specially set up for election propaganda.* ○ *A shortage of billboards has led to an increase in press advertising.* **3.** a short announcement which identifies an advertiser at the beginning, end, or in the breaks of a broadcast

billing /'bɪlɪŋ/ *noun* the work of writing invoices or bills

bill of entry /ˌbɪl əv 'entri/ *noun* the written details of goods that have to go through customs

bill of exchange /ˌbɪl əv ɪks'tʃeɪndʒ/ *noun* a document, signed by the person authorizing it, which tells another person or a financial institution to pay money unconditionally to a named person on a specific date (NOTE: Bills of exchange are usually used for payments in foreign currency.) □ **to accept a bill** to sign a bill of exchange to show that you promise to pay it □ **to discount a bill** to buy or sell a bill of exchange at a lower price than that written on it in order to cash it later □ **to retire a bill** to pay a bill of exchange when it is due

bill of lading /ˌbɪl əv ˈleɪdɪŋ/ *noun* a list of goods being shipped, which the transporter gives to the person sending the goods to show that the goods have been loaded

bill of sale /ˌbɪl əv ˈseɪl/ *noun* a document which the seller gives to the buyer to show that the sale has taken place

bill poster /ˈbɪl ˌpoʊstər/ *noun* a person who sticks up small posters. ◊ **fly poster**

bin /bɪn/ *noun* **1.** a large container **2.** a separate section of shelves in a warehouse

Bingo card /ˈbɪŋgoʊ kɑrd/ *noun* a printed card bound into a magazine, with a squared grid of numbers and letters which a reader can mark. The numbers refer to products advertised in the magazine, and the card is returned postage paid to the publisher, who passes the card to the advertiser for further response.

bipolar scale /ˌbaɪpoʊlər ˈskeɪl/ *noun* a scale used in questionnaires which contains two extreme points between which an interviewee can choose an answer

birth rate /ˈbɜrθ reɪt/ *noun* the number of children born per 1,000 of the population

black economy /ˌblæk ɪˈkɑnəmi/ *noun* goods and services which are paid for in cash, and therefore not declared for tax. Also called **hidden economy, parallel economy, shadow economy**

black list /ˈblæk lɪst/ *noun* a list of goods, people, or companies which have been banned

blacklist /ˈblæklɪst/ *verb* to put goods, people or a company on a black list ○ *Their firm was blacklisted by the government.*

black market /ˌblæk ˈmɑrkət/ *noun* the buying and selling of goods or cur-

rency in a way which is not allowed by law ○ *There is a flourishing black market in spare parts for cars.* □ **to pay black market prices** to pay high prices to get items which are not easily available

black-market economy /ˌblæk ˌmɑrkət ɪˈkɑnəmi/ *noun* an economy, or part of an economy, that functions by illegally trading goods that are normally subject to official controls

blank check /ˌblæŋk ˈtʃek/ *noun* a check with the amount of money and the payee left blank, but signed by the drawer

blanket agreement /ˌblæŋkɪt əˈgrimənt/ *noun* an agreement which covers many different items

blanket branding /ˌblæŋkɪt ˈbrændɪŋ/ *noun* giving a whole group or line of products the same brand name ○ *Blanket branding will make the brand a household name.*

blanket coverage /ˌblæŋkɪt ˈkʌv(ə)rɪdʒ/ *noun* advertising to the general public with no particular target audience in mind ○ *We will go for blanket coverage first and then see what kind of people buy the product.*

blanket insurance (cover) /ˌblæŋkɪt ɪnˈʃʊrəns ˌkʌvər/ *noun* insurance which covers various items such as a house and its contents

blanket refusal /ˌblæŋkɪt rɪˈfjuz(ə)l/ *noun* a refusal to accept many different items

bleed /blid/ *noun* an illustration or text which runs right to the edge of the printed page ■ *verb* to allow advertising space to run to the edge of a printed page

blind offer /ˌblaɪnd ˈɔfər/ *noun* a premium offer which is hidden away in an advertisement so as to find out how many readers read the advertisement

blindside /ˈblaɪndsaɪd/ *verb* to attack a competitor unexpectedly and in a way which is difficult to respond to

blind testing /ˌblaɪnd ˈtestɪŋ/ *noun* the practice of testing a product on consumers without telling them what brand it is

blister pack /ˈblɪstər pæk/ *noun* a type of packing where the item for sale is covered with a stiff plastic cover sealed to a card backing. Also called **bubble pack**

blitz /blɪts/ *noun* a marketing campaign which starts at full pressure, as opposed to a gradual build-up

blog /blɑg/ *noun* same as **web log** (*informal*)

blow-in /ˈbloʊ ɪn/ *noun* a postcard-size advertising card inserted in a magazine

blue-hair /ˌblu ˈher/ *adjective* referring to elderly women

blue-sky thinking /ˌblu ˌskaɪ ˈθɪŋkɪŋ/ *noun* extremely idealistic and often unconventional ideas

bluetooth /ˈblutuθ/ *trademark* a type of technology allowing for communication between cell phones, computers, and the Internet

blur /blɜr/ *noun* a period in which a great many important changes take place in an organization very quickly

blurb /blɜrb/ *noun* a brief description of a book, printed in a publisher's catalog or on the cover of the book itself

body copy /ˈbɑdi ˌkɑpi/ *noun* the main part of the text of an advertisement ○ *The body copy is OK, though the company's address doesn't need to be included.* ○ *The body copy on the poster is too long for passers-by to read it all.*

body language /ˈbɑdi ˌlæŋgwɪdʒ/ *noun* gestures, expressions, and movements which show what somebody's response is to a situation ○ *Trainee salespeople learn how to interpret a customer's body language.* ○ *The interviewer of prospective marketing managers observed the body language of the candidates very carefully.* ○ *The candidate claimed to be very confident about taking the job, but her body language was saying the opposite.*

bogof /ˈbɑgɔf/ *noun* the practice of giving free gifts to customers, e.g., one free item for each one bought. Full form **buy one get one free**

boilerplate /ˈbɔɪlərpleɪt/ *noun* a basic standard version of a contract that can be used again and again

bonded warehouse /ˌbɑndɪd ˈwerhaʊs/ *noun* a warehouse where goods are stored until excise duty has been paid

bonus /ˈboʊnəs/ *noun* an extra payment in addition to a normal payment

bonus offer /ˈboʊnəs ˌɔfər/ *noun* a special offer, especially one to launch a new product, which includes a bonus or free gift

bonus pack /ˈboʊnəs pæk/ *noun* a pack with extra contents or extra items for which no extra charge is made ○ *We are offering bonus packs in order to attract new customers to the product.*

bonus size /ˈboʊnəs saɪz/ *noun* an extra large size of pack sold at the usual price as a form of sales promotion ○ *Bonus size packs are 20% larger, but are sold at the normal price.*

bonus spot /ˈboʊnəs spɑt/ *noun* a free television or radio spot offered to an advertiser as part of an advertising package

book /bʊk/ *noun* **1.** a set of sheets of paper attached together □ **a company's books** the financial records of a company **2.** a statement of a dealer's exposure to the market, i.e. the amount which he or she is due to pay or has borrowed

book club /ˈbʊk klʌb/ *noun* a group of people who pay a small subscription and buy books regularly by mail order

booking /ˈbʊkɪŋ/ *noun* the act of reserving something such as a room or a seat ○ *Hotel bookings have fallen since the end of the tourist season.*

bookmark /ˈbʊkmɑrk/ *verb* to make a special mental note of somebody or something so that you remember them in the future ■ *noun* a software tool in a web browser that enables users to select and store webpages that they want to look at often and to access them quickly and conveniently

book sales /ˈbʊk seɪlz/ *plural noun* sales as recorded in the sales book

book token /'bʊk ˌtoʊkən/ *noun* a voucher bought in a store which is given as a present and which must be exchanged for books

book value /'bʊk ˌvælju/ *noun* the value of an asset as recorded in the company's balance sheet

boom /buːm/ *noun* a time when sales, production or business activity are increasing ○ *a period of economic boom* ○ *the boom of the 1990s* □ **the boom years** years when there is an economic boom ■ *verb* to expand or to become prosperous ○ *business is booming* ○ *sales are booming*

boom industry /'buːm ˌɪndəstri/ *noun* an industry which is expanding rapidly

booming /'buːmɪŋ/ *adjective* expanding or becoming prosperous ○ *a booming industry* or *company* ○ *Technology is a booming sector of the economy.*

boom share /'buːm ʃeə/ *noun* a share in a company which is expanding

BOP *abbreviation* balance of payments

borderless world /ˌbɔːdələs 'wɜːld/ *noun* the global economy in the age of the Internet, which is thought to have removed all the previous barriers to international trade

Boston Box /ˌbɒstən 'bɒks/ *noun* a system used to indicate a company's potential by analyzing the relationship between its market share and its growth rate (NOTE: The Boston Box was devised by the Boston Consulting Group in the 1970s to help companies decide which businesses they should invest in and which they should withdraw from. In this system businesses with a high market share and high growth rate are called stars, businesses with a low market share and low growth rate are called dogs, businesses with a high market share and a low growth rate are called cash cows and businesses with a low market share and a high growth rate are called question marks.)

Boston matrix /ˌbɒstən 'meɪtrɪks/ *noun* a type of product portfolio analysis, in which products are identified as stars, question marks, cash cows, or dogs. Full form **Boston Consulting Group Share/Growth Matrix**

bottle hanger /'bɒt(ə)l ˌhæŋər/ *noun* an advertisement in the form of a card which hangs round the neck of a bottle

bottleneck /'bɒt(ə)l,nek/ *noun* a situation which occurs when one section of an operation cannot cope with the amount of work it has to do, which slows down the later stages of the operation and business activity in general ○ *a bottleneck in the supply system* ○ *There are serious bottlenecks in the production line.*

bottom /'bɒtəm/ *noun* the lowest part or point □ **the bottom has fallen out of the market** sales have fallen below what previously seemed to be the lowest point □ **rock-bottom price** the lowest price of all ■ *verb* to reach the lowest point

bottom line /ˌbɒtəm 'laɪn/ *noun* **1.** the last line on a balance sheet indicating profit or loss **2.** the final decision on a matter ○ *The bottom line was that the work had to completed within budget.*

bottom price /'bɒtəm praɪs/ *noun* the lowest price

bounce back /ˌbaʊns 'bæk/ *verb* (*of emails*) to be returned to the sender because the address is incorrect or the user is not known at the mail server

bounce-back coupon /ˌbaʊns 'bæk ˌkuːpɒn/ *noun* a coupon offer made to existing customers in order to persuade them to continue purchasing the brand

box /bɒks/ *noun* a cardboard, wooden, or plastic container ○ *The goods were sent in thin cardboard boxes.* ○ *The watches are prepacked in plastic display boxes.* □ **paperclips come in boxes of two hundred** paperclips are packed two hundred to a box

boxed /bɒkst/ *adjective* put or sold in a box

box store /'bɒks stɔː/ *noun* a supermarket like a warehouse, with not much service or promotion, where goods are sold from their original packing cases ○

The school bought stationery in large quantities from the box store. ○ *With low overheads, box stores can offer cut-rate prices.*

boycott /'bɔɪkɑt/ *noun* a refusal to buy or to deal in certain products ○ *The union organized a boycott against* or *of imported cars.* ■ *verb* to refuse to buy or deal in a product ○ *We are boycotting all imports from that country.* □ **the management has boycotted the meeting** the management has refused to attend the meeting

brainstorming /'breɪnˌstɔrmɪŋ/ *noun* an intensive discussion by a small group of people as a method of producing new ideas or solving problems

brainstorming session /'breɪnˌstɔrmɪŋ ˌseʃ(ə)n/ *noun* a meeting to thrash out problems, where everyone puts forward different ideas

branch /bræntʃ/ *noun* the local office of a bank or large business, or a local store which is part of a large chain

    branch out *phrasal verb* to start a new but usually related type of business ○ *From car retailing, the company branched out into car leasing.*

branch manager /ˌbræntʃ 'mænɪdʒər/ *noun* a person in charge of a branch of a company

brand /brænd/ *noun* a make of product, which can be recognized by a name or by a design ○ *the top-selling brands of toothpaste* ○ *The company is launching a new brand of soap.*

brand awareness /'brænd əˌwernəs/ *noun* consciousness by the public of a brand's existence and qualities ○ *How can you talk about brand awareness when most people don't even know what the product is supposed to do?* ○ *Our sales staff must work harder to increase brand awareness in this area.*

brand building /'brænd ˌbɪldɪŋ/, **brand development** /'brænd dɪˌveləpmənt/ *noun* the expansion of the total awareness and sales of a brand in a given market

brand champion /'brænd ˌtʃæmpiən/ *noun* an executive who is passionate about a brand and promotes it vigorously worldwide

brand development index /ˌbrænd dɪˈveləpmənt ɪnˌdeks/ *noun* an index that compares the percentage of a brand's total sales in a given market to the percentage of the total population in the market. Abbreviation **BDI**

branded goods /ˌbrændɪd 'gʊdz/ *plural noun* goods sold under brand names

brand equity /'brænd ˌekwəti/ *noun* the extra value brought to a product by being a brand, both value as seen by the customer as well as financial value to the company

brand extension strategy /ˌbrænd ɪk'stenʃən ˌstrætədʒi/ *noun* the applying of an existing brand name to a new product

brand image /ˌbrænd 'ɪmɪdʒ/ *noun* an opinion of a product which people associate in their minds with the brand name. Brand image is developed and protected carefully by companies to make sure that their product or service is adopted by its target customers.

branding /'brændɪŋ/ *noun* the act of giving brand names to products or services. Branding is an important part of a marketing strategy as it helps organizations reach their key customers.

brand leader /ˌbrænd 'lidər/ *noun* the brand with the largest market share

brand life cycle /ˌbrænd 'laɪf ˌsaɪk(ə)l/ *noun* stages in the life of a brand in terms of sales and profitability, from its launch to its decline

brand loyalty /ˌbrænd 'lɔɪəlti/ *noun* the feeling of trust and satisfaction that makes a customer always buy the same brand of product

brand management /ˌbrænd 'mænɪdʒmənt/ *noun* directing the making and selling of a brand as an independent item

brand manager /ˌbrænd 'mænɪdʒər/ *noun* the manager or executive responsible for the marketing of a particular brand ○ *The brand manager and the production manager met to dis-*

cuss changes to be made to the company's leading brand of soap.

brand name /'brænd neɪm/ *noun* a name of a particular make of product

brand positioning /ˌbrænd pə 'zɪʃ(ə)nɪŋ/ *noun* the practice of placing a brand in a particular position in the market, so that it is recognizable to the public ○ *Intensive television advertising is a key part of our brand positioning strategy.* (NOTE: also called **product positioning**)

brand recognition /ˌbrænd ˌrekəg 'nɪʃ(ə)n/ *noun* the ability of the consumer to recognize a brand on sight

brand switching /'brænd ˌswɪtʃɪŋ/ *noun* the practice of changing from buying one brand to another, showing little brand loyalty ○ *We can't rely on steady sales with so much brand switching going on.* ○ *Brand switching makes shopping more fun for consumers.*

brand value /'brænd ˌvælju/ *noun* the value of a brand name

brand wagon /'brænd ˌwægən/ *noun* the tendency for marketers to see branding as the only way to promote a product

brandwidth /'brændwɪdθ/ *noun* the amount of customer recognition which a brand enjoys

brand X /ˌbrænd 'eks/ *noun* the anonymous brand used in TV commercials to compare with the named brand being advertised

breach /briːtʃ/ *noun* a failure to carry out the terms of an agreement

breach of contract /ˌbriːtʃ əv 'kɒntrækt/ *noun* the failure to do something which has been agreed upon in a contract

bread-and-butter line /ˌbred ən 'bʌtər laɪn/ *noun* a range of items which are found in all stores of one category, and which provide a solid basis of continuing sales

break /breɪk/ *noun* a pause between periods of work ○ *She keyboarded for two hours without a break.* ■ *verb* □ **break bulk** to split into small quantities for retail sale after having bought a large quantity □ **to break even** to balance

costs and receipts, but not make a profit ○ *Last year the company only just broke even.* ○ *We broke even in our first two months of trading.* (NOTE: [all verb senses] **breaking – broke – has broken**)

  break up *phrasal verb* to split something large into small sections ○ *The company was broken up and separate divisions sold off.*

breakeven analysis /ˌbreɪk'iːv(ə)n əˌnæləsɪs/ *noun* **1.** the analysis of fixed and variable costs and sales that determines at what level of production the break-even point will be reached ○ *The break-even analysis showed that the company will only break even if it sells at least 1,000 bicycles a month.* **2.** a method of showing the point at which a company's income from sales will be equal to its production costs so that it neither makes a profit nor makes a loss (NOTE: Break-even analysis is usually shown in the form of a chart and can be used to help companies make decisions, set prices for their products, and work out the effects of changes in production or sales volume on their costs and profits.)

breakeven point /ˌbreɪk'iːv(ə)n pɔɪnt/ *noun* the point or level of financial activity at which expenditure equals income, or the value of an investment equals its cost so that the result is neither a profit nor a loss. Abbreviation **BEP**

breaking bulk /ˌbreɪkɪŋ 'bʌlk/ *noun* the practice of buying in bulk and then selling in small quantities to many customers

break-up value /'breɪk ʌp ˌvælju/ *noun* **1.** the value of the material of a fixed asset ○ *What would the break-up value of our old machinery be?* ○ *Scrap merchants were asked to estimate the tractors' break-up value.* **2.** the value of various parts of a company taken separately

bricks-and-mortar /ˌbrɪks ən 'mɔrtər/ *adjective* conducting business in the traditional way in buildings such as stores and warehouses and not being involved in e-commerce. Compare **clicks-and-mortar**

bridge /brɪdʒ/ *verb* to print an advertisement across the center of a double-page spread in a magazine

brief /briːf/ *verb* to explain something to someone in detail ○ *The salespeople were briefed on the new product.* ○ *The managing director briefed the board on the progress of the negotiations.*

briefing /ˈbriːfɪŋ/ *noun* an act of telling someone details ○ *All sales staff have to attend a sales briefing on the new product.*

broadband /ˈbrɔːdbænd/ *noun* a data transmission system that allows large amounts of data to be transferred very quickly

broadcast /ˈbrɔːdkɑːst/ *noun* a radio or TV program ■ *verb* to send out on radio or TV

broadcasting media /ˈbrɔːdkɑːstɪŋ ˌmiːdiə/ *plural noun* media such as radio or TV

broadsheet /ˈbrɔːdʃiːt/ *noun* a large size of newspaper page (as opposed to tabloid). Compare **tabloid**

broadside /ˈbrɔːdsaɪd/ *noun* a large format publicity leaflet

brochure /brouˈʃʊr/ *noun* a publicity booklet ○ *We sent off for a brochure about vacations in Greece or about postal services.*

brochure site /ˈbrouʃə saɪt/ *noun* a website that gives details of a company's products and contact information

brochureware /ˈbrouʃʊrwer/ *noun* a website that provides information about products and services in the same way as a printed brochure (NOTE: The word is often used negatively to refer to electronic advertising for planned but nonexistent products.)

broken lot /ˌbroukən ˈlɑt/ *noun* an incomplete set of goods for sale ○ *We'll give you a discount since it is a broken lot, with two items missing.*

broker /ˈboukər/ *noun* **1.** a dealer who acts as a middleman between a buyer and a seller **2.** □ **(stock)broker** a person or firm that buys and sells shares or bonds on behalf of clients

brokerage /ˈbroukərɪdʒ/, **broker's commission** /ˌbroukərz kəˈmɪʃ(ə)n/ *noun* payment to a broker for a deal carried out

brown goods /ˈbraun gudz/ *plural noun* electrical equipment for home entertainment, e.g., television sets, hi-fi equipment. Compare **white goods**

browser /ˈbrauzər/ *noun* a piece of software that enables computer users to have access to the Internet and World Wide Web

bubble card /ˈbʌb(ə)l kɑrd/, **bubble pack** /ˈbʌb(ə)l pæk/ *noun* a type of packaging, where the item for sale is covered by a stiff plastic sheet sealed to a card backing

bubble pack /ˈbʌb(ə)l pæk/ *noun* same as **blister pack**

bubble wrap /ˈbʌb(ə)l ræp/ *noun* a sheet of clear plastic with bubbles of air in it, used as a protective wrapping material

bucket shop /ˈbʌkət ʃɑp/ *noun U.K.* **1.** a firm of brokers or dealers that sells shares that may be worthless **2.** a firm that sells cheap airline or other travel tickets (*informal*)

budget /ˈbʌdʒət/ *noun* **1.** a plan of expected spending and income for a period of time ○ *We have agreed on the budgets for next year.* **2.** □ **to balance the budget** to plan income and expenditure so that they balance ○ *The president is planning for a balanced budget.* ■ *adjective* cheap □ **budget prices** low prices ■ *verb* to plan probable income and expenditure ○ *We are budgeting for $10,000 of sales next year.*

budget account /ˈbʌdʒət əˌkaunt/ *noun* a bank account where you plan income and expenditure to allow for periods when expenditure is high, by paying a set amount each month

budgetary /ˈbʌdʒɪt(ə)ri/ *adjective* referring to a budget

budgetary control /ˌbʌdʒɪt(ə)ri kənˈtroul/ *noun* controlled spending according to a planned budget

budgetary policy /ˌbʌdʒɪt(ə)ri ˈpɑlɪsi/ *noun* the policy of planning income and expenditure

budgetary requirements /ˌbʌdʒɪt(ə)ri rɪˈkwaɪəməntz/ *plural noun* the rate of spending or income required to meet the budget forecasts

budget department /ˈbʌdʒət dɪˌpɑːtmənt/ *noun* a department in a large store which sells cheaper goods

budgeting /ˈbʌdʒətɪŋ/ *noun* the preparation of budgets to help plan expenditure and income

budget surplus /ˌbʌdʒət ˈsɜːpləs/ *noun* a situation where there is more revenue than was planned for in the budget

budget variance /ˌbʌdʒət ˈveəriəns/ *noun* the difference between the cost as estimated for a budget and the actual cost

building materials /ˈbɪldɪŋ məˌtɪriəlz/ *plural noun* materials used in building, e.g., bricks and cement

building permit /ˈbɪldɪŋ ˌpɜːmɪt/ *noun* an official document which allows someone to build on a piece of land

build-up approach /ˈbɪld ʌp əˌprəʊtʃ/ *noun* a method of calculating the budget for promotion by determining the tasks that have to be carried out and estimating the costs of performing them

built-in /ˌbɪlt ˈɪn/ *adjective* forming part of the system or of a machine ○ *The PC has a built-in modem.* ○ *The accounting system has a series of built-in checks.*

built-in obsolescence /ˈbɪlt ɪn ˌɒbsəˌles(ə)ns/ *noun* a method of ensuring continuing sales of a product by making it in such a way that it will soon become obsolete

bulk /bʌlk/ *noun* a large quantity of goods □ **in bulk** in large quantities ○ *to buy rice in bulk*

bulk breaking /ˈbʌlk ˌbreɪkɪŋ/ *noun* same as **breaking bulk**

bulk buying /ˌbʌlk ˈbaɪɪŋ/ *noun* the act of buying large quantities of goods at low prices

bulk carrier /ˌbʌlk ˈkæriər/ *noun* a ship which carries large quantities of loose goods such as corn or coal

bulk discount /ˌbʌlk ˈdɪskaʊnt/ *noun* a discount given to a purchaser who buys in bulk

bulk rate /ˈbʌlk reɪt/ *noun* a cheap rate offered to advertisers who take large amounts of advertising space

bulk shipment /ˌbʌlk ˈʃɪpmənt/ *noun* a shipment of large quantities of goods

bulky /ˈbʌlki/ *adjective* large and awkward ○ *The Post Office does not accept bulky packages.*

bulldog /ˈbʊldɒg/ *noun* the first edition of a daily newspaper

bulletin /ˈbʊlɪtɪn/ *noun* a short note, newsletter, or report, issued regularly ○ *Bulletins were regularly sent to the sales force.* ○ *The bulletin contained sales figures for the month.*

bulletin board /ˈbʊlɪtɪn bɔːd/ *noun* **1.** a board fixed to a wall where notices can be put up ○ *Did you see the new list of prices on the bulletin board?* **2.** a website that allows members of an interest group to exchange emails, chat online, and access software

bumper sticker /ˈbʌmpər ˌstɪkər/ *noun* an advertising sticker put onto the bumper of a car

bundle /ˈbʌnd(ə)l/ *verb* to market a package that contains various products or services at a special price

bundling /ˈbʌndlɪŋ/ *noun* putting several items together to form a package deal, especially offering software as part of the purchase of computer hardware

buppies /ˈbʌpiz/ *plural noun* young professional African-American people with relatively high incomes (NOTE: Short for **Black Upwardly-Mobile Professionals**)

burst /bɜːst/ *noun* a large number of advertisements for a product placed over a short period ○ *Shall we go for a burst or for a more prolonged campaign?*

business /ˈbɪznɪs/ *noun* **1.** work in buying, selling, or doing other things to make a profit ○ *We do a lot of business with Japan.* ○ *Business is expanding.* ○ *Business is slow.* ○ *Repairing cars is*

90% of our business. ○ *We did more business in the week before Christmas than we usually do in a month.* ○ *Strikes are very bad for business.* ○ *What's your line of business?* □ **to be in business** to run a commercial firm □ **on business** doing commercial work ○ *She had to go abroad on business.* ○ *The chairman is in Holland on business.* **2.** a commercial company ○ *He owns a small car repair business.* ○ *She runs a business from her home.* ○ *I set up in business as an insurance broker.* **3.** the affairs discussed ○ *The main business of the meeting was finished by 3 p.m.*

business address /ˈbɪznɪs əˌdres/ *noun* the details of number, street, and city or town where a company is located

business agent /ˈbɪznɪs ˌeɪdʒənt/ *noun* the chief local official of a labor union

business call /ˈbɪznɪs kɔl/ *noun* a visit to talk to someone about business

business card /ˈbɪznɪs kɑrd/ *noun* a card showing a businessperson's name and the name and address of the company he or she works for

business case /ˈbɪznɪs keɪs/ *noun* a statement that explains why a particular course of action would be advantageous or profitable to an organization (NOTE: A business case depends on the preparation and presentation of a viable business plan and is intended to weed out ideas that may seem promising but have no real long-term value to an organization.)

business center /ˈbɪznɪs ˌsentər/ *noun* the part of a town where the main banks, stores, and offices are located

business class /ˈbɪznɪs klæs/ *noun* a type of airline travel which is less expensive than first class and more comfortable than economy class

business community /ˈbɪznɪs kəˌmjunəti/ *noun* the business people living and working in the area

business computer /ˈbɪznɪs kəmˌpjutər/ *noun* a powerful small computer programmed for special business uses

business correspondence /ˈbɪznɪs kɔrɪˌspandəns/ *noun* letters concerned with a business

business correspondent /ˈbɪznɪs kɔrɪˌspandənt/ *noun* a journalist who writes articles on business news for newspapers

business cycle /ˈbɪznɪs ˌsaɪk(ə)l/ *noun* the period during which trade expands, slows down, and then expands again. Also called **trade cycle**

business efficiency exhibition /ˌbɪznɪs ɪˈfɪʃ(ə)nsi eksɪˌbɪʃ(ə)n/ *noun* an exhibition which shows products such as computers and word-processors which help businesses to be efficient

business environment /ˌbɪznɪs ɪnˈvaɪrənmənt/ *noun* the elements or factors outside a business organization which directly affect it, such as the supply of raw materials and product demand ○ *The unreliability of supplies is one of the worst features of our business environment.*

business equipment /ˈbɪznɪs ɪˌkwɪpmənt/ *noun* the machines used in an office

business expenses /ˈbɪznɪs ɪkˌspensɪz/ *plural noun* money spent on running a business, not on stock or assets

business game /ˈbɪznɪs geɪm/ *noun* a game, often run on a computer, in which individuals or teams compete to do business in an imaginary market ○ *Students on management courses are often asked to take part in business games to improve their decision-making skills.*

business gift /ˈbɪznɪs gɪft/ *noun* a present received by a customer, either attached to a product bought or given to him by the retailer or producer on proof of purchase of a minimum quantity of goods

business hours /ˈbɪznɪs ˌaʊrz/ *plural noun* the time when a business is open, usually 9.00 a.m. to 5.30 p.m.

business intelligence /ˈbɪznɪs ɪnˌtelɪdʒ(ə)ns/ *noun* information that may be useful to a business when it is planning its strategy

business letter /'bɪznɪs ˌletər/ *noun* a letter which deals with business matters

business mailing list /ˌbɪznɪs 'meɪlɪŋ lɪst/ *noun* a list of names and addresses of businesses

businessman /'bɪznɪsmæn/ *noun* a man engaged in business

business park /'bɪznɪs pɑrk/ *noun* same as **office park**

business plan /'bɪznɪs plæn/ *noun* a document drawn up to show how a business is planned to work, with cash flow forecasts, sales forecasts, etc., often used when trying to raise a loan, or when setting up a new business

business portfolio analysis /ˌbɪznɪs pɔrt'foʊlioʊ əˌnæləsɪs/ *noun* a method of categorizing a firm's products according to their relative competitive position and business growth rate in order to lay the foundations for sound strategic planning

business publication /'bɪznɪs ˌpʌblɪkeɪʃ(ə)n/ *noun* a magazine or newspaper which is only concerned with business matters, e.g., trade journals

business-to-business /ˌbɪznɪs tə 'bɪznɪs/ *adjective* full form of **B2B**

business-to-business advertising /ˌbɪznɪs tə 'bɪznɪs ˌædvərtaɪzɪŋ/ *noun* advertising aimed at businesses, not at households or private purchasers

business-to-consumer /ˌbɪznɪs tə kən'sumər/ *adjective* full form of **B2C**

business transaction /'bɪznɪs trænˌzækʃən/ *noun* an act of buying or selling

business unit /'bɪznɪs ˌjunɪt/ *noun* a unit within an organization that operates as a separate department, division, or stand-alone business and is usually treated as a separate profit center

businesswoman /'bɪznɪsˌwʊmən/ *noun* a woman engaged in business

busy season /'bɪzi ˌsiz(ə)n/ *noun* the period when a company is busy

buy /baɪ/ *verb* to get something by paying money ○ *to buy wholesale and sell retail* ○ *to buy for cash* ○ *She bought*

10,000 shares. ○ *The company has been bought by its leading supplier.* (NOTE: **buying – bought**) □ **buy one get one free** giving free gifts to customers such as one free item for each one bought. Abbreviation **bogof**

buy back *phrasal verb* to buy something which you sold earlier ○ *She sold the store last year and is now trying to buy it back.*

buy forward *phrasal verb* to buy foreign currency before you need it, in order to be sure of the exchange rate

buy in *phrasal verb* (*of a seller at an auction*) to buy the thing which you are trying to sell because no one will pay the price you want

buy-back agreement /'baɪ bæk əˌgrimənt/ *noun* an agreement that a producer will buy back goods from a distributor on a specific date if the distributor has not been able to sell them

buy classes /'baɪ ˌklæsɪz/ *plural noun* categories of buying based on how much the purchasing decisions of an organization have changed from the time of the previous purchase

buyer /'baɪər/ *noun* **1.** a person who buys □ **there were no buyers** no one wanted to buy **2.** a person who buys stock on behalf of a trading organization for resale or for use in production **3.** in B2B selling, a person who has made a commitment to buy, but has not finalized the deal

buyer expectation /ˌbaɪər ˌekspek'teɪʃ(ə)n/ *noun* same as **customer expectation**

buyer's guide /'baɪərz gaɪd/ *noun* a book or pamphlet which gives advice to purchasers on the prices, availability, and reliability of products or services

buyer's market /'baɪərz ˌmarkət/ *noun* a market where products are sold cheaply because there are few people who want to buy them. Opposite **seller's market**

buyer's risk /ˌbaɪərz 'rɪsk/ *noun* the risk taken by a buyer when accepting goods or services without a guarantee

buyer's surplus /ˌbaɪərz 'sɜrpləs/ *noun* an extra margin generated when an item is bought at a higher discount than usual ○ *When the brand manager realized how great the buyer's surplus was, she decided to lower the price of the product.*

buy grid /'baɪ grɪd/ *noun* a method used for objective assessment of competing products, especially when purchasing industrial supplies

buying /'baɪɪŋ/ *noun* the act of getting something for money

buying agent /'baɪɪŋ ‚eɪdʒənt/ *noun* a person who buys for a business or another person, and earns a commission ○ *Our buying agent is presently looking for materials in Panama.* ○ *The buying agent knows a whole network of suppliers around the country.*

buying department /'baɪɪŋ dɪ ‚pɑrtmənt/ *noun* the department in a company which buys raw materials or goods for use in the company

buying habits /'baɪɪŋ ‚hæbɪtz/ *plural noun* the general way in which some people select and buy goods

buying power /'baɪɪŋ ‚pauər/ *noun* the ability to buy ○ *The buying power of the dollar has fallen over the last five years.*

buying service /'baɪɪŋ ‚sɜrvɪs/ *noun* an agency which buys advertising space or time for its clients

buyout /'baɪaut/ *noun* the purchase of a controlling interest in a company

buy phases /'baɪ ‚feɪzɪz/ *plural noun* phases in the buying of industrial products. The main phases are the recognition of a want, the identification of a product, comparison with other competing products on the market, evaluation of possible courses of action, and final decision-making.

by-line /'baɪ laɪn/ *noun* the journalist's name which appears before a newspaper report

C

C2C commerce /ˌsi tə si ˈkɑmɜrs/ same as **consumer-to-consumer commerce**

CA *abbreviation* Consumers Association

cabinet /ˈkæbɪnət/ *noun* a display case for goods for sale, especially frozen food

cable television /ˌkeɪb(ə)l ˈtelɪvɪʒ(ə)n/, **cable TV** /ˌkeɪb(ə)l ˌti ˈvi/ *noun* a television service which a viewer receives via a cable from a particular station and pays for on subscription

caging /ˈkeɪdʒɪŋ/ *noun* the handling of cash and checks in a direct-mail operation

call /kɔl/ *noun* a visit ○ *The salespeople make six calls a day.* ■ *verb* □ **to call on someone** to visit someone ○ *Our salespeople call on their best accounts twice a month.*

> **call in** *phrasal verb* **1.** to visit ○ *Their sales representative called in twice last week.* **2.** to telephone to make contact ○ *We ask the reps to call in every Friday to report the week's sales.*

call bird /ˈkɔl bɜrd/ *noun* a low-priced product advertised to attract customers to the point-of-sale where they can then be sold more profitable goods ○ *We need a call bird to bring around more customers.*

call center /ˈkɔl ˌsentər/ *noun* a department or business that operates a large number of telephones and specializes in making calls to sell products or in receiving calls from customers to provide information or after-sales services (NOTE: A call center often acts as the central point of contact between an organization and its customers.)

call cycle /ˈkɔl ˌsaɪk(ə)l/ *noun* the time between a salesperson's visits to the same customer ○ *Because we now have more customers to deal with, call cycles are getting longer.*

call divert /ˌkɔl daɪˈvɜrt/ *noun* a telephone facility in which calls are automatically switched from one number to another

call frequency /ˈkɔl ˌfrikwənsi/ *noun* the number of times a salesperson visits a specific customer during a period of time

calling line identification /ˈkɔlɪŋ laɪn aɪˌdentɪfɪˌkeɪʃ(ə)n/ *noun* ♦ **computer telephony integration**

call letters /ˈkɔl ˌletərz/ *plural noun* a series of letters used to identify a radio station

call rate /ˈkɔl reɪt/ *noun* the number of calls per day or per week which a salesperson makes on customers

call report /ˈkɔl rɪˌpɔrt/ *noun* a report made by a salesperson after a visit to a customer ○ *In his call report, the sales rep explained why he was experiencing sales resistance.* ○ *The call reports have to be handed in each week to the sales manager.*

call to action /ˌkɔl tʊ ˈækʃən/ *noun* a prompt which encourages a potential Internet purchaser to do something such as click to see a range of colors

camp /kæmp/ *verb* □ **to camp on the line** to have to wait on hold for a long time until someone answers your telephone call

campaign /kæm'peɪn/ *noun* a series of coordinated activities to reach an objective

cancellation clause /ˌkænsə'leɪʃ(ə)n klɔːz/ *noun* a clause in a contract which states the terms on which the contract may be canceled

cancellation date /ˌkænsə'leɪʃ(ə)n deɪt/ *noun* the final date by which an advertisement must be canceled if the advertiser does not wish to proceed

canned presentation /ˌkænd prez(ə)n'teɪʃ(ə)n/ *noun* a standard sales presentation which some salespeople use all the time ○ *When trainee sales reps are not sure how to approach customers they fall back on canned presentations.* ○ *The sales manager feels that the artificiality of canned presentations makes them ineffective.*

cannibalization /ˌkænɪbəlaɪz(ə)m/, **cannibalism** *noun* a situation where a company launches a new product which sells well at the expense of another established product ○ *Though the new product sold well, the resultant cannibalization damaged the company's overall profits for the year.* ○ *Cannibalism became a real problem because the new product made the existing line seem obsolete.*

canvass /'kænvəs/ *verb* to visit people to ask them to buy goods, to vote, or to say what they think ○ *He's canvassing for customers for his hairdresser's store.* ○ *We've canvassed the staff about raising the prices in the staff restaurant.*

canvasser /'kænvəsər/ *noun* a person who canvasses

canvassing /'kænvəsɪŋ/ *noun* the practice of asking people to buy, to vote, or to say what they think ○ *door-to-door canvassing* ○ *canvassing techniques*

capital /'kæpɪt(ə)l/ *noun* **1.** the money, property, and assets used in a business ○ *a company with $10,000 capital* or *with a capital of $10,000* □ **capital structure of a company** the way in which a company's capital is made up from various sources **2.** money owned by individuals or companies, which they use for investment □ **movements of capital** changes of investments from one country to another □ **flight of capital** the rapid movement of capital out of one country because of lack of confidence in that country's economic future

capital account /'kæpɪt(ə)l ə,kaʊnt/ *noun* an account of dealings such as money invested in or taken out of the company by the owners of a company

capital allowances /ˌkæpɪt(ə)l ə'laʊənsɪz/ *plural noun* the allowances based on the value of fixed assets which may be deducted from a company's profits and so reduce its tax liability

capital assets /ˌkæpɪt(ə)l 'æsets/ *plural noun* the property, machines, and other assets which a company owns and uses but which it does not buy and sell as part of its regular trade. Also called **fixed assets**

capital city /ˌkæpɪt(ə)l 'sɪti/ *noun* the main city in a country, where the government is located

capital gain /ˌkæpɪt(ə)l 'geɪn/ *noun* an amount of money made by selling a fixed asset. Opposite **capital loss**

capital gains tax /ˌkæpɪt(ə)l 'geɪnz tæks/ *noun* a tax on the difference between the gross acquisition cost and the net proceeds when an asset is sold. Abbreviation **CGT**

capital goods /'kæpɪt(ə)l gʊdz/ *plural noun* machinery, buildings, and raw materials which are used to make other goods

capital-intensive industry /ˌkæpɪt(ə)l ɪn'tensɪv ,ɪndəstri/ *noun* an industry which needs a large amount of capital investment in plant to make it work

capitalism /'kæpɪt(ə)lɪz(ə)m/ *noun* the economic system in which each person has the right to invest money, to work in business, and to buy and sell, with no restrictions from the state

capitalist /'kæpɪt(ə)lɪst/ *adjective* working according to the principles of capitalism ○ *the capitalist system* ○ *the capitalist countries* or *world* ■ *noun* a person who invests capital in business enterprises

capitalist economy /ˌkæpɪt(ə)lɪst ɪ'kɑnəmi/ *noun* an economy in which each person has the right to invest money, to work in business, and to buy and sell, with no restrictions from the state

capitalize *verb*
capitalize on *phrasal verb* to make a profit from ○ *We are seeking to capitalize on our market position.*

capital levy /ˌkæpɪt(ə)l 'levi/ *noun* a tax on the value of a person's property and possessions

capital loss /ˌkæpɪt(ə)l 'lɔs/ *noun* a loss made by selling assets. Opposite **capital gain**

captain /'kæptɪn/ *noun* same as **channel captain**

caption /'kæpʃən/ *noun* a short description at the bottom of an illustration or photograph ○ *Having no caption at the bottom of the illustration created more reader interest in the product.* ○ *It took the copywriter days to think of a suitable caption for the photograph.*

captive audience /ˌkæptɪv 'ɔdiəns/ *noun* the people who cannot avoid being exposed to an advertisement ○ *Advertisers like to have their posters in subway stations where there is a large captive audience.*

captive market /ˌkæptɪv 'mɑrkət/ *noun* a market where one supplier has a monopoly and the buyer has no choice over the product which he or she must purchase

capture /'kæptʃə/ *verb* to take or get control of something □ **to capture 10% of the market** to sell hard, and so take a 10% market share □ **to capture 20% of a company's shares** to buy shares in a company rapidly and so own 20% of it

car assembly plant /ˌkɑr ə'sembli ˌplænt/ *noun* a factory where cars are put together from parts made in other factories

car card /'kɑr kɑrd/ *noun* an advertisement display card which is placed in a vehicle such as a bus, taxi, or train

card /kɑrd/ *noun* **1.** a small piece of cardboard or plastic, usually with information printed on it ○ *He showed his staff card to get a discount in the store.*

2. a printed piece of cardboard with information on it

card deck /'kɑrd dek/ *noun* a series of small cards, advertising different products or services, which are mailed as a pack in a plastic envelope to prospective customers

cardholder /'kɑrdˌhoʊldər/ *noun* an individual or company that has an account with a credit card company and whose name usually appears on the card

card-issuing bank /'kɑrd ɪʃuɪŋ ˌbæŋk/ *noun* same as **issuer**

card-not-present merchant account /ˌkɑrd nɑt ˌprez(ə)nt 'mɜrtʃənt əˌkaʊnt/ *noun* an account that enables businesses operating on the web to receive payments by credit card without the buyer or card being physically present when the transaction is made

card rate /'kɑrd reɪt/ *noun* an advertising charge which is based on the charges listed in a rate card, i.e. without any discounts. ◊ **escalator card, showcard**

careline /'kerlaɪn/ *noun* a telephone number which links people to services which can help them, such as social services departments, hospitals, or a similar service offered by stores to their customers

cargo /'kɑrgoʊ/ *noun* a load of goods which are sent in a ship or plane, etc. □ **the ship was taking on cargo** the ship was being loaded with goods □ **to load cargo** to put cargo on a ship

cargo liner /'kɑrgoʊ ˌlaɪnər/ *noun* a cargo ship with a regular schedule ○ *If the cargo liner's schedule doesn't suit us, we'll charter a ship.* ○ *The cargo liner makes regular trips between Manila and Seattle.*

cargo ship /'kɑrgoʊ ʃɪp/ *noun* a ship which carries cargo, not passengers

car mart /'kɑr mɑrt/ *noun* a second-hand car salesroom

carnet /'kɑrneɪ/ *noun* an international document which allows dutiable goods to cross several European countries by road without paying duty until the goods reach their final destination

carriage /'kærɪdʒ/ *noun* **1.** the transporting of goods from one place to another ○ *to pay for carriage* **2.** the cost of transportation of goods ○ *to allow 10% for carriage* ○ *Carriage is 15% of the total cost.* □ **carriage free** a deal where the customer does not pay for the shipping □ **carriage paid** a deal where the seller has paid for the shipping □ **carriage prepaid** a note showing that the transportation costs have been paid in advance

carrier /'kæriər/ *noun* **1.** a company which transports goods ○ *We only use reputable carriers.* **2.** a vehicle or ship which transports goods

carrier bag /'kæriər bæg/ *noun* a shopping bag made of strong paper

carrier's risk /ˌkæriərz 'rɪsk/ *noun* the responsibility of a carrier to pay for damage or loss of goods being shipped

carry /'kæri/ *verb* **1.** to take from one place to another ○ *a tanker carrying oil from the Gulf* ○ *The truck was carrying goods to the supermarket.* **2.** to keep in stock ○ *to carry a line of goods* ○ *We do not carry pens.* (NOTE: [all senses] **carries – carrying – carried**)

　　carry over *phrasal verb* **1.** □ **to carry over a balance** to take a balance from the end of one page or period to the beginning of the next **2.** □ **to carry over stock** to hold stock from the end of one stocktaking period to the beginning of the next

carrying /'kæriɪŋ/ *noun* transporting from one place to another ○ *carrying charges* ○ *carrying cost*

carry-over effect /ˌkæri 'oʊvər ɪˌfekt/ *noun* the effect of something after it has happened ○ *The carry-over effect of the currency devaluation was a good few years of lucrative exporting.* ○ *The political unrest in our key export markets had disastrous carry-over effects on our international marketing.*

cart /kɑrt/ *noun* an open vehicle or movable stand for goods

cartage /'kɑrtɪdʒ/ *noun* the activity of carrying goods by road

cartel /kɑr'tel/ *noun* a group of companies which try to fix the price or to regulate the supply of a product so that they can make more profit

carter /'kɑrtər/ *noun* a person who transports goods by road

carton /'kɑrt(ə)n/ *noun* a box made of cardboard ○ *a carton of milk*

case /keɪs/ *noun* **1.** a cardboard or wooden box for packing and carrying goods □ **six cases of wine** six boxes, each containing twelve bottles **2.** a typical example of something ○ *The company has had several cases of petty theft in the mail room.* **3.** reasons for doing something ○ *The negotiators put forward the union's case for a pay raise.*

case study /'keɪs ˌstʌdi/ *noun* a true or invented business situation used in business training to practice decision-making ○ *The marketing case study consisted of a long history of the company, the present situation, and a choice of strategic plans.* ○ *The case study was about territory-planning in a city in which there were a number of accounts of varying importance.*

cash /kæʃ/ *noun* **1.** money in the form of coins or notes **2.** the using of money in coins or notes □ **to pay cash down** to pay in cash immediately ■ *verb* □ **to cash a cheque** to exchange a check for cash

　　cash out *phrasal verb* to add up the cash in a store at the end of the day
　　cash up *phrasal verb U.K.* same as **cash out**

cashable /'kæʃəb(ə)l/ *adjective* able to be cashed ○ *A crossed check is not cashable at any bank.*

cash account /'kæʃ əˌkaʊnt/ *noun* an account which records the money which is received and spent

cash advance /ˌkæʃ əd'væns/ *noun* a loan in cash against a future payment

cash against documents /ˌkæʃ əgenst 'dɑkjəmənts/ *noun* a system whereby a buyer receives documents for the goods on payment of a bill of exchange

cash and carry /ˌkæʃ ən 'kæri/ *noun* a large store selling goods at low prices, where the customer pays cash and takes the goods away immediately

cashback

○ *We get our supplies every morning from the cash-and-carry.*

cashback /'kæʃbæk/ *noun* a discount system where a purchaser receives a cash discount on the completion of the purchase

cash balance /'kæʃ ˌbæləns/ *noun* a balance in cash, as opposed to amounts owed

cash book /'kæʃ bʊk/ *noun* a book in which all cash payments and receipts are recorded. In a double-entry book-keeping system, the balance at the end of a given period is included in the trial balance and then transferred to the balance sheet itself.

cash budget /'kæʃ ˌbʌdʒət/ *noun* a plan of cash income and expenditure

cash card /'kæʃ kɑrd/ *noun* a plastic card used to obtain money from an ATM

cash cow /'kæʃ kaʊ/ *noun* a product or subsidiary company that consistently generates good profits but does not provide growth

cash deal /ˌkæʃ 'dil/ *noun* a sale done for cash

cash desk /'kæʃ desk/ *noun U.K.* same as **checkout**

cash discount /ˌkæʃ 'dɪskaʊnt/ *noun* a discount given for payment in cash. Also called **discount for cash**

cash dispenser /'kæʃ dɪˌspensər/ *noun U.K.* same as **automated teller machine**

cash float /'kæʃ floʊt/ *noun* cash put into the cash box at the beginning of the day or week to allow change to be given to customers

cash flow /'kæʃ floʊ/ *noun* cash which comes into a company from sales (cash inflow) or the money which goes out in purchases or overhead expenditure (cash outflow) □ **the company is suffering from cash flow problems** cash income is not coming in fast enough to pay the expenditure going out

cash flow forecast /'kæʃ floʊ ˌfɔrkæst/ *noun* a forecast of when cash will be received or paid out

cash flow statement /'kæʃ floʊ ˌsteɪtmənt/ *noun* a record of a compa-

ny's cash inflows and cash outflows over a specific period of time, typically a year

cashier /kæ'ʃɪr/ *noun* **1.** a person who takes money from customers in a store or who deals with the money that has been paid **2.** a person who deals with customers in a bank and takes or gives cash at the counter

cash in hand /ˌkæʃ ɪn 'hænd/ *noun* money and notes, kept to pay small amounts but not deposited in the bank

cash items /'kæʃ ˌaɪtəmz/ *plural noun* goods sold for cash

cash offer /'kæʃ ˌɔfər/ *noun* an offer to pay in cash, especially an offer to pay cash when buying shares in a takeover bid

cash on delivery /ˌkæʃ ɑn dɪ'lɪv(ə)ri/ *noun* payment in cash when goods are delivered. Abbreviation **COD**

cash payment /'kæʃ ˌpeɪmənt/ *noun* payment in cash

cash purchase /'kæʃ ˌpɜrtʃɪs/ *noun* a purchase made for cash

cash register /'kæʃ ˌredʒɪstər/ *noun* a machine which shows and adds the prices of items bought, with a drawer for keeping the cash received

cash sale /'kæʃ seɪl/ *noun* a transaction paid for in cash

cash terms /'kæʃ tɜrmz/ *plural noun* lower terms which apply if the customer pays cash

cash till /'kæʃ tɪl/ *noun* same as **cash register**

cash transaction /'kæʃ trænˌzækʃən/ *noun* a transaction paid for in cash

cash voucher /'kæʃ ˌvaʊtʃər/ *noun* a piece of paper which can be exchanged for cash ○ *With every $20 of purchases, the customer gets a cash voucher for $2.*

catalog /'kætəlɔg/ *noun* a publication which lists items for sale, usually showing their prices ○ *an office equipment catalog* ○ *They sent us a catalog of their new range of products.* ■ *verb* to put an item into a catalog

catalog house /ˈkætəlɔg haʊs/ *noun* a company which mainly or solely sells by catalog

catalog price /ˈkætəlɔg praɪs/ *noun* a price as marked in a catalog or list

catalog store /ˈkætəlɔg stɔr/, **catalog showroom** /ˈkætəlɔg ˌʃoʊrʊm/ *noun* a store where customers can examine a catalog and choose goods from it

catchment area /ˈkætʃmənt ˌeriə/ *noun* the area around a store or shopping center, where the customers live

catchpenny /ˈkætʃpeni/ *noun* an article which has only superficial appeal, but which attracts buyers ○ *A closer look at the doll showed it to be just a shoddily made catchpenny.*

category extension /ˈkætɪg(ə)ri ɪk ˌstenʃən/ *noun* the applying of an existing brand name to a new product category

category management /ˈkætɪg(ə)ri ˌmænɪdʒmənt/ *noun* a system where managers have responsibility for the marketing of a particular category or line of products

cater /ˈkeɪtər/ *verb*
    cater for *phrasal verb* to deal with or provide for ○ *The store caters mainly for overseas customers.*

caterer /ˈkeɪtərər/ *noun* a person or company that supplies food and drink, especially for parties

catering /ˈkeɪtərɪŋ/ *noun* the activity of supplying food and drink for a party etc ■ *adjective* □ **catering for** providing for ○ *a store catering for overseas visitors*

catering trade /ˈkeɪtərɪŋ treɪd/ *noun* the food trade, especially businesses supplying food that is ready to eat

caveat emptor /ˌkæviæt ˈemptɔr/ *phrase* a Latin phrase meaning "let the buyer beware," which indicates that the buyer is responsible for checking that what he or she buys is in good order

CCTV /ˌsi si ti ˈvi/ *abbreviation* closed circuit television

ceiling /ˈsilɪŋ/ *noun* the highest point that something can reach, e.g., the highest rate of a pay increase ○ *to fix a ceiling for a budget* ○ *There is a ceiling of $100,000 on deposits.* ○ *Output reached its ceiling in June and has since fallen back.*

census /ˈsensəs/ *noun* an official count of a country's population, including such data as the age, sex, and occupation of individuals ○ *The market research department made a careful study of the census in different areas of the country to see where demand would be highest.* ◊ **distribution census**

center spread /ˌsentər ˈspred/ *noun* two facing pages in the center of a newspaper or magazine used by an advertiser for one advertisement ○ *The whole center spread for three days cost the advertiser $150,000.* ○ *The center spread was taken up with a large advertisement for a new model of car.*

central /ˈsentrəl/ *adjective* organized from one main point

centralize /ˈsentrəlaɪz/ *verb* to organize from a central point ○ *All purchasing has been centralized in our main office.* ○ *The company has become very centralized, and far more staff work at headquarters.*

centralized distribution /ˌsentrəlaɪzd ˌdɪstrɪˈbjuʃ(ə)n/ *noun* a system of distribution of goods to retail stores in a chain, from a central or local warehouse, so avoiding direct distribution from the manufacturer, and making stock control easier

centralized organizational structure /ˌsentrəlaɪzd ɔrgənaɪ ˌzeɪʃ(ə)n(ə)l ˈstrʌktʃər/ *noun* a method of organizing international advertising and promotion where all decisions are made in a company's central office ○ *The group benefits from a highly centralized organizational structure.*

centralized system /ˌsentrəlaɪzd ˈsɪstəm/ *noun* a system where advertising and other marketing activities are run from one central marketing department

central office /ˌsentrəl ˈɔfɪs/ *noun* the main office which controls all smaller offices

central purchasing /ˌsentrəl ˈpɜrtʃɪsɪŋ/ *noun* purchasing organized by a central office for all branches of a company

certificate of approval /səˌtɪfɪkət əv əˈpruːv(ə)l/ *noun* a document showing that an item has been approved officially

certificate of origin /sərˌtɪfɪkət əv ˈɔrɪdʒɪn/ *noun* a document showing where imported goods come from or were made

certified mail /ˌsɜrtɪfaɪd ˈmeɪl/ *noun* a mail service where the letters are signed for by the person receiving them ○ *We sent the documents (by) certified mail.*

certified public accountant /ˌsɜrtɪfaɪd ˌpʌblɪk əˈkaʊntənt/ *noun* an accountant who has passed the examinations of the AICPA and been given a certificate by a state, allowing him or her to practice in that state. Abbreviation **CPA**

CGT *abbreviation* capital gains tax

chain /tʃeɪn/ *noun* a series of stores or other businesses belonging to the same company ○ *a chain of hotels* or *a hotel chain* ○ *the chairman of a large do-it-yourself chain* ○ *He runs a chain of shoe shops.* ○ *She bought several garden centers and gradually built up a chain.*

chairman and managing director /ˌtʃermən ən ˌmænɪdʒɪŋ daɪ ˈrektər/ *noun* a managing director who is also chairman of the board of directors

challenger /ˈtʃælɪndʒər/ *noun* a company which challenges other companies which are already established in the marketplace

channel /ˈtʃæn(ə)l/ *noun* a means by which information or goods pass from one place to another □ **to go through the official channels** to deal with government officials, especially when making a request □ **channels of influence** the ways in which a company can influence consumers to buy their products, i.e. personal influence channels such as salesmen, or non-personal channels such as press advertising ○ *Owing to lack of capital there were not many channels of influence open to the company.* ○ *It was decided that personal selling was the most effective channel of influence for such a specialized product.*

channel captain /ˈtʃæn(ə)l ˌkæptɪn/ *noun* a business which controls or has the most influence in a distribution channel ○ *The production company became a channel captain by acquiring a number of important retail outlets.* ○ *Only businesses with enough financial resources to acquire other companies can become channel captains.*

channel communications /ˈtʃæn(ə)l kəmjunɪˌkeɪʃ(ə)ŋz/ *plural noun* communications to a marketing channel such as the company's sales force or to selected retailers

channel management /ˈtʃæn(ə)l ˌmænɪdʒmənt/ *noun* the managing of a marketing channel and the business partners which form part of it

channel members /ˈtʃæn(ə)l ˌmembərz/ *plural noun* the various companies which form a distribution channel

channel of distribution /ˌtʃæn(ə)l əv ˌdɪstrɪˈbjuʃ(ə)n/ *noun* same as **distribution channel**

channel power /ˈtʃæn(ə)l ˌpaʊər/ *noun* the influence which one company in a trading channel has over the other companies in the channel

channel strip /ˈtʃæn(ə)l strɪp/ *noun* the front edge of a shelf on which details of the products displayed can be put such as price, weight, code numbers

channel support /ˈtʃæn(ə)l səˌpɔrt/ *noun* support given to a marketing channel, that is to the people or companies that help to sell the product

character /ˈkærɪktər/ *noun* a letter, number, or sign used in typesetting, e.g., a letter of the alphabet, a number, or a punctuation mark

charge /tʃɑrdʒ/ *noun* **1.** money which must be paid, or the price of a service ○

to make no charge for delivery ○ to make a small charge for rental ○ There is no charge for this service or No charge is made for this service. □ **charges forward** charges which will be paid by the customer **2.** a debit on an account ○ It appears as a charge on the accounts. ■ verb **1.** to ask someone to pay for services later □ **to charge the packing to the customer, to charge the customer with the packing** the customer has to pay for packing **2.** to ask for money to be paid ○ to charge $5 for delivery ○ How much does he charge?

chargeable /'tʃɑrdʒəb(ə)l/ adjective able to be charged ○ repairs chargeable to the occupier

charge account /'tʃɑrdʒ ə,kaʊnt/ noun an arrangement which a customer has with a store to buy goods and to pay for them at a later date, usually when the invoice is sent at the end of the month (NOTE: The customer will make regular monthly payments into the account and is allowed credit of a multiple of those payments.)

charity /'tʃærəti/ noun an organization which offers free help or services to those in need ○ Because the organization is a charity it does not have to pay taxes. ○ The charity owes its success to clever marketing strategies in its fundraising.

charity shop /'tʃærəti ʃɑp/ noun U.K. a store organized by a charity, usually paying low rent and manned by volunteer staff, selling secondhand or specially bought products

chart /tʃɑrt/ noun a diagram displaying information as a series of lines, blocks, etc.

charter /'tʃɑrtər/ noun the action or business of hiring transport for a special purpose □ **boat on charter to Mr Smith** a boat which Mr. Smith has hired for a voyage. ■ verb to hire for a special purpose ○ to charter a plane or a boat or a bus

chartered /'tʃɑrtərd/ adjective □ **a chartered ship** or **bus** or **plane** a ship, bus or plane which has been hired for a special purpose

charterer /'tʃɑrtərər/ noun a person who hires a ship etc. for a special purpose

charter flight /'tʃɑrtər flaɪt/ noun a flight in an aircraft which has been hired for that purpose

chartering /'tʃɑrtərɪŋ/ noun the act of hiring for a special purpose

charter party /'tʃɑrtər ˌpɑrti/ noun a contract between the owner and the charterer of a ship

charter plane /'tʃɑrtər pleɪn/ noun a plane which has been chartered

cheap money /ˌtʃip 'mʌni/ noun money which can be borrowed at a low rate of interest

check /tʃek/ noun **1.** a list of charges in a restaurant **2.** a note to a bank asking them to pay money from your account to the account of the person whose name is written on the note ○ a check for $10 or a $10 check □ **check to the bearer** a check with no name written on it, so that the person who holds it can cash it □ **to endorse a check** to sign a check on the back to show that you accept it □ **to pay a check into your account** to deposit a check □ **the bank referred the check to the drawer** the bank returned the check to the person who wrote it because there was not enough money in the account to pay it □ **to sign a check** to sign on the front of a check to show that you authorize the bank to pay the money from your account □ **to stop a check** to ask a bank not to pay a check which has been signed and sent

checkbook /'tʃekbʊk/ noun a booklet with new blank checks

check card /'tʃek kɑrd/ noun a card issued by a bank to use in ATMs, but also used in some retail outlets

checking account /'tʃekɪŋ əˌkaʊnt/ noun an account in a bank from which the customer can withdraw money when he or she wants. Checking accounts do not always pay interest. ○ to pay money into a checking account

checklist /'tʃeklɪst/ noun a list of points which have to be checked before something can be regarded as finished, or as part of a procedure for evaluating something

checkout /'tʃekaʊt/ *noun* the place where goods are paid for in a store or supermarket ○ *We have opened two more checkouts to cope with the Saturday rush.*

checkout staff /'tʃekaʊt stæf/ *noun* the people who work at checkouts

check sample /'tʃek ˌsæmp(ə)l/ *noun* a sample to be used to see if a consignment is acceptable

cheque /tʃek/ *noun U.K.* same as **check**

cheque book /'tʃek bʊk/ *noun U.K.* same as **checkbook**

cheque card /'tʃek kɑːd/, **cheque guarantee card** /ˌtʃek ˌɡærənˈtiː kɑːd/ *noun U.K.* same as **check card**

cherry-picking /'tʃeri ˌpɪkɪŋ/ *noun* **1.** going from store to store or from supplier to supplier, looking for special bargains ○ *Cherry-picking has become so widespread that prices may be forced down.* **2.** the practice of choosing only the best or most valuable items from among a group

churn /tʃɜːn/ *verb* **1.** to persuade an investor to change the shares in his or her portfolio frequently because the broker is paid every time the investor buys a new share **2.** to be in a situation where many employees stay for only a short time and then leave and have to be replaced **3.** to buy many different products or services one after the other without showing loyalty to any of them (NOTE: Churning often happens when companies have competitive marketing strategies and continually undercut their rivals' prices. This encourages customers to switch brands constantly in order to take advantage of cheaper or more attractive offers.)

churn rate /'tʃɜːn reɪt/ *noun* **1.** a measurement of how often new customers try a product or service and then stop using it **2.** a measurement of how many stocks and bonds are traded in a brokerage account and how often they are traded

CIF, c.i.f. *abbreviation* cost, insurance, and freight

cinema advertising /'sɪnɪmə ˌædvətaɪzɪŋ/ *noun* advertising by short films or still messages on cinema screens

circular /'sɜːkjələr/ *adjective* sent to many people ■ *noun* a leaflet or letter sent to many people ○ *They sent out a circular offering a 10% discount.*

circularize /'sɜːkjələraɪz/ *verb* to send a circular to ○ *The committee has agreed to circularize the members of the society.* ○ *They circularized all their customers with a new list of prices.*

circular letter /ˌsɜːkjələr 'letər/ *noun* a letter sent to many people

circular letter of credit /ˌsɜːkjələr ˌletər əv 'kredɪt/ *noun* a letter of credit sent to all branches of the bank which issues it

circulate /'sɜːkjəleɪt/ *verb* **1.** □ **to circulate freely** (*of money*) to move about without restriction by the government **2.** to send information to ○ *They circulated a new list of prices to all their customers.* ○ *They circulated information about job vacancies to all colleges in the area.*

circulation /ˌsɜːkjə'leɪʃ(ə)n/ *noun* the number of readers of a newspaper or magazine. It is audited and is not the same as "readership."

circulation battle /ˌsɜːkjə'leɪʃ(ə)n ˌbæt(ə)l/ *noun* a competition between two papers to try to sell more copies in the same market

city /'səti/ *noun* a large town ○ *The largest cities in Europe are linked by hourly flights.*

city center /ˌsəti 'sentər/ *noun* the center of a large town, usually where the main shops and offices are situated

CKD *abbreviation* Completely Knocked Down products

claim form /'kleɪm fɔːm/ *noun* a form which has to be filled in when making an insurance claim

class /klæs/ *noun* a category or group into which things are classified

classification /ˌklæsɪfɪˈkeɪʃ(ə)n/ *noun* arrangement into classes or categories according to specific characteristics ○ *the classification of employees by ages or skills* ○ *Jobs in this organization fall into several classifications.*

classified advertisements /ˌklæsɪfaɪd ədˈvɜːtɪsmənts/, **classified ads** /ˌklæsɪfaɪd ˈædz/ *plural noun* advertisements listed in a newspaper under special headings such as "property for sale" or "jobs wanted" ○ *Look in the small ads to see if anyone has a filing cabinet for sale.*

classified catalog /ˌklæsɪfaɪd ˈkætəlɒg/ *noun* a catalog which groups articles into categories ○ *The classified catalog is divided into two sections, electrical and non-electrical products.* ○ *The department store publishes a classified catalog with a section for each department.* ○ *There is no entry for garden furniture in the classified catalog.*

classified directory /ˌklæsɪfaɪd daɪˈrekt(ə)ri/ *noun* a list of businesses grouped under various headings such as computer shops or newsagents

classified display advertising /ˌklæsɪfaɪd dɪsˈpleɪ ˌædvərtaɪzɪŋ/ *noun* advertising that, although it is classified, may also have individual features such as its own box border or the company logo

classify /ˈklæsɪfaɪ/ *verb* to put into classes or categories according to specific characteristics (NOTE: **classifies – classifying – classified**)

clause /klɔːz/ *noun* a section of a contract ○ *There are ten clauses in the contract of employment.* ○ *There is a clause in this contract concerning the employer's right to dismiss an employee.*

claused bill of lading /ˌklɔːzd bɪl əv ˈleɪdɪŋ/ *noun* a bill of lading stating that goods did not arrive on board in good condition

clean /kliːn/ *adjective* straightforward or with no complications

clean acceptance /ˌkliːn əkˈseptəns/ *noun* an unconditional acceptance of a bill of lading ○ *A clean accep-*tance ensures a quick and uncomplicated transaction.*

clean bill of lading /ˌkliːn bɪl əv ˈleɪdɪŋ/ *noun* a bill of lading with no note to say the shipment is faulty or damaged

clear /klɪr/ *verb* 1. to sell something cheaply in order to get rid of stock ○ *"Demonstration models to clear"* 2. to obtain a slot for broadcasting an advertisement

clearance /ˈklɪrəns/ *noun* 1. □ **to effect customs clearance** to clear goods through customs 2. □ **clearance of a cheque** the passing of a check through the banking system, transferring money from one account to another ○ *You should allow six days for check clearance.*

clearance sale /ˈklɪrəns seɪl/ *noun* a sale of items at low prices to get rid of stock

clear profit /ˌklɪr ˈprɒfɪt/ *noun* a profit after all expenses have been paid ○ *We made $6,000 clear profit on the deal.*

clerical error /ˌklerɪk(ə)l ˈerər/ *noun* a mistake made by someone doing office work

click /klɪk/ *verb* to press a key or button on a keyboard or mouse

clickable corporation /ˌklɪkəbl ˌkɔːpəˈreɪʃ(ə)n/ *noun* a company that operates on the Internet

click rate /ˈklɪk reɪt/ *noun* same as **click-through rate**

clicks and bricks /ˌklɪks ən ˈbrɪks/ *noun* a way of doing business that combines e-commerce and traditional shops

clicks-and-mortar /ˌklɪks ən ˈmɔːrtar/ *adjective* conducting business both through e-commerce and also in the traditional way in buildings such as stores and warehouses. Compare **bricks-and-mortar**

clicks-and-mortar business /ˌklɪks ən ˈmɔːrtər ˌbɪznɪs/ *noun* a business that uses both e-commerce and buildings such as stores to market its products

click-through /'klɪk θru/ *noun* an act of clicking on a banner or other on-screen advertising that takes the user through to the advertiser's website (NOTE: The number of times users click on an advertisement can be counted, and the total number of click-throughs is a way of measuring how successful the advertisement has been.)

click-through rate /'klɪk θru ˌreɪt/ *noun* a method of charging an advertiser for the display of a banner advertisement on a website. Each time a visitor clicks on a displayed advertisement which links to the advertiser's main site, the advertiser is charged a fee. A click-through rate of just a few percent is common and most advertisers have to pay per thousand impressions of their banner ad, sometimes written CTM (click-through per thousand). (NOTE: The click-through rate is expressed as a percentage of ad views and is used to measure how successful an advertisement has been.)

client /'klaɪənt/ *noun* a person with whom business is done or who pays for a service ○ *One of our major clients has defaulted on her payments.*

client base /'klaɪənt beɪs/ *noun* same as **client list**

clientele /ˌklaɪən'tel/ *noun* all the clients of a business or all the customers of a store

client list /'klaɪənt lɪst/ *noun* a list of clients of an advertising agency

clip /klɪp/ *noun* a short extract from a movie

clipping /'klɪpɪŋ/ *noun* a piece cut out from a publication which refers to an item of particular interest

clipping service /'klɪpɪŋ ˌsɜrvɪs/ *noun* the service of cutting out references to a client in newspapers or magazines and sending them to him

close *noun* the end of a sales negotiation ■ *verb* **1.** to bring something to an end □ **to close a sale** to end a sales negotiation and persuade a buyer to make a purchase **2.** (*business, store*) to stop doing business for the day ○ *The office closes at 5.30.* ○ *We close early on Sat-*

urdays. **3.** □ **to close a market** to restrict a market to one agent or distributor, and refuse to allow others to deal in the area **4.** to stop something being open

close down *phrasal verb* **1.** to shut a store, factory, or service for a long period or for ever ○ *The company is closing down its Denver office.* ○ *The accident closed down the station for a period.* **2.** (*of a store, factory, or service*) to stop doing business or operating

closed /kloʊzd/ *adjective* **1.** not open for business, or not doing business ○ *The office is closed on Mondays.* ○ *These warehouses are usually closed to the public.* **2.** restricted

closed circuit television /ˌkloʊzd ˌsɜrkɪt ˌtelɪ'vɪʒ(ə)n/ *noun* a system where TV is shown only to a small group of people within a limited area such as a building. Abbreviation **CCTV**

closed market /ˌkloʊzd 'mɑrkət/ *noun* a market where a supplier deals only with one agent or distributor and does not supply any others direct ○ *They signed a closed-market agreement with an Egyptian company.*

closing /'kloʊzɪŋ/ *adjective* **1.** final or coming at the end **2.** at the end of an accounting period ○ *At the end of the quarter the bookkeeper has to calculate the closing balance.* ■ *noun* □ **the closing of an account** the act of stopping supply to a customer on credit

closing bid /'kloʊzɪŋ bɪd/ *noun* the last bid at an auction, the bid which is successful

closing date /'kloʊzɪŋ deɪt/ *noun* the last date ○ *The closing date for tenders to be received is May 1st.*

closing-down sale /ˌkloʊzɪŋ 'daʊn ˌseɪl/ *noun* the sale of goods when a store is closing for ever

closing price /'kloʊzɪŋ praɪs/ *noun* the price of a share at the end of a day's trading

closing sentence /'kloʊzɪŋ ˌsentəns/ *noun* the last sentence in a marketing email which pushes the customer to take action

closing stock /ˌkloʊzɪŋ 'stɑk/ *noun* a business's remaining stock at the end of an accounting period. It includes finished products, raw materials, or work in progress and is deducted from the period's costs in the balance sheets. ○ *At the end of the month the closing stock was 10% higher than at the end of the previous month.*

closing technique /'kloʊzɪŋ tek ˌnik/ *noun* a special technique of persuasion used by salespeople to close sales ○ *The training manager demonstrated some presentation and closing techniques.* ○ *Most of our sales force develop their own selling methods, including closing techniques.*

closing time /'kloʊzɪŋ taɪm/ *noun* the time when a store or office stops work

closure /'kloʊʒər/ *noun* the act of closing

cluster /'klʌstər/ *noun* a group of things or people taken together

cluster analysis /'klʌstər ə ˌnæləsɪs/ *noun* a method whereby samples are classified into groups according to characteristics

cluster sampling /'klʌstər ˌsæmplɪŋ/ *noun* sampling on the basis of well-defined groups ○ *Cluster sampling was used in the survey since there were several very distinct groups in the population under study.*

clutter /'klʌtər/ *noun* a mass of advertising units shown together, so that any single advertisement or commercial tends to get lost

co-browsing /ˌkoʊ 'braʊzɪŋ/ *noun* the synchronization of two or more browsers so that their users can see the same web pages at the same time. Also called **page pushing**

code /koʊd/ *noun* a system of signs, numbers, or letters which mean something

code of practice /ˌkoʊd əv 'præktɪs/ *noun* the formally established ways in which members of a profession agree to work ○ *Advertisers have agreed to abide by the code of practice set out by the advertising council.*

coefficient of correlation /koʊɪ ˌfɪʃ(ə)nt əv ˌkɔrə'leɪʃ(ə)n/ *noun* a measurement of correlation or relationship between two sets of data on a continuum from −1 to +1

cognitive dissonance /ˌkɑgnətɪv 'dɪsənəns/ *noun* the feeling of dissatisfaction experienced by a person who cannot reconcile apparently contradictory information, as when making buying decisions or comparing purchases with the claims made for them in advertising

cognitive processing /ˌkɑgnətɪv 'prɑsesɪŋ/ *noun* the way in which a person changes external information into patterns of thought and how these are used to form judgments or choices

cold /koʊld/ *adjective* without being prepared

cold call /ˌkoʊld 'kɔl/ *noun* a telephone call or sales visit where the salesperson has no appointment and the client is not an established customer

cold list /'koʊld lɪst/ *noun* a list of names and addresses of people who have not been approached before by a seller

cold start /ˌkoʊld 'stɑrt/ *noun* the act of beginning a new business or opening a new store with no previous turnover to base it on

cold storage /ˌkoʊld 'stɔrɪdʒ/ *noun* the keeping of food in a cold store to prevent it or other goods from going bad

cold store /'koʊld stɔr/ *noun* a warehouse or room where food can be kept cold

collateral /kə'læt(ə)rəl/ *adjective* used to provide a guarantee for a loan ■ *noun* a security, such as negotiable instruments, shares, or goods, used to provide a guarantee for a loan

collateral services /kəˌlæt(ə)rəl 'sɜrvɪsɪz/ *plural noun* agencies which provide specialized services such as package design, production of advertising material, or marketing research

collect /kə'lekt/ *verb* **1.** to get money which is owed to you by making the person who owes it pay □ **to collect a debt** to go and make someone pay a debt **2.** to take things away from a place ○ *We have to collect the stock from the warehouse.* □ **letters are collected twice a day** postal workers take letters from the mail box to the post office for dispatch ■ *adverb, adjective* referring to a phone call which the person receiving the call agrees to pay for

collectibles /kə'lektɪb(ə)lz/ *plural noun* items which people collect, e.g., stamps, playing cards, or matchboxes

collecting agency /kə'lektɪŋ ˌeɪdʒənsi/ *noun* an agency which collects money owed to other companies for a commission

collocation hosting /ˌkɑlə ˌkeɪʃ(ə)n 'hoʊstɪŋ/ *noun* a (**hosting option**) in which a business places its own servers with a hosting company and controls everything that happens on its website. The hosting company simply provides an agreed speed of access to the Internet and an agreed amount of (**data transfer**), and ensures that the business's server is up and running.

color supplement /'kʌlər ˌsʌplɪmənt/ *noun* a magazine which accompanies a newspaper, usually with the weekend issue, printed in color ȯn art paper, and containing a lot of advertising ○ *The spring color supplements were mostly devoted to vacation advertising.* ○ *The clothing company bought advertising space on three pages of the color supplement.*

color swatch /'kʌlər swɑtʃ/ *noun* a small sample of color which the finished product must look like

color theory /'kʌlər ˌθɪəri/ *noun* knowledge about colors and their psychological effect on prospective customers

column /'kɑləm/ *noun* a section of printed words in a newspaper or magazine

combination commercial /ˌkɑmbɪ 'neɪʃ(ə)n kəˌmɜrʃ(ə)l/ *noun* a television advertisement which combines still pictures with action shots

combination rate /ˌkɑmbɪ'neɪʃ(ə)n reɪt/ *noun* a special rate or discount for advertising in two or more magazines

comfortable belongers /ˌkʌmf(ə)təb(ə)l bɪ'lɒŋərz/ *plural noun* a large group of consumers who are conservative in outlook and happy with their existence

commando selling /kə'mændoʊ ˌselɪŋ/ *noun* hard intensive selling ○ *Commando selling campaigns were started in all the new markets where the company's products were virtually unknown.* ○ *Commando selling is needed to obtain a reasonable market share in a market dominated by a powerful competitor.*

commerce /'kɑmɜrs/ *noun* the buying and selling of goods and services

commerce service provider /ˌkɑmɜrs 'sɜrvɪs prəˌvaɪdər/ *noun* an organization that provides a service that helps companies with some aspect of e-commerce, e.g., by acting as an Internet payment gateway

commercial /kə'mɜrʃ(ə)l/ *adjective* **1.** referring to business **2.** profitable □ **not a commercial proposition** not likely to make a profit ■ *noun* an advertisement on television

commercial agent /kəˌmɜrʃ(ə)l 'eɪdʒənt/ *noun* a person or business selling a company's products or services for a commission ○ *The commercial agent earned a 30% commission on sales he made.* ○ *As a commercial agent, she represents several companies.*

commercial aircraft /kəˌmɜrʃ(ə)l 'erkræft/ *noun* an aircraft used to carry cargo or passengers for payment

commercial artist /kəˌmɜrʃ(ə)l 'ɑrtɪst/ *noun* an artist who designs advertisements, posters, etc. for payment

commercial break /kəˌmɜrʃ(ə)l 'breɪk/ *noun* the time set aside for commercials on television ○ *The advertiser wished to specify exactly when in the commercial break the advertisements were to appear.* ○ *The advertising manager placed one advertisement in each commercial break of the day on the radio channel.*

commercial college /kə'mɜrʃ(ə)l ˌkɑlɪdʒ/ *noun* a college which teaches business studies

commercial counselor /kə
ˌmɜrʃ(ə)l ˈkaʊns(ə)lər/ *noun* a person
who advises on commercial matters in
an embassy ○ *The commercial counselor gave us sound advice on marketing
in the country he represented.*

commercial course /kəˈmɜrʃ(ə)l
kɔrs/ *noun* a course where business
skills are studied ○ *He took a commercial course by correspondence.*

commercial district /kəˈmɜrʃ(ə)l
ˌdɪstrɪkt/ *noun* the part of a town where
offices and shops are located

commercialization /kəˌmɜrʃ(ə)laɪ
ˈzeɪʃ(ə)n/ *noun* the act of making
something into a business run for profit
○ *the commercialization of museums*

commercialize /kəˈmɜrʃəlaɪz/ *verb*
to make something into a business ○ *The
vacation town has become unpleasantly
commercialized.*

commercial law /kəˌmɜrʃ(ə)l ˈlɔ/
noun the laws regarding business

commercial load /kəˌmɜrʃ(ə)l
ˈloʊd/ *noun* the amount of goods or
number of passengers which a bus,
train, or plane has to carry to make a
profit

commercially /kəˈmɜrʃ(ə)li/ *adverb*
in a business way □ **not commercially
viable** not likely to make a profit

commercial port /kəˌmɜrʃ(ə)l
ˈpɔrt/ *noun* a port which has only goods
traffic and no passengers

commercial protection /kə
ˌmɜrʃ(ə)l prəˈtekʃən/ *noun* the guarantee that rival products will not be advertised directly before or after a particular advertisement

commercial radio /kəˌmɜrʃ(ə)l
ˈreɪdioʊ/, **commercial TV** /kə
ˌmɜrʃ(ə)l tiˈvi/ *noun* a radio or TV station which broadcasts advertisements,
which help to pay for its programming
costs

commercial services /kəˌmɜrʃ(ə)l
ˈsɜrvɪsɪz/ *plural noun* services which
support trade, e.g., banking and advertising ○ *The recession has affected commercial services and the industries they
support and supply.*

commercial time /kəˈmɜrʃ(ə)l
taɪm/ *noun* the time that a television or
radio station devotes to advertising ○
*The TV station is extending its commer-
cial time in order to increase revenue.*

commercial traveler /kəˌmɜrʃ(ə)l
ˈtræv(ə)lər/ *noun* a salesperson who
travels round an area visiting customers
on behalf of his or her company (NOTE:
The modern term for a commercial
traveler is **sales representative**.)

commercial value /kəˌmɜrʃ(ə)l
ˈvælju/ *noun* the value that a thing
would have if it were offered for sale □
**"sample only – of no commercial val-
ue"** these goods are intended only as a
sample and would not be worth anything
if sold

commission /kəˈmɪʃ(ə)n/ *noun*
money paid to a salesperson or agent,
usually a percentage of the sales made ○
*She gets 10% commission on everything
she sells.* □ **he charges 10% commission** he asks for 10% of sales as his payment

commission agent /kəˈmɪʃ(ə)n
ˌeɪdʒənt/ *noun* an agent who is paid a
percentage of sales

commission rebating /kəˈmɪʃ(ə)n
ˌribeɪtɪŋ/ *noun* an advertising agency's
discounting of invoices for media costs
sent to clients, in effect taking them out
of its own commission or profit margin

commission rep /kəˈmɪʃ(ə)n rep/
noun a representative who is not paid a
salary but receives a commission on
sales

commitment /kəˈmɪtmənt/ *noun* **1.**
something which you have agreed to do
○ *The company has a commitment to
provide a cheap service.* **2.** money
which you have agreed to spend

commodity /kəˈmɑdəti/ *noun* something sold in very large quantities, especially a raw material such as a metal or
a food such as wheat

commodity exchange /kəˈmɑdəti
ɪksˌtʃeɪndʒ/ *noun* a place where commodities are bought and sold

commodity futures /kəˌmɑdəti
ˈfjutʃəz/ *plural noun* commodities
traded for delivery at a later date ○ *Sil-*

ver rose 5% on the commodity futures market yesterday.

commodity trader /kə'mɒdəti ˌtreɪdər/ *noun* a person whose business is buying and selling commodities

common /'kɒmən/ *adjective* **1.** happening frequently ○ *Unrealistic salary expectations in younger staff was a common problem they had to deal with.* **2.** belonging to several different people or to everyone

common carrier /ˌkɒmən 'kæriər/ *noun* a firm which carries goods or passengers, and which anyone can use

Common Market /ˌkɒmən 'mɑrkət/ *noun* an association of nations who join together in order to remove or reduce the barriers to trade between them

common ownership /ˌkɒmən 'oʊnəʃɪp/ *noun* a situation where a business is owned by the employees who work in it

common pricing /ˌkɒmən 'praɪsɪŋ/ *noun* the illegal fixing of prices by several businesses so that they all charge the same price

common stock /ˌkɒmən 'stɒk/ *noun* ordinary shares in a company, giving shareholders a right to vote at meetings and to receive dividends

communication /kəˌmjuːnɪ'keɪʃ(ə)n/ *noun* the passing on of views or information ○ *A house journal was started to improve communication between management and staff.* ○ *Customers complained about the lack of communication about the unexpected delay.* □ **to enter into communication with someone** to start discussing something with someone, usually in writing ○ *We have entered into communication with the relevant government department.*

communication objectives /kəˌmjuːnɪ'keɪʃ(ə)n əbˌdʒektɪvz/ *plural noun* objectives that a company tries to achieve through its advertising, e.g., creating awareness, knowledge, images, attitudes, preferences, or purchase intentions

communications /kəˌmjuːnɪ'keɪʃ(ə)nz/ *plural noun* **1.** the fact of being able to contact people or to pass messages ○ *After the flood all communications with the outside world were broken.* **2.** systems or technologies used for sending and receiving messages, e.g., postal and telephone networks **3.** messages sent from one individual or organization to another

communications channel /kəˌmjuːnɪ'keɪʃ(ə)nz ˌtʃæn(ə)l/ *noun* a means of passing messages from one individual or organization to another (NOTE: Communications channels include the spoken, written, and printed word, and media such as radio and television, telephones, video-conferencing and electronic mail.)

communication skills /kəˌmjuːnɪ'keɪʃ(ə)n skɪlz/ *plural noun* the ability to pass information to others easily and intelligibly

communications management /kəˌmjuːnɪ'keɪʃ(ə)nz ˌmænɪdʒmənt/ *noun* the managing of communications, so that advertising messages are sent efficiently to people who need to receive them

communications strategy /kəˌmjuːnɪ'keɪʃ(ə)nz ˌstrætədʒi/ *noun* planning the best way of communicating with potential customers

communication task /kəˌmjuːnɪ'keɪʃ(ə)n tæsk/ *noun* things that can be attributed to advertising, e.g., awareness, comprehension, conviction, and action, following the DAGMAR approach to setting advertising goals and objectives

communisuasion /kəˌmjuːnɪ'sweɪʒ(ə)n/ *noun* communication that is intended to persuade ○ *The sales reps are being trained in the subtleties of communisuasion.*

community /kə'mjuːnəti/ *noun* a group of people living or working in the same place

community initiative /kəˌmjuːnəti ɪ'nɪʃətɪv/ *noun* a particular scheme set up by a business organization with the aim of making a positive contribution to the life of the community by helping local people take practical action to solve their problems

community involvement /kə
ˌmjunəti ɪnˈvɒlvmənt/ *noun* the contribution that business organizations
make to the life of their local community in the form of community initiatives
(NOTE: Community involvement developed as a result of the growing emphasis on the social responsibility of business in the 1960s and 1970s and often
involves companies not only giving
money to finance local projects but
also sending trained staff to help set
them up.)

company /ˈkʌmp(ə)ni/ *noun* a business organization, a group of people organized to buy, sell, or provide a service,
usually for profit

company report /ˌkʌmp(ə)ni rɪ
ˈpɔːt/ *noun* a document that sets out in
detail what a company has done and
how well it has performed (NOTE: Companies are legally required to write annual reports and financial reports and
to submit them to the authorities in the
country where they are registered, but
they may also produce other reports
on specific subjects, for example, on
the environmental or social impact of a
project they are undertaking.)

comparative /kəmˈpærətɪv/ *adjective* which can be compared with something else

comparative advertising /kəm
ˌpærətɪv ˈædvətaɪzɪŋ/ *noun* advertising which compares a company's product with competing brands to its own advantage ○ *Disparaging remarks in comparative advertising were strongly
discouraged in the industry.* ○ *The company uses comparative advertising to
highlight the advantages of its products.*

comparative analysis /kəm
ˌpærətɪv əˈnæləsɪs/ *noun* an analysis
of different media and vehicle options
by an advertiser ○ *A tight advertising
budget made a thorough comparative
analysis essential.* ○ *Comparative analysis is difficult when the various media
offer such different advantages.*

comparative pricing /kəm
ˌpærətɪv ˈpraɪsɪŋ/ *noun* the indication
of a price by comparing it with another,
e.g., "15% reduction"

comparison /kəmˈpærɪs(ə)n/ *noun*
the act of comparing one thing with another ○ *Sales are down in comparison
with last year.*

comparison-shop /kəmˈpærɪs(ə)n
ʃɒp/ *verb* to compare prices and features of items for sale in different stores
to find the best deal

compete /kəmˈpiːt/ *verb* □ **to compete with someone** *or* **with a company**
to try to do better than another person or
another company ○ *We have to compete
with cheap imports from the Far East.* ○
*They were competing unsuccessfully
with local companies on their home territory.* □ **the two companies are competing for a market share** *or* **for a contract** each company is trying to win a
larger part of the market, trying to win
the contract

competence framework
/ˈkɒmpɪt(ə)ns ˌfreɪmwɜːk/ *noun* the
set of duties or tasks performed as part
of a job with the standards which should
be achieved in these duties

competing /kəmˈpiːtɪŋ/ *adjective*
which competes □ **competing firms**
firms which compete with each other □
competing products products from different companies which have the same
use and are sold in the same markets at
similar prices

competition /ˌkɒmpəˈtɪʃ(ə)n/ *noun*
1. a situation where companies or individuals are trying to do better than others, e.g., trying to win a larger share of
the market, or to produce a better or
cheaper product or to control the use of
resources □ **keen competition** strong
competition ○ *We are facing keen competition from European manufacturers.*
2. □ **the competition** companies which
are trying to compete with your product
○ *We have lowered our prices to beat
the competition.* ○ *The competition have
brought out a new range of products.*

competition-oriented pricing
/kɒmpəˌtɪʃ(ə)n ˌɔːrientɪd ˈpraɪsɪŋ/
noun the act of putting low prices on
goods so as to compete with other competing products

competitions /ˌkɒmpəˈtɪʃ(ə)nz/
noun a sales promotion which enables

consumers who can show that they have bought a minimum number of purchases to compete in a game ○ *The company uses competitions to sell off an excess supply of canned food.* ○ *Competitions involve prizes ranging from washing-machines to vacations abroad.* ○ *Competitions and free gifts make up a large part of the company's sales promotions.*

competitive /kəmˈpetətɪv/ *adjective* **1.** involving competition **2.** intended to compete with others, usually by being cheaper or better □ **competitive price** a low price aimed to compete with a rival product □ **competitive product** a product made or priced to compete with existing products

competitive advantage /kəmˌpetətɪv ədˈvæntɪdʒ/ *noun* same as **competitive edge**

competitive analysis /kəmˌpetətɪv əˈnæləsɪs/ *noun* analysis for marketing purposes that can include industry, customer, and competitor analysis and aims to discover how competitive an organization, project, or product is, especially by evaluating the capabilities of key competitors

competitive check /kəmˌpetətɪv ˈtʃek/ *noun* analyzing rival advertising levels and patterns, often conducted on the basis of data supplied by monitoring organizations

competitive demand /kəmˌpetətɪv dɪˈmænd/ *noun* demand for products that are competing for sales

competitive edge /kəmˌpetətɪv ˈedʒ/ *noun* an advantage that one company or product has over its rivals in the market ○ *Any competitive edge we have in this market is due to our good after-sales service.* ○ *Why does this product have the competitive edge over its rivals?* Also called **competitive advantage**

competitive forces /kəmˌpetətɪv ˈfɔrsɪz/ *plural noun* economic and business factors that force an organization to become more competitive if wants to survive and succeed

competitive intelligence /kəmˌpetətɪv ɪnˈtelɪdʒəns/ *noun* information, especially information concerning the plans, activities, and products of its competitors, that an organization gathers and analyzes in order to make itself more competitive (NOTE: Competitive intelligence may sometimes be gained through industrial espionage.)

competitively /kəmˈpetətɪvli/ *adverb* □ **competitively priced** sold at a low price which competes with the price of similar products from other companies

competitiveness /kəmˈpetətɪvnəs/ *noun* the fact of being competitive

competitiveness index /kəmˈpetətɪvnəs ˌɪndeks/ *noun* a list that uses economic and other data to rank countries in order according to the competitiveness of their industries and products

competitive parity /kəmˌpetətɪv ˈpærəti/ *noun* a method of budgeting marketing or promotional expenses according to the amounts being spent by competitors

competitive pricing /kəmˌpetətɪv ˈpraɪsɪŋ/ *noun* the practice of putting low prices on goods so as to compete with other products

competitive separation /kəmˌpetətɪv ˌsepəˈreɪʃ(ə)n/ *noun* a guarantee that rival products will not be advertised directly before or after a particular advertisement ○ *If our advertising campaign is to be really effective, we must insist on competitive separation.*

competitor /kəmˈpetɪtər/ *noun* a person or company that is competing with another ○ *Two German firms are our main competitors.*

competitor analysis /kəmˌpetɪtər əˈnæləsɪs/ *noun* the process of analyzing information about competitors and their products in order to build up a picture of where their strengths and weaknesses lie

competitor profiling /kəmˌpetɪtər ˈproʊfaɪlɪŋ/ *noun* same as **competitor analysis**

complaint /kəmˈpleɪnt/ *noun* a statement that you feel something is wrong ○ *complaints from the work force about conditions in the factory* ○ *She sent her* *letter of complaint to the managing director.*

complaints department /kəm'pleɪnts dɪˌpɑrtmənt/ *noun* a department in a company or store to which customers can send or bring complaints about its products or service

complaints management /kəm'pleɪnts ˌmænɪdʒmənt/ *noun* the management of complaints from customers

complementary /ˌkɑmplɪ'ment(ə)ri/ *adjective* which adds to or completes something else

complementary demand /ˌkɑmplɪment(ə)ri dɪ'mænd/ *noun* demand for two or more products that are needed together ○ *The demand for cars and gasoline was an example of complementary demand.*

complementary goods /ˌkɑmplɪment(ə)ri 'gʊdz/, **complementary products** /ˌkɑmplɪment(ə)ri 'prɑdʌkts/ *plural noun* a product for which demand is dependent on the demand for another product

complementary supply /ˌkɑmplɪment(ə)ri sə'plaɪ/ *noun* the supply of two or more products from the same production process

complementor /'kɑmplɪmentər/ *noun* a company that makes something that your product needs in order to function successfully. For example, software companies are complementors to computer companies. (NOTE: Software companies, for example, are complementors to computer companies.)

Completely Knocked Down products /kəmˌplit(ə)li nɑkt daʊn 'prɑdʌktz/ *plural noun* products which are sold in pieces, which the purchaser has to assemble, and are therefore sold at reasonably low prices ○ *Many low-income buyers buy CKD products.* ○ *CKD products are popular with DIY enthusiasts.* Abbreviation **CKD products**

compliance documentation /kəm'plaɪəns dɑkjˌmenˌteɪʃ(ə)n/ *noun* documents that a company has to publish when it issues shares in order to comply with the regulations governing share issues

compliance officer /kəm'plaɪəns ˌɔfɪsər/ *noun* an employee of a financial organization whose job is to make sure that the organization complies with the regulations governing its business

complimentary /ˌkɑmplɪ'ment(ə)ri/ *adjective* free

complimentary ticket /ˌkɑmplɪment(ə)ri 'tɪkət/ *noun* a free ticket, given as a present

compliments slip /'kɑmplɪmənts slɪp/ *noun* a piece of paper with the name of the company printed on it, sent with documents or gifts etc. instead of a letter

component /kəm'poʊnənt/ *noun* a piece of machinery or a part which will be put into a final product ○ *The assembly line stopped because the supply of a vital component was delayed.*

components factory /kəm'poʊnənts ˌfækt(ə)ri/ *noun* a factory which makes parts which are used in other factories to make finished products

composite demand /'kɑmpəzɪt dɪˌmænd/ *noun* the total demand for a product that has many uses ○ *Composite demand for the construction equipment came from construction companies and DIY enthusiasts.*

computer /kəm'pjutər/ *noun* an electronic machine which calculates or stores information and processes it automatically

computer bureau /kəm'pjutər ˌbjʊroʊ/ *noun* an office which offers to do work on its computers for companies which do not own their own computers

computer department /kəm'pjutər dɪˌpɑrtmənt/ *noun* a department in a company which manages the company's computers

computer error /kəmˌpjutər 'erər/ *noun* a mistake made by a computer

computer file /kəm'pjutər faɪl/ *noun* a section of information on a computer, e.g., the payroll, list of addresses, or list of customer accounts

computer hardware /kəmˌpjutər 'hɑrdwer/ *noun* machines used in data processing, including the computers and printers, but not the programs

computerize /kəmˈpjutəraɪz/ *verb* to change something from a manual system to one using computers ○ *We have computerized all our records.* ○ *Stock control is now completely computerized.*

computerized /kəmˈpjutəraɪzd/ *adjective* carried out by computers ○ *a computerized invoicing or filing system*

computer language /kəmˈpjutər ˌlæŋgwɪdʒ/ *noun* a system of signs, letters, and words used to instruct a computer

computer listing /kəmˌpjutər ˈlɪstɪŋ/ *noun* a printout of a list of items taken from data stored in a computer

computer magazine /kəmˈpjutər ˌmægəzin/ *noun* a magazine with articles on computers and programs

computer manager /kəmˈpjutər ˌmænɪdʒər/ *noun* a person in charge of a computer department

computer network /kəmˌpjutər ˈnetwɜrk/ *noun* a computer system where several PCs are linked so that they all draw on the same database

computer-readable /kəmˌpjutər ˈridəb(ə)l/ *adjective* able to be read and understood by a computer ○ *computer-readable codes*

computer run /kəmˈpjutər rʌn/ *noun* a period of work done by a computer

computer services /kəmˌpjutər ˈsɜrvɪsɪz/ *plural noun* work using a computer, done by a computer bureau

computer system /kəmˈpjutər ˌsɪstəm/ *noun* a set of programs, commands, etc., which run a computer

computer telephony integration /kəmˌpjutər təˌlefəni ˌɪntɪˈgreɪʃ(ə)n/ *noun* a technology that links computers and telephones and enables computers to dial telephone numbers and send and receive messages (NOTE: One product of computer telephony integration is calling line identification, which identifies the telephone number a customer is calling from, searches the customer database to identify the caller, and displays his or her account on a computer screen.)

computer time /kəmˈpjutər taɪm/ *noun* the time when a computer is being used, paid for at an hourly rate

computer worm /kəmˈpjutər wɜrm/ *noun* a type of computer (**virus**) that does damage by making as many copies of itself as it can as quickly in order to clog up communication channels on the Internet

computing /kəmˈpjutɪŋ/ *noun* the operating of computers

computing speed /kəmˈpjutɪŋ spid/ *noun* the speed at which a computer calculates

concentrated marketing /ˌkɑnsəntreɪtɪd ˈmɑrkətɪŋ/, **concentrated segmentation** /ˌkɑnsəntreɪtɪd ˌsegmənˈteɪʃ(ə)n/ *noun* niche marketing, the promotion of a product aimed at one particular area of the market ○ *When it became obvious that the general public were interested in our product, we switched from concentrated marketing to a much broader approach.* ◊ **differentiated marketing strategy, undifferentiated product**

concentration /ˌkɑnsənˈtreɪʃ(ə)n/ *noun* the degree to which a small number of businesses control a large section of the market ○ *Too much concentration created resentment among small businesses trying to enter the market.* ○ *Concentration has meant too little competition and therefore higher prices to the consumer.*

concept /ˈkɑnsept/ *noun* an idea

concept testing /ˈkɑnsept ˌtestɪŋ/ *noun* the evaluation of a new product idea, usually by consulting representatives from all the main departments in a company, and/or by interviewing a sample of consumers ○ *The new product idea did not survive concept testing because it didn't answer an existing demand.* ○ *After thorough concept testing the idea of a disposable pen was rejected as the company's production capacity was too limited.*

concession /kənˈseʃ(ə)n/ *noun* **1.** the right to use someone else's property for business purposes **2.** the right to be the only seller of a product in a place ○ *She runs a jewelry concession in a department store.* **3.** the act of allowing something to be done, which is not normally done ○ *The union obtained some important concessions from management during negotiations.*

concessionaire /kən͵seʃə'neər/ *noun* a person or business that has the right to be the only seller of a product in a place

concession close /kən'seʃ(ə)n klouz/ *noun* the act of offering a concession to a potential buyer in order to close a sale ○ *The trainee sales reps were told to resort to concession closes only when meeting with strong sales resistance.* ○ *A full morning's bargaining finally ended with a concession close.*

condition /kən'dɪʃ(ə)n/ *noun* something which has to be carried out as part of a contract or which has to be agreed before a contract becomes valid □ **on condition that** provided that ○ *They were granted the lease on condition that they paid the legal costs.*

conditional /kən'dɪʃ(ə)n(ə)l/ *adjective* provided that specific conditions are taken into account □ **to give a conditional acceptance** to accept, provided that specific things happen or that specific terms apply □ **the offer is conditional on the board's acceptance** the offer is only valid provided the board accepts

conditional offer /kən͵dɪʃ(ə)nəl 'ɔfər/ *noun* an offer to buy provided that specific terms apply

conditions of sale /kən͵dɪʃ(ə)nz əv 'seɪl/ *plural noun* agreed ways in which a sale takes place, e.g., discounts or credit terms

conference /'kɑnf(ə)rəns/ *noun* a meeting of people to discuss problems ○ *Many useful tips can be picked up at a sales conference.* ○ *The conference of HR managers included talks on payment and recruitment policies.* □ **to be in conference** to be in a meeting

conference call /'kɑnf(ə)rəns kɔl/ *noun* a telephone call that connects three or more lines so that people in dif-

ferent places can talk to one another (NOTE: Conference calls reduce the cost of meetings by making it unnecessary for the participants to spend time and money on getting together in one place.)

confidence /'kɑnfɪd(ə)ns/ *noun* the state of feeling sure or being certain ○ *The sales teams do not have much confidence in their manager.* ○ *The board has total confidence in the managing director.*

confidence level /'kɑnfɪd(ə)ns ͵lev(ə)l/ *noun* a measurement, shown as a percentage, of how reliable or accurate the results of a survey can be expected to be

confidentiality agreement /͵kɑnfɪdenʃi'æləti ə͵grimənt/ *noun* an agreement in which an organization that has important information about the plans and activities of another organization promises not to pass that information on to outsiders (NOTE: Confidentiality agreements are often used when someone is planning to buy a company and is given access to confidential information and in partnerships and benchmarking programs.)

confirm /kən'fɜrm/ *verb* to say again that something agreed before is correct ○ *to confirm a hotel reservation* or *a ticket* or *an agreement* or *a booking* □ **to confirm someone in a job** to say that someone is now permanently in the job

confirmation /͵kɑnfə'meɪʃ(ə)n/ *noun* **1.** the act of making certain □ **confirmation of a booking** the act of checking that a booking is certain **2.** a document which confirms something ○ *She received confirmation from the bank that the deeds had been deposited.*

confirmed credit /kən͵fɜrmd 'kredɪt/ *noun* credit that is official and binding

confirming house /kən'fɜrmɪŋ haʊs/ *noun* an organization that confirms a buyer's order with a supplier and makes transportation arrangements ○ *A reputable confirming house acted for the buyers of the machinery.* ○ *We will need a confirming house to arrange for* *a new supply of office furniture to be delivered to our store by December.*

conflict of interest /ˌkɒnflɪkt əv ˈɪntrəst/ *noun* a situation where a person or firm may profit personally from decisions taken in an official capacity

conglomerate /kənˈglɒmərət/ *noun* a group of subsidiary companies linked together and forming a group, each making very different types of products

conjoint analysis /kənˌdʒɔɪnt əˈnæləsɪs/ *noun* a research method aimed at discovering the best combination of features for a product or service, e.g., price and size

connectivity /ˌkɒnekˈtɪvəti/ *noun* the ability of an electronic product to connect with other similar products, or the extent to which individuals, companies and countries can connect with one another electronically

consign /kənˈsaɪn/ *verb* □ **to consign goods to someone** to send goods to someone for them to use or to sell for you

consignation /ˌkɒnsaɪˈneɪʃ(ə)n/ *noun* the act of consigning

consignee /ˌkɒnsaɪˈniː/ *noun* a person who receives goods from someone for their own use or to sell for the sender

consignment /kənˈsaɪnmənt/ *noun* the sending of goods to someone who will sell them for you □ **goods on consignment** goods kept for another company to be sold on their behalf for a commission

consignment note /kənˈsaɪnmənt nəʊt/ *noun* a note saying that goods have been sent

consignor /kənˈsaɪnər/ *noun* a person who consigns goods to someone

consolidate /kənˈsɒlɪdeɪt/ *verb* **1.** to include the accounts of several subsidiary companies as well as the holding company in a single set of accounts **2.** to group goods together for shipping

consolidated shipment /kənˌsɒlɪdeɪtɪd ˈʃɪpmənt/ *noun* a single shipment of goods from different companies grouped together

consolidation /kənˌsɒlɪˈdeɪʃ(ə)n/ *noun* the grouping together of goods for shipping

consolidator /kənˈsɒlɪdeɪtər/ *noun* a firm which groups together orders from different companies into one shipment

consortium /kənˈsɔːtiəm/ *noun* a group of companies which work together ○ *A consortium of Canadian companies* or *A Canadian consortium has tendered for the job.* (NOTE: The plural is **consortia**.)

conspicuous consumption /kənˌspɪkjuəs kənˈsʌmpʃən/ *noun* the consumption of goods for show or to get approval, rather than because they are useful

consult /kənˈsʌlt/ *verb* to ask an expert for advice ○ *We consulted our accountant about our tax.*

consultancy /kənˈsʌltənsi/ *noun* the act of giving specialist advice ○ *a consultancy firm* ○ *She offers a consultancy service.*

consultant /kənˈsʌltənt/ *noun* a specialist who gives advice ○ *an engineering consultant* ○ *a management consultant* ○ *a tax consultant*

consulting /kənˈsʌltɪŋ/ *adjective* giving specialist advice ○ *a consulting engineer*

consumable goods /kənˌsuːməb(ə)l ˈgʊdz/ *plural noun* goods which are bought by members of the public and not by companies. Also called **consumer goods, consumables**

consumables /kənˈsuːməb(ə)lz/ *plural noun* same as **consumable goods**

consumer /kənˈsuːmər/ *noun* a person or company that buys and uses goods and services ○ *Gas consumers are protesting at the increase in prices.* ○ *The factory is a heavy consumer of water.*

consumer advertising /kənˈsuːmər ˌædvətaɪzɪŋ/ *noun* advertising direct to individual consumers, as opposed to businesses

consumer cooperative /kən
ˌsuːmər koʊˈɑp(ə)rətɪv/ *noun* a retailing business owned by consumers who
share in its profits

consumer council /kənˌsuːmər
ˈkaʊns(ə)l/ *noun* a group representing
the interests of consumers

consumer credit /kənˌsuːmər
ˈkredɪt/ *noun* the credit given by shops,
banks, and other financial institutions to
consumers so that they can buy goods

consumer durables /kənˌsuːmər
ˈdjʊərəb(ə)lz/ *plural noun* items which
are bought and used by the public, e.g.,
washing machines, refrigerators, or ov-
ens

consumer goods /kənˌsjuːmər
ˈɡʊdz/ *plural noun* same as **consumable goods**

consumerism /kənˈsuːmərɪz(ə)m/
noun the activities concerned with protecting the rights and interests of consumers

consumer list /kənˈsuːmər lɪst/
noun a list of individuals who can be
mailed with details of a product or service, e.g., from the electoral register

consumer magazine /kənˈsuːmər
ˌmæɡəzɪn/ *noun* a magazine published
for consumers, giving details of product
tests, special legal problems regarding
services offered, etc.

consumer mailing list /kənˌsuːmər
ˈmeɪlɪŋ lɪst/ *noun* same as **consumer
list**

consumer market /kənˈsuːmər
ˌmɑːkət/ *noun* the customers who buy
consumer goods ○ *There is a growing
consumer market for construction materials owing to the increased popularity
of DIY.* ○ *Both consumer markets and
industrial markets have been affected by
the recession.*

consumer panel /kənˈsuːmər
ˌpæn(ə)l/ *noun* a group of consumers
who report on products they have used
so that the manufacturers can improve
them or use what the panel says about
them in advertising

Consumer Price Index /kən
ˌsuːmər ˈpraɪs ˌɪndeks/ *noun* an American index showing how prices of con-

sumer goods have risen over a period of
time, used as a way of measuring inflation and the cost of living. Abbreviation
CPI (NOTE: The U.K. term is **retail
prices index**.)

consumer profile /kənˌsuːmər
ˈproʊfaɪl/ *noun* a description of the relevant details of the average customer for
a product or service

consumer research /kənˌsuːmər rɪ
ˈsɜːtʃ/ *noun* research into why consumers buy goods and what goods they may
want to buy

consumer resistance /kənˌsuːmər
rɪˈzɪstəns/ *noun* a lack of interest by
consumers in buying a new product ○
*The new product met no consumer resis-
tance even though the price was high.*

Consumers Association /kən
ˈsuːmərz əsoʊsiˌeiʃ(ə)n/ *noun* an independent organization which protects
consumers and represents their interests, and reports on the quality of products and services in its regular magazine. Abbreviation **CA**

consumer society /kənˌsuːmər sə
ˈsaɪəti/ *noun* a type of society where
consumers are encouraged to buy goods

consumer sovereignty /kən
ˌsuːmər ˈsɑvrɪnti/ *noun* the power of
consumers to influence trends in production and marketing

consumer spending /kənˌsuːmər
ˈspendɪŋ/ *noun* spending by private
households on goods and services

consumer's surplus /kənˌsuːmərz
ˈsɜːpləs/ *noun* the difference between
what a consumer is willing to pay for
something and what he or she actually
does pay for it ○ *When the brand manager realized how big the consumer's
surplus was she decided to raise the
price of the product.*

consumer survey /kənˌsuːmər
ˈsɜːveɪ/ *noun* a survey of existing and
potential demand for a product

**consumer-to-consumer com-
merce** /kənˌsuːmər tə kənˈsuːmər
ˌkɑmɜːrs/ *noun* business, especially e-
business, done by one individual with
another and not involving any business
organization

consumption /kən'sʌmpʃən/ *noun* the act of buying or using goods or services ○ *a car with low gasoline consumption* ○ *The factory has a heavy consumption of coal.*

contain /kən'teɪn/ *verb* to hold something inside ○ *a barrel of oil contains 42 gallons* ○ *Each crate contains two computers and their peripherals.* ○ *We have lost a file containing important documents.*

container /kən'teɪnər/ *noun* **1.** a box, bottle, can, etc. which can hold goods ○ *The gas is shipped in strong metal containers.* ○ *The container burst during shipping.* **2.** a very large metal case of a standard size for loading and transporting goods on trucks, trains, and ships ○ *to ship goods in containers* □ **a container-load of spare parts** a shipment of spare parts sent in a container

containerization /kən,teɪnəraɪ'zeɪʃ(ə)n/ *noun* the act of shipping goods in containers

containerize /kən'teɪnəraɪz/ *verb* to put or ship goods in containers

content /'kɑntent/ *noun* the text, illustrations, and graphics of a piece of publicity

content management /'kɑntent ,mænɪdʒmənt/ *noun* the management of the textual and graphical material contained on a website (NOTE: Owners of large sites with thousands of pages often invest in a content management application system to help with the creation and organization of the content of these sites.)

contest /'kɑntest/ *noun* a type of promotion where prizes are given to people who give the right answers to a series of questions

contested takeover /kən,testɪd 'teɪkoʊvər/ *noun* a takeover bid where the board of the target company does not recommend it to the shareholders and tries to fight it. Also called **hostile bid**

context /'kɑntekst/ *noun* additional information about a product that is considered to be helpful to customers and is shown on a website. For example, reviews by other customers displayed on the site for a particular book.

contingency plan /kən'tɪndʒənsi plæn/ *noun* a plan which will be put into action if something unexpected happens

contingent liability /kən,tɪndʒənt ,laɪə'bɪləti/ *noun* a liability which may or may not occur, but for which provision is made in a company's accounts, as opposed to "provisions," where money is set aside for an anticipated expenditure

continuity /,kɑntɪ'nuəti/ *noun* the act of maintaining a continuous stable level of advertising activity ○ *Continuity must be the watchword of this promotional campaign to keep the product firmly in the minds of the target audience.* ○ *Should we aim for a sudden short blast of advertising or should continuity be the essence of our strategy?*

continuity program /,kɑntɪ'njuəti ,proʊɡræm/ *noun* a marketing program which offers a series of products which are sent to customers at regular intervals

continuous /kən'tɪnjuəs/ *adjective* with no end or with no breaks ○ *a continuous production line*

continuous process production /kən,tɪnjuəs 'prɑses prə,dʌkʃən/ *noun* automated production of many identical products

continuous research /kən,tɪnjuəs rɪ'sɜrtʃ/ *noun* regular ongoing market research ○ *Continuous research will tell us if sales are dropping off.*

contra /'kɑntrə/ *verb* □ **to contra an entry** to enter a similar amount in the opposite side of an account

contra account /'kɑntrə ə,kaʊnt/ *noun* an account which offsets another account, e.g., where a company's supplier is not only a creditor in that company's books but also a debtor because it has purchased goods on credit

contraband /'kɑntrəbænd/ *noun* goods brought into a country illegally, without paying customs duty

contract *noun* /'kɑntrækt/ **1.** a legal agreement between two parties ○ *to draw up a contract* ○ *to draft a contract*

○ *to sign a contract* □ **the contract is binding on both parties** both parties signing the contract must do what is agreed □ **under contract** bound by the terms of a contract ○ *The firm is under contract to deliver the goods by November.* □ **to void a contract** to make a contract invalid **2.** □ **by private contract** by private legal agreement **3.** an agreement for the supply of a service or goods ○ *to enter into a contract to supply spare parts* ○ *to sign a contract for $10,000 worth of spare parts* □ **to put work out to contract** to decide that work should be done by another company on a contract, rather than by employing members of staff to do it □ **to award a contract to a company, to place a contract with a company** to decide that a company shall have the contract to do work for you □ **to tender for a contract** to put forward an estimate of cost for work under contract ■ *verb* /kən'trækt/ to agree to do some work on the basis of a legally binding contract ○ *to contract to supply spare parts* or *to contract for the supply of spare parts* □ **the supply of spare parts was contracted out to Smith Inc.** Smith Inc. was given the contract for supplying spare parts. □ **to contract out of an agreement** to withdraw from an agreement with the written permission of the other party

contract carrier /'kɑntrækt ˌkæriər/ *noun* a carrier or transportation company which has special contracts with businesses ○ *a contract carrier which ships coffee beans from Brazil to coffee wholesalers in the United States*

contract hire /'kɑntrækt haɪr/ *noun* a system that allows organizations to hire equipment that they need to use for a long period, e.g., cars or office machines, from other organizations instead of buying it, on condition that they sign a contract for the hire with owners (NOTE: Contract hire agreements often include arrangements for maintenance and replacement.)

contracting company /kən ˌtræktɪŋ 'kʌmp(ə)ni/ *noun* an independent broadcasting company that sells advertising time ○ *With two new*

contracting companies being set up this year, advertisers will have more choice.

contracting party /kənˌtræktɪŋ 'pɑrti/ *noun* a person or company that signs a contract

contract manufacturing /ˌkɑntrækt ˌmænjə'fæktʃərɪŋ/ *noun* an agreement which allows an overseas manufacturer to manufacture or assemble your products in that country for sale there ○ *Under a contract manufacturing agreement a local company is making our cars in France.*

contract note /'kɑntrækt noʊt/ *noun* a note showing that shares have been bought or sold but not yet paid for, also including the commission

contractor /kən'træktər/ *noun* a person or company that does work according to a written agreement

contractual /kən'træktʃuəl/ *adjective* according to a contract ○ *contractual conditions* □ **to fulfil your contractual obligations** to do what you have agreed to do in a contract

contractual liability /kən ˌtræktʃuəl ˌlaɪə'bɪləti/ *noun* a legal responsibility for something as stated in a contract

contractually /kən'træktjuəli/ *adverb* according to a contract ○ *The company is contractually bound to pay our expenses.*

contractual obligation /kən ˌtræktʃuəl ˌɑblɪ'geɪʃ(ə)n/ *noun* something that a person is legally forced to do through having signed a contract to do □ **to fulfil your contractual obligations** to do what you have agreed to do in a contract □ **he is under no contractual obligation to buy** he has signed no agreement to buy

contract work /'kɑntrækt wɜrk/ *noun* work done according to a written agreement

contra deal /'kɑntrə ˌdil/ *noun* a deal between two businesses to exchange goods and services

contra entry /'kɑntrə ˌentri/ *noun* an entry made in the opposite side of an account to make an earlier entry worthless, i.e. a debit against a credit

contribute /kən'trɪbjut/ *verb* to give money or add to money ○ *We agreed to contribute 10% of the profits.* ○ *They had contributed to the pension fund for 10 years.*

contributed content website /kən,trɪbjutd ,kɒntent 'websaɪt/ *noun* a website that allows visitors to add their contributions to its content, e.g., to write reviews of books that are advertised on the site

contribution /,kɒntrɪ'bjuʃ(ə)n/ *noun* something that is contributed

contribution analysis /,kɒntrɪ'bjuʃ(ə)n ə,næləsɪs/ *noun* an analysis of how much each of a company's products contributes to fixed costs, based on its profit margin and sales ○ *Contribution analysis helps to streamline production and marketing.* ○ *Thorough contribution analysis led to six products being dropped from the product range.*

contribution margin /,kɒntrɪ'bjuʃ(ə)n ,mɑrdʒɪn/ *noun* a way of showing how much individual products or services contribute to net profit

contribution of capital /kɒntrɪ,bjuʃ(ə)n əv 'kæpɪt(ə)l/ *noun* money paid to a company as additional capital

contribution pricing /,kɒntrɪ'bjuʃ(ə)n ,praɪsɪŋ/ *noun* a pricing method based on maximizing the contribution of each product to fixed costs

contributor /kən'trɪbjutər/ *noun* a person who gives money □ **contributor of capital** person who contributes capital

control /kən'troʊl/ *noun* **1.** the power or ability to direct something ○ *The company is under the control of three shareholders.* □ **to lose control of a business** to find that you have less than 50% of the shares in a company, and so are no longer able to direct it ○ *The family lost control of its business.* **2.** the act of restricting or checking something or making sure that something is kept in check □ **under control** kept in check ○ *Expenses are kept under tight control.* ○ *The company is trying to bring its overheads back under control.* □ **out of control** not kept in check ○ *Costs have gotten ten out of control.* ■ *verb* **1.** □ **to control**

a business to direct a business ○ *The business is controlled by a company based in Luxembourg.* ○ *The company is controlled by the majority stockholder.* **2.** to make sure that something is kept in check or is not allowed to develop ○ *The government is fighting to control inflation* or *to control the rise in the cost of living.* (NOTE: **controlling – controlled**)

control group /kən'troʊl grup/ *noun* a small group which is used to check a sample group

controllable /kən'troʊləb(ə)l/ *adjective* which can be controlled

controllable variables /kən,troʊləb(ə)l 'veriəb(ə)lz/ *plural noun* factors that can be controlled, e.g., a company's marketing mix ○ *Because there were so few controllable variables the outcome of the marketing plan was very uncertain.*

controlled /kən'troʊld/ *adjective* ruled or kept in check

controlled circulation /kən,troʊld ,sɜrkjə'leɪʃ(ə)n/ *noun* the distribution of a publication to a specialist readership who are members of a particular organization or profession (often a free controlled circulation, where the magazine is distributed free to key executives, and is paid for by the advertisers) ○ *The professional institute publishes a quarterly magazine with a controlled circulation.* ○ *The newspaper has a controlled circulation and is suitable for advertisements for highly specialized products.*

controlled circulation magazine /kən,troʊld sɜrkjə,leɪʃ(ə)n 'mægəzin/ *noun* a magazine which is sent free to a limited number of readers, and is paid for by the advertising it contains

controlled economy /kən,troʊld ɪ'kɒnəmi/ *noun* an economy where most business activity is directed by orders from the government

control question /kən'troʊl ,kwestʃən/ *noun* a question in a questionnaire designed to check that answers are consistent ○ *A control question was included to check that respondents were* *not lying about their age.* ○ *If control questions show that answers are not honest, the interview is ended.*

control systems /kən'troʊl ˌsɪstəmz/ *plural noun* the systems used to check that a computer system is working correctly

convenience /kən'viniəns/ *noun* □ **at your earliest convenience** as soon as you find it possible

convenience food /kən'viniəns fud/ *noun* food which is prepared by the store before it is sold, so that it needs only heating to be made ready to eat

convenience goods /kən'viniəns gʊdz/ *plural noun* ordinary everyday products that people have to buy but which command little or no brand loyalty ○ *Price competition is very fierce in the convenience goods market.*

convenience store /kən'viniəns stɔr/ *noun* a small store selling food or housewares, open until late at night, or even 24 hours per day

convenient /kən'viniənt/ *adjective* suitable or handy ○ *A bank draft is a convenient way of sending money abroad.* ○ *Is 9.30 a convenient time for the meeting?*

conversion /kən'vɜrʃ(ə)n/ *noun* the action of converting a prospective customer into an actual purchaser

conversion rate /kən'vɜrʃ(ə)n reɪt/ *noun* the proportion of contacts, by mailing, advertising, or email marketing, who actually end up purchasing the product or service

convertible currency /kən ˌvɜrtəb(ə)l 'kʌrənsi/ *noun* a currency which can easily be exchanged for another

cooling-off laws /ˌkulɪŋ 'ɔf lɔz/ *plural noun* state laws allowing cancellation of an order within a specific period after signing an agreement ○ *Cooling-off laws are making buyers less hesitant about placing large orders.*

cooling-off period /ˌkulɪŋ 'ɔf ˌpɪriəd/ *noun* **1.** (*during an industrial dispute*) a period when negotiations have to be carried on and no action can be taken by either side **2.** a period during

which someone who is about to enter into an agreement may reflect on all aspects of the arrangement and change his or her mind if necessary ○ *New York has a three day cooling-off period for telephone sales.*

co-op /'koʊ ɑp/ *noun* same as **cooperative** *noun* 1

cooperate /ˌkoʊ'ɑpəreɪt/ *verb* to work together ○ *The regional governments are cooperating in the fight against piracy.* ○ *The two firms have cooperated on the computer project.*

cooperation /koʊˌɑpə'reɪʃ(ə)n/ *noun* the act of working together ○ *The project was completed ahead of schedule with the cooperation of the work force.*

cooperative /koʊ'ɑp(ə)rətɪv/ *adjective* willing to work together ○ *The work force has not been cooperative over the management's productivity plan.* ■ *noun* **1.** a business run by a group of employees who are also the owners and who share the profits ○ *The product is marketed by an agricultural cooperative.* ○ *They set up a workers' cooperative to run the factory.* **2.** a business which organizes cooperative mailing or advertising for different companies

cooperative advertising /koʊ ˌɑp(ə)rətɪv 'ædvərtaɪzɪŋ/ *noun* **1.** the sharing by two companies, often a producer and a distributor, of advertising costs ○ *A cooperative advertising agreement means that two companies can enjoy quantity discounts offered by the media.* **2.** mailing advertising material from different companies in the same mailing pack

cooperative marketing /koʊ ˌɑp(ə)rətɪv 'mɑrkətɪŋ/ *noun* an arrangement whereby various producers cooperate in the marketing of their products or services ○ *Cooperative marketing proved an economic method of selling for companies with few financial resources.*

cooperative movement /koʊ 'ɑp(ə)rətɪv ˌmuvmənt/ *noun* a movement that encourages the setting-up of cooperative businesses that are jointly owned by their members who share the profits and benefits they gain from trading among themselves (NOTE: The movement was founded in Rochdale, Lancashire, England, in 1844 by 28 weavers.)

co-opetition /koʊˌɑpəˈtɪʃ(ə)n/ *noun* cooperation between competing companies

copier /ˈkɑpiər/ *noun* a machine which makes copies of documents

copy /ˈkɑpi/ *verb* to make a second document which is like the first ○ *He copied the company report and took it home.* (NOTE: **copies – copying- copied**)

copy brief /ˈkɑpi brif/ *noun* the instructions from an advertiser to a copywriter explaining the objectives of an advertising campaign ○ *The copy brief made it clear that the advertisements were to be aimed at young people.* ○ *The advertisers blamed the agency for not paying enough attention to the copy brief.*

copy clearance /ˈkɑpi ˌklɪrəns/ *noun* the passing of an advertiser's copy as neither misleading nor offensive ○ *It is doubtful the advertisement will get copy clearance since it directly disparages the competition.* ○ *The advertisement has received copy clearance because all its claims can be substantiated.* ○ *You will not get copy clearance for this ad because the caption is sure to offend a lot of women readers.*

copy date /ˈkɑpi deɪt/ *noun* the date by which an advertisement must be delivered to the media concerned ○ *The creative teams are working flat out because the copy date is only one week away.* ○ *Let's work on the advertisements with the earliest copy dates.*

copy fitting /ˈkɑpi ˌfɪtɪŋ/ *noun* the arrangement of advertising text so it fits the space allowed for it

copying machine /ˈkɑpiɪŋ məˌʃin/ *noun* a machine which makes copies of documents

copy platform /ˈkɑpi ˌplætfɔrm/ *noun* the main theme of an advertisement's copy ○ *There is no point in discussing details until we decide on a copy platform.*

copyright /ˈkɑpiraɪt/ *noun* **1.** an author's legal right to publish his or her own work and not to have it copied, lasting seventy years after the author's death **2.** a legal right which protects the creative work of writers and artists and prevents others from copying or using it without authorization, and which also applies to such things as company logos and brand names ■ *adjective* covered by the laws of copyright ○ *It is illegal to photocopy a copyright work.*

copy testing /ˈkɑpi ˌtestɪŋ/ *noun* the act of testing the effectiveness of an advertisement's copy ○ *Copy testing led to the copywriter having to rethink the wording of the message.* ○ *Copy testing will tell us whether or not the advertisements are offensive to the public in general.*

copywriter /ˈkɑpiˌraɪtər/ *noun* a person who writes advertisements

core /kɔr/ *noun* the central or main part

core activity /ˈkɔr ækˌtɪvəti/ *noun* the central activity of a company, which is its basic product or service

core business /ˈkɔr ˌbɪznɪs/ *noun* the most important work that an organization does, that it is most expert at, that makes it different from other organizations, that contributes most to its success and, usually, that it was originally set up to do (NOTE: The concept of core business became prominent in the 1980s when attempts at diversification by large companies proved less successful than expected.)

core capability /ˌkɔr ˌkeɪpəˈbɪləti/ *noun* same as **core competence**

core competence /ˌkɔr ˈkɑmpɪt(ə)ns/ *noun* a skill or an area of expertise possessed by an organization that makes it particularly good at doing some things and makes an important contribution to its success by giving it competitive advantage over other organizations

core product /ˌkɔr ˈprɑdʌkt/ *noun* **1.** the main product which a company makes or sells **2.** a basic product, without added benefits such as credit terms, installation service, etc.

core values /ˌkɔr ˈvæljuz/ *plural noun* **1.** the main commercial and moral principles that influence the way an organization is run and the way it conducts its business, and that are supposed to be shared by everyone in the organization from senior management to ordinary employees (NOTE: Core values are often reflected in an organization's mission statement.) **2.** a set of concepts and ideals that guide someone's life and help them to make important decisions

corner /ˈkɔrnər/ *verb* □ **to corner the market** to own most or all of the supply of a commodity and so control the price ○ *The syndicate tried to corner the market in silver.*

corner store /ˈkɔrnər stɔr/ *noun* a small privately owned general store

corporate /ˈkɔrp(ə)rət/ *adjective* referring to corporations or companies, or to a particular company as a whole

corporate advertising /ˌkɔrp(ə)rət ˈædvərtaɪzɪŋ/ *noun* the advertising of an organization rather than a product ○ *Our corporate advertising is designed to present us as a caring organization.* ○ *No amount of corporate advertising will ever persuade the consumer that the company stands for quality.*

corporate brand /ˌkɔrp(ə)rət ˈbrænd/ *noun* the overall image that a company presents to the outside world, or the image of it that exists in the minds of its customers, its employees, and the public, and that encapsulates what it does and what it stands for

corporate communication /ˌkɔrp(ə)rət kəˌmjunɪˈkeɪʃ(ə)n/ *noun* the activities undertaken by an organization to pass on information both to its own employees and to its existing and prospective customers and the general public

corporate culture /ˌkɔrp(ə)rət ˈkʌltʃər/ *noun* the often unspoken beliefs and values that determine the way an organization does things, the atmosphere that exists within it, and the way people who work for it behave (NOTE:

The culture of an organization is often summed up as "the way we do things around here.")

corporate discount /ˌkɔrp(ə)rət ˈdɪskaʊnt/ *noun* a reduction in advertising charges calculated on the basis of the total advertising revenue from all the brands of a company

corporate hospitality /ˌkɔrp(ə)rət ˌhɒspɪˈtæləti/ *noun* entertainment provided by an organization, originally intended to help salespeople build relationships with customers, but now increasingly used as an incentive for staff and in team-building and training exercises for employees

corporate identity /ˌkɔrp(ə)rət aɪˈdentəti/ *noun* the way in which a corporation is distinguished from others

corporate image /ˌkɔrp(ə)rət ˈɪmɪdʒ/ *noun* an idea which a company would like the public to have of it

corporate name /ˌkɔrp(ə)rət ˈneɪm/ *noun* the name of a large corporation

corporate plan /ˌkɔrp(ə)rət ˈplæn/ *noun* a plan for the future work of a whole company

corporate planning /ˌkɔrp(ə)rət ˈplænɪŋ/ *noun* the process of planning the future work of a whole company

corporate portal /ˌkɔrp(ə)rət ˈpɔrt(ə)l/ *noun* a main website that allows access to all the information and software applications held by an organization and provides links to information from outside it (NOTE: A corporate portal is a development of intranet technology and, ideally, should allow users to access groupware, email, and desktop applications, and to customize the way information is presented and the way it is used.)

corporate profits /ˌkɔrp(ə)rət ˈprɑfɪts/ *plural noun* the profits of a corporation

corporate strategy /ˌkɔrp(ə)rət ˈstrætədʒi/ *noun* the plans for future action by a corporation

corporate vision /ˌkɔrp(ə)rət ˈvɪʒ(ə)n/ *noun* the overall aim or purpose of an organization that all its business activities are designed to help it achieve (NOTE: An organization's corporate vision is usually summed up in its vision statement.)

corporation /ˌkɔrpəˈreɪʃ(ə)n/ *noun* **1.** a large company **2.** a company which is incorporated in the United States

corporation income tax /ˌkɔrpəreɪʃ(ə)n ˈɪnkʌm tæks/ *noun* a tax on profits made by incorporated companies

corporation tax /ˌkɔrpəˈreɪʃ(ə)n tæks/ *noun* a tax on profits and capital gains made by companies, calculated before dividends are paid. Abbreviation **CT**

correlation /ˌkɔrəˈleɪʃ(ə)n/ *noun* the degree to which there is a relationship between two sets of data ○ *Is there any correlation between people's incomes and the amount they spend on clothing?* ◊ **coefficient of correlation, multiple correlation**

cosmetic /kɑzˈmetɪk/ *adjective* referring to the appearance of people or things ○ *We've made some cosmetic changes to our product line.* ○ *Packaging has both practical as well as cosmetic importance.*

cost /kɔst/ *noun* the amount of money which has to be paid for something ○ *What is the cost of a first class ticket to New York?* ○ *Computer costs are falling each year.* ○ *We cannot afford the cost of two cars.* □ **to cover costs** to produce enough money in sales to pay for the costs of production ○ *The sales revenue barely covers the costs of advertising* or *the advertising costs.* □ **to sell at cost** to sell at a price which is the same as the cost of manufacture or the wholesale cost ■ *verb* **1.** to have as its price ○ *How much does the machine cost?* ○ *This cloth costs $10 a yard.* **2.** □ **to cost a product** to calculate how much money will be needed to make a product, and so work out its selling price

cost, insurance, and freight /ˌkɔst ɪnˌʃʊrəns ən ˈfreɪt/ *noun* the estimate of a price, which includes the cost of the goods, the insurance, and the transportation charges. Abbreviation **CIF, c.i.f.**

cost accountant /ˈkɔst əˌkaʊntənt/ *noun* an accountant who gives managers information about their business costs

cost accounting /ˈkɔst əˌkaʊntɪŋ/ *noun* the process of preparing special accounts of manufacturing and sales costs

cost analysis /ˈkɔst əˌnæləsɪs/ *noun* the process of calculating in advance what a new product will cost

cost-benefit analysis /ˌkɔst ˈbenəfɪt əˌnæləsɪs/ *noun* the process of comparing the costs and benefits of various possible ways of using available resources. Also called **benefit-cost analysis**

cost center /ˈkɔst ˌsentər/ *noun* **1.** a person or group whose costs can be itemized and to which costs can be allocated in accounts **2.** a unit, a process, or an individual that provides a service needed by another part of an organization and whose cost is therefore accepted as an overhead of the business

cost-cutting /ˈkɔst ˌkʌtɪŋ/ *noun* the process of reducing costs ○ *As a result of cost-cutting, we have had to lay off half the staff.*

cost driver /ˈkɔst ˌdraɪvər/ *noun* a factor that determines how much it costs to carry out a particular task or project, e.g., the amount of resources needed for it, or the activities involved in completing it

cost-effective /ˌkɔstɪ ˈfektɪv/ *adjective* giving good value when compared with the original cost ○ *We find advertising in the Sunday newspapers very cost-effective.*

cost-effectiveness /ˌkɔst ɪˈfektɪvnəs/, **cost efficiency** /ˌkɔst ɪˈfɪʃənsi/ *noun* the quality of being cost-effective ○ *Can we calculate the cost-effectiveness of air freight against shipping by sea?*

cost factor /ˈkɔst ˌfæktər/ *noun* the problem of cost

costing /ˈkɔstɪŋ/ *noun* a calculation of the manufacturing costs, and so the selling price, of a product ○ *The costings give us a retail price of $2.95.* ○ *We* *cannot do the costing until we have details of all the production expenditure.*

costly /'kɔstli/ *adjective* costing a lot of money, or costing too much money ○ *Defending the court case was a costly process.* ○ *The mistakes were time-consuming and costly.*

cost of entry /ˌkɔst əv 'entri/ *noun* the cost of going into a market for the first time

cost of goods sold /ˌkɑst əv ˌɡʊdz 'soʊld/ *noun* same as **cost of sales**

cost-of-living increase /ˌkɔst əv 'lɪvɪŋ ˌɪnkriːs/ *noun* an increase in salary to allow it to keep up with the increased cost of living

cost-of-living index /ˌkɔst əv 'lɪvɪŋ ˌɪndeks/ *noun* a way of measuring the cost of living which is shown as a percentage increase on the figure for the previous year. It is similar to the consumer price index, but includes other items such as the interest on mortgages.

cost of sales /ˌkɔst əv 'seɪlz/ *noun* all the costs of a product sold, including manufacturing costs and the staff costs of the production department, before general overheads are calculated. Also called **cost of goods sold**

cost per acquisition /ˌkɔst pər ˌækwɪ'zɪʃ(ə)n/ *noun* the average cost for each acquisition of a new customer in response to an advertisement. Abbreviation **CPA**

cost per click-through /ˌkɔst pər 'klɪk θruː/ *noun* a method of pricing online advertising, based on the principle that the seller gets paid whenever a visitor clicks on an advertisement

cost per customer /ˌkɔst pər 'kʌstəmər/ *noun* a measure of cost-effectiveness based on the cost per sale generated

cost per inquiry /ˌkɔst pər ɪn 'kwaɪri/ *noun* the average cost for each inquiry in response to an advertisement

cost per order /ˌkɔst pər 'ɔrdər/ *noun* a measure used to determine the number of orders generated compared to the cost of running the advertisement. Abbreviation **CPO**

cost per thousand /ˌkɔst pər 'θaʊz(ə)nd/, **cost per mille** /ˌkɔst pər 'mɪl/ *noun* the cost of an advertisement, calculated as the cost for every thousand people reached or the cost of a thousand impressions for a website ○ *This newspaper has the highest cost per thousand but a very high proportion of its readers fall within our target audience.* Abbreviation **CPT, CPM**

cost plus /ˌkɔst 'plʌs/ *noun* a system of calculating a price, by taking the cost of production of goods or services and adding a percentage to cover the supplier's overheads and margin ○ *We are charging for the work on a cost plus basis.*

cost-plus pricing /ˌkɔst 'plʌs ˌpraɪsɪŋ/ *noun* a pricing method that involves basing the price on the production costs and adding a percentage for margin

cost price /'kɔst praɪs/ *noun* a selling price which is the same as the price, either the manufacturing price or the wholesale price, which the seller paid for the item

costs /kɔsts/ *plural noun* the expenses involved in a court case ○ *The judge awarded costs to the defendant.* ○ *Costs of the case will be borne by the prosecution.*

cottage industry /ˌkɑtɪdʒ 'ɪndəstri/ *noun* the production of goods or some other type of work, carried out by people working in their own homes

counter /'kaʊntər/ *noun* a long flat surface in a store for displaying and selling goods □ **glove counter** the section of a store where gloves are sold □ **goods sold over the counter** retail sales of goods in shops ○ *Some drugs are sold over the counter, but others need to be recommended by a doctor.* □ **under the counter** illegally

counter- /kaʊntə/ *prefix* against

counteradvertising /ˌkaʊntər 'ædvərtaɪzɪŋ/ *noun* advertising aimed as a reply to a competitor's advertisements

counter-argument /'kaʊntər ˌɑrɡjəmənt/ *noun* a response that is opposed to the position advocated in an advertising message

counterbid /'kaʊntəbɪd/ *noun* a higher bid in reply to a previous bid ○ *When I bid $20 she put in a counterbid of $25.*

counter-jumper /'kaʊntə ˌdʒʌmpər/ *noun* a person who sells goods over the counter (*informal*) ○ *He was a counter-jumper for many years before he became a manager.* ○ *Five years as a counter-jumper gave her plenty of experience of customer relations.*

countermand /ˌkaʊntə'mænd/ *verb* to say that an order must not be carried out ○ *to countermand an order*

counter-offer /'kaʊntər ˌɔfər/ *noun* a higher or lower offer made in reply to another offer ○ *Smith Inc. made an offer of $1m for the property, and Blacks replied with a counter-offer of $1.4m.*

counterpack /'kaʊntəpæk/ *noun* a box for the display of goods for sale, placed on the counter or on another flat surface in a store

counter-programming /'kaʊntər ˌproʊɡræmɪŋ/ *noun* the presenting of TV programs that are designed to appeal to the audience of competing programs run during at the same time

countersign /'kaʊntəsaɪn/ *verb* to sign a document which has already been signed by someone else ○ *All our checks have to be countersigned by the finance director.* ○ *The sales director countersigns all my orders.*

counter staff /'kaʊntər stæf/ *noun* sales staff who serve behind counters

country of origin /ˌkʌntri əv 'ɔrɪdʒɪn/ *noun* a country where a product is manufactured or where a food product comes from ○ *All produce must be labeled to show the country of origin.*

coupon /'kupɑn/ *noun* **1.** a piece of paper used in place of money **2.** a piece of paper which replaces an order form

coupon ad /'kupɑn æd/ *noun* an advertisement with a form attached, which you cut out and return to the advertiser with your name and address for further information

couponed /'kupɑnd/ *adjective* with a coupon attached ○ *The agency is using couponed direct response advertising.*

couponing /'kupɑnɪŋ/ *noun* a selling method using coupons delivered to homes, giving special discounts on some items

course /kɔrs/ *noun* a series of lessons or a program of instruction ○ *She has finished her secretarial course.* ○ *The company has paid for her to attend a course for trainee sales managers.* ○ *Management trainees all took a six-month course in business studies.* ○ *The training officer was constantly on the lookout for new courses in management studies.* ○ *The company sent her on a management course.*

courtesy /'kɜrtəsi/ *adjective* supplied free of charge ○ *A courtesy sample is sent with the sales literature.*

courtesy car /'kɜrtəsi kar/ *noun* the use of a car offered free to a customer

cover /'kʌvər/ *noun* **1.** the proportion of a target audience reached by advertising **2.** one of the outside pages of a publication. The four cover pages are front cover, inside front cover, inside back cover, and back cover. ○ *We could never afford to advertise on the cover of this magazine.*

coverage /'kʌv(ə)rɪdʒ/ *noun* the proportion of a target market that is reached by an advertisement ○ *The advertisement itself was effective but it had very poor coverage.* ○ *We must consider both the cost of the advertisement and its coverage before committing ourselves any further.*

cover charge /'kʌvər tʃardʒ/ *noun* (*in restaurants*) a charge for a place at the table in addition to the charge for food

covered market /ˌkʌvəd 'markət/ *noun* a market which is held in a special building

cover letter /'kʌvər ˌletər/ *noun* a letter sent with documents to say why they are being sent ○ *She sent a cover letter with her résumé, explaining why she wanted the job.* ○ *The job advertise-*

ment asked for a résumé and a cover letter.

cover note /'kʌvər noʊt/ noun **1.** a letter from an insurance company giving details of an insurance policy and confirming that the policy exists **2.** same as **cover letter**

cover page /'kʌvər peɪdʒ/ noun the front or back cover of a publication

cover price /'kʌvər praɪs/ noun the price of a newspaper or magazine which is printed on the cover and paid by the final purchaser

CPA abbreviation cost per acquisition

CPM abbreviation cost per mille

CPO abbreviation cost per order

CPT abbreviation cost per thousand

crash-test /'kræʃ test/ verb to establish the safety and reliability of something by testing it in different ways

creaming /'kriːmɪŋ/ noun the act of fixing a high price for a product in order to achieve high short-term profits

create /kri'eɪt/ verb to make something new ○ By acquiring small unprofitable companies he soon created a large manufacturing group. ○ The government program aims at creating new jobs for young people.

creative /kri'eɪtɪv/ adjective relating to the conceptual or artistic side of advertising ○ There are three copywriters and four illustrators in the agency's creative department. ○ He has had good experience working on both the creative and the administrative sides of advertising. ■ noun someone who works in the conceptual or artistic side of a business

creative boutique noun a highly specialized business offering creative customer advertising services ○ A group of copywriters and designers have left the agency to set up their own creative store. ○ The creative store made short advertising films and designed some press ads for us.

creative director /kri.eɪtɪv daɪ 'rektər/ noun an employee of an advertising agency who is in overall charge of finding the right words and images to promote the product during an advertising campaign

creative selling /kri.eɪtɪv 'selɪŋ/ noun a sales technique where the main emphasis is on generating new business

creative strategy /kri'eɪtɪv ˌstrætədʒi/ noun a strategy to determine what message an advertisement will communicate

creativity /ˌkrieɪ'tɪvəti/, **creative thinking** /kri.eɪtɪv 'θɪŋkɪŋ/ noun the ability to generate new ideas, especially by taking a fresh and imaginative approach to old problems or existing procedures (NOTE: Creativity is considered important not just in the development of new products and services, but also in organizational decision-making and problem-solving, and many organizations try to encourage it through their corporate culture and by using techniques such as brainstorming and lateral thinking.)

credere /'kreɪdəri/ noun ▸ **del credere agent**

credibility /ˌkredɪ'bɪləti/ noun the state of being trusted

credibility gap /ˌkredɪ'bɪləti gæp/ noun a discrepancy between claims for a product made by the manufacturer and acceptance of these claims by the target audience ○ The credibility gap that we face is partly due to our product's bad performance record. ◊ **source credibility**

credit /'kredɪt/ noun **1.** a period of time allowed before a customer has to pay a debt incurred for goods or services ○ to give someone six months' credit ○ to sell on good credit terms □ **to open a line of credit, a credit line** to make credit available to someone □ **on credit** without paying immediately ○ to live on credit ○ We buy everything on sixty days' credit. ○ The company exists on credit from its suppliers. **2.** an amount entered in accounts to show a decrease in assets or expenses or an increase in liabilities, revenue, or capital. In accounts, credits are entered in the right-hand column. ○ to enter $100 to someone's credit ○ to pay in $100 to the credit of Mr. Smith Compare **debit** □ **ac-**

count **in credit** an account where the credits are higher than the debits **3.** money set against a client's account because an advertisement was not run at the correct time

credit account /'kredɪt ə,kaʊnt/ *noun U.K.* same as **charge account**

credit agency /'kredɪt ,eɪdʒənsi/ *noun* a company which reports on the creditworthiness of customers to show whether they should be allowed credit

credit bank /'kredɪt bæŋk/ *noun* a bank which lends money

credit bureau /'kredɪt ,bjʊroʊ/ *noun* a company used by businesses and banks to assess the creditworthiness of people

credit card /'kredɪt kard/ *noun* a plastic card which allows you to borrow money and to buy goods without paying for them immediately. You must pay the balance to the credit card company at a later date.

credit card sale /'kredɪt kard ,seɪl/ *noun* the act of selling where the buyer uses a credit card to pay

credit column /'kredɪt ,kaləm/ *noun* the right-hand column in accounts showing money received

credit control /'kredɪt kən,troʊl/ *noun* a check that customers pay on time and do not owe more than their credit limit

credit entry /'kredɪt ,entri/ *noun* an entry on the credit side of an account

credit facilities /'kredɪt fə,sɪlətiz/ *plural noun* an arrangement with a bank or supplier to have credit so as to buy goods

credit freeze /'kredɪt friz/ *noun* a period when lending by banks is restricted by the government

credit history /'kredɪt ,hɪst(ə)ri/ *noun* a record of how a potential borrower has repaid his or her previous debts

credit limit /'kredɪt ,lɪmɪt/ *noun* the largest amount of money which a customer can borrow □ **he has exceeded his credit limit** he has borrowed more money than he is allowed to

credit memorandum /'kredɪt ,memərændəm/, **credit memo** /'kredɪt ,memoʊ/ *noun* a note showing that money is owed to a customer ○ *When the buyer paid too much money for the goods he was immediately sent a credit memorandum.* ○ *I hope we receive a credit memo from the suppliers for the money they owe us.*

credit note /'kredɪt noʊt/ *noun* a note showing that money is owed to a customer ○ *The company sent the wrong order and so had to issue a credit note.* Abbreviation **C/N**

creditor /'kredɪtər/ *noun* a person or company that is owed money, i.e. a company's creditors are its liabilities

creditors' meeting /'kredɪtərz ,mitɪŋ/ *noun* a meeting of all the people to whom an insolvent company owes money, to decide how to obtain the money owed

credit rating agency /'kredɪt reɪtɪŋ ,eɪdʒənsi/ *noun* a company used by businesses and banks to assess the creditworthiness of people

credit-reference agency /'kredɪt ,refər(ə)ns ,eɪdʒənsi/ *noun U.K.* same as **credit bureau**

credits /'kredɪts/ *plural noun* a list of the names of people who have worked on a movie, TV program, etc.

credit sale /'kredɪt seɪl/ *noun* a sale where the purchaser will pay for the goods bought at a later date

credit scoring /'kredɪt ,skɔrɪŋ/ *noun* a calculation made when assessing the creditworthiness of someone or something

credit side /'kredɪt saɪd/ *noun* the right-hand column of accounts showing money received

credit system /'kredɪt ,sɪstəm/ *noun* the system that governs the way that loans are made to people and organizations, especially the regulations that relate to loans and to organizations that provide loans

credit union /'kredɪt ,junjən/ *noun* a group of people who pay in regular deposits or subscriptions which earn interest and are used to make loans to other members of the group

creditworthiness /'kredɪtˌwɜːðɪnəs/ *noun* the ability of a customer to pay for goods bought on credit

creditworthy /'kredɪtwɜːði/ *adjective* having enough money to be able to buy goods on credit ○ *We will do some checks on her to see if she is creditworthy.*

crisis /'kraɪsɪs/ *noun* a serious situation where decisions have to be taken rapidly

crisis management /'kraɪsɪs ˌmænɪdʒmənt/ *noun* management of a business or a country's economy during a period of crisis

critical mass /ˌkrɪtɪk(ə)l 'mæs/ *noun* the point at which an organization or a project is generating enough income or has gained a large enough market share to be able to survive on its own or to be worth investing more money or resources in

critical path analysis /ˌkrɪtɪk(ə)l 'pæθ əˌnæləsɪs/ *noun* 1. an analysis of the way a project is organized in terms of the minimum time it will take to complete, calculating which parts can be delayed without holding up the rest of the project 2. same as **critical-path method**

critical-path method /ˌkrɪtɪk(ə)l 'pæθ ˌmeθəd/ *noun* a technique used in project management to identify the activities within a project that are critical to its success, usually by showing on a diagram or flow chart the order in which activities must be carried out so that the project can be completed in the shortest time and at the least cost

CRM *abbreviation* customer relations management *or* customer relationship management

cross /krɒs/ *verb* 1. to go across ○ *The Concorde only took three hours to cross the Atlantic.* ○ *To get to the bank, you turn left and cross the street at the post office.* 2. □ **to cross a cheque** to write two lines across a check to show that it has to be paid into a bank

crossed check /ˌkrɒst 'tʃek/ *noun* a check with two lines across it showing that it can only be deposited at a bank and not exchanged for cash

cross elasticity of demand /ˌkrɒs ɪlæˌstɪsəti əv dɪ'mænd/ *noun* changes in demand for an item depending on the selling price of a competing product

cross-media advertising /ˌkrɒs miːdiə 'ædvətaɪzɪŋ/ *noun* advertising the same product or service in several different types of media which are offered by a single-company media provider

cross-selling /ˌkrɒs 'selɪŋ/ *noun* 1. the act of selling two products which go with each other, by placing them side by side in a store 2. the selling of a new product which goes with another product a customer has already bought

cross-tracks /'krɒs træks/ *noun* a poster site next to a railroad track

cryptography /krɪp'tɒgrəfi/ *noun* the use of codes and ciphers, especially as a way of restricting access to part or all of a website, so that only a user with a key can read the information

CTM /ˌsiː tiː 'em/ *noun* ♦ **click-through rate**

CTR /kən'trəʊl/ *abbreviation* click-through rate

cume /kjuːm/ *noun* same as **cumulative audience** (*informal*)

cumulative /'kjuːmjəˌleɪtɪv/ *adjective* added to regularly over a period of time

cumulative audience /ˌkjuːmjələtɪv 'ɔːdiəns/ *noun* the number of people reached by an advertisement at least once over a period of time

cumulative interest /ˌkjuːmjəleɪtɪv 'ɪntrəst/ *noun* the interest which is added to the capital each year

cumulative quantity discount /ˌkjuːmjəleɪtɪv ˌkwɒntəti 'dɪskaʊnt/ *noun* a discount based on a quantity bought or the value of purchases over a period of time ○ *We have purchased only from these suppliers over the last few months in order to enjoy a cumulative quantity discount.*

cumulative reach /ˌkjumjəleɪtɪv 'ritʃ/ *noun* same as **cumulative audience**

curbside conference /ˌkɜrbsaɪd 'kɑnf(ə)rəns/ *noun* a discussion of selling techniques between a trainee salesperson and the person training them after making a sales call ○ *In the curbside conference, the sales trainer described a number of different approaches that might have been made to a particular customer.*

currency /'kʌrənsi/ *noun* money in coins and notes which is used in a particular country

currency backing /'kʌrənsi ˌbækɪŋ/ *noun* gold or government securities which maintain the strength of a currency

currency basket /'kʌrənsi ˌbæskət/ *noun* a group of currencies, each of which is weighted, calculated together as a single unit against which another currency can be measured

currency note /'kʌrənsi noʊt/ *noun* a bank bill

current /'kʌrənt/ *adjective* referring to the present time ○ *the current round of wage negotiations*

current account /'kʌrənt əˌkaʊnt/ *noun* **1.** an account of the balance of payments of a country relating to the sale or purchase of raw materials, goods, and invisibles **2.** *U.K.* same as **checking account**

current assets /ˌkʌrənt 'æsets/ *plural noun* the assets used by a company in its ordinary work, e.g., materials, finished goods, cash and monies due, and which are held for a short time only

current cost accounting /ˌkʌrənt 'kɔst əˌkaʊntɪŋ/ *noun* a method of accounting which notes the cost of replacing assets at current prices, rather than valuing assets at their original cost. Abbreviation **CCA**

current liabilities /ˌkʌrənt laɪə 'bɪlətiz/ *plural noun* the debts which a company has to pay within the next accounting period. In a company's annual accounts, these would be debts which must be paid within the year and are usually payments for goods or services received.

current price /ˌkʌrənt 'praɪs/ *noun* today's price

current rate of exchange /ˌkʌrənt reɪt əv ɪks'tʃeɪndʒ/ *noun* today's rate of exchange

current yield /ˌkʌrənt 'jild/ *noun* a dividend calculated as a percentage of the current price of a share on the stock market

curriculum vitae /kəˌrɪkjələm 'vitaɪ/ *noun* same as **résumé**

curve /kɜrv/ *noun* a line which is not straight, e.g., a line on a graph ○ *The graph shows an upward curve.*

custom /'kʌstəm/ *noun* **1.** a thing which is usually done ○ *It is the custom of the book trade to allow unlimited returns for credit.* □ **the customs of the trade** the general way of working in a trade **2.** *U.K.* same as **patronage** □ **to lose someone's custom** to do something which makes a regular customer go to another store

custom-built /'kʌstəm bɪlt/ *adjective* made specially for one customer ○ *He drives a custom-built Rolls Royce.*

customer /'kʌstəmər/ *noun* a person or company that buys goods ○ *The store was full of customers.* ○ *Can you serve this customer first please?* ○ *She's a regular customer of ours.* (NOTE: The customer may not be the consumer or end user of the product.)

customer appeal /'kʌstəmər əˌpil/ *noun* what attracts customers to a product

customer capital /ˌkʌstəmər 'kæpɪt(ə)l/ *noun* an organization's relationships with its customers considered as a business asset

customer care /ˌkʌstəmər 'ker/ *noun* the activity of looking after customers, so that they do not become dissatisfied

customer-centric model /ˌkʌstəmər 'sentrɪk ˌmɑd(ə)l/ *noun* a business model that is based on an assessment of what the customer needs

customer complaint /ˌkʌstəmər kəmˈpleɪnt/ *noun* same as **complaint**

customer expectation /ˌkʌstəmər ekspekˈteɪʃ(ə)n/ *noun* the ideas and feelings that a customer has about a product or service, based on what he or she needs from it and expects it to do (NOTE: Customer expectation can be created by previous experience, advertising, what other people say about it, awareness of competitors' products, and brand image. If customer expectations are met, then customer satisfaction results.)

customer flow /ˈkʌstəmər floʊ/ *noun* the number of customers in a store and the pattern of their movements around the store

customer focus /ˌkʌstəmər ˈfoʊkəs/ *noun* the aiming of all marketing operations toward the customer

customer loyalty /ˌkʌstəmər ˈlɔɪəlti/ *noun* the feeling of customers who always shop at the same store

customer profile /ˌkʌstəmər ˈproʊfaɪl/ *noun* a description of an average customer for a product or service ○ *The customer profile shows our average buyer to be male, aged 25–30, and employed in the service industries.*

customer profitability /ˌkʌstəmər ˌprɑfɪtəˈbɪləti/ *noun* the amount of profit generated by each individual customer. Usually a small percentage of customers generate the most profit.

customer relations /ˌkʌstəmər rɪˈleɪʃ(ə)nz/ *plural noun* relations between a company and its customers

customer relations management /ˌkʌstəmər rɪˈleɪʃ(ə)nʃɪp ˌmænɪdʒmənt/, **customer relationship management** *noun* the management of relations between a company and its customers, keeping them informed of new products or services and dealing sympathetically with their complaints or inquiries. Abbreviation **CRM**

customer retention /ˌkʌstəmər rɪˈtenʃən/ *noun* same as **retention**

customer satisfaction /ˌkʌstəmər ˌsætɪsˈfækʃən/ *noun* the act of making customers pleased with what they have bought

customer service /ˌkʌstəmər ˈsɜrvɪs/ *noun* a service given to customers once they have made their decision to buy, including delivery, after-sales service, installation, training, etc.

customer service department /ˌkʌstəmər ˈsɜrvɪs dɪˌpɑrtmənt/ *noun* a department which deals with customers and their complaints and orders

customization *noun* the process of making changes to products or services that enable them to satisfy the particular needs of individual customers

customize *verb* to change something to fit the special needs of a customer ○ *We use customized computer terminals.*

customized service /ˌkʌstəmaɪzd ˈsɜrvɪs/ *noun* a service that is specifically designed to satisfy the particular needs of an individual customer

custom publisher /ˈkʌstəm ˌpʌblɪʃər/ *noun* a company which creates a magazine for a company to use as publicity

customs /ˈkʌstəmz/ *plural noun* the government department which organizes the collection of taxes on imports, or an office of this department at a port or airport ○ *He was stopped by customs.* ○ *Her car was searched by customs.* □ **to go through customs** to pass through the area of a port or airport where customs officials examine goods □ **to take something through customs** to carry something illegal through a customs area without declaring it □ **the crates had to go through a customs examination** the crates had to be examined by customs officials

customs broker /ˈkʌstəmz ˌbroʊkər/ *noun* a person or company that takes goods through customs for a shipping company

customs clearance /ˈkʌstəmz ˌklɪrəns/ *noun* **1.** the act of passing goods through customs so that they can enter or leave the country **2.** a document given by customs to a shipper to show that customs duty has been paid and the goods can be shipped ○ *to wait for customs clearance*

customs declaration /ˈkʌstəmz dekləˌreɪʃ(ə)n/ *noun* a statement showing goods being imported on which duty will have to be paid ○ *to fill in a customs declaration form*

customs entry point /ˌkʌstəmz ˈentri pɔɪnt/ *noun* a place at a border between two countries where goods are declared to customs

customs invoice /ˈkʌstəmz ˌɪnvɔɪs/ *noun* a customs form containing a list of goods with their values in both the exporter's and importer's countries

customs seal /ˈkʌstəmz siːl/ *noun* a seal attached by a customs officer to a box, to show that the contents have not passed through customs

customs tariff /ˈkʌstəmz ˌtærɪf/ *noun* a list of taxes to be paid on imported goods

customs warehouse /ˈkʌstəmz ˌweəhaʊs/ *noun* a government-run warehouse where goods are stored until duty is paid ○ *The goods will remain in the customs warehouse until the buyer claims them.*

cut-off /ˈkʌt ɒf/ *noun* the time after which a spot cannot be broadcast, usually late at night

cut-price /ˌkʌt ˈpraɪs/ *adjective* cheaper than usual

cut-price store /ˌkʌt praɪs ˈstɔː/ *noun* a store selling cut-price goods

cut-throat competition /ˌkʌt θrəʊt ˌkɒmpəˈtɪʃ(ə)n/ *noun* sharp competition which cuts prices and offers high discounts

cutting /ˈkʌtɪŋ/ *noun* U.K. same as **clipping**

cutting-edge /ˌkʌtɪŋ ˈedʒ/ *adjective* using or involving the latest and most advanced techniques and technologies

CV *abbreviation* curriculum vitae ○ *Please apply in writing, enclosing a current CV.*

cybercrime /ˈsaɪbəkraɪm/ *noun* a crime committed using the Internet

cyber mall /ˈsaɪbər mɔl/ *noun* a website that provides information and links for a number of online businesses

cybermarketing /ˈsaɪbəˌmɑːkətɪŋ/ *noun* marketing that uses any kind of Internet-based promotion, e.g., targeted emails, bulletin boards, websites, or sites from which the customer can download files

cybershopping /ˈsaɪbəˌʃɒpɪŋ/ *noun* the activity of making purchases using the Internet

cycle /ˈsaɪk(ə)l/ *noun* a set of events which happen in a regularly repeated sequence

cycle models /ˈsaɪk(ə)l ˌmɒd(ə)lz/ *plural noun* models which are used to explain cyclical change ○ *Cycle models were used in the case study to show recent developments in retailing.*

cyclical /ˈsɪklɪk(ə)l/ *adjective* happening in cycles

cyclical factors /ˌsɪklɪk(ə)l ˈfæktəz/ *plural noun* the way in which a trade cycle affects businesses

D

DAGMAR /'dægmɑr/ *noun* a model showing stages in the effect of advertising on a consumer, e.g., awareness, comprehension, conviction, and action. Full form **defining advertising goals for measured advertising results**

DAR *abbreviation* day after recall test

data /'deɪtə/ *noun* information available on computer, e.g., letters or figures ○ *All important data on employees was fed into the computer.* ○ *To calculate the weekly wages, you need data on hours worked and rates of pay.* (NOTE: takes a singular or plural verb) □ **data bank, bank of data** a store of information in a computer

data acquisition /'deɪtə ækwɪ,zɪʃ(ə)n/ *noun* the act of gathering information about a subject

database /'deɪtəbeɪs/ *noun* a set of data stored in an organized way in a computer system ○ *We can extract the lists of potential customers from our database.*

database cleaning /'deɪtəbeɪs ,klinɪŋ/, **database cleansing** /'deɪtəbeɪs ,klenzɪŋ/ *noun* checking the details of a database to make sure they are correct

database management system /,deɪtəbeɪs 'mænɪdʒmənt ,sɪstəm/ *noun* a computer program that is specially designed to organize and process the information contained in a database

database marketing /'deɪtəbeɪs ,mɑrkɪtɪŋ/ *noun* using a database to market a product or service by building up a relationship with customers

database modeling /'deɪtəbeɪs ,mɑd(ə)lɪŋ/ *noun* using the information from a database to create a website or to forecast trends in a market

database publishing /'deɪtəbeɪs ,pʌblɪʃɪŋ/ *noun* the publishing of information selected from a database, either on-line where the user pays for it on a per-page inspection basis or as a CD-ROM

data capture /'deɪtə ,kæptʃər/, **data entry** /,deɪtə 'entri/ *noun* the act of putting information onto a computer by keyboarding or by scanning

data cleansing /'deɪtə ,klenzɪŋ/, **data cleaning** /'deɪtə ,klinɪŋ/ *noun* checking data to make sure it is correct

data mining /'deɪtə ,maɪnɪŋ/ *noun* the use of advanced software to search online databases and identify statistical patterns or relationships in the data that may be commercially useful

data protection /'deɪtə prə,tekʃən/ *noun* making sure that computerized information about people is not misused

data sheet /'deɪtə ʃit/ *noun* a leaflet with data *or* information about a product

data warehouse /'deɪtə ,werhaʊs/ *noun* a large collection data that is collected over a period of time from different sources and stored on a computer in a standard format so that is easy to retrieve. It can be used, e.g., to support managerial decision-making. (NOTE: Organizations often use data warehouses for marketing purposes, for example, in order to store and analyze customer information.)

date /deɪt/ *noun* the number of the day, month, and year ○ *I have received your letter of yesterday's date.* □ **date of receipt** the date when something is received

date coding /'deɪt ˌkoʊdɪŋ/ *noun* the act of showing the date by which a product should be consumed

date-in-charge /ˌdeɪt ɪn 'tʃɑrdʒ/ *noun* the date from which a poster site is charged ○ *We will have three weeks of exposure from the date-in-charge.*

day /deɪ/ *noun* **1.** a period of 24 hours ○ *There are thirty days in June.* ○ *The first day of the month is a public holiday.* □ **days of grace** the time given to a debtor to repay a loan, to pay the amount purchased using a credit card, or to pay an insurance premium ○ *Let's send the check at once since we have only five days of grace left.* ○ *Because the store owner has so little cash available, we will have to allow him additional days of grace.* **2.** one of the days of the week

day after recall test /ˌdeɪ æftər 'rɪkɔl test/ *noun* an advertising research test to see how much someone can remember of an advertisement, the day after it appeared or was broadcast. Abbreviation **DAR**

day in the sun /ˌdeɪ ɪn ðə 'sʌn/ *noun* the period of time during which a product is in demand and sells well in the marketplace (*informal*)

daypart /'deɪpɑrt/ *noun* a section of a day, used for measuring audience ratings on TV

DBS *abbreviation* direct broadcast by satellite

dead /ded/ *adjective* not working □ **the line went dead** the telephone line suddenly stopped working

dead account /ˌded ə'kaʊnt/ *noun* an account which is no longer used

dead freight /ˌded 'freɪt/ *noun* payment by a charterer for unfilled space in a ship or plane ○ *Too much dead freight is making it impossible for the company to continue to charter ships.*

deadline /'dedlaɪn/ *noun* the date by which something has to be done □ **to meet a deadline** to finish something in time □ **to miss a deadline** to finish something later than it was planned ○ *We've missed our October 1st deadline.*

dead loss /ˌded 'lɑs/ *noun* a total loss ○ *The car was written off as a dead loss.*

dead season /'ded ˌsiz(ə)n/ *noun* the time of year when there are few tourists about

deadweight /'dedweɪt/ *noun* heavy goods, e.g., coal, iron, or sand

deadweight cargo /ˌdedweɪt 'kɑrgoʊ/ *noun* a heavy cargo which is charged by weight, not by volume

deal /dil/ *noun* a business agreement, affair or contract ○ *The sales director set up a deal with a Russian bank.* ○ *The deal will be signed tomorrow.* ○ *They did a deal with an American airline.* □ **to call off a deal** to stop an agreement ○ *When the chairman heard about the deal he called it off.* ■ *verb* **1.** □ **to deal with** to organize something ○ *Leave it to the filing clerk – he'll deal with it.* □ **to deal with an order** to work to supply an order **2.** to buy and sell □ **to deal with someone** to do business with someone □ **to deal in leather** *or* **options** to buy and sell leather or options □ **he deals on the Stock Exchange** his work involves buying and selling shares on the Stock Exchange for clients

dealer /'dilər/ *noun* a person who buys and sells ○ *a used-car dealer*

dealer aids /'dilər eɪdz/ *plural noun* types of advertising material used by shops to stimulate sales

dealer's brand /'diləz brænd/ *noun* a brand owned by a distributor rather by a producer ○ *I bought the dealer's brand of soap since the store is well known for its high quality goods.*

dealership /'dilərʃɪp/ *noun* **1.** the authority to sell some products or services **2.** a business run by an authorized dealer

dealer tie-in /ˌdilər 'taɪ ɪn/ *noun* advertising which includes the names of local dealers that stock the product being advertised

deal in /'dil ɪn/ *noun* sales promotion to the trade

deal out /'dil aʊt/ *noun* sales promotion to consumers

dear money /'dɪr ˌmʌni/ *noun* same as **tight money**

death duty /'deθ ˌduti/ *noun* a tax paid on the property left by a dead person. Also called **death tax** (NOTE: The U.K. term is **inheritance tax**.)

death tax /'deθ tæks/ *noun* same as **death duty**

deaveraging /diˈæv(ə)rɪdʒɪŋ/ *noun* the act of treating customers in different ways according to the amount they buy, by rewarding the best and penalizing the worst

debit /'debɪt/ *noun* an amount entered in accounts which shows an increase in assets or expenses or a decrease in liabilities, revenue or capital. In accounts, debits are entered in the left-hand column. Compare **credit** ■ *verb* □ **to debit an account** to charge an account with a cost ○ *His account was debited with the sum of $25.*

debitable /'debɪtəb(ə)l/ *adjective* able to be debited

debit card /'debɪt kɑrd/ *noun* a plastic card, similar to a credit card, but which debits the holder's account immediately through an EPOS system

debit column /'debɪt ˌkɑləm/ *noun* the left-hand column in accounts showing the money paid or owed to others

debit entry /'debɪt ˌentri/ *noun* an entry on the debit side of an account

debit note /'debɪt noʊt/ *noun* a note showing that a customer owes money ○ *We undercharged Mr. Smith and had to send him a debit note for the extra amount.*

debits and credits /ˌdebɪts ən 'kredɪts/ *plural noun* money which a company owes and money it receives, or figures which are entered in the accounts to record increases or decreases in assets, expenses, liabilities, revenue, or capital

debt /det/ *noun* money owed for goods or services ○ *The company stopped trading with debts of over $1 million.* □ **to be in debt** to owe money □ **he is in debt to the tune of $250,000** he owes $250,000 □ **to get into debt** to start to borrow more money than you can pay back □ **the company is out of debt** the company does not owe money anymore □ **to pay back a debt** to pay all the money owed □ **to pay off a debt** to finish paying money owed □ **to service a debt** to pay interest on a debt ○ *The company is having problems in servicing its debts.* □ **debts due** money owed which is due for repayment

debt collection /'det kəˌlekʃən/ *noun* the act of collecting money which is owed

debt collector /'det kəˌlektər/ *noun* a person who collects debts

debtor /'detər/ *noun* a person who owes money

debtor side /'detər saɪd/ *noun* the debit side of an account

decentralize /diˈsentrəlaɪz/ *verb* to move power or authority or action from a central point to local areas

decentralized system /diˌsentrəlaɪzd 'sɪstəm/ *noun* a system where responsibility for marketing, advertising, and promotion lies with a product manager rather than a centralized department

deception /dɪˈsepʃən/ *noun* telling a lie in order to mislead a customer

decide /dɪˈsaɪd/ *verb* to make up your mind to do something ○ *to decide on a course of action* ○ *to decide to appoint a new managing director*

decider /dɪˈsaɪdər/ *noun* a person who makes decisions, especially the person who makes the decision to buy

deciding factor /dɪˌsaɪdɪŋ 'fæktər/ *noun* the most important factor which influences a decision ○ *A deciding factor in marketing our range of sports goods in the country was the rising standard of living there.*

decimal system /'desɪm(ə)l ˌsɪstəm/ *noun* a system of mathematics based on the number 10

decision /dɪˈsɪʒ(ə)n/ *noun* a choice made after thinking about what to do ○ *It took the committee some time to come to a decision* or *to reach a decision.*

decision-maker /dɪˈsɪʒ(ə)n ˌmeɪkər/ *noun* a person who takes decisions

decision-making /dɪˈsɪʒ(ə)n ˌmeɪkɪŋ/ *noun* the act of coming to a decision

decision-making unit /dɪˈsɪʒ(ə)n ˌmeɪkɪŋ ˌjuːnɪt/ *noun* a group of people who decide on the purchase of a product. For the purchase of a new piece of equipment, they would be the manager, the financial controller, and the operator who will use the equipment. Abbreviation **DMU**

decision theory /dɪˈsɪʒ(ə)n ˌθɪəri/ *noun* the mathematical methods for weighing the various factors in making decisions ○ *In practice it is difficult to apply decision theory to our planning.* ○ *Students study decision theory to help them suggest strategies in case-studies.*

decision tree /dɪˈsɪʒ(ə)n triː/ *noun* a model for decision-making, showing the possible outcomes of different decisions ○ *This computer program incorporates a decision tree.*

deck /dek/ *noun* a flat floor in a ship

deck cargo /ˈdek ˌkɑːɡəʊ/ *noun* the cargo carried on the open top deck of a ship

decline /dɪˈklaɪn/ *noun* **1.** a gradual fall ○ *the decline in the value of the dollar* ○ *a decline in buying power* ○ *The last year has seen a decline in real wages.* **2.** the final stage in the life cycle of a product when the sales and profitability are falling off and the product is no longer worth investing in ■ *verb* to fall slowly or decrease ○ *Shares declined in a weak market.* ○ *New job applications have declined over the last year.* ○ *The economy declined during the last government.*

decode /diːˈkəʊd/ *verb* to translate and interpret a coded message

deduplication /diːˌduːplɪˈkeɪʃ(ə)n/ *noun* removing duplicate entries from a database

deep-rooted demand /ˌdiːp ˌruːtɪd dɪˈmænd/ *noun* brand loyalty which survives even if the product no longer offers value for money ○ *There is deep-rooted demand for this product which is a household name.*

de facto standard /deɪ ˌfæktəʊ ˈstændəd/ *noun* a standard that is set by a product or service that is very successful in a particular market

defensive spending /dɪˌfensɪv ˈspendɪŋ/ *noun* a budget strategy that promotes areas where sales are currently strong rather than potential areas where sales could be made

defer /dɪˈfɜː/ *verb* to put back to a later date, to postpone ○ *We will have to defer payment until January.* ○ *The decision has been deferred until the next meeting.* (NOTE: **deferring – deferred**)

deferment /dɪˈfɜːmənt/ *noun* the act of leaving until a later date ○ *deferment of payment* ○ *deferment of a decision*

deferred /dɪˈfɜːd/ *adjective* put back to a later date

deferred creditor /dɪˌfɜːd ˈkredɪtər/ *noun* a person who is owed money by a bankrupt but who is paid only after all other creditors

deferred payment /dɪˌfɜːd ˈpeɪmənt/ *noun* **1.** money paid later than the agreed date **2.** payment for goods by installments over a long period

deferred rebate /dɪˌfɜːd ˈriːbeɪt/ *noun* a discount given to a customer who buys up to a specified quantity over a specified period

deferred shares /dɪˌfɜːd ˈʃeəz/, **deferred stock** /dɪˌfɜːd ˈstɒk/ *noun* shares which receive a dividend only after all other dividends have been paid

deficit /ˈdefɪsɪt/ *noun* the amount by which spending is higher than income □ **the accounts show a deficit** the accounts show a loss □ **to make good a deficit** to put money into an account to balance it

deficit financing /ˈdefɪsɪt ˌfaɪnænsɪŋ/ *noun* a type of financial planning by a government in which it borrows money to cover the difference between its tax income and its expenditure

deflate /diːˈfleɪt/ *verb* □ **to deflate the economy** to reduce activity in the economy by cutting the supply of money

deflation /diːˈfleɪʃ(ə)n/ *noun* a general reduction in economic activity as a result of a reduced supply of money and credit, leading to lower prices ○ *The oil crisis resulted in worldwide deflation.* Opposite **inflation**

deflationary /dɪˈfleɪʃ(ə)n(ə)ri/ *adjective* causing deflation ○ *The government has introduced some deflationary measures in the budget.*

delay /dɪˈleɪ/ *noun* the time when someone or something is later than planned ○ *There was a delay of thirty minutes before the AGM started* or *the AGM started after a thirty-minute delay.* ○ *We are sorry for the delay in supplying your order* or *in replying to your letter.* ■ *verb* to make someone or something late ○ *The company has delayed payment of all invoices.* ○ *She was delayed because her taxi was involved in an accident.*

delayed response /dɪˌleɪd rɪˈspɒns/ *noun* a slower than expected response by consumers to a company's promotion ○ *If there is a delayed response we will only reap the benefits next year.* ○ *A delayed response is not usual in such a new product.*

del credere agent /del ˈkreɪdərɪ ˌeɪdʒənt/ *noun* an agent who receives a high commission because he or she guarantees payment by customers

delegation /delɪˈɡeɪʃ(ə)n/ *noun* **1.** a group of delegates ○ *A Chinese trade delegation is visiting Washington.* ○ *The management met a union delegation.* **2.** an act of passing authority or responsibility to someone else

delete /dɪˈliːt/ *verb* to remove a product from a company's product range ○ *We have decided to delete three old products as the new ones are coming on stream.*

deletion /dɪˈliːʃ(ə)n/ *noun* the act of removing an old product from the market ○ *The product has lost market share and is a candidate for deletion.*

delight factor /dɪˈlaɪt ˌfæktər/ *noun* the customer's pleasure at making a purchase

deliver /dɪˈlɪvər/ *verb* to transport goods to a customer □ **goods delivered free** *or* **free delivered goods** goods transported to the customer's address at a price which includes transportation costs □ **goods delivered on board** goods transported free to the ship or plane but not to the customer's warehouse

delivered price /dɪˈlɪvəd praɪs/ *noun* a price which includes packing and transportation

delivery /dɪˈlɪv(ə)ri/ *noun* **1.** the transporting of goods to a customer ○ *allow 28 days for delivery* ○ *parcels awaiting delivery* ○ *free delivery* or *delivery free* ○ *a delivery date* ○ *Delivery is not included.* ○ *We have a pallet of parcels awaiting delivery.* □ **to take delivery of goods** to accept goods when they are delivered ○ *We took delivery of the stock into our warehouse on the 25th.* **2.** a consignment of goods being delivered ○ *We take in three deliveries a day.* ○ *There were four items missing in the last delivery.*

delivery note /dɪˈlɪv(ə)ri nəʊt/ *noun* a list of goods being delivered, given to the customer with the goods

delivery of goods /dɪˌlɪv(ə)ri əv ˈɡʊdz/ *noun* the transportation of goods to a customer's address

delivery order /dɪˈlɪv(ə)ri ˌɔrdər/ *noun* the instructions given by the customer to the person holding her goods, to tell her where and when to deliver them

delivery receipt /dɪˈlɪv(ə)ri rɪˌsiːt/ *noun* a delivery note when it has been signed by the person receiving the goods

delivery service /dɪˈlɪv(ə)ri ˌsɜrvɪs/ *noun* a transportation service organized by a supplier or a store to take goods to customers

delivery time /dɪˈlɪv(ə)ri taɪm/ *noun* the number of days before something will be delivered

delivery van /dɪˈlɪv(ə)ri væn/ *noun* a van for delivering goods to customers

delphi method /ˈdelfaɪ ˌmeθəd/ *noun* a method of forming strategies by soliciting individual estimates on the time-scale of projected developments and then inviting further estimates on the basis of all those already made until a consensus is reached

demand /dɪˈmænd/ *noun* an act of asking for payment □ **payable on demand** which must be paid when payment is asked for ■ *verb* **1.** the need that customers have for a product or their eagerness to buy it ○ *There was an active demand for oil shares on the stock market.* ○ *The factory had to cut production when demand slackened.* ○ *The office cleaning company cannot keep up with the demand for its services.* □ **there is not much demand for this item** not many people want to buy it □ **this book is in great demand** *or* **there is a great demand for this book** many people want to buy it □ **to meet** *or* **fill a demand** to supply what is needed ○ *The factory had to increase production to meet the extra demand.* **2.** to ask for something and expect to get it ○ *She demanded a refund.* ○ *The suppliers are demanding immediate payment of their outstanding invoices.* ○ *The store stewards demanded an urgent meeting with the managing director.*

demand bill /dɪˈmænd bɪl/ *noun* a bill of exchange which must be paid when payment is asked for

demand deposit /dɪˈmænd dɪ ˌpɑzɪt/ *noun* money in a deposit account which can be taken out when you want it by writing a check

demand forecasting /dɪˈmænd ˌfɔrkæstɪŋ/ *noun* estimating what demand would exist at various prices, used as a method of calculating prices

demand-led inflation /dɪˌmænd led ɪnˈfleɪʃ(ə)n/, **demand-pull inflation** /dɪˌmænd pʊl ɪnˈfleɪʃ(ə)n/ *noun* inflation caused by rising demand which cannot be met

demand price /dɪˈmænd praɪs/ *noun* the price at which a quantity of goods will be bought

demand schedule /dɪˈmænd ˌskedʒəl/ *noun* a table showing demand for a product or service at different prices

demand theory /dɪˈmænd ˌθiəri/ *noun* a branch of economics concerned with consumer buying habits and factors which determine demand

demarketing /diˈmɑrkətɪŋ/ *noun* the act of attempting to reduce the demand for a product ○ *Demarketing was the*

keynote in the industry when rationing was introduced.

demassifying /ˌdiˈmæsɪfaɪɪŋ/ *noun* the process of changing a mass medium into one that is customized to fit the needs of individual consumers

demographic /ˌdeməˈgræfɪk/ *adjective* referring to demography or demographics ○ *A full demographic study of the country must be done before we decide how to export there.*

demographic edition /ˌdemə ˈgræfɪk ɪˌdɪʃ(ə)n/ *noun* a special edition of a magazine targeted at a specific demographic group

demographics /deməˈgræfɪks/ *plural noun* the details of the population of a country, in particular its size, density, distribution, and the birth, death, and marriage rates, which affect marketing (NOTE: takes a singular verb)

demographic segmentation /deməˌgræfɪk ˌsegmenˈteɪʃ(ə)n/ *noun* the act of dividing a market up into segments according to the age, sex, income levels, etc. of the potential customers

demography /dɪˈmɑgrəfi/ *noun* the study of populations and population statistics such as size, density, distribution, and birth, death, and marriage rates

demonstrate /ˈdemənstreɪt/ *verb* to show how something works ○ *He was demonstrating a new tractor when he was killed.* ○ *The managers saw the new stock-control system being demonstrated.*

demonstration /ˌdemənˈstreɪʃ(ə)n/ *noun* an act of showing or explaining how something works ○ *We went to a demonstration of new laser equipment.*

demonstration effect /ˌdemən ˈstreɪʃ(ə)n ɪˌfekt/ *noun* the theory stating that people buy products to impress or keep up with their neighbors ○ *The promotion of luxury goods is intended to exploit the demonstration effect.*

demonstration model /ˌdemən ˈstreɪʃ(ə)n ˌmɑd(ə)l/ *noun* a piece of equipment used in demonstrations and later sold off cheaply

demonstrator /'demənstreɪtər/ *noun* **1.** a person who demonstrates pieces of equipment **2.** same as **demonstration model**

demurrage /dɪ'mʌrɪdʒ/ *noun* money paid to a customer when a shipment is delayed at a port or by customs

department /dɪ'pɑːtmənt/ *noun* **1.** a specialized section of a large organization ○ *Trainee managers work for a while in each department to get an idea of the organization as a whole.* **2.** a section of a large store selling one type of product ○ *You will find beds in the furniture department.*

departmental manager /ˌdipɑːtment(ə)l 'mænɪdʒər/ *noun* the manager of a department

departmental system /ˌdipɑːt'ment(ə)l ˌsɪstəm/ *noun* a way of organizing an advertising agency into departments such as creative, media, administration, etc.

depend /dɪ'pend/ *verb* **1.** □ **to depend on** to need someone or something to exist ○ *The company depends on efficient service from its suppliers.* ○ *We depend on government grants to pay the salary bill.* **2.** to happen because of something ○ *The success of the launch will depend on the publicity campaign.* □ **depending on** which varies according to something

dependent /dɪ'pendənt/ *adjective* supported financially by someone else ○ *Employees may be granted leave to care for dependent relatives.*

dependent variable /dɪˌpendənt 'veriəb(ə)l/ *noun* a variable or factor which changes as a result of a change in another (the "independent variable") ○ *We are trying to understand the effects of several independent variables on one dependent variable, in this case, sales.*

deposit /dɪ'pɑzɪt/ *noun* money given in advance so that the thing which you want to buy will not be sold to someone else ○ *to pay a deposit on a watch* ○ *to leave $10 as deposit*

depot /'dipoʊ/ *noun* a central warehouse or storage area for goods, or a place for keeping vehicles used for transportation ○ *a goods depot* ○ *an oil storage depot* ○ *a freight depot* ○ *a bus depot*

depreciate /dɪ'priʃieɪt/ *verb* **1.** to reduce the value of assets in accounts ○ *We depreciate our company cars over three years.* **2.** to lose value ○ *a share which has depreciated by 10% over the year* ○ *The pound has depreciated by 5% against the dollar.*

COMMENT: Various methods of depreciating assets are used, such as the "straight line method", where the asset is depreciated at a constant percentage of its cost each year and the "reducing balance method", where the asset is depreciated at a constant percentage which is applied to the cost of the asset after each of the previous years' depreciation has been deducted.

depreciation /dɪˌpriʃi'eɪʃ(ə)n/ *noun* **1.** a reduction in value of an asset **2.** a loss of value ○ *a share which has shown a depreciation of 10% over the year* ○ *the depreciation of the pound against the dollar*

depreciation rate /dɪˌpriʃi'eɪʃ(ə)n reɪt/ *noun* the rate at which an asset is depreciated each year in the company accounts

depress /dɪ'pres/ *verb* to reduce something ○ *Reducing the money supply has the effect of depressing demand for consumer goods.*

depressed area /dɪˌprest 'eriə/ *noun* a part of a country suffering from depression

depressed market /dɪˌprest 'mɑrkət/ *noun* a market where there are more goods than customers

depression /dɪ'preʃ(ə)n/ *noun* a period of economic crisis with high unemployment and loss of trade ○ *The country entered a period of economic depression.*

depth /depθ/ *noun* the variety in a product line

depth interview /'depθ ˌɪntərvju/ *noun* an interview with no preset questions and following no fixed pattern, but which can last a long time and allows the respondent time to express personal views and tastes ○ *Depth interviews* *elicited some very original points of view.*

deregulation /diˌregjəˈleɪʃ(ə)n/ *noun* the reduction of government control over an industry ○ *the deregulation of the airlines*

derived demand /dɪˌraɪvd dɪ ˈmænd/ *noun* a demand for a product because it is needed to produce another product which is in demand

describe /dɪˈskraɪb/ *verb* to say what someone or something is like ○ *The leaflet describes the services the company can offer.* ○ *The managing director described the difficulties the company was having with cash flow.*

description /dɪˈskrɪpʃən/ *noun* a detailed account of what something is like □ **false description of contents** the act of wrongly stating the contents of a packet to trick customers into buying it

design /dɪˈzaɪn/ *noun* **1.** the planning or drawing of a product before it is built or manufactured **2.** the planning of the visual aspect of an advertisement ■ *verb* to plan or to draw something before it is built or manufactured ○ *He designed a new car factory.* ○ *She designs garden furniture.*

designate /ˈdezɪgneɪt/ *verb* to identify something or someone in a particular way

designated market area /ˌdezɪgneɪtɪd ˈmɑrkət ˌeriə/ *noun* geographic areas used in measuring the size of an audience. Abbreviation **DMA**

design audit /dɪˈzaɪn ˌɔdɪt/ *noun* the checking and evaluating of design, especially in advertising materials or on a website

design consultancy /dɪˈzaɪn kənˌsʌltənsi/ *noun* a firm which gives specialist advice on design

design department /dɪˈzaɪn dɪ ˌpɑrtmənt/ *noun* the department in a large company which designs the company's products or its advertising

designer /dɪˈzaɪnər/ *noun* a person who designs ○ *She is the designer of the new computer.* ■ *adjective* expensive and fashionable ○ *designer jeans*

designer product /dɪˌzaɪnər ˈprɑdʌkt/ *noun* a fashionable product created by a well-known designer ○ *Recent wealth in the cities has increased the demand for designer products.* ○ *Jeans and sportswear are only some of our designer products.*

design factor /dɪˈzaɪn ˌfæktər/ *noun* the ratio of sampling error of a complex sample or sample design to that of a completely random sample

design for manufacturability /dɪˈzaɪn fə ˌmænjʊfæktʃərəˈbɪləti/ *noun* the process of adapting the design of a product so that it fits as well as possible into the manufacturing system of an organization, thus reducing the problems of bringing the product to market (NOTE: The manufacturing issues that need to be taken into account in design for manufacturability include selecting appropriate materials, making the product easy to assemble, and minimizing the number of machine set-ups required.)

design protection /dɪˈzaɪn prəˌtekʃən/ *noun* making sure that a design is not copied by an unauthorized user

design studio /dɪˈzaɪn ˌstudioʊ/ *noun* an independent firm which specializes in creating designs

desire /dɪˈzaɪə/ *noun* the wish to do something

desire to purchase /dɪˌzaɪr tər ˈpɜrtʃɪs/ *noun* the feeling of a customer that he or she needs to purchase a product. ◊ **AIDA**

desk /desk/ *noun* a writing table in an office, usually with drawers for stationery ○ *a desk diary* ○ *a desk drawer* ○ *a desk light*

desk research /ˈdesk rɪˌsɜrtʃ/ *noun* the process of looking for information which is in printed sources such as directories

desk researcher /ˈdesk rɪˌsɜrtʃər/ *noun* a person who carries out desk research

devaluation /ˌdivæljuˈeɪʃ(ə)n/ *noun* a reduction in the value of a currency against other currencies ○ *the devaluation of the rand*

devalue /di'vælju/ *verb* to reduce the value of a currency against other currencies ○ *The dollar was devalued by 7%.*

develop /dɪ'veləp/ *verb* **1.** to plan and produce ○ *to develop a new product* **2.** to plan and build an area ○ *to develop an industrial estate*

developed country /dɪ,veləpt 'kʌntri/ *noun* a country which has an advanced manufacturing system

developing country /dɪ,veləpɪŋ 'kʌntri/, **developing nation** /dɪ ,veləpɪŋ 'neɪʃ(ə)n/ *noun* a country which is not fully industrialized

development /dɪ'veləpmənt/ *noun* the work of planning the production of a new product and constructing the first prototypes ○ *We spend a great deal on research and development.*

development cycle /dɪ'veləpmənt ,saɪk(ə)l/ *noun* the various stages which are involved in the development of a product from the initial concept to its manufacture and marketing

deviation /,divi'eɪʃ(ə)n/ *noun* a change of route or strategy ○ *Advertising in the tabloids will mean a deviation from our normal marketing strategy.*

diadic test /daɪ,ædɪk 'test/ *noun* a product test in which respondents compare two products

diagram /'daɪəgræm/ *noun* a drawing which presents information visually ○ *a diagram showing sales locations* ○ *a diagram of the company's organizational structure* ○ *The first diagram shows how our decision-making processes work.*

diagrammatic /,daɪəgrə'mætɪk/ *adjective* □ **in diagrammatic form** in the form of a diagram

diagrammatically /,daɪəgrə 'mætɪkli/ *adverb* using a diagram ○ *The chart shows the sales pattern diagrammatically.*

dial /'daɪəl/ *verb* to call a telephone number on a telephone ○ *to dial a number* ○ *to dial the operator*

dial-and-smile /,daɪəl ən 'smaɪl/ *verb* to try to appear pleasant when cold-calling potential customers

diary /'daɪəri/ *noun U.K.* same as **appointment book**

diary method /'daɪəri ,meθəd/ *noun* a market research method whereby respondents keep a regular written account of advertising noticed or purchases made or products used

diary panel /'daɪəri ,pæn(ə)l/ *noun* a group of people who are asked to keep notes of their purchases on a daily basis

dice /daɪs/ *verb* to cut food into small cubes

dichotomous question /daɪ ,kɒtəməs 'kwestʃən/ *noun* a question in a questionnaire that can only be answered by "yes" or "no"

differential /,dɪfə'renʃəl/ *adjective* showing a difference ■ *noun* □ **to erode wage differentials** to reduce differences in salary gradually

differential advantage /,dɪfərenʃəl əd'væntɪdʒ/ *noun* an advantage that one product has over rival products in the market ○ *We are confident that our toothpaste has a differential advantage.*

differential pricing /,dɪfərenʃəl 'praɪsɪŋ/ *noun* the act of giving different products in a range of different prices so as to distinguish them from each other

differential tariffs /,dɪfərenʃəl 'tærɪfs/ *plural noun* different tariffs for different classes of goods as, e.g., when imports from some countries are taxed more heavily than similar imports from other countries

differentiated marketing strategy /dɪfə,renʃeɪtɪd 'mɑrkɪtɪŋ ,strætɪdʒi/ *noun* a method of marketing where the product is modified to suit each potential market. ◊ **concentrated marketing, undifferentiated product**

differentiation /,dɪfərenʃi'eɪʃ(ə)n/ *noun* the act of ensuring that a product has some unique features that distinguish it from competing products ○ *We are adding some extra features to our watches in the interest of product differ-*

entiation. ○ *The aim of differentiation should be to catch the customer's eye.*

diffusion /dɪˈfjuːʒ(ə)n/ *noun* the process by which a product is gradually adopted by consumers

diffusion curve /dɪˈfjuːʒ(ə)n kɜːrv/ *noun* the geographic representation of how many consumers adopt a product at different times. ◊ **exponential diffusion**

digerati /ˌdɪdʒəˈrɑːti/ *plural noun* people who claim to have a sophisticated understanding of Internet or computer technology (*slang*)

digital /ˈdɪdʒɪt(ə)l/ *adjective* converted into a form that can be processed by computers and accurately reproduced

digital cash /ˌdɪdʒɪt(ə)l ˈkæʃ/ *noun* a form of digital money that can be used like physical cash to make online purchases and is anonymous because there is no way of obtaining information about the buyer when it is used

digital color proof /ˌdɪdʒɪt(ə)l ˈkʌlər pruːf/ *noun* a color proof taken from digital files prior to film output at high or low resolution

digital economy /ˌdɪdʒɪt(ə)l ɪˈkɑnəmi/ *noun* an economy that is based on electronic commerce, e.g., trade on the Internet

digital goods /ˌdɪdʒɪt(ə)l ˈɡʊdz/ *plural noun* goods that are sold and delivered electronically, usually over the Internet

digital money /ˌdɪdʒɪt(ə)l ˈmʌni/ *noun* a series of numbers that has a value equivalent to a sum of money in a physical currency

digital nervous system /ˌdɪdʒɪt(ə)l ˈnɜrvəs ˌsɪstəm/ *noun* a digital information system that gathers, manages, and distributes knowledge in a way that allows an organization to respond quickly and effectively to events in the outside world

digital TV /ˌdɪdʒɪt(ə)l tiˈviː/ *noun* TV where the picture has been changed into a form which a computer can process

digital wallet /ˌdɪdʒɪt(ə)l ˈwɒlət/ *noun* a piece of personalized software

on the hard drive of a user's computer that contains, in coded form, such items as credit card information, digital cash, a digital identity certificate, and standardized shipping information, and can be used when paying for a transaction electronically. Also called **e-purse, electronic purse**

digitizable /ˈdɪdʒɪtaɪzəb(ə)l/ *adjective* able to be converted into digital form for distribution via the Internet or other networks

Dinkies /ˈdɪŋkiz/ *plural noun* couples who are both wage-earners and have no children (NOTE: short for **Double Income No Kids**)

direct /daɪˈrekt/ *verb* to manage or organize something ○ *He directs our Southeast Asian operations.* ○ *She was directing the development unit until last year.* ■ *adjective* straight or without interference ■ *adverb* with no third party involved ○ *We pay income tax direct to the government.* □ **to dial direct** to contact a phone number yourself without asking the operator to do it for you ○ *You can dial New York direct from London if you want.*

direct-action advertising /daɪˌrekt ˌækʃən ˈædvərtaɪzɪŋ/ *noun* advertising which aims to get a quick response ○ *We'll need some direct-action advertising if we're not to fall behind our competitors this spring.* ○ *Direct-action advertising will only help us in the short term.*

direct-action marketing /daɪˌrekt ˌækʃən ˈmɑrkətɪŋ/ *noun* same as **direct response advertising**

direct broadcast by satellite /daɪˌrekt ˌbrɔdkæst baɪ ˈsætəlaɪt/ *noun* TV and radio signals broadcast over a wide area from an earth station via a satellite, received with a dish antenna. Abbreviation **DBS**

direct channel /daɪˌrekt ˈtʃæn(ə)l/ *noun* a marketing channel where a producer and consumer deal directly with one another

direct close /daɪˌrekt ˈkloʊz/ *noun* the act of ending a sale by asking the customer if they want to buy

direct demand /daɪˌrekt dɪˈmænd/ *noun* demand for a product or service for its own sake, and not for what can be derived from it

direct export /daɪˌrekt ˈekspɔːt/ *noun* selling a product direct to the overseas customer without going through a middleman ○ *Direct export is the only way to keep down the retail price.* ○ *Our overseas marketing consists mainly of direct export to German department stores.*

direct headline /daɪˌrekt ˈhedlaɪn/ *noun* an eye-catching headline that presents its message directly to its target audience

direction /daɪˈrekʃən/ *noun* **1.** the process of organizing or managing ○ *He took over the direction of a multinational group.* **2.** □ **directions for use** instructions showing how to use something

directional /daɪˈrekʃən(ə)l/ *adjective* pointing in a specific direction

directional medium /daɪˌrekʃən(ə)l ˈmiːdiəm/ *noun* an advertising medium that tells potential customers where to find products or services, e.g., a directory

directive interview /daɪˌrektɪv ˈɪntəvjuː/ *noun* an interview using preset questions and following a fixed pattern

direct labor /daɪˌrekt ˈleɪbər/ *noun* the cost of the workers employed which can be allocated to a product, not including materials or overheads

directly /daɪˈrektli/ *adverb* with no third party involved ○ *We deal directly with the manufacturer, without using a wholesaler.*

direct mail /daɪˌrekt ˈmeɪl/ *noun* the practice of selling a product by sending publicity material to possible buyers through the mail ○ *These calculators are only sold by direct mail.* ○ *The company runs a successful direct-mail operation.*

direct-mail advertising /daɪˌrekt meɪl ˈædvətaɪzɪŋ/ *noun* advertising by sending leaflets to people through the mail

direct mailing /daɪˌrekt ˈmeɪlɪŋ/ *noun* the sending of publicity material by mail to possible buyers

direct mail preference service /daɪˌrekt meɪl ˈpref(ə)rəns ˌsɜːvɪs/ *noun* a service where an addressee can have his or her name removed from a mailing list

direct marketing /daɪˌrekt ˈmɑːkətɪŋ/ *noun* same as **direct response advertising**

direct-marketing media /daɪˌrekt ˈmɑːkətɪŋ ˌmiːdiə/ *plural noun* media that are used for direct marketing, e.g., direct mail, telemarketing, and TV

director /daɪˈrektər/ *noun* **1.** a senior employee appointed by the shareholders to help run a company, who is usually in charge of one or other of its main functions, e.g., sales or human relations, and usually, but not always, a member of the board of directors **2.** the person who is in charge of a project, an official institute, or other organization ○ *the director of the government research institute* ○ *She was appointed director of the trade association.*

directorate /daɪˈrekt(ə)rət/ *noun* a group of directors

directorship /daɪˈrektəʃɪp/ *noun* the post of director ○ *She was offered a directorship with Smith Inc.*

directors' report /daɪˌrektəz rɪˈpɔːt/ *noun* the annual report from the board of directors to the shareholders

directory /daɪˈrekt(ə)ri/ *noun* a reference book containing information on companies and their products

direct response advertising /daɪˌrekt rɪˈspɒns ˌædvətaɪzɪŋ/ *noun* advertising in such a way as to get customers to send in inquiries or orders directly by mail

direct response agency /daɪˌrekt rɪˈspɒns ˌeɪdʒənsi/ *noun* a company which provides direct marketing services to its clients such as database management, direct mail, and response collecting

direct response marketing /daɪˌrekt rɪˈspɒns ˌmɑːkətɪŋ/ *noun* same as **direct response advertising**

direct selling /daɪˌrekt 'selɪŋ/ *noun* the work of selling a product direct to the customer without going through a store

direct services /daɪˌrekt 'sɜːvɪsɪz/ *plural noun* personal services to the public, e.g., catering, dentistry, or hairdressing ○ *There is little manufacturing industry in the area, and direct services account for most of the wealth.*

dirty /'dɜːti/ *adjective* not clean

dirty bill of lading /ˌdɜːti bɪl əv 'leɪdɪŋ/ *noun* a bill of lading stating that the goods did not arrive on board in good condition. Also called **foul bill of lading**

disclosure of information /dɪs ˌkləʊʒər əv ˌɪnfər'meɪʃ(ə)n/ *noun* the passing on of information that was intended to be kept secret or private to someone else

discount *noun* /'dɪskaʊnt/ **1.** the percentage by which the seller reduces the full price for the buyer ○ *to give a discount on bulk purchases* □ **to sell goods at a discount** *or* **at a discount price** to sell goods below the normal price □ **10% discount for cash** *or* **10% cash discount** you pay 10% less if you pay in cash **2.** the amount by which something is sold for less than its value ■ *verb* /dɪs 'kaʊnt/ **1.** □ **to discount bills of exchange** to buy or sell bills of exchange for less than the value written on them in order to cash them later **2.** to react to something which may happen in the future, such as a possible takeover bid or currency devaluation □ **shares are discounting a rise in the dollar** shares have risen in advance of a rise in the dollar price

discountable /'dɪskaʊntəb(ə)l/ *adjective* possible to discount ○ *These bills are not discountable.*

discounted cash flow /ˌdɪskaʊntɪd 'kæʃ fləʊ/ *noun* the calculation of the forecast return on capital investment by discounting future cash flows from the investment, usually at a rate equivalent to the company's minimum required rate of return. Abbreviation **DCF**

discounted value /ˌdɪskaʊntɪd 'vælju/ *noun* the difference between the face value of a share and its lower market price

discounter /'dɪskaʊntər/ *noun* a person or company that discounts bills or invoices, or sells goods at a discount

discount for cash /ˌdɪskaʊnt fər 'kæʃ/ *noun* same as **cash discount**

discount house /'dɪskaʊnt haʊs/ *noun* **1.** a financial company which specializes in discounting bills **2.** a store which specializes in selling cheap goods bought at a high discount

discount price /'dɪskaʊnt praɪs/ *noun* the full price less a discount

discount rate /'dɪskaʊnt reɪt/ *noun* the rate charged by a central bank on any loans it makes to other banks

discount store /'dɪskaʊnt stɔr/ *noun* a store which specializes in cheap goods bought at a high discount

discount table /'dɪskaʊnt ˌteɪb(ə)l/ *noun* same as **table of discounts**

discrepancy /dɪ'skrepənsi/ *noun* a lack of agreement between figures in invoices or accounts

discretion /dɪ'skreʃ(ə)n/ *noun* the ability to decide what should be done □ **I leave it to your discretion** I leave it for you to decide what to do □ **at the discretion of someone** according to what someone decides ○ *Membership is at the discretion of the committee.*

discretionary /dɪ'skreʃ(ə)n(ə)ri/ *adjective* possible if someone wants □ **the minister's discretionary powers** powers which the minister could use if he or she thought it necessary

discretionary income /dɪ ˌskreʃ(ə)n(ə)ri 'ɪnkʌm/ *noun* income left after fixed payments have been made and whose spending is therefore subject to advertising influence ○ *Discretionary incomes generally increase in a recession.*

discrimination test /dɪˌskrɪmɪ 'neɪʃ(ə)n test/ *noun* a product test designed to show how one product differs from another ○ *The discrimination test* *showed our product to be superior to that of our closest competitor.*

discussion board /dɪ'skʌʃ(ə)n bɔrd/, **discussion group** /dɪ'skʌʃ(ə)n grup/ *noun* a group of people who discuss something by sending emails to the group and where each member can respond and see the responses of other members

discussion list /dɪ'skʌʃ(ə)n lɪst/ *noun* a list of addresses of members of a discussion board

diseconomies of scale /dɪsɪ,kɑnəmiz əv 'skeɪl/ *plural noun* a situation where increased production leads to a higher production cost per unit or average production cost

disequilibrium /,dɪsikwɪ'lɪbriəm/ *noun* an imbalance in the economy when supply does not equal demand

dishoarding /dɪs'hɔrdɪŋ/ *noun* putting goods back onto the market when they have been hoarded or stored for some time

dishonor /dɪs'ɑnər/ *verb* □ **to dishonour a bill** not to pay a bill (NOTE: The U.K. spelling is **dishonour**.)

dishonored check /dɪs,ɑnərd 'tʃek/ *noun* a check which the bank will not pay because there is not enough money in the account to pay it

disintegration /dɪs,ɪntɪ'greɪʃ(ə)n/ *noun* the decision to stop producing some goods or supplies and to buy them in instead ○ *Disintegration has meant we now have to buy all of our plastic parts.* ○ *Part of the company's disintegration policy involved selling off the factories.*

disintermediation /dɪs,ɪntəmidi'eɪʃ(ə)n/ *noun* the removal of any intermediaries from a process so that, e.g., manufacturers sell direct to consumers instead of selling their products through wholesalers and retailers

disparage /dɪ'spærɪdʒ/ *verb* to criticize

disparaging copy /dɪ,spærɪdʒɪŋ 'kɑpi/ *noun* advertising copy which is critical of another company's products ○ *Their disparaging copy has given*

them a bad name in the industry. Also called **knocking copy**

dispatch /dɪ'spætʃ/ *noun* **1.** the sending of goods to a customer ○ *Production difficulties held up dispatch for several weeks.* **2.** goods which have been sent ○ *The weekly dispatch went off yesterday.* ■ *verb* to send goods to customers ○ *The goods were dispatched last Friday.*

dispatch department /dɪ'spætʃ dɪ,pɑrtmənt/ *noun* the department which deals with the packing and sending of goods to customers

dispatcher /dɪ'spætʃər/ *noun* a person who sends goods to customers

dispatch note /dɪ'spætʃ noʊt/ *noun* a note saying that goods have been sent

dispatch rider /dɪ'spætʃ ,raɪdər/ *noun* a motorcyclist who delivers messages or parcels in a town

dispenser /dɪ'spensər/ *noun* a machine which automatically provides something such as an object, a drink, or an item of food, often when money is put in ○ *an automatic dispenser* ○ *a towel dispenser*

dispersion /dɪ'spɜrʃ(ə)n/ *noun* the attempt by a distributor to distribute a product to a market

display /dɪ'spleɪ/ *noun* the showing of goods for sale ○ *an attractive display of kitchen equipment* ○ *The store has several car models on display.* ■ *verb* to show ○ *The company was displaying three new car models at the show.*

display advertisement /dɪ'spleɪ əd,vɜrtɪsmənt/, **display ad** /dɪ'spleɪ æd/ *noun* an advertisement which is well designed or printed in bold type to attract attention

display advertising /dɪ'spleɪ ,ædvərtaɪzɪŋ/ *noun* advertising that has individual features such as photographs, its own box border, or the company logo in addition to text

display material /dɪ'spleɪ mə,tɪriəl/ *noun* material used to attract attention to goods which are for sale, e.g., posters and photographs

display outer /dɪ'spleɪ ,aʊtər/ *noun* a container for protecting goods in transit which can also be used as an attractive display container for the goods in a store

display panel /dɪ'spleɪ ˌpæn(ə)l/ *noun* a flat area for displaying goods in a store window

disposable /dɪ'spəʊzəb(ə)l/ *adjective* which can be used and then thrown away ○ *The machine serves soup in disposable paper cups.*

disposable income /dɪˌspəʊzəb(ə)l 'ɪnkʌm/, **disposable personal income** /dɪˌspəʊzəb(ə)l ˌpɜːs(ə)nəl 'ɪnkʌm/ *noun* the income left after tax has been deducted

disposal /dɪ'spəʊz(ə)l/ *noun* a sale ○ *a disposal of securities* ○ *The company has started a systematic disposal of its property portfolio.* □ **lease *or* business for disposal** a lease or business for sale

dispose /dɪ'spəʊz/ *verb* □ **to dispose of** to get rid of or to sell, especially cheaply ○ *to dispose of excess stock* ○ *He is planning to dispose of his business in the new year.*

disrewarding /ˌdɪsrɪ'wɔːdɪŋ/ *noun* the penalizing of bad customers to allow the company to give special terms to the best customers

dissonance/attribution model /ˌdɪsənəns ˌætrɪ'bjuːʃ(ə)n ˌmɒd(ə)l/ *noun* a response model which follows the opposite sequence from normal: consumers first act in a specific way, then develop feelings as a result of their behavior, and then look for information that supports their attitude and behavior

dissonance reduction /'dɪsənəns rɪˌdʌkʃən/ *noun* a reduction in worries experienced by the purchaser after a product has been purchased, by increasing their awareness of the positive features of the product and reducing their fears about its negative features. ◊ **cognitive dissonance**

distance freight /'dɪstəns freɪt/ *noun* freight charges based on the distance over which the goods are transported

distinctive competence /dɪˌstɪŋktɪv 'kɒmpɪt(ə)ns/ *noun* an advantage that one company or producer has over competitors in the market ○

Our distinctive competence is a highly professional sales force. ○ *The company could not survive with high costs and no distinctive competence.*

distress merchandise /dɪ'stres ˌmɜːtʃəndaɪs/ *noun* goods sold cheaply to pay a company's debts

distress sale /dɪ'stres seɪl/ *noun* a sale of goods at low prices to pay a company's debts

distress selling /dɪ'stres ˌselɪŋ/ *noun* the sale of goods cheaply in order to pay off debts ○ *Difficult circumstances forced the producers to resort to distress selling.*

distribute /dɪ'strɪbjuːt/ *verb* **1.** to share out dividends ○ *Profits were distributed among the shareholders.* **2.** to send out goods from a manufacturer's warehouse to retail shops ○ *Smith Inc. distributes for several smaller companies.* ○ *All orders are distributed from our warehouse near Oxford.*

distribution /ˌdɪstrɪ'bjuːʃ(ə)n/ *noun* **1.** the act of sending goods from the manufacturer to the wholesaler and then to retailers ○ *Stock is held in a distribution center which deals with all order processing.* ○ *Distribution costs have risen sharply over the last 18 months.* ○ *She has several years' experience as distribution manager.* **2.** the act of sharing something among several people

distribution census /ˌdɪstrɪ'bjuːʃ(ə)n ˌsensəs/ *noun* official statistics regarding the number of distributors and their businesses ○ *Using the distribution census, we drew up a list of wholesalers who were worth approaching.*

distribution center /ˌdɪstrɪ'bjuːʃ(ə)n ˌsentər/ *noun* a place where goods are collected and stored temporarily but whose main function is to send them on to wholesalers, retailers, or consumers

distribution channel /ˌdɪstrɪ'bjuːʃ(ə)n ˌtʃæn(ə)l/ *noun* the route by which a product or service reaches a customer after it leaves the producer or supplier (NOTE: A distribution channel usually consists of a chain of intermediaries, for example wholesalers and retailers, that is designed to move goods from the point of production to the point of consumption in the most efficient way.)

distribution management /ˌdɪstrɪ 'bjuːʃ(ə)n ˌmænɪdʒmənt/ *noun* the management of the efficient transfer of goods from the place where they are manufactured to the place where they are sold or used (NOTE: Distribution management involves such activities as warehousing, materials handling, packaging, stock control, order processing, and transportation.)

distribution network /ˌdɪstrɪ 'bjuːʃ(ə)n ˌnetwɜːk/ *noun* a series of points or small warehouses from which goods are sent all over a country

distribution resource planning /dɪstrɪˌbjuːʃ(ə)n rɪˈsɔːs ˌplænɪŋ/ *noun* planning, especially using a computerized system, that is intended to ensure the most efficient use of the resources used in distributing goods (NOTE: Effective distribution resource planning integrates distribution with manufacturing and synchronizes supply and demand by identifying requirements for finished goods and by producing schedules for the movement of goods along the distribution chain so that they reach the customer as soon as possible.)

distributive /dɪˈstrɪbjʊtɪv/ *adjective* referring to distribution

distributive trades /dɪˈstrɪbjʊtɪv ˌtreɪdz/ *plural noun* all businesses involved in the distribution of goods

distributor /dɪˈstrɪbjətər/ *noun* a company which sells goods for another company which makes them □ **a network of distributors** a number of distributors spread all over a country

distributor's brand /dɪˈstrɪbjətərz ˌbrænd/ *noun* goods specially packed for a store with the store's name printed on them ○ *I bought the distributor's brand of soap because it was the cheapest.*

distributorship /dɪˈstrɪbjətərʃɪp/ *noun* the position of being a distributor for a company

distributor support /dɪˌstrɪbjətər səˈpɔːt/ *noun* the action of a supplier of a product or service in providing help to distributors, by offering training, promotional material, etc.

divergent marketing /daɪˌvɜːdʒənt ˈmɑːkətɪŋ/ *noun* a separate marketing treatment for each of a company's products ○ *Divergent marketing is giving way to a more coordinated and integrated marketing effort.*

diversification /daɪˌvɜːsɪfɪˈkeɪʃ(ə)n/ *noun* the process of adding another quite different type of business to a firm's existing trade

diversify /daɪˈvɜːsɪfaɪ/ *verb* **1.** to add new types of business to existing ones ○ *The company is planning to diversify into new products.* **2.** to invest in different types of shares or savings so as to spread the risk of loss

divert /daɪˈvɜːt/ *verb* **1.** to send to another place or in another direction **2.** to buy stock in a special offer and then sell it on to customers living outside the special-offer area

divestment /daɪˈvestmənt/ *noun* the dropping or sale of a whole product line, to allow the company to concentrate on other products

division /dɪˈvɪʒ(ə)n/ *noun* **1.** the main section of a large company ○ *the marketing division* ○ *the production division* ○ *the retail division* ○ *the hotel division of the leisure group* **2.** a company which is part of a large group ○ *Smith's is now a division of the Brown group of companies.* **3.** the act of separating a whole into parts ○ *the division of responsibility between managers*

divisional /dɪˈvɪʒ(ə)n(ə)l/ *adjective* referring to a division ○ *a divisional director* ○ *the divisional headquarters*

DM *abbreviation* direct marketing

DMA /ˌdiː em ˈeɪ/ *abbreviation* designated market area

DMU *abbreviation* decision-making unit

document /ˈdɒkjəmənt/ *noun* a paper, especially an official paper, with written information on it ○ *He left a file* *of documents in the taxi.* ○ *She asked to see the documents relating to the case.*

documentary /ˌdɑkjə'ment(ə)ri/ *adjective* in the form of documents ○ *documentary evidence*

documentation /ˌdɑkjəmen'teɪʃ(ə)n/ *noun* all the documents referring to something ○ *Please send me the complete documentation concerning the sale.*

document of title /ˌdɑkjəmənt əv 'taɪt(ə)l/ *noun* a document allowing the holder to handle goods as if they own them

documents against acceptance /ˌdɑkjəmənts əˌgenst ək'septəns/ *noun* an arrangement whereby buyers receive documents for the goods on their acceptance of a bill of exchange

documents against cash /ˌdɑkjəmənts əˌgenst 'kæʃ/, **documents against presentation** /ˌdɑkjəmənts əˌgenst prez(ə)n'teɪʃ(ə)n/ *noun* an arrangement whereby a buyer receives documents for the goods on payment of a bill of exchange

dog /dɔg/ *noun* a product that has a low market share and a low growth rate, and so is likely to be dropped from the company's product line

dog-eat-dog /ˌdɑg ɪt 'dɑg/ *noun* marketing activity where everyone fights for their own product and attacks competitors mercilessly (*informal*)

do-it-yourself /ˌduː ɪt jə'self/ *adjective* done by an ordinary person, not by a skilled worker. Abbreviation **DIY**

do-it-yourself conveyancing /ˌduː ɪt jəˌself kən'veɪənsɪŋ/ *noun* the drawing up of a legal conveyance by the person selling a property, without the help of a lawyer

do-it-yourself magazine /ˌduː ɪt jə'self ˌmægəziːn/ *noun* a magazine with articles on work which the average person can do to repair or paint his or her house

do-it-yourself store /ˌduː ɪt jə'self ˌstɔr/ *noun* a large store specializing in selling materials for the repair and improvement of houses, for gardening and for light car maintenance

domestic /də'mestɪk/ *adjective* **1.** referring to the home market or the market of the country where the business is situated ○ *Domestic sales have increased over the last six months.* **2.** for use in the home ○ *Glue which is intended for both domestic and industrial use.*

domestic appliances /dəˌmestɪk ə'plaɪənsɪz/ *plural noun* electrical machines which are used in the home, e.g., washing machines

domestic consumption /dəˌmestɪk kən'sʌmpʃən/ *noun* use in the home country ○ *Domestic consumption of oil has fallen sharply.*

domestic market /dəˌmestɪk 'mɑrkət/ *noun* the market in the country where a company is based ○ *They produce goods for the domestic market.*

domestic production /dəˌmestɪk prə'dʌkʃən/ *noun* the production of goods for use in the home country

door /dɔr/ *noun* the piece of wood, metal, or other material which closes the entrance to a building or room ○ *The finance director knocked on the chairman's door and walked in.* □ **the store opened its doors on June 1st** the store started doing business on June 1st

door drop /'dɔr drɑp/ *noun* a delivery of promotional literature by hand to all the houses in an area

door-to-door /ˌdɔr tə 'dɔr/ *adjective* going from one house to the next, asking the occupiers to buy something or to vote for someone ○ *door-to-door canvassing* ○ *We have 200 door-to-door salesmen.* ○ *Door-to-door selling is banned in this town.*

door-to-door salesman /ˌdɔr tə dɔr 'seɪlzmən/ *noun* a man who goes from one house to the next, asking people to buy something

door-to-door service /ˌdɔr tə dɔr 'sɜrvɪs/ *noun* a transportation service that takes goods directly to the buyer's address

dormant /'dɔrmənt/ *adjective* no longer active or no longer operating

dormant account /ˌdɔrmənt ə'kaʊnt/ *noun* a bank account which is no longer used

dot.com /ˌdɑtˈkɑm/, **dot-com** /dɑt kɑm/ *noun* a business that markets its products through the Internet, rather than by using traditional marketing channels

double /ˈdʌb(ə)l/ *adjective* twice as large or two times the size ○ *Their turnover is double ours.* □ **to be on double time** to earn twice the usual wages for working on Sundays or other holidays ■ *verb* to become twice as big, or make something twice as big ○ *We have doubled our profits this year* or *our profits have doubled this year.* ○ *The company's borrowings have doubled.*

double column /ˌdʌb(ə)l ˈkɑləm/ *noun* two columns spanned by an advertisement

double crown /ˌdʌb(ə)l ˈkraʊn/ *noun* a basic poster size, 30 inches deep by 20 inches wide

double-decker /ˌdʌb(ə)l ˈdekə/ *noun* two advertising panels, one on top of the other

double-digit /ˌdʌb(ə)l ˈdɪdʒɪt/ *adjective* more than 10 and less than 100 ○ *double-digit inflation*

double opt-in /ˌdʌb(ə)l ˈɑpt ˌɪn/ *noun* a method by which users who want to receive information or services from a website can register themselves as subscribers

double-page spread /ˌdʌb(ə)l peɪdʒ ˈspred/ *noun* two facing pages in a magazine or newspaper, used by an advertiser

double-pricing /ˌdʌb(ə)l ˈpraɪsɪŋ/ *noun* the practice of showing two prices on a product, to make buyers think there has been a price reduction

double-spotting /ˌdʌb(ə)l ˈspɑtɪŋ/ *noun* running an advertising spot twice

down /daʊn/ *adverb, preposition* in a lower position or to a lower position ○ *The inflation rate is gradually coming down.* ○ *Shares are slightly down on the day.* ○ *The price of gasoline has gone down.* □ **to pay money down** to pay a deposit ○ *They paid $50 down and the rest in monthly installments.*

  down tools *phrasal verb* to stop working ○ *The entire work force*

downed tools in protest.

downmarket /ˌdaʊnˈmɑrkət/ *adverb, adjective* cheaper or appealing to a less wealthy section of the population ○ *The company has adopted a downmarket image.*

downside /ˈdaʊnsaɪd/ *noun* □ **the sales force have been asked to give downside forecasts** they have been asked for pessimistic forecasts

downside factor /ˈdaʊnsaɪd ˌfæktər/, **downside potential** /ˌdaʊnsaɪd pəˈtenʃ(ə)l/ *noun* the possibility of making a loss in an investment

downturn /ˈdaʊntɜrn/ *noun* the movement toward lower prices, sales, or profits ○ *a downturn in the market price* ○ *The last quarter saw a downturn in the economy.*

draft /dræft/ *noun* an order for money to be paid by a bank ○ *We asked for payment by banker's draft.* □ **to make a draft on a bank** to ask a bank to pay money for you

draw /drɔ/ *verb* **1.** to take money away ○ *to draw money out of an account* □ **to draw a salary** to have a salary paid by the company ○ *The chairman does not draw a salary.* **2.** to write a check ○ *She paid the invoice with a check drawn on a Canadian bank.* (NOTE: **drawing – drew – has drawn**)

drawback /ˈdrɔbæk/ *noun* **1.** something which is not convenient or which is likely to cause problems ○ *One of the main drawbacks of the plan is that it will take six years to complete.* **2.** a rebate on customs duty for imported goods when these are then used in producing exports

drawee /drɔˈi/ *noun* the person or bank asked to make a payment by a drawer

drawer /ˈdrɔər/ *noun* the person who writes a check or a bill asking a drawee to pay money to a payee □ **the bank returned the cheque to drawer** the bank would not pay the check because the person who wrote it did not have enough money in the account to pay it

drawing account /ˈdrɔɪŋ əˌkaʊnt/ *noun* a checking account, or any account from which the customer may take money when he or she wants

drilling down /ˌdrɪlɪŋ 'daʊn/ *noun* the action of sorting data into hierarchies, each of which is more detailed than the previous one

drip /'drɪp kæmˌpeɪn/, **drip campaign**, **drip method** /'drɪp ˌmeθəd/ *noun* the placing of advertisements for a product at fairly long intervals, making a long-drawn-out advertising campaign

drive /draɪv/ *noun* an energetic way of doing things □ **She has a lot of drive** she is very energetic in business

driver /'draɪvər/ *noun* something or someone that provides an impetus for something to happen

driver's license /'draɪvərz ˌlaɪs(ə)ns/ *noun* the official document which shows someone is legally allowed to drive a car, truck, or other vehicle ○ *Applicants for the job should hold a valid driver's license.* (NOTE: The U.K. term is **driving license**.)

drive time /'draɪv taɪm/ *noun* the time when people are most likely to be listening to the radio in their cars, hence a good time for broadcasting commercials

drop /drɑp/ *noun* a fall ○ *a drop in sales* ○ *Sales show a drop of 10%.* ○ *The drop in prices resulted in no significant increase in sales.* ■ *verb* **1.** to fall ○ *Sales have dropped by 10% or have dropped 10%.* ○ *The pound dropped three points against the dollar.* **2.** not to keep in a product range ○ *We have dropped these items from the catalog because they've been losing sales steadily for some time.* (NOTE: **dropping – dropped**)

    drop ship *phrasal verb* to deliver a large order direct to a customer

drop shipment /'drɑp ˌʃɪpmənt/ *noun* the delivery of a large order from the manufacturer direct to a customer's store or warehouse without going through an agent or wholesaler

dud /dʌd/ *noun, adjective* referring to a coin or banknote which is false or not good, or something which does not do

what it is supposed to do (*informal*) ○ *The $50 bill was a dud.*

dud check /ˌdʌd 'tʃek/ *noun* a check which cannot be cashed because the person writing it does not have enough money in the account to pay it

due /du/ *adjective* **1.** owed ○ *a sum due from a debtor* □ **to fall** *or* **become due** to be ready for payment □ **bill due on May 1st** a bill which has to be paid on May 1st □ **balance due to us** the amount owed to us which should be paid **2.** expected to arrive **3.** correct and appropriate in the situation □ **in due form** written in the correct legal form ○ *a receipt in due form* ○ *a contract drawn up in due form* □ **after due consideration of the problem** after thinking seriously about the problem □ **due to** caused by ○ *The company pays the wages of staff who are absent due to illness.*

dues /duz/ *plural noun* orders taken but not supplied until new stock arrives □ **to release dues** to send off orders which had been piling up while a product was out of stock ○ *We have recorded thousands of dues for that item and our supplier cannot supply it.*

dummy /'dʌmi/ *noun* an imitation product to test the reaction of potential customers to its design

dummy pack /'dʌmi pæk/ *noun* an empty pack for display in a store

dump /dʌmp/ *verb* □ **to dump goods on a market** to get rid of large quantities of excess goods cheaply in an overseas market

dump bin /'dʌmp bɪn/ *noun* a display container like a large box which is filled with goods for sale

dump display /'dʌmp dɪˌspleɪ/ *noun* goods on special display in a container for purchasers to select themselves in a store ○ *We will use dump displays with price reductions clearly marked.* ○ *There are several dump displays near the counters in the supermarket.*

dumping /'dʌmpɪŋ/ *noun* the act of getting rid of excess goods cheaply in an overseas market ○ *The government has passed anti-dumping legislation.* ○

Dumping of goods on the European market is banned.

duopoly /duˈɑpəli/ *noun* the existence of only two producers or suppliers in a market ○ *The duopoly meant that the two businesses collaborated to keep prices at very high levels.* ○ *When they took over their only competitor in the market, the duopoly became a monopoly.* Compare **monopoly**

duplication /ˌduplɪˈkeɪʃ(ə)n/ *noun* running an advertisement twice to the same audience

durable /ˈdjʊrəb(ə)l/ *adjective* □ **durable effects** effects which will be felt for a long time ○ *These demographic changes will have durable effects on the economy.*

durable goods /ˈdjʊrəb(ə)l ɡʊdz/ *plural noun* goods which will be used for a long time, e.g., washing machines or refrigerators

Dutch auction /ˌdʌtʃ ˈɔkʃən/ *noun* an auction in which the auctioneer offers an item for sale at a high price and then gradually reduces the price until someone makes a bid

duty /ˈduti/ *noun* **1.** a tax which has to be paid ○ *Traders are asking the government to take the duty off alcohol or to put a duty on cigarettes.* □ **goods which are liable to duty** goods on which customs or excise tax has to be paid **2.** a moral or legal obligation ○ *the employee's duty to his employer* ○ *He felt he*

had a duty to show his successor how the job was done.

duty-free /ˌduti ˈfri/ *adjective, adverb* sold with no duty to be paid ○ *She bought duty-free perfume at the airport.* ○ *He bought the watch duty-free.*

duty-free store /ˌdjuti ˈfri stɔr/ *noun* a store at an airport or on a ship where goods can be bought without paying duty

duty-paid goods /ˌduti ˈpeɪd ɡʊdz/ *plural noun* goods where the duty has been paid

dyadic communication /daɪˌædɪk kəˌmjunɪˈkeɪʃ(ə)n/ *noun* direct conversation between two people such as a salesperson and a customer

Dynamic HTML /daɪˌnæmɪk ˌeɪtʃ ti em ˈel/ *noun* a tool for creating limited animated graphics on a website that can be viewed by most browsers. Its major advantage is that it does not require a plug-in to be viewed by users. Abbreviation **DHTML**

dynamic obsolescence /daɪˌnæmɪk ˌɑbsəˈles(ə)ns/ *noun* the redesigning of a company's product in order to make previous models and other products on the market obsolete

dynamic pricing /daɪˌnæmɪk ˈpraɪsɪŋ/ *noun* pricing that changes when the demand for something increases or decreases

E

e-alliance /'i ə,laɪəns/ *noun* a partnership between organizations that do business over the web. Studies show that the most successful e-alliances have been those that link traditional off-line businesses with businesses that specialize in operating online entities.

e. & o.e. *abbreviation* errors and omissions excepted

ear /ɪr/ *noun* a space at the top left or right corner of the front page of a newspaper, set aside for advertising

early /'ɜrli/ *adjective, adverb* before the usual time ○ *The mail arrived early.* □ **at an early date** very soon

early adopters /,ɜrli ə'dɑptərz/ *plural noun* the category of buyers of a product who use it or buy it later than innovators, but earlier than the late majority

early majority /,ɜrli mə'dʒɔrəti/ *noun* a category of buyers of a product who buy it later than the early adopters

earned rate /,ɜrnd 'reɪt/ *noun* the actual rate for a printed advertising space after taking discounts into account

earnest /'ɜrnɪst/ *noun* money paid as an initial payment by a buyer to a seller, to show commitment to the contract of sale

earning potential /'ɜrnɪŋ pə,tenʃəl/ *noun* **1.** the amount of money a person should be able to earn in his or her professional capacity **2.** the amount of dividend which a share is capable of earning

easy terms /,izi 'tɜrmz/ *plural noun* financial terms which are not difficult to accept ○ *The store is rented on very easy terms.*

e-business /'i ,bɪznəs/ *noun* **1.** business activities, e.g., buying and selling, servicing customers, and communicating with business partners, that are carried out electronically, especially on the Internet. Also called **electronic commerce 2.** a company that does its business using the Internet

ecoconsumer /'ikoʊkən,sumər/ *noun* a customer who will buy goods that have been produced in a way that does not harm the environment

ecolabel /'ikoʊleɪb(ə)l/ *noun* a label used to mark products that are produced and can be used and disposed of in a way that does not harm the environment

e-commerce /'i ,kɑmɜrs/ *noun* the exchange of goods, information, products, or services via an electronic medium such as the Internet. Also called **electronic commerce** (NOTE: Although e-commerce was originally limited to buying and selling, it has now evolved and includes such things as customer service, marketing, and advertising.)

e-commerce mall /'i kɑmɜrs mɔl/ *noun* same as **cyber mall**

e-company /'i ,kʌmp(ə)ni/ *noun* a company that does all its business using the Internet

econometrics /ɪ,kɑnə'metrɪks/ *plural noun* the study of the statistics of economics, using computers to analyze these statistics and make forecasts using mathematical models

economic /,ikə'nɑmɪk/ *adjective* **1.** providing enough money to make a profit ○ *The apartment is rented for an economic sum.* ○ *It is hardly economic for the company to run its own warehouse.* **2.** referring to the financial state of a country ○ *economic planning* ○ *economic trends* ○ *Economic planners are expecting a consumer-led boom.* ○ *The government's economic policy is in ruins after the devaluation.* ○ *The economic situation is getting worse.* ○ *The country's economic system needs more regulation.*

economical /ˌikəˈnamɪk(ə)l/ *adjective* saving money or materials or being less expensive ○ *This car is very economical.* □ **economical car** a car which does not use much gasoline □ **an economical use of resources** the fact of using resources as carefully as possible

economic development /ˌikənamɪk dɪˈveləpmənt/ *noun* the expansion of the commercial and financial situation ○ *The government has offered tax incentives to speed up the economic development of the region.* ○ *Economic development has been relatively slow in the north, compared with the rest of the country.*

economic growth /ˌikənamɪk ˈɡroʊθ/ *noun* the rate at which a country's national income grows

economic indicator /ˌikənamɪk ˈɪndɪkeɪtəz/ *noun* various statistics, e.g., for the unemployment rate or overseas trade, which show how the economy is going to perform in the short or long term

economic infrastructure /ˌikənamɪk ˈɪnfrəstrʌktʃər/ *noun* the road and rail systems of a country

economic model /ˌikənamɪk ˈmad(ə)l/ *noun* a computerized plan of a country's economic system, used for forecasting economic trends

economic order quantity /ˌikənamɪk ˈɔrdər ˌkwantəti/ *noun* the quantity of stocks which a company should hold, calculated on the basis of the costs of warehousing, of lower unit costs because of higher quantities purchased, the rate at which stocks are used, and the time it takes for suppliers to deliver new orders. Abbreviation **EOQ**

economic planning /ˌikənamɪk ˈplænɪŋ/ *noun* the process of planning the future financial state of the country for the government

economics /ˌikəˈnamɪks/ *noun* the study of the production, distribution, selling and use of goods and services ■ *plural noun* the study of financial structures to show how a product or service is costed and what returns it produces ○ *I do not understand the economics of the coal industry.* (NOTE: [all senses] takes a singular verb)

economic stagnation /ˌikənamɪk stæɡˈneɪʃ(ə)n/ *noun* a lack of expansion in the economy

economic trend /ˌikənamɪk ˈtrend/ *noun* the way in which a country's economy is moving

economies of scale /ɪˌkanəmiz əv ˈskeɪl/ *plural noun* measures taken so that a product is made more profitable, as by manufacturing it in larger quantities so that each unit costs less to make. Compare **diseconomies of scale**

economist /ɪˈkanəmɪst/ *noun* a person who specializes in the study of economics ○ *Government economists are forecasting a growth rate of 3% next year.* ○ *An agricultural economist studies the economics of the agriculture industry.*

economy /ɪˈkanəmi/ *noun* **1.** an action which is intended to stop money or materials from being wasted, or the quality of being careful not to waste money or materials □ **to introduce economies** *or* **economy measures into the system** to start using methods to save money or materials **2.** the financial state of a country, or the way in which a country makes and uses its money ○ *The country's economy is in ruins.*

economy car /ɪˈkanəmi kar/ *noun* a car which does not use much gasoline

economy drive /ɪˈkanəmi draɪv/ *noun* a vigorous effort to save money or materials

economy measure /ɪˈkanəmi ˌmeʒər/ *noun* an action to save money or materials

economy size /ɪˈkanəmi saɪz/ *noun* a large size or large packet which is cheaper than usual

EDI *abbreviation* electronic data interchange

editing /'edɪtɪŋ/ *noun* **1.** the process of checking the results of a survey to confirm that data has been collected correctly **2.** the process of modifying or correcting a text or movie ○ *This sales literature needs editing to make it less long-winded.*

edition /ɪ'dɪʃ(ə)n/ *noun* an issue of a publication such as a newspaper, trade magazine, or book ○ *We are too late to advertise in this month's edition.* ○ *There will be too many competing advertisements in that edition.*

editorial /ˌedɪ'tɔːriəl/ *adjective* referring to editors or to editing ■ *noun* the main article in a newspaper, written by the editor

editorial advertisement /edɪˌtɔːriəl əd'vɜːtɪsmənt/ *noun* an advertisement in the form of text material in a magazine

editorial board /edɪˌtɔːriəl 'bɔːd/ *noun* a group of editors on a newspaper or other publication

editorial environment /edɪˌtɔːriəl ɪn'vaɪrənmənt/ *noun* the general editorial tone and philosophy of a medium

editorial matter /edɪˌtɔːriəl ˌmætər/ *noun* the text of a magazine which is written by journalists, and not part of an advertisement

editorial publicity /edɪˌtɔːriəl pʌ'lɪsəti/ *noun* free publicity which is given to a product by a newspaper or magazine in an editorial or article, rather than in an advertisement which must be paid for

educational advertising /edjʊ ˌkeɪʃ(ə)nəl 'ædvətaɪzɪŋ/ *noun* advertising that informs consumers about a product, particularly important when the product has only recently been introduced ○ *Educational advertising has made the public aware that our product is just as safe as more traditional devices on the market.*

e-economy /'iː ɪˌkɑnəmi/ *noun* an economy in which the use of the Internet and information technology plays a major role

effect /ɪ'fekt/ *noun* **1.** a result ○ *The effect of the pay increase was to raise productivity levels.* **2.** an operation □ **terms of a contract which take effect** *or* **come into effect from January 1st** terms which start to operate on January 1st □ **prices are increased 10% with effect from January 1st** new prices will apply from January 1st □ **to remain in effect** to continue to be applied **3.** meaning □ **a clause to the effect that** a clause which means that □ **we have made provision to this effect** we have put into the contract terms which will make this work ■ *verb* to carry out □ **to effect a payment** to make a payment □ **to effect customs clearance** to clear something through customs □ **to effect a settlement between two parties** to bring two parties together and make them agree to a settlement

effective /ɪ'fektɪv/ *adjective* **1.** actual, as opposed to theoretical **2.** □ **a clause effective as from January 1st** a clause which starts to be applied on January 1st **3.** producing results ○ *Advertising in the Sunday papers is the most effective way of selling.* ○ *She is an effective marketing manager.* ◊ **cost-effective**

effective cover /ɪˌfektɪv 'kʌvər/ *noun* a situation where consumers in the target audience will have seen the advertisement at least four times on average

effective date /ɪ'fektɪv deɪt/ *noun* the date on which a rule or contract starts to be applied, or on which a transaction takes place

effective demand /ɪˌfektɪv dɪ 'mænd/ *noun* the actual demand for a product which can be paid for

effectiveness /ɪ'fektɪvnəs/ *noun* the quality of working successfully or producing results ○ *I doubt the effectiveness of television advertising.* ◊ **cost-effectiveness**

effective reach /ɪˌfektɪv 'riːtʃ/ *noun* the actual number of people who will see an advertisement once

effective sample size /ɪˌfektɪv 'sæmpəl ˌsaɪz/ *noun* the size of a sample after all irrelevant factors have been removed

effectual /ɪˈfektʃuəl/ *adjective* which produces a correct result

ego /ˈegoʊ/ *noun* the psychological term for a person's consciousness of himself or herself ○ *We are designing clothes to boost men's egos.* ○ *Glamorous advertising appeals to the customer's ego.*

eighty/twenty law /ˌeɪti ˈtwenti ˌrul/, **80/20 law** *noun* the rule that a small percentage of customers may account for a large percentage of sales. ◊ **Pareto's Law**

elastic /ɪˈlæstɪk/ *adjective* able to expand or contract easily because of small changes in price

elastic demand /ɪˌlæstɪk dɪˈmænd/ *noun* demand which experiences a comparatively large percentage change in response to a change in price

elasticity /ˌɪlæˈstɪsəti/ *noun* the ability to change easily in response to a change in circumstances □ **elasticity of supply and demand** changes in supply and demand of an item depending on its market price

elastic supply /ɪˌlæstɪk səˈplaɪ/ *noun* supply which experiences a comparatively large percentage change in response to a change in price

electronic /ɪlekˈtrɑnɪk/ *adjective* referring to computers and electronics

electronic cash /ˌɪlektrɑnɪk ˈkæʃ/ *noun* same as **digital cash**

electronic catalog /ˌelektrɑnɪk ˈkætəlɔg/ *noun* a catalog of the goods that a supplier has for sale, which can be viewed in an electronic format, e.g., on a website

electronic commerce /ˌelektrɑnɪk ˈkɑmɜrs/ *noun* same as **e-commerce**

electronic data capture /ˌɪlektrɑnɪk ˈdeɪtə ˌkæptʃər/ *noun* the use of data-processing equipment to collect data, especially the use of electronic point-of-sale equipment to collect, validate, and submit data when credit or debit cards are used in transactions

electronic data interchange /ˌɪlektrɑnɪk ˈdeɪtə ˌɪntətʃeɪndʒ/ *noun* a standard format used when business documents such as invoices and purchase orders are exchanged over electronic networks such as the Internet. Abbreviation **EDI**

electronic data processing /ˌelektrɑnɪk ˈdeɪtə ˌprɑsesɪŋ/ *noun* the process of selecting and examining data stored in a computer to produce information. Abbreviation **EDP**

electronic funds transfer at point of sale /ˌelektrɑnɪk ˌfʌndz ˌtrænsfɜr ət ˌpɔɪnt əv ˈseɪl/ *noun* the payment for goods or services by a bank customer using a card that is swiped through an electronic reader on the register, thereby transferring the cash from the customer's account to the retailer's or service provider's account. Abbreviation **EFTPOS**

electronic mail /ˌelektrɑnɪk ˈmeɪl/ *noun* same as **email** *noun* 1

electronic media /ˌelektrɑnɪk ˈmidiə/ *plural noun* electronic-based media, e.g., television and radio ○ *Advertising in the electronic media would certainly increase sales, but we can only afford to advertise in the press.*

electronic payment system /ˌelektrɑnɪk ˈpeɪmənt ˌsɪstəm/ *noun* a means of making payments over an electronic network such as the Internet

electronic point of sale /ˌelektrɑnɪk pɔɪnt əv ˈseɪl/ *noun* a system where sales are charged automatically to a customer's credit card and stock is controlled by the store's computer. Abbreviation **EPOS**

electronic purse /ˌelektrɑnɪk ˈpɜrs/ *noun* same as **digital wallet**

electronic shopping /ˌelektrɑnɪk ˈʃɑpɪŋ/ *noun* shopping for goods or services which takes place over an electronic network such as the Internet

eliminate /ɪˈlɪmɪneɪt/ *verb* to remove ○ *to eliminate defects in the system* ○ *Using a computer should eliminate all possibility of error.* ○ *We have decided to eliminate this series of old products from our range.* ○ *Most of the candidates were eliminated after the first batch of tests.*

elimination /ɪˌlɪmɪˈneɪʃ(ə)n/ *noun* the act of removing something

email /ˈiːmeɪl/, **e-mail** /ˈiː meɪl/ *noun* **1.** a system of sending messages from one computer terminal to another, using a modem and telephone lines ○ *You can contact me by phone or email if you want.* **2.** a message sent electronically ○ *I had six emails from him today.* ■ *verb* to send a message from one computer to another, using a modem and telephone lines ○ *She emailed her order to the warehouse.* ○ *I emailed him about the meeting.*

email campaign /ˈiːmeɪl kæmˌpeɪn/ *noun* a series of emails which deliver marketing messages to individuals

email mailing list /ˌiːmeɪl ˈmeɪlɪŋ ˌlɪst/ *noun* a marketing technique that involves contacting a group of people from anywhere in the world and inviting them to discuss a particular topic and share information and experience by email (NOTE: An email mailing list is run by a moderator who compiles a list of email addresses for possible members, mails them with the theme for discussion, collects their contributions, and publishes them by email so that other members of the group can respond to them.)

e-marketplace /ˌiː ˈmɑːkɪtpleɪs/ *noun* a network of connections that brings business-to-business buyers and sellers together on the Internet and enables them to trade more efficiently online

embargo /ɪmˈbɑːgoʊ/ *noun* **1.** a government order which stops a type of trade □ **to lay** *or* **put an embargo on trade with a country** to say that trade with a country must not take place ○ *The government has put an embargo on the export of computer equipment.* □ **to lift an embargo** to allow trade to start again ○ *The government has lifted the embargo on the export of computers.* □ **to be under an embargo** to be forbidden **2.** a period of time during which specific information in a press release must not be published (NOTE: The plural is **embargoes.**) ■ *verb* **1.** to stop trade, or not to allow something to be traded ○ *The gov-*ernment has embargoed trade with countries that are in breach of international agreements. **2.** not to allow publication of information for a period of time ○ *The news of the merger has been embargoed until next Wednesday.*

e-money /ˈiː ˌmʌni/ *noun* same as **digital money**

emotional appeal /ɪˌmoʊʃ(ə)n(ə)l əˈpiːl/ *noun* an attempt by advertising to persuade through an emotional rather than a rational message ○ *The charity used the emotional appeal of starving children to raise funds.* ○ *Emotional appeal was an obvious feature in all the political parties' campaign films.*

empirical data /ɪmˌpɪrɪk(ə)l ˈdeɪtə/ *noun* data or information which comes from actual observation or which can be proved ○ *We have no empirical data concerning our competitors' sales last year.*

employer's association /ɪmˌplɔɪərz əˌsoʊsiˈeɪʃ(ə)n/ *noun* same as **employers' organization**

employers' liability insurance /ɪmˌplɔɪərz ˌlaɪəˈbɪləti ɪnˌʃʊrəns/ *noun* insurance to cover accidents which may happen at work, and for which the company may be responsible

employers' organization /ɪmˈplɔɪərz ˌɔːrgənaɪzeɪʃ(ə)n/, **employers' association** /ɪmˌplɔɪərz əˌsoʊsiˈeɪʃ(ə)n/ *noun* a group of employers with similar interests

employment agency /ɪmˈplɔɪmənt ˌeɪdʒənsi/ *noun* an office which finds jobs for staff

emporium /ɪmˈpɔːriəm/ *noun* a large store (NOTE: The plural is **emporia.**)

emptor /ˈemptər/ *noun* ♦ **caveat emptor**

empty nesters /ˌempti ˈnestərz/ *plural noun* couples whose children have grown up and left the home

emulator /ˈemjʊleɪtər/ *noun* someone who is trying to become an achiever

enc, encl *abbreviation* enclosure

enclose /ɪnˈkloʊz/ *verb* to put something inside an envelope with a letter ○ *to enclose an invoice with a letter* ○ *I am* *enclosing a copy of the contract.* ○ *Please find the check enclosed herewith.* ○ *Please enclose a recent photograph with your résumé.*

enclosure /ɪnˈkloʊʒər/ *noun* a document enclosed with a letter or package ○ *The enclosure turned out to be a free sample of perfume.* ○ *Sales material on other products was sent out as an enclosure.*

encode /ɪnˈkoʊd/ *verb* to write something in a code so that it cannot be read or used by other people

end /end/ *noun* the final point or last part ○ *at the end of the contract period*

end consumer /ˌend kənˈsumər/ *noun* a person who uses a product ○ *The survey was designed to assess the attitudes of end consumers to the product.*

end of season sale /ˌend əv ˈsiz(ə)n seɪl/ *noun* a sale of goods at a lower price when the season in which they would be used is over, such as summer clothes sold cheaply in the fall

endorse /ɪnˈdɔrs/ *verb* to say that a product is good □ **to endorse a bill** *or* **a cheque** to sign a bill or check on the back to show that you accept it

endorsee /ˌendɔrˈsi/ *noun* a person whose name is written on a bill or check as having the right to cash it

endorsement /ɪnˈdɔrsmənt/ *noun* **1.** the act of endorsing **2.** a signature on a document which endorses it

endorsement advertising /ɪnˈdɔrsmənt ˌædvərtaɪzɪŋ/ *noun* same as **product endorsement**

endorser /ɪnˈdɔrsər/ *noun* a person who endorses a bill or check which is then paid to him or her

end user /ˌend ˈjuzər/ *noun* a person who actually uses a product

enhancement /ɪnˈhænsmənt/ *noun* increase or improvement in quality of service, value for money, etc.

ent /ent/ *noun* a test of number sequences for large quantities of data

enterprise /ˈentərpraɪz/ *noun* **1.** a system of carrying on a business **2.** a business

enterprise portal /ˌentərpraɪz ˈpɔrt(ə)l/ *noun* a website that contains a wide variety of information and services useful to the employees of a particular organization for their work (NOTE: The essential difference between an enterprise portal and an intranet is that an enterprise portal also provides external content that may be useful, e.g., specialist news feeds and access to industry research reports.)

enterprise zone /ˈentərpraɪz zoʊn/ *noun* an area of the country where businesses are encouraged to develop by offering special conditions such as easy planning permission for buildings or a reduction in the business rate

entrant /ˈentrənt/ *noun* a company which goes into a market for the first time

entrepot port /ˈɑntrəpoʊ pɔrt/ *noun* a town with a large international commercial port dealing in re-exports

entrepot trade /ˈɑntrəpoʊ treɪd/ *noun* the exporting of imported goods

entrepreneur /ˌɑntrəprəˈnɜr/ *noun* a person who directs a company and takes commercial risks

entrepreneurial /ˌɑntrəprəˈnɜrriəl/ *adjective* taking commercial risks ○ *an entrepreneurial decision*

entry barrier /ˈentri ˌbæriə/ *noun* same as **barrier to entry**

envelope stuffer /ˈenvəloʊp ˌstʌfər/ *noun* advertising material which is mailed in an envelope

environment /ɪnˈvaɪrənmənt/ *noun* the area in which an organization works

environmental analysis /ɪnˌvaɪrənˈment(ə)l əˈnæləsɪs/ *noun* the analysis of factors outside an organization such as demography or politics, in order to make strategic planning more effective ○ *Our environmental analysis must cover all the countries we sell in.* ○ *Environmental analysis made clear that some markets were too unstable to enter.*

environmental management /ɪnˌvaɪrənˈment(ə)l ˈmænɪdʒmənt/ *noun* a planned approach to minimizing an organization's impact on the environment

epos /'ipɑs/, **EPOS, EPoS** *abbreviation* electronic point of sale

e-purse /'i pɜrs/ *noun* same as **digital wallet**

equilibrium /,ikwɪ'lɪbriəm/ *noun* the state of balance in the economy where supply equals demand or a country's balance of payments is neither in deficit nor in excess

equity capital /'ekwəti ,kæpɪt(ə)l/ *noun* the nominal value of the shares owned by the ordinary shareholders of a company (NOTE: Preference shares are not equity capital. If the company were wound up, none of the equity capital would be distributed to preference shareholders.)

e-retailer /'i ,riteɪlər/ *noun* a business that uses an electronic network such as the Internet to sell its goods or services

erode /ɪ'roʊd/ *verb* to wear away gradually □ **to erode wage differentials** to reduce gradually differences in salary between different grades

error /'erər/ *noun* a mistake ○ *He made an error in calculating the total.* ○ *Someone must have made a keyboarding error.*

error rate /'erər reɪt/ *noun* the number of mistakes per thousand entries or per page

escalate /'eskəleɪt/ *verb* to increase steadily

escalation /,eskə'leɪʃ(ə)n/ *noun* a steady increase ○ *an escalation of wage demands* ○ *The union has threatened an escalation in strike action.* □ **escalation of prices** a steady increase in prices

escalation clause /,eskə'leɪʃ(ə)n klɔz/ *noun* same as **escalator clause**

escalator /'eskəleɪtər/ *noun* a moving staircase

escalator card /'eskəleɪtər kɑrd/ *noun* an advertisement on either side of an escalator in subway stations ○ *The media buyer compared the cost of posters and escalator cards.*

escalator clause /'eskəleɪtər klɔz/ *noun* a clause in a contract allowing for regular price increases because of increased costs, or regular wage increases because of the increased cost of living

escrow /'eskroʊ/ *noun* an agreement between two parties that something should be held by a third party until conditions are fulfilled □ **in escrow** held in safekeeping by a third party □ **document held in escrow** a document given to a third party to keep and to pass on to someone when money has been paid

escrow account /'eskroʊ ə,kaʊnt/ *noun* an account where money is held in escrow until a contract is signed or until goods are delivered

essential /ɪ'senʃəl/ *adjective* very important ○ *It is essential that an agreement be reached before the end of the month.* ○ *The factory is lacking essential spare parts.*

essential goods /ɪ,senʃəl 'gʊdz/, **essential products** /ɪ,senʃəl 'prɑdʌktz/ *plural noun* basic goods or products necessary for everyday life

estate duty /ɪ'steɪt ,duti/ *noun* a tax paid on the property left by a dead person (NOTE: now called **inheritance tax**)

estimate *noun* /'estɪmət/ **1.** a calculation of the probable cost, size, or time of something ○ *Can you give me an estimate of how much time was spent on the job?* □ **these figures are only an estimate** these are not the final accurate figures **2.** a calculation by a contractor or seller of a service of how much something is likely to cost, given to a client in advance of an order ○ *You should ask for an estimate before committing yourselves.* ○ *Before we can give the grant we must have an estimate of the total costs involved.* ○ *Unfortunately the final bill was quite different from the estimate.* □ **to put in an estimate** to give someone a written calculation of the probable costs of carrying out a job ○ *Three firms put in estimates for the job.* ■ *verb* /'estɪmeɪt/ **1.** to calculate the probable cost, size, or time of something ○ *to estimate that it will cost $1m* or *to estimate costs at $1m* ○ *We estimate current sales at only 60% of last year.* **2.** □ **to estimate for a job** to state in writing the future costs of carrying out a piece of work so that a client can make an order ○ *Three firms estimated for the refitting of the offices.*

estimated /'estɪmeɪtɪd/ *adjective* calculated approximately ○ *estimated sales* ○ *Costs were slightly more than the estimated figure.*

estimation /ˌestɪ'meɪʃ(ə)n/ *noun* an approximate calculation

estimator /'estɪmeɪtər/ *noun* a person whose job is to calculate estimates for carrying out work

e-tailer /'i teɪlər/ *noun* same as **e-retailer**

e-tailing /'i teɪlɪŋ/ *noun* **1.** the selling of goods and services using an electronic network such as the Internet **2.** same as **e-commerce**

ethics /'eθɪks/ *noun* the moral aspects of decision-making ○ *Whether or not we use such aggressive sales tactics is a matter of ethics.* (NOTE: takes a singular verb)

ethnic /'eθnɪk/ *adjective* relating to people who share the same race, culture, and traditions

ethnic media /ˌeθnɪk 'miːdiə/ *plural noun* magazines or TV stations which appeal to ethnic audiences

ethnic monitoring /ˌeθnɪk 'mɒnɪt(ə)rɪŋ/ *noun* the recording of the racial origins of employees or customers in order to ensure that all parts of the population are represented

ethnocentric stage /ˌeθnoʊ 'sentrɪk steɪdʒ/ *noun* an early stage in a company's marketing when goods are sent overseas with no concessions to local needs or tastes

e-ticket /'i tɪkɪt/ *noun* a reservation, especially for air travel, made on the Internet for which no paper ticket is issued to the customer

European Union /ˌjʊərəpiən 'juːnjən/ *noun* a group of European countries linked together by the Treaty of Rome. The European Community was set up in 1957 and changed its name to the European Union when it adopted the single market. It has now grown to include twenty-five member states. These are: Austria, Belgium, Cyprus, the Czech Republic, Denmark, Estonia, Finland, France, Germany, Greece, Hungary, Ireland, Italy, Latvia, Lithuania, Luxembourg, Malta, the Netherlands, Poland, Portugal, Slovakia, Slovenia, Spain, Sweden and the United Kingdom. The member states of the EU are linked together by the Treaty of Rome in such a way that trade is more free, that money can be moved from one country to another freely, that people can move from one country to another more freely and that people can work more freely in other countries of the group (the four fundamental freedoms). Abbreviation **EU**

evaluate /ɪ'væljueɪt/ *verb* to examine something to see how good it is

evaluation /ɪˌvælju'eɪʃ(ə)n/ *noun* the examination of a product to see how good it is

evaluative /ɪ'væljuətɪv/ *adjective* referring to the calculation of value

evaluative criteria /ɪˌvæljuətɪv kraɪ'tɪriə/ *plural noun* the criteria used to compare different products or services

even number /ˌiːv(ə)n 'nʌmbər/ *noun* a number which can be divided by two, e.g., 24 or 80

event /ɪ'vent/ *noun* a thing which happens, e.g., a sports competition, a flower show

event marketing /ɪ'vent ˌmɑːkətɪŋ/ *noun* promotional activity to advertise an event

event sponsorship /ɪ'vent ˌspɒnsəʃɪp/ *noun* a promotional deal by which a company sponsors a particular event such as a concert, sporting event, or other activity, on a regular basis

evoke /ɪ'voʊk/ *verb* to call up an image

evoked set /ɪˌvoʊkt 'set/ *noun* the various brands which are identified by a consumer as possible purchases and which he or she considers during the alternative evaluation process

ex /eks/ *prefix* out of or from □ **price ex warehouse** a price for a product which is to be collected from the manufacturer's or agent's warehouse and so does not include delivery □ **price ex works**, **ex factory** a price not including transportation from the maker's factory ■ *adverb* without

ex- /eks/ *prefix* former ○ *an ex-director of the company*

excess /'ekses/; /ɪk'ses/ *noun, adjective* an amount which is more than what is allowed ○ *an excess of expenditure over revenue*

excess baggage /ˌekses 'bægɪdʒ/ *noun* an extra payment at an airport for taking baggage which is heavier than the normal passenger's allowance

excess capacity /ˌekses kə'pæsəti/ *noun* spare capacity which is not being used

excess demand /ˌekses dɪ'mænd/ *noun* more demand at the present price than sellers can satisfy ○ *Much more machinery and labor must be acquired to meet excess demand.*

excess profit /ˌekses 'prɑfɪt/ *noun* a profit which is higher than what is thought to be normal

excess supply /ˌekses sə'plaɪ/ *noun* more supply at the present price than buyers want to buy

exchange /ɪks'tʃeɪndʒ/ *noun* 1. the act of giving one thing for another □ **exchange of contracts** the point in the sale of property when the buyer and the seller both sign the contract of sale which then becomes binding 2. a market for shares, commodities, futures, etc. ■ *verb* 1. □ **to exchange something (for something else)** to give one thing in place of something else ○ *He exchanged his motorcycle for a car.* ○ *Hang on to your sales slip in case you need to exchange the items you bought.* 2. □ **to exchange contracts** to sign a contract when buying a property, carried out by both buyer and seller at the same time 3. to change money of one country for money of another ○ *to exchange euros for dollars*

exchangeable /ɪks'tʃeɪndʒəb(ə)l/ *adjective* possible to exchange

exchange control /ɪks'tʃeɪndʒ kən-ˌtroʊl/ *noun* the control by a govern-

ment of the way in which its currency may be exchanged for foreign currencies

exchange controls /ɪks'tʃeɪndʒ kənˌtroʊlz/ *plural noun* government restrictions on changing the local currency into foreign currency ○ *The government had to impose exchange controls to stop the rush to buy dollars.* ○ *They say the government is going to lift exchange controls.*

exchange dealer /ɪks'tʃeɪndʒ ˌdilər/ *noun* a person who buys and sells foreign currency

exchange dealings /ɪks'tʃeɪndʒ ˌdilɪŋz/ *plural noun* the buying and selling of foreign currency

exchange economy /ɪks'tʃeɪndʒ ɪˌkɑnəmi/ *noun* an economy based on the exchange of goods and services

exchange premium /ɪks'tʃeɪndʒ ˌprimiəm/ *noun* an extra cost above the usual rate for buying a foreign currency

exchanger /ɪks'tʃeɪndʒər/ *noun* a person who buys and sells foreign currency

exchange rate /ɪks'tʃeɪndʒ reɪt/ *noun* a figure that expresses how much a unit of one country's currency is worth in terms of the currency of another country

exchange transaction /ɪks-'tʃeɪndʒ trænˌzækʃən/ *noun* a purchase or sale of foreign currency

excise duty /'eksaɪz ˌduti/ *noun* a tax on goods such as alcohol and gasoline which are produced in the country

exclusion clause /ɪk'skluʒ(ə)n klɔz/ *noun* a clause in an insurance policy or warranty which says which items or events are not covered

exclusive /ɪk'sklusɪv/ *adjective* 1. limited to one person or group □ **to have exclusive right to market a product** to be the only person who has the right to market a product 2. □ **exclusive of** not including ○ *The invoice is exclusive of tax.* ■ *noun* the exclusive rights to a news story or the story itself

exclusive agreement /ɪkˌsklusɪv ə-'grimənt/ *noun* an agreement where a person is made sole agent for a product in a market

exclusivity /ˌeksklu'sɪvəti/ *noun* the exclusive right to market a product

ex dividend /ˌeks 'dɪvɪdend/, **ex div** /ˌeks 'dɪv/ *adjective* referring to a share price not including the right to receive the next dividend ○ *The shares went ex dividend yesterday.* Abbreviation **xd**

exempt /ɪg'zempt/ *adjective* not forced to do something, especially not forced to obey a particular law or rule, or not forced to pay something ○ *Anyone over 65 is exempt from charges* □ **exempt from tax** not required to pay tax ○ *As a nonprofit organization we are exempt from tax.*

exempt rating /ɪg'zempt ˌreɪtɪŋ/ *noun U.K.* the legal right of a business not to add VAT to the prices of some products or services

exempt supplies /ɪgˌzempt sə 'plaɪz/ *plural noun U.K.* products or services on which the supplier does not have to charge VAT, e.g., the purchase of, or rent on, real estate and financial services

ex gratia /ˌeks 'greɪʃə/ *adjective* as an act of favor, without obligation

ex gratia payment /eks ˌgreɪʃə 'peɪmənt/ *noun* a payment made as a gift, with no other obligations

exhibit /ɪg'zɪbɪt/ *noun* **1.** a thing which is shown ○ *The buyers admired the exhibits on our stand.* **2.** a single section of an exhibition ○ *the British Trade Exhibit at the International Computer Fair* ■ *verb* □ **to exhibit at the Motor Show** to display new models of cars at the Motor Show

exhibition /ˌeksɪ'bɪʃ(ə)n/ *noun* an occasion for the display of goods so that buyers can look at them and decide what to buy ○ *The government has sponsored an exhibition of good design.* ○ *We have a stand at the Ideal Home Exhibition.* ○ *The agricultural exhibition grounds were crowded with visitors.*

exhibition stand /ˌeksɪ'bɪʃ(ə)n stænd/ *noun* a separate section of an exhibition where a company exhibits its products or services

exhibitor /ɪg'zɪbɪtər/ *noun* a person or company that shows products at an exhibition

exorbitant /ɪg'zɔrbɪtənt/ *adjective* unreasonably high in price ○ *$10,000 a minute, that's exorbitant and totally unjustified.* ○ *Their fees may seem exorbitant, but their costs are very high.*

expand /ɪk'spænd/ *verb* to get bigger, or make something bigger ○ *an expanding economy* ○ *The company is expanding fast.* ○ *We have had to expand our sales force.*

expansion /ɪk'spænʃən/ *noun* an increase in size ○ *The expansion of the domestic market.* ○ *The company had difficulty in financing its current expansion program.*

expect /ɪk'spekt/ *verb* to hope that something is going to happen ○ *We are expecting him to arrive at 10:45.* ○ *They are expecting a check from their agent next week.* ○ *The house was sold for more than the expected price.*

expectation /ˌekspek'teɪʃ(ə)n/ *noun* **1.** what someone believes will happen, especially concerning their future prosperity **2.** what someone believes about an item or service to be purchased, which is one of the reasons for making the purchase

expected price /ɪk'spektɪd praɪs/ *noun* the price of a product which consumers consider corresponds to its true value

expense /ɪk'spens/ *noun* money spent ○ *It is not worth the expense.* ○ *The expense is too much for my bank balance.* ○ *The likely profits do not justify the expense of setting up the project.* ○ *It was well worth the expense to get really high-quality equipment.*

expense account /ɪk'spens ə ˌkaʊnt/ *noun* an allowance of money which a business pays for an employee to spend on traveling and entertaining clients in connection with that business

expenses /ɪk'spensɪz/ *plural noun* money paid to cover the costs incurred by someone when doing something ○ *The salary offered is $10,000 plus expenses.* □ **all expenses paid** with all costs paid by the company ○ *The company sent him to San Francisco all expenses paid.* □ **to cut down on expenses** to reduce spending

expensive /ɪkˈspensɪv/ *adjective* which costs a lot of money ○ *First-class air travel is becoming more and more expensive.*

experience /ɪkˈspɪriəns/ *noun* knowledge or skill that comes from having had to deal with many different situations ○ *She has a lot of experience of dealing with German companies.* ○ *I gained most of my experience abroad.* ○ *Considerable experience is required for this job.* ○ *The applicant was pleasant, but did not have any relevant experience.* ■ *verb* to live through a situation ○ *The company experienced a period of falling sales.*

experience curve /ɪkˈspɪriəns kɜrv/ *noun* a graph showing the relationship between the cumulative amount of products produced and the production cost per unit ○ *The experience curve shows how increasing efficiency has brought down our costs.*

experienced /ɪkˈspɪriənst/ *adjective* referring to a person who has lived through many situations and has learned from them ○ *You are the most experienced negotiator I know.* ○ *We have appointed a very experienced candidate as sales director.* ○ *Our more experienced staff will have dealt with a crisis like this before.*

experience effect /ɪkˈspɪriəns ɪˌfekt/ *noun* the role of experience in improving business efficiency ○ *The experience effect is evident in the rise in our profits as our work force becomes more skilled.*

experiencer /ɪkˈspɪriənsər/ *noun* in the VALS lifestyle classification system, a young person who likes new and unusual things and spends a lot of money on hobbies and socializing

experiential /ekˌspɪriˈenʃəl/ *noun* a lifestyle segment according to VALS, people who are attracted to others

experiential advertising /ekˌspɪrienʃəl ˈædvərtaɪzɪŋ/ *noun* adver-

tising which conveys to the customer the real sensation of using the product

experimental method /ekˌsperɪˈment(ə)l ˌmeθəd/ *noun* the use of controlled experiments to discover the influence of various variables in marketing such as types of promotion and sales training

expert /ˈekspɜrt/ *noun* a person who knows a lot about something ○ *an expert in the field of electronics* or *an electronics expert* ○ *The company asked a financial expert for advice* or *asked for expert financial advice.* □ **expert's report** a report written by an expert

expertise /ˌekspəˈtiz/ *noun* specialist knowledge or skill in a particular field ○ *We hired Mr. Smith because of his financial expertise* or *because of his expertise in finance.* ○ *With years of experience in the industry, we have plenty of expertise to draw on.* ○ *Lack of marketing expertise led to low sales figures.*

expert system /ˈekspɜrt ˌsɪstəm/ *noun* a computer program that is designed to imitate the way a human expert in a particular field thinks and makes decisions (NOTE: Expert systems, which are an application of artificial intelligence, are used for a wide variety of tasks including medical diagnostics and financial decision-making and can be used by non-experts to solve well-defined problems when human experts are unavailable.)

exploit /ɪkˈsplɔɪt/ *verb* to use something to make a profit ○ *The company is exploiting its contacts in the Trade Office.* ○ *We hope to exploit the oil resources in the China Sea.*

exponential diffusion /ekspəˌnenʃ(ə)l dɪˈfjuʒ(ə)n/, **exponential growth** /ekspə,nenʃ(ə)l ˈɡroʊθ/ *noun* a typical growth pattern of new products that involves a slow start, followed by acceleration and finally a slowing down

exponential smoothing /ekspəˌnenʃ(ə)l ˈsmuðɪŋ/ *noun* a technique for working out averages while allowing for recent changes in values by moving forward the period under consideration at regular intervals

export noun /'ekspɔrt/ the practice or business of sending goods to foreign countries to be sold ○ *50% of the company's profits come from the export trade* or *the export market.* ◊ **exports** ■ verb /ɪk'spɔrt/ to send goods to foreign countries for sale ○ *50% of our production is exported.* ○ *The company imports raw materials and exports the finished products.*

export agent /'ekspɔrt ˌeɪdʒənt/ noun a person who sells overseas on behalf of a company and earns a commission ○ *An export agent is developing our business in West Africa.* ○ *She is working in New York as an export agent for a French company.*

exportation /ˌekspɔ'teɪʃ(ə)n/ noun the act of sending goods to foreign countries for sale

export bounty /'ekspɔrt ˌbaʊnti/ noun a government payment to businesses to encourage specific types of export

export department /'ekspɔrt dɪ ˌpɑrtmənt/ noun the section of a company which deals in sales to foreign countries

export duty /'ekspɔrt ˌduti/ noun a tax paid on goods sent out of a country for sale

exporter /ɪk'spɔrtər/ noun a person, company, or country that sells goods in foreign countries ○ *a major furniture exporter* ○ *Canada is an important exporter of oil* or *an important oil exporter.*

export house /'ekspɔrt haʊs/ noun a company which specializes in the export of goods manufactured by other companies

exporting /ek'spɔrtɪŋ/ adjective sending goods out of a country □ **oil-exporting countries** countries which produce oil and sell it to other countries

export license /'ekspɔrt ˌlaɪs(ə)ns/ noun a government permit allowing something to be exported ○ *The government has refused an export license for computer parts.*

export manager /'ekspɔrt ˌmænɪdʒər/ noun the person in charge of an export department in a company ○ *The export manager planned to set up a sales force in Southern Europe.* ○ *Sales managers from all export markets report to our export manager.*

exports /'ekspɔrts/ plural noun goods sent to a foreign country to be sold ○ *Exports to Africa have increased by 25%.* (NOTE: Usually used in the plural, but the singular form is used before a noun.)

exposition /ˌekspə'zɪʃ(ə)n/ noun same as **exhibition**

exposure /ɪk'spoʊʒər/ noun publicity given to an organization or product ○ *Our company has achieved more exposure since we decided to advertise nationally.*

express /ɪk'spres/ adjective rapid or very fast ○ *an express letter* ■ verb to send something very fast ○ *We expressed the order to the customer's warehouse.*

expressage /ɪk'spresɪdʒ/ noun a very fast transportation service

express delivery /ɪk.spres dɪ 'lɪv(ə)ri/ noun a very fast delivery

extend /ɪk'stend/ verb **1.** to offer something ○ *to extend credit to a customer* **2.** to make something longer ○ *Her contract of employment was extended for two years.* ○ *We have extended the deadline for making the appointment by two weeks.*

extended credit /ɪk.stendɪd 'kredɪt/ noun credit allowing the borrower a very long time to pay ○ *We sell to Australia on extended credit.*

extended guarantee /ɪk.stendɪd gærən'ti/ noun a guarantee, offered by a dealer on durable goods such as dishwashers, which goes beyond the time specified in the manufacturer's guarantee

extension /ɪk'stenʃən/ noun a longer time allowed for something than was originally agreed □ **to get an extension of credit** to get more time to pay back □ **extension of a contract** the continuing of a contract for a further period

extension strategy /ɪk'stenʃən ˌstrætədʒi/ noun a marketing strategy aimed at extending the life of a product either by making small changes in it, finding new uses for it, or finding new markets ○ *An extension strategy is needed to ensure demand for another few years.* ○ *The extension strategy consisted in providing a greater choice of colors and upholstery for the range of cars.*

extensive /ɪk'stensɪv/ *adjective* very large or covering a wide area ○ *an extensive network of sales outlets*

extensive marketing /ɪk,stensɪv 'mɑːkətɪŋ/ *noun* the practice of using a wide network of distributors and a great variety of promotional activities to gain as large a section of the market as possible ○ *Only a company with vast resources could embark on this type of extensive marketing.*

extensive problem-solving /ɪk ,stensɪv 'prɒbləm ,sɒlvɪŋ/ *noun* detailed research and decision-making by a buyer who needs to examine carefully all options open to him or her

external /ɪk'stɜːn(ə)l/ *adjective* **1.** outside a country. Opposite **internal 2.** outside a company

external analysis /ɪk,stɜːn(ə)l ə 'næləsɪs/ *noun* the analysis of an organization's customers, market segments, competitors, and marketing environment

external audience /ɪk,stɜːn(ə)l 'ɔːdiəns/ *noun* people, such as the general public, who do not belong to an organization

external audit /ɪk,stɜːn(ə)l 'ɔːdɪt/ *noun* an evaluation of the effectiveness of a company's public relations carried out by an outside agency

external communication /ɪk ,stɜːn(ə)l kə,mjuːnɪ'keɪʃ(ə)n/ *noun* the exchange of information and messages between an organization and other organizations, groups, or individuals that are not part of it (NOTE: External communication includes the fields of public relations, media relations, advertising, and marketing management.)

external desk research /ɪk ,stɜːn(ə)l 'desk rɪ,sɜːtʃ/ *noun* research based on material outside the company's own records, e.g., in libraries or government departments

external search /ɪk,stɜːn(ə)l 'sɜːtʃ/ *noun* a method of finding information from external sources such as advertising, or from the web using a search engine

external search engine /ɪk ,stɜːn(ə)l 'sɜːtʃ ,endʒɪn/ *noun* a search engine that allows the user to search millions of Internet pages rapidly

external trade /ɪk,stɜːn(ə)l 'treɪd/ *noun* trade with foreign countries. Opposite **internal trade**

extra /'ekstrə/ *adjective* which is added or which is more than usual ○ *to charge 10% extra for postage* ○ *There is no extra charge for heating.* ○ *Service is extra.* ○ *We get $25 extra pay for working on Sunday.*

extranet /'ekstrənet/ *noun* a closed network of websites and email systems that is accessible to the people who belong to an organization and to some others who do not, and that allows the outsiders access to the organization's internal applications or information—usually subject to some kind of signed agreement (NOTE: Like intranets, extranets provide all the benefits of Internet technology (browsers, web servers, HTML, etc.) with the added benefit of security, since the network cannot be used by the general public.)

extraordinary items /ɪk 'strɔːd(ə)n(ə)ri ,aɪtəmz/ *plural noun* formerly, large items of income or expenditure which did not arise from usual trading and which did not occur every year. They were shown separately in the P&L account, after taxation.

extrapolation /ɪk,stræpə'leɪʃ(ə)n/ *noun* a forecasting technique which involves projecting past trends into the future ○ *We are using extrapolation to forecast demand for a new product based on the demand for a similar product over the last five years.*

extras /'ekstrəz/ *plural noun* items which are not included in a price ○ *Packing and postage are extras.*

eyeballing /'aɪbɔlɪŋ/ *nouń* simply looking at statistical data to make a quick and informal assessment of the results (*informal*)

eyeballs /'aɪbɔlz/ *plural noun* a measure of the number of visits made to a website (*slang*)

eye candy /'aɪ ˌkændi/ *noun* visually attractive material (*slang*)

eye-movement test /'aɪ ˌmuvmənt ˌtest/, **eye tracking** /'aɪ ˌtrækɪŋ/ *noun* an advertising research test which involves recording the movement of a person's eyes as they look at an advertisement to see which parts are of special interest ○ *The eye-movement test will tell us what to highlight in future advertisements.*

e-zine /'i zin/ *noun* a publication on a particular topic that is distributed regularly in electronic form, mainly via the web but also by email

F

face-lift /'feɪslɪft/ *noun* an improvement to the design of products and packaging or of an organization's image ○ *These products need a face-lift if they are going to retain their appeal.*

face out /'feɪs aʊt/ *adverb* used to refer to the displaying of books on bookstore shelves, showing the front cover

face-to-face selling /ˌfeɪs tə feɪs 'selɪŋ/ *noun* person-to-person or direct selling, involving a meeting between seller and buyer ○ *Six months of face-to-face selling will give trainees direct experience of the market.* ○ *We need confident outgoing people to do our face-to-face selling.*

face value /ˌfeɪs 'vælju/ *noun* the value written on a coin, banknote, or share certificate

facia /'feɪʃə/ *noun* another spelling of **fascia**

facilities /fə'sɪlətiz/ *plural noun* services, equipment, or buildings which make it possible to do something ○ *Our storage facilities are the best in the region.* ○ *Transport facilities in the area are not satisfactory.* ○ *There are no facilities for disabled visitors.*

facility /fə'sɪləti/ *noun* **1.** the total amount of credit which a lender will allow a borrower **2.** a single large building ○ *We have opened our new warehouse facility.*

facing /'feɪsɪŋ/ *adjective* opposite

facing matter /'feɪsɪŋ ˌmætər/, **facing text matter** /ˌfeɪsɪŋ 'tekst ˌmætər/ *noun* an advertisement on a page opposite to one containing editorial matter

facing page /'feɪsɪŋ peɪdʒ/ *noun* the page opposite

facsimile /fæk'sɪmɪli/ *noun* an exact copy of a text or illustration

fact /fækt/ *noun* a piece of information ○ *The chairman asked to see all the facts on the income tax claim.* ○ *The sales director can give you the facts and figures about the African operation.*

fact book /'fækt bʊk/ *noun* data put together about a product on the market that can be used for reference by the producers or by an advertising agency

fact-finding mission /'fækt faɪndɪŋ ˌmɪʃ(ə)n/ *noun* a visit by a person or group of people, usually to another country, to obtain information about a specific issue ○ *The trade official went on a fact-finding tour of the region.*

factor /'fæktər/ *noun* **1.** something which is important, or which is taken into account when making a decision ○ *The drop in sales is an important factor in the company's lower profits.* ○ *Motivation was an important factor in drawing up the new payment plan.* **2.** a person who sells for a business or another person and earns a commission ■ *verb* to buy debts from a company at a discount

factorage /'fæktərɪdʒ/ *noun* a commission earned by a factor ○ *What percentage is the factorage?*

factor analysis /'fæktər ə,næləsɪs/ *noun* a process of identifying key factors that influence the results in an attitude research program

factoring /'fæktərɪŋ/ *noun* the business of buying debts from a firm at a discount and then getting the debtors to pay

factoring agent /'fæktərɪŋ ˌeɪdʒənt/ *noun* a person who sells for a business or another person and earns a commission

factoring charges /ˈfæktərɪŋ ˌtʃɑːdʒɪz/ *plural noun* the cost of selling debts to a factor for a commission

factory /ˈfækt(ə)ri/ *noun* a building where products are manufactured ○ *a car factory* ○ *a shoe factory* ○ *The company is proposing to close three of its factories with the loss of 200 jobs.*

factory gate price /ˌfækt(ə)ri ˈɡeɪt praɪs/ *noun* the actual cost of manufacturing goods before any mark-up is added to give profit (NOTE: The factory gate price includes direct costs such as labor, raw materials, and energy, and indirect costs such as interest on loans, plant maintenance, or rent.)

factory outlet /ˈfækt(ə)ri ˌaʊt(ə)let/ *noun* a store where merchandise is sold direct to the public from the factory, usually at wholesale prices

factory unit /ˈfækt(ə)ri ˌjuːnɪt/ *noun* U.K. a single building in an industrial park

fact sheet /ˈfækt ʃiːt/ *noun* a sheet of paper giving information about a product or service which can be used for publicity purposes

fad /fæd/ *noun* a short-lived fashion or craze

failure /ˈfeɪljə/ *noun* the fact of not doing something which you promised to do

failure fee /ˈfeɪljər fiː/ *noun* a fee charged by a distributor to the manufacturer of a product whose sales are less than those agreed upon in advance

fair /fer/ *noun* same as **trade fair** ○ *The computer fair runs from April 1st to 6th.* ■ *adjective* reasonable, with equal treatment

fair deal /ˌfer ˈdiːl/ *noun* an arrangement where both parties are treated equally ○ *The employees feel they did not get a fair deal from the management.*

fair price /ˌfer ˈpraɪs/ *noun* a good price for both buyer and seller

fair trade /ˌfer ˈtreɪd/ *noun* an international business system where countries agree not to charge import duties on some items imported from their trading partners

fall /fɔːl/ *noun* a sudden reduction or loss of value ○ *a fall in the exchange rate* ○ *a fall in the price of gold* ○ *a fall on the Stock Exchange* ○ *Profits showed a 10% fall.* ■ *verb* **1.** to be reduced suddenly to a lower price or value ○ *Shares fell on the market today.* ○ *Gold shares fell 10% or fell 45 cents on the Stock Exchange.* ○ *The price of gold fell for the second day running.* ○ *The dollar fell against the euro.* **2.** to happen or to take place ○ *The public holiday falls on a Tuesday.* □ **payments which fall due** payments which are now due to be made

fall away *phrasal verb* to become less ○ *Hotel bookings have fallen away since the tourist season ended.*

fall back *phrasal verb* to become lower or cheaper after rising in price ○ *Shares fell back in light trading.*

fall back on *phrasal verb* to have to use something kept for emergencies ○ *to fall back on cash reserves* ○ *The management fell back on the usual old excuses.*

fall behind *phrasal verb* to be late in doing something ○ *They fell behind with their mortgage repayments.*

fall off *phrasal verb* to become lower, cheaper, or less ○ *Sales have fallen off since the tourist season ended.*

fall out *phrasal verb* □ **the bottom has fallen out of the market** sales have fallen below what previously seemed to be their lowest point

fall through *phrasal verb* not to happen or not to take place ○ *The plan fell through at the last moment.*

fall-back price /ˈfɔːl bæk ˌpraɪs/ *noun* the lowest price which a seller will accept ○ *The buyer tries to guess the seller's fall-back price.* ○ *The fall-back price must not be any lower or there won't be any profit in the deal.*

falling /ˈfɔːlɪŋ/ *adjective* becoming smaller or dropping in price

falling market /ˌfɔːlɪŋ ˈmɑːkət/ *noun* a market where prices are coming down

false /fɔːls/ *adjective* not true or not correct ○ *to make a false claim for a product* ○ *to make a false entry in the balance sheet*

false claim /fɔls 'kleɪm/ *noun* an untrue or exaggerated claim made in the advertising of a product ○ *A voluntary control body was set up to discourage false claims in the advertising business.*

false weight /ˌfɔls 'weɪt/ *noun* a weight as measured on a store scales which is wrong and so cheats customers

falsification /ˌfɔlsɪfɪ'keɪʃ(ə)n/ *noun* the act of making false entries in accounts

falsify /'fɔlsɪfaɪ/ *verb* to change something to make it wrong ○ *They were accused of falsifying the accounts.*

family /'fæm(ə)li/ *noun* **1.** a group of products which are linked by a brand name or by their packaging **2.** a group of people, formed of parents and children

family branding /ˌfæm(ə)li 'brændɪŋ/ *noun* the practice of selling a variety of different products under the same brand name

family life cycle /ˌfæm(ə)li 'laɪf ˌsaɪk(ə)l/ *noun* the stages through which consumers pass in their lives, as they have families, e.g., "young singles," "young marrieds," "young couples with small children," "couples with adolescent children still at home" and "retired couples," which correspond to different types of buying behavior

family packaging /ˌfæm(ə)li 'pækɪdʒɪŋ/ *noun* the practice of selling a whole range of products in similar packaging ○ *We hope that family packaging will make for a clear company image.*

fancy goods /'fænsi gʊdz/ *plural noun* small attractive items

fascia /'feɪʃə/, **facia** /'feɪʃə/ *noun* **1.** a board over a store on which the name of the store is written **2.** a board above an exhibition stand on which the name of the company represented is written

fast /fæst/ *adjective, adverb* quick or quickly ○ *The train is the fastest way of getting to our supplier's factory.* ○ *Home computers sell fast in the pre-Christmas period.*

fast food /fæst 'fʊd/ *noun* food that can be cooked and sold quickly to customers, often using franchises, e.g., hamburgers and pizzas

fastmarketing /'fæstˌmækətɪŋ/ *noun* the concept of concentrating all promotions into a short space of time, so that customers cannot avoid being affected

fast-moving consumer goods /ˌfæst ˌmuvɪŋ kən'sumər ˌgʊdz/ *plural noun* essential low-price goods which get repeat orders ○ *He couldn't work in FMCGs because his only experience was in industrial selling.* Abbreviation **FMCGs**

fast-selling item /ˌfæst ˌselɪŋ 'aɪtəm/ *noun* an item which sells quickly

favorable /'feɪv(ə)rəb(ə)l/ *adjective* giving an advantage (NOTE: The U.K. spelling is **favourable**.) □ **on favorable terms** on especially good terms ○ *The store is rented on very favorable terms.*

favorable balance of trade /ˌfeɪv(ə)rəb(ə)l ˌbæləns əv 'treɪd/, **favorable trade balance** /ˌfeɪv(ə)rəb(ə)l 'treɪd ˌbæləns/ *noun* a situation where a country's exports are larger than its imports

fax /fæks/ *noun* **1.** a system for sending the exact copy of a document via telephone lines ○ *Can you confirm the booking by fax?* **2.** a document sent by this method ○ *We received a fax of the order this morning.* ■ *verb* to send a message by fax ○ *The details of the offer were faxed to the brokers this morning.* ○ *I've faxed the documents to our New York office.*

faxback /'fæksbæk/ *noun* a system of responding by fax, e.g., by downloading pages from a website direct to a fax machine, or where customers dial a fax number and get a fax back on their fax machine

fear /fɪr/ *noun* the feeling of being afraid

fear appeal /'fɪr əˌpil/ *noun* an advertising message that makes the reader anxious about something, especially about not doing something

feasibility report /ˌfizəˈbɪləti rɪ
ˌpɔrt/ *noun* a document which says if it
is worth undertaking something

feasibility study /ˌfizəˈbɪləti ˌstʌdi/
noun the careful investigation of a
project to see whether it is worth undertaking ○ *We will carry out a feasibility
study to decide whether it is worth setting up an agency in South America.*

feasibility test /ˌfizəˈbɪləti test/
noun a test to see if something is possible

feature /ˈfitʃər/ *noun* an article in a
newspaper or magazine that deals with
one subject in depth ○ *There is a feature
in the next issue describing the history
of our company.*

features /ˈfitʃəz/ *plural noun* the particular important aspects of a product or
service which are advertised as an at-
traction to the purchaser, as opposed to
"benefits" which show how the product
or service will improve the quality of
life of the purchaser

Federal Trade Commission
/ˌfed(ə)rəl ˈtreɪd kəˌmɪʃ(ə)n/ *noun* a
federal agency established to keep business competition free and fair

feed /fid/ *verb* to give information or
tips to another salesperson regarding
promising customers or areas for sales ○
*I can feed you some interesting sales
leads.* (NOTE: **feeding- fed**)

feedback /ˈfidbæk/ *noun* information, especially about the result of an activity which allows adjustments to be
made to the way it is done in future ○ *We
are getting positive feedback about our
after-sales service.* ○ *It would be useful
to have some feedback from people who
had a test drive but didn't buy the car.* ○
*Are we getting any feedback on custom-
er reaction to our new product?*

field /fild/ *noun* **1.** an area of study or
interest □ **first in the field** being the first
company to bring out a product or to
start a service ○ *Smith Inc. has a great
advantage in being first in the field with
a reliable electric car.* **2.** □ **in the field**
outside the office, among the customers
○ *We have sixteen reps in the field.*

field of experience /ˌfild əv ɪk
ˈspɪrəns/ *noun* the general experience
that a sender and receiver of a message
use in considering the message

field research /ˈfild rɪˌsɜrtʃ/ *noun*
the process of looking for information
that is not yet published and must be obtained in surveys ○ *They had to do a lot
of fieldwork before they found the right
market for the product.* ○ *Field research
is carried out to gauge potential demand.*

field sales force /ˌfild ˈseɪlz ˌfɔrs/
noun salespeople working outside the
company's offices, in the field ○ *After
working for a year in the field sales
force, she became field sales manager.* ○
*The field sales force operates in three
main areas.*

field sales manager /fild ˈseɪlz
ˌmænɪdʒər/ *noun* the manager in
charge of a group of salespeople

field trial /ˈfild traɪəl/, **field test** /ˈfild
tests/ *noun* a test of a new product or of
something such as an advertisement on
real customers

field work /ˈfild wɜrk/ *noun* same as
field research ○ *They had to do a lot of
field work to find the right market for the
product.*

filing system /ˈfaɪlɪŋ ˌsɪstəm/ *noun*
a way of putting documents in order for
easy reference

filler /ˈfɪlər/ *noun* something which
fills a space

filter /ˈfɪltə/ *noun* a process of analysis
applied to incoming information in order to identify any material that could be
of interest to an organization

filter question /ˈfɪltər ˌkwestʃən/
noun a question in a questionnaire designed to separate respondents who are
worth questioning further from those
who are not

finance /ˈfaɪnæns/ *noun* **1.** money
used by a company, provided by the
shareholders or by loans ○ *Where will
they get the necessary finance for the
project?* **2.** the business of managing
money ■ *verb* to provide money to pay
for something ○ *They plan to finance the
operation with short-term loans.*

finance department /'faɪnæns dɪ ˌpɑːtmənt/, **finance committee** /'faɪnæns kəˌməti/ *noun* the department or committee which manages the money used in an organization

finance market /'faɪnæns ˌmɑːkət/ *noun* a place where large sums of money can be lent or borrowed

finances /'faɪnænsɪz/ *plural noun* money or cash which is available ○ *the bad state of the company's finances*

financial /faɪ'nænʃəl/ *adjective* concerning money

financial advertising /faɪˌnænʃəl 'ædvətaɪzɪŋ/ *noun* advertising by companies in the field of financial investment

financial audit /faɪˌnænʃəl 'ɔːdɪt/ *noun* an examination of the books and accounts of an advertising agency

financial correspondent /faɪ ˌnænʃəl ˌkɒrɪs'pɒndənt/ *noun* a journalist who writes articles on money matters for a newspaper

financial institution /faɪˌnænʃəl ˌɪnstɪ'tjuːʃ(ə)n/ *noun* a bank, investment trust, or insurance company whose work involves lending or investing large sums of money

financially /fɪ'nænʃəli/ *adverb* regarding money □ **a company which is financially sound** a company which is profitable and has strong assets

financial position /faɪˌnænʃəl pə 'zɪʃ(ə)n/ *noun* the state of a person's or company's bank balance in terms of assets and debts ○ *She must think of her financial position.*

financial resources /faɪˌnænʃəl rɪ 'zɔːsɪz/ *plural noun* the supply of money for something ○ *a company with strong financial resources*

financial risk /faɪˌnænʃəl 'rɪsk/ *noun* the possibility of losing money ○ *The company is taking a considerable financial risk in manufacturing 25 million units without doing any market research.* ○ *There is always some financial risk in selling on credit.*

financial statement /faɪˌnænʃəl 'steɪtmənt/ *noun* a document which shows the financial situation of a company ○ *The accounts department has prepared a financial statement for the shareholders.*

financier /faɪ'nænsiər/ *noun* a person who lends large amounts of money to companies or who buys shares in companies as an investment

financing /'faɪnænsɪŋ/ *noun* the act of providing money for a project ○ *The financing of the project was done by two international banks.*

find time /'faɪnd taɪm/ *noun* the time taken by a customer to find what he or she wants in a store

fine /faɪn/ *adverb* very thin or very small □ **we are cutting our margins very fine** we are reducing our margins to the smallest possible amount

finished goods /ˌfɪnɪʃt 'gʊdz/ *plural noun* manufactured goods which are ready to be sold

fire-fight /'faɪə faɪt/ *verb* to fight bad publicity for a client ○ *The agency has done fire-fighting work for the egg producers.*

fire sale /'faɪə seɪl/ *noun* **1.** a sale of fire-damaged goods **2.** a sale of anything at a very low price

firm /fɜːm/ *noun* a company, business or partnership ○ *a manufacturing firm* ○ *an important publishing firm* ○ *She is a partner in a law firm.* ■ *adjective* **1.** unchangeable ○ *to make a firm offer for something* ○ *to place a firm order for two aircraft* **2.** not dropping in price and possibly going to rise ○ *Shares remained firm.* ■ *verb* to remain at a price and seem likely to rise ○ *The shares firmed at $1.50.*

  firm up *phrasal verb* to agree on the final details of something ○ *We expect to firm up the deal at the next trade fair.*

firm price /ˌfɜːm 'praɪs/ *noun* a price which will not change ○ *They are quoting a firm price of $1.23 a unit.*

first choice /ˌfɜːst 'tʃɔɪs/ *noun* a prospective customer who chooses the first option available, as opposed to a "tirekicker" who wants to examine every option before coming to a decision

firsthand /ˌfɜrst ˈhænd/ *adjective* **1.** coming directly from the original source **2.** new or unused ○ *I actually bought the TV firsthand, but at a secondhand price.*

firsthand information /ˌfɜrst hænd ˌɪnfərˈmeɪʃ(ə)n/ *noun* information from an original source ○ *We had a firsthand account of what happened at the sales meeting from one of the sales representatives who was there.*

first-line management /ˌfɜrst laɪn ˈmænɪdʒmənt/ *noun* the managers who have immediate contact with the work force

first mover /ˌfɜrst ˈmuvər/ *noun* a person or company that is the first to launch a product in a market

first mover advantage /fɜrst ˈmuvər ədˌvæntɪdʒ/ *noun* the advantage a company gets in being the first to enter a market

first-run syndication /ˌfɜrst rʌn sɪndɪˈkeɪʃ(ə)n/ *noun* material produced specifically for the syndication market

fishy-back freight /ˈfɪʃi bæk ˌfreɪt/ *noun* the transportation of trucks or freight-train cars on ferries or barges (NOTE: compare **piggy-back freight**)

fix /fɪks/ *verb* **1.** to arrange or to agree to ○ *to fix a budget* ○ *to fix a meeting for 3 p.m.* ○ *The date has still to be fixed.* ○ *The price of gold was fixed at $300.* ○ *The mortgage rate has been fixed at 5%.* **2.** to mend ○ *The technicians are coming to fix the phone system.* ○ *Can you fix the photocopier?*

fixed /fɪkst/ *adjective* unable to be changed or removed

fixed assets /ˌfɪkst ˈæsets/ *plural noun* property or machinery which a company owns and uses, but which the company does not buy or sell as part of its regular trade, including the company's investments in shares of other companies

fixed break /fɪkst ˈbreɪk/ *noun* the placing of a television or radio advertisement in a specific commercial break on a specific day, at the advertiser's insistence

fixed costs /ˌfɪkst ˈkɔsts/ *plural noun* business costs which do not change with the quantity of the product made

fixed expenses /ˌfɪkst ɪkˈspensɪz/ *plural noun* expenses which do not vary with different levels of production, e.g., rent, secretaries' salaries, and insurance

fixed-fee arrangement /fɪkst ˈfi ə ˌreɪndʒmənt/ *noun* a way of agreeing on the fees for an agency before the agency starts work on a project

fixed position /fɪkst pəˈzɪʃ(ə)n/ *noun* the placing of an advertisement in a specific location in a publication, or running a commercial at a fixed time of day, at the advertiser's insistence

fixed-price agreement /fɪkst ˈpraɪs əˌgrimənt/ *noun* an agreement where a company provides a service or a product at a price which stays the same for the whole period of the agreement

fixed rate /ˌfɪkst ˈreɪt/ *noun* a rate, e.g., an exchange rate, which does not change

fixed scale of charges /ˌfɪkst skeɪl əv ˈtʃɑrdʒɪz/ *noun* a rate of charging which does not change

fixed spot /fɪkst ˈspɑt/ *noun* the placing of a TV or radio commercial in a specific position, at the advertiser's insistence

fixing /ˈfɪksɪŋ/ *noun* **1.** arranging ○ *the fixing of charges* ○ *the fixing of a mortgage rate* **2.** a regular meeting to set a price

flagship /ˈflægʃɪp/ *noun* the key product in a range, on which the reputation of the producer most depends

flagship store /ˈflægʃɪp stɔr/, **flagship hotel** /ˈflægʃɪp hoʊˌtel/ *noun* the main store or hotel in a chain

flash pack /ˈflæʃ pæk/ *noun* a pack or package which shows a price reduction very clearly in order to attract customers ○ *Flash packs are displayed at eye-level on the supermarket shelves to attract the attention of passing customers.*

flat rate /ˌflæt ˈreɪt/ *noun* a charge which always stays the same ○ *a flat-*

rate increase of 10% ○ We pay a flat rate for electricity each quarter. ○ He is paid a flat rate of $2 per thousand.

flier /ˈflaɪər/ *noun* a promotional leaflet

flight /flaɪt/ *verb* to arrange a scheduling pattern for something

flighting by number /ˌflaɪtɪŋ baɪ ˈnʌmbər/ *noun* scheduling things in a series of groups, with the same number in each group

floating population /ˌfloʊtɪŋ ˌpɒpjəˈleɪʃ(ə)n/ *noun* people who move from place to place

flood /flʌd/ *noun* a large quantity ○ We received a flood of orders. ○ Floods of tourists filled the hotels. ■ *verb* to fill with a large quantity of something ○ The market was flooded with cheap imitations. ○ The sales department is flooded with orders or with complaints.

floor /flɔr/ *noun* **1.** the part of the room which you walk on **2.** all the rooms on one level in a building ○ Her office is on the 26th floor. (NOTE: In the U.S., the floor at street level is the **first floor**, but In the U.K., it is the **ground floor**. Each floor in the U.K. is one number lower than the same floor in USA.)

floor manager /ˈflɔr ˌmænɪdʒər/ *noun* a person in charge of the sales staff in a department store

floor space /ˈflɔr speɪs/ *noun* an area of floor in an office or warehouse ○ We have 3,500 square meters of floor space to rent.

floor stand /ˈflɔr stænd/ *noun* a display stand which stands on the floor, as opposed to one which stands on a table or counter

floorwalker /ˈflɔrwɔkər/ *noun* an employee of a department store who advises customers, and supervises the store assistants in a department

flop /flɑp/ *noun* a failure, or something which has not been successful ○ The new model was a flop. ■ *verb* to fail or not be a success ○ The launch of the new shampoo flopped badly. (NOTE: **flopping – flopped**)

flow chart /ˈfloʊtʃɑrt/, **flow diagram** /ˈfloʊ ˌdaɪəɡræm/ *noun* a chart which shows the arrangement of work processes in a series

fluff /flʌf/ *noun* □ **fluff it and fly it** give a product an attractive appearance and then sell it (*informal*)

fluidity /fluˈɪdəti/ *noun* ease of movement or change

fluidity of labor /fluˌɪdəti əv ˈleɪbə/ *noun* the extent to which employees move from one place to another to work or from one occupation to another

fly poster /ˈflaɪ ˌpoʊstər/ *noun* a poster which is pasted to a site without permission and without being paid for

fly-posting /ˈflaɪ ˌpoʊstɪŋ/ *noun* the practice of sticking posters up illegally, without permission of the site owner and without making any payment

FMCGs *abbreviation* fast-moving consumer goods

focus group /ˈfoʊkəs ɡrup/ *noun* a group of people who are brought together to discuss informally a market-research question

fold-out /ˈfoʊld aʊt/ *noun* a folded page in a publication, which opens out to show a much larger advertisement

follow /ˈfɑloʊ/ *verb* to come behind or to come afterward ○ The samples will follow by surface mail. ○ We will pay $10,000 down, with the balance to follow in six months' time.

follow up *phrasal verb* to examine something further ○ I'll follow up your idea of targeting our address list with a special mailing. □ **to follow up an initiative** to take action once someone else has decided to do something

follower /ˈfɑloʊər/ *noun* a company which follows others into a market

following reading matter /ˌfɑloʊɪŋ ˈridɪŋ ˌmætər/ *noun* a good position for an advertisement, which follows an interesting article in a newspaper or magazine

font /fɑnt/ *noun* a set of characters all of the same size and face

foot /fʊt/ *verb* □ **to foot the bill** to pay the costs

footer /'futə/ *noun* a section at the bottom of a web page, which usually contains any essential links and information on how to contact the organization that owns the page and on its copyright and privacy policy

footfall /'futfɔl/ *noun* the number of customers who come into and walk round a store

force /fɔrs/ *noun* **1.** strength □ **to be in force** to be operating or working ○ *The rules have been in force since 1986.* □ **to come into force** to start to operate or work ○ *The new regulations will come into force on January 1st.* **2.** a group of people ■ *verb* to make someone do something ○ *Competition has forced the company to lower its prices.* ○ *After the takeover several of the managers were forced to take early retirement.*

force down *phrasal verb* to make something such as prices become lower □ **to force prices down** to make prices come down ○ *Competition has forced prices down.*

force up *phrasal verb* to make something become higher □ **to force prices up** to make prices go up ○ *The war forced up the price of oil.*

forced consumption /ˌfɔrst kən'sʌmpʃən/ *noun* the attempt to impose a rate or type of consumption on consumers

forced sale /ˌfɔrst 'seɪl/ *noun* a sale which takes place because a court orders it or because it is the only way to avoid a financial crisis

force majeure /ˌfɔrs mæ'ʒɜr/ *noun* something which happens which is out of the control of the parties who have signed a contract, e.g., a strike, war, or storm

forecast /'fɔrkæst/ *noun* a description or calculation of what will probably happen in the future ○ *The chairman did not believe the sales director's forecast of higher turnover.* ■ *verb* to calculate or to say what will probably happen in the future ○ *She is forecasting sales of $2m.* ○ *Economists have forecast a fall in the exchange rate.* (NOTE: **forecasting – forecast**)

forecasting /'fɔrkæstɪŋ/ *noun* the process of calculating what will probably happen in the future ○ *Manpower planning will depend on forecasting the future levels of production.*

foreign /'fɔrɪn/ *adjective* not belonging to your own country ○ *Foreign cars have flooded our market.* ○ *We are increasing our trade with foreign countries.*

foreign currency /ˌfɔrɪn 'kʌrənsi/ *noun* money of another country

foreign currency account /ˌfɔrɪn 'kʌrənsi əˌkaʊnt/ *noun* a bank account in the currency of another country, e.g., a dollar account in a British bank

foreign currency reserves /ˌfɔrɪn 'kʌrənsi rɪˌzɜrvz/ *plural noun* a country's reserves held in currencies of other countries. Also called **foreign exchange reserves, international reserves**

foreigner /'fɔrɪnər/ *noun* a person from another country

foreign exchange market /ˌfɔrɪn ɪks'tʃeɪndʒ ˌmarkət/ *noun* **1.** a market where people buy and sell foreign currencies ○ *She trades on the foreign exchange market.* **2.** dealings in foreign currencies ○ *Foreign exchange markets were very active after the dollar devalued.*

foreign exchange reserves /ˌfɔrɪn ɪks'tʃeɪndʒ rɪˌzɜrvz/ *plural noun* foreign money held by a government to support its own currency and pay its debts

foreign exchange transfer /ˌfɔrɪn ɪks'tʃeɪndʒ ˌtrænsfɜr/ *noun* the sending of money from one country to another

foreign goods /ˌfɔrɪn 'gʊdz/ *plural noun* goods manufactured in other countries

foreign investments /ˌfɔrɪn ɪn'vestmənts/ *plural noun* money invested in other countries

forfeit /'fɔrfɪt/ *noun* the fact of having something taken away as a punishment □ **the goods were declared forfeit** the court said that the goods had to be taken away from the person who was holding them ■ *verb* to have something taken away as a punishment □ **to forfeit a deposit** to lose a deposit which was left for an item because you have decided not to buy that item

forfeit clause /'fɔrfɪt klɔz/ *noun* a clause in a contract which says that goods or a deposit will be taken away if the contract is not obeyed

forfeiture /'fɔrfɪtʃər/ *noun* the act of forfeiting a property

form /fɔrm/ *noun* 1. □ **form of words** words correctly laid out for a legal document □ **receipt in due form** a correctly written receipt 2. an official printed paper with blank spaces which have to be filled in with information ○ *You have to fill in form A20.* ○ *Each passenger was given a customs declaration form.* ○ *The reps carry pads of order forms.*

forma /'fɔrmə/ *noun* ♦ **pro forma**

format /'fɔrmæt/ *noun* 1. the general page design or size of a publication 2. the general style of an email or electronic marketing piece

form utility /'fɔrm juˌtɪləti/ *noun* a use for a product created by the introduction of the product

forty-eight sheet /ˌfɔrti 'eɪt ʃiːt/ *noun* a large poster-sized sheet of paper

forum /'fɔrəm/ *noun* an online area where Internet users can read, post, and respond to messages

forward /'fɔrwərd/ *adjective* in advance or to be paid at a later date ■ *adverb* 1. □ **to date a cheque forward** to put a later date than the present one on a check 2. □ **to sell forward** to sell foreign currency, commodities, etc., for delivery at a later date 3. □ **balance brought forward, carried forward** balance which is entered in an account at the end of a period and is then taken to be the starting point of the next period ■ *verb* □ **to forward something to someone** to send something to someone ○ *to forward a consignment to Nigeria* □ **"please forward", "to be forwarded"** words written on an envelope, asking the person receiving it to send it on to the person whose name is written on it

forward contract /'fɔrwərd ˌkɑntrækt/ *noun* a one-off agreement to buy foreign currency or shares or commodities for delivery at a later date at a specific price

forward exchange rate /ˌfɔrwərd ɪks'tʃeɪndʒ reɪt/, **forward rate** *noun* a rate for purchase of foreign currency at a fixed price for delivery at a later date ○ *What are the forward rates for the pound?*

forwarding /'fɔrwərdɪŋ/ *noun* the act of arranging shipping and customs documents

forwarding address /'fɔrwərdɪŋ əˌdres/ *noun* the address to which a person's mail can be sent on

forwarding agent /'fɔrwərdɪŋ ˌeɪdʒənt/ *noun* a person or company which arranges shipping and customs documents

forward integration /ˌfɔwərd ˌɪntə'greɪʃ(ə)n/ *noun* a process of expansion in which a company becomes its own distributor or takes over a company in the same line of business as itself ○ *Forward integration will give the company greater control over its selling.* ○ *Forward integration has brought the company closer to its consumers and has made it aware of their buying habits.* Compare **backward integration**

forward market /ˌfɔrwərd 'mɑrkət/ *noun* a market for purchasing foreign currency, oil, or commodities for delivery at a later date

forward price /'fɔrwərd praɪs/ *noun* a price of goods which are to be delivered in the future

forward sales /'fɔrwərd seɪlz/ *plural noun* the sales of shares, commodities, or foreign exchange for delivery at a later date

foul bill of lading /ˌfaʊl bɪl əv 'leɪdɪŋ/ *noun* a bill of lading which says that the goods were in bad condition when received by the shipper

four-color process /ˌfɔr kʌlər 'prɑses/ *noun* a printing process where the three primary colors and black are used to create a wide range of shades

four Cs /ˌfɔr 'siz/ *plural noun* a simple way of referring to the four important points regarding customers: value to the Customer, Cost, Convenience for the customer, and Communication between seller and buyer

four O's /ˌfɔr 'oʊz/ *plural noun* a simple way of summarizing the essentials of a marketing operation, which are Objects, Objectives, Organization, and Operations

four-plus cover /ˌfɔr 'plʌs ˌkʌvər/ *noun* a situation where consumers in the target audience will have seen an advertisement at least four times on average

four P's /ˌfɔr 'piz/ *plural noun* a simple way of summarizing the essentials of the marketing mix, which are Product, Price, Promotion, and Place

fraction /'frækʃən/ *noun* a part of a whole

fragile /'frædʒaɪl/ *adjective* which can be easily broken ○ *There is an extra premium for insuring fragile goods in shipment.*

fragment /fræg'ment/ *verb* to split into sections

fragmentation /ˌfrægmən'teɪʃ(ə)n/ *noun* the use of a variety of media for a publicity campaign

fragmented market /fræg,mentɪd 'mɑrkət/ *noun* a market which is split into many small segments, which are more difficult to sell into

frame /freɪm/ *noun* same as **sampling frame**

franchise /'fræntʃaɪz/ *noun* a license to trade using a brand name and paying a royalty for it ○ *He's bought a printing franchise* or *a pizza franchise.* ■ *verb* to sell licenses for people to trade using a brand name and paying a royalty ○ *His sandwich bar was so successful that he decided to franchise it.*

franchise agreement /'fræntʃaɪz əˌgrimənt/, **franchise contract** /'fræntʃaɪz ˌkɑntrækt/ *noun* a legal contract to trade using a brand name and paying a royalty for it

franchise-building promotion /'fræntʃaɪz ˌbɪldɪŋ prəˌmoʊʃ(ə)n/ *noun* a sales promotion aimed at building up long-term repeat sales and customer loyalty

franchise chain /'fræntʃaɪz tʃeɪn/ *noun* a series of retail stores or fast-food outlets which are operated as franchises from the main operator

franchisee /ˌfræntʃaɪ'zi/ *noun* a person who runs a franchise

franchiser /'fræntʃaɪzər/ *noun* a person who licenses a franchise

franchising /'fræntʃaɪzɪŋ/ *noun* the act of selling a license to trade as a franchise ○ *She runs her sandwich chain as a franchising operation.*

franchisor /'fræntʃaɪzər/ *noun* another spelling of **franchiser**

franco /'fræŋkoʊ/ *adverb* free

fraudulent misrepresentation /ˌfrɔdjələnt mɪsˌreprɪzen'teɪʃ(ə)n/ *noun* the act of making a false statement with the intention of tricking a customer

free /fri/ *adjective, adverb* **1.** not costing any money ○ *I have been given a free ticket to the exhibition.* ○ *The price includes free delivery.* ○ *All goods in the store are delivered free.* ○ *A catalog will be sent free on request.* □ **free alongside ship** referring to a price that includes all costs up to delivery of goods next to the ship on the quay □ **free docks** referring to a price that includes all costs up to delivery of goods to the docks □ **free of charge** with no payment to be made □ **free on quay** referring to a price that includes all costs up to delivery of goods next to the ship on the quay □ **free overboard, free overside** referring to a price that includes all costs up to arrival of the ship at a port **2.** with no restrictions □ **free of tax** with no tax having to be paid ○ *Interest is paid free of tax.* □ **free of duty** with no duty to be paid ○ *to import wine free of duty* **3.** not busy or not occupied ○ *Are there any free tables in the restaurant?* ○ *I will be free in a few minutes.* ○ *The chairman always keeps Friday afternoon free for a game of bridge.* ■ *verb* to make something available or easy ○ *The government's decision has freed millions of dollars for investment.*

free advertisement /fri əd
'vɜrtɪsmənt/ *noun* an advertisement
shown without any charge to the advertiser ○ *The newspaper agreed to place a
free advertisement for the charity on the
back page.*

freebie /'fribi/ *noun* a product or service supplied free of charge, especially a
gift to an agent or journalist (*informal*)

free collective bargaining /ˌfri kə
ˌlektɪv 'bɑrɡɪnɪŋ/ *noun* negotiations
between management and trade unions
about wage increases and working conditions

free competition /ˌfri ˌkɑmpə
'tɪʃ(ə)n/ *noun* the fact of being free to
compete without government interference

free currency /ˌfri 'kʌrənsi/ *noun* a
currency which is allowed by the government to be bought and sold without
restriction

free delivery area /fri dɪ'lɪv(ə)ri
ˌeriə/ *noun* an area within which a seller
will deliver purchases free ○ *The total
price will be low as the goods are being
delivered in a free delivery area.*

free enterprise /ˌfri 'entəpraɪz/
noun a system of business free from
government interference

free gift /ˌfri 'ɡɪft/ *noun* a present giv-
en by a store to a customer who buys a
specific amount of goods ○ *There is a
free gift worth $25 to any customer buy-
ing a washing machine.*

free market /ˌfri 'mɑrkət/ *noun* a
market in which there is no government
control of supply and demand, and the
rights of individuals and organizations
to physical and intellectual property are
upheld

free market economy /ˌfri ˌmɑrkət
ɪ'kɑnəmi/ *noun* a system where the
government does not interfere in business activity in any way

free on board /ˌfri ɑn 'bɔrd/ *adjective* **1.** including in the price all the seller's costs until the goods are on the ship
for transportation. Abbreviation **f.o.b.**
2. including in the price all the seller's
costs until the goods are delivered to a
place

free paper /ˌfri 'peɪpər/ *noun* a newspaper which is given away free, and
which relies for its income on its advertising

freephone /'frifoʊn/, **freefone** *noun*
a system where you can telephone to reply to an advertisement, to place an order, or to ask for information and the
seller pays for the call

free port /'fri pɔrt/ *noun* a port where
there are no customs duties to be paid

freepost /'frifoʊst/ *noun* a system
where someone can write to an advertiser to place an order or to ask for information to be sent, without paying for a
stamp. The company paying for the
postage on receipt of the envelope.

free sample /ˌfri 'sæmpəl/ *noun* a
sample given free to advertise a product

freesheet /'friʃit/ *noun* same as **free
paper**

free-standing insert /ˌfri stændɪŋ
'ɪnsɜrt/ *noun* advertising material on
one or more pages which is inserted into
a newspaper. Abbreviation **FSI**

free trade /ˌfri 'treɪd/ *noun* a system
where goods can go from one country to
another without any restrictions

free trader /ˌfri 'treɪdər/ *noun* a person who is in favor of free trade

free trade zone /ˌfri 'treɪd ˌzoʊn/
noun an area where there are no customs duties

free trial /ˌfri 'traɪəl/ *noun* an opportunity to test a machine or product with
no payment involved

freeware /'friwer/ *noun* free software
programs

freeze /friz/ *verb* to keep something
such as money or costs at their present
level and not allow them to rise ○ *to
freeze wages and prices* ○ *to freeze credits* ○ *to freeze company dividends* ○ *We
have frozen expenditure at last year's
level.* (NOTE: **freezing – froze – frozen**)

    freeze out *phrasal verb* □ **to freeze
out the competition** to trade successfully and cheaply and so prevent
competitors from operating

freight /freɪt/ *noun* **1.** the cost of transporting goods by air, sea, or land ○ *At an auction, the buyer pays the freight.* **2.** goods which are transported □ **to take on freight** to load goods onto a ship, train, or truck ■ *verb* □ **to freight goods** to send goods ○ *We freight goods to all parts of the country.*

freightage /ˈfreɪtɪdʒ/ *noun* the cost of transporting goods

freight collect /ˈfreɪt kəˌlekt/ *noun* an arrangement whereby the customer pays for transporting the goods

freight costs /ˈfreɪt kɔsts/ *plural noun* money paid to transport goods

freight depot /ˈfreɪt ˌdepoʊ/ *noun* a central point where goods are collected before being shipped

freight elevator /ˈfreɪt ˌeləveɪtər/ *noun* a strong elevator for carrying goods up and down inside a building

freighter /ˈfreɪtər/ *noun* **1.** an aircraft or ship which carries goods **2.** a person or company that organizes the transportation of goods

freight forward /ˌfreɪt ˈfɔrwərd/ *noun* a deal where the customer pays for transporting the goods

freight forwarder /ˈfreɪt ˌfɔrwərdər/ *noun* a person or company that arranges shipping and customs documents for several shipments from different companies, putting them together to form one large shipment

freight plane /ˈfreɪt pleɪn/ *noun* an aircraft which carries goods, not passengers

frequency /ˈfrikwənsi/ *noun* **1.** the number of times something happens **2.** the number of times an advertisement appears in a specific period ○ *The plan is to have larger advertisements but less frequency.* **3.** the number of times a person sees an advertisement during a campaign ○ *We feel that a frequency of two showings per night is enough for the first week of the campaign.*

frequency analysis /ˈfrikwənsi əˌnæləsɪs/ *noun* analysis of frequency distribution statistics

frequency discount /ˈfrikwənsi ˌdɪskaʊnt/ *noun* reduced rates offered for frequent use of a advertising medium

frequency distribution /ˈfrikwənsi dɪstrɪˌbjuʃ(ə)n/ *noun* statistics, usually in the form of a graph, showing how often a sample group responded in a certain way to a questionnaire

frequent /ˈfrikwənt/ *adjective* which comes, goes or takes place often ○ *There is a frequent ferry service between England and France.* ○ *We send frequent faxes to New York.* ○ *How frequent are the planes to Birmingham?*

frequently /ˈfrikwəntli/ *adverb* often ○ *The photocopier is frequently out of use.* ○ *We email our New York office very frequently – at least four times a day.*

friction-free market /ˌfrɪkʃən fri ˈmɑrkɪt/ *noun* a market in which there are few differences between competing products, so that the customer has an exceptionally free choice

fringe account /ˈfrɪndʒ əˌkaʊnt/ *noun* accounts or customers that are not very profitable for the supplier ○ *The salespeople are not giving priority to these fringe accounts.* ○ *It is hoped that some of these fringe accounts will soon start buying in larger quantities.*

fringe benefit /ˈfrɪndʒ ˌbenəfɪt/ *noun* an extra item given by a company to employees in addition to a salary, e.g., company cars or health club membership ○ *The fringe benefits make up for the poor pay.* ○ *Use of the company recreation facilities is one of the fringe benefits of the job.*

fringe time /ˈfrɪndʒ taɪm/ *noun* TV time around prime time where there is usually more availability

front /frʌnt/ *noun* a part of something which faces away from the back ○ *The front of the office building is on Main Street.* ○ *Our ad appeared on the front page of the newspaper.* ○ *There is a photograph of the managing director on the front page of the company report.*

frontage /ˈfrʌntɪdʒ/ *noun* the width of a store which faces onto the street

front cover /frʌnt 'kʌvər/ *noun* the front outside page of a publication, as opposed to the back cover

front end /'frʌnt end/ *noun* the part of an organization that meets and deals with customers face-to-face

front-line management /ˌfrʌnt laɪn 'mænɪdʒmənt/ *noun* managers who have immediate contact with the employees

frontload /'frʌntˌloʊd/ *verb* to plan a publicity campaign where most costs are incurred in the early stages. Compare **backload**

front man /'frʌnt mæn/ *noun* a person who seems honest but is hiding an illegal trade

front of book /ˌfrʌnt əv 'bʊk/ *noun* the first few pages of a magazine

FSI *abbreviation* free-standing insert

fudge /fʌdʒ/ *noun* a mistake made in an advertisement

fulfill /fʊl'fɪl/ *verb* to complete something in a satisfactory way ○ *The clause regarding payments has not been fulfilled.* (NOTE: **fulfilling- fulfilled**The U.K. spelling is **fulfil**.) □ **to fulfill an order** to supply the items which have been ordered ○ *We are so understaffed that we cannot fulfill anymore orders before Christmas.*

fulfillment /fʊl'fɪlmənt/ *noun* the act of carrying something out in a satisfactory way (NOTE: The U.K. spelling is **fulfilment**.)

fulfillment house /fʊl'fɪlmənt haʊs/ *noun* a company which supplies orders on behalf of a mail-order company

full /fʊl/ *adjective* **1.** complete, including everything □ **we are working at full capacity** we are doing as much work as possible **2.** □ **in full** completely ○ *a full refund* or *a refund paid in full* ○ *Give your full name and address* or *your name and address in full.* ○ *He accepted all our conditions in full.*

full cost pricing /ˌfʊl kɔst 'praɪsɪŋ/ *noun* a pricing method based on assessing the full production cost of each product unit and adding a profit margin

full costs /ˌfʊl 'kɔsts/ *plural noun* all the costs of manufacturing a product, including both fixed and variable costs

full cover /ˌfʊl 'kʌvər/ *noun* insurance cover against all risks

full employment /ˌfʊl ɪm'plɔɪmənt/ *noun* a situation where all the people who can work have jobs

full-function wholesaler /ˌfʊl fʌŋkʃ(ə)n 'hoʊlseɪlər/ *noun* a distributor performing all the normal functions of a wholesaler such as storage and transportation ○ *There is room for only one full-function wholesaler dealing with this product in the Tucson area.*

full-line forcing /ˌfʊl laɪn 'fɔrsɪŋ/ *noun* a situation where a supplier pressures a customer to buy from that supplier only ○ *If the supplier succeeds in full-line forcing, he will probably raise prices.*

full nester /ˌfʊl 'nestər/ *noun* an older customer who has their own home and who is interested in a good quality of life, eats in restaurants, buys new gadgets, and is not influenced by advertising. ◊ **empty nesters**

full page /'fʊl peɪdʒ/ *noun* a size of advertisement taking up one complete page

full price /ˌfʊl 'praɪs/ *noun* a price with no discount ○ *She bought a full-price ticket.*

full rate /ˌfʊl 'reɪt/ *noun* the full charge, with no reductions

full repairing lease /ˌfʊl rɪ'perɪŋ ˌlis/ *noun* a lease where the tenant has to pay for all repairs to the property

full-scale /'fʊl skeɪl/ *adjective* complete or very thorough ○ *The bank ordered a full-scale review of credit terms.*

full-service advertising agency /ˌfʊl ˌsɜrvɪs 'ædvərtaɪzɪŋ ˌeɪdʒənsi/, **full-service agency** /fʊl ˌsɜrvɪs 'eɪdʒənsi/ *noun* an advertising agency offering a full range of services such as sales promotion, design of house style, advice on public relations and market research, and creating stands for exhibitions ○ *We have so little marketing expertise, we'll need a full-service advertising agency.*

full-time /'fʊl taɪm/ *adjective, adverb* working all the usual working time, i.e. about eight hours a day, five days a week ○ *She has full-time work* or *She works full-time.* ○ *He is one of our full-time staff.*

full-timer /ˌfʊl 'taɪmər/ *noun* a person who works full-time

fully connected world /ˌfʊli kə 'nektɪd wɜrld/ *noun* a world where most people and organizations are linked by the Internet or similar networks

function /'fʌŋkʃən/ *noun* a duty or job ■ *verb* to work ○ *The advertising campaign is functioning smoothly.* ○ *The new management structure does not seem to be functioning very well.*

functional /'fʌŋkʃən(ə)l/ *adjective* which can function properly

functional consequences /ˌfʌŋkʃən(ə)l 'kɑnsɪkwensɪz/ *plural noun* the tangible effects of a product or service which a customer experiences directly

functional discount /ˌfʌŋkʃən(ə)l 'dɪskaʊnt/ *noun* a discount offered on goods sold to distributors

functional product differentiation /ˌfʌŋkʃən(ə)l 'prɑdʌkt dɪfərenʃi ˌeɪʃ(ə)n/ *noun* the process of ensuring that a product has some functional features that distinguish it from competing ones

functional title /'fʌŋkʃən(ə)l ˌtaɪt(ə)l/ *noun* a job title, the description of a person's job which is used as part of his or her address, e.g.,"marketing manager" or "head buyer"

fund /fʌnd/ *noun* money set aside for a special purpose

future /'fjutʃər/ *adjective* referring to time to come or to something which has not yet happened ■ *noun* the time which has not yet happened ○ *Try to be more careful in the future.* ○ *In the future all reports must be sent to Australia by air.*

future delivery /ˌfjutʃər dɪ'lɪv(ə)ri/ *noun* delivery at a later date

futurology /ˌfjutʃə'rɑlədʒi/ *noun* the prediction and study of future trends

G

gable end /'geɪb(ə)l end/ *noun* the end of a building which is used as a poster site

gain /geɪn/ *noun* **1.** an increase, or the act of becoming larger □ **gain in experience** the act of getting more experience □ **gain in profitability** the act of becoming more profitable **2.** an increase in profit, price, or value ○ *Oil shares showed gains on the Stock Exchange.* ○ *Property shares put on gains of 10%-15%.* ■ *verb* **1.** to get or to obtain ○ *She gained some useful experience working in a bank.* □ **to gain control of a business** to buy more than 50% of the shares so that you can direct the business **2.** to rise in value ○ *The dollar gained six points on the foreign exchange markets.*

galleria /ˌgælə'riə/ *noun* a large shopping complex with many different stores under one roof, usually built around a large open space, with fountains, plants, etc.

galley /'gæli/, **galley proof** /'gæli pruf/ *noun* the first proof of typesetting, before the text is made up into pages

galloping inflation /ˌgæləpɪŋ ɪn'fleɪʃ(ə)n/ *noun* very rapid inflation which is almost impossible to reduce

game /geɪm/ *noun* a form of promotional material where people have a chance of winning a prize

game theory /'geɪm ˌθɪəri/ *noun* a mathematical method of analysis used in operational research to predict the outcomes of games of strategy and conflicts of interest. It is used to assess the likely strategies that people will adopt in situations governed by a particular set of rules and to identify the best approach to a particular problem or conflict.

gap /gæp/ *noun* an empty space □ **gap in the market** an opportunity to make a product or provide a service which is needed but which no one has sold before ○ *to look for* or *to find a gap in the market* ○ *This laptop has filled a real gap in the market.*

gap analysis /'gæp əˌnæləsɪs/ *noun* analysis of a market to try to find a particular area that is not at present being satisfied ○ *Gap analysis showed that there was a whole area of the market we were not exploiting.* ○ *The computer performed a gap analysis and came up with suggestions for a medium-priced machine suitable for the small business market.*

gatefold /'geɪtfoʊld/ *noun* a double-page spread in which both pages are folded over, and which open out like a gate to give a spread of almost four pages

general cargo /ˌdʒen(ə)rəl 'kɑrgoʊ/ *noun* a cargo made up of various types of goods ○ *The ship left the port with a general cargo bound for various destinations.*

general delivery /ˌdʒen(ə)rəl dɪ'lɪv(ə)ri/ *noun* a system where letters can be addressed to someone at a post office, where they can be collected ○ *They received the mail-order items via general delivery.* (NOTE: The U.K. term is **poste restante**.)

general preplanning input /ˌdʒen(ə)rəl pri'plænɪŋ ˌɪnpʊt/ *noun* market research which can be used to prepare the initial stages of an advertising campaign

general store /ˌdʒen(ə)rəl 'stɔr/ *noun* a small country store which sells a large range of goods

general trading /ˌdʒen(ə)rəl ˈtreɪdɪŋ/ *noun* dealing in all types of goods

general wholesaler /ˌdʒen(ə)rəl ˈhoʊlseɪlər/ *noun* a wholesaler selling a variety of goods

generation /ˌdʒenəˈreɪʃ(ə)n/ *noun* a stage in the development of a product. Each new generation is a new version of the product with certain technical improvements on the preceding version.

Generation X /ˌdʒenəreɪʃ(ə)n ˈeks/ *noun* the generation of people who were born between 1963 and 1981 and began their working lives from the 1980s onward (NOTE: The people who belong to Generation X are said to have challenged traditional corporate expectations by not being solely motivated by money. Instead they want to establish a balance between their professional and personal lives, being in favor of flexible working practices and valuing opportunities for learning and self-advancement.)

generic /dʒəˈnerɪk/ *adjective* which is shared by a group, and does not refer to one individual ■ *noun* **1.** a product sold without a brand name ○ *Generics are cheap since they have no name to advertise.* **2.** a brand name which is now given to a product rather than to a particular brand, e.g., kleenex or thermos

generic product /dʒəˌnerɪk ˈprɑdʌkt/ *noun* same as **generic** *noun* 1 ○ *Next to the brightly packaged branded goods the generic products on display were easily overlooked.*

generic term /dʒəˌnerɪk ˈtɜrm/, **generic name** /dʒəˌnerɪk ˈneɪm/ *noun* same as **generic** *noun* 2

gentleman's agreement /ˈdʒent(ə)lmənz əˌgrimənt/ *noun* a verbal agreement between two parties who trust each other

geocentric stage /ˌdʒioʊˈsentrɪk steɪdʒ/ *noun* an advanced stage in a company's international marketing when there is great coordination of overseas marketing activities

geographic /ˌdʒiəˈgræfɪk/ *adjective* referring to an area

geographic concentration /dʒiəˌgræfɪk ˌkɑnsənˈtreɪʃ(ə)n/ *noun* the degree to which consumers in a market are concentrated or dispersed in a country or area ○ *The number of sales personnel needed will depend on the geographic concentration of the market.*

geographic information system /ˌdʒiəgræfɪk ˌɪnfərˈmeɪʃ(ə)n ˌsɪstəm/ *noun* a type of database which is sorted on geographic data, such as a census, or one which provides maps onscreen. Abbreviation **GIS**

geographic segmentation /dʒiəˌgræfɪk ˌsegmənˈteɪʃ(ə)n/ *noun* the division of a market according to areas or regions

geographic weighting /dʒiəˌgræfɪk ˈweɪtɪŋ/ *noun* a statistical process which gives more importance to some geographic areas than others in the process of reaching a final figure or result

gestation period /dʒeˈsteɪʃ(ə)n ˌpɪriəd/ *noun* the period of time between the initial inquiry about a product and the placing of an order ○ *The long gestation period is due to inefficient decision-making procedures in the buying company.*

GHI *abbreviation* guaranteed homes impressions

ghosting /ˈgoʊstɪŋ/ *noun* the practice of showing a little of the product itself by removing a small part of the packaging

GHR *abbreviation* guaranteed homes ratings

giant retailer /ˌdʒaɪənt ˈriteɪlər/ *noun* a very large retailing group, e.g., a department store or chain store

GIF /gɪf/ *noun* a common file format for web graphics and banners. Full form **graphic interchange format**

GIF89 /ˌgɪf eɪti ˈnaɪn/ *noun* a commonly used version of GIF

gift coupon /ˈgɪft ˌkupɑn/, **gift certificate** /ˈgɪft sɜrˌtɪfɪkət/ *noun* a card that can be used to buy specified goods up to the value printed on it, often issued by chain stores. The person receiving the voucher is able to redeem it in any store in the chain. ○ *We gave her a gift certificate for her birthday.*

gift-wrap /ˈgɪft ræp/ *verb* to wrap a present in attractive paper ○ *Do you want this book gift-wrapped?* (NOTE: **gift-wrapping – gift-wrapped**)

gimmick /ˈgɪmɪk/ *noun* a clever idea or trick ○ *a publicity gimmick*

give /gɪv/ *verb*

  give away *phrasal verb* to give something as a free present ○ *We are giving away a pocket calculator with each $10 of purchases.*

giveaway /ˈgɪvəweɪ/ *adjective* □ **to sell at giveaway prices** to sell at very cheap prices ■ *noun* something which is given as a free gift when another item is bought

giveaway paper /ˈgɪvəweɪ ˌpeɪpər/ *noun* a newspaper which is given away free, and which relies for its income on its advertising

global /ˈgloʊb(ə)l/ *adjective* referring to the whole world ○ *We offer a 24-hour global delivery service.*

global advertising /ˌgloʊb(ə)l ˈædvərtaɪzɪŋ/ *noun* using the same advertising message to advertise the same product internationally

global brand /ˌgloʊb(ə)l ˈbrænd/ *noun* a famous brand name which is recognized and sold all over the world

globalization /ˌgloʊbələˈzeɪʃ(ə)n/ *noun* the process of making something international or worldwide, especially the process of expanding business interests, operations, and strategies to countries all over the world (NOTE: Globalization is due to technological developments that make global communications possible, political developments such as the fall of communism, and developments in transportation that make traveling faster and more frequent. It can benefit companies by opening up new markets, giving access to new raw materials and investment opportunities, and enabling them to take advantage of lower operating costs in other countries.)

global marketing /ˌgloʊb(ə)l ˈmɑrkətɪŋ/ *noun* using a common mar-

keting plan to sell the same product or services everywhere in the world

global product /ˌgloʊb(ə)l ˈprɑdʌkt/ *noun* a product with a famous brand name which is recognized and sold all over the world

global retailer /ˌgloʊb(ə)l ˈriteɪlər/ *noun* a company which sells its products all over the world

glocalization /ˌgloʊkələaɪˈzeɪʃ(ə)n/ *noun* the process of adapting globalized products or services to fit the needs of different local markets and communities around the world (NOTE: The word is a combination of globalisation and localisation.)

glue /glu/ *noun* something such as information that unifies organizations, supply chains, and other commercial groups

glut /glʌt/ *noun* □ **a glut of produce** too much produce, which is then difficult to sell ○ *a coffee glut* or *a glut of coffee* □ **a glut of money** a situation where there is too much money available to borrowers ■ *verb* to fill the market with something which is then difficult to sell ○ *The market is glutted with cheap cameras.* (NOTE: **glutting – glutted**)

goal /goʊl/ *noun* something which you try to achieve ○ *Our goal is to break even within twelve months.* ○ *The company achieved all its goals.*

going rate /ˌgoʊɪŋ ˈreɪt/ *noun* the usual or current rate of payment ○ *We pay the going rate for typists.* ○ *The going rate for offices is $10 per square meter.*

gondola /ˈgɑndələ/ *noun* a free-standing display in a supermarket which shoppers can walk round

gone aways /ˈgɑn əˌweɪz/ *plural noun* people who have moved away from the address they have in a mailing list

good industrial relations /gʊd ɪnˌdʌstriəl rɪˈleɪʃ(ə)nz/ *plural noun* a situation where management and employees understand each others' problems and work together for the good of the company

goods /gʊdz/ *plural noun* **1.** □ **goods and chattels** movable personal possessions □ **goods in progress** the value of goods being manufactured which are not complete at the end of an accounting period ○ *Our current assets are made up of stock, goods in progress, and cash.* □ **goods sold loose** goods sold by weight, not prepacked in bags **2.** items which can be moved and are for sale

goods depot /'gʊdz ˌdepoʊ/ *noun* a central warehouse where goods can be stored until they are moved

goods train /'gʊdz treɪn/ *noun* a train for carrying freight

goodwill /gʊd'wɪl/ *noun* good feeling toward someone ○ *To show goodwill, the management increased the terms of the offer.*

GOTS *abbreviation* gross opportunity to see

government contractor /ˌgʌv(ə)nmənt kən'træktər/ *noun* a company which supplies the government with goods by contract

government-controlled /ˌgʌv(ə)nmənt kən'troʊld/ *adjective* under the direct control of the government ○ *Advertisements cannot be placed in the government-controlled newspapers.*

government economic indicators /ˌgʌv(ə)nmənt ˌikənɑmɪk 'ɪndɪkeɪtərz/ *plural noun* statistics which show how the country's economy is going to perform in the short or long term

government organization /ˌgʌv(ə)nmənt ˌɔrgənaɪ'zeɪʃ(ə)n/ *noun* an official body run by the government

grade /greɪd/ *noun* a level or rank ○ *to reach the top grade in the civil service* ■ *verb* **1.** to sort something into different levels of quality ○ *to grade coal* **2.** to make something rise in steps according to quantity □ **graded advertising rates** rates which become cheaper as you take more advertising space

graded hotel /ˌgreɪdɪd hoʊ'tel/ *noun* a good-quality hotel

graded tax /ˌgreɪdɪd 'tæks/ *noun* **1.** a tax which rises according to income **2.** a tax on property which is higher if the property has not been kept in a good state by the owner

grade level /'greɪd ˌlev(ə)l/ *noun* the classification of a product's quality written on a label attached to the product ○ *Many consumers do not properly understand the grade levels.*

grand /grænd/ *adjective* important □ **grand plan** *or* **grand strategy** a major plan ○ *They explained their grand plan for redeveloping the factory site.* ■ *noun* one thousand dollars (*informal*) ○ *They offered him fifty grand for the information.*

grand total /ˌgrænd 'toʊt(ə)l/ *noun* the final total made by adding several subtotals

grapevine /'greɪpvaɪn/ *noun* an informal and unofficial communications network within an organization that passes on information by word of mouth (NOTE: A grapevine may distort information or spread gossip and rumor, but it can also back up the official communications network, provide feedback, and strengthen social relationships within the organization.)

graph /grɑf/ *noun* a diagram which shows the relationship between two sets of quantities or values, each of which is represented on an axis ○ *A graph was used to show salary increases in relation to increases in output.* ○ *According to the graph, as average salaries have risen so has absenteeism.* ○ *We need to set out the results of the questionnaire in a graph.*

graphics /'græfɪks/ *plural noun* designs and illustrations in printed work, especially designs which are created by computers ○ *In this series of advertisements the graphics do not do justice to the copy.*

graph paper /'græf ˌpeɪpər/ *noun* a special type of paper with many little squares, used for drawing graphs

gratis /'grætɪs/ *adverb* free or not costing anything ○ *We got into the exhibition gratis.*

gray market /'greɪ ˌmɑrkət/ *noun* **1.** the unofficial legal buying and selling of scarce, highly priced goods ○ *If the government puts a ceiling on prices for these products the gray market will become a black market.* **2.** a market formed of people over 60 years of age. ◊ **silver market**

green issues /'grin ˌɪʃuz/ *plural noun* same as **environmental management**

green marketing /'grin ˌmɑrkətɪŋ/ *noun* marketing products and services on the basis of their environmental acceptability

grid /grɪd/ *noun* a graph with lines crossing at right angles and items written in the boxes, used for comparison

gross /groʊs/ *adverb* with no deductions ○ *My salary is paid gross.* ■ *verb* to make as a gross profit or earn as gross income ○ *The group grossed $25m in 1999.*

gross audience /groʊs 'ɔrdiəns/ *noun* the total number of people who have seen an advertisement, multiplied by the number of times it has been run

gross circulation /ˌgroʊs ˌsɜrkjə'leɪʃ(ə)n/ *noun* the total sales of a publication before adjusting for error or discounting unsold copies

gross cover /groʊs 'kʌvər/ *noun* the number of times a television or radio spot has been seen based on television ratings

gross domestic product /ˌgroʊs də,mestɪk 'prɑdʌkt/ *noun* the annual value of goods sold and services paid for inside a country. Abbreviation **GDP**

gross earnings /ˌgroʊs 'ɜrnɪŋz/ *plural noun* total earnings before tax and other deductions

gross impressions /groʊs ɪm 'preʃ(ə)nz/ *plural noun* the total number of people who have seen an advertisement, multiplied by the number of times it has been run. ◊ **guaranteed homes impressions**

gross margin /ˌgroʊs 'mɑrdʒɪn/ *noun* the percentage difference between the received price and the unit manufac-

turing cost or purchase price of goods for resale. Abbreviation **GM**

gross national product /ˌgroʊs ˌnæʃ(ə)nəl 'prɑdʌkt/ *noun* the annual value of goods and services in a country including income from other countries. Abbreviation **GNP**

gross opportunity to see /ˌgroʊs ˌɑpərtjunəti tə 'si/ *noun* the number of opportunities that an average member of the target audience will have to see the advertisements in an advertising campaign. Abbreviation **GOTS**

gross profit /ˌgroʊs 'prɑfɪt/ *noun* a profit calculated as sales income less the cost of the goods sold, i.e. without deducting any other expenses

gross rating point /ˌgroʊs 'reɪtɪŋ ˌpɔɪnt/ *noun* a way of calculating the effectiveness of outdoor advertising, where each point represents one per cent of the population in a specific market. Abbreviation **GRP**

gross reach /groʊs 'ritʃ/ *noun* the total number of opportunities for people to see a company's advertisements in a campaign, i.e. the total number of publications sold multiplied by the number of advertisements appearing in each one

gross receipts /ˌgroʊs rɪ'sits/ *plural noun* the total amount of money received before expenses are deducted

gross sales /ˌgroʊs 'seɪlz/ *plural noun* money received from sales before deductions for goods returned, special discounts, etc. ○ *Gross sales are impressive since many buyers seem to be ordering more than they will eventually need.*

gross weight /ˌgroʊs 'weɪt/ *noun* the weight of both the container and its contents

ground transportation /'graʊnd trænspɔ,teɪʃ(ə)n/ *noun* the means of transportation available to take passengers from an airport to the town, e.g., buses, taxis, or trains

group /grup/ *noun* **1.** several things or people together ○ *A group of managers has sent a memo to the chairman complaining about noise in the office.* ○ *The respondents were interviewed in groups* *of three or four, and then singly.* **2.** several companies linked together in the same organization ○ *the group chairman* or *the chairman of the group* ○ *group turnover* or *turnover for the group* ○ *the Granada Group* ■ *verb* □ **to group together** to put several items together ○ *Sales from six different agencies are grouped together under the heading "European sales."*

group discussion /ˌgrup dɪˈskʌʃ(ə)n/ *noun* a survey method in which a focus group is brought together to discuss informally a market-research question ○ *The group discussion was taken over by one or two strong personalities.* ○ *A sample of young people took part in a group discussion on the new shampoo.*

group interview /ˌgrup ˈɪntərvju/ *noun* an interview with a group of respondents such as a family in order to discover the views of the group as a whole ○ *There were group interviews with all the classes in the school in order to gauge reactions to the new educational program.*

group results /ˌgrup rɪˈzʌlts/ *plural noun* the results of a group of companies taken together

group system /ˈgrup ˌsɪstəm/ *noun* a system of organizing an advertising agency in groups, each group having specialists in creative, media, marketing services, and other areas, and each group dealing with particular accounts

groupware /ˈgrupwer/ *noun* software that enables a group of people who are based in different locations to work together and share information (NOTE: Groupware usually provides communal diaries, address books, work planners, bulletin boards, and newsletters in electronic format on a closed network.)

grow /groʊ/ *verb* to cause something such as a business to develop or expand

growth /groʊθ/ *noun* **1.** the fact of becoming larger or increasing □ **the company is aiming for growth** the company is aiming to expand rapidly **2.** the second stage in a product life cycle, fol-

lowing the launch, when demand for the product increases rapidly

growth area /ˈgroʊθ ˌeriə/ *noun* an area where sales are increasing rapidly

growth index /ˈgroʊθ ˌɪndeks/ *noun* an index showing how something has grown

growth industry /ˈgroʊθ ˌɪndəstri/ *noun* an industry that is expanding or has the potential to expand faster than other industries

growth market /ˈgroʊθ ˌmɑrkət/ *noun* a market where sales are increasing rapidly ○ *We plan to build a factory in the Far East, which is a growth market for our products.*

growth rate /ˈgroʊθ reɪt/ *noun* the speed at which something grows

growth share matrix /ˈgroʊθ ʃer ˌmeɪtrɪks/ *noun* a model for a marketing strategy with various categories of product based on present performance and growth rate ○ *The growth share matrix helped to decide what products needed extra marketing efforts.*

growth vector matrix /ˈgroʊθ ˌvektər ˌmeɪtrɪks/ *noun* a model for a marketing strategy with various choices and combinations of strategy based on product and market development

GRP *abbreviation* gross rating point

guarantee /ˌgærənˈti/ *noun* **1.** a legal document in which the producer agrees to compensate the buyer if the product is faulty or becomes faulty before a specific date after purchase ○ *a certificate of guarantee* or *a guarantee certificate* ○ *The guarantee lasts for two years.* ○ *It is sold with a twelve-month guarantee.* □ **the car is still under guarantee** the car is still covered by the maker's guarantee **2.** a promise that someone will pay another person's debts □ **to go guarantee for someone** to act as security for someone's debts **3.** something given as a security ○ *to leave share certificates as a guarantee* ■ *verb* **1.** to give a promise that something will happen □ **to guarantee a debt** to promise that you will pay a debt made by someone else □ **to guarantee an associate company** to promise that an associate company will pay its debts □ **to guarantee a bill of exchange** to promise that the bill will be paid **2.** □ **the product is guaranteed for twelve months** the manufacturer says that the product will work well for twelve months, and will mend it free of charge if it breaks down

guaranteed circulation /ˌɡærəntɪd ˌsɜrkjəˈleɪʃ(ə)n/ *noun* the audited circulation of a magazine which is used as a basis for calculating advertising rates

guaranteed homes impressions /ˌɡærəntɪd ˈhoʊmz ɪmˌpreʃ(ə)nz/, **guaranteed homes ratings** /ˌɡærəntɪd ˈhoʊmz ˌreɪtɪŋz/ *plural noun* an advertising package offered by television companies which guarantees the advertisers that their advertising will reach a specified number of people, but leaves it to the TV company to choose the number and timing of the spots. Abbreviation **GHI, GHR**

guaranteed prices /ˌɡærəntɪd ˈpraɪsɪz/ *plural noun* minimum prices guaranteed to an industry by the government, with the payment of a subsidy to make up for market prices that fall below this level ○ *Guaranteed prices help*

bring some security to a notoriously unstable industry.

guaranteed wage /ˌɡærəntɪd ˈweɪdʒ/ *noun* a wage which a company promises will not fall below a specific figure

guarantor /ˌɡærənˈtɔr/ *noun* a person who promises to pay someone's debts ○ *She stood guarantor for her brother.*

guard book /ˈɡɑrd bʊk/ *noun* a hardcover album which allows pages to be inserted into it, e.g., for showing samples or advertising material

guerrilla marketing /ɡəˈrɪlə ˌmɑrkətɪŋ/ *noun* a form of unconventional flexible marketing, adapted to the products or services sold, or to the type of customer targeted

guesstimate /ˈɡestɪmət/ *noun* a rough calculation (*informal*)

gutter /ˈɡʌtər/ *noun* the area where the two pages meet in a book or magazine. It can be left blank as a center margin, or can be printed across to form a double-page spread.

H

habit /ˈhæbɪt/ *noun* the practice of doing something regularly ○ *Most consumers continue to buy the same brands from force of habit.*

habit buying /ˈhæbɪt ˌbaɪɪŋ/ *noun* the practice of buying a particular product again and again out of habit, without making any conscious decision to buy

haggle /ˈhæg(ə)l/ *verb* to discuss prices and terms and try to reduce them ○ *to haggle about* or *over the details of a contract* ○ *After two days' haggling the contract was signed.*

half-price sale /ˌhæf praɪs ˈseɪl/ *noun* a sale of items at half the usual price

hallmark /ˈhɔlmɑrk/ *noun* a mark put on gold or silver items to show that the metal is of the correct quality ■ *verb* to put a hallmark on a piece of gold or silver ○ *a hallmarked spoon*

hallmark of excellence /ˌhɔlmɑrk əv ˈeksələns/ *noun* the reputation that a brand name has for high quality

hall test /ˈhɔl test/ *noun* a market-research test where respondents are asked to go into a public building or central place to answer questions or to test new products ○ *The hall test was conducted in the town's main school.*

halo effect /ˈheɪlou ɪˌfekt/ *noun* a series of positive impressions of a product which consumers retain and which can be revealed by a respondent when questioned in a survey

hand /hænd/ *noun* **1.** the part of the body at the end of each arm □ **to shake hands** to hold someone's hand when meeting to show you are pleased to meet them, or to show that an agreement has been reached ○ *The two negotiating teams shook hands and sat down at the conference table.* □ **to shake hands on a deal** to shake hands to show that a deal has been agreed **2.** □ **in hand** kept in reserve ○ *we have $10,000 in hand* □ **balance in hand**, **cash in hand** cash held to pay small debts and running costs □ **work in hand** work which is in progress but not finished

handbill /ˈhændbɪl/ *noun* a sheet of printed paper handed out to members of the public as an advertisement

handbook /ˈhændbʊk/ *noun* a book which gives instructions on how to use something ○ *The handbook does not say how you open the photocopier.*

handed-overs /ˈhændɪd ˌoʊvərz/ *plural noun* sales leads which have been passed on to the client to pursue

handle /ˈhænd(ə)l/ *verb* **1.** to deal with something or to organize something ○ *The accounts department handles all the cash.* ○ *We can handle orders for up to 15,000 units.* ○ *They handle all our overseas orders.* **2.** to sell or to trade in a type of product ○ *We do not handle foreign cars.* ○ *They will not handle goods produced by other firms.*

handling /ˈhændlɪŋ/ *noun* the process of receiving, storing and sending off goods

handling charge /ˈhændlɪŋ tʃɑrdʒ/ *noun* money to be paid for packing, invoicing, and dealing with goods which are being shipped

handout /ˈhændaʊt/ *noun* a free gift, especially of money ○ *The company exists on handouts from the government.*

hard cash /ˌhɑrd ˈkæʃ/ *noun* money in notes and coins, as opposed to checks or credit cards

hard currency /ˌhɑrd ˈkʌrənsi/ *noun* the currency of a country which has a strong economy, and which can be changed into other currencies easily ○ *to pay for imports in hard currency* ○ *to sell raw materials to earn hard currency* Also called **scarce currency**. Opposite **soft currency**

hardening /ˈhɑrd(ə)nɪŋ/ *adjective* (*of a market*) slowly moving upward □ **a hardening of prices** prices which are becoming settled at a higher level

hardness /ˈhɑrdnəs/ *noun* □ **hardness of the market** the state of the market when it is strong and not likely to fall

hard sell /ˌhɑrd ˈsel/ *noun* □ **to give a product the hard sell** to make great efforts to persuade people to buy a product □ **he tried to give me the hard sell** he put a lot of effort into trying to make me buy

hard selling /ˌhɑrd ˈselɪŋ/ *noun* the act of selling by using great efforts ○ *A lot of hard selling went into that deal.*

hardware /ˈhɑrdwer/ *noun* **1.** machines used in data processing, including the computers and printers, but not the programs **2.** solid goods for use in the house, e.g., frying pans or hammers ○ *a hardware store*

harvesting /ˈhɑrvɪstɪŋ/ *noun* the practice of cutting marketing investment on a particular product prior to withdrawing it from the market

haulage /ˈhɔlɪdʒ/ *noun* the cost of transporting goods by road ○ *Haulage is increasing by 5% per annum.*

haulage contractor /ˈhɔlɪdʒ kən ˌtræktər/ *noun* a company which transports goods by contract

hawk /hɔk/ *verb* to sell goods from door to door or in the street □ **to hawk something round** to take a product, an idea, or a project to various companies to see if one will accept it ○ *He hawked his idea for a plastic car body around to all the major car manufacturers.*

hawker /ˈhɔkər/ *noun* a person who sells goods from door to door or in the street

head buyer /ˌhed ˈbaɪər/ *noun* the most important buyer in a store

headhunt /ˈhedhʌnt/ *verb* to look for managers and offer them jobs in other companies □ **she was headhunted** she was approached by a headhunter and offered a new job

headhunter /ˈhedhʌntər/ *noun* a person or company whose job is to find suitable top managers to fill jobs in companies

headline /ˈhedlaɪn/ *noun* the heading of an article or advertisement, which is set in much larger type than the rest

head-on position /ˈhed ɑn pə ˌzɪʃ(ə)n/ *noun* a poster site directly facing traffic ○ *Let's try to obtain a head-on position in the central part of town.*

heads of agreement /ˌhedz əv ə ˈgrimənt/ *plural noun* the most important parts of a commercial agreement

heat sealing /ˈhit ˌsilɪŋ/ *noun* a method of closing plastic food containers

COMMENT: Air is removed from a plastic bag with the food inside. The bag is then pressed by a hot plate which melts the plastic and seals the contents in the vacuum.

heavy /ˈhevi/ *adjective* large or in large quantities ○ *a program of heavy investment overseas* ○ *He suffered heavy losses on the Stock Exchange.* ○ *The government imposed a heavy tax on luxury goods.* □ **heavy costs** *or* **heavy expenditure** large sums of money that have to be spent

heavy half /ˌhevi ˈhæf/ *noun* a situation where a small number of customers make up more than half of the total demand for a product

heavy industry /ˌhevi ˈɪndəstri/ *noun* an industry which deals in heavy raw materials such as coal or makes large products such as ships or engines

heavy user /ˌhevi ˈjuzər/ *noun* a consumer who buys more of a product than average ○ *Heavy users will be particularly affected by the price increase.*

heavy viewer /ˌhevi ˈvjuər/ *noun* a person who watches a lot of television, and is part of the target audience for commercials ○ *Heavy viewers gave us the most interesting comments on our advertising.*

helicopter view /'helɪkɑptər vju/ *noun* a general or broad view of a problem as a whole, which does not go into details (*slang*)

helpline /'helplaɪn/ *noun* a telephone number which links people to services that can give them specialist advice, or a similar service offered by stores to their customers. Also called **careline**

heterogeneous /ˌhetərou'dʒiniəs/ *adjective* varied

heterogeneous shopping goods /ˌhetəroudʒiniəs 'ʃɑpɪŋ ˌgudz/ *plural noun* goods which vary in quality and style from brand to brand and which consumers spend time in choosing. Compare **homogeneous shopping goods**

heuristics /hju'rɪstɪks/ *noun* simple decision rules used by ordinary customers when choosing what to buy, e.g., buying whatever is cheapest

hidden economy /ˌhɪd(ə)n ɪ 'kɑnəmi/ *noun* same as **black economy**

hierarchy /'haɪərɑrki/ *noun* a series of items ranged in order of importance □ **hierarchy of needs** the theory that needs of individuals are arranged in an order based on their importance, such as safety, social needs, esteem, etc.

hierarchy of effects /ˌhaɪərɑrki əv ɪ'fekts/ *noun* a model showing the stages in the effect of advertising on a consumer such as awareness, knowledge, liking, preference, conviction, and purchase

high /haɪ/ *adjective* **1.** tall ○ *The shelves are 30 cm high.* ○ *The door is not high enough to let us get the machines into the building.* ○ *They are planning a 30-storey-high office building.* **2.** large, not low ○ *High overhead costs increase the unit price.* ○ *High prices put customers off.* ○ *They are budgeting for a high level of expenditure.* ○ *High interest rates are crippling small businesses.* □ **high sales** a large amount of revenue produced by sales □ **high taxation** taxation which imposes large taxes on incomes or profits □ **highest tax bracket** the group which pays

the most tax □ **high volume (of sales)** a large number of items sold **3.** □ **the highest bidder** the person who offers the most money at an auction ○ *The tender will be awarded to the highest bidder.* ○ *The property was sold to the highest bidder.* ■ *adverb* □ **prices are running high** prices are above their usual level ■ *noun* a point where prices or sales are very large ○ *Prices have dropped by 10% since the high of January 2nd.* □ **sales volume has reached an all-time high** the sales volume has reached the highest point it has ever been at

high concept /ˌhaɪ 'kɑnsept/ *noun* an important and persuasive idea expressed clearly and in few words

high-end /'haɪ end/ *adjective* more expensive, more advanced, or more powerful than the other items in a range of things, e.g., computers

high finance /ˌhaɪ 'faɪnæns/ *noun* the lending, investing, and borrowing of very large sums of money organized by financiers

high-grade /'haɪ greɪd/ *adjective* of very good quality ○ *high-grade gasoline* □ **high-grade trade delegation** a delegation made up of very important people

high-involvement product /ˌhaɪ ɪn'vɑlvmənt ˌprɑdʌkt/ *noun* a high-priced or high-tech product that is carefully considered by a consumer before being bought

high pressure /ˌhaɪ 'preʃə/ *noun* a strong insistence that somebody should do something □ **working under high pressure** working very hard, with a manager telling you what to do and to do it quickly, or with customers asking for supplies urgently

high-pressure salesman /ˌhaɪ ˌpreʃər 'seɪlzmən/, **high-pressure saleswoman** *noun* a salesman or saleswoman who forces a customer to buy something he or she does not really want

high-pressure sales technique /ˌhaɪ ˌpreʃər 'seɪlz tekˌnik/ *noun* an attempt to force a customer to buy something he or she does not really want

high-quality /ˌhaɪ ˈkwɑləti/ *adjective* of very good quality ○ *high-quality goods* ○ *a high-quality product*

high season /ˌhaɪ ˈsiːz(ə)n/ *noun* the period when there are the most travelers and tourists

high street /ˈhaɪ striːt/ *noun* the main shopping street in a British town ○ *the high street shops* ○ *a high street bookstore*

hire purchase /ˌhaɪr ˈpɜːtʃɪs/ *noun U.K.* same as **installment plan** ○ *to buy a refrigerator on installment plan* □ **to sign a hire-purchase agreement** to sign a contract to pay for something by installments

hire-purchase company /ˌhaɪr ˈpɜːtʃɪs ˌkʌmp(ə)ni/ *noun U.K.* a company which provides money for installment plan

histogram /ˈhɪstəɡræm/ *noun* same as **bar chart**

historic /hɪˈstɒrɪk/, **historical** /hɪˈstɒrɪk(ə)l/ *adjective* dating back over a period of time

historical figures /hɪˌstɒrɪk(ə)l ˈfɪɡəz/ *plural noun* figures which were current in the past

historical trend /hɪˌstɒrɪk(ə)l ˈtrend/ *noun* a trend detected in the past on the basis of historical data ○ *Historical trends may help us to predict how the economy will develop in the future.* ○ *It is difficult to detect any clear historical trends in consumer reaction to our past product launches.*

historic cost /hɪˌstɒrɪk ˈkɒst/, **historical cost** /hɪˌstɒrɪk(ə)l ˈkɒst/ *noun* the actual cost of purchasing something which was bought some time ago

hit /hɪt/ *noun* **1.** a response to a request sent from an Internet browser (NOTE: When a browser conducts a search, the number of hits it gets is the number of websites, files, or images it finds that fit the criteria set for the search.) **2.** a successful match or search of a database

hit rate /ˈhɪt reɪt/ *noun* the rate at which a target is reached such as the number of mail shots needed before a customer makes an order for a product

advertised on them, or the number of customers who reply to a mail shot compared to the total number of customers mailed

hive /haɪv/ *verb*
  hive off *phrasal verb* to split off part of a large company to form a smaller subsidiary ○ *The new managing director hived off the retail sections of the company.*

hoard /hɔːd/ *verb* **1.** to buy and store goods in case of need **2.** to keep cash instead of investing it

hoarder /ˈhɔːdər/ *noun* a person who buys and stores goods in case of need

hoarding /ˈhɔːdɪŋ/ *noun* **1.** □ **hoarding of supplies** the buying of large quantities of goods to keep in case of need **2.** a large wooden board for posters

home audit /ˌhoʊm ˈɔːdɪt/ *noun* a survey method whereby a panel of householders keeps records of purchases so that these can be regularly checked for quantity and brand ○ *The home audit showed that although wholesalers were buying the product in large quantities, consumers were not.* ○ *The home audit suggested that there is little brand loyalty for this type of product.*

home country /ˌhoʊm ˈkʌntri/ *noun* a country where a company is based

homegrown /ˈhoʊmɡroʊn/ *adjective* which has been developed in a local area or in a country where the company is based ○ *a homegrown computer industry* ○ *India's homegrown car industry*

home industry /ˌhoʊm ˈɪndəstri/ *noun* productive work carried out by people at home ○ *In third world countries there are still many home industries.* ○ *Home industries are disappearing as mass production takes over.*

home market /ˌhoʊm ˈmɑːkət/ *noun* the market in the country where the selling company is based ○ *Sales in the home market rose by 22%.*

homepage /ˈhoʊmpeɪdʒ/ *noun* the first page that is displayed when you visit a site on the Internet

home-produced product /ˌhoʊm prəˌduːst ˈprɒdʌkt/ *noun* a product manufactured in the country where the company is based

home shopping /hoʊm ˈʃɑpɪŋ/ *noun* buying items direct from the customer's house, using a computer linked to the telephone which is linked to the store's ordering department

home trade /ˌhoʊm ˈtreɪd/ *noun* trade in the country where a company is based

homeward /ˈhoʊmwərd/ *adjective* going toward the home country ○ *The ship is carrying homeward freight.* ○ *The liner left Buenos Aires on her homeward journey.*

homewards /ˈhoʊmwərdz/ *adverb* toward the home country ○ *cargo homewards*

homogeneous /ˌhoʊmoʊˈdʒiniəs/ *adjective* uniform or unvaried

homogeneous shopping goods /ˌhoʊmoʊdʒiniəs ˈʃɑpɪŋ gʊdz/ *plural noun* goods which vary little in style and quality from brand to brand and which consumers spend little time choosing. Compare **heterogeneous shopping goods**

homogenization /həˌmɑdʒənaɪˈzeɪʃ(ə)n/ *noun* the tendency for different products, markets and cultures to lose their characteristic differences and become the same (NOTE: Globalisation is often blamed for homogenisation.)

horizontal /ˌhɔrɪˈzɑnt(ə)l/ *adjective* at the same level or with the same status ○ *Her new job is a horizontal move into a different branch of the business.*

horizontal communication /ˌhɔrɪzɑnt(ə)l kəˌmjuːnɪˈkeɪʃ(ə)n/ *noun* communication between employees at the same level

horizontal cooperative advertising /ˌhɔrɪzɑnt(ə)l koʊˈɑp(ə)rətɪv ˈædvərtaɪzɪŋ/ *noun* cooperative advertising where the advertising is sponsored by a group of retailers

horizontal industrial market /ˌhɔrɪzɑnt(ə)l ɪnˌdʌstriəl ˈmɑrkət/ *noun* a market in which a product is used by many industries

horizontal integration /ˌhɔrɪzɑnt(ə)l ˌɪntɪˈgreɪʃ(ə)n/ *noun* the process of joining similar companies or taking over a company in the same line of business as yourself

horizontal marketing system /ˌhɔrɪzɑnt(ə)l ˈmɑrkətɪŋ ˌsɪstəm/ *noun* cooperation between or merger of two or more companies whose assets are complementary and who therefore all gain from coming together

horizontal publication /ˌhɔrɪzɑnt(ə)l ˌpʌblɪˈkeɪʃ(ə)n/ *noun* a publication which is aimed at people in similar levels of occupation in different industries

horizontal rotation /ˌhɔrɪzɑnt(ə)l roʊˈteɪʃ(ə)n/ *noun* distributing broadcast spots on different days of the week at the same time of day

horse trading /ˈhɔrs ˌtreɪdɪŋ/ *noun* hard bargaining which ends with someone giving something in return for a concession from the other side

hostess party selling /ˌhoʊstes ˈpɑrti ˌselɪŋ/ *noun* a method of selling certain items such as housewares directly by the manufacturer's agent at a party to which potential customers are invited

hostile bid /ˌhɑstaɪl ˈbɪd/ *noun* same as **contested takeover**

hosting /ˈhoʊstɪŋ/ *noun* the business of putting websites onto the Internet so that people can visit them. ◊ **hosting option**

hosting option /ˈhoʊstɪŋ ˈɑpʃən/ *noun* any of the different kinds of hosting that a business may use when putting a website on the Internet and that are usually provided by specialist hosting companies. ◊ **collocation hosting, managed hosting, non-virtual hosting, virtual hosting**

host service /ˈhoʊst ˌsɜrvɪs/, **hosting service provider** /ˈhoʊstɪŋ ˌsɜrvɪs prəˌvaɪdər/ *noun* a company that provides connections to the Internet and storage space on its computers, which can store the files for a user's website

hot button /ˈhɑt ˌbʌt(ə)n/ *noun* the immediate interest a customer has in a product or service offered for sale

hoteling /hoʊˈtelɪŋ/ *noun* the practice of using a desk or workspace in an office belonging to someone who is not your employer. Hoteling is normally carried out by consultants or sales people, who spend more time with their customers than at their base.

hotline /ˈhɑtlaɪn/ *noun* a special telephone ordering service set up for a special period ○ *a Christmas hotline*

hot money /ˌhɑt ˈmʌni/ *noun* money which is moved from country to country to get the best returns

house /haʊs/ *noun* **1.** the building in which someone lives **2.** a company ○ *the largest London finance house* ○ *a publishing house*

house advertisment /ˈhaʊs æd/, **house ad** *noun* an advertisement in a publication which is placed by the publication itself, e.g., one offering a readers' advice service or selling back numbers of the publication

house agency /ˈhaʊz ˌeɪdʒənsi/ *noun* an advertising agency owned and used by a large company, and which other companies may also use

house agent /ˈhaʊz ˌeɪdʒənt/ *noun* a real estate agent who deals in buying or selling houses or apartments

house brand /ˈhaʊs brænd/ *noun* a brand owned by a retailer rather than by the producer

household /ˈhaʊshoʊld/ *noun* a unit formed of all the people living together in a single house or apartment, whether it is a single person living alone, a married couple, or a large family

household appliances /ˌhaʊshoʊld əˈplaɪənsɪz/ *plural noun* appliances which are used in carrying out day-to-day work in the house, e.g., dishwashers and refrigerators

household name /ˌhaʊshoʊld neɪm/ *noun* a brand name which is recognized by a large number of consumers

households using television /ˌhaʊshoʊldz ˌjuzɪŋ ˌteliˈvɪʒ(ə)n/ *noun* the percentage of homes watching television during a specific time period and within a specific area. Abbreviation **HUT**

house journal /ˈhaʊs ˌdʒɜrn(ə)l/, **house magazine** /ˈhaʊs ˌmægəzin/ *noun* a magazine produced for the employees or shareholders in a company to give them news about the company

house property /ˈhaʊs ˌprɑpərti/ *noun* private houses or apartments, not stores, offices, or factories

house style /ˌhaʊs ˈstaɪl/ *noun* a company's own design which is used in all its products, including packaging and stationery

house-to-house /ˌhaʊs tə ˈhaʊs/ *adjective* going from one house to the next, asking people to buy something or to vote for someone ○ *house-to-house canvassing* ○ *He trained as a house-to-house salesman.* ○ *House-to-house selling is banned in this area.*

housewares /ˈhaʊswerz/ *plural noun* items which are used in the home

housing market /ˈhaʊzɪŋ ˌmɑrkət/ *noun* the sale of houses. Also called **property market**

HTML /ˌeɪtʃ ti em ˈel/ *noun* the standard computer code used to build and develop webpages

human resources /ˌhjumən rɪˈsɔrsɪz/ *plural noun* the employees which an organization has available ○ *Our human resources must be looked after and developed if we are to raise productivity successfully.* Abbreviation **HR**. Also called **personnel**

human resources department /ˌhjumən rɪˈzɔrsɪz dɪˌpɑrtmənt/ *noun* the section of the company which deals with its staff

human resources officer /ˌhjumən rɪˈzɔrsɪz ˌɒfɪsər/ *noun* a person who deals with the staff in a company, especially interviewing candidates for new positions

hunch marketing /ˈhʌntʃ ˌmɑrkətɪŋ/ *noun* the process of making marketing decisions following a hunch, rather than relying on market research

HUT *abbreviation* households using television

hype /haɪp/ *noun* excessive claims made in advertising ○ *all the hype sur-*

rounding the launch of the new soap ○ *Many consumers were actually put off by all the media hype surrounding the launch of the new magazine.* ■ *verb* to make excessive claims in advertising

hyperlink /ˈhaɪpəlɪŋk/ *noun* **1.** an image or a piece of text that a user clicks on in order to move directly from one webpage to another (NOTE: Hyperlinks can be added to webpages by using simple HTML commands; they can also be used in email messages, for example, to include the address of a company's website.) **2.** a series of commands attached to a button or word on one webpage that link it to another page, so that if a user clicks on the button or word, the hyperlink will move the user to another position or display another page

hypermarket /ˈhaɪpəmɑːkət/ *noun* a very large supermarket, usually outside a large town, with car-parking facilities

hypertext /ˈhaɪpətekst/ *noun* a system of organizing information in which certain words in a document link to other documents and display the text when the word is selected

hypertext link /ˈhaɪpətekst lɪŋk/ *noun* same as **hyperlink**

hypertext markup language /ˌhaɪpətekst ˈmɑːkʌp ˌlæŋɡwɪdʒ/ *noun* full form of **HTML**

hypoing /ˈhaɪpəʊɪŋ/ *noun* using special promotions to increase the audience of a TV station during the sweep periods and so affect the ratings

hypothesis /haɪˈpɒθəsɪs/ *noun* an assumption or theory which must be tested to be confirmed or proved correct ○ *Let us assume, as a working hypothesis, that we can win a 5% market share within two years of the launch.* ○ *Surveys proved that our original hypothesis about likely consumer behavior was by and large correct.* (NOTE: The plural is **hypotheses**)

I

iceberg principle /'aɪsbɜrg ˌprɪnsɪp(ə)l/ *noun* the principle that strong needs and desires lie deep in the human personality and that advertising must work at this level if it is to be effective

ident /'aɪdent/ *noun* a short TV image which identifies a channel

image /'ɪmɪdʒ/ *noun* the general idea that the public has of a product, brand, or company ○ *They are spending a lot of advertising money to improve the company's image.* ○ *The company has adopted a downmarket image.* □ **to promote the corporate image** to publicize a company so that its reputation is improved

image advertising /'ɪmɪdʒ ˌædvərtaɪzɪŋ/ *noun* advertising with the aim of making a brand or company name easily remembered

image-maker /'ɪmɪdʒ ˌmeɪkər/ *noun* someone who is employed to create a favorable public image for an organization, product, or public figure

image manipulation /'ɪmɪdʒ mə ˌnɪpjʊleɪʃ(ə)n/ *noun* alteration of digital images using special computer software

image setter /'ɪmɪdʒ ˌsetər/ *noun* a typesetting device that can process a PostScript page and produce a high-resolution output

image transfer /'ɪmɪdʒ ˌtrænsfɜr/ *noun* the technique of transferring images from one medium to another, e.g., from a photograph to a computer disc

IMF *abbreviation* International Monetary Fund

imitate /'ɪmɪteɪt/ *verb* to do what someone else does ○ *They imitate all our sales gimmicks.*

imitation /ˌɪmɪ'teɪʃ(ə)n/ *noun* something which is a copy of an original □ **beware of imitations** be careful not to buy low-quality goods which are made to look like other more expensive items

immediate /ɪ'midiət/ *adjective* happening at once ○ *We wrote an immediate letter of complaint.* ○ *Your order will receive immediate attention.*

immediate environment /ɪˌmidiət ɪn'vaɪrənmənt/ *noun* elements or factors outside a business organization which directly affect its work, such as the supply of raw materials and demand for its products ○ *The unreliability of our suppliers is one of the worst features of our immediate environment.*

impact /'ɪmpækt/ *noun* a shock or strong effect ○ *the impact of new technology on the cotton trade* ○ *The new design has made little impact on the buying public.*

impactaplan /ɪm'pæktəplæn/ *noun* an extensive poster advertising campaign

impact scheduling /'ɪmpækt ˌʃedjulɪŋ/ *noun* the practice of running advertisements for the same product close together so as to make a strong impression on the target audience ○ *Impact scheduling can achieve rapid brand awareness.*

imperfect /ɪm'pɜrfɪkt/ *adjective* having defects ○ *They are holding a sale of imperfect items.* ○ *Check the batch for imperfect products.*

imperfect competition /ɪm ˌpɜrfɪkt ˌkɑmpə'tɪʃ(ə)n/ *noun* the degree of competition in a market which is somewhere between a monopoly at one extreme and perfect competition at the other. Also called **monopolistic competition**

imperfection /ˌɪmpəˈfekʃən/ *noun* a defect in something ○ *to check a batch for imperfections*

implied close /ɪmˌplaɪd ˈkloʊz/ *noun* an act of ending a sale by assuming that the customer will make the purchase

import /ɪmˈpɔrt/ *verb* to bring goods from abroad into a country for sale ○ *The company imports television sets from Japan.* ○ *This car was imported from France.*

importation /ˌɪmpɔˈteɪʃ(ə)n/ *noun* the act of importing ○ *The importation of arms is forbidden.* ○ *The importation of livestock is subject to very strict controls.*

import ban /ˈɪmpɔrt bæn/ *noun* an order forbidding imports ○ *The government has imposed an import ban on arms.*

import duty /ˈɪmpɔrt ˌduti/ *noun* a tax on goods imported into a country

importer /ɪmˈpɔrtər/ *noun* a person or company that imports goods ○ *a cigar importer* ○ *The company is a big importer of foreign cars.*

import-export /ˌɪmpɔrt ˈekspɔrt/ *adjective, noun* referring to business which deals with both bringing foreign goods into a country and sending locally made goods abroad ○ *Rotterdam is an important center for the import-export trade.* ○ *She works in import-export.*

importing /ɪmˈpɔrtɪŋ/ *adjective* bringing goods into a country ○ *oil-importing countries* ○ *an importing company* ■ *noun* the act of bringing foreign goods into a country for sale ○ *The importing of arms into the country is illegal.*

import levy /ˈɪmpɔrt ˌlevi/ *noun* a tax on imports, especially in the EU a tax on imports of farm produce from outside the EU

import license /ˈɪmpɔrt ˌlaɪs(ə)ns/, **import permit** *noun* an official document which allows goods to be imported

import quota /ˈɪmpɔrt ˌkwoʊtə/ *noun* a fixed quantity of a particular type of goods which the government allows to be imported ○ *The government has imposed a import quota on cars.*

imports /ˈɪmpɔrts/ *plural noun* goods brought into a country from abroad for sale ○ *Imports from Poland have risen to $1m a year.* (NOTE: Usually used in the plural, but the singular is used before a noun.)

import surcharge /ˈɪmpɔrt ˌsɜrtʃɑrdʒ/ *noun* the extra duty charged on imported goods, to try to stop them from being imported and to encourage local manufacture

impression /ɪmˈpreʃ(ə)n/ *noun* **1.** one person's single exposure to an advertisement ○ *One impression can be enough to induce a consumer to buy.* ○ *Too many impressions can put consumers off.* **2.** the number of times an ad banner is displayed

impression cover /ɪmˈpreʃ(ə)n ˌkʌvər/ *noun* the amount of advertising necessary to ensure the required number of impressions

impulse /ˈɪmpʌls/ *noun* a sudden decision □ **to do something on impulse** to do something because you have just thought of it, not because it was planned

impulse buyer /ˈɪmpʌls ˌbaɪər/ *noun* a person who buys something on impulse, not because he or she intended to buy it

impulse buying /ˈɪmpʌls ˌbaɪɪŋ/ *noun* the practice of buying items which you have just seen, not because you had planned to buy them

impulse purchase /ˈɪmpʌls ˌpɜrtʃɪs/ *noun* something bought as soon as it is seen

incentive /ɪnˈsentɪv/ *noun* something which encourages a customer to buy, or employees to work better

incentive-based system /ɪnˈsentɪv beɪst ˌsɪstəm/ *noun* a payment system by which an advertising agency's commission depends on how well it performs

incentive marketing /ɪn'sentɪv ˌmɑːkətɪŋ/ *noun* any additional incentives to buy apart from advertising, e.g., free gifts ○ *We will have to use incentive marketing to break down sales resistance.*

incentive program /ɪn'sentɪv ˌprəʊɡræm/ *noun* a plan to encourage better work by paying higher commission or bonuses ○ *Incentive programs are boosting production.*

inch rate /'ɪnʃ reɪt/ *noun* an advertising rate for periodicals, calculated on a normal column width, one inch in depth

inclusive charge /ɪnˌkluːsɪv 'tʃɑːdʒ/, **inclusive sum** /ɪnˌkluːsɪv 'sʌm/ *noun* a charge which includes all items or costs

income /'ɪnkʌm/ *noun* money which a person receives as salary or dividends □ **lower income bracket, upper income bracket** the groups of people who earn low or high salaries considered for tax purposes

income distribution /'ɪnkʌm dɪstrɪˌbjuːʃ(ə)n/ *noun* the way in which the national income is distributed among the various classes and occupations in a country

income effect /'ɪnkʌm ɪˌfekt/ *noun* the effect that a change in a person's income has on his or her spending

incomes policy /'ɪnkʌmz ˌpɒlɪsi/ *noun* the government's ideas on how incomes should be controlled

income statement /'ɪnkʌm ˌsteɪtmənt/ *noun* same as **profit and loss account**

incorrectly labeled parcel /ˌɪnkərekt(ə)li ˌleɪb(ə)ld 'pɑːs(ə)l/ *noun* a parcel with the wrong information on the label

indemnity /ɪn'demnəti/ *noun* a guarantee of payment after a loss ○ *She had to pay an indemnity of $100.*

indent *noun* /'ɪndent/ **1.** an order placed by an importer for goods from overseas ○ *They put in an indent for a new stock of soap.* **2.** a line of typing which starts several spaces from the left-hand margin ■ *verb* /ɪn'dent/ **1.** □ **to indent for something** to put in an order for something ○ *The department has indented for a new computer.* **2.** to start a line of typing several spaces from the left-hand margin ○ *Indent the first line three spaces.*

independent /ˌɪndɪ'pendənt/ *adjective* not under the control or authority of anyone else

independent company /ˌɪndɪpendənt 'kʌmp(ə)ni/ *noun* a company which is not controlled by another company

independents /ˌɪndɪ'pendənts/ *plural noun* shops or companies which are owned by private individuals or families

independent trader /ˌɪndɪpendənt 'treɪdər/, **independent store** /ˌɪndɪpendənt 'stɔː/ *noun* a store which is owned by an individual proprietor, not by a chain

independent variable /ˌɪndɪpendənt 'veriəb(ə)l/ *noun* a factor whose value, when it changes, influences one or more other variables called "dependent variables" ○ *In this model personal income is the independent variable and expenditure the dependent variable.*

index /'ɪndeks/ *noun* a regular statistical report which shows rises and falls in prices, values, or levels

indexation /ˌɪndek'seɪʃ(ə)n/ *noun* the linking of something to an index

indexation of wage increases /ˌɪndekseɪʃ(ə)n əv 'weɪdʒ ˌɪnkrɪsɪz/ *noun* the linking of wage increases to the percentage rise in the cost of living

indexing /'ɪndeksɪŋ/ *noun* a method of showing changes in a value over time by starting with a simple base point such as 100, which then serves as a reference point for future years ○ *Indexing is used to show the rise in the cost of living over a ten-year period.*

index-linked /ˌɪndeks 'lɪŋkt/ *adjective* rising automatically by the percentage increase in the cost of living ○ *index-linked government bonds* ○ *Inflation did not affect her as she has an index-linked pension.*

indicate /ˈɪndɪkeɪt/ *verb* to show something ○ The latest figures indicate a fall in the inflation rate. ○ Our sales for last year indicate a move from the home market to exports.

indicator /ˈɪndɪkeɪtər/ *noun* something which indicates

indicia /ɪnˈdɪsɪə/ *noun* a stamp printed on an envelope to show that postage has been paid by the sender

indifference curve /ɪnˈdɪf(ə)rəns kɜrv/ *noun* a line on a graph that joins various points, each point representing a combination of two commodities, each combination giving the customer equal satisfaction

indigenous /ɪnˈdɪdʒɪnəs/ *adjective* belonging to a particular country or area ○ Cocoa is not indigenous to the area, but has been grown there for some years.

indirect /ˌɪndaɪˈrekt/ *adjective* not direct

indirect channel /ˌɪndaɪrekt ˈtʃæn(ə)l/ *noun* a marketing channel where intermediaries such as wholesalers and retailers are used to sell a product, as opposed to using a direct sales force

indirect exporting /ˌɪndaɪrekt ˈekspɔːtɪŋ/ *noun* selling products to a customer overseas through a middleman in your own country ○ There is no need for indirect exporting as we can sell directly to the major department stores in Spain. ○ Indirect exporting saved the company from having to worry about export documentation and transportation.

indirect headline /ˌɪndaɪrekt ˈhedlaɪn/ *noun* a headline which does not directly try to sell a product or service but rather tries to attract the customer's attention or plays on his or her emotions

indirect labor costs /ˌɪndaɪrekt ˈleɪbər ˌkɔsts/ *plural noun* the cost of paying employees not directly involved in making a product such as cleaners or cafeteria staff. Such costs cannot be allocated to a cost center.

individual /ˌɪndɪˈvɪdʒuəl/ *noun* one single person ○ a savings plan tailored to the requirements of the private individual ■ *adjective* single or belonging to one person ○ a pension plan designed to meet each person's individual requirements ○ We sell individual portions of ice cream.

individual demand /ˌɪndɪvɪdʒuəl dɪˈmænd/ *noun* demand from one single consumer

industrial /ɪnˈdʌstriəl/ *adjective* referring to manufacturing work □ **to take industrial action** to go on strike or go-slow

industrial advertising /ɪnˌdʌstriəl ˈædvərtaɪzɪŋ/ *noun* advertising to businesses, not to private individuals

industrial capacity /ɪnˌdʌstriəl kəˈpæsəti/ *noun* the amount of work which can be done in a factory or several factories

industrial center /ɪnˈdʌstriəl ˌsentər/ *noun* a large town with many industries

industrial consumer /ɪnˌdʌstriəl kənˈsumər/ *noun* a business which buys industrial goods

industrial design /ɪnˌdʌstriəl dɪˈzaɪn/ *noun* the design of products made by machines such as cars and refrigerators

industrial development /ɪnˌdʌstriəl dɪˈveləpmənt/ *noun* the planning and building of new industries in special areas

industrial espionage /ɪnˌdʌstriəl ˈespiənɑrʒ/ *noun* the practice of trying to find out the secrets of a competitor's work or products, usually by illegal means

industrial expansion /ɪnˌdʌstriəl ɪkˈspænʃən/ *noun* the growth of industries in a country or a region

industrial goods /ɪnˌdʌstriəl ˈgʊdz/, **industrial products** /ɪnˌdʌstriəl ˈprɑdʌkts/ *plural noun* **1.** goods or products bought by producers to be used in production processes ○ Our industrial products are advertised in the specialized press. ○ He is an engineer by profession and sells industrial *goods to factories.* **2.** goods produced for use by industry, which include processed or raw materials and goods such as machinery and equipment that are used to produce other goods

industrial injury /ɪnˌdʌstriəl ˈɪndʒəriz/ *noun* an injury to an employee that occurs in the workplace

industrialist /ɪnˈdʌstriəlɪst/ *noun* an owner or director of a factory

industrialization /ɪnˌdʌstriəlaɪˈzeɪʃ(ə)n/ *noun* the process of change by which an economy becomes based on industrial production rather than on agriculture

industrialize /ɪnˈdʌstriəˌlaɪz/ *verb* to set up industries in a country which had none before

industrialized society /ɪnˌdʌstriəlaɪzd səˈsaɪəti/ *noun* a country which has many industries

industrial market /ɪnˈdʌstriəl ˌmɑrkət/ *noun* customers who buy goods to be used in production

industrial marketing /ɪnˌdʌstriəl ˈmɑrkətɪŋ/ *noun* the marketing of industrial products ○ *After doing a course in industrial marketing, I got a job selling machinery to aircraft manufacturers.*

industrial market research /ɪnˌdʌstriəl mɑrkət rɪˈsɜrtʃ/ *noun* market research into selling to businesses as opposed to private individuals

industrial services marketing /ɪnˌdʌstriəl ˈsɜrvɪsɪz ˌmɑrkətɪŋ/ *noun* the marketing to business customers of such services as debt collection, office cleaning, etc.

industrial user /ɪnˌdʌstriəl ˈjuzər/ *noun* a customer who buys industrial products to use in production

industry /ˈɪndəstri/ *noun* **1.** all factories, companies, or processes involved in the manufacturing of products ○ *All sectors of industry have shown rises in output.* **2.** a group of companies making the same type of product or offering the same type of service ○ *the aircraft industry* ○ *the food-processing industry* ○ *the petroleum industry* ○ *the advertising industry*

inelastic demand /ˌɪniˌlæstɪk dɪˈmænd/ *noun* demand which experiences a comparatively small percentage change in response to a percentage change in price ○ *Where a product is a household necessity, you almost always find an inelastic demand.*

inelastic supply /ˌɪniˌlæstɪk səˈplaɪ/ *noun* supply which experiences a comparatively small percentage change in response to a percentage change in price

inertia selling /ɪˈnɜrʃə ˌselɪŋ/ *noun* a method of selling items by sending them when they have not been ordered and assuming that if the items are not returned, the person who has received them is willing to buy them

inferior /ɪnˈfɪriər/ *adjective* not as good as others ○ *products of inferior quality*

inferior product /ɪnˌfɪriər ˈprɑdʌkt/ *noun* a product which consumers buy less of as their incomes rise ○ *Margarine was clearly an inferior product before it came to be considered healthier than butter.* ○ *As the recession hit, sales of inferior products soared.*

inflation /ɪnˈfleɪʃ(ə)n/ *noun* a greater increase in the supply of money or credit than in the production of goods and services, resulting in higher prices and a fall in the purchasing power of money ○ *to take measures to reduce inflation* ○ *High interest rates tend to increase inflation.* □ **we have 3% inflation** *or* **inflation is running at 3%** prices are 3% higher than at the same time last year

inflationary /ɪnˈfleɪʃ(ə)n(ə)ri/ *adjective* tending to increase inflation ○ *inflationary trends in the economy* □ **the economy is in an inflationary spiral** the economy is in a situation where price increases encourage higher wage demands which in turn make prices rise

inflight advertising /ˌɪnflaɪt ˈædvərtaɪzɪŋ/ *noun* advertising on TV screens inside a plane

inflight audience /ˌɪnflaɪt ˈɔdiəns/ *noun* travelers, especially business executives, seen as a market for advertisers

influencer /ˈɪnfluənsər/ *noun* an expert in the decision-making unit who advises on technical aspects of the product or service under consideration

infoholic /ˌɪnfoʊˈhɑlɪk/ *noun* a person who is obsessed with obtaining information, especially on the Internet (*slang*)

infomediary /ˈɪnfoʊˌmidiəri/ *noun* a business or website that collects information about customers for use by other companies (NOTE: The plural is **infomediaries**.)

infomercial /ˌɪnfoʊˈmɜrʃ(ə)l/ *noun* a TV commercial that is longer than the normal 30 seconds, and contains information about the product or service being sold

inform /ɪnˈfɔrm/ *verb* to tell someone officially ○ *I regret to inform you that your tender was not acceptable.* ○ *We are pleased to inform you that you have been selected for interview.* ○ *We have been informed by the Department that new regulations are coming into force.*

informant /ɪnˈfɔrmənt/ *noun* a person who answers questions in a survey ○ *So far only two informants have said that they never buy the product.*

information /ˌɪnfərˈmeɪʃ(ə)n/ *noun* details which explain something ○ *to disclose a piece of information* ○ *to answer a request for information* ○ *Please send me information on* or *about vacations in the Southwest.* ○ *Have you any information on* or *about deposit accounts?* ○ *I enclose this leaflet for your information.* ○ *For further information, please write to Department 27.* □ **disclosure of confidential information** the act of telling someone information which should be secret

informational appeal /ɪnfər ˌmeɪʃ(ə)n(ə)l əˈpil/ *noun* same as **rational appeal**

information and communications technologies /ɪnfər ˌmeɪʃ(ə)n ən kəˌmjunɪˈkeɪʃ(ə)nz tek ˌnɑlədʒiz/ *plural noun* computer and telecommunications technologies considered together (NOTE: It is the coming together of information and communications technology that has made possible such things as the Internet, videoconferencing, groupware, intranets, and third-generation cell phones.)

information architecture /ˌɪnfə ˌmeɪʃ(ə)n ˈɑrkɪtektʃə/ *noun* the methods used in designing the navigation, search and content layout for a website

information management /ˌɪnfərmeɪʃ(ə)n ˈmænɪdʒmənt/ *noun* the task of controlling information and the flow of information within an organization, which involves acquiring, recording, organizing, storing, distributing, and retrieving it (NOTE: Good information management has been described as getting the right information to the right person in the right format at the right time.)

information officer /ˌɪnfər ˈmeɪʃ(ə)n ˌɒfɪsər/ *noun* **1.** a person whose job is to give information about a company, an organization or a government department to the public **2.** a person whose job is to give information to other departments in the same organization

information processing model /ˌɪnfərmeɪʃ(ə)n ˈprɑsesɪŋ ˌmɑd(ə)l/ *noun* a way of evaluating the effect of advertising by seeing the receiver of the message as someone who processes information and deals with problems

information retrieval /ˌɪnfərmeɪʃ(ə)n rɪˈtriv(ə)l/ *noun* the finding of stored data in a computer

infotainment /ˌɪnfoʊˈteɪnmənt/ *noun* entertainment that is informative, especially television programs that deal with serious issues or current affairs in an entertaining way

ingredient /ɪnˈgridiənt/ *noun* material or a substance which goes to make something

ingredient sponsored cooperative advertising /ɪnˌgridiənt spɑnsəd koʊˌɑp(ə)rətɪv ˈædvərtaɪzɪŋ/ *noun* advertising sponsored by the producers of raw materials which aims to encourage the production of products that use these raw materials

inherent drama /ɪnˌhɪrənt ˈdrɑrmə/ *noun* advertising that emphasizes the benefits of purchasing a product or service and the vital interest which the user has in the product such as the speed of a car, the nutrition value of cereals, etc.

inherent vice /ɪnˌhɪrənt ˈvaɪs/ *noun* the tendency of some goods to spoil during transportation ○ *Inherent vice discouraged us from importing tropical fruit.*

in-home selling /ˌɪn hoʊm ˈselɪŋ/, **in-home retailing** /ˌɪn hoʊm ˈriːteɪlɪŋ/ *noun* selling to a customer in his or her home, either by direct contact or by telephone ○ *In-home selling is the national strategy for our products.* ○ *In-home selling is useful when housewives are the target market.*

in-house /ˌɪn ˈhaʊs/ *adverb, adjective* done by someone employed by a company on their premises, not by an outside contractor ○ *the in-house staff* ○ *We do all our data processing in-house.*

in-house agency /ˌɪn haʊs ˈeɪdʒənsi/ *noun* an advertising agency which is owned and operated by a company and is responsible for the company's advertising program

in-house newsletter /ˌɪn haʊs ˈnuːzletər/ *noun* same as **newsletter**

initial /ɪˈnɪʃ(ə)l/ *adjective* first or starting ○ *The initial response to the TV advertising has been very good.*

initial capital /ɪˌnɪʃ(ə)l ˈkæpɪt(ə)l/ *noun* capital which is used to start a business

initial sales /ɪˌnɪʃ(ə)l ˈseɪlz/ *plural noun* the first sales of a new product

ink-jet printing /ˈɪŋk dʒet ˌprɪntɪŋ/, **ink-jet imaging** /ˈɪŋk dʒet ˌɪmɪdʒɪŋ/ *noun* a printing process where text is reproduced by projecting dots of electronically charged ink onto the paper

inland port /ˌɪnlənd ˈpɔːrt/ *noun* a port on a river or canal

innovate /ˈɪnoʊveɪt/ *verb* to bring in new ideas or new methods

innovation /ˌɪnəˈveɪʃ(ə)n/ *noun* the development of new products or new ways of selling

innovation-adoption model /ˌɪnəˌveɪʃ(ə)n əˈdɑpʃ(ə)n ˌmɑd(ə)l/ *noun* a model that shows the stages in the adoption process for a new product by a consumer, which are: awareness, interest, evaluation, trial, and adoption

innovative /ˈɪnəveɪtɪv/ *adjective* referring to a person or thing which is new and makes changes

innovator /ˈɪnəveɪtər/ *noun* **1.** a person or company that brings in new ideas and methods **2.** a person who buys a new product first

in-pack /ˈɪn pæk/ *noun* something placed inside the packaging with the product ○ *In-pack promotion may include information on other products in the same line.*

input tax /ˈɪnpʊt tæks/ *noun* VAT which is paid by a company on goods or services bought

inquiry /ɪnˈkwaɪəri/ *noun* a request for information about a product

inquiry test /ɪŋˈkwaɪəri test/ *noun* a measuring of the effectiveness of advertising based on responses following the advertisement such as requests for information, phone calls, or the number of coupons redeemed

insert *noun* /ˈɪnsɜrt/ a form or leaflet which is put inside something, usually a magazine or newspaper □ **an insert in a magazine mailing, a magazine insert** an advertising sheet put into a magazine when it is mailed ■ *verb* /ɪnˈsɜrt/ to put something in ○ *to insert a clause into a contract* ○ *to insert a publicity piece into a magazine mailing*

insertion /ɪnˈsɜrʃ(ə)n/ *noun* the act of putting an advertisement into a magazine or newspaper

insertion rate /ɪnˈsɜrʃ(ə)n reɪt/ *noun* the rate charged for a single insertion of an advertisement

inset /ˈɪnset/ *abbreviation* in-service training. Same as **insert**

inside back cover /ˌɪnsaɪd bæk ˈkʌvər/ *noun* the page on the inside of the back cover used for advertising ○ *We have advertised on the inside back cover of every issue this year.* ○ *The survey is trying to establish how much notice readers take of the inside back cover.*

inside front cover /ˌɪnsaɪd ˌfrʌnt ˈkʌvər/ *noun* the page on the inside of the front cover of a magazine, used for advertisements

instability /ˌɪnstəˈbɪləti/ *noun* the state of being unstable or moving up and down □ **a period of instability in the money markets** a period when currencies fluctuate rapidly

install /ɪnˈstɔl/ *verb* **1.** to put a machine into an office or into a factory ○ *We are planning to install the new machinery over the weekend.* ○ *They must install a new data processing system because the old one cannot cope with the mass of work involved.* **2.** to set up a piece of machinery or equipment, e.g., a new computer system, so that it can be used **3.** to configure a new computer program to the existing system requirements

installation /ˌɪnstəˈleɪʃ(ə)n/ *noun* **1.** the act of putting new machines into an office or a factory ○ *to supervise the installation of new equipment* **2.** machines, equipment and buildings ○ *Harbor installations were picketed by striking dockers.* ○ *The fire seriously damaged the oil installations.* **3.** the act of setting up a piece of equipment

installment /ɪnˈstɔlmənt/ *noun* a part of a payment which is paid regularly until the total amount is paid ○ *The first installment is payable on signature of the agreement.* (NOTE: The U.K. spelling is **instalment**.) □ **the final instalment is now due** the last of a series of payments should be paid now □ **to pay $50 down and monthly instalments of $40** to pay a first payment of $50 and the rest in payments of $40 each month □ **to miss an instalment** not to pay an installment at the right time

installment plan /ɪnˈstɔlmənt plæn/, **installment sales** /ɪnˈstɔlmənt seɪlz/, **installment buying** /ɪnˈstɔlmənt ˈbaɪɪŋ/, **installment credit** *noun* a system of buying something by paying a sum regularly each month ○ *to buy a car on the installment plan* (NOTE: The U.K. term is **hire purchase**.)

institution /ˌɪnstɪˈtuːʃ(ə)n/ *noun* an organization or society set up for a particular purpose. ◊ **financial institution**

institutional /ˌɪnstɪˈtuːʃ(ə)n(ə)l/ *adjective* referring to an institution, especially a financial institution

institutional advertising /ˌɪnstɪtuʃ(ə)n(ə)l ˈædvərtaɪzɪŋ/ *noun* advertising an organization rather than a product

institutional investor /ˌɪnstɪtuʃ(ə)n(ə)l ɪnˈvestər/ *noun* a financial institution which invests money in securities

in-store /ˈɪn stɔr/ *adjective* inside a store

in-store bakery /ˌɪn stɔr ˈbeɪkəri/ *noun* a bakery in a large supermarket, where bread is baked fresh for the customers

in-store demonstration /ˌɪn stɔr ˌdemənˈstreɪʃ(ə)n/ *noun* a demonstration of a product such as a piece of kitchen equipment inside a store

in-store media /ˌɪn stɔr ˈmidiə/ *noun* promotional material used inside a store, e.g., POS material, display banners, and advertisements on shopping carts

in-store promotion /ˌɪn stɔr prəˈmouʃ(ə)n/ *noun* a promotion of a product inside a store, e.g., by demonstrations or special gift counters

instrument /ˈɪnstrʊmənt/ *noun* a legal document

instrumental conditioning /ˌɪnstrʊment(ə)l kənˈdɪʃ(ə)nɪŋ/ *noun* same as **operant conditioning**

insurance rates /ɪnˈʃʊrəns reɪts/ *plural noun* the amount of premium which has to be paid per $1000 of insurance

intangible assets /ɪnˌtændʒɪb(ə)l ˈæsets/, **intangibles** /ɪnˈtændʒɪb(ə)lz/ *plural noun* assets which have a value, but which cannot be seen, e.g., goodwill, or a patent or a trademark

integrate /ˈɪntɪɡreɪt/ *verb* to link things together to form one whole group

integrated information response model /ˌɪntɪɡreɪtɪd ˌɪnfərmeɪʃ(ə)n rɪˈspɑns ˌmɑd(ə)l/ *noun* a model showing the response process to an advertising message which suggests that advertising leads to a low acceptance rate of information, but that after trials of the product the acceptance rate increases and this in turn leads to brand loyalty

integrated lifestyle segment /ˌɪntɪgreɪtɪd ˈlaɪfstaɪl ˌsegmənt/ *noun* according to VALS, the group of people in society who are satisfied with their way of life

integrated marketing /ˌɪntɪgreɪtɪd ˈmɑːkɪtɪŋ/ *noun* coordination of all of a company's marketing activities in establishing marketing strategies such as packaging, media promotion, POS material, or after-sales service ○ *The separation of departments makes integrated marketing difficult to achieve.*

integrated marketing communications concept /ˌɪntɪgreɪtɪd ˌmɑːkɪtɪŋ kəˌmjuːnɪˈkeɪʃ(ə)nz ˌkɒnsept/ *noun* the concept or principle that a company should link all its promotions, either of its own image or of the products and services it sells, in a consistent way on several different levels

integrated marketing communications objectives /ˌɪntɪgreɪtɪd ˌmɑːkɪtɪŋ kəˌmjuːnɪˈkeɪʃ(ə)nz əb ˌdʒektɪvz/ *plural noun* the listed objectives of an integrated marketing communications program such as communication tasks, anticipated sales, and increased market share

integrated processes /ˌɪntɪgreɪtɪd ˈprɒsesɪz/ *plural noun* the processes by which knowledge of products, and beliefs about their excellence, combine to help the purchaser evaluate alternate products

integration /ˌɪntɪˈgreɪʃ(ə)n/ *noun* the act of bringing several businesses together under a central control

intellectual property /ˌɪntɪˌlektjuəl ˈprɒpərti/ *noun* ideas, designs, and inventions, including copyrights, patents, and trademarks, that were created by and legally belong to an individual or an organization (NOTE: Intellectual property is protected by law in most countries, and the World Intellectual Prop-

erty Organization is responsible for harmonizing the law in different countries and promoting the protection of intellectual property rights.)

intensive distribution /ɪnˌtensɪv ˌdɪstrɪˈbjuːʃ(ə)n/ *noun* the use by a producer of as wide a network of distributors as possible to sell products ○ *Without intensive distribution we cannot hope to achieve these ambitious sales targets.* ○ *Intensive distribution makes us rely on too many retailers and wholesalers.*

intention to buy /ɪnˌtenʃ(ə)n tə ˈbaɪ/ *noun* a statement by a respondent that he or she intends to buy a product or service, which may or may not be true

interactive /ˌɪntərˈæktɪv/ *adjective* allowing the customer and seller to influence the presentation of information or the development of strategies

interactive marketing /ˌɪntəræktɪv ˈmɑːkətɪŋ/ *noun* marketing strategies which are developed as a result of decisions taken by both salespeople and customers

interactive media /ˌɪntəræktɪv ˈmiːdiə/ *plural noun* media that allow the customer to interact with the source of the message, receiving information and replying to questions, etc.

interactive voice response /ˌɪntəræktɪv ˈvɔɪs rɪˌspɒns/ *noun* a telephone or Internet system which is activated by the voice of the caller and responds to the caller's queries. Abbreviation **IVR**

intercompany comparison /ˌɪntəkʌmpəni kəmˈpærɪs(ə)n/, **interfirm comparison** /ˌɪntəfɜːm kəm ˈpærɪs(ə)n/ *noun* a comparison of different companies to see how much they spend on promotion, what their return on investment is, etc.

interconnect /ˌɪntəkəˈnekt/ *noun* two or more cable systems joined together for advertising purposes so as to give a wider geographic spread

interest /ˈɪntrəst/ *noun* **1.** special attention ○ *The buyers showed a lot of interest in our new product range.* **2.** payment made by a borrower for the use of money, calculated as a percentage of the capital borrowed ■ *verb* to attract someone's attention ○ *She tried to interest several companies in her new invention.* ○ *The company is trying to interest a wide range of customers in its products.*

interest   charges   /ˈɪntrəst ˌtʃɑːdʒɪz/ *plural noun* money paid as interest on a loan

interest rate /ˈɪntrəst reɪt/ *noun* a figure which shows the percentage of the capital sum borrowed or deposited which is to be paid as interest. Also called **rate of interest**

intermedia   comparison /ˌɪntəmiːdiə kəmˈpærɪs(ə)n/ *noun* a comparison of different media to decide how suitable they are for advertising ○ *We will carry out intermedia comparisons before deciding on our promotional strategy.* Compare **intramedia comparison**

intermediate goods /ˌɪntəmiːdiət ˈɡʊdz/ *plural noun* goods bought for use in the production of other goods

internal /ɪnˈtɜːn(ə)l/ *adjective* **1.** inside a company □ **we decided to make an internal appointment** we decided to appoint an existing member of staff to the position, and not bring someone in from outside the company **2.** inside a country or a region

internal   analysis /ɪnˌtɜːn(ə)l əˈnæləsɪs/ *noun* detailed examination and reports on the product or service offered and the company itself

internal   communication /ɪnˌtɜːn(ə)l kəˌmjuːnɪˈkeɪʃ(ə)n/ *noun* communication between employees or departments of the same organization (NOTE: Internal communication can take various forms such as team briefings, interviewing, employee councils, meetings, memos, an intranet, newsletters, [suggestion box]es, the grapevine, and reports.)

internal desk research /ɪnˌtɜːn(ə)l ˈdesk rɪˌsɜːtʃ/ *noun* research based on information in a company's own records such as customer accounts and sales reports

internal   flight /ɪnˌtɜːn(ə)l ˈflaɪt/ *noun* a flight to a town inside the same country

internalization /ɪnˌtɜːnəlaɪˈzeɪʃ(ə)n/ *noun* a process by which individuals identify information which is relevant to them personally and so acquire values and norms which allow them to make decisions

internally /ɪnˈtɜːn(ə)li/ *adverb* inside a company ○ *The job was advertised internally.*

internal   marketing /ɪnˌtɜːn(ə)l ˈmɑːkətɪŋ/ *noun* marketing conducted inside a large organization, where independent departments sell goods or services to each other

Internal   Revenue   Service /ɪn ˌtɜːn(ə)l ˈrevənjuː ˌsɜːvɪs/ *noun* in the United States, the branch of the federal government charged with collecting the majority of federal taxes. Abbreviation **IRS**

internal search /ɪnˌtɜːn(ə)l ˈsɜːtʃ/ *noun* the process by which a consumer acquires information from past experience or something he or she has remembered

internal   telephone /ɪnˌtɜːn(ə)l ˈtelɪfoʊn/ *noun* a telephone which is linked to other telephones in an office

internal trade /ɪnˌtɜːn(ə)l ˈtreɪd/ *noun* trade between various parts of a country. Opposite **external trade**

international /ˌɪntəˈnæʃ(ə)nəl/ *adjective* working between countries

international   marketing /ˌɪntənæʃ(ə)nəl ˈmɑːkətɪŋ/ *noun* the marketing of a company's products abroad ○ *Our international marketing so far consists of exporting to three countries.* ○ *The next stage in the company's international marketing was the setting up of factories overseas.*

international   media /ˌɪntənæʃ(ə)nəl ˈmiːdiə/ *plural noun* advertising media that cover several countries and can be used to reach audiences in them

International   Monetary   Fund /ˌɪntənæʃ(ə)nəl ˈmʌnɪt(ə)ri ˌfʌnd/ *noun* a type of bank which is part of the

United Nations and helps member states in financial difficulties, gives financial advice to members, and encourages world trade. Abbreviation **IMF**

international monetary system /ˌɪntənæʃ(ə)nəl ˈmʌnɪt(ə)ri ˌsɪstəm/ *noun* methods of controlling and exchanging currencies between countries

international postal reply coupon /ˌɪntənæʃ(ə)nəl ˌpoʊst(ə)l rɪ ˈplaɪ kuˌpɒn/ *noun* a coupon which can be used in another country to pay the postage of replying to a letter ○ *She enclosed an international reply coupon with her letter.*

international reserves /ˌɪntə ˌnæʃ(ə)nəl rɪˈzɜrvs/ *plural noun* same as **foreign currency reserves**

international trade /ˌɪntənæʃ(ə)nəl ˈtreɪd/ *noun* trade between different countries

Internet /ˈɪntənet/ *noun* the global, public network of computers and telephone links that houses websites, allows email to be sent, and is accessed with the aid of a modem ○ *Much of our business is done on the Internet.* ○ *Internet sales form an important part of our turnover.* ○ *He searched the Internet for information on cheap tickets to Russia.*

Internet commerce /ˈɪntənet ˌkɑmɜrs/ *noun* the part of e-commerce that consists of commercial business transactions conducted over the Internet

Internet marketing /ˈɪntənet ˌmɑrkətɪŋ/ *noun* the marketing of products or services over the Internet

Internet merchant /ˈɪntənet ˌmɜrtʃənt/ *noun* a businessman or businesswoman who sells a product or service over the Internet

Internet payment system /ˌɪntənet ˈpeɪmənt ˌsɪstəm/ *noun* any mechanism that enables funds to be transferred from a customer to seller or from one business to another via the Internet

Internet security /ˌɪntənet sɪ ˈkjʊrəti/ *noun* the means used to protect websites and other electronic files against attacks by hackers and viruses

and to ensure that business can be safely conducted over the Internet

interpolation /ɪnˌtɜrpəˈleɪʃ(ə)n/ *noun* a method of estimating a value between two established values

interstate commerce /ˌɪntəsteɪt ˈkɑmɜrs/ *noun* commerce between different states which is therefore subject to federal government control

interstitial /ˌɪntəˈstɪʃ(ə)l/ *noun* a page of advertising which is inserted into a website

interview /ˈɪntəvjuː/ *noun* a meeting in order to talk to a person who is applying for a job to find out whether they are suitable for it ○ *We called six people for interview.* ○ *I have an interview next week or I am going for an interview next week.* ■ *verb* to talk to a person applying for a job to see if they are suitable ○ *We interviewed ten candidates, but found no one suitable.*

interviewee /ˌɪntəvjuˈiː/ *noun* the person who is being interviewed ○ *The interviewer did everything to put the interviewee at ease.* ○ *The interviewees were all nervous as they waited to be called into the interview room.*

interviewer /ˈɪntəvjuər/ *noun* the person who is conducting an interview

intramedia comparison /ˌɪntrərmidiə kəmˈpærɪs(ə)n/ *noun* a comparison of different advertising options within the same medium ○ *After extensive intramedia comparison we now know all the possibilities of TV advertising.* Compare **intermedia comparison**

intranet /ˈɪntrənet/ *noun* a network of computers and telephone links that uses Internet technology but is accessible only to the employees of a particular organization

intransient /ɪnˈtrænziənt/ *adjective* referring to an advertisement which the target audience can keep and look at again, e.g., in a newspaper or magazine, as opposed to a transient advertisement on TV or radio

intrinsic value /ɪnˌtrɪnsɪk ˈvælju/ *noun* the material value of something ○ *These objects have sentimental value,* *but no intrinsic value at all. ○ The intrinsic value of jewelry makes it a good investment.*

introduce /ˌɪntrəˈdus/ *verb* to make someone get to know somebody or something □ **to introduce a client** to bring in a new client and make them known to someone □ **to introduce a new product on the market** to produce a new product and launch it on the market

introductory offer /ˌɪntrədʌkt(ə)ri ˈɔfər/ *noun* a special price offered on a new product to attract customers

inventory /ˈɪnvənt(ə)ri/ *noun* **1.** *especially U.S.* all the stock or goods in a warehouse or store ○ *to carry a high inventory* ○ *to aim to reduce inventory* Also called **stock 2.** a list of the contents of a building such as a house for sale or an office for rent ○ *to draw up an inventory of fixtures and fittings* **3.** advertising time or space which is not used and is available ■ *verb* to make a list of stock or contents

inventory control /ˈɪnvənt(ə)ri kən ˌtroʊl/ *noun* the process of making sure that the correct level of inventory is maintained, to be able to meet demand while keeping the costs of holding inventory to a minimum (NOTE: The U.K. term is **stock control.**)

investment /ɪnˈvestmənt/ *noun* the placing of money so that it will produce interest and increase in value ○ *They called for more government investment in new industries.* ○ *She was advised to make investments in oil companies.*

investment advertising /ɪn ˈvestmənt ˌædvərtaɪzɪŋ/ *noun* large expenditure on advertising to achieve long-term objectives

investment spending /ɪn ˈvestmənt ˌspendɪŋ/ *noun* spending more than normal on advertising with the expectation of increased sales and profits

investor relations research /ɪn ˌvestər rɪˈleɪʃ(ə)nz rɪˌsɜrtʃ/ *noun* research that allows a company to see how financial institutions such as merchant banks view the company

invisible /ɪnˈvɪzɪb(ə)l/ *adjective* not recorded or reflected in economic statistics

invisible assets /ɪnˌvɪzɪb(ə)l ˈæsets/ *plural noun* assets which have a value but which cannot be seen, e.g., goodwill or patents

invisible exports /ɪnˌvɪzəb(ə)l ˈeksports/ *plural noun* services such as banking, insurance, or tourism which do not involve selling a product and which are provided to foreign customers and paid for in foreign currency. Opposite **visible exports**

invisible imports /ɪnˌvɪzɪb(ə)l ˈɪmports/ *noun* services such as banking, insurance, or tourism which do not involve selling a product and which are provided by foreign companies and paid for in local currency

invisibles /ɪnˈvɪzɪb(ə)lz/ *plural noun* invisible imports and exports

invitation to tender /ˌɪnvɪteɪʃ(ə)n tə ˈtendər/ *noun* a formal request, sent to a small number of suppliers, asking them to submit a detailed proposal for completing a particular piece of work

invoice /ˈɪnvɔɪs/ *noun* a note asking for payment for goods or services supplied ○ *your invoice dated November 10th* ○ *to make out an invoice for $250* ○ *to settle* or *to pay an invoice* ○ *They sent in their invoice six weeks late.* □ **the total is payable within thirty days of invoice** the total sum has to be paid within thirty days of the date on the invoice ■ *verb* to send an invoice to someone ○ *to invoice a customer* □ **we invoiced you on November 10th** we sent you the invoice on November 10th

invoice clerk /ˈɪnvɔɪs klɑrk/ *noun* an office employee who deals with invoices

invoice price /ˈɪnvɔɪs praɪs/ *noun* the price as given on an invoice, including any discount and tax

invoicing /ˈɪnvɔɪsɪŋ/ *noun* the work of sending invoices ○ *All our invoicing is done by computer.* □ **invoicing in triplicate** the preparation of three copies of invoices

invoicing department /ˈɪnvɔɪsɪŋ dɪˌpɑrtmənt/ *noun* the department in a company which deals with preparing and sending invoices

inward /'ɪnwəd/ *adjective* toward the home country

inward bill /ˌɪnwəd 'bɪl/ *noun* a bill of lading for goods arriving in a country

inward mission /ˌɪnwəd 'mɪʃ(ə)n/ *noun* a visit to your home country by a group of foreign businesspeople

IP address /aɪ 'pi əˌdres/ *noun* a unique 32-bit number that defines the precise location of a computer connected to a network or the Internet

irrevocable /ɪ'revəkəb(ə)l/ *adjective* unchangeable

irrevocable acceptance /ɪˌrevəkəb(ə)l ək'septəns/ *noun* an acceptance which cannot be withdrawn

island display /'aɪlənd dɪsˌpleɪ/ *noun* same as **island site**

island position /ˌaɪlənd pə'zɪʃ(ə)n/ *noun* advertising space separated from other advertising space in a newspaper or magazine ○ *An island position is expensive but will attract great attention.*

island site /'aɪlənd saɪt/, **island display** /'aɪlənd dɪsˌpleɪ/ *noun* an exhibition stand separated from others ○ *There are only two island sites at the exhibition and we have one of them.* ○ *An island site means that visitors can approach the stand from several directions.*

issue /'ɪʃu/ *noun* the number of a newspaper or magazine ○ *We have an ad in the January issue of the magazine.* ■ *verb* to put out or to give out ○ *to issue a letter of credit* ○ *to issue shares in a new company* ○ *to issue a writ against*

someone ○ *The government issued a report on air traffic.*

issue life /'ɪʃu laɪf/ *noun* the time between one issue of a publication and another ○ *The reason the magazine's advertising rates are so expensive is because it has an issue life of three months.*

issuer /'ɪʃuər/ *noun* a financial institution that issues credit and debit cards and maintains the systems for billing and payment

ITC *abbreviation* Independent Television Commission

item /'aɪtəm/ *noun* **1.** something for sale □ **we are holding orders for out-of-stock items** we are holding orders for goods which are not in stock ○ *Please find enclosed an order for the following items from your catalog.* **2.** a piece of information ○ *items on a balance sheet* □ **item of expenditure** goods or services which have been paid for and appear in the accounts **3.** a point on a list □ **we will now take item four on the agenda** we will now discuss the fourth point on the agenda

itemize /'aɪtəmaɪz/ *verb* to make a detailed list of things ○ *Itemizing the sales figures will take about two days.*

itemized account /ˌaɪtəmaɪzd ə'kaʊnt/ *noun* a detailed record of money paid or owed

itemized invoice /ˌaɪtəmaɪzd 'ɪnvɔɪs/ *noun* an invoice which lists each item separately

itinerary /aɪ'tɪnərəri/ *noun* a list of places to be visited on one journey ○ *a sales representative's itinerary*

IVR *abbreviation* interactive voice response

J

jargon /'dʒɑrgən/ *noun* a special sort of language used by a trade or profession or particular group of people

JIT *abbreviation* just-in-time

job /dʒɑb/ *noun* an order being worked on ○ *We are working on six jobs at the moment.* ○ *The shipyard has a big job starting in August.*

jobber /'dʒɑbər/ *noun* a wholesaler

jobbing /'dʒɑbɪŋ/ *noun* the practice of doing small pieces of work

jobbing printer /'dʒɑbɪŋ ˌprɪntər/ *noun* a person who does small printing jobs

jobbing production /'dʒɑbɪŋ prə ˌdʌkʃən/ *noun* the production of several different articles, each to individual requirements

job classification /'dʒɑb klæsɪfɪ ˌkeɪʃ(ə)n/ *noun* the process of describing jobs listed in various groups

job description /'dʒɑb dɪˌskrɪpʃən/ *noun* a description of what a job consists of and what skills are needed for it ○ *The letter enclosed an application form and a job description.*

job lot /ˌdʒɑb 'lɑt/ *noun* a group of miscellaneous items sold together ○ *They sold the household furniture as a job lot.*

job opening /'dʒɑb ˌoʊp(ə)nɪŋ/ *noun* a job which is empty and needs filling ○ *We have job openings for office staff.*

job opportunities /'dʒɑb əpə ˌtunətiz/ *plural noun* new jobs which are available ○ *The increase in export orders has created hundreds of job opportunities.*

job satisfaction /'dʒɑb sætɪs ˌfækʃən/ *noun* an employee's feeling that he or she is happy at work and pleased with the work he or she does

job specification /'dʒɑb ˌspesɪfɪkeɪʃ(ə)n/ *noun* a very detailed description of what is involved in a job

joined-up /'dʒɔɪnd ʌp/ *adjective* involving two or more individuals or organizations who share information and coordinate their activities in order to achieve their aims more effectively

joint account /'dʒɔɪnt əˌkaʊnt/ *noun* a bank or savings and loan association account shared by two people ○ *Many married couples have joint accounts so that they can pay for household expenses.*

Joint Photographics Experts Group *noun* full form of **JPEG**

journal /'dʒɜrn(ə)l/ *noun* **1.** a book with the account of sales and purchases made each day **2.** a magazine

journalist /'dʒɜrn(ə)lɪst/ *noun* a person who writes for a newspaper

journey /'dʒɜrni/ *noun* a long trip, especially a trip made by a salesperson ○ *She planned her journey so that she could visit all her accounts in two days.*

journey mapping /'dʒɜrni ˌmæpɪŋ/ *noun* a method of calculating how many people pass a poster site ○ *Journey mapping allows us to pinpoint the ten key sites we will be renting for the next three months.*

journey order /'dʒɜrni ˌɔrdər/ *noun* an order given by a storekeeper to a salesperson when they call

journey planning /'dʒɜrni ˌplænɪŋ/ *noun* the act of planning what calls a salesperson will make and how they will be reached most efficiently, giving priority to the more profitable accounts ○ *The sales manager will stress how good journey planning will save precious time.* ○ *Inefficient journey planning means miles of unnecessary traveling for the sales force every day.*

JPEG /'dʒeɪ peg/ *noun* a file format used to compress and store photographic images for transfer over the Internet

judgement /'dʒʌdʒmənt/, **judgment** *noun* an assessment or evaluation of the quality of someone or something

judgement forecasting /'dʒʌdʒmənt ˌfɔːkæstɪŋ/ *noun* forecasting based on judgement rather than on any scientific techniques ○ *We need more precise information so that we can extrapolate rather than use judgement forecasting.* ○ *Market research departments find judgement forecasting too subjective and unreliable.*

judgement sampling /'dʒʌdʒmənt ˌsɑːmplɪŋ/ *noun* the choosing of a sample for a survey based on judgement of what criteria would be especially significant rather than applying any scientific techniques ○ *Judgement sampling can produce an insufficiently representative sample.*

jumbo /'dʒʌmboʊ/ *adjective* very large ○ *jumbo-sized pack* or *jumbo pack*

junk mail /'dʒʌŋk meɪl/ *noun* **1.** unsolicited advertising material sent through the mail and usually thrown away immediately by the people who receive it **2.** unsolicited advertising material sent by email

jury of executive opinion /ˌdʒʊri əv ɪgˌzekjʊtɪv əˈpɪnjən/ *noun* a panel of executives used to contribute to forecasting

just-in-time /ˌdʒʌst ɪn 'taɪm/ *noun* a system in which goods are made or purchased just before they are needed, so as to avoid carrying high levels of inventory. Abbreviation **JIT**

K

KAM *abbreviation* key account management

keen /kin/ *adjective* **1.** eager or active □ **keen competition** strong competition ○ *We are facing some keen competition from European manufacturers.* □ **keen demand** wide demand ○ *There is a keen demand for home computers.* **2.** □ **keen prices** prices which are kept low so as to be competitive ○ *Our prices are the keenest on the market.*

kerbside conference /ˌkɜrbsaɪd ˈkɑnf(ə)rəns/ *noun* U.K. spelling of **curbside conference**

key /ki/ *adjective* important ○ *a key factor* ○ *key industries* ○ *key personnel* ○ *a key member of our management team* ○ *She has a key post in the organization.* ○ *We don't want to lose any key staff in the reorganization.*

key account /ˈki əˌkaʊnt/ *noun* an important account or client, e.g., of an advertising agency

key account management /ˈki əˌkaʊnt ˌmænɪdʒmənt/ *noun* the management of the small number of key accounts which represent the bulk of a company's business. Abbreviation **KAM**

keyboard /ˈkibɔrd/ *noun* the part of a computer or other device with keys which are pressed to make letters or figures ■ *verb* to press the keys on a keyboard to type something ○ *She is keyboarding our address list.*

keyboarder /ˈkibɔrdər/ *noun* a person who types information into a computer

keyboarding /ˈkibɔrdɪŋ/ *noun* the act of typing on a keyboard ○ *Keyboarding costs have risen sharply.*

key code /ˈki koʊd/ *noun* a letter and number code printed on mailshots so that the respondents can be identified

keyed advertisement /ˌkid ədˈvɜrtɪsmənt/ *noun* an advertisement which asks people to write to a specially coded address which will indicate where they saw it, thus helping the advertisers to evaluate the effectiveness of advertising in that particular newspaper or magazine

key number /ˈki ˌnʌmbər/ *noun* the number used in a keyed advertisement

keypad /ˈkipæd/ *noun* a set of keys on a computer

key prospects /ˌki ˈprɑspekts/ *plural noun* potential customers ○ *In this sales campaign we will be concentrating on key prospects.* ○ *This is bad journey planning since it does not allow sufficient time to visit all the key prospects.*

keyword /ˈkiwɜrd/ *noun* a word used by a search engine to help it locate a particular type of website (NOTE: Companies need to think very carefully about the keywords they place in their webpages in order to attract relevant search-engine traffic.)

keyword search /ˌkiwɜrd ˈsɜrtʃ/ *noun* a search for documents containing one or more words that are specified by a search-engine user

kickback /ˈkɪkbæk/ *noun* an illegal commission paid to someone, especially a government official, who helps in a business deal

Kimball tag /ˈkɪmb(ə)l tæg/ *noun* a paper tag attached to an item for sale, which is removed when the item has been sold and is kept by the store so that it can be used for inventory control

king-size /'kıŋ saız/ *adjective* **1.** referring to an extra large container of a product, usually comparatively economical to buy **2.** referring to a very large size of poster

kiosk /'kiɑsk/ *noun* a small wooden shelter, for selling goods out of doors ○ *She had a newspaper kiosk near the station for 20 years.*

KISS /kıs/ *noun* the need to make sure your advertising is clear and concise so as to improve its chances of getting a response. Full form **keep it simple, stupid**

knock /nɑk/ *verb* □ **to knock the competition** to hit competing firms hard by vigorous selling

    knock down *phrasal verb* □ **to knock something down to a bidder** to sell something to somebody at an auction ○ *The furniture was knocked down to him for $100.*

    knock off *phrasal verb* to reduce a price by a particular amount ○ *She knocked $10 off the price for cash.*

knockdown /'nɑkdaʊn/ *noun* □ **knockdown goods** goods sold in parts, which must be assembled by the buyer

knockdown price /ˌnɑkdaʊn 'praɪs/ *noun* a very low price ○ *He sold me the car at a knockdown price.*

knocking copy /'nɑkıŋ ˌkɑpi/ *noun* advertising material which criticizes competing products

know-how /'noʊ haʊ/ *noun* knowledge or skill in a particular field ○ *to acquire computer know-how*

knowledge capital /'nɑlıdʒ ˌkæpıt(ə)l/ *noun* knowledge, especially specialist knowledge, that a company and its employees possess and that can be put to profitable use

knowledge management /'nɑlıdʒ ˌmænıdʒmənt/ *noun* **1.** the task of coordinating the specialist knowledge possessed by employees so that it can be exploited to create benefits and competitive advantage for the organization **2.** same as **information management**

L

label /'leɪb(ə)l/ *noun* a piece of paper or card attached to something to show its price or an address or instructions for use ■ *verb* to attach a label to something (NOTE: **labeling- labeled**)

labeling /'leɪb(ə)lɪŋ/ *noun* the act of putting a label on something

labeling department /'leɪb(ə)lɪŋ dɪ ˌpɑrtmənt/ *noun* a section of a factory where labels are attached to the product

laboratory test /lə'bɑrət(ə)ri test/ *noun* a test carried out under controlled conditions, e.g., of the reactions of consumers to advertising

labor-intensive industry /ˌleɪbər ɪnˌtensɪv 'ɪndəstri/ *noun* an industry which needs large numbers of employees and where labor costs are high in relation to turnover

labor market /'leɪbər ˌmɑrkət/ *noun* the number of people who are available for work ○ *25,000 graduates have just come on to the labor market.*

lading /'leɪdɪŋ/ *noun* the work of putting goods on a ship

laggards /'lægədz/ *plural noun* a category of buyers of a product who are the last to buy it or use it

laissez-faire economy /ˌleseɪ 'fer ɪ ˌkɑnəmi/ *noun* an economy where the government does not interfere because it believes it is right to let the economy run itself

land /lænd/ *verb* to put goods or passengers onto land after a voyage by sea or by air ○ *The ship landed some goods at Mombasa.* ○ *The plane stopped for thirty minutes at the local airport to land passengers and mail.*

landed costs /ˌlændɪd 'kɔsts/ *plural noun* the costs of goods which have been delivered to a port, unloaded, and passed through customs

landing card /'lændɪŋ kɑrd/ *noun* a card given to passengers who have passed through customs and can land from a ship or an aircraft

landing charges /'lændɪŋ ˌtʃɑrdʒɪz/ *plural noun* payments for putting goods on land and paying customs duties

landing order /'lændɪŋ ˌɔrdər/ *noun* a permit which allows goods to be unloaded into a bonded warehouse without paying customs duty

landing page /'lændɪŋ peɪdʒ/ *noun* the page on a website where the user arrives, in particular the page you arrive on when directed by a hyperlink

landscape /'lændskeɪp/ *noun* an illustration, page, or book whose width is greater than its height. Compare **portrait**

laser printer /'leɪzər ˌprɪntər/ *noun* a computer printer which uses a laser source to print high-quality dot matrix characters on paper

laser printing /'leɪzər ˌprɪntɪŋ/ *noun* printing using a laser printer

late /leɪt/ *adjective* **1.** after the time stated or agreed ○ *We apologize for the late arrival of the plane from Amsterdam.* □ **there is a penalty for late delivery** if delivery is later than the agreed date, the supplier has to pay a fine **2.** at the end of a period of time □ **latest date for signature of the contract** the last acceptable date for signing the contract ■ *adverb* after the time stated or agreed ○ *The shipment was landed late.* ○ *The plane was two hours late.*

late majority /ˌleɪt məˈdʒɑrəti/ *noun* a category of buyers of a product who buy it later than the early majority but before the laggards

latent /ˈleɪt(ə)nt/ *adjective* present but not yet developed □ **latent market** a potential market which has not so far been touched

latent demand /ˌleɪt(ə)nt dɪˈmænd/ *noun* a situation where there is demand for a product but potential customers are unable to pay for it ○ *We will have to wait for the economy to improve in countries where there is latent demand.* ○ *Situation analysis has shown that there is only latent demand.*

lateral /ˈlæt(ə)rəl/ *adjective* at the same level or with the same status ○ *Her transfer to Marketing was something of a lateral move.*

lateral diversification /ˌlæt(ə)rəl daɪˌvɜrsɪfɪˈkeɪʃ(ə)n/ *noun* the act of diversifying into a very different type of business

lateral integration /ˌlæt(ə)rəl ɪntəˈgreɪʃ(ə)n/ *noun* the act of joining similar companies or taking over a company in the same line of business as yourself ○ *Lateral integration will allow a pooling of resources.* ○ *Lateral integration in the form of a merger will improve the efficiency of both businesses involved.*

lateral thinking /ˌlæt(ə)rəl ˈθɪŋkɪŋ/ *noun* an imaginative approach to problem-solving which involves changing established patterns of thinking to help make a breakthrough ○ *Lateral thinking resulted in finding a completely new use for an existing product.* ○ *Brainstorming sessions encourage lateral thinking and originality.*

latest /ˈleɪtɪst/ *adjective* most recent ○ *He always drives the latest model of car.* ○ *Here are the latest sales figures.*

launch /lɔntʃ/ *verb* to put a new product on the market, usually spending money on advertising it ○ *They launched their new car model at the motor show.* ○ *The company is spending thousands of pounds on launching a new brand of soap.* ■ *noun* the act of putting a new product on the market ○ *The launch of the new model has been put*

back three months. ○ *The management has decided on a September launch date.* ○ *The company is geared up for the launch of its first microcomputer.*

launching /ˈlɔntʃɪŋ/ *noun* the act of putting a new product on the market

launching costs /ˈlɔntʃɪŋ kɔsts/ *plural noun* the costs of publicity for a new product

launching date /ˈlɔntʃɪŋ deɪt/ *noun* the date when a new product is officially shown to the public for the first time

launching party /ˈlɔntʃɪŋ ˌpɑrti/ *noun* a party held to advertise the launching of a new product

law /lɔ/ *noun* a rule governing some aspect of human activity made and enforced by the state

law of diminishing returns /ˌlɔr əv dɪˌmɪnɪʃɪŋ rɪˈtɜrnz/ *noun* a general rule that as more factors of production such as land, labor, and capital are added to the existing factors, so the amount they produce is proportionately smaller

law of inertia of large numbers /ˌlɔr əv ɪˌnɜrʃər əv ˌlɑrdʒ ˈnʌmbərz/ *noun* a general rule that larger samples are more likely to be representative of the population than small ones

law of statistical regularity /ˌlɔr əv stəˌtɪstɪk(ə)l ˌregjəˈlærəti/ *noun* a general rule that a group of people or objects taken from a larger group of people or objects will tend to resemble the larger group

law of supply and demand /ˌlɔr əv səˌplaɪ ən dɪˈmænd/ *noun* a general rule that the amount of a product which is available is related to the needs of potential customers

layout /ˈleɪaʊt/ *noun* **1.** the arrangement of the inside space of a building or its contents ○ *They have altered the layout of the offices.* **2.** the arrangement of words and pictures on a printed page, in an advertisement, on an email advertising message, etc., including the headline, illustrations, text, and trademarks ○ *I like the illustration and the copy but not the layout.* ○ *The layout needs to be changed so that other features are highlighted.*

lead /lid/ *verb* to be the main person in a group ○ *She will lead the trade mission to Nigeria.* ○ *The tour of American factories will be led by the minister of industry.* (NOTE: **leading – led**) ■ *noun* **1.** information which may lead to a sale ○ *It has been difficult starting selling in this territory with no leads to follow up.* ○ *I was given some useful leads by the sales rep who used to cover this territory.* **2.** a prospective purchaser who is the main decision-maker when buying a product or service

leader /'lidər/ *noun* **1.** a person who manages or directs others ○ *the leader of the construction workers' union* or *the construction workers' leader* ○ *She is the leader of the trade mission to Nigeria.* ○ *The minister was the leader of the party of industrialists on a tour of American factories.* **2.** a product which sells best

leader pricing /'lidər ˌpraɪsɪŋ/ *noun* the practice of cutting prices on some goods in the hope that they attract customers to the store where more profitable sales can be made

lead generation /'lid dʒenə ˌreɪʃ(ə)n/ *noun* the process of finding prospective purchasers

leading question /ˌlidɪŋ 'kweʃtʃən/ *noun* a question in a questionnaire which, by its phrasing, suggests a certain answer ○ *Interviewers were trained to avoid bias and leading questions.* ○ *The leading question pressured the respondent into answering untruthfully.*

lead partner /'lid ˌpɑrtnər/ *noun* the organization that takes the leading role in a business alliance

lead sourcing /'lid ˌsɔrsɪŋ/ *noun* searching through online databases to find the addresses of potential customers

leaflet /'liflət/ *noun* a sheet of paper giving information, used to advertise something ○ *to mail leaflets advertising a new hairdressing salon* ○ *They are handing out leaflets describing the financial services they offer.* ○ *We made a leaflet mailing to 20,000 addresses.*

leakage /'likɪdʒ/ *noun* an amount of goods lost in storage, e.g., by going bad or by being stolen or by leaking from the container

learning curve /'lɜrnɪŋ kɜrv/ *noun* a process of learning something that starts slowly and then becomes faster

learning disability /'lɜrnɪŋ ˌdɪsəbɪləti/ *noun* a condition which prevents someone from learning basic skills or assimilating information as easily as other people (NOTE: The plural is **learning disabilities.**)

learning organization /'lɜrnɪŋ ɔrgənaɪˌzeɪʃ(ə)n/ *noun* an organization whose employees are willing and eager to share information with each other, to learn from each other, and to work as a team to achieve their goals

lease /lis/ *noun* a written contract for leasing or renting a building, a piece of land, or a piece of equipment for a period against payment of a fee ○ *to rent office space on a twenty-year lease* □ **the lease expires next year** *or* **the lease runs out next year** the lease comes to an end next year

leave leaflet /'liv ˌliflət/ *noun* a promotional leaflet left by a salesperson with a prospective customer

ledger /'ledʒər/ *noun* a book in which accounts are written

legal /'lig(ə)l/ *adjective* **1.** according to the law or allowed by the law **2.** referring to the law □ **to take legal action** to sue someone or to take someone to court □ **to take legal advice** to ask a lawyer to advise about a legal problem

legal adviser /ˌlig(ə)l əd'vaɪzər/ *noun* a person who advises clients about the law

legal currency /ˌlig(ə)l 'kʌrənsi/ *noun* money which is legally used in a country

legality /lɪ'gæləti/ *noun* the fact of being allowed by law ○ *There is doubt about the legality of the company's action in dismissing him.*

legalization /ˌligəlaɪ'zeɪʃ(ə)n/ *noun* the act of making something legal ○ *the campaign for the legalization of cannabis*

legalize /'ligəlaɪz/ *verb* to make something legal

legally /'liːgəli/ *adverb* according to the law □ **the contract is legally binding** according to the law, the contract has to be obeyed □ **the directors are legally responsible** the law says that the directors are responsible

legend /'ledʒənd/ *noun* a short note printed underneath an illustration to explain it

legislation /ˌledʒɪ'sleɪʃ(ə)n/ *noun* laws

legs /legz/ *plural noun* the ability of an advertising campaign, a movie, a book, or other usually short-lived product to interest people for a much longer time than normal (*informal*)

leisure market /'leʒər ˌmɑːrkət/ *noun* people who have plenty of leisure time and are willing to buy products or services to occupy their time

lemon /'lemən/ *noun* **1.** a product, especially a car, that is defective in some way **2.** an investment that is performing poorly

lending limit /'lendɪŋ ˌlɪmɪt/ *noun* a restriction on the amount of money a bank can lend

letter /'letər/ *noun* a piece of writing sent from one person or company to another to ask for or to give information

COMMENT: First names are commonly used between business people in the U.S. and U.K.; they are less often used in other European countries (France and Germany), for example, where business letters tend to be more formal.

letterhead /'letəhed/ *noun* the name and address of a company printed at the top of a piece of stationery

letter of acknowledgement /ˌletər əv ək'nɑlɪdʒmənt/ *noun* a letter which says that something has been received

letter of advice /ˌletər əv əd'vaɪs/ *noun* same as **advice note** ○ *The letter of advice stated that the goods would be at Miami on the morning of the 6th.* ○ *The letter of advice reminded the customer of the agreed payment terms.*

letter of agreement /ˌletər əv ə'grimənt/ *noun* a document that sets out what has been agreed between two

people or organizations and acts as a simple form of contract

letter of complaint /ˌletər əv kəm'pleɪnt/ *noun* a letter in which someone complains

letter of credit /ˌletər əv 'kredɪt/ *noun* a document issued by a bank on behalf of a customer authorizing payment to a supplier when the conditions specified in the document are met. Abbreviation **L/C**

letter of indemnity /ˌletər əv ɪn'demnəti/ *noun* a letter promising payment as compensation for a loss

letter of inquiry /ˌletər əv ɪn'kwaɪəri/ *noun* a letter from a prospective buyer to a supplier inquiring about products and their prices ○ *The letter of inquiry requested us to send our catalogs and price lists.* ○ *We received a letter of inquiry concerning possible trade discounts.*

lettershop /'letəʃɑp/ *noun* a company that puts together the various elements of a direct mailing shot, and sorts the envelopes by addresses

letters of administration /ˌletəz əv ədˌmɪnɪ'streɪʃ(ə)n/ *plural noun* a letter given by a court to allow someone to deal with the estate of a person who has died

letters patent /ˌletəz 'peɪtənt/ *plural noun* the official term for a patent

level /'lev(ə)l/ *noun* the position of something compared to others ○ *low levels of productivity* or *low productivity levels* ○ *to raise the level of employee benefits* ○ *to lower the level of borrowings*

level playing field /ˌlev(ə)l 'pleɪɪŋ fild/ *noun* a situation in which the same rules apply for all competitors and none of them has any special advantage over the others

levy /'levi/ *noun* money which is demanded and collected by the government □ **levies on luxury items** taxes on luxury items

liabilities /ˌlaɪə'bɪlətiz/ *plural noun* the debts of a business, including dividends owed to shareholders ○ *The balance sheet shows the company's assets* *and liabilities.* □ **he was not able to meet his liabilities** he could not pay his debts □ **to discharge your liabilities in full** to pay everything which you owe

liability /ˌlaɪə'bɪləti/ *noun* **1.** a legal responsibility for damage, loss, or harm □ **to accept liability for something** to agree that you are responsible for something □ **to refuse liability for something** to refuse to agree that you are responsible for something **2.** responsibility for a payment such as the repayment of a loan

liable /'laɪəb(ə)l/ *adjective* □ **liable for** legally responsible for ○ *The customer is liable for breakages.* ○ *The chairman was personally liable for the company's debts.*

license¹ /'laɪs(ə)ns/ *noun* an official document which allows someone to do something (NOTE: The U.K. spelling is **licence**.) □ **goods manufactured under licence** goods made with the permission of the owner of the copyright or patent

license² /'laɪs(ə)ns/ *verb* to give someone official permission to do something for a fee, e.g., when a company allows another company to manufacture its products abroad ○ *licensed to sell beers, wines and spirits* ○ *to license a company to manufacture spare parts* ○ *She is licensed to run an employment agency.*

license agreement /'laɪs(ə)ns ə,grimənt/ *noun* a legal document which comes with a software product and defines how you can use the software and how many people are allowed to use it

licensee /ˌlaɪs(ə)n'si/ *noun* a person who has a license, especially a license to sell alcohol or to manufacture something

licensing /'laɪs(ə)nsɪŋ/ *adjective* referring to licenses ○ *a licensing agreement* ○ *licensing laws*

licensing agreement /'laɪs(ə)nsɪŋ ə,grimənt/ *noun* an agreement where a person or company is granted a license to manufacture something or to use something, but not an outright sale

licensing hours /'laɪs(ə)nsɪŋ ,aʊrz/ *plural noun* the hours of the day when alcohol can be sold

licensing laws /'laɪs(ə)nsɪŋ ,lɔz/ *plural noun* the laws which control when and where alcohol can be sold

licensor /'laɪsensər/ *noun* a person who licenses someone

lien /'liən/ *noun* the legal right to hold someone's goods and keep them until a debt has been paid

life /laɪf/ *noun* the period of time for which something or someone exists

life cycle /'laɪf ,saɪk(ə)l/ *noun* a concept used for charting the different stages in the life of people, animals, or products

life expectancy /'laɪf ɪk,spektənsi/ *noun* the number of years a person is likely to live

lifestyle /'laɪfstaɪl/ *noun* the way of living of a particular section of society ○ *These upmarket products appeal to people with an extravagant lifestyle.* ○ *The magazine ran a series of articles on the lifestyles of some successful businessmen.*

lifestyle segmentation /'laɪfstaɪl segmen,teɪʃ(ə)n/ *noun* the dividing of a market into segments according to the way in which customers live. ◊ **VALS**

lifetime /'laɪftaɪm/ *noun* the time when you are alive

lifetime customer value /ˌlaɪftaɪm 'kʌstəmər ,vælju/, **lifetime value** /'laɪftaɪm ,vælju/ *noun* the value of a customer to a firm during the customer's lifetime, which can be charted using technology and market research

light /laɪt/ *adjective* not heavy, not very busy or active

light industry /ˌlaɪt 'ɪndəstri/ *noun* an industry making small products such as clothes, books, or calculators

light pen /'laɪt pen/ *noun* a type of electronic pen that directs a beam of light which, when passed over a bar code, can read it and send information back to a computer

light viewer /laɪt 'vjuər/ *noun* a person who watches little television ○ *If too* many of the target audience are light viewers, the impact of the commercials will be wasted.

limit /'lɪmɪt/ *noun* the point at which something ends or the point where you can go no further □ **to set limits to imports, to impose import limits** to allow only a specific amount of imports ■ *verb* **1.** to stop something from going beyond a specific point, to restrict the number or amount of something □ **the banks have limited their credit** the banks have allowed their customers only a specific amount of credit □ **each agent is limited to twenty-five units** each agent is allowed only twenty-five units to sell **2.** to restrict the number or amount of something

limitation /ˌlɪmɪ'teɪʃ(ə)n/ *noun* the act of allowing only a specific quantity of something ○ *The contract imposes limitations on the number of cars which can be imported.* □ **limitation of liability** the fact of making someone liable for only a part of the damage or loss

limited /'lɪmɪtɪd/ *adjective* restricted

limited company /ˌlɪmɪtɪd 'kʌmp(ə)ni/ *noun* a company where each stockholder is responsible for the company's debts only to the amount that he or she has invested in the company. Limited companies must be formed by at least two directors. Abbreviation **Ltd**. Also called **limited liability company**

limited function wholesaler /ˌlɪmɪtɪd 'fʌŋkʃən ˌhoʊlseɪlər/ *noun* a distributor performing only some of the functions of a wholesaler ○ *As a limited function wholesaler the dealer did not provide a delivery service to retailers.*

limited liability /ˌlɪmɪtɪd laɪə'bɪləti/ *noun* a situation where someone's liability for debt is limited by law

limited liability company /ˌlɪmɪtɪd laɪəˌbɪləti 'kʌmp(ə)ni/ *noun* same as **limited company**

limited market /ˌlɪmɪtɪd 'mɑrkət/ *noun* a market which can take only a specific quantity of goods

limiting /'lɪmɪtɪŋ/ *adjective* not allowing something to go beyond a point, restricting ○ *a limiting clause in a con-*

tract ○ *The short tourist season is a limiting factor on the hotel trade.*

line /laɪn/ *noun* **1.** a long mark printed or written on paper ○ *paper with thin blue lines* ○ *I prefer notepaper without any lines.* ○ *She drew a thick line before the column of figures.* **2.** a row of letters or figures on a page **3.** a series of things, one after another **4.** same as **product line 5.** a short letter

lineage /'lɪniɪdʒ/ *noun* a method of measuring a classified advertisement by counting the lines, used for charging purposes

linear /'lɪniər/ *adjective* calculated by length

linear measurement /ˌlɪniə 'meʒərmənt/, **linear footage** /ˌlɪniə 'fʊtɪdʒ/ *noun* a measurement of how long something is such as the length of shelving available for a display

line block /'laɪn blɑk/ *noun* a printing block for line drawings

line chart /'laɪn tʃɑrt/ *noun* a chart or graph using lines to indicate values

line divestment /'laɪn daɪ ˌvestmənt/ *noun* the dropping or selling of an entire product line so as to concentrate on other products

line drawing /'laɪn ˌdrɔɪŋ/, **line illustration** /'laɪn ɪləˌstreɪʃ(ə)n/ *noun* a drawing or illustration consisting only of lines and no tones. Shades are shown by lines drawn close together.

line extension /'laɪn ɪkˌstenʃən/ *noun* the adding of another product to a product line

line filling /'laɪn ˌfɪlɪŋ/ *noun* the filling of gaps in a product line

line management /'laɪn ˌmænɪdʒmənt/ *noun* U.K. the organization of a company where each manager is responsible for doing what their superior tells them to do. Also called **line organization**

line of credit /ˌlaɪn əv 'kredɪt/ *noun* **1.** the amount of money made available to a customer by a bank as an overdraft □ **to open a line of credit** or **a credit line** to make credit available to someone **2.** the borrowing limit on a credit card

line rate /ˈlaɪn reɪt/ *noun* the rate charged for advertising space, based on the line space used in a newspaper or magazine

line simplification /ˈlaɪn sɪmplɪfɪˌkeɪʃ(ə)n/ *noun* the removal of some products from a product line to make the whole line more easily manageable

link /lɪŋk/ *noun* same as **hyperlink**

linking /ˈlɪŋkɪŋ/ *noun* the process of connecting two or more websites or documents by inserting links that enable users to move from one to the other

liquid assets /ˌlɪkwɪd ˈæsets/ *plural noun* cash, or investments which can be quickly converted into cash

liquor license /ˈlɪkər ˌlaɪs(ə)ns/ *noun* a government document allowing someone to sell alcohol

liquor store /ˈlɪkə stɔr/ *noun* a store which sells alcohol for drinking at home

list /lɪst/ *noun* **1.** several items written one after the other ○ *They have an attractive list of products* or *product list.* ○ *I can't find that item on our stock list.* ○ *Please add this item to the list.* ○ *She crossed the item off her list.* **2.** a catalog ■ *verb* to write a series of items one after the other ○ *to list products by category* ○ *to list representatives by area* ○ *to list products in a catalog* ○ *The catalog lists ten models of fax machine.*

list broker /ˈlɪst ˌbroʊkər/ *noun* a person who arranges to sell mailing lists to users, but who does not own the lists

list building /ˈlɪst ˌbɪldɪŋ/ *noun* finding names and addresses and entering them into a database for direct marketing purposes

list cleaning /ˈlɪst ˌklinɪŋ/ *noun* checking the details of a mailing list to make sure they are correct

listen /ˈlɪs(ə)n/ *verb* to pay attention to someone who is talking or to something which you can hear

listening area /ˈlɪs(ə)nɪŋ ˌeriə/ *noun* the area covered by a radio station's signal

listening share /ˈlɪs(ə)nɪŋ ʃer/ *noun* the share of the total audience enjoyed by a radio station

list host /ˈlɪst hoʊst/ *noun* a company that provides connections to the Internet and storage space on its computers which can store the files for a user's website (NOTE: also called a "host service *or* hosting service provider")

list maintenance /ˈlɪst ˌmeɪntənəns/ *noun* the process of keeping a mailing list up to date

list manager /ˈlɪst ˌmænɪdʒər/ *noun* a person who promotes a mailing list to potential users

list price /ˈlɪst praɪs/ *noun* the price for something as given in a catalog

list rental /ˈlɪst ˌrent(ə)l/ *noun* the action of renting a mailing list

list renting /ˈlɪst ˌrentɪŋ/ *noun* an arrangement in which a company that owns a direct mail list lets another company use it for a fee

literature /ˈlɪt(ə)rətʃər/ *noun* written information about something ○ *Please send me literature about your new product range.*

lithography /lɪˈθɑɡrəfi/ *noun* a printing process by which a design is applied to a smooth flat surface with greasy ink or a crayon. The surface is wetted and ink will adhere to the greasy parts, but not to the wet parts.

livery /ˈlɪvəri/ *noun* a company's own special design and colors, used e.g., on uniforms, office decoration, and vehicles

living /ˈlɪvɪŋ/ *noun* □ **she does not earn a living wage** she does not earn enough to pay for essentials such as food, heat, and rent

load /loʊd/ *noun* an amount of goods which are transported in a particular vehicle or aircraft □ **the load of a lorry** *or* **of a container** the goods carried by a truck or in a container □ **maximum load** the largest weight of goods which a truck or plane can carry ■ *verb* **1.** □ **to load a lorry, a ship** to put goods into a truck or a ship for transporting ○ *to load cargo onto a ship* ○ *a truck loaded with boxes* ○ *a ship loaded with iron* □ **a fully loaded ship** a ship which is full of cargo **2.** (*of a ship*) to take on cargo ○ *The ship is loading a cargo of wood.* **3.** to put a program into a computer ○ *Load the word-processing program before you start keyboarding.* **4.** to add extra charges to a price

load-carrying capacity /ˈloʊd ˌkæriɪŋ kəˌpæsəti/ *noun* the amount of goods which a truck is capable of carrying

loaded price /ˌloʊdɪd ˈpraɪs/ *noun* a price which includes an unusually large extra payment for some service ○ *That company is notorious for loading its prices.*

loading /ˈloʊdɪŋ/ *noun* the process of assigning work to workers or machines ○ *The production manager has to ensure that careful loading makes the best use of human resources.*

loading dock /ˈloʊdɪŋ dak/ *noun* the part of a harbor where ships can load or unload

load time /ˈloʊd taɪm/ *noun* in computing, the time it takes for a page of data to open completely in a window

lobby /ˈlɑbi/ *noun* a pressure group that tries to persuade a government or law-makers to support a particular cause or interest

local /ˈloʊk(ə)l/ *adjective* located in or providing a service for a restricted area

local advertising /ˌloʊk(ə)l ˈædvərtaɪzɪŋ/ *noun* advertising in the area where a company is based

localization /ˌgloʊkələaɪˈzeɪʃ(ə)n/ *noun* **1.** the process of restricting something to a particular area or adapting it for use in a particular area **2.** the translation of a website into a language or idiom that can be easily understood by the target user

localized /ˈloʊkəlaɪzd/ *adjective* which occurs in one area only

localized advertising strategy /ˌloʊkəlaɪzd ˈædvərtaɪzɪŋ ˌstrætədʒi/ *noun* planning an advertising campaign for a particular country or area of a market rather than a global campaign

local media /ˌloʊk(ə)l ˈmidiə/ *plural noun* newspapers and radio and TV stations in a small area of the country

local newspaper /ˌloʊk(ə)l ˈnuzpeɪpər/ *noun* a newspaper which is sold only in a restricted area, and mainly carries news about that area

local press /ˌloʊk(ə)l ˈpres/ *noun* newspapers which are sold in a small area of the country ○ *The product was only advertised in the local press as it was only being distributed in that area of the country.*

local radio station /ˌloʊk(ə)l ˈreɪdioʊ ˌsteɪʃ(ə)n/ *noun* a radio station which broadcasts over a small area of the country

location /loʊˈkeɪʃ(ə)n/ *noun* **1.** a place where something is **2.** a place, especially a site where still photographs or films are made ○ *We still have to decide on locations for the advertisements.*

logical models /ˌlɑdʒɪk(ə)l ˈmɑd(ə)lz/ *plural noun* models of buyer decision-making which assume that purchasing is the result of a set of rational decisions made by the purchaser ○ *Logical models do not allow for the unpredictable side of buying behavior.*

logistics /ləˈdʒɪstɪks/ *noun* the task or science of managing the movement, storage, and processing of materials and information in a supply chain (NOTE: Logistics includes the acquisition of raw materials and components, manufacturing or processing, and the distribution of finished products to the end user.)

logistics management /ləˈdʒɪstɪks ˌmænɪdʒmənt/ *noun* the management of the distribution of products to the market

logo /ˈloʊgoʊ/ *noun* a symbol, design, or group of letters used by a company as a mark on its products and in advertising

London gold fixing /ˌlʌndən ˈɡoʊld ˌfɪksɪŋ/ *noun* a system where the world price for gold is set each day in London

long lease /ˌlɑŋ ˈlis/ *noun* a lease which runs for fifty years or more ○ *to take an office building on a long lease*

long-range /ˌlɑŋ ˈreɪndʒ/ *adjective* for a long period of time in the future □ **long-range economic forecast** a forecast which covers a period of several years

long-standing /ˌlɒŋ 'stændɪŋ/ *adjective* which has been arranged for a long time ○ *a long-standing agreement* □ **long-standing customer**, **customer of long standing** a person who has been a customer for many years

long-term /ˌlɒŋ 'tɜrm/ *adjective* ○ *The management projections are made on a long-term basis.* ○ *Sound long-term planning will give the company more direction.* ○ *It is in the company's long-term interests to have a contented staff.* □ **on a long-term basis** continuing for a long period of time □ **long-term debts** debts which will be repaid many years later □ **long-term forecast** a forecast for a period of over three years □ **long-term loan** a loan to be repaid many years later □ **long-term objectives** aims which will take years to achieve

look and feel /ˌlʊk ən 'fil/ *noun* the appeal of the design, layout, and ease of use of a website to potential customers and the way the site fits the image the company is trying to put across

loose /lus/ *adjective* not attached

loose insert /lus 'ɪnsɜrt/ *noun* a sheet of advertising material slipped between the pages of a publication

lorry-load /'lɑri loʊd/ *noun U.K.* same as **truckload** ○ *They delivered six lorry-loads of coal.*

lose /luz/ *verb* not to have something anymore □ **to lose an order** not to get an order which you were hoping to get ○ *During the strike, the company lost six orders to South American competitors.* □ **to lose customers** to have fewer customers ○ *Their service is so slow that they have been losing customers.* □ **the company is losing sales**, **is losing market share** the company has fewer sales or a smaller share of the market than before

lose out *phrasal verb* to suffer as a result of something ○ *The company has lost out in the rush to make cheap computers.* ○ *We lost out to a Japanese company who put in a lower tender for the job.*

loss /lɒs/ *noun* **1.** the state or process of not having something anymore □ **loss of customers** not keeping customers because of bad service, high prices, etc. □ **loss of an order** not getting an order which was expected □ **the company suffered a loss of market penetration** the company found it had a smaller share of the market **2.** the state of having less money than before or of not making a profit □ **the company suffered a loss** the company did not make a profit □ **to report a loss** not to show a profit in the accounts at the end of the year ○ *The company reported a loss of $1m on the first year's trading.* □ **the car was written off as a dead loss** *or* **a total loss** the car was so badly damaged that the insurers said it had no value □ **at a loss** making a loss, not making any profit ○ *The company is trading at a loss.* ○ *We sold the store at a loss.* □ **to cut your losses** to stop doing something which is losing money **3.** the state of being worth less or having a lower value ○ *Shares showed losses of up to 5% on the Stock Exchange.* **4.** the state of weighing less □ **loss in weight** goods which weigh less than when they were packed □ **loss in transport** the amount of weight which is lost while goods are being transported

low-grade /'loʊ greɪd/ *adjective* **1.** not very important ○ *a low-grade official from the Department of Commerce* **2.** not of very good quality ○ *The car runs best on low-grade gasoline.*

low-hanging fruit /ˌloʊ hæŋɪŋ 'frut/ *noun* an easy short-term sales or market opportunity which provides a quick profit without too much effort (*informal*)

low-involvement hierarchy /ˌloʊ ɪn'vɒlvmənt ˌhaɪrɑrki/ *noun* a hierarchy of response to advertising where the customer is relatively indifferent to the product or service and only responds to repeated marketing

low-involvement product /ˌloʊ ɪn'vɒlvmənt ˌprɒdʌkt/ *noun* a low-priced product for everyday use that is bought by consumers without giving much thought to brands

low-pressure /ˌloʊ ˈpreʃər/ *adjective* □ **low-pressure sales** sales where the salesperson does not force someone to buy, but only encourages them to do so

low-quality /ˌloʊ ˈkwɑləti/ *adjective* not of good quality ○ *They tried to sell us some low-quality steel.*

low season /ˌloʊ ˈsiːz(ə)n/ *noun* a period when there are few travelers ○ *Air fares are cheaper in the low season.*

loyal /ˈlɔɪəl/ *adjective* always buying the same brand or using the same store ○ *The aim of the advertising is to keep the customers loyal.*

loyalty /ˈlɔɪəlti/ *noun* the state of being faithful to someone or something

loyalty card /ˈlɔɪəlti kɑrd/ *noun* a special plastic card which gives discounts to customers over a period of time and so encourages them to remain as customers

lull /lʌl/ *noun* a quiet period ○ *After last week's hectic trading this week's lull was welcome.*

lump sum /ˌlʌmp ˈsʌm/ *noun* money paid in one single amount, not in several small sums ○ *When he retired he was given a lump-sum bonus.* ○ *She sold her house and invested the money as a lump sum.*

luxury /ˈlʌkʃəri/ *noun, adjective* referring to an expensive thing which is not necessary but which is good to have ○ *a black market in luxury articles* ○ *Luxury items are taxed very heavily.*

luxury goods /ˈlʌkʃəri gʊdz/, **luxury items** /ˈlʌkʃəri ˌaɪtəmz/ *plural noun* expensive items which are not basic necessities

luxury product /ˈlʌkʃəri ˌprɑdʌkt/ *noun* a product which people buy more of as their incomes rise ○ *Luxury products such as caviar are selling poorly since the slump.* ○ *The company has gone upmarket and is now selling luxury products.*

M

Ma and Pa shop /ˌmɑ ən ˈpɑ ʃɑp/ *noun U.K.* same as **mom-and-pop operation**

macro- /ˈmækroʊ/ *prefix* very large, covering a wide area

macroeconomics /ˌmækroʊikəˈnɑmɪks/ *plural noun* a study of the economics of a whole area, a whole industry, a whole group of the population, or a whole country, in order to help in economic planning. Compare **microeconomics** (NOTE: takes a singular verb) □ **macroeconomic conditions** factors that influence the state of the overall economy, e.g., changes in gross national product, interest rates, inflation, recession, and employment levels

macroenvironment /ˈmækroʊ ɪnˌvaɪrənmənt/ *noun* **1.** the general environmental factors that affect an organization, such as legislation or the country's economy ○ *We must develop a flexible planning system to allow for major changes in the macroenvironment.* **2.** factors outside the area of marketing which cannot be influenced by the marketing effort, including demographics, the natural environment, etc.

macromarketing /ˈmækroʊ ˌmɑrkətɪŋ/ *noun* the study of trading activity within a whole economic system such as a country, with its political, economic, and social implications

Macromedia Flash™ /ˌmækroʊmidiə ˈflæʃ/ *noun* a trade name for a type of animation software used on the Web, which is characterized by small file sizes, easy scalability and the use of streaming technology

Madam Chairman /ˌmædəm ˈtʃermən/, **Madam Chairwoman** /ˌmædəm ˈtʃerˌwʊmən/ *noun* a way of speaking to a female chairman of a committee or meeting

made-to-measure /ˌmeɪd tə ˈmeʒər/ *adjective* made to fit the requirements of the customer ○ *made-to-measure kitchen cabinets* ○ *a made-to-measure suit*

magazine /ˈmægəzin/ *noun* **1.** a paper, usually with pictures and printed on glossy paper, which comes out regularly, every month or every week **2.** a special type of newspaper, usually published only weekly or monthly, often with a glossy cover and often devoted to a particular subject □ **magazine insert** an advertising sheet put into a magazine when it is mailed or sold □ **to insert a leaflet in a specialist magazine** to put an advertising leaflet into a magazine before it is mailed or sold

magazine mailing /ˈmægəzin ˌmeɪlɪŋ/ *noun* the sending of copies of a magazine by mail to subscribers

magazine network /ˈmægəzin ˌnetwɜrk/ *noun* a group of magazines owned by one publisher and offering advertisers the possibility of buying space in several publications as a packaged deal

mail /meɪl/ *noun* **1.** a system of sending letters and parcels from one place to another ○ *The check was lost in the mail.* ○ *The invoice was put in the mail yesterday.* ○ *Mail to some of the islands in the Pacific can take six weeks.* □ **by mail** using the postal services, not sending something by hand or by messenger □ **to send a package by surface mail** to send a package by land or sea, not by air □ **by sea mail** sent by mail abroad, using a ship □ **by air mail** sent by mail abroad, using a plane □ **we sent the order by**

first-class mail we sent the order by the most expensive mail service, designed to be faster **2.** letters sent or received ○ *Has the mail arrived yet?* ○ *The first thing I do is open the mail.* ○ *The receipt was in this morning's mail.* **3.** same as **email** ■ *verb* **1.** to send something by post ○ *to mail a letter* ○ *We mailed our order last Wednesday.* ○ *They mailed their catalog to three thousand customers in Europe.* **2.** to send something by mail

mail drop /ˈmeɪl drɒp/ *noun* the mailing of promotional material to a large number of addresses

mailer /ˈmeɪlər/ *noun* packaging made of folded cardboard, used to mail items which need protection ○ *a diskette mailer*

mailing /ˈmeɪlɪŋ/ *noun* the sending of something by mail ○ *the mailing of publicity material* □ **to buy a mailing list** to pay a society or other organization money to buy the list of members so that you can use it to mail publicity material

mailing house /ˈmeɪlɪŋ haʊs/ *noun* a company which specializes in carrying out mailings for other companies

mailing list /ˈmeɪlɪŋ lɪst/ *noun* a list of names and addresses of people who might be interested in a product, or a list of names and addresses of members of a society ○ *to build up a mailing list* ○ *Your name is on our mailing list.*

mailing tube /ˈmeɪlɪŋ tub/ *noun* a stiff cardboard or plastic tube, used for mailing large pieces of paper such as posters

mail interview /ˈmeɪl ˌɪntərvjuː/, **mail survey** /ˈmeɪl ˌsɜrveɪ/ *noun* the sending of a questionnaire to respondents by mail for a survey ○ *Not enough consumers responded to the mail interview.* ○ *To encourage people to cooperate in the mail survey we'll include a free sample with the questionnaire.*

mail merge /ˈmeɪl mɜrdʒ/ *noun* a word-processing program that allows a standard form letter to be printed out to a series of different names and addresses

mail order /ˌmeɪl ˈɔrdər/ *noun* a system of buying and selling from a catalog, placing orders, and sending goods by mail ○ *We bought our kitchen units by mail order.*

mail-order catalog /ˈmeɪl ɔrdər ˌkætəlɒg/ *noun* a catalog from which a customer can order items to be sent by mail

mail-order selling /ˈmeɪl ɔrdər ˌselɪŋ/ *noun* a method of selling in which orders are taken and products are delivered by mail

mail out /ˌmeɪl ˈaʊt/ *verb* to send promotional material by mail

mailout /ˈmeɪlaʊt/ *noun* a piece of promotional material sent by direct mail, usually accompanied by a letter which may be personalized

mail room /ˈmeɪl rum/ *noun* a room in a building where the mail is sorted and sent to each department or collected from each department for sending

mail shot /ˈmeɪl ʃɑt/ *noun* **1.** leaflets sent by mail to possible customers. Also called **mailing shot 2.** a single mailing of direct-mail advertising literature

mailsort /ˈmeɪlsɔrt/ *noun* computer software used by mailing companies to sort mailings before they are sent to the post office, usually by using special labels with bar codes

Main Street /ˈmeɪn strit/ *noun* the most important street in a town, where the shops and banks usually are

majority /məˈdʒɔrəti/ *noun* more than half of a group

major selling idea /ˌmeɪdʒər ˈselɪŋ aɪˌdiə/ *adjective* the central theme in an advertising campaign

make /meɪk/ *noun* a brand or type of product manufactured ○ *Japanese makes of cars* ○ *a standard make of equipment* ○ *What make is the new computer system* or *What's the make of the new computer system?* ■ *verb* **1.** to produce or to manufacture ○ *The employees spent ten weeks making the table.* ○ *The factory makes three hundred cars a day.* **2.** □ **to make a profit** to have more money after a deal

make out *phrasal verb* to write something ○ *to make out an invoice* ○ *The bill is made out to Smith Inc.* □

to make out a cheque to someone to write someone's name on a check

makegood /ˈmeɪkɡʊd/ *noun* an advertisement placed again in a magazine or newspaper free of charge, because a mistake was made in it when it was previously published

maker /ˈmeɪkər/ *noun* in the VALS lifestyle classification, a practical, independent person who is interested in products that are good value but not necessarily fashionable

make-to-order /ˌmeɪk tʊ ˈɔrdər/ *noun* the making of goods or components to fulfill an existing order (NOTE: Make-to-order products are made to the customer's specification, and are often processed in small batches.)

manage /ˈmænɪdʒ/ *verb* **1.** to direct or to be in charge of something ○ *to manage a branch office* **2.** □ **to manage property** to look after rented property for the owner **3.** □ **to manage to** to be able to do something ○ *Did you manage to see the head buyer?* ○ *She managed to write six orders and take three phone calls all in two minutes.*

manageable /ˈmænɪdʒəb(ə)l/ *adjective* which can be dealt with ○ *The problems which the company faces are too large to be manageable by one person.*

managed economy /ˌmænɪdʒd ɪˈkɑnəmi/ *noun* an economy that is controlled by a government

managed hosting /ˌmænɪdʒd ˈhoʊstɪŋ/ *noun* a hosting option in which the hosting company is mainly responsible for a client's servers, often supplying and managing not only the hardware but the software as well

management /ˈmænɪdʒmənt/ *noun* **1.** the process of directing or running a business ○ *a management graduate* or *a graduate in management* ○ *She studied management in college.* ○ *Good management* or *efficient management is essential in a large organization.* ○ *Bad management* or *inefficient management can ruin a business.* **2.** a group of managers or directors ○ *The management has decided to give everyone a pay increase.* (NOTE: Where **management**

refers to a group of people it is sometimes followed by a plural verb.)

management accountant /ˈmænɪdʒmənt əˌkaʊntənt/ *noun* an accountant who prepares financial information for managers so that they can take decisions

management accounting /ˈmænɪdʒmənt əˌkaʊntɪŋ/ *noun* the preparation and use of financial information to support management decisions

management accounts /ˈmænɪdʒmənt əˌkaʊnts/ *plural noun* financial information prepared for a manager so that decisions can be made, including monthly or quarterly financial statements, often in great detail, with analysis of actual performance against the budget

management buyout /ˌmænɪdʒmənt ˈbaɪaʊt/ *noun* the takeover of a company by a group of employees, usually senior managers and directors. Abbreviation **MBO**

management by exception /ˌmænɪdʒmənt baɪ ɪkˈsepʃən/ *noun* a management system whereby deviations from plans are located and corrected

management by objectives /ˌmænɪdʒmənt baɪ əbˈdʒektɪvz/ *noun* a way of managing a business by planning work for the managers to do and testing if it is completed correctly and on time

management consultant /ˈmænɪdʒmənt kənˌsʌltənt/ *noun* a person who gives advice on how to manage a business

management course /ˈmænɪdʒmənt kɔrs/ *noun* a training course for managers

management development /ˈmænɪdʒmənt dɪˌveləpmənt/ *noun* the selection and training of potential managers

management team /ˈmænɪdʒmənt tim/ *noun* all the managers who work in a particular company

management technique /'mænɪdʒmənt tek,nik/ *noun* a way of managing a business

manager /'mænɪdʒər/ *noun* **1.** the head of a department in a company ○ *She's a department manager in an engineering company.* ○ *Go and see the human resources manager if you have a problem.* ○ *The production manager has been with the company for only two weeks.* ○ *Our sales manager started as a rep in London.* **2.** the person in charge of a branch or store ○ *Mr. Smith is the manager of our local Eastern Bank.* ○ *The manager of our London branch is in Boston for a series of meetings.*

managerial /,mænə'dʒɪriəl/ *adjective* referring to managers ○ *All the managerial staff are sent for training every year.* □ **to be appointed to a managerial position** to be appointed a manager □ **decisions taken at managerial level** decisions taken by managers

managership /'mænɪdʒəʃɪp/ *noun* the job of being a manager ○ *After six years, she was offered the managership of a branch in Scotland.*

managing director /,mænədʒɪŋ daɪ'rektər/ *noun* the director who is in charge of a whole company. Abbreviation **MD**

mandatory /'mændət(ə)ri/ *adjective* required by law or stipulated in a contract

mandatory blurb /,mændət(ə)ri 'blɜrb/, **mandatory copy** /,mændət(ə)ri 'kɑpi/ *noun* certain words which are required by law to be included in an advertisement, e.g., a health warning on cigarette advertisements

manifest /'mænɪfest/ *noun* a list of goods in a shipment

mannequin /'mænɪkɪn/ *noun* a model of a person, used to display clothes in a store window or inside a store

manpower /'mænpaʊər/ *noun* the number of employees in an organization, industry, or country (NOTE: **manpower** does not mean only men.)

manpower forecasting /'mænpaʊər ,fɔrkæstɪŋ/ *noun* the process of calculating how many employees will be needed in the future, and how many will actually be available

manpower planning /'mænpaʊər ,plænɪŋ/ *noun* the process of planning to obtain the right number of employees in each job

manpower requirements /'mænpaʊər rɪ,kwaɪəmənts/, **manpower needs** /'mænpaʊər nidz/ *plural noun* the number of employees needed

manufacture /,mænjʊ'fæktʃə/ *verb* to make a product for sale, using machines ○ *The company manufactures spare parts for cars.* ■ *noun* the making of a product for sale, using machines □ **products of foreign manufacture** products made in foreign countries

manufactured goods /,mænjufæktʃəd 'gʊdz/ *plural noun* items which are made by machine

manufacturer /,mænjʊ'fæktʃərər/ *noun* a person or company that produces machine-made products ○ *a big Indian cotton manufacturer* ○ *Foreign manufacturers have set up factories here.*

manufacturer's agent /mænjʊ ,fæktʃərəz 'eɪdʒənt/ *noun* a person who sells on behalf of a manufacturer and earns a commission

manufacturer's brand /mænjʊ ,fæktʃərəz 'brænd/ *noun* a brand which belongs to the manufacturer and has the same name

manufacturer's recommended price /,mænjufæktʃərəz ,rekəmendɪd 'praɪs/ *noun* a price at which the manufacturer suggests the product should be sold on the retail market, which is often reduced by the retailer ○ *"All china – 20% off the manufacturer's recommended price"* Abbreviation **MRP**

manufacturing /,mænjʊ'fæktʃərɪŋ/ *noun* the production of machine-made products for sale ○ *We must try to reduce the manufacturing overheads.* ○ *Manufacturing processes are continually being updated.*

manufacturing capacity /,mænjʊ 'fæktʃərɪŋ kə,pæsəti/ *noun* the

2

amount of a product which a factory is capable of making

manufacturing industries /ˌmænjʊˈfæktʃərɪŋ ˌɪndəstriz/ *plural noun* industries which take raw materials and make them into finished products

map /mæp/ *noun* a chart which shows a geographic area

mapping /ˈmæpɪŋ/ *noun* the drawing up of a map of an area

margin /ˈmɑrdʒɪn/ *noun* **1.** the difference between the money received when selling a product and the money paid for it □ **we are cutting our margins very fine** we are reducing our margins to the smallest possible in order to be competitive □ **our margins have been squeezed** profits have been reduced because our margins have to be smaller to stay competitive **2.** extra space or time allowed

marginal /ˈmɑrdʒɪn(ə)l/ *adjective* **1.** hardly worth the money paid **2.** not very profitable ○ *a marginal return on investment*

marginal cost /ˌmɑrdʒɪn(ə)l ˈkɒst/ *noun* the cost of making a single extra unit above the number already planned

marginal cost pricing /ˌmɑrdʒɪn(ə)l ˈkɒst ˌpraɪsɪŋ/ *noun* a pricing method that involves fixing a price per unit that covers marginal costs and makes an acceptable contribution to fixed costs

marginal land /ˌmɑrdʒɪn(ə)l ˈlænd/ *noun* land which is almost not worth farming

marginal pricing /ˌmɑrdʒɪn(ə)l ˈpraɪsɪŋ/ *noun* the practice of basing the selling price of a product on its variable costs of production plus a margin, but excluding fixed costs

marginal productivity /ˌmɑrdʒɪn(ə)l prɒdʌkˈtɪvəti/ *noun* extra productivity achieved by the use of one more factor of production

marginal purchase /ˌmɑrdʒɪn(ə)l ˈpɜrtʃɪs/ *noun* something which a buyer feels is only just worth buying

marginal rate of tax /ˌmɑrdʒɪn(ə)l reɪt əv ˈtæks/, **marginal rate of taxa-tion** /ˌmɑrdʒɪn(ə)l reɪt əv tæks ˈeɪʃ(ə)n/ *noun* the percentage of tax which a taxpayer pays at the top rate, which he or she therefore pays on every further dollar or pound he or she earns

marginal revenue /ˌmɑrdʒɪn(ə)l ˈrevenju/ *noun* the income from selling a single extra unit above the number already sold

marginal tax rate /ˌmɑrdʒɪn(ə)l ˈtæks reɪt/ *noun* same as **marginal rate of tax**

marginal utility /ˌmɑrdʒɪn(ə)l ju ˈtɪləti/ *noun* satisfaction gained from using one more unit of a product

margin of error /ˌmɑrdʒɪn əv ˈerər/ *noun* the number of mistakes which can be accepted in a document or in a calculation

marine /məˈrin/ *adjective* referring to the sea

marine insurance /məˌrin ɪnˈʃʊrəns/ *noun* the insurance of ships and their cargoes

marine underwriter /məˌrin ˈʌndərraɪtər/ *noun* a person or company that insures ships and their cargoes

maritime /ˈmærɪtaɪm/ *adjective* referring to the sea

maritime lawyer /ˌmærɪtaɪm ˈlɔjər/ *noun* a lawyer who specializes in legal matters concerning ships and cargoes

maritime trade /ˌmærɪtaɪm ˈtreɪd/ *noun* the transporting of commercial goods by sea

mark /mɑrk/ *noun* **1.** a sign put on an item to show something **2.** a former unit of currency in Germany ○ *The price was twenty-five marks.* ○ *The mark rose against the dollar.* (NOTE: Usually written **DM** after a figure: 25DM.) ■ *verb* to put a sign on something ○ *to mark a product "for export only"* ○ *an article marked at $1.50* ○ *She used a black pen to mark the price on the book.*

mark down *phrasal verb* to make the price of something lower

mark up *phrasal verb* to make the price of something higher

mark-down /ˈmɑrk daʊn/ *noun* **1.** a reduction of the price of something to less than its usual price **2.** the percentage amount by which a price has been lowered ○ *There has been a 30% mark-down on all goods in the sale.*

marked price /mɑrkt 'praɪs/ *noun* the price which is marked on or attached to an article for sale

market /'mɑrkət/ *noun* **1.** a place, often in the open air where farm produce and housewares are sold ○ *The fish market is held every Thursday.* ○ *The open-air market is held in the central square.* ○ *Here are this week's market prices for sheep.* **2.** an area where a product might be sold or the group of people who might buy a product ○ *There is no market for this product.* ○ *Our share of the Far eastern market has gone down.* **3.** the possible sales of a specific product or demand for a specific product ○ *There's no market for word processors* ○ *The market for home computers has fallen sharply.* ○ *We have 20% of the British car market.* **4.** □ **to pay black market prices** to pay high prices to get items which are not easily available **5.** □ **to go up market, to go down market** to make products which appeal to a wealthy section of the market or to a wider, less wealthy section of the market **6.** □ **to be in the market for second-hand cars** to look for secondhand cars to buy □ **to come on to the market** to start to be sold ○ *This soap has just come on to the market.* □ **to put something on the market** to start to offer something for sale ○ *They put their house on the market.* ○ *I hear the company has been put on the market.* □ **the company has priced itself out of the market** the company has raised its prices so high that its products do not sell ■ *verb* to sell a product, or to present and promote a product in a way which will help to sell it ○ *This product is being marketed in all European countries.*

marketable /'mɑrkɪtəb(ə)l/ *adjective* easily sold

market analysis /,mɑrkət ə 'næləsɪs/ *noun* the detailed examination and report of a market

market area /'mɑrkət ,eriə/ *noun* a geographic area which represents a particular market, e.g., a TV viewing area or a representative's territory

market build-up method /,mɑrkət 'bɪld ʌp ,meθəd/ *noun* a method of assessing the sales potential of a product by adding up the number of potential buyers in each market segment

market challenger strategy /,mɑrkət 'tʃælɪndʒər ,strætədʒi/ *noun* a strategy adopted by a company which is challenging the market leaders through pricing, promotion, or product design ○ *It's a new aggressive company adopting a market challenger strategy.*

market coverage /,mɑrkət 'kʌv(ə)rɪdʒ/ *noun* a market share or measurement of what proportion of the sales of an article is accounted for by a particular brand ○ *The marketing director's brief was to increase market coverage by at least ten per cent.*

market day /'mɑrkət deɪ/ *noun* the day when a market is regularly held ○ *Tuesday is market day, so the streets are closed to traffic.*

market demand /,mɑrkət dɪ 'mænd/ *noun* the total demand for a product in the market ○ *Market demand for this product is falling, as fashions have changed.*

market development /,mɑrkət dɪ 'veləpmənt/ *noun* a strategy involving the search for and exploitation of new markets for a product ○ *Market development for our tractors is part of the company's growth strategy.*

market-driven /'mɑrkɪt ,drɪv(ə)n/ *adjective* which is driven by market forces

market dues /,mɑrkət 'duz/ *plural noun* the rent to be paid for a stall in a market

market economist /,mɑrkət ɪ 'kɑnəmɪst/ *noun* a person who specializes in the study of financial structures and the return on investments in the stock market

market economy /,mɑrkət ɪ 'kɑnəmi/ *noun* same as **free market economy**

marketeer /,mɑrkɪ'tɪr/ *noun* same as **marketer**

marketer /'mɑrkɪtər/ *noun* a person or company that carries out marketing activities ○ *The company has been in manufacturing for ten years, and is now becoming a marketer of its own products as well.* ○ *Most direct marketers support the Post Office, which is almost the sole channel for their services.*

marketface /ˈmɑrkɪtfeɪs/ *noun* the point of contact between suppliers and their customers

market-facing enterprise /ˈmɑrkɪt feɪsɪŋ ˌentəpraɪz/ *noun* an organization that is sensitive to the needs of its markets and customers and arranges its activities with them in mind

market factor analysis /ˌmɑrkət ˌfæktər əˈnæləsɪs/ *noun* a forecasting method which concentrates on key market factors that are believed to affect demand

market follower strategy /ˌmɑrkət ˈfɑloʊər ˌstrætədʒi/ *noun* a strategy of a company which does not directly challenge the market leaders, but attempts to benefit from their innovations and gain a profitable corner of the market ○ *Adopting a market follower strategy greatly reduces expenditure on research and development.*

market forces /ˌmɑrkət ˈfɔrsɪz/ *plural noun* the influences on the sales of a product which bring about a change in prices

market forecast /ˌmɑrkət ˈfɔrkæst/ *noun* a forecast of prices on the stock market

market fragmentation /ˌmɑrkət ˌfrægmənˈteɪʃ(ə)n/ *noun* the splitting of a market into many small segments, which are more difficult to sell into

market gap /ˌmɑrkət ˈgæp/ *noun* an opportunity to sell a product or service which is needed but which no one has sold before. ◊ **gap**

market hall /ˈmɑrkət hɔl/ *noun* the building in which a market is held regularly

marketing /ˈmɑrkətɪŋ/ *noun* **1.** the business of presenting and promoting goods or services in such a way as to make customers want to buy them **2.** the

techniques used in selling a product, such as packaging and advertising

marketing agreement /ˈmɑrkətɪŋ əˌgriːmənt/ *noun* a contract by which one company will market another company's products

marketing audit /ˈmɑrkətɪŋ ˌɔdɪt/ *noun* an examination of the effectiveness of a company's marketing plans

marketing board /ˈmɑrkətɪŋ bɔrd/ *noun* an organization set up by the government or by a group of producers to help market a certain type of product

marketing budget /ˈmɑrkətɪŋ ˌbʌdʒət/ *noun* money set aside by an organization for its marketing activities

marketing channels /ˈmɑrkətɪŋ ˌtʃæn(ə)lz/ *plural noun* the means of communicating a message involved in the process of marketing

marketing communications /ˌmɑrkətɪŋ kəˌmjuːnɪˈkeɪʃ(ə)nz/ *plural noun* all methods of communicating used in marketing, e.g., television, radio, and sales literature

marketing concept /ˈmɑrkətɪŋ ˌkɑnsept/ *noun* a business idea or philosophy based on the importance of profit, consumer satisfaction, and the welfare of the general public

marketing consultancy /ˈmɑrkətɪŋ kənˌsʌltənsi/ *noun* a firm which gives specialist advice on marketing

marketing department /ˈmɑrkətɪŋ dɪˌpɑrtmənt/ *noun* the section of a company dealing with marketing and sales

marketing director /ˈmɑrkətɪŋ daɪ ˌrektər/ *noun* a director who is responsible for an organization's marketing activities

marketing information system /ˌmɑrkətɪŋ ˌɪnfərˈmeɪʃ(ə)n ˌsɪstəm/ *noun* computer software which analyzes marketing information and produces material on which marketers can make decisions

marketing intelligence /ˈmɑrkətɪŋ ɪnˌtelɪdʒəns/ *noun* information about a market that can help a marketing effort

marketing management /'mɑrkətɪŋ ˌmænɪdʒmənt/ *noun* the organizing of a company's marketing

marketing manager /'mɑrkətɪŋ ˌmænɪdʒər/ *noun* a person in charge of a marketing department ○ *The marketing manager has decided to start a new advertising campaign.*

marketing mix /'mɑrkətɪŋ mɪks/ *noun* the combination of all the elements that make up marketing such as price, distribution, and advertising ○ *Personal selling is a vital part of the company's marketing mix.*

marketing model /'mɑrkətɪŋ ˌmɑd(ə)l/ *noun* an overview of the entire marketing process which can be shown graphically, often using a computer, and used to solve problems

marketing myopia /ˌmɑrkətɪŋ maɪ'oʊpiə/ *noun* a problem which occurs when a business is "nearsighted" and only views the world from its own perspective, and fails to see the point of view of the customer

marketing objectives /'mɑrkətɪŋ əb,dʒektɪvz/ *plural noun* aims set for an organization's marketing program, including sales, market share, and profitability

marketing plan /'mɑrkətɪŋ plæn/ *noun* a plan, usually annual, for a company's marketing activities, specifying expenditure and expected revenue and profits ○ *Has this year's marketing plan been drawn up yet?* ○ *The marketing plan is flexible enough to allow for an increase in advertising costs.*

marketing planning /'mɑrkətɪŋ ˌplænɪŋ/ *noun* making a plan for a company's marketing activities, specifying expenditure and expected revenue and profits

marketing policy /'mɑrkətɪŋ ˌpɑlɪsi/ *noun* the basic attitudes underlying a company's marketing activities

marketing research /ˌmɑrkətɪŋ rɪ'sɜrtʃ/ *noun* all research carried out in the interests of successful marketing, including market research, media research, and product research

marketing services /'mɑrkətɪŋ ˌsɜrvɪsɪz/ *plural noun* marketing functions other than selling, e.g., market research and advertising ○ *Our sales drive is supported by well-developed and effective marketing services.*

marketing strategy /'mɑrkətɪŋ ˌstrætədʒi/ *noun* a strategy or plan for marketing activities ○ *What marketing strategy should be adopted to reach these long-term objectives?* ○ *The marketing strategy was one of expansion through diversification and market development.*

market intelligence /'mɑrkət ɪnˌtelɪdʒəns/ *noun* information about a market that can help a marketing effort

market leader /ˌmɑrkət 'lidər/ *noun* the company with the largest market share ○ *We are the market leader in home computers.*

market leader strategy /ˌmɑrkət 'lidər ˌstrætədʒi/ *noun* a strategy of a company which is a market leader and wants to maintain a dominant market share or to keep its reputation as an innovator

marketmaker /'mɑrkɪtmeɪkər/ *noun* a person who buys or sells shares on the stock market and offers to do so. A marketmaker operates a book, listing the securities he or she is willing to buy or sell, and makes his or her money by charging a commission on each transaction.

market map /'mɑrkət mæp/ *noun* a graph showing the structure of a market in terms of the number and type of consumers and the activity of competitors ○ *One look at the market map shows we are aiming at the wrong target market.*

market niche /'mɑrkət niʃ/ *noun* a particular segment or specialized area of a market ○ *In producing this unusual product, the company has found itself a market niche.*

market opening /'mɑrkət ˌoʊp(ə)nɪŋ/ *noun* the possibility of starting to do business in a new market

market opportunity /ˌmɑrkət ˌɑpər'tunəti/ *noun* the possibility of going into a market for the first time

market penetration /ˌmɑrkət ˌpenɪˈtreɪʃ(ə)n/ *noun* the percentage of a total market which the sales of a company cover

market penetration pricing /ˌmɑrkət penɪˈtreɪʃ(ə)n ˌpraɪsɪŋ/ *noun* pricing a product low enough to achieve market penetration

marketplace /ˈmɑrkɪtpleɪs/ *noun* **1.** the open space in the middle of a town where a market is held ○ *You can park in the marketplace when there is no market.* **2.** the situation and environment in which goods are sold ○ *Our salespeople find life difficult in the marketplace.* ○ *What's the reaction to the new car in the marketplace?* ○ *What's the marketplace reaction to the new car?*

market position /ˌmɑrkət pəˈzɪʃ(ə)n/ *noun* the place a company holds in a market

market potential /ˌmɑrkət pəˈtenʃəl/ *noun* the sales of a product that should be achieved with the right kind of marketing effort ○ *The product is promising but has not yet achieved its full market potential.*

market power /ˈmɑrkət ˌpaʊər/ *noun* the power of a business within a market, usually based on the firm's market position

market price /ˈmɑrkət praɪs/ *noun* the price at which a product can be sold

market profile /ˌmɑrkət ˈproʊfaɪl/ *noun* the basic characteristics of a particular market

market rate /ˌmɑrkət ˈreɪt/ *noun* the usual price in the market ○ *We pay the market rate for executive assistants* or *We pay executive assistants the market rate.*

market research /ˌmɑrkət rɪˈsɜrtʃ/ *noun* the process of examining the possible sales of a product and the possible customers for it before it is put on the market

market sector /ˌmɑrkət ˈsektər/ *noun* a particular section of a market, especially an area into which a firm sells

market segment /ˌmɑrkət ˈsegmənt/ *noun* a group of consumers in a market who are definable by their particular needs

market segmentation /ˌmɑrkət ˌsegmenˈteɪʃ(ə)n/ *noun* the division of the market or consumers into categories according to their buying habits ○ *Our strategy is based on satisfying the demands of many different types of buyer and therefore requires thorough market segmentation.*

market share /ˌmɑrkət ˈʃer/ *noun* the percentage of a total market which the sales of a company's product cover ○ *We hope our new product range will increase our market share.*

market specialist /ˌmɑrkət ˈspeʃəlɪst/ *noun* a person who concentrates on a few markets, and has an expertise in the media industry in these markets

market stall /ˈmɑrkət stɔl/ *noun* a light wooden stand where a trader sells goods in a market

market structure /ˌmɑrkət ˈstrʌktʃər/ *noun* the way in which a market is organized, including the concentration of suppliers or consumers, the ease of entry or barriers to entry, and the competitiveness of players in the market

market survey /ˌmɑrkət ˈsɜrveɪ/ *noun* a survey or general report on market conditions ○ *The market survey suggests that there is no longer much demand for this type of product.*

market targeting /ˌmɑrkət ˈtɑrgətɪŋ/ *noun* planning how to sell a product or service into a particular market

market test /ˌmɑrkət ˈtest/ *noun* an examination to see if a sample of a product will sell in a market

market trends /ˌmɑrkət ˈtrendz/ *plural noun* gradual changes taking place in a market

market value /ˌmɑrkət ˈvælju/ *noun* the value of an asset, a share, a product, or a company if sold today

mark-up /ˈmɑrk ʌp/ *noun* **1.** an increase in price ○ *We put into effect a 10% mark-up of all prices in June.* ○ *Since I was last in the store they have* *put at least a 5% mark-up on the whole range of items.* **2.** the difference between the cost of a product or service and its selling price □ **we work to a 3.5 times mark-up** *or* **to a 350% mark-up** we take the unit cost and multiply by 3.5 to give the selling price

mark-up percentage /'mɑrk ʌp pə ˌsentɪdʒ/ *noun* the mark-up expressed as a percentage either of the cost or of the selling price ○ *What's the mark-up percentage on these items?*

marque /mɑrk/ *noun* a famous brand name for a car, e.g., Jaguar, MG, or Ferrari

mart /mɑrt/ *noun* a place where things are sold

mass /mæs/ *noun* **1.** a large group of people **2.** a large number ○ *We have a mass of letters* or *masses of letters to write.* ○ *They received a mass of orders* or *masses of orders after the TV commercials.*

mass customization /ˌmæs ˌkʌstəmaɪˈzeɪʃ(ə)n/ *noun* a process that allows a standard, mass-produced item, e.g., a bicycle, to be altered to fit the specific requirements of individual customers

mass market /mæs ˈmɑrkət/ *noun* the whole market, consisting of a very large number of customers

mass marketing /ˌmæs ˈmɑrkətɪŋ/ *noun* marketing which aims at reaching large numbers of people

mass media /ˌmæs ˈmidiə/ *noun* the means of communication by which large numbers of people are reached, e.g., radio, television, or newspapers

mass-produce /ˌmæs prəˈdus/ *verb* to manufacture identical products in large quantities ○ *to mass-produce cars*

master /'mæstər/ *adjective* main or original □ **master budget** a budget prepared by amalgamating budgets from various profit and cost centers such as sales, production, marketing, or administration in order to provide a main budget for the whole company □ **the master copy of a file** the main copy of a computer file, kept for security purposes

master franchise /'mæstər ˌfræntʃaɪz/ *noun* a franchise given to a single entrepreneur who then sells subsidiary franchises to others

master sample /'mæstər ˌsɑrmpəl/ *noun* a collection of basic sampling units (such as parliamentary constituencies) compiled by research organizations to help a company's market research

masthead /'mɑrsthed/ *noun* the area at the top of a webpage, which usually contains the logo of the organization that owns the page, and often a search box and a set of links to important areas of the website

matched sample /ˌmætʃd 'sɑrmpəl/ *noun* the use of two samples of people with the same characteristics to compare reactions to different products in tests

material /məˈtɪriəl/ *noun* a substance which can be used to make a finished product □ **materials control** a system to check that a company has enough materials in stock to do its work □ **materials handling** the moving of materials from one part of a factory to another in an efficient way

matrix /'meɪtrɪks/ *noun* an arrangement of data in horizontal and vertical columns (NOTE: The plural is **matrices**)

matrix management /'meɪtrɪks ˌmænɪdʒmənt/ *noun* management that operates both through the hierarchical chain of command within the organization, and through relationships at the same level with other managers working in other locations or on different products or projects

mature /məˈtʃʊr/ *adjective* □ **mature economy** a fully developed economy ■ *verb* to become due □ **bills which mature in three weeks' time** bills which will be due for payment in three weeks

mature market /məˌtʃʊr 'mɑrkət/ *noun* a well-established market, with little potential for increased sales

maturity /məˈtʃʊrəti/ *noun* the third stage in a product life cycle when a product is well established in the market though no longer enjoying increasing sales, after which sooner or later it will start to decline

maximal awareness /ˌmæksɪməl ə 'wernəs/ *noun* the point at which a consumer is convinced enough by a product's advertising to buy the product ○ *The marketing director considered the advertisement's message too weak to achieve maximal awareness.*

maximization /ˌmæksɪmaɪ 'zeɪʃ(ə)n/ *noun* the process of making something as large as possible ○ *profit maximization* or *maximization of profit*

maximize /'mæksɪmaɪz/ *verb* to make something as large as possible ○ *Our aim is to maximize profits.* ○ *The cooperation of the work force will be needed if we are to maximize production.* ○ *She is paid on results, and so has to work flat out to maximize her earnings.*

maximum /'mæksɪməm/ *noun* the largest possible number, price or quantity ○ *It is the maximum the insurance company will pay.* (NOTE: The plural is **maximums** or **maxima**.) □ **up to a maximum of $30** no more than $30 □ **to increase exports to the maximum** to increase exports as much as possible ■ *adjective* largest possible ○ *40% is the maximum income tax rate* or *the maximum rate of tax.* ○ *The maximum load for the truck is one ton.* ○ *Maximum production levels were reached last week.* □ **to increase production to the maximum level** to increase it as much as possible

maximum price /ˌmæksɪməm 'praɪs/ *noun* the highest legal price for a product ○ *The government insists on such a low maximum price that we'll never break even.* ○ *Demand for the product is so low that no company is charging the maximum price.*

M.B.A. /ˌem bi 'eɪ/ *noun* a degree awarded to graduates who have completed a further course in business studies. Full form **Master of Business Administration**

m-commerce /'em ˌkɑmɜrs/ *noun* marketing functions other than selling, e.g., market research and advertising

mean /min/ *adjective* average ○ *The mean annual increase in sales is 3.20%.*
■ *noun* the average or number calculated by adding several quantities together and dividing by the number of quantities added ○ *Unit sales are over the mean for the first quarter* or *above the first-quarter mean.*

means /minz/ *noun* a way of doing something ○ *Do we have any means of copying all these documents quickly?* ○ *Bank transfer is the easiest means of payment.* (NOTE: The plural is **means**.)
■ *plural noun* money or resources ○ *The company has the means to launch the new product.* ○ *Such a level of investment is beyond the means of a small private company.*

means test /'minz test/ *noun* an inquiry into how much money someone earns to see if they are eligible for state benefits

mechanical /mɪ'kænɪk(ə)l/ *adjective* worked by a machine ○ *a mechanical pump*

mechanical data /mɪˌkænɪk(ə)l 'deɪtə/ *noun* information regarding the printing of newspapers or magazines, e.g., format or column width

media /'midiə/ *noun* the means of communicating a message about a product or service to the public (NOTE: **media** is followed by a singular or plural verb.)

media broker /'midiə ˌbroʊkər/ *noun* a business which offers organizations a media-buying service and possibly additional services such as media planning

media buyer /'midiə ˌbaɪər/ *noun* a person in an advertising agency who places advertisements in the media on behalf of clients

media buying /'midiə ˌbaɪɪŋ/ *noun* the placing of advertisements in the media on behalf of an organization ○ *Efficient media buying is impossible without a good knowledge of comparative media costs.*

media class /'midiə klɑrs/ *noun* a basic type of medium, e.g., TV, radio, or the press

media coverage /ˈmidiə ˌkʌv(ə)rɪdʒ/ *noun* reports about something in the media ○ *We got good media coverage for the launch of the new model.*

media data form /ˌmidiə ˈdeɪtə fɔrm/ *noun* a document giving basic data or information about a publication such as circulation, readership, and geographic distribution

media event /ˌmidiə ɪˈvent/ *noun* a happening which is staged by or organized so as to attract the attention of the mass media

media independent /ˌmidiə ˌɪndɪˈpendənt/, **media shop** /ˈmidiə ʃɑp/ *noun* a business which offers organizations a media-buying service, but without the creative services usually offered by advertising agencies

median /ˈmidiən/ *noun* the middle number in a list of numbers

media objectives /ˌmidiə əbˈdʒektɪvz/ *plural noun* aims which an advertiser has in advertising through the media

media option /ˈmidiə ˌɑpʃən/ *noun* a single unit of advertising space or time

media organizations /ˈmidiə ɔrɡənaɪˌzeɪʃ(ə)nz/ *plural noun* organizations whose aim is to provide information or entertainment to their subscribers, viewers, or readers while at the same offering marketers a way of reaching audiences with print and broadcast messages

media owner /ˈmidiə ˌoʊnər/ *noun* a person or company that owns a magazine or newspaper or radio or TV station

media plan /ˈmidiə plæn/ *noun* a plan showing what type of media will be used and how much advertising will be done and when

media planner /ˈmidiə ˌplænər/ *noun* a person who deals with media planning

media planning /ˈmidiə ˌplænɪŋ/ *noun* a strategy concerned with what type of media should be used and how much advertising should be done and when ○ *The marketing manager and media buyer are having a media plan-*

ning session. ○ *Proper media planning avoids overexpenditure on promotion.*

media research /ˈmidiə rɪˌsɜrtʃ/ *noun* the study or evaluation of a target audience in order to improve an organization's promotional activities

media schedule /ˈmidiə ˌskedʒəl/ *noun* all the details of advertising to be used in a promotional campaign, e.g., the timing and positioning of advertisements

media selection /ˈmidiə sɪˌlekʃən/ *noun* the process of choosing the right type of media for a promotional campaign ○ *The agency will give us guidance on media selection.*

media service /ˈmidiə ˌsɜrvɪs/ *noun* an organization which provides the full range of media functions to its clients

media shop /ˈmidiə ʃɑp/ *noun* same as **media independent**

media strategy /ˈmidiə ˌstrætədʒi/ *noun* action plans for achieving media objectives

media vehicle /ˈmidiə ˌviɪk(ə)l/ *noun* the specific program or publication used to carry an advertising message

medium /ˈmidiəm/ *noun* one particular means of communicating information to the public (NOTE: The plural is **media**)

medium-term /ˌmidiəm ˈtɜrm/ *adjective* referring to a point between short term and long term □ **medium-term forecast** a forecast for two or three years

megastore /ˈmeɡəstɔr/ *noun* a very large store

mentee /menˈti/ *noun* a less experienced employee who is offered special guidance and support by a respected and trusted person with more experience (a mentor)

mercantile /ˈmɜrkəntaɪl/ *adjective* commercial □ **mercantile country** a country which earns income from trade □ **mercantile law** laws relating to business

mercantile agent /ˈmɜrkəntaɪl ˌeɪdʒənt/ *noun* a person who sells on behalf of a business or another person and earns a commission

mercantile marine /ˌmɜrkəntaɪl məˈrin/ *noun* all the commercial ships of a country

mercantile paper /ˈmɜrkəntaɪl ˌpeɪpər/ *noun* a negotiable document used in commerce

merchandise /ˈmɜrtʃəndaɪz/ *noun* goods which are for sale or which have been sold ○ *The merchandise is shipped through two ports.* ■ *verb* to sell goods by a wide variety of means, such as display, advertising, or sending samples ○ *to merchandise a product*

merchandiser /ˈmɜrtʃəndaɪzər/ *noun* a person or company that organizes the display and promotion of goods

merchandising /ˈmɜrtʃ(ə)nˌdaɪzɪŋ/ *noun* the process of organizing the display and promotion of goods in retail outlets ○ *the merchandising of a product* ○ *the merchandising department*

merchant /ˈmɜrtʃənt/ *noun* a businessperson who buys and sells, especially one who buys imported goods in bulk for retail sale ○ *a coal merchant* ○ *a wine merchant*

merchantable /ˈmɜrtʃəntəb(ə)l/ *adjective* of good enough quality for sale and use

merchant account /ˈmɜrtʃənt əˌkaʊnt/ *noun* an account opened by an e-merchant at a financial institution to receive the proceeds of credit-card transactions

merchant bank /ˈmɜrtʃənt bæŋk/ *noun* a bank which arranges loans to companies, deals in international finance, buys and sells shares and launches new companies on the Stock Exchange, but does not provide banking services to the general public

merchanting /ˈmɜrtʃəntɪŋ/ *noun* the action of buying and selling

merchantman /ˈmɜrtʃəntmən/ *noun* a commercial ship

merchant marine /ˌmɜrtʃənt məˈrin/, **merchant navy** /ˌmɜrtʃənt ˈneɪvi/ *noun* all the commercial ships of a country

merge /mɜrdʒ/ *verb* to join together ○ *The two companies have merged.* ○ *The firm merged with its main competitor.*

merge-purge /mɜrdʒ pɜrdʒ/ *noun* combining two mailing lists and checking to remove duplicate addresses

merger /ˈmɜrdʒər/ *noun* the joining together of two or more companies ○ *As a result of the merger, the company is now the largest in the field.*

message /ˈmesɪdʒ/ *noun* **1.** a piece of news which is sent to someone ○ *He says he never received the message.* ○ *I'll leave a message with her assistant.* **2.** an idea that is communicated by promotion ○ *The agency was given clear instructions as to what message the advertisement should convey.* ○ *Few people interviewed in the survey knew what the advertisement's message was supposed to be.* ○ *The message on the poster was conveyed in only three words.*

message effect /ˈmesɪdʒ ɪˌfekt/ *noun* the effect of an advertisement's message on the target audience ○ *The message effect was lost because so many people didn't understand the joke used in the advertisement.* ○ *After the campaign we'll try to assess what the message effect has been.*

metadata /ˈmetədeɪtə/ *noun* essential information contained in a document or web page, e.g., its publication date, author, keywords, title, and summary, which is used by search engines to find relevant websites in response to a search request from a user. ◊ **meta-tag** (NOTE: takes a singular or plural verb)

metamarketing /ˈmetəmɑrkətɪŋ/ *noun* marketing applied to all kinds of organizations, such as hospitals, churches, and religions, as well as to profit-making concerns

meta-tag /ˈmetə tæg/ *noun* a keyword or description command used on a web page to enable it to be found by search engines

me-too product /ˌmi ˈtu ˌprɑdʌkt/ *noun* a product which is a very similar to an existing market leader

metro area /ˈmetroʊ ˌeriə/ *noun* the central part of a large city

micro- /'maɪkroʊ/ *prefix* very small

microeconomics /'maɪkroʊ ikə
ˌnɑmɪks/ *plural noun* the study of the
economics of people or single companies. Compare **macroeconomics**
(NOTE: takes a singular verb) □ **micro-
economic trends** trends in a country's
economy, e.g., consumer income and
patterns of spending, wages, savings, or
debt

microenvironment /'maɪkroʊɪn
ˌvaɪrənmənt/ *noun* the elements or factors outside a business organization
which directly affect it, such as supply
of raw materials, demand for its products, and rival companies ○ *Unreliability of suppliers is one the greatest problems in our microenvironment.*

micromarketing /'maɪkroʊ
ˌmɑrkətɪŋ/ *prefix* the study of the marketing strategy of an individual business

middleman /'mɪd(ə)l,mæn/ *noun* a
businessperson who buys from the manufacturer and sells to retailers or to the
public ○ *We sell direct from the factory
to the customer and cut out the middleman.* (NOTE: The plural is **middlemen**.)

milk /mɪlk/ *verb* to make as much profit for as long as possible from a particular product or service ○ *We intend to
milk the product hard for the next two
years, before it becomes obsolete.*

mindset /'maɪndset/ *noun* a way of
thinking or general attitude to things

mindshare /'maɪndʃer/ *noun* the
density of the interconnects found by a
search engine, that is the number of pages that have links to a website

minicontainer /'mɪnikən,teɪnər/
noun a small container

minimarket /'mɪni,mɑrkət/ *noun* a
very small self-service store

minimum frequency /,mɪnɪməm
'frikwənsi/ *noun* the minimum number
of exposures for an advertisement to be
effective

mining concession /'maɪnɪŋ kən
ˌseʃ(ə)n/ *noun* the right to dig a mine on
a piece of land

miscellaneous /,mɪsə'leɪniəs/ *adjective* various, mixed, or not all of the
same sort ○ *miscellaneous items on the
agenda* ○ *a box of miscellaneous pieces
of equipment* ○ *Miscellaneous expenditure is not itemized in the accounts.*

misrepresentation /,mɪs,reprɪzen
'teɪʃ(ə)n/ *noun* the act of making a
wrong statement in order to persuade
someone to enter into a contract such as
one for buying a product or service

mission /'mɪʃ(ə)n/ *noun* a group of
people going on a journey for a special
purpose

missionary sales /'mɪʃ(ə)n(ə)ri
seɪlz/ *plural noun* a sales pitch where a
salesperson emphasizes support services rather than taking orders

missionary salesperson
/'mɪʃ(ə)n(ə)ri ,seɪlzpɜrs(ə)n/ *noun* a
salesperson who approaches a new market with a product

missionary selling /'mɪʃ(ə)n(ə)ri
ˌselɪŋ/ *noun* the act of approaching new
customers with a product ○ *We have
never sold there before, so be prepared
for missionary selling.* ○ *Some sales
reps are not aggressive enough for missionary selling.*

mission statement /'mɪʃ(ə)n
ˌsteɪtmənt/ *noun* a short statement of
the reasons for the existence of an organization

mix /mɪks/ *noun* an arrangement of
different things together

mixed /mɪkst/ *adjective* made up of
different sorts or of different types of
things together

mixed economy /,mɪkst ɪ'kɑnəmi/
noun a system which contains both nationalized industries and private enterprise

mixed media /,mɪkst 'midiə/ *plural
noun* various types of media used together in a promotional campaign

mnemonic /nɪ'mɑnɪk/ *noun* a word,
sentence, or little poem which helps you
remember something

mobile /'moʊbaɪl/ *adjective* which
can move about

mock-up /'mɑk ʌp/ *noun* the model
of a new product for testing or to show

to possible buyers ○ *The sales team were shown a mock-up of the new car.*

mode /moʊd/ *noun* a way of doing something □ **mode of payment** the way in which payment is made, e.g., cash or check

model /'mɑd(ə)l/ *noun* **1.** a small copy of something made to show what it will look like when finished ○ *They showed us a model of the new office building.* **2.** a style or type of product ○ *This is the latest model.* ○ *The model on display is last year's.* ○ *I drive a 2001 model Range Rover.* **3.** a person whose job is to wear new clothes to show them to possible buyers **4.** a description in the form of mathematical data ■ *adjective* which is a perfect example to be copied ○ *a model agreement* ■ *verb* to wear new clothes to show them to possible buyers ○ *She has decided on a career in modeling.* (NOTE: **modeling – modeled**)

modem /'moʊdem/ *noun* a device which links a computer to a telephone line, allowing data to be sent from one computer to another

modification /,mɑdɪfɪ'keɪʃ(ə)n/ *noun* a change ○ *The board wanted to make* or *to carry out modifications to the plan.* ○ *The new model has had several important modifications.* ○ *The client pressed for modifications to the contract.*

modified rebuy /,mɑdɪfaɪd 'ribaɪ/ *noun* a buying decision where either the product or the supplier has changed from the time of the previous purchase

modify /'mɑdɪfaɪ/ *verb* to change or to make something fit a different use ○ *The management modified its proposals.* ○ *This is the new modified agreement.* ○ *The car will have to be modified to pass the government tests.* ○ *The refrigerator was considerably modified before it went into production.* (NOTE: **modifies – modifying – modified**)

modular /'mɑdʒələr/ *adjective* made of various sections

mom-and-pop operation /,mɑm ən 'pɑp ɑpə,reɪʃ(ə)n/ *noun* a small business owned and run by a couple

monadic test /mɑ'nædɪk test/ *noun* a product test involving only one product

monetary /'mʌnɪt(ə)ri/ *adjective* referring to money or currency

monetary policy /,mʌnɪt(ə)ri 'pɑlɪsi/ *noun* the government's policy relating to finance, e.g., bank interest rates, taxes, government expenditure, and borrowing

monetary standard /,mʌnɪt(ə)ri 'stændəd/ *noun* a fixed exchange rate for a currency

money /'mʌni/ *noun* coins and bills used for buying and selling □ **to earn money** to have a wage or salary □ **to earn good money** to have a large wage or salary □ **to lose money** to make a loss, not to make a profit □ **the company has been losing money for months** the company has been working at a loss for months □ **to get your money back** to make enough profit to cover your original investment □ **to make money** to make a profit □ **to put money into the bank** to deposit money into a bank account □ **to put money into a business** to invest money in a business ○ *She put all her severance pay into a store.* □ **to put money down** to pay cash, especially as a deposit ○ *We put $25 down and paid the rest in installments.* □ **money up front** payment in advance ○ *They are asking for $10,000 up front before they will consider the deal.* ○ *He had to put money up front before he could clinch the deal.*

money-back guarantee /,mʌni 'bæk gærən,ti/, **money-back offer** /,mʌni 'bæk ,ɔfər/ *noun* a guarantee that money will be paid back to customers who are not satisfied with their purchases

money-making /'mʌni ,meɪkɪŋ/ *adjective* able to turn over a profit ○ *a money-making plan*

money-off coupon /,mʌni 'ɔf ,kupən/ *noun* a coupon in a newspaper or on a package which can be cut off and used to claim a discount on the next purchase

money order /ˈmʌni ˌɔrdər/ *noun* a document which can be bought as a way of sending money through the mail

money rates /ˈmʌni reɪts/ *plural noun* rates of interest for borrowers or lenders

money-spinner /ˈmʌni ˌspɪnər/ *noun* an item which sells very well or which is very profitable ○ *The home-delivery service has proved to be a real money-spinner.*

money supply /ˈmʌni səˌplaɪ/ *noun* the amount of money which exists in a country

monies /ˈmʌniz/ *plural noun* sums of money ○ *monies owing to the company* ○ *to collect monies due*

monopolist /məˈnɑpəlɪst/ *noun* a business which is the sole seller in a market

monopolistic competition /mənɑpəˌlɪstɪk ˌkɑmpəˈtɪʃ(ə)n/ *noun* a situation where there are only a few producers who therefore control the market between them ○ *With only three suppliers of cotton in the country it was a clear case of monopolistic competition.* Also called **imperfect competition**

monopolization /məˌnɑpəlaɪˈzeɪʃ(ə)n/ *noun* the process of making a monopoly

monopolize /məˈnɑpəlaɪz/ *verb* to create a monopoly or to get control of all the supply of a product

monopoly /məˈnɑpəli/ *noun* a situation where one person or company is the only supplier of a particular product or service ○ *to be in a monopoly situation* ○ *The company has the monopoly of imports of Brazilian wine.* ○ *The factory has the absolute monopoly of jobs in the town.*

monopoly profit /məˈnɑpəli ˌprɑfɪt/ *noun* profit earned by a business through having a monopoly

monopsonist /məˈnɑpsənɪst/ *noun* a sole buyer of a particular product or service

monopsony /məˈnɑpsəni/ *noun* a situation where there is only one buyer

for a particular product or service ○ *Monopsony gives the buyer leverage in demanding a low price.*

monthly /ˈmʌnθli/ *noun* a magazine which is published each month ○ *The vacations were advertised in all the monthlies.* (NOTE: The plural is **monthlies.**)

monthly sales report /ˌmʌnθli ˈseɪlz rɪˌpɔrt/ *noun* a report made every month showing the number of items sold or the amount of money a company has received for selling stock

morphological analysis /mɔrfə ˌlɑdʒɪk(ə)l əˈnæləsɪs/ *noun* a method of identifying the most profitable market segments by exploring various dimensions such as countries and market types

most favored nation /ˌmoʊst ˌfeɪvərd ˈneɪʃ(ə)n/ *noun* a foreign country to which the home country allows the best trade terms. Abbreviation **MFN**

motivate /ˈmoʊtɪveɪt/ *verb* to encourage someone to do something, especially to work or to sell □ **highly motivated sales staff** sales staff who are very eager to sell

motivation /ˌmoʊtɪˈveɪʃ(ə)n/ *noun* **1.** an encouragement to staff **2.** eagerness to work well or sell large quantities of a product □ **the sales staff lack motivation** the sales staff are not eager enough to sell

motivation research /ˌmoʊtɪ ˈveɪʃən rɪˌsɜrtʃ/, **motivational research** /moʊtɪˌveɪʃən(ə)l rɪˈsɜrtʃ/ *noun* research designed to find out the consumer's motives for purchasing a product or service

motive /ˈmoʊtɪv/ *noun* something that forces someone to take a particular action

move /muv/ *verb* to be sold, or to sell ○ *Over Christmas the stock hardly moved at all but with the January sales it is finally starting to sell.* ○ *The sales staff will have to work hard if they want to move all that stock by the end of the month.*

moving averages /ˌmuvɪŋ ˈæv(ə)rɪdʒɪz/ *plural noun* a method for working out averages while allowing for seasonal variations, in which the period under consideration is moved forward at regular intervals

multi- /mʌlti/ *prefix* referring to many things

multi-channel /ˌmʌltɪ ˈtʃæn(ə)l/ *adjective* using both online and offline methods of communication to do business

multi-channel system /ˈmʌltɪ ˌtʃæn(ə)l ˌsɪstəm/ *noun* a distribution system used by a producer which makes use of more than one distribution channel

multi-dimensional scaling /ˌmʌltɪ daɪˌmenʃ(ə)nəl ˈskeɪlɪŋ/ *noun* a method of carrying out market research, in which the respondents are given a scale (usually 1 to 5) on which they base their replies

multilateral /ˌmʌltiˈlæt(ə)rəl/ *adjective* between several organizations or countries ○ *a multilateral agreement* □ **multilateral trade** trade between several countries

multilevel marketing /mʌltɪ ˈlev(ə)l ˌmɑrkətɪŋ/ *noun* same as **network marketing**

multimagazine deal /ˌmʌltɪ ˈmæɡəzin ˌdil/ *plural noun* a deal where different publishers offer advertisers the opportunity to buy space in their magazines at the same time

multimedia /ˌmʌltiˈmidiə/ *adjective* referring to several media used in a project ○ *We are going for an all-out multimedia advertising campaign.*

multimedia document /ˌmʌltɪ ˈmidiə ˌdɑkjəmənt/ *noun* an electronic document that contains interactive material from a range of different media such as text, video, sound, graphics, and animation

multinational /ˌmʌltiˈnæʃ(ə)nəl/ *noun, adjective* (a company) which has branches or subsidiary companies in several countries ○ *The company has been bought by one of the big multinationals.* Also called **transnational**

multi-pack offer /ˈmʌlti pæk ˌɔfər/ *noun* a special promotional offer in which an extra pack is offered free, or at a reduced price, for each pack bought at full price

multiple /ˈmʌltɪp(ə)l/ *adjective* many ■ *noun* a company with stores in several different towns

multiple choice question /ˌmʌltɪp(ə)l ˈtʃɔɪs ˌkwetʃən/ *noun* a type of question used in a survey which allows the respondent to choose a single answer from several possible ones ○ *The questionnaire had eight multiple choice questions, two dichotomous questions, and one open question.*

multiple correlation /ˌmʌltɪp(ə)l kɑrəˈleɪʃ(ə)n/ *noun* a method for measuring the effect of several independent variables on one dependent variable

multiple discriminant analysis /ˌmʌltɪp(ə)l dɪˈskrɪmɪnənt əˌnæləsɪs/ *noun* a method for assessing products by separating out their various attributes, and estimating the relative values of these attributes to different market segments. The whole process produces an assessment of the general potential of a product.

multiple pricing /ˌmʌltɪp(ə)l ˈpraɪsɪŋ/ *noun* the practice of fixing the same price for several different products

multiple regression analysis /ˌmʌltɪp(ə)l rɪˈɡreʃ(ə)n əˌnæləsɪs/ *noun* a method for discovering the relationship between several independent variables and one dependent variable

multiple store /ˈmʌltɪp(ə)l stɔr/ *noun* one store in a chain of stores

multiplexing /ˈmʌltɪpleksɪŋ/ *noun* an arrangement where several TV channels are transmitted by one cable network, or where several messages are combined in the same transmission medium

multi-stage sample /mʌlti ˌsteɪdʒ ˈsɑrmpəl/ *noun* a sample selected by ensuring equal proportions of various categories existing in the population and then using random sampling to select respondents within these categories

multitasking /'mʌlti,tæskɪŋ/ *noun* the action of performing several different tasks at the same time

mystery /'mɪst(ə)ri/ *noun* something which cannot be explained

mystery shopper /'mɪst(ə)ri ,ʃɑpər/ *noun* a person employed by a market-research company to visit stores anonymously to test the quality of service

mystery shopping /'mɪst(ə)ri ,ʃɑpɪŋ/ *noun* shopping done by anonymous employees of a market-research company to test staff reactions, etc.

N

N *abbreviation* naira

name /neɪm/ *noun* the word used for referring to a person, animal, or thing ○ *I cannot remember the name of the managing director of Smith Inc.* ○ *His first name is John, but I am not sure of his other names.* □ **under the name of** using a particular name □ **trading under the name of "Best Foods"** using the name "Best Foods" as a commercial name, and not the name of the company

named /neɪmd/ *adjective* □ **the person named in the policy** the person whose name is given on an insurance policy as the person insured

narrowcasting /ˈnærəʊkɑːstɪŋ/ *noun* the act of reaching only a small special audience through an electronic medium such as cable television

nation /ˈneɪʃ(ə)n/ *noun* a country and the people living in it

national /ˈnæʃ(ə)nəl/ *adjective* referring to the whole of a particular country □ **national advertising** advertising in every part of a country, not just in the capital ○ *We took national advertising to promote our new 24-hour delivery service.* □ **national campaign** a sales or publicity campaign in every part of a country

national account /ˌnæʃ(ə)nəl ə ˈkaʊnt/ *noun* a customer with branches or offices all over the country

national advertiser /ˌnæʃ(ə)nəl ˈædvərtaɪzər/ *noun* a company that advertises in every part of a country, not just in the capital city

national brand /ˈnæʃ(ə)nəl brænd/ *noun* a brand which is recognized throughout a whole country, not just in a local area

National Debt /ˌnæʃ(ə)nəl ˈdet/ *noun* money borrowed by a government

national income /ˌnæʃ(ə)nəl ˈɪnkʌm/ *noun* the value of income from the sales of goods and services in a country

nationalization /ˌnæʃ(ə)nəlaɪ ˈzeɪʃ(ə)n/ *noun* the taking over of private industry by the state

national launch /ˌnæʃ(ə)nəl ˈlɔːntʃ/ *noun* a launch of a product over the whole country at the same time, as opposed to launching it in some areas only

national newspaper /ˌnæʃ(ə)nəl ˈnuːzpeɪpər/ *noun* a newspaper which is sold throughout a whole country and carries national and international news

national press /ˌnæʃ(ə)nəl ˈpres/ *noun* newspapers which sell in all parts of the country ○ *The new car has been advertised in the national press.*

national retailer /ˌnæʃ(ə)nəl ˈriteɪlər/ *noun* a retailing company which has branches throughout a country

nationwide /ˈneɪʃənwaɪd/ *adjective* all over a country ○ *We offer a nationwide delivery service.* ○ *The new car is being launched with a nationwide sales campaign.*

natural /ˈnætʃ(ə)rəl/ *adjective* **1.** found in the earth ○ *The offices are heated by natural gas.* **2.** not made by people ○ *They use only natural fibers for their best cloths.* **3.** normal ○ *It was only natural that the storekeeper should feel annoyed when the hypermarket was built close to his store.* ○ *It was natural for the workers to feel aggrieved when production methods were changed without consultation.*

natural break /ˌnætʃ(ə)rəl 'breɪk/ *noun* a convenient or reasonable point in a TV program for a commercial break

natural resources /ˌnætʃ(ə)rəl rɪ'zɔːsɪz/ *plural noun* raw materials which are found in the earth, e.g., coal, gas, or iron

navigation /ˌnævɪ'geɪʃ(ə)n/ *noun* the action of guiding and steering, in particular the graphics which lead users to different websites

necessity /nə'sesəti/ *noun* something which is vitally important, without which nothing can be done or no one can survive ○ *Being unemployed makes it difficult to afford even the basic necessities.* (NOTE: The plural is **necessities**.)

necessity product /nə'sesəti ˌprɒdʌkt/ *noun* an ordinary everyday product which consumers tend not to buy much more of as their incomes rise ○ *Consumers find shopping for necessity products boring.* ○ *Fancy packaging will not increase sales of necessity products.*

negative /'negətɪv/ *adjective* meaning "no" □ **the answer was in the negative** the answer was "no"

negative cash flow /ˌnegətɪv 'kæʃ fləʊ/ *noun* a situation where more money is going out of a company than is coming in

negative demand /ˌnegətɪv dɪ'mænd/ *noun* firm decisions by consumers not to buy a particular product ○ *Negative demand was due to offensive advertising.*

negative variance /ˌnegətɪv 'veriəns/ *noun* a difference between a financial plan and its outcome that means a less favorable profit than expected ○ *The unexpected increase in raw material prices meant a negative variance of $5,000.* ○ *A sudden fall in revenue resulted in a negative variance for the year as a whole.*

negotiable /nɪ'goʊʃiəb(ə)l/ *adjective* transferable from one person to another or exchanged for cash □ **not negotiable** which cannot be exchanged for cash □ **"not negotiable"** words written on a check to show that it can be paid only to a specific person □ **negotiable cheque** a check made payable to bearer, i.e. to anyone who holds it

negotiable instrument /nɪˌgoʊʃiəb(ə)l 'ɪnstrʊmənt/ *noun* a document which can be exchanged for cash, e.g., a bill of exchange or a check

negotiable paper /nɪˌgoʊʃiəb(ə)l 'peɪpər/ *noun* a document which can be transferred from one owner to another for cash

negotiate /nɪ'goʊʃieɪt/ *verb* □ **to negotiate with someone** to discuss a problem or issue formally with someone, so as to reach an agreement ○ *The management refused to negotiate with the union.* □ **to negotiate terms and conditions** *or* **a contract** to discuss and agree upon the terms of a contract □ **he negotiated a $250,000 loan with the bank** he came to an agreement with the bank for a loan of $250,000

negotiated commission /nɪˌgoʊʃieɪtɪd kə'mɪʃ(ə)n/ *noun* a commission agreed with an advertising agency before work starts, and which may be different from standard commissions

negotiation /nɪˌgoʊʃi'eɪʃ(ə)n/ *noun* the discussion of terms and conditions in order to reach an agreement □ **contract under negotiation** a contract which is being discussed □ **a matter for negotiation** something which must be discussed before a decision is reached □ **to enter into** *or* **to start negotiations** to start discussing a problem □ **to resume negotiations** to start discussing a problem again, after talks have stopped for a time □ **to break off negotiations** to stop discussing a problem □ **to conduct negotiations** to negotiate □ **negotiations broke down after six hours** discussions stopped because no agreement was possible

negotiator /nɪ'goʊʃieɪtər/ *noun* **1.** a person who discusses a problem with the aim of achieving agreement between different people or groups of people **2.** a person who works in an estate agency

nester /'nestər/ *noun* a person who has left the family home and is buying his or her own home

net /net/ *adjective* referring to a price, weight, pay, etc., after all deductions have been made ■ *verb* to make a true profit ○ *to net a profit of $10,000* (NOTE: **netting – netted**)

net assets /net 'æsets/ *plural noun* same as **net worth**

net cash flow /ˌnet 'kæʃ ˌfloʊ/ *noun* the difference between the money coming in and the money going out

net circulation /ˌnet ˌsɜrkjə 'leɪʃ(ə)n/ *noun* the total sales figure of a publication after adjusting for error and discounting unsold copies

net cover /net 'kʌvər/ *noun* the proportion of a target audience exposed to an advertisement at least once

Net imperative /ˌnet ɪm'perətɪv/ *noun* the idea that an ability to use the Internet for business purposes is vital for organizations that wish to be successful in the future

net loss /ˌnet 'lɑs/ *noun* an actual loss, after deducting overheads

net margin /ˌnet 'mɑrdʒɪn/ *noun* the percentage difference between received price and all costs, including overheads

net names /net 'neɪmz/ *plural noun* the names left in a mailing list after a merge-purge has removed the duplicate entries

net national product /ˌnet ˌnæʃ(ə)nəl 'prɑdʌkt/ *noun* the gross national product less investment on capital goods and depreciation. Abbreviation **NNP**

net price /ˌnet 'praɪs/ *noun* the price of goods or services which cannot be reduced by a discount

net profit /ˌnet 'prɑfɪt/ *noun* the amount by which income from sales is larger than all expenditure. Also called **profit after tax**

net reach /net 'ritʃ/ *noun* the total number of people who have seen an advertisement at least once

net receipts /ˌnet rɪ'sits/ *plural noun* receipts after deducting commission, tax, discounts, etc.

net sales /ˌnet 'seɪlz/ *plural noun* the total amount of sales less damaged or returned items and discounts to retailers

net weight /ˌnet 'weɪt/ *noun* the weight of goods after deducting the packing material and container

network /'netwɜrk/ *noun* a system which links different points together ■ *verb* to link together in a network □ **to network a television programme** to send out the same television program through several TV stations

network analysis /'netwɜrk ə ˌnæləsɪs/ *noun* an analysis of a project that charts the individual activities involved, each with the time needed for its completion, so that the timing of the whole can be planned and controlled

networked system /ˌnetwɜrkt 'sɪstəm/ *noun* a computer system where several PCs are linked together so that they all draw on the same database or use the same server

networking /'netwɜrkɪŋ/ *noun* the practice of keeping in contact with former colleagues, school friends, etc., so that all the members of the group can help each other in their careers

network marketing /'netwɜrk ˌmɑrkətɪŋ/ *noun* a marketing campaign carried out through a complete magazine network

network programming /ˌnetwɜrk 'proʊgræmɪŋ/ *noun* the practice of scheduling TV programs over the whole network

network society /'netwɜrk sə ˌsaɪəti/ *noun* a society that regularly uses global networks for the purposes of work, communication, and government

net worth /ˌnet 'wɜrθ/ *noun* the value of all the property of a person or company after taking away what the person or company owes ○ *The upmarket product is targeted at individuals of high net worth.*

net yield /ˌnet 'jild/ *noun* the profit from investments after deduction of tax

neural network /ˌnʊrəl 'netwɜrk/ *noun* a computer system designed to imitate the nerve patterns of the human brain

neurolinguistic programming /ˌnʊroʊlɪŋɡwɪstɪk 'proʊɡræmɪŋ/ *noun* a theory of behavior and communication based on how people avoid change and how to help them to change. Abbreviation **NLP**

never-never /ˌnevə 'nevər/ *noun* U.K. buying on credit (*informal*) ○ *She bought her car on the never-never.*

new /nu/ *adjective* recent or not old

new buy /ˌnu 'baɪ/ *noun* a type of organizational buying in which a completely new product is bought

new entrant /ˌnu 'entrənt/ *noun* a company which is going into a market for the first time

new issues department /nu 'ɪʃuz dɪˌpɑrtmənt/ *noun* the section of a bank which deals with issues of new shares

new product committee /nu 'prɑdʌkt kəˌməti/ *noun* a group of people from different departments in a company who work together on a new product development project ○ *The new product committee met regularly to monitor the progress in the product's development.*

new product development /ˌnju 'prɑdʌkt dɪˌveləpmənt/ *noun* the process of developing completely new products or improving existing ones ○ *The company fell behind because it failed to invest enough in new product development.* Abbreviation **NPD**

news /nuz/ *noun* information about things which have happened ○ *She always reads the business news* or *financial news first in the paper.* ○ *Financial markets were shocked by the news of the devaluation.*

news agency /'nuz ˌeɪdʒənsi/ *noun* an office which distributes news to newspapers and television stations

new season /nu 'siz(ə)n/ *noun* the start of the TV "year," usually taken to be the fall and winter programming season

newsletter /'nuzletər/ *noun* □ **company newsletter** a printed sheet or small newspaper giving news about a company

newspaper /'nuzpeɪpər/ *noun* a regular publication, usually daily or weekly, which gives items of general news, sold to the general public

news release /'nuz rɪˌlis/ *noun* a sheet giving information about a new event which is sent to newspapers and TV and radio stations so that they can use it ○ *The company sent out a news release about the new product launch.*

news stand /'nuz stænd/ *noun* a small wooden store on a sidewalk, for selling newspapers

new technology /ˌnu tek'nɑlədʒi/ *noun* electronic devices which have recently been invented

next matter /'nekst ˌmætər/, **next-to-reading matter** /ˌnekst tə 'ridɪŋ ˌmætər/ *noun* advertising material placed next to editorial matter in a publication

niche /nɪtʃ/ *noun* a special place in a market, occupied by one company (a "niche company") ○ *They seem to have discovered a niche in the market.*

niche market /ˌnɪtʃ 'mɑrkət/ *noun* a small specialty market, where there is little competition

niche marketing /ˌnɪtʃ 'mɑrkətɪŋ/ *noun* the promotion of a product aimed at one particular area of the market. ◊ **concentrated marketing**

Nielsen Index /'nilsən ˌɪndeks/ *noun* an American publication belonging to A.C. Nielsen, with a number of different retail and wholesale audit services referring to various types of outlet and different areas of the country

night rate /'naɪt reɪt/ *noun* a cheap rate for telephone calls at night

nixies /'nɪksiz/ *plural noun* (*informal*) **1.** records that do not match a file correctly **2.** mail returned as unable to be delivered

NLP *abbreviation* neurolinguistic programming

no-change discount /noʊ 'tʃeɪndʒ ˌdɪskaʊnt/ *noun* a reduction in the price of an advertisement which uses the same artwork as a previous one

noise /nɔɪz/ *noun* a random signal present in addition to any wanted signal, caused by static, temperature, power supply, magnetic or electric fields, and also from stars and the sun

noise level /'nɔɪz ˌlev(ə)l/ *noun* the amount of unwanted information found when searching the Internet

nominal ledger /ˌnamɪn(ə)l 'ledʒər/ *noun* a book which records a company's transactions in the various accounts

nominal value /ˌnamɪn(ə)l 'vælju/ *noun* same as **face value**

non- /nɑn/ *prefix* not

non-acceptance /ˌnɑn ək'septəns/ *noun* a situation in which the person who is to pay a bill of exchange does not accept it

non-business organization /nɑn ˌbɪznɪs ˌɔrgənaɪ'zeɪʃ(ə)n/ *noun* an organization (such as a club) which is not allowed by law to make a profit ○ *Though only a non-business organization, the charity used highly sophisticated marketing techniques.* ○ *He became a fundraiser for a non-business organization.*

non-delivery /ˌnɑn dɪ'lɪv(ə)ri/ *noun* the failure to deliver goods that have been ordered

non-directive interview /nɑn daɪ'rektɪv ˌɪntərvju/, **non-directed interview** /nɑn daɪ'rektɪd ˌɪntərvju/ *noun* an interview in which the questions are not set in advance and no fixed pattern is followed ○ *Non-directed interviews give candidates a good chance to show their creative potential.*

non-durables /ˌnɑn 'djʊrəb(ə)lz/, **non-durable goods** /ˌnɑn 'djʊrəb(ə)l gʊdz/ *plural noun* goods which are used up soon after they have been bought, e.g., food or newspapers

non-franchise-building promotion /nɑn ˌfræntʃaɪz ˌbɪldɪŋ prə'moʊʃ(ə)n/ *noun* sales promotion aimed at increasing sales in the short term, without increasing customer loyalty or repeat sales

nonnegotiable instrument /ˌnɑnnɪˌgoʊʃəb(ə)l 'ɪnstrʊmənt/ *noun* a document which cannot be exchanged for cash, e.g., a crossed check

non-payment /ˌnɑn 'peɪmənt/ *noun* □ **non-payment of a debt** the act of not paying a debt that is due

non-personal /ˌnɑn 'pɜrs(ə)n(ə)l/ *adjective* which does to apply to an individual person

non-personal channels /nɑn ˌpɜrs(ə)n(ə)l 'tʃæn(ə)lz/ *plural noun* channels that carry a message without involving any contact between the advertiser and an individual customer

non-price competition /ˌnɑn 'praɪs kɑmpəˌtɪʃ(ə)n/ *noun* an attempt to compete in a market through other means than price such as quality of product and promotion

nonprofit organization /ˌnɑn ˌprɑfɪtmeɪkɪŋ ˌɔrgənaɪ'zeɪʃən/, **nonprofit organization** /nɑn 'prɑfɪt ɔrgənaɪˌzeɪʃ(ə)n/ *noun* an organization which is not allowed by law to make a profit ○ *Nonprofitmaking organizations are exempted from tax.* (NOTE: Nonprofit organizations include charities, professional associations, labor unions, and religious, arts, community, research, and campaigning bodies.)

non-refundable /ˌnɑn rɪ'fʌndəb(ə)l/ *adjective* not possible to refund ○ *You will be asked to make a non-refundable deposit.*

non-returnable /ˌnɑn rɪ'tɜrnəb(ə)l/ *adjective* which cannot be returned

non-returnable packing /nɑn rɪˌtɜrnəb(ə)l 'pækɪŋ/ *noun* packing which is to be thrown away when it has been used and not returned to the sender

non-statistical error /nɑn stəˌtɪstɪk(ə)l 'erər/ *noun* a distortion of the results of a survey owing to bias and mistakes made in conducting the survey

non-store retailing /ˌnɑn stɔr 'riteɪlɪŋ/ *noun* the selling of goods and services electronically without setting up a physical store

non-tariff barriers /ˌnɑn ˌtærɪf ˈbæriərz/ *noun* barriers to international trade other than tariffs. They include over-complicated documentation; verification of goods for health and safety reasons and blocked deposits payable by importers to obtain foreign currency. Abbreviation **NTBs**

non-traditional media /ˌnɑn trə ˌdɪʃ(ə)n(ə)l ˈmidiə/ *noun* ♦ **support media**

non-verbal communication /nɑn ˌvɜrb(ə)l kəˌmjunɪˈkeɪʃ(ə)n/ *noun* any form of communication that is not expressed in words (NOTE: Non-verbal communication, which includes, for example, body language, silence, failure or slowness to respond to a message, and lateness in arriving for a meeting, is estimated to make up 65–90% of all communication.)

non-virtual hosting /ˌnɑn ˌvɜrtjuəl ˈhoʊstɪŋ/ *noun* the most basic type of hosting option, often provided free, in which clients do not have their own domain names, but attach their names to the web address of the hosting company (NOTE: This hosting option is only suitable for small companies and has the disadvantage that clients cannot change their hosting company without changing their web address.)

no returns policy /noʊ rɪˈtɜrnz ˌpɑlɪsi/ *noun* a trading policy where the supplier will not take back unsold merchandise in exchange for credit, and in return allows the retailer an extra discount

normal /ˈnɔrm(ə)l/ *adjective* usual or which happens regularly ○ *Normal deliveries are made on Tuesdays and Fridays.* ○ *Now that supply difficulties have been resolved we hope to resume normal service as soon as possible.* □ **under normal conditions** if things work in the usual way ○ *Under normal conditions a package takes ten days to get to Copenhagen.*

normal distribution /ˌnɔrm(ə)l ˌdɪstrɪˈbjuʃ(ə)n/ *noun* a term used in sampling theory, referring to the results of a sample and meaning a symmetrical distribution of values around a mean or average, so that you can be confident that the sample is properly representative of the people being surveyed in a study

normal price /ˌnɔrm(ə)l ˈpraɪs/ *noun* the price that can be expected for a product under normal market conditions

normal product /ˌnɔrm(ə)l ˈprɑdʌkt/ *noun* a product which people buy more of as their incomes rise and less of as their incomes fall

normal profit /ˌnɔrm(ə)l ˈprɑfɪt/ *noun* a minimum profit that can motivate a business to carry on a type of production or selling

note /noʊt/ *noun* a short document or piece of writing, or a short piece of information ○ *to send someone a note* ○ *I left a note on her desk.* ■ *verb* to notice an advertisement in a publication but not necessarily read or understand it

notice /ˈnoʊtɪs/ *noun* **1.** an official warning that a contract is going to end or that terms are going to be changed □ **until further notice** until different instructions are given ○ *You must pay $200 on the 30th of each month until further notice.* **2.** the time allowed before something takes place ○ *We require three months' notice* □ **at short notice** with very little warning ○ *The bank manager will not see anyone at short notice.* □ **you must give seven days' notice of withdrawal** you must ask to take money out of the account seven days before you want it

noticeboard /ˈnoʊtɪsbɔrd/ *noun* U.K. same as **bulletin board** ○ *Did you see the new list of prices on the noticeboard?*

noting /ˈnoʊtɪŋ/ *noun* the act of noticing, though not necessarily reading and understanding, an advertisement in a publication

noting score /ˈnoʊtɪŋ skɔr/ *noun* the percentage of total readers who note an advertisement ○ *The amount of advertising we will need to do depends on the anticipated noting score.*

novelty /ˈnɑv(ə)lti/ *noun* an original amusing article which is often bought as a gift ○ *A novelty store provided paper hats for parties.*

NPD *abbreviation* new product development

NTBs *abbreviation* non-tariff barriers

null /nʌl/ *adjective* **1.** with no meaning **2.** which cannot legally be enforced □ **the contract was declared null and void** the contract was said to be not valid □ **to render a decision null** to make a decision useless or to cancel it

nullification /ˌnʌlɪfɪˈkeɪʃ(ə)n/ *noun* an act of making something invalid

nullify /ˈnʌlɪfaɪ/ *verb* to make something invalid or to cancel something (NOTE: **nullifying- nullified**)

numeric /nuˈmerɪk/, **numerical** /nuˈmerɪk(ə)l/ *adjective* referring to numbers

numeric data /nuˌmerɪk ˈdeɪtə/ *noun* data in the form of figures

numeric keypad /nuˌmerɪk ˈkipæd/ *noun* the part of a computer keyboard which is a programmable set of numbered keys

O

O & M *abbreviation* organization and methods

objective /əbˈdʒektɪv/ *noun* something which you hope to achieve ○ *The company has achieved its objectives.* ○ *We set the sales forces specific objectives.* ■ *adjective* considered from a general point of view rather than from that of the person involved ○ *You must be objective in assessing the performance of the staff.* ○ *They have been asked to carry out an objective survey of the market.*

objective and task method /əb ˌdʒektɪv ən ˈtæsk ˌmeθəd/ *noun* a method of calculating an advertising appropriation by setting objectives, deciding what tasks are needed to achieve them and then calculating the actual costs involved

obligation /ˌɑblɪˈɡeɪʃ(ə)n/ *noun* **1.** a duty to do something ○ *There is no obligation to help out in another department* ○ *There is no obligation to buy.* □ **two weeks' free trial without obligation** the customer can try the item at home for two weeks without having to buy it at the end of the test □ **to be under an obligation to do something** to feel it is your duty to do something □ **he is under no contractual obligation to buy** he has signed no contract which forces him to buy **2.** a debt □ **to meet your obligations** to pay your debts

observation method /ˌɑbzər ˈveɪʃən ˌmeθəd/, **observational research** /ˌɑbzəˌveɪʃ(ə)n(ə)l rɪˈsɜrtʃ/ *noun* a market research method that obtains information through personal observation, rather than interviews ○ *The observation method does not tell you*

anything about the consumers' attitudes to the product.

obsolescence /ˌɑbsəˈles(ə)ns/ *noun* the process of a product going out of date because of progress in design or technology, and therefore becoming less useful or valuable

obsolescent /ˌɑbsəˈles(ə)nt/ *adjective* becoming out of date

obsolete /ˌɑbsəˈlit/ *adjective* no longer used ○ *Computer technology changes so fast that hardware soon becomes obsolete.*

odd /ɑd/ *adjective* one of a group □ **we have a few odd boxes left** we have a few boxes left out of the total shipment □ **to do odd jobs** to do various pieces of work

odd-even pricing /ˌɑd ˈiv(ə)n ˌpraɪsɪŋ/ *noun* the practice of using odd numbers such as 0.95 or 0.99 or even numbers such as 1.00 or 2.50 when pricing, because this seems to be most effective psychologically in persuading customers to buy ○ *Students can study the psychological bases of odd-even pricing.*

odd lot /ˌɑd ˈlɑt/ *noun* a group of miscellaneous items for sale at an auction

oddments /ˈɑdmənts/ *plural noun* **1.** items left over **2.** left-over pieces of large items, sold separately

odd number /ˌɑd ˈnʌmbər/ *noun* a number which cannot be divided by two, e.g., 17 or 33 ○ *Buildings with odd numbers are on the south side of the street*

odd size /ˌɑd ˈsaɪz/ *noun* a size which is not usual

off /ɔf/ *adjective* not working or not in operation ○ *to take three days off* ○ *The* *agreement is off.* ○ *They called the strike off.* ○ *We give the staff four days off at Christmas.* ○ *It's my day off tomorrow.* ■ *adverb* lower than a previous price ○ *The shares closed 2% off.* ■ *preposition* subtracted from ○ *to take $25 off the price* ○ *We give 10% off our usual prices.*

off-card rate /ˌɒf 'kɑrd ˌreɪt/ *noun* a specially arranged price, lower than that on the rate card, for advertising space or time ○ *The newspaper offered us an off-card rate for space which was still empty the day before publication.*

offensive spending /əˌfensɪv 'spendɪŋ/ *noun* spending on advertising which aims to attract users of a rival brand or to attack the competition

offer /'ɒfər/ *noun* **1.** a statement that you are willing to give or do something, especially to pay a specific amount of money to buy something ○ *to make an offer for a company* ○ *We made an offer of $10 a share.* ○ *We made a written offer for the house.* ○ *$1,000 is the best offer I can make.* ○ *We accepted an offer of $1,000 for the car.* □ **the house is under offer** someone has made an offer to buy the house and the offer has been accepted provisionally □ **we are open to offers** we are ready to discuss the price which we are asking □ **or near offer, or best offer** or an offer of a price which is slightly less than the price asked ○ *The car is for sale at $2,000 or near offer.* **2.** a statement that you are willing to sell something □ **offer for sale** a situation where a company advertises new shares for sale to the public as a way of launching the company on the Stock Exchange. The other ways of launching a company are a "tender" or a "placing." **3.** a statement that you are willing to employ someone □ **she received six offers of jobs** *or* **six job offers** six companies told her she could have a job with them ■ *verb* **1.** to say that you are willing to pay a specific amount of money for something ○ *to offer someone $100,000 for their house* ○ *She offered $10 a share.* **2.** to say that you are willing to sell something ○ *We offered the house for sale.* ○ *They are offering spe-*

cial prices on winter vacations in Europe.

office park /'bɪznɪs pɑrk/ *noun* a group of small factories or warehouses, especially near a town ○ *He has rented a unit in the local office park.*

official receiver /əˌfɪʃ(ə)l rɪ'siːvər/ *noun* a government official who is appointed to run a company which is in financial difficulties, to pay off its debts as far as possible and to close it down ○ *The company is in the hands of the official receiver.*

off-licence /'ɒf ˌlaɪs(ə)ns/ *noun U.K.* **1.** same as **liquor store 2.** a license to sell alcohol for drinking away from the place where you buy it

offline /ˌɒf 'laɪn/ *adverb* not connected to a network or central computer

offload /ɒf'loʊd/ *verb* to pass something which you do not want to someone else □ **to offload excess stock** to try to sell excess inventory □ **to offload costs onto a subsidiary company** to try to get a subsidiary company to pay some charges so as to reduce tax

off-peak /ˌɒf 'piːk/ *adjective* not during the most busy time

off-peak period /ɒf 'piːk ˌpɪriəd/ *noun* the time when business is less busy

off-price label /ɒf 'praɪs ˌleɪb(ə)l/ *noun* a label on a product which shows a reduced price

off-season /'ɒf ˌsiːz(ə)n/ *noun* the less busy season for travel, usually during the winter ○ *Air fares are cheaper in the off-season.*

offset /'ɒfset/ *noun* a method of printing from a plate to a rubber surface and then to paper

offset lithography /ˌɒfset lɪ'θɑgrəfi/ *noun* a printing process used for printing books, where the ink sticks to image areas on the plate and is transferred to an offset cylinder from which it is printed on to the paper

off-the-page buying /ˌɒf ðə 'peɪdʒ ˌbaɪɪŋ/ *noun* the buying of items which have been advertised in magazines or newspapers

off-the-rack /ˌɔf ðə ˈræk/ *adjective, adverb* ready made in standard sizes, and not fitted specially ○ *She buys all her clothes off-the-rack.*

off-the-rack research /ˌɔf ðə ræk rɪˈsɜrtʃ/ *noun* the practice of taking research which has already been carried out in another context, and using it as the basis for taking particular decisions

oil-exporting country /ˈɔɪl ɪkˌspɔrtɪŋ ˌkʌntri/ *noun* a country which produces oil and sells it to others

oligopoly /ˌɑlɪˈɡɑpəli/ *noun* a situation where only a few sellers control the market ○ *An oligopoly means that prices can be kept high.*

oligopsony /ˌɑlɪˈɡɑpsəni/ *noun* a situation where only a few buyers control the market

omnibus advertisement /ˈɑmnɪbəs ədˌvɜrtɪsmənt/ *noun* an advertisement which covers several different products

omnibus agreement /ˈɑmnɪbəs əˌɡrimənt/ *noun* an agreement which covers many different items

omnibus research /ˈɑmnɪbəs rɪˌsɜrtʃ/, **omnibus survey** /ˈɑmnɪbəs ˌsɜrveɪ/ *noun* a survey to which several companies subscribe, each adding specific questions of its own

oncosts /ˈɑnkɔsts/ *plural noun* money spent in producing a product, which does not rise with the quantity of the product made. Also called **fixed costs**

one-sided /ˌwʌn ˈsaɪdɪd/ *adjective* favoring one side and not the other in a negotiation

one-sided message /wʌn ˌsaɪdɪd ˈmesɪdʒ/ *noun* a message which only gives the benefits of a product or service

one-step approach /ˌwʌn step ə ˈproʊtʃ/ *noun* a form of direct marketing where advertisements are used to obtain orders directly

one-stop /ˈwʌn stɑp/ *adjective* offering a wide range of services to a customer, not necessarily services which are related to the product or services which the company normally sells

one-stop shopping center /ˌwʌn stɑp ˈʃɑpɪŋ ˌsentər/ *noun* a shopping center with a comprehensive choice of stores and supermarkets, designed to cover all of a customer's shopping needs

one-time order /ˌwʌn taɪm ˈɔrdər/ *noun* an order for an advertising spot for a particular time which is not scheduled to be repeated

one-time rate /wʌn ˈtaɪm reɪt/ *noun* a special rate for an advertisement that is only placed once

one-to-one /ˌwʌn tə ˈwʌn/ *adjective* where one person has to deal with one other person only

one-to-one marketing /ˌwʌn tə wʌn ˈmɑrkətɪŋ/ *noun* marketing through a website which aims to establish a personal relationship with a customer, selling to each customer as an individual and trying to differentiate between customers

on-hold advertising /ɑn ˈhoʊld ˌædvərtaɪzɪŋ/ *noun* advertising to telephone callers while they are waiting to be connected to the person they want to speak to, usually involving voice messages about the firm and its products

online /ɑnˈlaɪn/; /ˈɑnlaɪn/ *adjective, adverb* linked via a computer directly to another computer, a computer network or, especially, the Internet; on the Internet ○ *The sales office is online to the warehouse.* ○ *We get our data online from the stock control department.*

online community /ɑnˌlaɪn kəˈmjuniti/ *noun* a network of people who communicate with one another and with an organization through interactive tools such as e-mail, discussion boards and chat systems

online shopping /ˌɑnlaɪn ˈʃɑpɪŋ/ *noun* same as **electronic shopping**

online shopping mall /ˌɑnlaɪn ˈʃɑpɪŋ mɔl/ *noun* same as **cyber mall**

on-pack promotion /ɑn ˈpæk prəˌmoʊʃ(ə)n/ *noun* advertising material on the outside of packaged goods ○ *We use on-pack promotion to stimulate buying at the point-of-sale.* ○ *Our on-pack promotion is designed to complement the TV advertising campaign.*

op-ed /ˌɑp 'ed/ *noun* in a newspaper, a page that has signed articles expressing personal opinions, usually found opposite the editorial page

open /'oʊpən/ *adjective* ready to accept something □ **the job is open to all applicants** anyone can apply for the job □ **open to offers** ready to accept a reasonable offer □ **the company is open to offers for the empty factory** the company is ready to discuss an offer which is lower than the suggested price ∎ *verb* to start a new business ○ *She has opened a store on Main Street.* ○ *We have opened a branch in London.*

> **open up** *phrasal verb* □ **to open up new markets** to work to start business in markets where such business has not been done before

open account /ˌoʊpən ə'kaʊnt/ *noun* an account where the supplier offers the purchaser credit without security

open-air market /ˌoʊpən er 'mɑrkət/ *noun* a market which is held on stalls in the open air

open check /ˌoʊpən 'tʃek/ *noun* same as **uncrossed check**

open communication /ˌoʊpən kə-ˌmjunɪ'keɪʃ(ə)n/ *noun* a policy intended to ensure that employees are able to find out everything they want to know about their organization

open credit /ˌoʊpən 'kredɪt/ *noun* credit given to good customers without security

open dating /ˌoʊpən 'deɪtɪŋ/ *noun* the practice of putting the expiration date on a packet in an uncoded form which can be understood by the consumers ○ *Open dating is considered by many to be an important feature of consumer protection in food products.*

open-door policy /ˌoʊpən 'dɔr ˌpɑlɪsi/ *noun* a policy in which a country accepts imports from all other countries on equal terms

open-end /ˌoʊpən 'end/ *adjective* with no fixed limit or with some items not specified

open-ended /ˌoʊpən 'endɪd/ *adjective* with no fixed limit or with some items not specified ○ *They signed an open-ended agreement.* ○ *The candidate was offered an open-ended contract with a good career plan.* Same as **open-end**

open-ended question /ˌoʊpən endɪd 'kwestʃən/ *noun* a question in a questionnaire which allows respondents to answer in some detail as they like without having simply to say "yes" or "no" ○ *Open-ended questions elicit answers that are original but hard to evaluate.* ○ *An open-ended question is needed here, since the question involves the respondent's personal feelings.*

open general license /ˌoʊpən ˌdʒen(ə)rəl 'laɪs(ə)ns/ *noun* an import license for all goods which are subject to special import restrictions

opening /'oʊp(ə)nɪŋ/ *noun* **1.** the act of starting a new business ○ *the opening of a new branch* ○ *the opening of a new market* or *of a new distribution network* **2.** an opportunity to do something ∎ *adjective* being at the beginning, or the first of several

opening balance /'oʊp(ə)nɪŋ ˌbæləns/ *noun* a balance at the beginning of an accounting period

opening bid /ˌoʊp(ə)nɪŋ 'bɪd/ *noun* the first bid at an auction

opening entry /'oʊp(ə)nɪŋ ˌentri/ *noun* the first entry in an account

opening hours /'oʊp(ə)nɪŋ aʊrz/ *plural noun* the hours when a store or business is open

opening sentence /ˌoʊp(ə)nɪŋ 'sentəns/ *noun* the first sentence in an email

opening stock /ˌoʊp(ə)nɪŋ 'stɑk/ *noun U.K.* same as **beginning inventory**

open market /ˌoʊpən 'mɑrkət/ *noun* a market where anyone can buy or sell

open pricing /ˌoʊpən 'praɪsɪŋ/ *noun* the attempt by companies to achieve some cooperation and conformity in pricing ○ *Representatives from the major companies in the industry are meeting to establish an open-pricing policy.*

open rate /'oʊpən reɪt/ *noun* an advertising rate where discounts are available for frequent or bulk orders

open standard /,oʊpən 'stændəd/ *noun* a standard that allows computers and similar pieces of equipment made by different manufacturers to operate with each other

operant conditioning /'apərənt kən,dɪʃ(ə)nɪŋ/ *noun* a learning theory stating that behavior can be modified by stimuli and also by the consequences which follow on from the behavior itself. Also called **instrumental conditioning**

operate /'apəreɪt/ *verb* **1.** to be in force ○ *The new terms of service will operate from January 1st.* ○ *The rules operate on domestic postal services only.* **2.** to make something work or function □ **to operate a machine** to make a machine work ○ *He is learning to operate the new telephone switchboard.*

operating /'apəreɪtɪŋ/ *noun* the general running of a business or of a machine

operating budget /'apəreɪtɪŋ ,bʌdʒət/ *noun* a forecast of income and expenditure over a period of time

operating manual /'apəreɪtɪŋ ,mænjuəl/ *noun* a book which shows how to work a machine

operating statement /'apəreɪtɪŋ ,steɪtmənt/ *noun* a financial statement which shows a company's expenditure and income and consequently its final profit or loss ○ *The operating statement shows unexpected electricity costs.* ○ *Let's look at the operating statement to find last month's expenditure.*

operating supplies /'apəreɪtɪŋ sə ,plaɪz/ *plural noun* low-priced industrial products that are normally bought by producers ○ *Production came to a standstill for lack of operating supplies.* ○ *We are now ordering operating supplies for next month's production.*

operating system /'apəreɪtɪŋ ,sɪstəm/ *noun* the main program which operates a computer

operation /,apə'reɪʃ(ə)n/ *noun* an activity or a piece of work, or the task of running something ○ *the company's operations in West Africa* ○ *He heads up the operations in Northern Europe.*

operational /,apə'reɪʃ(ə)nəl/ *adjective* **1.** referring to the day-to-day activities of a business or to the way in which something is run **2.** working or in operation

operational budget /,apəreɪʃ(ə)nəl 'bʌdʒət/ *noun* a forecast of expenditure on running a business

operational costs /,apəreɪʃ(ə)nəl 'kɔsts/ *plural noun* the costs of running a business

operational planning /,apəreɪʃ(ə)nəl 'plænɪŋ/ *noun* the planning of how a business is to be run

operational research /,apəreɪʃ(ə)nəl rɪ'sɜrtʃ/ *noun* a study of a company's way of working to see if it can be made more efficient and profitable

operations review /,apəreɪʃ(ə)nz rɪ'vju/ *noun* an act of examining the way in which a company or department works to see how it can be made more efficient and profitable

opinion-former /ə'pɪnjən ,fɔrmər/, **opinion-leader** /ə'pɪnjən ,lidər/ *noun* someone well known whose opinions influence others in society ○ *A pop-star is the ideal opinion-leader if we are aiming at the teenage market.* ○ *The celebrity used in the sales promotion campaign was not respected enough to be a true opinion-former.*

opinion-leader research /ə ,pɪnjən lidər rɪ'sɜrtʃ/ *noun* research into the attitudes of opinion-leaders

opinion poll /ə'pɪnjən poʊl/ *noun* the activity of asking a sample group of people what their opinion is, so as to guess the opinion of the whole population ○ *Opinion polls showed that the public preferred butter to margarine.* ○ *Before starting the new service, the company carried out nationwide opinion polls.*

opinion shopping /ə'pɪnjən ,ʃapɪŋ/ *noun* the practice of trying to find an auditor who interprets the law in the same way that the company does, is likely to view the company's actions sympathetically, and will approve the company's financial statements, even if the company has been involved in dealings that other auditors might consider questionable

opportunities to see /ɑpər ˌtjunətiz tə ˈsi/ *plural noun* the number of opportunities an average member of the target audience will have to see an advertisement. Abbreviation **OTS**

opportunity /ˌɑpərˈtunəti/ *noun* a chance to do something successfully

opportunity and threat analysis /ɑpərˌtunəti ən ˈθret əˌnæləsɪs/ *noun* a company's analysis of both the advantages and disadvantages in its situation, done in order to ensure sound strategic planning

opportunity cost /ˌɑpərˈtjunɪtɪ kɔst/ *noun* the cost of a business initiative in terms of profits that could have been gained through an alternate plan ○ *It's a good investment plan and we will not be deterred by the opportunity cost.*

optimal /ˈɑptɪm(ə)l/ *adjective* best

optimal balance /ˌɑptɪm(ə)l ˈbæləns/ *noun* the best combination of elements or activities that can be achieved in a marketing mix ○ *If it achieves optimal balance the company will soon be a market leader.*

opt-in /ˈɑpt ɪn/ *noun* a method by which users can register with a website if they want to receive particular information or services from it. In opt-in, users must provide their e-mail addresses, so that the website owner can send them e-mails.

opt-in mailing list /ˌɑpt ɪn ˈmeɪlɪŋ lɪst/ *noun* a list of email addresses in which each recipient has specifically asked to receive advertising email messages, normally so that they can keep up to date with a topic or industry

option /ˈɑpʃən/ *noun* the opportunity to buy or sell something within a fixed period of time at a fixed price □ **to have first option on something** to have the right to be the first to have the possibili-

ty of deciding something □ **to grant someone a six-month option on a product** to allow someone six months to decide if they want to manufacture the product □ **to take up an option** *or* **to exercise an option** to accept the option which has been offered and to put it into action ○ *They exercised their option or they took up their option to acquire sole marketing rights to the product.* □ **I want to leave my options open** I want to be able to decide what to do when the time is right

optional /ˈɑpʃən(ə)l/ *adjective* able to be done or not done, taken or not taken, as a person chooses ○ *The insurance cover is optional.*

optional extra /ˌɑpʃən(ə)l ˈekstrə/ *noun* an item that is not essential but can be added if wanted

opt out /ˌɑpt ˈaʊt/ *noun* the action of asking not to receive advertising email messages and being removed from an email list

OR *abbreviation* operational research

orange goods /ˈɑrɪndʒ ɡʊdz/ *plural noun* goods which are not bought as often as fast-moving items but are replaced from time to time, e.g., clothing. Compare **red goods, yellow goods**

orbit /ˈɔrbɪt/ *noun* the practice of rotating advertisements among different programs on a TV station

order /ˈɔrdər/ *noun* **1.** an official request for goods to be supplied ○ *to give someone an order* or *to place an order with someone for twenty filing cabinets* □ **to fill an order, to fulfil an order** to supply items which have been ordered ○ *We are so understaffed we cannot fulfill anymore orders before Christmas.* □ **items available to order only** items which will be manufactured only if someone orders them □ **on order** ordered but not delivered ○ *This item is out of stock, but is on order.* **2.** an item which has been ordered ○ *The order is to be delivered to our warehouse.* **3.** an instruction **4.** a document which allows money to be paid to someone ○ *She sent us an order on the Bank of America.* **5.** □ **pay to Mr Smith or order** pay money to Mr. Smith or as he orders. □ **pay to**

the order of Mr Smith pay money directly to Mr. Smith or to his account. ■ *verb* **1.** to ask for goods to be supplied ○ *They ordered a new BMW for the managing director.* **2.** to give an official request for something to be done or for something to be supplied ○ *to order twenty filing cabinets to be delivered to the warehouse*

order book /ˈɔrdər bʊk/ *noun* a book which records orders received

order confirmation /ˈɔrdər kɑnf ˌmeɪʃ(ə)n/ *noun* an email message informing a purchaser that an order has been received

order form /ˈɔrdər fɔrm/ *noun* a pad of blank forms for orders to be written on

order fulfillment /ˈɔrdər fʊl ˌfɪlmənt/ *noun* the process of supplying items which have been ordered

order number /ˈɔrdər ˌnʌmbər/ *noun* the reference number printed on an order

order picking /ˈɔrdər ˌpɪkɪŋ/ *noun* the process of collecting various items in a warehouse in order to make up an order to be sent to a customer

order taking /ˈɔrdər ˌteɪkɪŋ/ *noun* the action of taking an order, the main responsibility of the salesperson

organization /ˌɔrgənaɪˈzeɪʃ(ə)n/ *noun* **1.** a way of arranging something so that it works efficiently ○ *the organization of the head office into departments* ○ *The chairman handles the organization of the AGM.* ○ *The organization of the group is too centralized to be efficient.* **2.** a group or institution which is arranged for efficient work

organizational buying /ˌɔrgənaɪ ˈzeɪʃ(ə)nəl ˌbaɪɪŋ/ *noun* buying by a large organization, such as a company or government department, as opposed to purchases by individual consumers

organizational chart /ˌɔrgənaɪ ˈzeɪʃ(ə)n(ə)l tʃɑrt/ *noun* a chart showing the hierarchical relationships between employees in a company

organization and methods /ˌɔrgənaɪzeɪʃ(ə)n ən ˈmeθədz/ *noun* a process of examining how an office

works, and suggesting how it can be made more efficient. Abbreviation **O & M**

organization chart /ˌɔrgənaɪ ˈzeɪʃ(ə)n tʃɑrt/ *noun* same as **organizational chart**

organize /ˈɔrgənaɪz/ *verb* to set up a system for doing something ○ *The company is organized into six profit centers.* ○ *The group is organized by sales areas.*

organized market /ˌɔrgənaɪzd ˈmɑrkət/ *noun* a market controlled by regulations set down by government or an official organization ○ *The government feels that an organized market is not conducive to business initiative.*

orientation /ˌɔriənˈteɪʃ(ə)n/ *noun* the main interest or type of activity ○ *The company's orientation is toward production and it has little marketing experience.*

oriented /ˈɔrientɪd/, **orientated** /ˈɔriənteɪtɪd/ *adjective* interested in or involved with ○ *Our strategy is oriented toward achieving further growth in the export market.* ○ *The promotion is entirely product-oriented.*

origin /ˈɔrɪdʒɪn/ *noun* the place where something or someone originally comes from ○ *spare parts of European origin*

original /əˈrɪdʒən(ə)l/ *adjective* which was used or made first ○ *They sent a copy of the original invoice.* ○ *He kept the original receipt for reference.* ■ *noun* the first copy made ○ *Send the original and file two copies.*

originally /əˈrɪdʒən(ə)li/ *adverb* first or at the beginning

original purchase /əˌrɪdʒən(ə)l ˈpɜrtʃɪs/ *noun* a copy of a magazine or newspaper which is actually bought by the reader, rather than simply read by them

OS *abbreviation* outsize

O/S *abbreviation* out of stock

OTO *abbreviation* one time only

OTS *abbreviation* opportunities to see

outbid /aʊtˈbɪd/ *verb* to offer a better price than someone else ○ *We offered $100,000 for the warehouse, but anoth-*

er company outbid us. (NOTE: **outbidding – outbid**)

outdoor /aʊt'dɔr/ *adjective* in the open air

outdoor advertising /ˌaʊtdɔrr 'ædvərtaɪzɪŋ/ *noun* **1.** advertising on the outside of a building or in the open air, using posters on billboards or neon signs **2.** advertising in the open air, including advertising in public transportation, on roadsides, at bus stops, skywriting, etc.

outer /'aʊtər/ *noun* a piece of packaging which covers items which already are in packages

outer pack /'aʊtər pæk/ *noun* a container which holds a number of smaller packaged items ○ *The goods are sold in outer packs, each containing twenty packets.*

outlet /'aʊtlet/ *noun* a place where something can be sold

out-of-date /ˌaʊt əv 'deɪt/ *adjective, adverb* old-fashioned or no longer modern ○ *Their computer system is years out of date.* ○ *They're still using out-of-date equipment.*

out-of-home advertising /ˌaʊt əv hoʊm 'ædvərtaɪzɪŋ/ *noun* outdoor advertising including transportation, skywriting, etc.

out of stock /ˌaʊt əv 'stɑk/ *adjective, adverb* with no stock left ○ *Those books are temporarily out of stock.* ○ *Several out-of-stock items have been on order for weeks.* Abbreviation **O/S**

output /'aʊtpʊt/ *noun* the amount which a company, person, or machine produces ○ *Output has increased by 10%.* ○ *25% of our output is exported.*

output bonus /'aʊtpʊt ˌboʊnəs/, **output-based bonus** /ˌaʊtpʊt beɪst 'boʊnəs/ *noun* an extra payment for increased production

output per hour /ˌaʊtpʊt pər 'aʊr/ *noun* the amount of something produced in one hour

output tax /'aʊtpʊt tæks/ *noun* VAT charged by a company on goods or services sold, and which the company pays to the government

outsell /aʊt'sel/ *verb* to sell more than someone ○ *The company is easily outselling its competitors.* (NOTE: **outselling – outsold**)

outside broadcast /ˌaʊtsaɪd 'brɔdkɑrst/ *noun* a program not transmitted from a studio

outside director /ˌaʊtsaɪd daɪ 'rektər/ *noun* a director who is not employed by the company, a non-executive director

outside poster /ˌaʊtsaɪd 'poʊstə/ *noun* a poster on public transportation such as buses, taxis, trains, and the subway

outsize /'aʊtsaɪz/ *noun* a size which is larger than usual. Abbreviation **OS** □ **outsize order** a very large order

outsource /'aʊtˌsɔrs/ *verb* to use a source outside a company or business to do the work that is needed

outsourcing /'aʊtsɔrsɪŋ/ *noun* the transfer of work previously done by employees of an organization to another organization, usually one that specializes in that type of work (NOTE: Things that have usually been outsourced in the past include legal services, transportation, catering, and security, but nowadays IT services, training, and public relations are often added to the list.)

outstanding /aʊt'stændɪŋ/ *adjective* not yet paid or completed □ **outstanding debts** debts which are waiting to be paid □ **outstanding orders** orders received but not yet supplied □ **what is the amount outstanding?** how much money is still owed? □ **matters outstanding from the previous meeting** questions which were not settled at the previous meeting

outward mission /ˌaʊtwəd 'mɪʃ(ə)n/ *noun* a visit by a group of businesspeople to a foreign country

over- /oʊvər/ *prefix* more than □ **shop which caters to the over-60s** a store which has goods which appeal to people who are more than sixty years old

overall /ˌoʊvər'ɔl/ *adjective* covering or including everything □ **the company reported an overall fall in profits** the company reported a general fall in profits □ **overall plan** a plan which covers everything

overcharge *noun* /'oʊvətʃɑrdʒ/ a charge which is higher than it should be ○ *to pay back an overcharge* ■ *verb* /ˌoʊvə'tʃɑrdʒ/ to ask someone for too much money ○ *They overcharged us for our meals.* ○ *We asked for a refund because we'd been overcharged.*

overhead *noun* the indirect costs of the day-to-day running of a business, i.e. not money spent on producing goods, but money spent on such things as renting or maintaining buildings and machinery ○ *The sales revenue covers the manufacturing costs but not the overhead.* (NOTE: The U.K. term is **overheads.**)

overhead budget /ˌoʊvərhed 'bʌdʒət/ *noun* a plan of probable overhead costs

overhead costs /ˌoʊvərhed 'kɔsts/, **overhead expenses** /ˌoʊvərhed ɪk'spensɪz/ *plural noun* same as **overhead**

overheads /'oʊvərhedz/ *plural noun* U.K. same as **overhead**

overkill /'oʊvərkɪl/ *noun* a very intensive and expensive marketing campaign which has the effect of putting potential customers off

overlay /'oʊvəleɪ/ *noun* a transparent plastic sheet placed over artwork with instructions for changing it, or showing the artwork is to be printed

overmatter /'oʊvərmætər/, **oversetting** /'oʊvərsetɪŋ/ *noun* text which, when it is typeset, is too long for the space available

overpayment /ˌoʊvər'peɪmənt/ *noun* an act of paying too much

overprice /ˌoʊvər'praɪs/ *verb* to give a higher price to something than seems reasonable

overpricing /ˌoʊvər'praɪsɪŋ/ *noun* the charging of a higher price than is justified by demand ○ *Overpricing led to the producer being priced out of the market.*

overprint /ˌoʊvər'prɪnt/ *verb* to print text on paper which already contains printed matter ○ *The retailer's name and address is overprinted on the catalog.* ○ *We will overprint the catalog with the retailer's name and address.*

overproduce /ˌoʊvərprə'dus/ *verb* to produce too much of a product

overproduction /ˌoʊvərprə'dʌkʃən/ *noun* the manufacturing of too much of a product

overrider /'oʊvəraɪdər/, **overriding commission** /ˌoʊvəraɪdɪŋ kə'mɪʃ(ə)n/ *noun* a special extra commission which is above all other commissions

overseas *adjective* /'oʊvəsiz/, *adverb* /ˌoʊvə'siz/ across the sea, or to or in foreign countries ○ *Management trainees knew that they would be sent overseas to learn about the export markets.* ○ *Some workers are going overseas to find new jobs.* ■ *noun* /ˌoʊvə'siz/ foreign countries ○ *The profits from overseas are far higher than those of the home division.*

overseas call /ˌoʊvərsiz 'kɔl/ *noun* a call to another country

overseas division /ˌoʊvərsiz dɪ'vɪʒ(ə)n/ *noun* the section of a company dealing with trade with other countries

overseas markets /ˌoʊvərsiz 'mɑrkɪts/ *plural noun* markets in foreign countries

oversell /ˌoʊvər'sel/ *verb* to sell more than you can produce □ **he is oversold** he has agreed to sell more product than he can produce □ **the market is oversold** stock-market prices are too low, because there have been too many sellers

overspend /ˌoʊvər'spend/ *verb* to spend too much

overstock /ˌoʊvər'stɑk/ *verb* to have a bigger stock, or inventory, of something than is needed □ **to be overstocked with spare parts** to have too many spare parts in stock

overstocks /'oʊvərstɑks/ *plural noun* more stock than is needed to supply orders ○ *We will have to sell off the overstocks to make room in the warehouse.*

over-the-counter sales /ˌoʊvər ðə 'kaʊntər ˌseɪlz/ *plural noun* the legal selling of shares which are not listed in

the official Stock Exchange list, usually
carried out by telephone

overweight /ˌoʊvərˈweɪt/ *adjective*
□ **the package is sixty grams overweight** the package weighs sixty grams
too much

own brand /ˌoʊn ˈbrænd/ *noun* the
name of a store which is used on products which are specially packed for that
store

own-brand goods /ˌoʊn brænd
ˈɡʊdz/ *plural noun* products specially
packed for a store with the store's name
on them

owner /ˈoʊnər/ *noun* a person who
owns something ○ *The owners of a company are its shareholders.* □ **goods sent
at owner's risk** a situation where the
owner has to insure the goods while they
are being transported

own label /ˌoʊn ˈleɪb(ə)l/ *noun* goods
specially produced for a store with the
store's name on them

own-label goods /ˌoʊn ˌleɪb(ə)l
ˈɡʊdz/ *plural noun* goods specially produced for a store with the store's name
on them

P

P2P /ˌpi tə ˈpi/ *adjective* referring to direct communications or dealings between one computer to another without a central server being involved (NOTE: Full form **peer-to-peer**)

pack /pæk/ *noun* items put together in a container or shrink-wrapped for selling □ **items sold in packs of 200** items sold in boxes containing 200 items □ **blister pack, bubble pack** a type of packing where the item for sale is covered with a stiff plastic cover sealed to a card backing ■ *verb* to put things into a container for selling or sending ○ *to pack goods into cartons* ○ *Your order has been packed and is ready for shipping.* ○ *The biscuits are packed in plastic wrappers.*

package /ˈpækɪdʒ/ *noun* **1.** goods packed and wrapped for sending by mail ○ *The Post Office does not accept bulky packages.* ○ *The goods are to be sent in airtight packages.* **2.** a group of different items joined together in one deal **3.** a group of TV or radio programs or commercial spots offered with a discount by a station ■ *verb* **1.** □ **to package goods** to wrap and pack goods in an attractive way **2.** □ **to package holidays** to sell a vacation package including travel, hotels, and food

packaged /ˈpækɪdʒd/ *adjective* put into a package ○ *packaged goods*

package deal /ˌpækɪdʒ ˈdil/ *noun* an agreement which covers several different things at the same time ○ *They agreed on a package deal which involves the construction of the factory, training of staff, and purchase of the product.*

package tour /ˈpækɪdʒ tʊr/, **package trip** /ˈpækɪdʒ trɪp/ *noun* a vacation

whose price includes transportation and accommodation, and sometimes also meals ○ *The travel company is arranging a package tour to the international trade fair.*

packaging /ˈpækɪdʒɪŋ/ *noun* **1.** the act of putting things into packages **2.** material used to protect goods which are being packed ○ *bubble wrap and other packaging material* ○ *The fruit is sold in airtight packaging.* **3.** material used to wrap goods for display

packer /ˈpækər/ *noun* a person who packs goods

packet /ˈpækət/ *noun* a small box of goods for selling ○ *Can you get me a packet of cigarettes?* ○ *She bought a packet of cookies.* ○ *We need two packets of filing cards.* □ **item sold in packets of 20** items are sold in boxes containing 20 items each

packing /ˈpækɪŋ/ *noun* **1.** the act of putting goods into boxes and wrapping them for shipping ○ *What is the cost of the packing?* ○ *Packing is included in the price.* **2.** material used to protect goods ○ *packed in airtight packing* ○ *The fruit is packed in airtight packing.*

packing case /ˈpækɪŋ keɪs/ *noun* a large wooden box for carrying items which can be easily broken

packing charges /ˈpækɪŋ ˌtʃɑrdʒɪz/ *plural noun* money charged for putting goods into boxes

packing station /ˈpækɪŋ ˌsteɪʃ(ə)n/ *noun* a place where goods are packed for transportation ○ *From the production line the goods are taken directly to the packing station.* ○ *The company has three packing stations, each one dealing with goods for a particular part of the world.*

page /peɪdʒ/ *noun* one side of a sheet of printed paper in a book, newspaper, or magazine

page impressions /'peɪdʒ ɪm ˌpreʃ(ə)nz/ *plural noun* the number of customers who land on a webpage, e.g., in an ad view

page make-up /peɪdʒ 'meɪk ʌp/ *noun* the arranging of material into pages in a publication

page proof /'peɪdʒ pruf/ *noun* a proof after the text has been made up into pages, ready for checking before printing

page pushing /'peɪdʒ ˌpʊʃɪŋ/ *noun* same as **co-browsing**

page rate /'peɪdʒ reɪt/ *noun* the cost of a whole page of advertising space ○ *What's the page rate in that paper?* ○ *The page rate is lower in August when circulation is at its lowest.*

page traffic /'peɪdʒ ˌtræfɪk/ *noun* the proportion of readers of a publication who read a particular page ○ *Let's find out the page traffic before we decide to advertise on page two.*

page view /'peɪdʒ vju/ *noun* the number of times a page containing an advertisement is seen or how many times a page is displayed

paid circulation /ˌpeɪd ˌsɜrkjə 'leɪʃ(ə)n/ *noun* the number of copies of a newspaper or magazine which have been bought. ◊ **controlled circulation, subscribed circulation**

pallet /'pælət/ *noun* a flat wooden base on which goods can be stacked for easy handling by a fork-lift truck, and on which they remain for the whole of their transportation

palletize /'pælətaɪz/ *verb* to put goods on pallets ○ *palletized cartons*

palmtop /'pɑrmtɒp/ *noun* a very small computer which can be held in your hand and which usually has a character recognition screen instead of a keyboard

pamphlet /'pæmflət/ *noun* a small booklet of advertising material or of information

panel /'pæn(ə)l/ *noun* **1.** a flat vertical surface **2.** a group of people who give advice on a problem ○ *a panel of experts*

panel study /'pæn(ə)l ˌstʌdi/ *noun* a study that collects and analyzes the opinions of a selected group of people over a period of time

panic buying /'pænɪk ˌbaɪɪŋ/ *noun* a rush to buy something at any price because stocks may run out

pantry check /'pæntri tʃek/, **pantry audit** /'pæntri ˌɒdɪt/ *noun* a survey method where a panel or sample of householders keep records of purchases so that these can be regularly checked for quantity and brand ○ *The pantry check suggests that there is little brand loyalty for that type of product.*

paper /'peɪpər/ *noun* **1.** a document which can represent money, e.g., a bill of exchange or a promissory note **2.** a newspaper

paper loss /ˌpeɪpər 'lɔs/ *noun* a loss made when an asset has fallen in value but has not been sold

paper profit /ˌpeɪpər 'prɑfɪt/ *noun* a profit on an asset which has increased in price but has not been sold ○ *He is showing a paper profit of $25,000 on his investment.* Also called **paper gain, unrealised profit**

parallel billboard /ˌpærəlel 'bɪlbɔrd/ *noun* a billboard which is parallel to a main road

parallel economy /ˌpærəlel ɪ 'kɒnəmi/ *noun* same as **black economy**

parcel /'pɑrs(ə)l/ *noun* goods wrapped up in paper or plastic to be sent by mail ○ *to do up goods into parcels* □ **to tie up a parcel** to fasten a parcel with string □ **parcel rates** the charges for sending parcels by mail ■ *verb* to wrap and tie up in a parcel ○ *to package up a consignment of books* (NOTE: **parceling – parceled**)

parcel delivery service /ˌpɑrs(ə)l dɪ'lɪv(ə)ri ˌsɜrvɪs/ *noun* a private company which delivers parcels within a specific area

parcel post /ˈpɑrs(ə)l poʊst/ *noun* a mail service for sending parcels ○ *Send the order by parcel post.*

parcels office /ˈpɑrs(ə)lz ˌɔfɪs/ *noun* an office where parcels can be handed in for sending by mail

Pareto's Law /pəˈritoʊz lɔ/, **Pareto Effect** /pəˈritoʊ ɪˌfekt/ *noun* the theory that incomes are distributed in the same way in all countries, whatever tax regime is in force, and that a small percentage of a total is responsible for a large proportion of value or resources. Also called **eighty/twenty law**

part exchange /ˌpɑrt ɪksˈtʃeɪndʒ/ *noun* the act of giving an old product as part of the payment for a new one ○ *to take a car in part exchange*

participation /pɑrˌtɪsɪˈpeɪʃ(ə)n/ *noun* taking part in something, e.g., when advertisers buy commercial time on TV

partnering /ˈpɑrtnərɪŋ/ *noun* same as **strategic partnering**

partnership /ˈpɑrtnərʃɪp/ *noun* a business set up by two or more people who make a contract with each other agreeing to share the profits and losses (NOTE: A partnership is not an incorporated company and the individual partners are responsible for decisions and debts.)

part payment /ˌpɑrt ˈpeɪmənt/ *noun* the paying of part of a whole payment ○ *I gave him $250 as part payment for the car.*

party /ˈpɑrti/ *noun* **1.** a person or organization involved in a legal dispute or legal agreement ○ *How many parties are there to the contract?* ○ *The company is not a party to the agreement.* **2.** a group of people who meet to celebrate something or to enjoy themselves

party-plan selling /ˈpɑrti plæn ˌselɪŋ/ *noun* selling by salespeople who present their products at parties organized in their homes ○ *Party-plan selling provides a relaxed atmosphere in which people are more inclined to buy the products being shown.*

par value /ˌpɑ ˈvælju/ *noun* same as **face value**

pass /pɑs/ *verb*

  pass off *phrasal verb* □ **to pass something off as something else** to pretend that something is another thing in order to cheat a customer ○ *She tried to pass off the wine as French, when in fact it came from Romania.*

pass-along readership /ˈpæs əˌlɔŋ ˌridərʃɪp/ *noun* the number of people who read a publication who have not bought it, but have borrowed it from a purchaser ○ *We know the magazine's circulation, but will have to estimate the level of pass-along readership.* (NOTE: The U.K. term is **pass-on readership**.)

passenger manifest /ˌpæsɪndʒər ˈmænɪfest/ *noun* a list of passengers on a ship or plane

passing trade /ˌpɑsɪŋ ˈtreɪd/ *noun* selling to people who go past the store without intending to buy

patent /ˈpeɪtənt, ˈpætənt/ *noun* an official document showing that a person has the exclusive right to make and sell an invention ○ *to take out a patent for a new type of light bulb* ○ *to apply for a patent for a new invention* □ **"patent applied for"**, **"patent pending"** words on a product showing that the inventor has applied for a patent for it □ **to forfeit a patent** to lose a patent because payments have not been made □ **to infringe a patent** to make and sell a product which works in the same way as a patented product and not pay a royalty for it □ **to file a patent application** to apply for a patent ■ *verb* □ **to patent an invention** to register an invention with the patent office to prevent other people from copying it

patent agent /ˈpeɪtənt ˌeɪdʒənt/ *noun* a person who advises on patents and applies for patents on behalf of clients

patented /ˈpeɪtəntɪd, ˈpætəntɪd/ *adjective* which is protected by a patent

patentee /ˌpeɪtənˈti/ *noun* a person or business that has acquired a patent ○ *We shall have to obtain the patentee's permission to manufacture the product.*

patent medicine /ˌpeɪtənt
ˈmed(ə)sɪn/ *noun* a medicine which is
registered as a patent

patent office /ˈpeɪtənt ˌɒfɪs/ *noun* a
government office which grants patents
and supervises them

patent rights /ˈpeɪtənt raɪts/ *plural
noun* the rights which an inventor holds
because of a patent

patron /ˈpeɪtrən/ *noun* **1.** a regular
customer, e.g., of a hotel, restaurant, etc.
○ *The parking lot is for the use of hotel
patrons only.* **2.** a person who gives an
organization or charity financial support
○ *She is a patron of several leading
charities.*

patronage /ˈpætrənɪdʒ/ *noun* the use
of a store by regular shoppers □ **to lose
someone's patronage** to do something
which makes a regular customer go to
another store

patronize /ˈpætrənaɪz/ *verb* to be a
regular customer ○ *I stopped patroniz-
ing that restaurant when their prices
went up.*

pattern /ˈpæt(ə)n/ *noun* the general
way in which something usually happens ○ *The pattern of sales* or *The sales
pattern is very different this year.*

pattern advertising /ˈpæt(ə)n
ˌædvərtaɪzɪŋ/ *noun* an advertising
campaign that follows a general global
approach

pattern book /ˈpæt(ə)n bʊk/ *noun* a
book showing examples of design

patterned interview /ˌpæt(ə)nd
ˈɪntərvjuː/ *noun* an interview using
questions set in advance and following a
fixed pattern

pay /peɪ/ *verb* **1.** to give money to buy
an item or a service ○ *to pay $1,000 for
a car* ○ *How much did you pay to have
the office cleaned?* (NOTE: **paying –
paid**) □ **"pay cash"** words written on a
crossed check to show that it can be paid
in cash if necessary □ **to pay in advance**
to pay before you receive the item
bought or before the service has been
completed ○ *We had to pay in advance
to have the new telephone system installed.* □ **to pay in instalments** to pay
for an item by giving small amounts reg-

ularly ○ *We are buying the van by paying installments of $500 a month.* □ **to
pay cash** to pay the complete sum in
cash □ **to pay by cheque** to pay by giving a check, not by using cash or credit
card □ **to pay by credit card** to pay using a credit card, not a check or cash **2.**
to give money which is owed or which
has to be paid ○ *He was late paying the
bill.* ○ *We phoned to ask when they were
going to pay the invoice.* ○ *You will have
to pay duty on these imports.* ○ *She pays
tax at the highest rate.* (NOTE: **paying –
paid**) □ **to pay on demand** to pay money when it is asked for, not after a period
of credit □ **please pay the sum of $10**
please give $10 in cash or by check

pay down *phrasal verb* □ **to pay
money down** to make a deposit ○
*They paid $50 down and the rest in
monthly installments.*

payable /ˈpeɪəb(ə)l/ *adjective* due to
be paid □ **payable in advance** which
has to be paid before the goods are delivered □ **payable on delivery** which
has to be paid when the goods are delivered □ **payable on demand** which must
be paid when payment is asked for □
payable at sixty days which has to be
paid by sixty days after the date on the
invoice □ **cheque made payable to
bearer** a check which will be paid to the
person who has it, not to any particular
name written on it □ **shares payable on
application** shares which must be paid
for when you apply to buy them

payback period /ˈpeɪbæk ˌpɪriəd/
noun the length of time it will take to
earn back the money invested in a
project

paycheck /ˈpeɪtʃek/ *noun* a monthly
check by which an employee is paid
(NOTE: The U.K. spelling is **pay
cheque**.)

payee /peɪˈiː/ *noun* a person who receives money from someone, or the person whose name is on a check

payer /ˈpeɪər/ *noun* a person who
gives money to someone

payload /ˈpeɪloʊd/ *noun* the cargo or
passengers carried by a ship, train, or
plane for which payment is made

payment /'peɪmənt/ *noun* **1.** the act of giving money in exchange for goods or a service ○ *We always ask for payment in cash* or *cash payment and not payment by check.* ○ *The payment of interest* or *the interest payment should be made on the 22nd of each month.* □ **payment after delivery** paying for goods at an agreed date after delivery ○ *There is a 10% discount for payment on delivery, but none for payment after delivery.* □ **payment on account** paying part of the money owed □ **payment on delivery** paying for goods when they are delivered ○ *Some customers won't agree to payment on delivery and want more time to settle up.* □ **payment on invoice** paying money as soon as an invoice is received □ **payment in kind** paying by giving goods or food, but not money □ **payment by results** money given which increases with the amount of work done or goods produced □ **payment supra protest** payment of a bill of exchange by a third party to protect the debtor's honor **2.** money paid □ **repayable in easy payments** repayable with small sums regularly

payment gateway /'peɪmənt ˌɡeɪtweɪ/ *noun* software that processes online credit-card payments. It gets authorization for the payment from the credit-card company and transfers money into the retailer's bank account.

payment terms /'peɪmənt tɜrmz/ *plural noun* the conditions laid down by a business regarding when it should be paid for goods or services that it supplies, e.g., cash with order, payment on delivery, or payment within a particular number of days of the invoice date

pay package /'peɪ ˌpækɪdʒ/ *noun* the salary and other benefits offered with a job ○ *The job carries an attractive pay package.*

pay-per-click /ˌpeɪ pe 'klɪk/ *noun* same as **pay-per-view**

pay-per-play /ˌpeɪ pe 'pleɪ/ *noun* a website where the user has to pay to play an interactive game over the Internet

pay-per-view /ˌpeɪ pər 'vju/ *noun* a website where the user has to pay to see digital information, e.g., an e-book or e-magazine. Also called **pay-per-click**

pay television /'peɪ teliˌvɪʒ(ə)n/, **pay TV** /'peɪ ti ˌvi/ *noun* a television service that is paid for by regular subscriptions

PC *abbreviation* personal computer

PD *abbreviation* physical distribution

peak /pik/ *noun* the highest point ○ *The shares reached their peak in January.* ○ *The share index has fallen 10% since the peak in January.* ○ *Withdrawals from bank accounts reached a peak in the week before Christmas.* ○ *He has reached the peak of his career.* ■ *verb* to reach the highest point ○ *Productivity peaked in January.* ○ *Shares have peaked and are beginning to slip back.* ○ *He peaked early and never achieved his ambition of becoming managing director.* ○ *Demand peaks in August, after which sales usually decline.*

peak output /ˌpik 'aʊtpʊt/ *noun* the highest output

peak period /'pik ˌpɪriəd/ *noun* the time of the day when something is at its highest point, e.g., when most commuters are traveling or when most electricity is being used

peak time /'pik taɪm/ *noun* the time during the day when the greatest number of people are watching television ○ *For the price of a 30-second spot at peak time we can get two minutes in mid-morning.*

peak year /ˌpik 'jɪr/ *noun* the year when the largest quantity of products was produced or when sales were highest

pedestrian precinct /pəˌdestriən 'prisɪŋkt/ *noun* the part of a town which is closed to traffic so that people can walk about and shop

peer group /'pɪr ˌɡrup/ *noun* the class of people that a person can respect or identify with, because they belong to the same age group, social class, or have the same opinions ○ *Consumers are found to be especially influenced by the tastes and opinions of those in their peer groups.*

peer-to-peer /ˌpɪr tə ˈpɪr/ *adjective* full form of **P2P**

peg /peg/ *verb* to maintain or fix something at a specific level ∎ *noun* a hook to hang clothes on

pen /pen/ *noun* an instrument for writing with, using ink

penalty clause /ˈpen(ə)lti klɔz/ *noun* a clause which lists the penalties which will be imposed if the terms of the contract are not fulfilled ○ *The contract contains a penalty clause which fines the company 1% for every week the completion date is late.*

penetrate /ˈpenɪtreɪt/ *verb* □ **to penetrate a market** to get into a market and capture a share of it

penetrated market /ˌpenɪtreɪtɪd ˈmɑrkət/ *noun* a market where more of a company's products are sold, shown as a percentage of the total market, using aggressive pricing and advertising

penetration /ˌpenɪˈtreɪʃ(ə)n/ *noun* **1.** the percentage of a target market that accepts a product **2.** the percentage of a target audience reached by an advertisement

penetration pricing /ˌpenɪ ˈtreɪʃ(ə)n ˌpraɪsɪŋ/ *noun* the practice of pricing a product low enough to achieve market penetration ○ *Penetration pricing is helping us acquire a bigger market share at the expense of short-term profits.*

penetration strategy /ˌpenɪ ˈtreɪʃ(ə)n ˌstrætədʒi/ *noun* selling more of a company's products into a market segment, shown as a percentage of the total market, by aggressive pricing and advertising. ◊ **market penetration**

per annum /pər ˈænəm/ *adverb* in a year ○ *What is their turnover per annum?* ○ *What is his total income per annum?* ○ *She earns over $100,000 per annum.*

per capita /pər ˈkæpɪtə/ *adjective, adverb* for each person

per-capita expenditure /pər ˌkæpɪtə ɪkˈspendɪtʃər/ *noun* the total money spent divided by the number of people involved

per capita income /pər ˌkæpɪtə ˈɪnkʌm/ *noun* the average income of each member of a particular group of people, e.g., the citizens of a country

percentage bounced back /pə ˌsentɪdʒ baʊnst ˈbæk/ *noun* the number of email messages returned as undeliverable, shown as a percentage of the total sent

percentile /pərˈsentaɪl/ *noun* one of a series of ninety-nine figures below which a percentage of the total falls

perception /pərˈsepʃən/ *noun* the way in which something is viewed and assessed by a person

perceptual map /pəˌseptʃuəl ˈmæp/ *noun* a map or diagram which represents how consumers view various comparative products on the basis of specific factors or attributes ○ *Thorough analysis of perceptual maps was followed by decisions on changes in product design and marketing strategy.*

perfect *adjective* /ˈpɜrfɪkt/ completely correct with no mistakes ○ *We check each batch to make sure it is perfect.* ○ *She did a perfect keyboarding test.* ∎ *verb* /pəˈfekt/ to develop or improve something until it is as good as it can be ○ *They perfected the process for making high-grade steel.*

perfect competition /ˌpɜrfɪkt ˌkɑmpəˈtɪʃ(ə)n/ *noun* (*in economic theory*) the ideal market, where all products are equal in price and all customers are provided with all information about the products. Also called **atomistic competition**

perfect market /ˌpɜrfɪkt ˈmɑrkət/ *noun* an imaginary market where there is perfect competition

performance review /pəˈfɔrməns rɪˌvju/ *noun* a yearly interview between a manager and each employee to discuss how the employee has worked during the year

periodical /ˌpɪriˈɑdɪk(ə)l/ *noun* a magazine which comes out regularly, usually once a month or once a week

perishable /ˈperɪʃəb(ə)l/ *adjective* which can go bad or become rotten easily ○ *perishable goods* ○ *perishable items* ○ *a perishable cargo*

perishables /'perɪʃəb(ə)lz/ *plural noun* goods which can go bad easily

permanent /'pɜrmənənt/ *adjective* which will last for a long time or for ever ○ *the permanent staff and part-timers* ○ *She has found a permanent job.* ○ *She is in permanent employment.*

permanent-income hypothesis /ˌpɜrmənənt 'ɪnkʌm haɪˌpɑθəsɪs/ *noun* the theory that people spend according to the average income they expect to receive in their lifetime

permission marketing /pə'mɪʃ(ə)n ˌmɑrkətɪŋ/ *noun* any form of online direct marketing that requires the seller to get permission from each recipient, usually through an opt-in, before sending him or her any promotional material

permit *noun* /'pɜrmɪt/ an official document which allows someone to do something ■ *verb* /pə'mɪt/ to allow someone to do something ○ *This document permits you to export twenty-five computer systems.* ○ *The ticket permits three people to go into the exhibition.* ○ *Will we be permitted to use her name in the advertising copy?* ○ *Smoking is not permitted in the design studio.* (NOTE: **permitting – permitted**)

persistent demand /pəˌsɪstənt dɪ'mænd/ *noun* a continuous or stable demand for a product ○ *Persistent demand for the product means that there is very little pressure to adapt it.* ○ *The product is so useful that it is not surprising there is a persistent demand for it.*

personal /'pɜrs(ə)n(ə)l/ *adjective* referring to one person

personal call /'pɜrs(ə)n(ə)l kɔl/ *noun* **1.** a telephone call where you ask the operator to connect you with a particular person **2.** a telephone call not related to business ○ *Staff are not allowed to make personal calls during office hours.*

personal computer /ˌpɜrs(ə)n(ə)l kəm'pjutə/ *noun* a small computer which can be used by one person in the home or office. Abbreviation **PC**

Personal Identification Number /ˌpɜrs(ə)n(ə)l aɪˌdentɪfɪ'keɪʃ(ə)n ˌnʌmbər/ *noun* a unique number allocated to the holder of an ATM card or credit card, by which he or she can enter an automatic banking system, to withdraw cash from an ATM or to pay in a store. Abbreviation **PIN**

personal interview /ˌpɜrs(ə)n(ə)l 'ɪntərvju/ *noun* an act of questioning respondents in a survey directly, by meeting them ○ *The advantage of a personal interview is that we have the chance to explain the questions.* ○ *It's possible that interviewers' bias may influence results in a personal interview.*

personality /ˌpɜrsə'næləti/ *noun* **1.** a famous person, usually connected with television or sports **2.** the character, especially the tone, of an advertising email, e.g., serious, cheerful, etc.

personality advertising /ˌpɜrsə'nælɪti ˌædvərtaɪzɪŋ/, **personality promotion** /ˌpɜrsə'nælɪti prəˌmoʊʃ(ə)n/ *noun* a promotion which makes use of a famous person to endorse a product ○ *Personality promotion is a tried and tested method of promoting beauty products.* ○ *A famous pop star was chosen for the personality promotion because of her widespread popularity among the target audience.*

personalization /ˌpɜrs(ə)nəlaɪ'zeɪʃ(ə)n/ *noun* **1.** the process by which a website presents customers with information that is selected and adapted to meet their specific needs **2.** using personal information such as the addressee's first name in a mailing campaign

personalized /'pɜrs(ə)nəlaɪzd/ *adjective* with the name or initials of a person printed on it ○ *She has a personalized briefcase.*

personalized mailing /ˌpɜrs(ə)nəlaɪzd 'meɪlɪŋ/ *noun* a mailing of letters addressed to particular people by name

personal selling /'pɜrs(ə)n(ə)l ˌselɪŋ/ *noun* selling to a customer by personal contact, either face to face or by telephone ○ *Personal selling allows any doubts the prospective customer*

may have to be cleared up by the sales-
man.

persuade /pə'sweɪd/ *verb* to talk to someone and get them to do what you want ○ *We could not persuade the French company to sign the contract.*

persuasibility /pə,sweɪzɪ'bɪləti/ *noun* the degree to which a target audience can be persuaded through advertising that a product has good qualities ○ *Persuasibility will depend on consumers' experience with products similar to the ones we are promoting.*

persuasion /pə'sweɪʒ(ə)n/ *noun* the act of persuading

persuasion matrix /pə'sweɪʒ(ə)n ,meɪtrɪks/ *noun* a planning model which shows how responses are affected by the communications they receive

PESTLE /'pes(ə)l/ *noun* analysis of the various outside influences on a firm, shown as Political, Environmental, Social, Technological, Legislative, and Economic

photoengraving /,foʊtoʊɪn 'greɪvɪŋ/ *noun* a process of producing a metal plate for printing, by photographing an image onto the plate which is then etched in such a way that prints can be taken from it

photogravure /,foʊtoʊgrə'vjʊr/ *noun* a type of photoengraving where the design is etched into the metal rather than in relief

photo opportunity /'foʊtoʊ ,ɑpərtunəti/ *noun* an arranged situation where a famous person can be filmed or photographed by journalists

phototypesetting /,foʊtoʊ 'taɪpsetɪŋ/ *noun* typesetting by photographic means rather than by using metal type

physical distribution /,fɪzɪk(ə)l ,dɪstrɪ'bjuʃ(ə)n/ *noun* the process of moving goods from the producer to the wholesaler, then to the retailer and so to the end user ○ *Physical distribution is always a problem because of high transportation costs.* Abbreviation **PD**

physical inventory /,fɪzɪk(ə)l 'ɪnvənt(ə)ri/ *noun* an act of counting actual items of inventory

physical retail shopping /,fɪzɪk(ə)l 'riteɪl ,ʃɑpɪŋ/ *noun* shopping that involves visiting actual stores rather than buying online

physical stock /,fɪzɪk(ə)l 'stɑk/ *noun* the actual items of stock, or inventory, held in a warehouse

picking /'pɪkɪŋ/ *noun* the selecting of a product according to its packaging or place on the shelf, rather than by making a conscious decision to buy

picking list /'pɪkɪŋ lɪst/ *noun* a list of items in an order, listed according to where they can be found in the warehouse

pickup /'pɪkʌp/ *noun* a type of small van for transporting goods

pickup and delivery service /,pɪkʌp ən dɪ'lɪv(ə)ri ,sɜrvɪs/ *noun* **1.** a service which takes goods from the warehouse and delivers them to the customer **2.** a service which takes something away for cleaning or servicing and returns it to the owner when finished

picture messaging /'pɪktʃər ,mesɪdʒɪŋ/ *noun* the transmission of images and photographs from one cell phone to another

pieceworker /'piswɜrkər/ *noun* a person who is employed at a piece rate

piggy-back advertising /'pɪgi bæk prə,moʊʃ(ə)n/, **piggy-back promotion** *noun* the sales promotion for one product which accompanies promotion for another product made by the same company

piggy-back freight /,pɪgi bæk 'freɪt/ *noun* the transportation of loaded trucks on freight trains. Compare **fishy-back freight**

pilferage /'pɪlfərɪdʒ/, **pilfering** /'pɪlfərɪŋ/ *noun* the stealing of small amounts of money or small items from an office or store

pilot /'paɪlət/ *adjective* used as a test, which if successful will then be expanded into a full operation ○ *The company set up a pilot project to see if the proposed manufacturing system was efficient.* ○ *The pilot factory has been built to test the new production processes.* ○ *She is directing a pilot program for* *training unemployed young people.* ■ *verb* to test a project on a small number of people, to see if it will work in practice ■ *noun* **1.** a trial episode of a proposed TV series **2.** a test project, undertaken to see whether something is likely to be successful or profitable

pilot survey /'paɪlət ˌsɜrveɪ/ *noun* a preliminary survey carried out to see if a full survey would be worthwhile

PIN /pɪn/ *abbreviation* Personal Identification Number

pink advertising /ˌpɪŋk 'ædvərtaɪzɪŋ/ *noun* advertising aimed specifically at the gay and lesbian market

pink dollar /ˌpɪŋk 'dɑlər/ *noun* money spent by gay and lesbian customers

pink market /'pɪŋk ˌmɑrkət/ *noun* the market that consists of gay and lesbian people

pioneer /ˌpaɪə'nɪr/ *verb* to be the first to do something ○ *The company pioneered developments in the field of electronics.*

pioneer selling /ˌpaɪə'nɪr ˌselɪŋ/ *noun* hard intensive selling in new markets ○ *A campaign of pioneer selling was organized to educate the public in the use of the new product.* ○ *There was a lot of consumer resistance to pioneer selling, since few customers had heard of the product or thought they needed it.*

pipeline /'paɪplaɪn/ *noun* a distribution channel from the manufacturer through wholesalers and retailers to the customer ○ *How many different businesses are involved in the product's pipeline?*

piracy /'paɪrəsi/ *noun* the copying of patented inventions or copyright works

pirate /'paɪrət/ *noun* a person who copies a patented invention or a copyright work and sells it ■ *verb* to copy a copyright work ○ *a pirated book* ○ *The designs for the new dress collection were pirated in the Far East.* ■ *adjective* copied without permission ○ *a pirate copy of a book*

pitch /pɪtʃ/ *noun* a presentation by an advertising agency to a potential customer

pix /pɪks/ *plural noun* pictures used in advertising or design (*informal*)

pixel /'pɪksəl/ *noun* the smallest single unit or point on a display or on a printer whose color or brightness can be controlled. A monitor normally has a resolution of 72 pixels per inch, whereas a laser printer has a resolution of 300–600 pixels (also called dots) per inch.

placard /'plækɑrd/ *noun* **1.** a poster of double crown size (i.e. 30 inches deep by 20 inches wide) **2.** a large advertisement on a stiff card

placement test /'pleɪsmənt test/ *noun* a test where different versions of a new product are tested in different places and with different types of consumer (as opposed to market tests, where the new product is actually sold through normal distribution channels in the test areas)

placement testing /'pleɪsmənt ˌtestɪŋ/ *noun* the practice of sending a product to different places for trial and then interviewing the users on its performance ○ *Placement testing revealed that the product was too easily breakable.*

place utility /'pleɪs juˌtɪləti/ *noun* the usefulness to a customer of receiving a product at a particular place

plain cover /ˌpleɪn 'kʌvər/ *noun* □ **to send something under plain cover** to send something in an ordinary envelope with no company name printed on it

plan /plæn/ *noun* an idea of how something should be done, which has been decided on and organized in advance ■ *verb* to decide on and organize something in advance (NOTE: **planning – planned**)

planned obsolescence /ˌplænd ˌɑbsə'les(ə)ns/ *adjective* built-in obsolescence ○ *Planned obsolescence was condemned by the consumer organization as a cynical marketing ploy.*

planning /'plænɪŋ/ *noun* the process of organizing how something should be done in the future ○ *Setting up a new incentive program with insufficient planning could be a disaster.* ○ *The long-*

term planning or *short-term planning of the project has been completed.*

plans board /'plænz bɔrd/ *noun* a group of senior managers that meets to discuss campaign strategy ○ *The plans board will meet on Monday to discuss the latest sales figures.* ○ *The plans board has decided to concentrate the campaign in those areas where there are most sales representatives.*

plastic /'plæstɪk/ *noun* a plastic card, especially a credit or debit card, for use as a means of payment

plateau /plæ'toʊ/ *noun* a level point, e.g., when sales or costs stop increasing

plateau pricing /plæ'toʊ ˌpraɪsɪŋ/ *noun* the setting of a medium price for a product where the raw materials used in making it are likely to change a lot in price

platform /'plætfɔrm/ *noun* a basic product that can be added to in order to develop more complex products

Plc, PLC, plc *abbreviation* public limited company

PLC *abbreviation* product life cycle

ploy /plɔɪ/ *noun* a trick or gimmick, used to attract customers

plug /plʌɡ/ *noun* □ **to give a plug to a new product** to publicize a new product ■ *verb* □ to publicize or advertise ○ *They ran six commercials plugging vacations in Spain.* (NOTE: **plugging- plugged**)

point /pɔɪnt/ *noun* a place or position

point of action /ˌpɔɪnt əv 'ækʃən/ *noun* a place in a presentation that encourages the prospective purchaser to take action. Abbreviation **POA**

point of purchase /ˌpɔɪnt əv 'pɜrtʃɪs/ *noun* **1.** a place where a product is bought, which is usually the same as point of sale, though not always, as in the case of mail-order purchases. Abbreviation **POP 2.** same as **point of sale**

point-of-purchase advertising /ˌpɔɪnt əv ˌpɜrtʃɪs 'ædvərtaɪzɪŋ/ *noun* advertising at the place where the products are bought, e.g., posters or dump bins. Abbreviation **POPA**

point-of-purchase display /ˌpɔɪnt əv ˌpɜrtʃɪs dɪs'pleɪ/ *noun* an arrangement of products and marketing material at the place where an item is bought, which is designed to encourage sales

point of sale /ˌpɔɪnt əv 'seɪl/ *noun* **1.** a place where a product is sold, e.g., a store. Abbreviation **POS 2.** the place where a product is bought by the customer (NOTE: The point of sale can be a particular store, or a display case or even a particular shelf inside a store.)

point-of-sale material /ˌpɔɪnt əv 'seɪl məˌtɪriəl/ *noun* a display material to advertise a product where it is being sold, e.g., posters or dump bins. Abbreviation **POS material**

policy /'pɑlɪsi/ *noun* **1.** a course of action or set of principles determining the general way of doing something ○ *a company's trading policy* ○ *The country's economic policy seems to lack any direction.* ○ *Our policy is to submit all contracts to the legal department.* □ **company policy** the company's agreed plan of action or the company's way of doing things ○ *What is the company policy on credit?* ○ *It is against company policy to give more than thirty days' credit.* **2.** a course of action or set of principles **3.** a contract for insurance

poll /poʊl/ *noun* same as **opinion poll** ■ *verb* □ **to poll a sample of the population** to ask a sample group of people what they feel about something

poly bag /ˌpɑli 'bæɡ/ *noun* a plastic bag used in packaging

polycentric stage /pɑli'sentrɪk steɪdʒ/ *noun* the stage in a company's international marketing when there is a separate marketing planning unit for each country ○ *It's an expanding multinational in its polycentric stage.*

POP /pɑp/ *abbreviation* point of purchase

POPA *abbreviation* point-of-purchase advertising

popular /'pɑpjələr/ *adjective* liked by many people ○ *This is our most popular model.* ○ *The South Coast is the most popular area for vacations.*

popular price /ˌpɑpjələr ˈpraɪs/ *noun* a price which is low and therefore liked

popular pricing /ˌpɑpjələr ˈpraɪsɪŋ/ *noun* a pricing method which tries to fix prices that will be popular with customers ○ *Our competitor's popular pricing strategy is a serious threat to our sales.*

population /ˌpɑpjʊˈleɪʃ(ə)n/ *noun* **1.** all the people living in a particular country or area ○ *Paris has a population of over three million.* ○ *Population statistics show a rise in the 18–25 age group.* ○ *Population trends have to be taken into account when drawing up economic plans.* ○ *The working population of the country is getting older.* **2.** the group of items or people in a survey or study

population forecast /ˌpɑpjə ˈleɪʃ(ə)n ˌfɔrkæst/ *noun* a calculation of how many people will be living in a country or in a town at some point in the future

pop-under ad /ˈpɑp ʌndər ˌæd/ *noun* a web advertisement that appears in a separate browser window from the rest of a website

port /pɔrt/ *noun* a harbor where ships come to load or unload ○ *the port of Rotterdam* □ **to call at a port** to stop at a port to load or unload cargo

portal /ˈpɔrt(ə)l/ *noun* a website that provides access and links to other sites and pages on the web (NOTE: Search engines and directories are the most common portal sites.)

port authority /ˈpɔrt ɔˌθɑrəti/ *noun* an organization which runs a port

portfolio /pɔrtˈfoʊlioʊ/ *noun* a folder containing a selection of samples ○ *The student brought a portfolio of designs to show the design department manager.*

port installations /ˌpɔrt ɪnstəˈleɪʃ(ə)nz/ *plural noun* the buildings and equipment of a port

port of call /ˌpɔrt əv ˈkɔl/ *noun* a port at which a ship often stops

portrait /ˈpɔrtrɪt/ *noun* an illustration, page, or book whose height is greater than its width. Compare **landscape**

position /pəˈzɪʃ(ə)n/ *noun* **1.** a situation or state of affairs □ **what is the cash position?** what is the state of the company's checking account? **2.** a point of view

positioning /pəˈzɪʃ(ə)nɪŋ/ *noun* **1.** the creation of an image for a product in the minds of consumers **2.** the placing of an advertisement in a specific place on a specific page of a magazine **3.** the promotion of a product in a particular area of a market

positive /ˈpɑzətɪv/ *adjective* meaning "yes" ○ *The board gave a positive reply.*

positive appeal /ˌpɑzətɪv əˈpil/ *noun* advertising which shows why a product is attractive

positive cash flow /ˌpɑzətɪv ˈkæʃ floʊ/ *noun* a situation where more money is coming into a company than is going out

positive variance /ˌpɑzətɪv ˈveriəns/ *noun* a difference between a financial plan and its outcome, that means a more favorable profit than expected ○ *The managing director is pleased because costs this year show a $60,000 positive variance.*

possession utility /pəˈzeʃ(ə)n ju ˌtɪləti/ *noun* same as **marginal utility**

post /poʊst/ *noun* **1.** *U.K.* a system of sending letters and parcels from one place to another ○ *to send an invoice by post* ○ *He put the letter in the post.* ○ *The check was lost in the post.* □ **to send a reply by return of post** to reply to a letter immediately □ **post free** without having to pay any postage ○ *The game is obtainable post free from the manufacturer.* **2.** *U.K.* letters sent or received ○ *Has the post arrived yet?* ○ *The first thing I do is open the post.* ○ *The receipt was in this morning's post.* ○ *The letter didn't arrive by the first post this morning.* (NOTE: British English uses both **mail** and **post** but American English only uses **mail**) ■ *verb U.K.* to send something by post ○ *to post a letter* or *to post a package*

post- /poʊst/ *prefix* after

postage /ˈpoʊstɪdʒ/ *noun* payment for sending a letter or package by mail ○

What is the postage for this airmail packet to China? □ **"postage paid"** words printed on an envelope to show that the sender has paid the postage even though there is no stamp on it

postal /ˈpoʊst(ə)l/ *adjective* referring to the mail

postal interview /ˌpoʊst(ə)l ˈɪntərvjuː/ *noun* same as **postal survey**

postal order /ˈpoʊst(ə)l ˌɔːrdər/ *noun* a document bought at a post office, used as a method of paying small amounts of money by mail

postal packet /ˈpoʊst(ə)l ˌpækət/ *noun* a small container of goods sent by mail

postal sales /ˈpoʊst(ə)l seɪlz/ *plural noun* sales of products by mail, through advertisements in the press ○ *The company carried out postal sales from a big warehouse in the north.*

postal survey /ˌpoʊst(ə)l ˈsɜːrveɪ/ *noun* a survey in which questionnaires are sent by mail for respondents to fill in and send back ○ *Not enough consumers responded to the postal survey.*

postcode /ˈpoʊstkoʊd/ *noun U.K.* same as **ZIP code**

poster /ˈpoʊstər/ *noun* a large eye-catching notice or advertisement which is stuck up outdoors or placed prominently inside a store

poster site /ˈpoʊstər saɪt/ *noun* a billboard, wall, or other surface, where posters are put up ○ *We want a poster site in a busy street.* ○ *I wish we could afford a prime poster site for our fund-raising campaign.* ◊ **bill poster, fly poster**

postpaid /poʊstˈpeɪd/ *adjective* with the postage already paid ○ *The price is $5.95 postpaid.*

post-purchase /ˌpoʊst ˈpɜːrtʃɪs/ *adjective* after a purchase has been made

post-purchase advertising /ˌpoʊst pɜːrtʃɪs ˈædvərtaɪzɪŋ/ *noun* advertising designed to minimize post-purchase anxiety

post-purchase anxiety /ˌpoʊst pɜːrtʃɪs æŋˈzaɪəti/ *noun* feelings of doubt about a purchase after it has been made

post-purchase assessment /ˌpoʊst pɜːrtʃɪs əˈsesmənt/ *noun* the assessment of a product by the purchaser after it has been bought and used

post room /ˈpoʊst rum/ *noun* same as **mail room**

post-test /ˈpoʊst test/ *noun* an evaluation of an advertising campaign after it has taken place, or of a product after it has been launched ○ *The post-test showed that an unnecessary amount of money had been spent.*

post-testing /ˈpoʊst ˌtestɪŋ/ *noun* the evaluation of an advertising campaign after it has been run, or of a product after it has been launched

potential /pəˈtenʃəl/ *adjective* possible □ **potential customers** people who could be customers □ **potential market** a market which could be exploited □ **the product has potential sales of 100,000 units** the product will possibly sell 100,000 units □ **she is a potential managing director** she is the sort of person who could become managing director ■ *noun* the possibility of becoming something □ **a product with considerable sales potential** a product which is likely to have very large sales □ **to analyse the market potential** to examine the market to see how large it possibly is

potential demand /pəˌtenʃəl dɪ ˈmænd/ *noun* a situation where there is no demand as yet for a product but there is money to buy it ○ *Though there is no interest in our product in Saudi Arabia as yet, there is considerable potential demand.*

power /ˈpaʊər/ *noun* the ability to control people or events

power brand /ˈpaʊər brænd/ *noun* a very powerful brand which covers several best-selling products and is known worldwide

PR *abbreviation* public relations ○ *A PR firm is handling all our publicity.* ○ *She works in PR.* ○ *The PR people gave away 100,000 balloons.*

preapproach /ˈpriːəˌproʊtʃ/ *noun* the stage in a salesperson's preparation for a sale devoted to planning actual meetings with customers ○ *Preapproach sessions cover techniques in assessing customers and their needs.*

precinct /'prisɪŋkt/ *noun* a separate area

pre-coding /pri 'koʊdɪŋ/ *noun* the process of assigning codes to items on questionnaires in order to facilitate reference and evaluation ○ *Much time was lost in the survey through a confusing pre-coding system.* ○ *Freelance interviewers should be given a complete explanation of the pre-coding of questionnaires.*

predatory /'predət(ə)ri/ *adjective* which tries to attack □ **a predatory pricing policy** a policy of reducing prices as low as possible to try to get market share from weaker competitors

preempt /ˌpri'empt/ *verb* to stop something happening or stop someone doing something by taking action quickly before anyone else can ○ *They staged a management buyout to preempt a takeover bid.*

preemption /ˌpri'empʃən/ *noun* getting an advantage by doing something quickly before anyone else

preempt selling /ˌpri'empt ˌselɪŋ/ *noun* the practice of selling television advertising time at a lower rate with the proviso that another advertiser can take it over if the full rate is offered ○ *As we're on a tight advertising budget we'll have to go for preempt selling.*

preferred position /prɪˌfɜrd pə'zɪʃ(ə)n/ *noun* the place in a publication where an advertiser asks for the advertisement to be put

preferred position rate /prɪˌfɜrd pə'zɪʃ(ə)n reɪt/ *noun* a higher rate charged for placing an advertisement in the position requested

prelaunch /'prilɔntʃ/ *adjective* before a launch

prelaunch period /'prilɔntʃ ˌpɪriəd/ *noun* the period before the launch of a new product

premium /'primiəm/ *noun* **1.** the amount added to a normal price or rate for a product or service **2.** free gift offered to a prospective purchaser as an inducement to make a purchase

premium offer /'primiəm ˌɔfə/ *noun* a free gift offered to attract more customers

premium pricing /'primiəm ˌpraɪsɪŋ/ *noun* the act of giving products or services high prices either to give the impression that the product is worth more than it really is, or as a means of offering customers an extra service

prepack /pri'pæk/, **prepackage** /pri'pækɪdʒ/ *verb* to pack something before putting it on sale ○ *The fruit are prepacked in plastic trays.* ○ *The watches are prepacked in attractive display boxes.*

prepaid /pri'peɪd/ *adjective* paid in advance

prepaid reply card /ˌpripeɪd rɪ'plaɪ kɑrd/ *noun* a stamped addressed card which is sent to someone so that they can reply without paying the postage

preparatory set /prɪ'pærət(ə)ri set/ *noun* the principle that people have preconceived ideas about brands which influence their buying decisions

prepay /pri'peɪ/ *verb* to pay something in advance (NOTE: **prepaying – prepaid**)

prepayment /pri'peɪmənt/ *noun* a payment in advance, or the act of paying in advance □ **to ask for prepayment of a fee** to ask for the fee to be paid before the work is done

pre-press /pri 'pres/ *adjective* before going to press

pre-press work /pri 'pres wɜrk/ *noun* the work needed to change original copy and artwork into the form required for printing

prequalification /ˌprikwɑlɪfɪ'keɪʃ(ə)n/ *noun* researching the value of a potential customer, especially one who wants to take out a loan, or a contractor for a project

presence /'prez(ə)ns/ *noun* a measurement of an advertisement's real audience as opposed to its potential audience ○ *With an impressive presence our advertisement should have considerable effect.*

present /ˈprez(ə)nt/; /prɪˈzent/ *vti* to give a talk about or demonstration of something ○ *I've been asked to present at the sales conference.* ○ *The HR director will present the new staff structure to the Board.*

presentation /ˌprez(ə)nˈteɪʃ(ə)n/ *noun* **1.** the showing of a document □ **cheque payable on presentation** a check which will be paid when it is presented □ **free admission on presentation of this card** you do not pay to go in if you show this card **2.** a demonstration or exhibition of a proposed plan ○ *The distribution company gave a presentation of the services they could offer.* ○ *We have asked two PR firms to make presentations of proposed publicity campaigns.*

press /pres/ *noun* newspapers and magazines ○ *We plan to give the product a lot of press publicity.* ○ *There was no mention of the new product in the press.*

press advertising /ˈpres ˌædvərtaɪzɪŋ/ *noun* advertising in newspapers and magazines

press clipping /ˈpres ˌklɪpɪŋ/ *noun* a copy of a news item kept by a company because it contains important business information or is a record of news published about the company ○ *We have kept a file of press clippings about the new car.*

press clipping agency /ˈpres ˌklɪpɪŋ ˌeɪdʒənsi/ *noun* a company which cuts out references to clients from newspapers and magazines and sends them on to them

press communications /ˌpres kəˌmjuːnɪˈkeɪʃ(ə)nz/ *plural noun* communications which increase the awareness of journalists of a product or firm, e.g., press releases or news flashes

press conference /ˈpres ˌkɒnf(ə)rəns/ *noun* a meeting where newspaper and TV reporters are invited to hear news of something such as a new product or a takeover bid

press cutting /ˈpres ˌkʌtɪŋ/ *noun* U.K. same as **press clipping**

press date /ˈpres deɪt/ *noun* the date on which a publication is printed

press relations /pres rɪˈleɪʃ(ə)nz/ *plural noun* part of the public relations activity of an organization, aimed at building up good relations with the press ○ *If the company image is to improve we must first improve our press relations.*

press release /ˈpres rɪˌliːs/ *noun* a sheet giving news about something which is sent to newspapers and TV and radio stations so that they can use the information ○ *The company sent out a press release about the launch of the new car.*

pressure /ˈpreʃə/ *noun* something which forces you to do something

pressure group /ˈpreʃər gruːp/ *noun* a group of people who try to influence the government or some other organization

prestige /preˈstiʒ/ *noun* **1.** importance because of factors such as high quality or high value □ **prestige product** an expensive luxury product □ **prestige offices** expensive offices in a good area of the town **2.** status achieved because of being successful, wealthy, or powerful

prestige advertising /preˈstiʒ ˌædvərtaɪzɪŋ/ *noun* advertising in high-quality magazines to increase a company's reputation

prestige pricing /preˈstiʒ ˌpraɪsɪŋ/ *noun* same as **premium pricing**

pretax profit /ˌpriːtæks ˈprɒfɪt/ *noun* the amount of profit a company makes before taxes are deducted ○ *The dividend paid is equivalent to one quarter of the pretax profit.* Also called **profit before tax, profit on ordinary activities before tax**

pretest /ˈpriːtest/ *noun* evaluation of an advertising campaign before it is run

pre-testing /ˈpriː testɪŋ/ *noun* the testing or evaluation of a product or advertising campaign before it is launched or run ○ *Pre-testing has shown that the product would do well in the country as a whole.* ○ *The area chosen for pre-testing may not be representative enough of the whole country.*

preview /'priːvjuː/ *noun* a showing of a movie, a television commercial, or an exhibition to a specially invited audience before the general public sees it

price /praɪs/ *noun* money which has to be paid to buy something □ **competitive price** a low price aimed to compete with a rival product □ **to sell goods off at half price** to sell goods at half the price at which they were being sold before □ **cars in the $18–19,000 price range** cars of different makes, selling for between $18,000 and $19,000 □ **price ex ship** the price that includes all costs up to the arrival of the ship at port □ **price ex warehouse** the price for a product which is to be collected from the manufacturer's or agent's warehouse and so does not include delivery □ **to increase in price** to become more expensive ○ *Gasoline has increased in price* or *the price of gasoline has increased.* □ **to increase prices, to raise prices** to make items more expensive □ **we will try to meet your price** we will try to offer a price which is acceptable to you □ **to cut prices** to reduce prices suddenly □ **to lower prices, to reduce prices** to make items cheaper ■ *verb* to give a price to a product ○ *We have two used cars for sale, both priced at $5,000.* □ **competitively priced** sold at a low price which competes with that of similar goods from other companies □ **the company has priced itself out of the market** the company has raised its prices so high that its products do not sell

price band /'praɪs bænd/ *noun* a method of grouping articles within a narrow range of prices

price ceiling /'praɪs ˌsiːlɪŋ/ *noun* the highest price which can be reached

price competition /'praɪs kɑmpə ˌtɪʃ(ə)n/ *noun* the attempt to compete in a market through skillful pricing

price controls /'praɪs kənˌtroʊlz/ *plural noun* legal measures to prevent prices rising too fast

price cutting /'praɪs ˌkʌtɪŋ/ *noun* a sudden lowering of prices

price-cutting war /'praɪs ˌkʌtɪŋ wɔr/ *noun* same as **price war**

price differential /'praɪs dɪfə ˌrenʃəl/ *noun* the difference in price between products in a range

price differentiation /'praɪs dɪfərenʃiˌeɪʃ(ə)n/ *noun* a pricing strategy in which a company sells the same product at different prices in different markets

price discrimination /'praɪs dɪskrɪmɪˌneɪʃ(ə)n/ *noun* the practice of charging different prices in different markets or to different types of customer ○ *Price discrimination has caused some ill-feeling among customers.*

price effect /'praɪs ɪˌfekt/ *noun* the result of a change in price on a person's buying habits ○ *Before fixing the price, we'll have to carry out a survey to determine the price effect.*

price elasticity /'praɪs ɪlæˌstɪsəti/ *noun* a situation where a change in price has the effect of causing a big change in demand

price escalation clause /ˌpraɪs ˌeskəˈleɪʃ(ə)n ˌklɔz/ *noun* a clause in a contract that permits the seller to raise prices if its costs increase

price fixing /'praɪs ˌfɪksɪŋ/ *noun* an illegal agreement between companies to charge the same price for competing products

price-insensitive /ˌpraɪs ɪn ˈsensətɪv/ *adjective* used to describe a good or service for which sales remain constant no matter what its price because it is essential to buyers

price leadership /'praɪs ˌlidərʃɪp/ *noun* a situation where the producers model their prices on those of one leading producer

price level /'praɪs ˌlev(ə)l/ *noun* the average price of a particular product in a country at a particular time

price list /'praɪs lɪst/ *noun* a sheet giving prices of goods for sale

price maintenance /'praɪs ˌmeɪntənəns/ *noun* an agreement between producers or distributors on a minimum price for a product

price-off label /ˌpraɪs 'ɔf ˌleɪb(ə)l/ *noun* a label on a product showing a reduced price

price pegging /'praɪs ˌpegɪŋ/ *noun* the practice of maintaining prices at a specific level

price point /'praɪs pɔɪnt/ *noun* the exact price for a range of different products which is psychologically important for the customer, since if an article is given a higher price it will discourage sales ○ *We must have a meeting to determine price points for our products.*

price range /'praɪs reɪndʒ/ *noun* a series of prices for similar products from different suppliers

price ring /'praɪs rɪŋ/ *noun* a group of producers or distributors who agree to control prices and market conditions in their industry

price-sensitive /ˌpraɪs 'sensətɪv/ *adjective* referring to a product for which demand will change significantly if its price is increased or decreased

price tag /'praɪs tæg/ *noun* **1.** a label attached to an item being sold that shows its price **2.** the value of a person or thing ○ *The takeover bid put a $2m price tag on the company.*

price ticket /'praɪs ˌtɪkət/ *noun* a piece of paper showing a price

price war /'praɪs wɔr/ *noun* a competition between companies to get a larger market share by cutting prices. Also called **price-cutting war**

pricing /'praɪsɪŋ/ *noun* the act of giving a price to a product

pricing policy /'praɪsɪŋ ˌpɑlisi/ *noun* a company's policy in giving prices to its products ○ *Our pricing policy aims at producing a 35% gross margin.*

primacy /'praɪməsi/ *noun* the fact of being in first place or being the most important

primacy effect theory /'praɪməsi ɪfekt ˌθɪri/ *noun* the theory that the first information in a message is most likely to be remembered

primary /'praɪməri/ *adjective* basic

primary brand /'praɪməri brænd/ *noun* a brand owned by a distributor

rather than by a producer. Compare **private brand**

primary commodities /ˌpraɪməri kə'mɑdətiz/ *plural noun* raw materials or food

primary data /ˌpraɪməri 'deɪtə/, **primary information** *noun* data or information which has not yet been published and must therefore be found by field research ○ *The company's market research proved very expensive since it needed so much primary data.*

primary demand /ˌpraɪməri dɪ'mænd/ *noun* demand for a product in general, as opposed to demand for a particular brand ○ *The main producer companies are cooperating to create primary demand since this type of product is very new to the public.*

primary industry /ˌpraɪməri 'ɪndəstri/ *noun* an industry dealing with basic raw materials such as coal, wood, or farm produce

primary products /ˌpraɪməri 'prɑdʌkts/ *plural noun* products which are basic raw materials, e.g., wood, milk, or fish

prime /praɪm/ *adjective* most important ■ *noun* same as **prime rate**

prime cost /ˌpraɪm 'kɔst/ *noun* the cost involved in producing a product, excluding overheads

prime rate /'praɪm reɪt/ *noun* the best rate of interest at which a bank lends to its customers. Also called **prime**

prime time /'praɪm taɪm/ *noun* the most expensive advertising time for TV commercials ○ *We are putting out a series of prime-time commercials.*

principal /'prɪnsɪp(ə)l/ *noun* a person or company that is represented by an agent ○ *The agent has come to Chicago to see his principals.* ■ *adjective* most important ○ *The principal shareholders asked for a meeting.* ○ *The country's principal products are paper and wood.* ○ *The company's principal asset is its design staff.*

print /prɪnt/ *noun* the action of marking letters or pictures on paper by a machine, and so producing a book, leaflet, newspaper, etc.

printed matter /'prɪntɪd ˌmætər/ noun printed items, e.g., books, newspapers, and publicity sheets

print farming /'prɪnt ˌfɑrmɪŋ/ noun organizing the printing by outside printers of printed material required by an organization, such as advertising leaflets, catalogs, letterheads, etc.

print media /ˌprɪntɪd 'midiə/ plural noun advertising media, e.g., magazines and newspapers

print run /'prɪnt rʌn/ noun the number of copies of a publication or piece of advertising material which are printed ○ The company has ordered a print run of 100,000 for their new catalog.

privacy /'praɪvəsi/ noun a situation of not being disturbed by other people, especially the knowledge that communications are private and cannot be accessed by others

private /'praɪvət/ adjective belonging to a single person or to individual people, not to a company or the state □ **a letter marked "private and confidential"** a letter which must not be opened by anyone other than the person it is addressed to

private brand /'praɪvət brænd/ noun a brand owned by a distributor rather than by a producer. Compare **primary brand**

private enterprise /ˌpraɪvət 'entərpraɪz/ noun businesses which are owned privately, not nationalized ○ The project is completely funded by private enterprise.

private label /'praɪvət ˌleɪb(ə)l/ noun a brand name which is owned by a store, rather than the producer

private label goods /'praɪvət ˌleɪb(ə)l gʊdz/ plural noun goods with a brand name which is owned by the store, rather than the producer

private limited company /ˌpraɪvət ˌlɪmɪtɪd 'kʌmp(ə)ni/ noun **1.** a company with a small number of shareholders, whose shares are not traded on the Stock Exchange **2.** a subsidiary company whose shares are not listed on the Stock

Exchange, while those of its parent company are ▶ abbreviation **Pty Ltd**

privately /'praɪvətli/ adverb away from other people ○ The deal was negotiated privately.

private means /ˌpraɪvət 'minz/ plural noun income from dividends, interest, or rent which is not part of someone's salary

private property /ˌpraɪvət 'prɑpəti/ noun property which belongs to a private person, not to the public

private sector /'praɪvət ˌsektər/ noun all companies which are owned by private shareholders, not by the state ○ The expansion is completely funded by the private sector. ○ Salaries in the private sector have increased faster than in the public sector.

privatization /ˌpraɪvətaɪ'zeɪʃ(ə)n/ noun the process of selling a nationalized industry to private owners

privatize /'praɪvətaɪz/ verb to sell a nationalized industry to private owners

probability /ˌprɑbə'bɪləti/ noun the likelihood that something will happen, expressed mathematically

probability sampling /ˌprɑbə'bɪləti ˌsɑrmplɪŋ/ noun the choosing of samples for testing without any special selection method

probable /'prɑbəb(ə)l/ adjective likely to happen ○ They are trying to prevent the probable collapse of the company. ○ It is probable that the company will collapse if a rescue package is not organized before the end of the month.

probing /'proʊbɪŋ/ noun an attempt by an interviewer to get the interviewee to develop an answer ○ No amount of probing would induce the homemaker to say why she did not like the new laundry detergent.

problem children /'prɑbləm ˌtʃɪldr(ə)n/ plural noun in the Boston matrix, products which are not very profitable, and have a low market share and a high growth rate ○ The problem children in our range make very little contribution to the company profits. Also called **question marks, wild**

cats (NOTE: the singular is **problem child**)

procurement /prə'kjʊrmənt/ *noun* the act of buying equipment or raw materials for a company ○ *Procurement of raw materials is becoming very complicated with the entry of so many new suppliers into the market.*

produce *noun* /'prɒdjus/ products from farms and gardens, especially fruit and vegetables ○ *home produce* ○ *agricultural produce* ○ *farm produce* ■ *verb* /prə'djus/ to make or manufacture something ○ *The factory produces cars or engines.*

producer /prə'djusə/ *noun* a person, company, or country that manufactures ○ *a country which is a producer of high-quality watches* ○ *The company is a major car producer.* Also called **supplier**

producer market /prə'dusər ˌmɑrkət/ *noun* customers who buy goods to be used in production

producer's surplus /prəˌdjusəz 'sɜrpləs/ *noun* the amount by which the actual price of a product is more than the minimum which the producer would accept for it ○ *There is a considerable producer's surplus because the product is in short supply.* ○ *If our customer knew the producer's surplus she would have offered much less than the asking price.*

product /'prɒdʌkt/ *noun* **1.** something which is made or manufactured **2.** a manufactured item for sale

product abandonment /ˌprɒdʌkt ə'bændənmənt/ *noun* the stopping of production and selling of a product

product acceptance /ˌprɒdʌkt ək'septəns/ *noun* the degree to which a product is accepted by the market and so sells well ○ *We do not know what product acceptance will be in such an unknown market.*

product advertising /'prɒdʌkt ˌædvərtaɪzɪŋ/ *noun* the advertising of a particular named product, not the company which makes it

product analysis /ˌprɒdʌkt ə'næləsɪs/ *noun* an examination of each separate product in a company's range to find out why it sells, who buys it, etc.

product assortment /ˌprɒdʌkt ə'sɔrtmənt/ *noun* a collection of different products for sale

product churning /'prɒdʌkt ˌtʃɜrnɪŋ/ *noun* the practice of putting many new products onto the market in the hope that one of them will become successful (NOTE: Product churning is especially prevalent in Japan.)

product concept /'prɒdʌkt ˌkɑnsept/ *noun* same as **product idea**

product deletion /ˌprɒdʌkt dɪ'liʃ(ə)n/ *noun* the removal of old products from the market as new ones are added to the company's range ○ *Product deletion was caused by poor sales.* ○ *If production costs continue to rise then product deletion will be the only answer.*

product design /'prɒdʌkt dɪˌzaɪn/ *noun* the design of consumer products

product development /ˌprɒdʌkt dɪ'veləpmənt/ *noun* the process of improving an existing product line to meet the needs of the market. ◊ **new product development**

product development cycle /ˌprɒdʌkt dɪ'veləpmənt ˌsaɪk(ə)l/ *noun* the stages in the development of a new product

product differentiation /ˌprɒdʌkt dɪfəˌrenʃi'eɪʃ(ə)n/ *noun* the process of ensuring that a product has some unique features that distinguish it from competing ones ○ *We are adding some extra features to our watches in the interest of product differentiation.*

product elimination /ˌprɒdʌkt ɪlɪmɪ'neɪʃ(ə)n/ *noun* same as **product deletion**

product endorsement /'prɒdʌkt ɪnˌdɔrsmənt/ *noun* advertising which makes use of famous or qualified people to endorse a product ○ *Which celebrities have agreed to contribute to our endorsement advertising?* ○ *Product endorsement will, we hope, help our fundraising campaign.*

product family /'prɒdʌkt ˌfæm(ə)li/ *noun* a group of interrelated products made by the same manufacturer

product idea /ˈprɒdʌkt aɪˌdɪə/ *noun* an idea for a totally new product or an adaptation of an existing one

product idea testing /ˌprɒdʌkt aɪ ˈdɪə ˌtestɪŋ/ *noun* the evaluation of a new product idea, usually by consulting representatives from all main departments in a company and interviewing a sample of consumers

product image /ˈprɒdʌkt ˌɪmɪdʒ/ *noun* the general idea which the public has of a product ○ *We need a huge promotional campaign to create the desired product image.*

production /prəˈdʌkʃən/ *noun* the work of making or manufacturing goods for sale ○ *We are hoping to speed up production by installing new machinery.*

production cost /prəˈdʌkʃən kɒst/ *noun* the cost of making a product

production department /prə ˈdʌkʃən dɪˌpɑːtmənt/ *noun* the section of a company which deals with the making of the company's products

production line /prəˈdʌkʃən laɪn/ *noun* a system of making a product, where each item such as a car moves slowly through the factory with new sections added to it as it goes along ○ *He works on the production line.* ○ *She is a production-line employee.*

production manager /prəˈdʌkʃən ˌmænɪdʒər/ *noun* the person in charge of the production department

production standards /prə ˈdʌkʃən ˌstændədz/ *plural noun* the quality levels relating to production

production target /prəˈdʌkʃən ˌtɑːgət/ *noun* the amount of units a factory is expected to produce

production unit /prəˈdʌkʃən ˌjuːnɪt/ *noun* a separate small group of employees producing a product

productive /prəˈdʌktɪv/ *adjective* producing something, especially something useful □ **productive discussions** useful discussions which lead to an agreement or decision

productive capital /prəˌdʌktɪv ˈkæpɪt(ə)l/ *noun* capital which is invested to give interest

productivity /ˌprɒdʌkˈtɪvəti/ *noun* the rate of output per employee or per machine in a factory ○ *Bonus payments are linked to productivity.* ○ *The company is aiming to increase productivity.* ○ *Productivity has fallen* or *risen since the company was taken over.*

productivity agreement /ˌprɒdʌk ˈtɪvəti əˌgriːmənt/ *noun* an agreement to pay a productivity bonus

productivity bonus /ˌprɒdʌk ˈtɪvəti ˌbəʊnəs/ *noun* an extra payment made to employees because of increased production per employee

productivity drive /ˌprɒdʌkˈtɪvəti draɪv/ *noun* an extra effort to increase productivity

product launch /ˈprɒdʌkt lɔːntʃ/ *noun* the act of putting a new product on the market

product leader /ˌprɒdʌkt ˈliːdər/ *noun* the person who is responsible for managing a product line

product liability /ˌprɒdʌkt ˌlaɪə ˈbɪləti/ *noun* the liability of the maker of a product for negligence in the design or production of the product

product life cycle /ˌprɒdʌkt ˈlaɪf ˌsaɪk(ə)l/ *noun* stages in the life of a product in terms of sales and profitability, from its launch to its decline ○ *Growth is the first stage in the product life cycle.* ○ *The machine has reached a point in its product life cycle where we should be thinking about a replacement for it.*

product line /ˈprɒdʌkt laɪn/ *noun* a series of different products which form a group, all made by the same company ○ *We do not stock that line.* ○ *Computers are not one of our best-selling lines.* ○ *They produce an interesting line in garden tools.*

product management /ˌprɒdʌkt ˈmænɪdʒmənt/ *noun* the process of directing the making and selling of a product as an independent item

product manager /ˌprɒdʌkt ˈmænɪdʒər/ *noun* the manager or executive responsible for the marketing of a particular product ○ *To coordinate the selling of our entire range we need more* *consultation between product managers.*

product market /ˌprɒdʌkt 'mɑrkət/ *noun* a group of consumers for a product which is different from other groups to which the product is also sold

product-market strategies /ˌprɒdʌkt ˌmɑrkət 'strætɪdʒiz/ *plural noun* basic marketing strategies consisting of either market penetration, market development, product development, or diversification

product mix /'prɒdʌkt mɪks/ *noun* a range of different products which a company has for sale

product placement /'prɒdʌkt ˌpleɪsmənt/ *noun* placing products as props on TV shows or in films as a form of advertising

product-plus /'prɒdʌkt plʌs/ *noun* features of a product which make it particularly attractive

product portfolio /ˌprɒdʌkt pɔrt'fouliou/ *noun* a collection of products made by the same company

product portfolio analysis /ˌprɒdʌkt pɔrt'fouliou əˌnæləsɪs/ *noun* a model for a marketing strategy with various categories of product based on present performance and growth rate, which can help a business to plan its product development and strategy ○ *Product portfolio analysis showed that some products were neither performing well nor showing any signs of increasing their market share.*

product positioning /'prɒdʌkt pəˌzɪʃ(ə)nɪŋ/ *noun* the placing of a product in the market so that it is recognizable to the public

product range /'prɒdʌkt reɪndʒ/ *noun* **1.** a series of products from which the customer can choose **2.** a series of different products made by the same company which form a group

product recall /ˌprɒdʌkt 'rikɔl/ *noun* the removal from sale of products that may constitute a risk to consumers because of contamination, sabotage, or faults

product research /ˌprɒdʌkt rɪ'sɜrtʃ/ *noun* research carried out to ex-

amine various competing products in a market and the potential market for such products

product strategy /'prɒdʌkt ˌstrætədʒi/ *noun* the various elements which a company has to take into account when developing a product, e.g., price, design, and availability

product testing /'prɒdʌkt ˌtestɪŋ/ *noun* the testing of a product by allowing a sample of consumers to use it without knowing which brand it is ○ *Product testing showed that unfortunately consumers preferred two other brands to this one.*

profile /'proufaɪl/ *noun* a brief description of the characteristics of something or someone ○ *They asked for a profile of the possible partners in the joint venture.* ○ *Her résumé provided a profile of her education and career to date.*

profit /'prɒfɪt/ *noun* money gained from a sale which is more than the money spent on making the item sold or on providing the service offered □ **profit after tax** profit after tax has been paid □ **to take your profit** to sell shares at a higher price than was paid for them, and so realize the profit, rather than to keep them as an investment □ **to show a profit** to make a profit and state it in the company accounts ○ *We are showing a small profit for the first quarter.* □ **to make a profit** to have more money as a result of a deal □ **to move into profit** to start to make a profit ○ *The company is breaking even now, and expects to move into profit within the next two months.* □ **to sell at a profit** to sell at a price which gives you a profit □ **healthy profit** a good or large profit

profitability /ˌprɒfɪtə'bɪləti/ *noun* **1.** the ability to make a profit ○ *We doubt the profitability of the project.* **2.** the amount of profit made as a percentage of costs

profitable /'prɒfɪtəb(ə)l/ *adjective* making a profit ○ *She runs a very profitable employment agency.*

profit and loss account /ˌprɒfɪt ən 'lɔs əˌkaunt/, **profit and loss statement** /ˌprɒfɪt ən 'lɔs ˌsteɪtmənt/

noun the accounts for a company showing expenditure and income over a period of time, usually one calendar year, balanced to show a final profit or loss. Also called **P&L account**

profit center /ˈprɑfɪt ˌsentər/ *noun* a person, unit, or department within an organization which is considered separately for the purposes of calculating a profit ○ *We count the kitchen equipment division as a single profit center.*

profiteer /ˌprɑfɪˈtɪr/ *noun* a person who makes too much profit, especially when goods are rationed or in short supply

profiteering /ˌprɑfɪˈtɪrɪŋ/ *noun* the practice of making too much profit

profit-making /ˈprɑfɪt ˌmeɪkɪŋ/ *adjective* making a profit ○ *The whole project was expected to be profit-making by 2001 but it still hasn't broken even.* ○ *We hope to make it into a profit-making concern.*

profit margin /ˈprɑfɪt ˌmɑrdʒɪn/ *noun* the percentage difference between sales income and the cost of sales

profit maximization /ˈprɑfɪt ˌmæksɪmaɪˌzeɪʃ(ə)n/ *noun* a business strategy or policy based on achieving as high a profit as possible ○ *The company considers profit maximization a socially irresponsible policy.*

profit on ordinary activities before tax /ˌprɑfɪt ɑn ˌɔrd(ə)n(ə)ri æk ˌtɪvətiz bɪˌfɔr ˈtæks/ *noun* same as **pretax profit**

pro forma /ˌproʊ ˈfɔrmə/ *noun* a document issued before all relevant details are known, usually followed by a final version

pro forma invoice /ˌproʊ ˌfɔrmə ˈɪnvɔɪs/, **pro forma** /ˌproʊ ˈfɔrmə/ *noun* an invoice sent to a buyer before the goods are sent, so that payment can be made or so that goods can be sent to a consignee who is not the buyer ○ *They sent us a pro forma invoice.* ○ *We only supply that account on pro forma.*

progress report /ˈproʊgres rɪˌpɔrt/ *noun* a document which describes what progress has been made

project /ˈprɑdʒekt/ *noun* **1.** a plan ○ *She has drawn up a project for developing new markets in Europe.* **2.** a particular job of work which follows a plan ○ *We are just completing an engineering project in North Africa.* ○ *The company will start work on the project next month.*

project analysis /ˈprɑdʒekt əˌnæləsɪs/ *noun* the examination of all the costs or problems of a project before work on it is started

projected /prəˈdʒektɪd/ *adjective* planned or expected □ **projected sales** a forecast of sales ○ *Projected sales next year should be over $1m.*

projection /prəˈdʒekʃən/ *noun* a forecast of something which will happen in the future ○ *Projection of profits for the next three years.* ○ *The sales manager was asked to draw up sales projections for the next three years.*

project management /ˈprɑdʒekt ˌmænɪdʒmənt/ *noun* the coordination of the financial, material, and human resources needed to complete a project and the organization of the work that the project involves

project manager /ˌprɑdʒekt ˈmænɪdʒər/ *noun* the manager in charge of a project

promissory note /ˈprɑmɪsəri ˌnoʊt/ *noun* a document stating that someone promises to pay an amount of money on a specific date

promote /prəˈmoʊt/ *verb* to advertise a product □ **to promote a new product** to increase the sales of a new product by a sales campaign, by TV commercials or free gifts, or by giving discounts

promotion /prəˈmoʊʃ(ə)n/ *noun* all means of conveying the message about a product or service to potential customers, e.g., publicity, a sales campaign, TV commercials or free gifts ○ *Our promotion budget has been doubled.* ○ *The promotion team has put forward plans for the launch.* ○ *We are offering free vacations in Mexico as part of our special in-store promotion.* ○ *We a running a special promotion offering two for the price of one.*

promotional /prə'mouʃ(ə)l/ *adjective* used in an advertising campaign ○ *The admen are using balloons as promotional material.*

promotional allowance /prə,mouʃ(ə)l ə'lauəns/ *noun* a discount which is offered to a buyer in return for some promotional activity in connection with the product sold

promotional budget /prə,mouʃ(ə)l 'bʌdʒət/ *noun* a forecast of the cost of promoting a new product

promotional discount /prə,mouʃ(ə)l 'dɪskaunt/ *noun* a special discount offered as part of the promotion for a product

promotional mix /prə,mouʃ(ə)l 'mɪks/ *noun* the combination of all the elements that make up a company's promotion ○ *Our promotional mix consists of an extended TV and radio advertising campaign.* ○ *The exact promotional mix will depend on the costs of the various media available.*

promotional price /prə'mouʃ(ə)l praɪs/ *noun* a reduced price offered in order to maximize sales (often when a product is launched)

promotional products /prə'mouʃ(ə)l ,prɑdʌkts/ *plural noun* premium offers, gifts, prizes, etc.

promotional tools /prə'mouʃ(ə)l tulz/ *plural noun* material used in promotion, e.g., display material and sales literature ○ *A draw for a free vacation on the exhibition stand is one of the best promotional tools I know.* ○ *The sales reps are armed with a full range of promotional tools.*

promotools /'proumoutulz/ *plural noun* same as **promotional tools** (*informal*)

prompt /prɑmpt/ *adjective* rapid or done immediately ○ *We got very prompt service at the complaints desk.* ○ *Thank you for your prompt reply to my letter.* □ **prompt payment** payment made rapidly □ **prompt supplier** a supplier who delivers orders rapidly ■ *noun* information or an idea offered to people to help them answer a question in a survey ■ *verb* to give someone help in answering

a question ○ *In order to avoid influencing the answers, the interviewer must prompt the respondent only when it is really necessary.*

prompted awareness test /,prɑmptɪd ə'wernəs test/ *noun* a test where the respondents are asked if they know the named product

prompted recall /,prɑmptɪd 'rikɔl/ *noun* a test to see how well people can remember an advertisement in which the respondents are given some help such as a picture which they might associate with the advertisement ○ *After a prompted recall test, the company and its advertising agency decided to change the advertisement.*

proof /pruf/ *noun* evidence which shows that something is true

proof of purchase /,pruf əv 'pɜrtʃɪs/ *noun* evidence, e.g., a sales slip, to show that an article has been purchased, used in order to claim some benefit such as a free gift, or in order to claim reimbursement

propaganda /,prɑpə'gændə/ *noun* an attempt to spread an idea through clever use of the media and other forms of communication ○ *The charity has been criticized for spreading political propaganda.*

propensity /prə'pensəti/ *noun* a tendency

propensity to consume /prə,pensəti tə kən'sum/ *noun* the ratio between consumers' needs and their expenditure on goods

propensity to import /prə,pensəti tə ɪm'pɔrt/ *noun* the ratio between changes in the national income and changes in expenditure on imports

propensity to invest /prə,pensəti tə ɪn'vest/ *noun* the tendency of producers to invest in capital goods

propensity to save /prə,pensəti tə 'seɪv/ *noun* the tendency of consumers to save instead of spending on consumer goods

property developer /'prɑpərti dɪ,veləpər/ *noun* a person who buys old buildings or empty land and plans and builds new houses or factories for sale or rent

property market /'prɑpərti ˌmɑrkət/ *noun* same as **housing market**

proprietary goods /prə'praɪət(ə)ri gʊdz/ *plural noun* brands of a product such as medicines that are owned by the company which makes them

prospect /'prɑspekt/ *noun* **1.** a chance or possibility that something will happen in the future □ **prospects for the market, market prospects are worse than those of last year** sales in the market are likely to be lower than they were last year **2.** a person who may become a customer ○ *The sales force were looking out for prospects.*

prospecting /prə'spektɪŋ/ *noun* the act of looking for new customers

prospective /prə'spektɪv/ *adjective* possibly happening in the future □ **a prospective buyer** someone who may buy in the future ○ *There is no shortage of prospective buyers for the computer.*

prospects /'prɑspekts/ *plural noun* the possibilities for the future

prospectus /prə'spektəs/ *noun* a document which gives information to attract buyers or customers ○ *The restaurant has people handing out prospectuses in the street.*

protectionism /prə'tekʃənɪz(ə)m/ *noun* the practice of protecting producers in the home country against foreign competitors by banning or taxing imports or by imposing import quotas

protest *noun* /'prəʊtest/ an official document which proves that a bill of exchange has not been paid ■ *verb* /prə'test/ □ **to protest a bill** to draw up a document to prove that a bill of exchange has not been paid

prototype /'prəʊtətaɪp/ *noun* the first model of a new product before it goes into production ○ *a prototype car* ○ *a prototype plane* ○ *The company is showing the prototype of the new model at the exhibition.*

provisional /prə'vɪʒ(ə)n(ə)l/ *adjective* temporary, not final or permanent ○

She was given a provisional posting to see ○ *The sales department has been asked to make a provisional forecast of sales.* ○ *The provisional budget has been drawn up for each department.* ○ *They faxed their provisional acceptance of the contract.*

prune /prun/ *verb* to reduce a product range by deleting old products ○ *The new marketing director insisted on pruning the product line to streamline the company's functions.*

psychogalvanometer /ˌsaɪkoʊgælvə'nɑmɪtər/ *noun* an instrument used to measure emotional reactions to advertising by checking the degree of sweating on the palms of the hands ○ *The results of the psychogalvanometer test suggested that the ad was so dull it had no effect whatever on the public.*

psychographics /ˌsaɪkoʊ'græfɪks/ *noun* the study of the life style of different sectors of society for marketing purposes ○ *Psychographics can help define the market segment we should be aiming for with our product.* (NOTE: takes a singular verb)

psychographic segmentation /ˌsaɪkoʊgræfɪk ˌsegmən'teɪʃ(ə)n/ *noun* the division of a market into segments according to the lifestyles of the customers

public /'pʌblɪk/ *adjective* referring to all the people in general ■ *noun* □ **the public, the general public** the people

publication /ˌpʌblɪ'keɪʃ(ə)n/ *noun* **1.** the act of making something public by publishing it ○ *the publication of the latest trade figures* **2.** a printed document which is to be sold or given to the public ○ *We asked the library for a list of government publications.*

public image /ˌpʌblɪk 'ɪmɪdʒ/ *noun* an idea which the people have of a company or a person ○ *The mayor is trying to improve her public image.*

publicity /pʌ'blɪsəti/ *noun* the process of attracting the attention of the public to products or services by mentioning them in the media

publicity budget /pʌ'blɪsəti ˌbʌdʒət/ *noun* money allowed for expenditure on publicity

publicity copy /pʌ'blɪsəti ˌkɑpi/ *noun* the text of a proposed advertisement before it is printed ○ *She writes publicity copy for a travel firm.*

publicity department /pʌ'blɪsəti dɪˌpɑrtmənt/ *noun* the section of a company which organizes the company's publicity

publicity expenditure /pʌ'blɪsəti ɪkˌspendɪtʃər/ *noun* money spent on publicity

publicity handout /pʌ'blɪsəti ˌhændaʊt/ *noun* an information sheet which is given to members of the public

publicity manager /pʌ'blɪsəti ˌmænɪdʒər/ *noun* the person in charge of a publicity department

publicity matter /pʌ'blɪsəti ˌmætər/ *noun* sheets, posters, or leaflets used for publicity

publicity slogan /pʌ'blɪsəti ˌsloʊɡən/ *noun* a group of words which can be easily remembered and which is used in publicity for a product ○ *We are using the slogan "Smiths can make it" on all our publicity.*

publicize /'pʌblɪsaɪz/ *verb* to attract people's attention to a product for sale, a service, or an entertainment ○ *The campaign is intended to publicize the services of the tourist board.* ○ *We are trying to publicize our products by advertisements on buses.*

public limited company /ˌpʌblɪk ˌlɪmɪtɪd 'kʌmp(ə)ni/ *noun* a company whose shares can be bought on the Stock Exchange. Abbreviation **Plc, PLC, plc**. Also called **public company**

public opinion /ˌpʌblɪk ə'pɪnjən/ *noun* what people think about something

public relations /ˌpʌblɪk rɪ'leɪʃ(ə)nz/ *plural noun* the practice of building up and keeping good relations between an organization and the public, or an organization and its employees, so that people know and think well of what the organization is doing ○ *She works in public relations.* ○ *A public relations firm handles all our publicity.* Abbreviation **PR** (NOTE: takes a singular verb)

public relations consultancy /ˌpʌblɪk rɪ'leɪʃ(ə)nz kənˌsʌltənsi/ *noun* a firm which advises on public relations

public relations department /ˌpʌblɪk rɪ'leɪʃ(ə)nz dɪˌpɑrtmənt/ *noun* the section of a company which deals with relations with the public. Abbreviation **PR department**

public relations exercise /ˌpʌblɪk rɪ'leɪʃ(ə)nz ˌeksəsaɪz/ *noun* a campaign to improve public relations

public relations officer /ˌpʌblɪk rɪ'leɪʃ(ə)nz ˌɒfɪsər/ *noun* a person in an organization who is responsible for public relations activities. Abbreviation **PRO**

publics /'pʌblɪks/ *plural noun* groups of people that are identified for marketing purposes ○ *What publics is this product likely to appeal to?* ○ *Different marketing messages need to be aimed at different publics.*

public sector /'pʌblɪk ˌsektər/ *noun* nationalized industries and services ○ *a report on wage increases in the public sector* or *on public-sector wage increases* Also called **government sector**

public service advertising /ˌpʌblɪk 'sɜrvɪs ˌædvərtaɪzɪŋ/ *noun* the advertising of a public service or cause such as famine relief

public transportation /ˌpʌblɪk ˌtrænspər'teɪʃ(ə)n/ *noun* transportation which is used by any member of the public, e.g., buses and trains

public transportation system /ˌpʌblɪk ˌtrænspər'teɪʃ(ə)n ˌsɪstəm/ *noun* a system of trains, buses, etc., used by the general public

public warehouse /ˌpʌblɪk 'werhaʊs/ *noun* a warehouse which stores goods which are awaiting shipment or which have just been landed

puff /pʌf/ *noun* a claim made for a product or an organization in order to promote it ○ *The magazine article was supposed to be about telecommunications, but was just a puff for a new modem.*

puffery /ˈpʌfəri/ *noun* advertising which praises the product or service being sold in an exaggerated way, without any specific factual data

puff piece /ˈpʌf pis/ *noun* a supposedly objective newspaper or magazine article about a product or service, which reads as if it were written by an in-house publicity department and may in fact be written by advertising people on behalf of a client

pull-push strategy /ˌpʊl ˈpʊʃ ˌstrætədʒi/ *noun* a combination of both pull and push strategies

pull strategy /ˈpʊl ˌstrætədʒi/ *noun* an attempt by a producer to use heavy advertising to persuade final users to buy a product, so "pulling" the product through the distribution channel to the point of sale ○ *We must develop a better pull strategy to allow retailers to sell off their excess stocks.*

pump priming /ˈpʌmp ˌpraɪmɪŋ/ *noun* government investment in new projects which it hopes will benefit the economy

purchase /ˈpɜrtʃɪs/ *noun* a product or service which has been bought □ **to make a purchase** to buy something ■ *verb* to buy something □ **to purchase something for cash** to pay cash for something

purchase book /ˈpɜrtʃɪs bʊk/ *noun* a book in which purchases are recorded

purchase history /ˈpɜrtʃɪs ˌhɪst(ə)ri/ *noun* a record of purchases which a customer has made in the past, or of sales made by a retail outlet, or of sales of a product over a specific period

purchase ledger /ˈpɜrtʃɪs ˌledʒər/ *noun* a book in which expenditure is noted

purchase order /ˈpɜrtʃɪs ˌɔrdər/ *noun* an official order made out by a purchasing department for goods which a company wants to buy ○ *We cannot supply you without a purchase order number.*

purchase price /ˈpɜrtʃɪs praɪs/ *noun* a price paid for something

purchaser /ˈpɜrtʃɪsər/ *noun* a person or company that purchases ○ *The company has found a purchaser for its warehouse.* □ **the company is looking for a purchaser** the company is trying to find someone who will buy it

purchase tax /ˈpɜrtʃɪs tæks/ *noun* a tax paid on things which are bought

purchasing /ˈpɜrtʃɪsɪŋ/ *noun, adjective* buying

purchasing department /ˈpɜrtʃɪsɪŋ dɪˌpɑrtmənt/ *noun* the section of a company which deals with the buying of stock, raw materials, equipment, etc.

purchasing manager /ˈpɜrtʃɪsɪŋ ˌmænɪdʒər/ *noun* the head of a purchasing department

purchasing officer /ˈpɜrtʃɪsɪŋ ˌɔfɪsər/ *noun* a person in a company or organization who is responsible for buying stock, raw materials, equipment, etc.

purchasing opportunity /ˈpɜrtʃɪsɪŋ ɑpərˌtunəti/ *noun* a possibility for a customer to make a purchase

pure competition /ˌpjʊr ˌkɑmpɪˈtɪʃ(ə)n/ *noun* a hypothetical model of a market where all products of a particular type are identical, where there is complete information about market conditions available to buyers and sellers, and complete freedom for sellers to enter or leave the market

push /pʊʃ/ *noun* the action of making something move forward ◇ **push the envelope** to go beyond normal limits and try to do something that is new and sometimes risky (*slang*)

push money /ˈpʊʃ ˌmʌni/ *noun* cash given to a sales force to encourage them to promote a product

push-pull strategy /ˌpʊʃ ˈpʊl ˌstrætɪdʒi/ *noun* same as **pull-push strategy**

push strategy /ˈpʊʃ ˌstrætədʒi/ *noun* **1.** an attempt by a manufacturer to push the product toward the customer **2.** an attempt by a producer to persuade distributors to take part in the marketing of a product, so "pushing" it through the distribution channel

put /pʊt/ *verb*
  put down *phrasal verb* to make a deposit ○ *to put down money on a*

house
put in *phrasal verb* □ **to put in a bid
for something** to offer to buy something, usually in writing □ **to put in
an estimate for something** to give
someone a written calculation of the
probable costs of carrying out a job □
to put in a claim for damage to ask
an insurance company to pay for
damage

pyramid selling /ˈpɪrəmɪd ˌselɪŋ/
noun an illegal way of selling goods or
investments to the public, where each
selling agent pays for the franchise to
sell the product or service, and sells that
right on to other agents together with
stock, so that in the end the person who
makes the most money is the original
franchiser, and sub-agents or investors
may lose all their investments

Q

quad crown /'kwɑd kraʊn/ *noun* a poster size corresponding to twice a double crown

qualified prospects /ˌkwɑlɪfaɪd 'prɑspekts/ *plural noun* prospective customers who can make buying decisions

qualitative /'kwɑlɪtətɪv/ *adjective* referring to quality

qualitative audit /ˌkwɑlɪtətɪv 'ɔdɪt/ *noun* examining an advertising agency's work in planning and developing a client's advertising program

qualitative data /ˌkwɑlɪtətɪv 'deɪtə/ *noun* data found in qualitative research

qualitative research /ˌkwɑlɪtətɪv rɪ'sɜrtʃ/ *noun* research based on finding the opinions and attitudes of respondents rather than any scientifically measurable data ○ *Qualitative research can be used to ascertain consumers' attitudes to a new advertising campaign.* ○ *Qualitative research will not give objective information.*

quality /'kwɑləti/ *noun* what something is like or how good or bad something is ○ *The poor quality of the service led to many complaints.* ○ *There is a market for good-quality secondhand computers.* □ **we sell only quality farm produce** we sell only farm produce of the best quality □ **high quality, top quality** of the very best quality ○ *The store specializes in high-quality imported items.*

quality control /'kwɑləti kən,troʊl/ *noun* the process of making sure that the quality of a product is good

quality controller /'kwɑləti kən,troʊlər/ *noun* a person who checks the quality of a product

quality label /'kwɑləti ˌleɪb(ə)l/ *noun* a label which states the quality of something

quality press /'kwɑləti pres/ *noun* newspapers aiming at the upper end of the market ○ *We advertise in the quality press.*

quantitative /'kwɑntɪtətɪv/ *adjective* referring to quantity

quantitative data /ˌkwɑntɪtətɪv 'deɪtə/ *noun* data gathered in quantitative research

quantitative research /ˌkwɑntɪtətɪv rɪ'sɜrtʃ/ *noun* research based on measurable data gathered by sampling ○ *Quantitative research will provide a firm basis for strategy decisions.*

quantity /'kwɑntəti/ *noun* **1.** the amount or number of items ○ *a small quantity of illegal drugs* ○ *She bought a large quantity of spare parts.* **2.** an amount, especially a large amount

quantity discount /ˌkwɑntəti 'dɪskaʊnt/ *noun* a discount given to people who buy large quantities

quantity purchase /'kwɑntəti ˌpɜrtʃɪs/ *noun* a large quantity of goods bought at one time ○ *The company offers a discount for quantity purchase.*

quarterly /'kwɔrtərli/ *noun* a newspaper or magazine which appears four times a year ○ *We're advertising in a medical quarterly.*

quasi- /kweɪzaɪ/ *prefix* almost or which seems like ○ *a quasi-official body*

quasi-retailing /ˌkweɪzaɪ ˈriteɪlɪŋ/ *prefix* retailing relating to the provision of services, as in restaurants or hair salons

quay /ki/ *noun* the place in a port where ships can tie up □ **price ex quay**, **price ex dock** price of goods after they have been unloaded, not including transportation from the harbor

question marks /ˈkwestʃən mɑrks/ *plural noun* same as **problem children**

questionnaire /ˌkwestʃəˈner/ *noun* a printed list of questions aiming at collecting data in an unbiased way, especially used in market research ○ *We'll send out a questionnaire to test the opinions of users of the system.* ○ *We were asked to answer or to fill in a questionnaire about vacations abroad.*

quota /ˈkwoʊtə/ *noun* a limited amount of something which is allowed to be produced, imported, etc.

quota sample /ˈkwoʊtə ˌsæmpəl/ *noun* a sample which is preselected on the basis of specific criteria so as best to represent the group of people sampled ○ *The quota sample was used to represent the various ethnic groupings in their correct proportions.*

quota system /ˈkwoʊtə ˌsɪstəm/ *noun* a system where imports or supplies are regulated by fixed maximum amounts

quotation /kwoʊˈteɪʃ(ə)n/ *noun* an estimate of how much something will cost ○ *They sent in their quotation for the job.* ○ *Our quotation was much lower than all the others.* ○ *We accepted the lowest quotation.*

quote /kwoʊt/ *verb* **1.** to repeat words or a reference number used by someone else ○ *He quoted figures from the annual report.* ○ *In reply please quote this number.* ○ *When making a complaint please quote the batch number printed on the box.* ○ *She replied, quoting the number of the account.* **2.** to estimate what a cost or price is likely to be ○ *to quote a price for supplying stationery* ○ *Their prices are always quoted in dollars.* ○ *He quoted me a price of $1,026.* ○ *Can you quote for supplying 20,000 envelopes?* ■ *noun* an estimate of how much something will cost (*informal*) ○ *to give someone a quote for supplying computers* ○ *We have asked for quotes for refitting the store.* ○ *Her quote was the lowest of three.* ○ *We accepted the lowest quote.*

R

rack /ræk/ *noun* a frame to hold items for display ○ *a magazine rack* ○ *Put the birthday-card display rack near the checkout.* ○ *We need a bigger display rack for these magazines.*

rack board /'ræk bɔrd/ *noun* a board on which items can be displayed, showing the names and prices of products

rack jobber /'ræk ˌdʒɑbər/ *noun* a wholesaler who sells goods by putting them on racks in retail shops

radio button /'reɪdioʊ ˌbʌt(ə)n/ *noun* a device on a computer screen that can be used to select an option from a list

rail /reɪl/ *noun* a railroad system ○ *Six million commuters travel to work by rail each day.* ○ *We ship all our goods by rail.* ○ *Rail travelers are complaining about rising fares.* ○ *Rail travel is cheaper than air travel.* □ **free on rail (FOR)** a price including all the seller's costs until the goods are delivered to the railroad for shipment

railhead /'reɪlhed/ *noun* the end of a railroad line ○ *The goods will be sent to the railhead by truck.*

railroad /'reɪlroʊd/ *noun* a system using trains to carry passengers and goods ○ *The country's railroad network is being modernized.*

railway /'reɪlweɪ/ *noun* U.K. same as **railroad**

rake-off /'reɪk ɔf/ *noun* a person's share of profits from a deal, especially if obtained illegally ○ *The group gets a rake-off on all the company's sales.* ○ *He got a $100,000 rake-off for introducing the new business.* (NOTE: The plural is **rake-offs**.)

R&D *abbreviation* research and development

random /'rændəm/ *adjective* done without making any special selection □ **at random** without special selection ○ *The director picked out two sales reports at random.*

random check /ˌrændəm 'tʃek/ *noun* a check on items taken from a group without any special selection

random error /ˌrændəm 'erər/ *noun* a computer error for which there is no special reason

random fluctuation /ˌrændəm ˌflʌktʃu'eɪʃ(ə)n/ *noun* unforeseeable deviation from an expected trend

random observation method /ˌrændəm ˌɑbzə'veɪʃ(ə)n ˌmeθəd/ *noun* same as **activity sampling**

random sample /ˌrændəm 'sæmpəl/ *noun* a sample taken without any selection

random sampling /ˌrændəm 'sæmplɪŋ/ *noun* the action of choosing samples for testing without any special selection

random walk /ˌrændəm 'wɔk/ *noun* a sampling technique which allows for random selection within specific limits set up by a non-random technique

range /reɪndʒ/ *noun* **1.** a series of items ○ *Their range of products or product range is too narrow.* ○ *We offer a wide range of sizes or range of styles.* **2.** a spread of sizes or amounts within fixed limits ○ *We make shoes in a wide range of prices.* **3.** a set of activities or products of the same general type or variety ○ *This falls within the company's range of activities.* ■ *verb* to be within a group of sizes or amounts falling within fixed limits ○ *The company sells prod-ucts ranging from cheap downmarket pens to imported luxury items.* ○ *The company's salary scale ranges from $10,000 for a trainee to $150,000 for the managing director.* ○ *Our activities range from mining in the USA to com-puter services in Scotland.*

rapport /ræ'pɔr/ *noun* good commu-nication and understanding between two people ○ *The interviewer managed to establish a good rapport with the inter-viewees.* ○ *Co-ordination is difficult ow-ing to lack of rapport between the mar-keting manager and the managing di-rector.*

rate /reɪt/ *noun* **1.** the money charged for time worked or work completed **2.** the value of one currency against anoth-er ○ *What is today's rate* or *the current rate for the dollar?* □ **to calculate costs on a fixed exchange rate** to calculate costs on an exchange rate which does not change **3.** an amount, number or speed compared with something else ○ *the rate of increase in lay-offs* ○ *The rate of absenteeism* or *The absenteeism rate always increases in fine weather.*

rate card /'reɪt kɑrd/ *noun* a list of charges for advertising issued by a newspaper or magazine

rate of exchange /ˌreɪt əv ɪks 'tʃeɪndʒ/ *noun* same as **exchange rate** ○ *The current rate of exchange is $1.60 to the pound.*

rate of interest /ˌreɪt əv 'ɪntrəst/ *noun* same as **interest rate**

rate of return /ˌreɪt əv rɪ'tɜrn/ *noun* the amount of interest or dividend which comes from an investment, shown as a percentage of the money invested

rate of sales /ˌreɪt əv 'seɪlz/ *noun* the speed at which units are sold

rate of turnover /ˌreɪt əv 'tɜrnoʊvər/ *noun* the length of time taken from the purchase of an item of stock to its replacement after being sold ○ *The rate of turnover is so low that some articles have been in the store for more than a year.*

rate of unemployment /ˌreɪt əv ˌʌnɪm'plɔɪmənt/ *noun* same as **unem-ployment rate**

rating /'reɪtɪŋ/ *noun* the act of giving something a value, or the value given

ratings /'reɪtɪŋz/ *plural noun* the esti-mated number of people who watch TV programs ○ *The show is high in the rat-ings, which means it will attract good publicity.*

ratings point /'reɪtɪŋz pɔɪnt/ *noun* one percentage point of a TV audience in a given area

ratio /'reɪʃioʊ/ *noun* a proportion or quantity of something compared to something else ○ *the ratio of successes to failures* ○ *Our product outsells theirs by a ratio of two to one.*

rational /'ræʃ(ə)n(ə)l/ *adjective* sen-sible, based on reason

rational appeal /ˌræʃ(ə)n(ə)l ə'pil/ *noun* advertising appeal to a prospective customer that uses logical arguments to show that the product satisfies the cus-tomer's practical needs (as opposed to an emotional appeal)

rationalize /'ræʃ(ə)nəlaɪz/ *verb* to make something more efficient ○ *The rail company is trying to rationalize its freight services.*

raw /rɔ/ *adjective* in the original state or not processed

raw data /ˌrɔ 'deɪtə/ *noun* data as it is put into a computer, without being ana-lyzed

raw materials /ˌrɔ mə'tɪriəlz/ *plural noun* basic materials which have to be treated or processed in some way before they can be used, e.g., wood, iron ore, or crude petroleum

reach /ritʃ/ *verb* to get to something ■ *noun* the actual number of people who will see an advertisement once (as op-posed to the frequency, which is the number of times one person sees an ad-vertisement over a given period of time) ○ *The success of an advertisement de-pends on its reach.*

readability /ˌridə'bɪləti/ *noun* the fact of being easy to read (either copy for an advertisement or the advertisement itself)

reader /'ridər/ noun a person who reads a newspaper or magazine

reader advertisement /'ridər əd,vɜrtɪsmənt/ noun an advertisement in the form of editorial matter

reader loyalty /,ridər 'lɔɪəlti/ noun the inclination of a person to keep reading and buying the same publication

readership /'ridərʃɪp/ noun all the people who read a particular publication ○ *Our readership has increased since we included more feature articles in the magazine.*

reader's inquiry card /,ridərz ɪn 'kwaɪri kɑrd/, **reader's service card** /,ridərz 'sɜrvɪs kɑrd/ noun a card bound into a magazine which contains a matrix of numbers and letters on which readers can mark codes for products they wish to have further information about. The card is returned to the publisher, who gets the advertiser to send the relevant information to the reader.

reading and noting /,ridɪŋ ən 'noʊtɪŋ/ noun a research statistic showing the proportion of the readership of a publication who actually read a given advertisement

readvertise /ri'ædvərtaɪz/ verb to advertise again ○ *All the candidates failed the test so we will just have to readvertise.* □ **to readvertise a post** to put in a second advertisement for a vacant position

readvertisement /,riəd 'vɜrtɪsmənt/ noun a second advertisement for a vacant position ○ *The readvertisement attracted only two new applicants.*

ready /'redi/ adjective **1.** fit to be used or to be sold ○ *The order will be ready for delivery next week.* ○ *The driver had to wait because the shipment was not ready.* **2.** quick □ **these items find a ready sale in the Middle East** these items sell rapidly or easily in the Middle East

ready cash /,redi 'kæʃ/ noun money which is immediately available for payment

ready-made /,redi 'meɪd/, **ready-to-wear** /,redi tə 'wer/ adjective referring to clothes which are mass-produced and not made for each customer personally ○ *The ready-to-wear trade has suffered from foreign competition.*

ready market /,redi 'mɑrkət/ noun a market with a high turnover of goods ○ *Distribution has to be good in such a ready market.*

ready money /,redi 'mʌni/ noun cash or money which is immediately available

ready sale /,redi 'seɪl/ noun a sale that is easily achieved ○ *Lengthy negotiations are a trial for salespeople used to ready sales.*

real /rɪəl/ adjective **1.** genuine and not an imitation ○ *His briefcase is made of real leather* or *he has a real leather briefcase.* ○ *That car is a real bargain at $300.* **2.** (*of prices or amounts*) shown in terms of money adjusted for inflation □ **in real terms** actually or really ○ *Salaries have gone up by 3% but with inflation running at 5% that is a fall in real terms.*

realized profit /,rɪəlaɪzd 'prɑfɪt/ noun an actual profit made when something is sold, as opposed to paper profit

real time credit card processing /,rɪəl taɪm 'kredɪt kɑrd ,prɑsesɪŋ/ noun online checking of a credit card that either approves or rejects it for use during a transaction

real time transaction /,rɪəl taɪm træn'zækʃən/ noun an Internet payment transaction that is either approved or rejected immediately when the customer completes the online order form

rebate /'ribeɪt/ noun **1.** a reduction in the amount of money to be paid ○ *We are offering a 10% rebate on selected goods.* **2.** money returned to someone because they have paid too much ○ *She got a tax rebate at the end of the year.*

rebating /ri'beɪtɪŋ/ noun the offering of a rebate

rebound /rɪ'baʊnd/ verb to go back up again quickly ○ *The market rebounded with the news of the government's decision.*

rebuy /'ribaɪ/ *noun* the act of buying a product again

recall /rɪ'kɔl/ *verb* (*of a manufacturer*) to ask for products to be returned because of possible faults ○ *They recalled 10,000 washing machines because of a faulty electrical connection.* ■ *noun* the ability to remember an advertisement

recall test /'rikɔl test/ *noun* in advertising, a research test that checks how well someone can remember an advertisement ○ *A disappointing number of respondents in the recall test failed to remember the advertisement.*

receipt /rɪ'sit/ *noun* a piece of paper showing that money has been paid or that something has been received ○ *He kept the customs receipt to show that he had paid duty on the goods.* ○ *She lost her taxi receipt.* ○ *Keep the receipt for items purchased in case you need to change them later.*

receipts /rɪ'sits/ *plural noun* money taken in sales ○ *to itemize receipts and expenditure* ○ *Receipts are down against the same period of last year.*

recession /rɪ'seʃ(ə)n/ *noun* a period where there is a decline in trade or in the economy ○ *The recession has reduced profits in many companies.* ○ *Several firms have closed factories because of the recession.*

recipient /rɪ'sɪpiənt/ *noun* a person who receives something ○ *She was the recipient of an allowance from the company.* ○ *He was the recipient of the award for salesperson of the year.* ○ *A registered letter must be signed for by the recipient.*

reciprocal /rɪ'sɪprək(ə)l/ *adjective* done by one person, company, or country to another one, which does the same thing in return ○ *We signed a reciprocal agreement* or *a reciprocal contract with a Russian company.*

reciprocal holdings /rɪ,sɪprək(ə)l 'houldɪŋz/ *plural noun* a situation where two companies own shares in each other to prevent takeover bids

reciprocal trade /rɪ,sɪprək(ə)l 'treɪd/ *noun* trade between two countries

reciprocate /rɪ'sɪprəkeɪt/ *verb* to do the same thing for someone as that person has done for you ○ *They offered us an exclusive agency for their cars and we reciprocated with an offer of the agency for our buses.*

recognition /,rekəg'nɪʃ(ə)n/ *noun* the act of recognizing something or somebody

recognition test /,rekəg'nɪʃ(ə)n test/ *noun* a research test in advertising that checks to see how well someone can remember an advertisement either with or without prompting or aided recall

recognize /'rekəgnaɪz/ *verb* **1.** to know someone or something because you have seen or heard them before ○ *I recognized his voice before he said who he was.* ○ *Do you recognize the handwriting on the application form?* **2.** □ **to recognize a union** to agree that a union can act on behalf of employees in a company ○ *Although more than half the staff had joined the union, the management refused to recognize it.*

recognized agent /,rekəgnaɪzd 'eɪdʒənt/ *noun* an agent who is approved by the company for which they act

recommended retail price /,rekəmendɪd 'riteɪl ,praɪs/ *noun* the price at which a manufacturer suggests a product should be sold on the retail market, though this may be reduced by the retailer. Abbreviation **RRP**. Also called **administered price**

record *noun* /'rekɔrd/ **1.** a description of what has happened in the past ○ *the salesperson's record of service* or *service record* ○ *the company's record in industrial relations* **2.** a success which is better than anything before ○ *Last year was a record year for the company.* ○ *Our top sales rep has set a new record for sales per call.* □ **we broke our record for June** we sold more than we have ever sold before in June ○ *Sales last year equaled the record set in 1997.* ■ *verb* /rɪ'kɔrd/ to note or report some-

thing ○ *The company has recorded an-*
other year of increased sales.

record-breaking /'rekɔrd ˌbreɪkɪŋ/
adjective better or worse than anything
which has happened before ○ *We are*
proud of our record-breaking profits in
2000.

recorded delivery /rɪˌkɔrdɪd dɪ
'lɪv(ə)ri/ *noun U.K.* same as **certified**
mail

recording /rɪ'kɔrdɪŋ/ *noun* the act of
making a note of something ○ *the re-*
cording of an order or *of a complaint*

records /'rekɔrdz/ *plural noun* documents which give information ○ *The*
names of customers are kept in the com-
pany's records. ○ *We find from our*
records that our invoice number 1234
has not been paid.

recruit /rɪ'krut/ *verb* □ **to recruit new**
staff to search for and appoint new staff
to join a company ○ *We are recruiting*
staff for our new store.

recruitment /rɪ'krutmənt/, **recruit-**
ing /rɪ'krutɪŋ/ *noun* □ **the recruitment**
of new staff the process of looking for
new staff to join a company

recruitment advertising /rɪ
'krutmənt ˌædvərtaɪzɪŋ/ *noun* the advertising of jobs ○ *A sudden need for la-*
bor has led to a huge demand for re-
cruitment advertising.

recycle /rɪ'saɪk(ə)l/ *verb* to take waste
material and process it so that it can be
used again

recycled paper /rɪˌsaɪk(ə)ld
'peɪpər/ *noun* paper made from waste
paper

redeem /rɪ'dim/ *verb* to exchange a
voucher, coupon, or stamp for a gift or a
reduction in price

redemption /rɪ'dempʃən/ *noun* the
exchanging of vouchers, coupons, or
stamps for a gift or a reduction in price

red goods /'red gʊdz/ *plural noun*
fast-selling convenience goods, especially food items. Compare **orange**
goods, yellow goods

reduced rate /rɪˌdjust 'reɪt/ *noun* a
specially cheap charge

reduction /rɪ'dʌkʃən/ *noun* an act of
making something smaller or less ○ *Re-*
duction in demand has led to the cancel-
lation of several new projects. ○ *The*
company was forced to make reductions
in its advertising budget. ○ *Price reduc-*
tions have had no effect on our sales.

re-export /ˌriek'spɔrt/ *noun* the exporting of goods which have been imported ○ *The port is a center for the re-*
export trade. ○ *We import wool for re-*
export. ○ *The value of re-exports has in-*
creased. ■ *verb* to export something
which has been imported

reexportation /riˌekspɔr'teɪʃ(ə)n/
noun the exporting of goods which have
been imported

refer /rɪ'fɜr/ *verb* □ **the bank referred**
the cheque to drawer the bank returned
the check to person who wrote it because there was not enough money in
the account to pay it

reference group /'ref(ə)rəns ˌgrup/
noun a group of people who share some
interest or aim and are used by consumers as a model to be imitated

reference site /'ref(ə)rəns saɪt/
noun a customer site where a new technology is being used successfully

refund *noun* /'rifʌnd/ money paid
back ○ *The shoes don't fit – I'm going to*
ask for a refund. ○ *She got a refund after*
complaining to the manager. ■ *verb* /rɪ
'fʌnd/ to pay back money ○ *to refund*
the cost of postage ○ *All money will be*
refunded if the goods are not satisfacto-
ry.

refundable /rɪ'fʌndəb(ə)l/ *adjective*
possible to pay back ○ *We ask for a re-*
fundable deposit of $20. ○ *The entrance*
fee is refundable if you purchase $5
worth of goods.

refusal /rɪ'fjuz(ə)l/ *noun* an act of
saying no

regiocenter stage /'ridʒioʊsentər
ˌsteɪdʒ/ *noun* the stage in a company's
international marketing when a region
consisting of several countries is treated
as one market

registered /'redʒɪstəd/ *adjective*
having been noted on an official list ○ *a*
registered share transaction

registered design /ˌredʒɪstəd dɪ
'zaɪn/ *noun* a design which is legally
registered to protect the owner against
unauthorized use of it by others

registered letter /ˌredʒɪstəd 'letər/,
registered parcel /ˌredʒɪstəd
'pɑrs(ə)l/ *noun* a letter or parcel which
is noted by the post office before it is
sent, so that the sender can claim compensation if it is lost

registered trademark /ˌredʒɪstəd
'treɪdmɑrk/ *noun* a name, design, or
symbol which has been registered by the
manufacturer and which cannot be used
by other manufacturers. It is an intangible asset. ○ *You can't call your beds
"Softn'kumfi" – it is a registered trademark.*

registration /ˌredʒɪ'streɪʃ(ə)n/ *noun*
the act of having something noted on an
official list ○ *the registration of a trademark or of a share transaction*

registration fee /ˌredʒɪ'streɪʃ(ə)n
fi/ *noun* **1.** money paid to have something registered **2.** money paid to attend
a conference

registration number /ˌredʒɪ
'streɪʃ(ə)n ˌnʌmbər/ *noun* an official
number, e.g., the number of a car

regression analysis /rɪ'greʃ(ə)n ə
ˌnæləsɪs/, **regression model** /rɪ
'greʃ(ə)n ˌmɑd(ə)l/ *noun* a method of
discovering the ratio of one dependent
variable and one or more independent
variables, so as to give a value to the dependent variable

regular /'regjələr/ *adjective* ordinary
or standard ○ *The regular price is $1.25,
but we are offering them at 99 cents.*

regular customer /ˌregjələr
'kʌstəmər/ *noun* a customer who always buys from the same store

regular model /ˌregjələr 'mɑd(ə)l/
noun the main product in a company's
product range ○ *We estimate that 65% of
the customers interested in our product
range will buy the regular model.*

regular size /'regjələr saɪz/ *noun*
the standard size (smaller than economy
size or family size)

regular staff /ˌregjələr 'stæf/ *noun*
the full-time staff

regulate /'regjʊleɪt/ *verb* **1.** to adjust
something so that it works well or is correct **2.** to change or maintain something
by law □ **prices are regulated by supply and demand** prices are increased or
lowered according to supply and demand □ **government-regulated price** a
price which is imposed by the government

regulation /ˌregjə'leɪʃ(ə)n/ *noun* **1.** a
law or rule ○ *the new government regulations on housing standards* ○ *Fire regulations or Safety regulations were not
observed at the restaurant.* ○ *Regulations concerning imports and exports
are set out in this leaflet.* **2.** the use of
laws or rules stipulated by a government
or regulatory body, such as the Securities and Exchange Commission, to provide orderly procedures and to protect
consumers and investors ○ *government
regulation of trading practices*

regulations /ˌregjʊ'leɪʃ(ə)nz/ *noun*
laws or rules ○ *the new government regulations on housing standards* ○ *Fire
regulations or Safety regulations were
not observed at the restaurant.* ○ *Regulations concerning imports and exports
are set out in this leaflet.*

regulator /'regjəleɪtər/ *noun* a person whose job it is to see that regulations
are followed

reimport *noun* /riˈɪmpɔrt/ the importing of goods which have been exported
from the same country ■ *verb* /ˌriɪm
'pɔrt/ to import goods which have already been exported

reimportation /ˌriɪmpɔ'teɪʃ(ə)n/
noun the importing of goods which have
already been exported

reinforcement advertising /ˌriɪn
'fɔrsmənt ˌædvərtaɪzɪŋ/ *noun* advertising aimed at making the positive features of a product stronger in order to re-
assure people who have already purchased it

reject /'ridʒekt/ *noun, adjective*
something which has been thrown out
because it is not of the usual standard ○
sale of rejects or *of reject items* ○ *to sell
off reject stock*

reject store /'ridʒekt stɔr/ *noun* a
store which specializes in the sale of

goods which have not passed all of their producers quality-control tests, but which are still suitable for sale at a reduced price

relational database /rɪ,leɪʃ(ə)n(ə)l 'deɪtəbeɪs/ noun a computer database in which different types of data are linked for analysis

relationship /rɪ'leɪʃ(ə)nʃɪp/ noun a link or connection

relationship building /rɪ 'leɪʃ(ə)nʃɪp ,bɪldɪŋ/ noun taking actions to develop a long-term relationship with the customer

relationship management /rɪ 'leɪʃ(ə)nʃɪp ,mænɪdʒmənt/ noun the management of customers so as to build long-term relationships with them

relationship marketing /rɪ 'leɪʃ(ə)nʃɪp ,mɑːkətɪŋ/ noun a long-term marketing strategy to build relationships with individual customers

relative /'relətɪv/ adjective compared to something else

relative cost /,relətɪv 'kɒst/ noun the relationship between the cost of advertising space and the size of the audience

relaunch noun /'riːlɔːnʃ/ the act of putting a product back on the market again, after adapting it to changing market conditions ○ The relaunch is scheduled for August. ■ verb /riː'lɔːntʃ/ to put a product on the market again ○ The product will be relaunched with some minor modifications next fall.

release /rɪ'liːs/ noun 1. the act of setting someone free or of making someone or something no longer subject to an obligation or restriction ○ release from a contract ○ the release of goods from customs 2. the act of making something public, or a public announcement 3. □ new release a new CD or a piece of software put on the market ■ verb to put something on the market ○ They released several new CDs this month. □ to release dues to send off orders which had been piling up while a product was out of stock

remainder /rɪ'meɪndər/ verb □ to remainder books to sell new books off

cheaply ○ The store was full of piles of remaindered books.

remainder merchant /rɪ'meɪndər ,mɜːtʃənt/ noun a book dealer who buys unsold new books from publishers at a very low price

remainders /rɪ'meɪndərz/ plural noun new books sold cheaply

reminder /rɪ'meɪndər/ noun a letter to remind a customer that he or she has not paid an invoice ○ to send someone a reminder

reminder advertising /rɪ'meɪndər ,ædvərtaɪzɪŋ/ noun advertising designed to remind consumers of a product already advertised ○ Reminder advertising is particularly important in a highly competitive market.

reminder line /rɪ'meɪndər laɪn/ noun a little advertising gimmick, e.g., a giveaway pen with the company's name on it

remnant /'remnənt/ noun an odd piece of a large item such as, a carpet or fabric sold separately ○ a sale of remnants or a remnant sale

remnant space /'remnənt speɪs/ noun odd unsold advertising space, which is usually available at a discount

render /'rendər/ verb □ to render an account to send in an account ○ Please find enclosed payment per account rendered.

rental list /'rent(ə)l lɪst/ noun a mailing list of names and addresses which can be rented

reorder /riː'ɔːdər/ noun a further order for something which has been ordered before ○ The product has only been on the market ten days and we are already getting reorders. ■ verb to place a new order for something ○ We must reorder these items because stock is getting low.

reorder level /riː'ɔːdər ,lev(ə)l/ noun a minimum amount of an item which a company holds in stock, such that, when stock falls to this amount, the item must be reordered

rep /rep/ noun same as **representative** (informal) ○ to hold a reps' meeting ○ Our reps make on average six calls a day.

repack /riˈpæk/ *verb* to pack again

repacking /riˈpækɪŋ/ *noun* the act of packing again

repeat /rɪˈpiːt/ *verb* □ **to repeat an order** to order something again

repeat business /rɪˌpiːt ˈbɪznɪs/ *noun* business which involves a new order for something which has been ordered before

repeat order /rɪˌpiːt ˈɔːdər/ *noun* a new order for something which has been ordered before ○ *The product has been on the market only ten days and we are already flooded with repeat orders.*

repeat purchasing /rɪˌpiːt ˈpɜːtʃɪsɪŋ/ *noun* **1.** the purchasing of the same product a second time **2.** the frequent buying of a low-priced item that is for everyday use such as soap or bread

repertory grid technique /ˌrepət(ə)ri ˈɡrɪd tekˌnik/ *noun* a market-research technique in which a test is first run to discover what the respondents' main criteria are in judging product brands. This is followed by another test in which the respondents evaluate brands on the basis of these established criteria.

reply /rɪˈplaɪ/ *noun* an answer ○ *the company's reply to the takeover bid* ○ *There was no reply to my letter* or *to my phone call.* ○ *I am writing in reply to your letter of the 24th.* ■ *verb* to answer ○ *We forgot to reply to our lawyer's letter.* ○ *The company has replied to the takeover bid by offering the shareholders higher dividends.* (NOTE: **replies-replying- replied**)

reply coupon /rɪˈplaɪ ˌkuːpɒn/ *noun* a form attached to a coupon ad which has to be filled in and returned to the advertiser

report /rɪˈpɔːt/ *noun* **1.** a statement describing what has happened or describing a state of affairs ○ *to make a report* or *to present a report* or *to send in a report on market opportunities in the Far East* ○ *The accountants are drafting a report on salary scales.* ○ *The sales manager reads all the reports from the sales team.* ○ *The chairman has re-*ceived a report from the insurance company. **2.** an official document from a government committee ○ *The government has issued a report on the credit problems of exporters.* ■ *verb* **1.** to make a statement describing something ○ *The sales force reported an increased demand for the product.* ○ *He reported the damage to the insurance company.* ○ *We asked the bank to report on his financial status.* **2.** □ **to report to someone** to be responsible to or to be under someone ○ *She reports directly to the vice president.* ○ *The sales force reports to the sales director.*

reposition /ˌriːpəˈzɪʃ(ə)n/ *verb* to change the position of a product or company in the market

repositioning /ˌriːpəˈzɪʃ(ə)nɪŋ/ *noun* a change or adjustment to the position of a product in the market, or the consumers' idea of it, by changing its design or by different advertising ○ *If this spring's promotional campaign doesn't achieve a repositioning of the product, sales will continue to fall.*

repossess /ˌriːpəˈzes/ *verb* to take back an item which someone is buying under an installment plan, or a property which someone is buying under a mortgage, because the purchaser cannot continue the payments

represent /ˌreprɪˈzent/ *verb* to work for a company, showing goods or services to possible buyers ○ *He represents an American car firm in Europe.* ○ *Our French distributor represents several other competing firms.*

representation /ˌreprɪzenˈteɪʃ(ə)n/ *noun* the right to sell goods for a company, or a person or organization that sells goods on behalf of a company ○ *We offered them exclusive representation in the USA.* ○ *They have no representation in Europe.*

representative /ˌreprɪˈzentətɪv/ *adjective* which is an example of what all others are like ○ *We displayed a representative selection of our product range.* ○ *The sample chosen was not representative of the whole batch.* ■ *noun* **1.** a company which works for another company, selling their goods ○ *We* *have appointed Smith & Co our exclusive representatives in Europe.* **2.** same as **salesperson**

resale /'riseɪl/ *noun* the selling of goods which have been bought ○ *to purchase something for resale* ○ *The contract forbids resale of the goods to Canada.*

resale price maintenance /ˌriseɪl 'praɪs ˌmeɪntənəns/ *noun* a system in which the price for an item is fixed by the manufacturer, and the retailer is not allowed to sell it at a lower price. Abbreviation **RPM**

research /rɪ'sɜːtʃ/ *noun* the process of trying to find out facts or information ■ *verb* to study or try to find out information about something ○ *They are researching the market for their new product.*

research and development /rɪ ˌsɜːtʃ ən dɪ'veləpmənt/ *noun* **1.** a scientific investigation which leads to making new products or improving existing products ○ *The company spends millions on research and development.* Abbreviation **R&D 2.** activities that are designed to produce new knowledge and ideas and to develop ways in which these can be commercially exploited by a business (NOTE: Research and development activities are often grouped together to form a separate division or department within an organization.)

COMMENT: Research costs can be divided into (a) applied research, which is the cost of research leading to a specific aim, and (b) basic, or pure, research, which is research carried out without a specific aim in mind: these costs are written off in the year in which they are incurred. Development costs are the costs of making the commercial products based on the research.

research brief /rɪ'sɜːtʃ briːf/ *noun* the basic objectives and instructions concerning a market-research project

research department /rɪ'sɜːtʃ dɪˌpɑːtmənt/ *noun* the section of a company which carries out research

researcher /rɪ'sɜːtʃər/ *noun* a person who carries out research ○ *Government statistics are a useful source of information for the desk researcher.*

research unit /rɪ'sɜːtʃ ˌjuːnɪt/ *noun* a separate small group of research workers

research worker /rɪ'sɜːtʃ ˌwɜːkər/ *noun* a person who works in a research department

resell /riː'sel/ *verb* to sell something which has just been bought ○ *The car was sold in June and the buyer resold it to an dealer two months later.* (NOTE: **reselling – resold**)

reseller /riː'selər/ *noun* somebody in the marketing chain who buys to sell to somebody else, e.g., wholesalers, distributors, and retailers

reseller market /riː'selər ˌmɑːkət/ *noun* a market in which customers buy products in order to resell them as wholesalers or retailers ○ *Fewer and fewer consumers are buying the product, so prices are falling in the reseller market.*

reserved market /rɪˌzɜːvd 'mɑːkət/ *noun* a market in which producers agree not to sell more than a specific amount in order to control competition. Also called **restricted market**

reserve price /rɪ'zɜːv praɪs/ *noun* the lowest price which a seller will accept, e.g., at an auction or when selling securities through a broker ○ *The painting was withdrawn when it failed to reach its reserve price.*

resistance /rɪ'zɪstəns/ *noun* opposition felt or shown by people to something ○ *There was a lot of resistance from the team to the new plan.* ○ *The chairman's proposal met with strong resistance from the banks.* ○ *There was a lot of resistance from the shareholders to the new plan.*

resources /rɪ'sɔːsɪz/ *plural noun* **1.** a supply of something □ **we are looking for a site with good water resources** a site with plenty of water available **2.** the money available for doing something □ **the cost of the new project is easily within our resources** we have more than enough money to pay for the new project

respond /rɪ'spɒnd/ *verb* to reply to a question

respondent /rɪˈspɒndənt/ *noun* a person who answers questions in a survey ○ *Some of the respondents' answers were influenced by the way the questions were asked.*

response /rɪˈspɒns/ *noun* a reply or reaction ○ *There was no response to our mailing shot.* ○ *We got very little response to our complaints.*

response booster /rɪˈspɒns ˌbuːstər/ *noun* anything that will help increase the response rate

response function /rɪˈspɒns ˌfʌŋkʃən/ *noun* a figure which represents the value of a particular quantity of advertising impressions on a person

response level /rɪˈspɒns ˌlevəl/, **response rate** /rɪˈspɒns reɪt/ *noun* the proportion of people approached in a survey who agree to answer questions ○ *The response rate has been very disappointing.*

response marketing /rɪˈspɒns ˌmɑːkətɪŋ/ *noun* in e-marketing, the process of managing responses or leads from the time they are received through to conversion to sale

response mechanism /rɪˈspɒns ˌmekənɪz(ə)m/ *noun* a method of showing a response to an Internet advertisement, or the way in which a customer can reply to an advertisement or direct mailshot, such as sending back a coupon or a faxback sheet

response rate /rɪˈspɒns reɪt/ *noun* the proportion of people who respond to a questionnaire or survey

re-sticker /ˌriː ˈstɪkər/ *verb* to put new stickers on stock, e.g., when increasing the price

restock /riːˈstɒk/ *verb* to order more stock or inventory ○ *to restock after the Christmas sales*

restocking /riːˈstɒkɪŋ/ *noun* the ordering of more stock or inventory

restraint /rɪˈstreɪnt/ *noun* control

restraint of trade /rɪˌstreɪnt əv ˈtreɪd/ *noun* **1.** a situation where employees are not allowed to use their knowledge in another company on changing jobs **2.** an attempt by companies to fix prices, create monopolies, or reduce competition, which could affect free trade

restrict /rɪˈstrɪkt/ *verb* to limit something or to impose controls on something ○ *to restrict credit* ○ *to restrict the flow of trade* or *to restrict imports* ○ *We are restricted to twenty staff by the size of our offices.*

restricted market /rɪˌstrɪktɪd ˈmɑːkət/ *noun* same as **reserved market**

restriction /rɪˈstrɪkʃən/ *noun* a limit or control ○ *import restrictions* or *restrictions on imports* □ **to impose restrictions on imports** *or* **credit** to start limiting imports or credit □ **to lift credit restrictions** *or* **import restrictions** to allow credit to be given freely or imports to enter the country freely

restrictive /rɪˈstrɪktɪv/ *adjective* not allowing something to go beyond a point, limiting

restrictive trade practices /rɪˌstrɪktɪv ˈtreɪd ˌpræktɪsɪz/, **restrictive practices** /rɪˌstrɪktɪv ˈpræktɪsɪz/ *plural noun* an arrangement between companies to fix prices or to share the market in order to restrict trade

résumé /ˈrezuˌmeɪ/, **resume** /rɪˈzjuːm/ *noun* a summary of a person's work experience and qualifications sent to a prospective employer by someone applying for a job ○ *Candidates should send a letter of application with a résumé to the HR manager.* ○ *The résumé listed all the candidate's previous jobs and her reasons for leaving them.* (NOTE: The U.K. term is **curriculum vitae**.)

retail /ˈriːteɪl/ *noun* the sale of small quantities of goods to the general public □ **the goods in stock have a retail value of $1m** the value of the goods if sold to the public is $1m, before discounts and other factors are taken into account ■ *adverb* □ **he buys wholesale and sells retail** he buys goods in bulk at a wholesale discount and sells in small quantities to the public ■ *verb* **1.** □ **to retail goods** to sell goods direct to the public **2.** to sell for a price □ **these items retail**

at *or* **for $2.50** the retail price of these items is $2.50

retail audit /'riteɪl ˌɔdɪt/ *noun* a market research method by which a research company regularly checks a sample of retailers for unit sales and inventory levels of different brands ○ *Since subscribing to the retail audit we've been able to compare our performance with that of our competitors.*

retail cooperative /'riteɪl koʊ ˌɑp(ə)rətɪv/ *noun* an organization whose business is the buying and selling of goods that is run by a group of people who share the profits between them (NOTE: Retail cooperatives were the first offshoot of the cooperative movement.)

retail dealer /'riteɪl ˌdilər/ *noun* a person who sells to the general public

retailer /'riteɪlər/ *noun* a person who runs a retail business, selling goods direct to the public

retailer cooperative /'riteɪlər koʊ ˌɑp(ə)rətɪv/ *noun* a group of retailers who buy together from suppliers so as to be able to enjoy quantity discounts

retailing /'riteɪlɪŋ/ *noun* the selling of full-price goods to the public ○ *From car retailing the company branched out into car leasing.*

retail management /ˌriteɪl 'mænɪdʒmənt/ *noun* managing the retail side of a business such as points of sale, stock control, and just-in-time purchasing

retail media /'riteɪl ˌmidiə/ *noun* advertising media in retail outlets, e.g., ads on shopping carts

retail outlet /'riteɪl ˌaʊtlet/ *noun* a store which sells to the general public

retail price /'riteɪl ˌpraɪs/ *noun* the price at which the retailer sells to the final customer

retail price index /ˌriteɪl 'praɪs ˌɪndeks/, **retail prices index** /ˌriteɪl 'praɪsɪz ˌɪndeks/ *noun U.K.* same as **Consumer Price Index**

retail trade /'riteɪl treɪd/ *noun* all people or businesses selling goods retail

retention /rɪ'tenʃən/ *noun* the act of keeping the loyalty of existing customers, as opposed to acquisition, which is the act of acquiring new customers. Both can be aims of advertising campaigns.

retrenchment /rɪ'trentʃmənt/ *noun* a reduction of expenditure or of new plans ○ *The company is in for a period of retrenchment.*

return /rɪ'tɜrn/ *noun* **1.** the act of sending something back □ **he replied by return of post** he replied by the next mail service back **2.** an official statement or form that has to be sent in to the authorities ■ *verb* to send back ○ *to return unsold stock to the wholesaler* ○ *to return a letter to sender*

returnable /rɪ'tɜrnəb(ə)l/ *adjective* which can be returned ○ *These bottles are not returnable.*

return address /rɪ'tɜrn əˌdres/ *noun* the address to which you send back something

returns /rɪ'tɜrnz/ *plural noun* unsold goods, especially books, newspapers, or magazines, sent back to the supplier

revenue /'revənju/ *noun* money received ○ *revenue from advertising* or *advertising revenue* ○ *Oil revenues have risen with the rise in the dollar.*

revenue accounts /'revənju əˌkaʊnts/ *plural noun* accounts of a business which record money received as sales, commission, etc.

reverse /rɪ'vɜrs/ *adjective* opposite or in the opposite direction

reverse engineering /rɪˌvɜrs ˌendʒɪ'nɪrɪŋ/ *noun* the taking apart of a product in order to find out how it was put together (NOTE: Reverse engineering can help a company redesign a product, but it can also enable competitors to analyze how their rivals' products are made.)

reverse takeover /rɪˌvɜrs 'teɪkoʊvər/ *noun* a takeover where the company which has been taken over ends up owning the company which has taken it over. The acquiring company's shareholders give up their shares in exchange for shares in the target company.

revocable /'revəkəb(ə)l/ *adjective* which can be revoked

revocable letter of credit /ˌrevəkəb(ə)l ˌletər əv 'kredɪt/ *noun* a letter of credit that can be canceled

revoke /rɪ'voʊk/ *verb* to cancel something ○ *to revoke a decision* or *a clause in an agreement* ○ *The quota on luxury items has been revoked.*

revolving credit /rɪˌvɑlvɪŋ 'kredɪt/ *noun* a system where someone can borrow money at any time up to an agreed amount, and continue to borrow while still paying off the original loan. Also called **open-ended credit**

risk /rɪsk/ *noun* **1.** possible harm or a chance of danger □ **to run a risk** to be likely to suffer harm □ **to take a risk** to do something which may make you lose money or suffer harm **2.** □ **at owner's risk** a situation where goods shipped or stored are insured by the owner, not by the transportation company or the storage company ○ *Goods left here are at owner's risk.* ○ *The shipment was sent at owner's risk.* **3.** loss or damage against which you are insured **4.** □ **he is a good** *or* **bad risk** it is not likely or it is very likely that the insurance company will have to pay out against claims where he is concerned

risk analysis /'rɪsk əˌnæləsɪs/ *noun* analysis of how much can be lost and gained through various marketing strategies ○ *After protracted risk analysis a very ambitious strategy was adopted.* ○ *Our risk analysis must concentrate on competitor activity.*

risk-averse /ˌrɪsk ə'vɜrs/ *adjective* not wanting to take risks

risk capital /'rɪsk ˌkæpɪt(ə)l/ *noun* same as **venture capital**

risk-free /ˌrɪsk 'fri/, **riskless** /'rɪskləs/ *adjective* with no risk involved ○ *a risk-free investment*

risky /'rɪski/ *adjective* dangerous or which may cause harm ○ *We lost all our money in some risky ventures in South America.*

rival /'raɪv(ə)l/ *noun* a person or company that competes in the same market ○ *a rival company* ○ *to undercut a rival*

rival brand /ˌraɪv(ə)l 'brænd/, **rival product** /ˌraɪv(ə)l 'prɑdʌkt/ *noun* a brand or product that is competing for sales with another brand or product ○ *We are analyzing the rival brands on the market.*

road /roʊd/ *noun* a way used by cars, trucks, etc. to move from one place to another ○ *to send* or *to ship goods by road* ○ *The main office is on Park Road.* ○ *Use the Park Road entrance to get to the buying department.* (NOTE: in addresses, **Road** is usually shortened to **Rd.**) □ **on the road** traveling ○ *The sales force is on the road thirty weeks a year.* ○ *We have twenty salesmen on the road.*

road haulage /'roʊd ˌhɔlɪdʒ/ *noun* the moving of goods by road

road haulage depot /roʊd 'hɔlɪdʒ ˌdepoʊ/ *noun* a center for goods which are being moved by road, and the trucks which carry them

road hauler /'roʊd ˌhɔlər/ *noun* a company which transports goods by road

ROB *abbreviation* run of book

rock bottom /ˌrɑk 'bɑtəm/ *noun* □ **sales have reached rock bottom** sales have reached the lowest point possible

rocket /'rɑkət/ *verb* to rise fast ○ *Investors are rushing to cash in on rocketing share prices.* ○ *Prices have rocketed on the commodity markets.*

roll /roʊl/ *verb*

    roll over *phrasal verb* □ **to roll over a credit** to make credit available over a continuing period □ **to roll over a debt** to allow a debt to stand after the repayment date

rolling /'roʊlɪŋ/ *adjective* continuing with no break

rolling launch /ˌroʊlɪŋ 'lɔntʃ/ *noun* a gradual launch of a new product onto the market by launching it in different areas over a period

rolling plan /ˌroʊlɪŋ 'plæn/ *noun* a plan which runs for a period of time and is updated regularly for the same period

roll out /ˌroʊl 'aʊt/ *verb* to extend a company's marketing of a product from its original test marketing area to the whole country

rollout /'roulaut/ *noun* **1.** extending the marketing of a product from the original test marketing area to the whole country **2.** same as **rolling launch**

RON *abbreviation* run of network

ROP *abbreviation* run of paper

ROS *abbreviation* **1.** run of site **2.** run of station

rough /rʌf/ *noun* the outline plan of an illustration for an advertisement ○ *The agency sent the rough to the advertisers for approval.* ○ *The advertising department will consider the rough carefully before telling the agency to go ahead and run the advertisement.*

> **rough out** *phrasal verb* to make a draft or a general design of something, which may be changed later ○ *The finance director roughed out a plan of investment.*

ROW *abbreviation* run of week

royalties /'rɔɪəltiz/ *plural noun* a proportion of the income from the sales of a product such as a new invention, a book, or a piece of music that is paid to its creator

royalty /'rɔɪəlti/ *noun* money paid to an inventor, writer, or the owner of land for the right to use their property, usually a specific percentage of sales, or a specific amount per sale ○ *The country will benefit from rising oil royalties.* ○ *He is still receiving substantial royalties from his invention.*

RPI *abbreviation* retail price index

RPM *abbreviation* resale price maintenance

RRP *abbreviation* recommended retail price

run /rʌn/ *noun* a period of time during which a machine is working □ **a cheque run** a series of checks processed through a computer

> **run down** *phrasal verb* **1.** to reduce a quantity gradually ○ *We decided to run down stocks* or *to let stocks run down at the end of the financial year.* **2.** to slow down the business activities of a company before it is going to be closed ○ *The company is being run down.*

running total /ˌrʌnɪŋ 'təʊt(ə)l/ *noun* the total carried from one column of figures to the next

run of book /ˌrʌn əv 'bʊk/, **run of paper** /ˌrʌn əv 'peɪpər/ *noun* an advertiser's order to the advertising department of a publication that buys advertising space at the basic rate and does not specify the position of the advertisement in the publication. Abbreviation **ROB**, **ROP**

run of network /ˌrʌn əv 'netwɜːrk/ *noun* banner advertising that runs across a network of websites. Abbreviation **RON**

run of site /ˌrʌn əv 'saɪt/ *noun* banner advertising that runs on one single website. Abbreviation **ROS**

run of station /ˌrʌn əv 'steɪʃ(ə)n/ *noun* TV advertising for which a particular time period has not been requested. Abbreviation **ROS**

run of week /ˌrʌn əv 'wiːk/ *noun* an advertiser's order to the advertising department of a publication that buys advertising space at the basic rate and does not specify the issue it will appear in. Abbreviation **ROW**

run-on /'rʌn ɒn/ *noun* copies of a publication printed in addition to the original print order, as in the case of a leaflet whose setting-up costs have been covered. More copies of it can be printed at a relatively cheap unit cost.

S

sachet /'sæʃeɪ/ *noun U.K.* a small package or envelope containing a product in the form of liquid or powder ○ *If you are traveling, buy sachets of shampoo.* ○ *The magazine came with a free sachet of skin cream attached.* ○ *Sachets of instant coffee were provided.*

sack /sæk/ *noun* a large bag made of strong cloth or plastic ○ *a sack of potatoes* ○ *We sell onions by the sack.*

salability /ˌseɪləˈbɪləti/, **saleability** *noun* a quality in an item which makes it easy to sell

salable /'seɪləb(ə)l/, **saleable** *adjective* which can easily be sold ○ *The company is not readily salable in its present state.*

salary check /'sæləri tʃek/ *noun* a monthly check by which an employee is paid

salary package /'sæləri ˌpækɪdʒ/ *noun* same as **pay package**

salary structure /'sæləri ˌstrʌktʃə/ *noun* the organization of salaries in a company with different rates of pay for different types of job

sale /seɪl/ *noun* **1.** an act of giving an item or doing a service in exchange for money, or for the promise that money will be paid □ **for sale** ready to be sold □ **to offer something for sale** *or* **to put something up for sale** to announce that something is ready to be sold ○ *They put the factory up for sale.* ○ *His store is for sale.* ○ *These items are not for sale to the general public.* □ **sale as seen** a sale with no guarantee of quality ○ *If the equipment is for sale as seen, we shall have no comeback if it breaks down.* □ **sale by description** a sale on condition that the goods match the description of

them given by the seller □ **sale or return** a system where the retailer sends goods back if they are not sold, and pays the supplier only for goods sold ○ *We have taken 4,000 items on sale or return.* **2.** an act of selling goods at specially low prices ○ *The store is having a sale to clear old stock.* ○ *The sale price is 50% of the usual price.*

sale and lease-back /ˌseɪl ən 'lis bæk/ *noun* the sale of an asset, usually a building, to somebody else who then leases it back to the original owner

saleroom /'seɪlrum/ *noun* a room where an auction takes place

sales /seɪlz/ *plural noun* □ **the sales** period when major stores sell many items at specially low prices ○ *I bought this in the sales* or *at the sales* or *in the January sales.*

sales agent /'seɪlz ˌeɪdʒənt/ *noun* a person who sells for a business or another person and earns a commission ○ *How many sales agents do we have in this area?* ○ *She's a competent sales agent representing several non-competing companies.*

sales aids /'seɪlz eɪdz/ *plural noun* various tools used for selling, e.g., samples, display cases, and sales literature ○ *The sales manager gave a talk on new sales aids which had just become available.* ○ *An exhibition of sales aids was held at the sales conference.*

sales analysis /'seɪlz əˌnæləsɪs/ *noun* an examination of the reports of sales to see why items have or have not sold well

sales appeal /'seɪlz əˌpil/ *noun* a quality in a product which makes customers want to buy it

sales assistant /'seɪlz ə,sɪstənt/ *noun* a person in a store who sells goods to customers

sales audit /'seɪlz ,ɔdɪt/ *noun* an analysis of a company's sales in terms of such factors as product, revenue, and area

sales book /'seɪlz bʊk/ *noun* a record of sales

sales budget /'seɪlz ,bʌdʒət/ *noun* a plan of probable sales

sales call /'seɪlz kɔl/ *noun* a visit by a salesperson to a prospective customer in order to make a sale ○ *How many sales calls does the manager expect us to make each day?* ○ *She kept reports on all her sales calls.*

sales campaign /'seɪlz kæm,peɪn/ *noun* a series of planned activities to achieve higher sales

sales channel /'seɪlz ,tʃæn(ə)l/ *noun* any means by which products can be brought into the marketplace and offered for sale, either directly to the customer or indirectly through retailers or dealers

sales chart /'seɪlz tʃɑrt/ *noun* a diagram showing how sales vary from month to month

sales clerk /'seɪlz klɑrk/ *noun* a person who sells goods to customers in a store

sales contest /'seɪlz ,kɑntest/ *noun* an incentive program that rewards the salesperson who has the best results

sales contract /'seɪlz ,kɑntrækt/ *noun* a contract between a buyer and a seller, whereby the buyer agrees to pay money to the seller in return for goods ○ *The sales contract was signed after lengthy negotiations over price and delivery.* ○ *The sales contract commits us to the purchase.*

sales department /'seɪlz dɪ ,pɑrtmənt/ *noun* the section of a company which deals with selling the company's products or services

sales director /'seɪlz daɪ,rektər/ *noun* a director who is responsible for an organization's sales

sales drive /'seɪlz draɪv/ *noun* a vigorous effort to increase sales

sales executive /'seɪlz ɪg,zekjʊtɪv/ *noun* a person in a company or department in charge of sales

sales force /'seɪlz fɔrs/ *noun* a group of sales staff

sales forecast /'seɪlz ,fɔrkæst/ *noun* an estimate of future sales

sales incentive /'seɪlz ɪn,sentɪv/ *noun* something offered to encourage higher sales, e.g., paying the salespeople a higher commission or bonuses, or giving them prizes such as vacations for increased sales

sales interview /'seɪlz ,ɪntərvju/ *noun* a meeting between a salesperson and a prospective customer in which the customer obtains all information about a product necessary for them to be able to make a buying decision ○ *At the beginning of the sales interview, the salesperson established exactly what the prospective customer's needs were.*

sales lead /'seɪlz lid/ *noun* a piece of information about a potential customer which may lead to a sale ○ *It has been difficult approaching this territory with no sales leads to follow up.* ○ *I was given some useful sales leads by the sales rep who used to operate here.*

sales ledger /'seɪlz ,ledʒər/ *noun* a book in which sales to each customer are entered

sales ledger clerk /'seɪlz ,ledʒər ,klɑrk/ *noun* an office employee who deals with the sales ledger

sales letter /'seɪlz ,letər/ *noun* a letter sent to prospective customers, especially as part of a direct-mail operation

sales literature /'seɪlz ,lɪt(ə)rətʃər/ *noun* printed information which helps sales, e.g., leaflets or prospectuses

salesman /'seɪlzmən/ *noun* **1.** a man who sells an organization's products or services to customers, especially to retail shops ○ *He is the head salesman in the carpet department.* ○ *His only experience is as a used-car salesman.* **2.** a man who represents a company, selling its products or services to retail shops ○ *We have six salesmen calling on ac-*

counts in central Florida. (NOTE: The plural is **salesmen**.)

sales manager /'seɪlz ˌmænɪdʒər/ *noun* a person in charge of a sales department

salesmanship /'seɪlzmənʃɪp/ *noun* the art of selling or of persuading customers to buy

sales network /'seɪlz ˌnetwɜrk/ *noun* the network of retailers, distributors, and agents who all contribute to selling a product

sales office /'seɪlz ˌɔfɪs/ *noun* a local office of a large organization, which deals only with sales

sales outlet /'seɪlz ˌaʊt(ə)let/ *noun* a store which sells to the general public

salesperson /'seɪlzˌpɜrs(ə)n/ *noun* **1.** a person who sells goods or services to members of the public **2.** a person who sells products or services to retail shops on behalf of a company (NOTE: The plural is **salespeople**.)

sales pitch /'seɪlz pɪtʃ/ *noun* a talk by a salesperson to persuade someone to buy

sales plan /'seɪlz plæn/ *noun* a plan that sets out the future aims of a sales department and shows ways in which it can improve its performance and increase sales

sales potential /'seɪlz pəˌtenʃəl/ *noun* the maximum market share that can be achieved by a product

sales presentation /'seɪlz prez(ə)nˌteɪʃ(ə)n/ *noun* a demonstration by a salesperson of a product

sales promotion /'seɪlz prəˌmoʊʃ(ə)n/ *noun* promotional and sales techniques aimed at short-term increases in sales, e.g., free gifts, competitions, and price discounts ○ *We need some good sales promotion to complement our advertising campaign.* ○ *Let's hope this sales promotion will help us sell off our stock.*

sales promotion agency /'seɪlz prəˌmoʊʃ(ə)n ˌeɪdʒənsi/ *noun* an agency that specializes in the planning of promotions such as games, premium offers, and other incentives

sales promotion trap /'seɪlz prəˌmoʊʃ(ə)n træp/ *noun* a problem that occurs when a number of competing firms use promotions, with the result that there is no advantage to any of them

sales quota /'seɪlz ˌkwoʊtə/ *noun* a sales target given to salespeople which is based on either unit sales or revenue ○ *The sales manager intends to introduce sales quotas, in order to put extra pressure on the sales force.*

sales representative /'seɪlz reprɪˌzentətɪv/, **sales rep** /'seɪlz rep/ *noun* same as **salesperson** ○ *We have six sales representatives in Europe.* ○ *They have vacancies for sales representatives to call on accounts in the Midwest.*

sales resistance /'seɪlz rɪˌzɪstəns/ *noun* a lack of willingness by the public to buy a product

sales response /'seɪlz rɪˌspɑns/ *noun* the degree to which customers buy a product in response to the promotion of it ○ *There was a very poor sales response to the advertising campaign.* ○ *Although the product was not spectacular, the sales response was enormous.*

sales revenue /'seɪlz ˌrevənju/ *noun* the income from sales of goods or services

sales statistics /'seɪlz stəˌtɪstɪks/ *plural noun* figures relating a company's sales

sales target /'seɪlz ˌtɑrgət/ *noun* the amount of sales a sales representative is expected to achieve

sales tax /'seɪlz tæks/ *noun* a tax which is paid on each item sold and is collected when the purchase is made. Also called **turnover tax**

sales team /'seɪlz tim/ *noun* all representatives, sales staff, and sales managers working in a company

sales technique /'seɪlz tekˌnik/ *noun* a method used by a salesperson to persuade customers to buy, e.g., presentation of goods, demonstrations, and closing of sales

sales territory /'seɪlz ˌterɪt(ə)ri/ *noun* an area visited by a salesman

saleswoman /'seɪlzwʊmən/ *noun* **1.** a woman who sells an organization's products or services to customers **2.** a woman in a store who sells goods to customers (NOTE: The plural is **saleswomen**.)

salutation /ˌsælju'teɪʃ(ə)n/ *noun* the way of addressing an email to a customer

sample /'sæmpəl/ *noun* **1.** a small part of an item which is used to show what the whole item is like ○ *Can you provide us with a sample of the cloth* or *a cloth sample?* **2.** a small group which is studied in order to show what a larger group is like ○ *We interviewed a sample of potential customers.* ■ *verb* **1.** to test or to try something by taking a small amount of it ○ *to sample a product before buying it* **2.** to ask a representative group of people questions to find out what the reactions of a much larger group would be ○ *They sampled 2,000 people at random to test the new drink.*

sample size /'sɑrmpəl saɪz/ *noun* the number of individuals included in a statistical survey

sample survey /'sɑrmpəl ˌsɜrveɪ/ *noun* a statistical study of a selected group of individuals designed to collect information on specific subjects such as their buying habits or voting behavior

sampling /'sɑrmplɪŋ/ *noun* **1.** the testing of a product by taking a small amount ○ *a sampling of European Union produce* **2.** the testing of the reactions of a small group of people to find out the reactions of a larger group of consumers

sampling error /'sɑrmplɪŋ ˌerər/ *noun* the difference between the results achieved in a survey using a small sample and what the results would be if you used the entire population

sampling fraction /'sɑrmplɪŋ ˌfrækʃən/ *noun* a proportion of a group of people being surveyed that is chosen as a sample ○ *The sampling fraction will have to be small since we cannot afford many interviews with respondents.*

sampling frame /'sɑrmplɪŋ freɪm/ *noun* the definition of the group of people being surveyed out of which a sample is to be taken

sampling point /'sɑrmplɪŋ pɔɪnt/ *noun* a place where sampling is carried out ○ *The sampling point was just outside the main railroad station.*

sandwich board /'sændwɪtʃ bɔrd/ *noun* a pair of boards with advertisements on them that is suspended from shoulder straps in front of and behind the person wearing them

sandwich man /'sændwɪdʒ mæn/ *noun* a man who carries a sandwich board

satellite television /ˌsæt(ə)laɪt 'telɪvɪʒ(ə)n/ *noun* a television service which is broadcast from a satellite, and which the viewer receives using a special antenna

satisfaction /ˌsætɪs'fækʃən/ *noun* a good feeling of happiness and contentment ○ *He finds great satisfaction in the job even though the pay is bad.*

satisfy /'sætɪsfaɪ/ *verb* **1.** to give satisfaction or to please (NOTE: **satisfies – satisfying – satisfied**) □ **to satisfy a client** to make a client pleased with what they have purchased □ **a satisfied customer** a customer who has gotten what they wanted **2.** to fill the requirements for a job (NOTE: **satisfies – satisfying – satisfied**) □ **to satisfy a demand** to fill a demand ○ *We cannot produce enough to satisfy the demand for the product.*

satisfying /'sætɪsfaɪɪŋ/ *noun* the act of making satisfactory profits and maintaining an acceptable market share rather than making maximum profits at all costs

saturate /'sætʃəreɪt/ *verb* to fill something completely ○ *They are planning to saturate the market with cheap cell phones.* ○ *The market for home computers is saturated.*

saturation /ˌsætʃə'reɪʃ(ə)n/ *noun* **1.** the process of filling completely □ **saturation of the market, market saturation** a situation where the market has taken as much of the product as it can buy □ **the market has reached saturation point** the market is at a point where it cannot buy anymore of the product **2.** the fourth stage in a product's life cycle where sales level off

saturation advertising /ˌsætʃə 'reɪʃ(ə)n ˌædvətaɪzɪŋ/ *noun* a highly intensive advertising campaign ○ *Saturation advertising is needed when there are large numbers of rival products on the market.*

savings account /'seɪvɪŋz əˌkaʊnt/ *noun* an account where you put money in regularly and which pays interest, often at a higher rate than a deposit account

SBU *abbreviation* strategic business unit

scale /skeɪl/ *noun* a system which is graded into various levels □ **scale of charges** *or* **scale of prices** a list showing various prices

   scale down *phrasal verb* to lower something in proportion

   COMMENT: If a share issue is oversubscribed, applications may be scaled down; by doing this, the small investor is protected. So, in a typical case, all applications for 1,000 shares may receive 300; all applications for 2,000 shares may receive 500; applications for 5,000 shares receive 1,000, and applications for more than 5,000 shares will go into a ballot.

   scale up *phrasal verb* to increase something in proportion

scaling technique /'skeɪlɪŋ tek ˌniːk/ *noun* the use of a scale in questionnaires to make interpretation of results easier ○ *The scaling technique was so complicated that the respondents did not understand the questions.*

scarce /skers/ *adjective* not easily found or not common ○ *scarce raw materials* ○ *Reliable trained staff are scarce.*

scarceness /'skersnəs/, **scarcity** /'skersɪti/ *noun* the state of being scarce ○ *There is a scarcity of trained staff.*

scarcity value /'skersəti ˌvæljuː/ *noun* the value something has because it is rare and there is a large demand for it

scatter /'skætər/ *noun* a strategy by which an advertising message is put out

through several different vehicles at the same time

scattered market /ˌskætərd 'mɑrkət/ *noun* a market which is spread around a wide area, and therefore can only be reached by a company with an efficient distribution system

scenario /sɪ'neriou/ *noun* the way in which a situation may develop, or a description or forecast of possible future developments

scenario planning /sɪ'neriou ˌplænɪŋ/ *noun* a planning technique in which the planners write down several different descriptions of what they think might happen in the future and how future events, good or bad, might affect their organization (NOTE: Scenario planning can help managers to prepare for changes in the business environment, to develop strategies for dealing with unexpected events, and to choose between alternate strategic options.)

schedule /'skedʒəl/ *noun* **1.** a timetable, a plan of how time should be spent, drawn up in advance ○ *The managing director has a busy schedule of appointments.* ○ *Her assistant tried to fit us into her schedule.* □ **on schedule** at the time or stage set down in the schedule ○ *The launch took place on schedule.* **2.** a list, especially a list forming an additional document attached to a contract ○ *the schedule of territories to which a contract applies* ○ *Please find enclosed our schedule of charges.* ○ *See the attached schedule* or *as per the attached schedule.*

science /'saɪəns/ *noun* study or knowledge based on observing and testing

science park /'saɪəns pɑrk/ *noun* an area near a town or university set aside for technological industries

scientific /ˌsaɪən'tɪfɪk/ *adjective* referring to science

scientific management /ˌsaɪəntɪfɪk 'mænɪdʒmənt/ *noun* a theory of management which believes in the rational use of resources in order to maximize output, thus motivating workers to earn more money

scope /skoʊp/ *noun* an opportunity or possibility ○ *There is considerable scope for expansion into the export market.* □ **there is scope for improvement in our sales performance** the sales performance could be improved

scrambled merchandising /ˌskræmbəld ˈmɜrtʃəndaɪzɪŋ/ *noun* the displaying and selling of products which are unrelated to most of the others in the store such as groceries or sandwiches in a drugstore

screen /skrin/ *noun* **1.** a glass surface on which computer information or TV pictures can be shown ○ *She brought up the information on the screen.* ○ *I'll just call up details of your account on the screen.* **2.** a grid of dots or lines placed between the camera and the artwork, which has the effect of dividing the picture up into small dots, creating an image which can be used for printing ■ *verb* to examine something carefully to evaluate or assess it □ **to screen candidates** to examine candidates to see if they are completely suitable

screening /ˈskrinɪŋ/ *noun* **1.** □ **the screening of candidates** the examining of candidates to see if they are suitable **2.** the act of evaluating or assessing new product ideas ○ *Representatives from each department concerned will take part in the screening process.* ○ *Screening showed the product idea to be unrealistic for our production capacity.*

screensaver /ˈskrinˌseɪvər/ *noun* a program that shows moving images on the screen when a computer is not being used, because a static image can damage the monitor by burning itself into the phosphor coating on the inside of the screen

script /skrɪpt/ *noun* the written text of a commercial

SDRs *abbreviation* special drawing rights

seal /sil/ *noun* **1.** a special symbol, often one stamped on a piece of wax, which is used to show that a document is officially approved by the organization that uses the symbol □ **contract under seal** a contract which has been legally approved with the seal of the company

2. a piece of paper, metal, or wax attached to close something, so that it can be opened only if the paper, metal, or wax is removed or broken ■ *verb* to close something tightly ○ *The computer disks were sent in a sealed container.*

sealed bid price /ˌsild ˈbɪd ˌpraɪs/ *noun* a price of goods or a service for which suppliers are invited to submit bids. The bids are considered together by the buyer who then chooses the lowest bidder.

sealed tender /ˌsild ˈtendər/ *noun* a tender sent in a sealed envelope which will be opened with others at a specific time

seal of approval /ˌsil əv əˈpruv(ə)l/ *noun* a certificate from an organization to show that a product has been officially approved

seaport /ˈsipɔrt/ *noun* a port by the sea

search /sɜrtʃ/ *noun* the facility that enables visitors to a website to look for the information they want

search engine /ˈsɜrtʃ ˌendʒɪn/ *noun* a computer program that searches through a number of documents, especially on the Internet, for particular keywords and provides the user with a list of the documents in which those keywords appear

search engine registration /ˈsɜrtʃ ˌendʒɪn redʒɪˌstreɪʃ(ə)n/ *noun* the process of registering a website with a search engine, so that the site can be selected when a user requests a search

season /ˈsiz(ə)n/ *noun* **1.** one of four parts into which a year is divided, i.e. spring, summer, fall, and winter **2.** a period of time when some activity usually takes place ○ *the selling season*

seasonal /ˈsiz(ə)n(ə)l/ *adjective* which lasts for a season or which only happens during a particular season ○ *seasonal variations in sales patterns* ○ *The demand for this item is very seasonal.*

seasonal adjustment /ˌsiz(ə)n(ə)l əˈdʒʌstmənt/ *noun* a change made to figures to take account of seasonal variations

seasonal business /ˌsiz(ə)n(ə)l ˈbɪznɪs/ *noun* trade that varies depending on the time of the year, e.g., trade in goods such as suntan products or Christmas trees

seasonal demand /ˌsiz(ə)n(ə)l dɪˈmænd/ *noun* a demand which exists only during the high season

seasonal discount /ˌsiz(ə)n(ə)l ˈdɪskaʊnt/ *noun* a discount offered at specific times of the year during periods of slack sales, such as by media owners to advertisers

seasonally adjusted /ˌsiz(ə)nəli əˈdʒʌstɪd/ *adjective* referring to statistics which are adjusted to take account of seasonal variations

seasonal product /ˈsiz(ə)n(ə)l ˌprɒdʌkt/ *noun* a product such as skis or New Year cards which is only bought for use at a specific time of year

seasonal variation /ˌsiz(ə)n(ə)l veriˈeɪʃ(ə)n/ *noun* variation in data that happens at particular times of the year, e.g., during the winter months or a tourist season

second /ˈsekənd/ *noun, adjective* the thing which comes after the first

secondary /ˈsekənd(ə)ri/ *adjective* second in importance

secondary audience /ˌsekənd(ə)ri ˈɔdiəns/, **secondary readership** /ˌsekənd(ə)ri ˈridərʃɪp/ *noun* people who do not buy a newspaper or magazine themselves, but read a copy after the original purchaser has finished with it

secondary bank /ˌsekənd(ə)ri ˈbæŋks/ *noun* a finance company which provides money for installment-plan deals

secondary data /ˈsekənd(ə)ri ˌdeɪtə/ *noun* data or information which has already been compiled and is therefore found through desk research ○ *All this secondary data can be found in our files.* ○ *We found the secondary data in the embassy library.*

secondary industry /ˈsekənd(ə)ri ˌɪndəstri/ *noun* an industry which uses basic raw materials to produce manufactured goods

secondary meaning /ˌsekənd(ə)ri ˈminɪŋ/ *noun* a nickname given to a brand deliberately by the producer or by the consumer

secondary products /ˈsekənd(ə)ri ˌprɒdʌkts/ *plural noun* products which have been processed from raw materials (as opposed to primary products)

second-class /ˌsekənd ˈklɑrs/ *adjective, adverb* referring to a less expensive or less comfortable way of traveling ○ *The group will travel second-class to Holland.* ○ *The price of a second-class ticket is half that of a first class.*

second-generation product /ˌsekənd ˌdʒenəreɪʃ(ə)n ˈprɒdʌkt/ *noun* a product which has been developed from another

second half-year /ˌsekənd ˌhæf ˈjɪr/ *noun* the six-month period from July to the end of December

secondhand /ˌsekəndˈhænd/ *adjective, adverb* which has been owned by someone before ○ *a secondhand car* ○ *the market in secondhand computers* or *the secondhand computer market* ○ *to buy something secondhand*

secondhand dealer /ˌsekəndhænd ˈdilər/ *noun* a dealer who buys and sells secondhand items

seconds /ˈsekəndz/ *plural noun* items which have been turned down by the quality controller as not being top quality ○ *The store has a sale of seconds.*

second season /ˌsekənd ˈsiz(ə)n/ *noun* the period when a second series of a network television program is shown

sector /ˈsektər/ *noun* a part of the economy or the business organization of a country ○ *All sectors of the economy suffered from the fall in the exchange rate.* ○ *Technology is a booming sector of the economy.*

secured loan /sɪˈkjʊrd loʊn/ *noun* a loan which is guaranteed by the borrower giving assets as security

secure server /sɪˌkjʊr ˈsɜrvər/ *noun* a combination of hardware and software that makes e-commerce credit card transactions safe by stopping unauthorized people from gaining access to credit card details online

secure sockets layer /sɪ,kjʊə 'sɒkɪts ,leɪər/ *noun* full form of **SSL**

secure website /sɪ,kjʊə 'websaɪt/ *noun* a website on the Internet that encrypts the messages between the visitor and the site to ensure that no hacker or eavesdropper can intercept the information

security /sɪ'kjʊrəti/ *noun* the fact of being protected against attack.

seed /siːd/ *noun* details of the address of the person who owns a list, put into a rented mailing list to check if it is being used correctly ■ *verb* to put the names and addresses of the mailers into a rented mailing list to check that it is being used correctly

see-safe /'siː seɪf/ *adverb* under an agreement where a supplier will give credit for unsold goods at the end of a period if the retailer cannot sell them ○ *We bought the stock see-safe.*

segment /'segmənt/ *noun* a part of the sales of a large business defined by specific criteria ■ *verb* /seg'ment/ to divide a potential market into different segments

segmentation /,segmən'teɪʃ(ə)n/ *noun* the division of the market or consumers into categories according to their buying habits

select /sɪ'lekt/ *adjective* of top quality or specially chosen ○ *The firm offers a select range of merchandise.* ○ *Our customers are a select group.* ■ *verb* to choose ○ *The board will meet to select three candidates for a second interview.* □ **selected items are reduced by 25%** some items have been reduced by 25%

selection /sɪ'lekʃən/ *noun* **1.** a choice **2.** a thing which has been chosen ○ *Here is a selection of our product line.*

selection procedure /sɪ'lekʃən prə ,siːdʒər/ *noun* the general method of choosing a candidate for a job

selective /sɪ'lektɪv/ *adjective* choosing carefully

selective attention /sɪ,lektɪv pər 'sepʃən/, **selective perception** *noun* an individual's tendency to unconsciously select what they want from an advertisement ○ *We must take selective perception into account when deciding what to stress in the advertising.*

selective demand /sɪ,lektɪv dɪ 'mænd/ *noun* demand for a particular brand

selective demand advertising /sɪ ,lektɪv dɪ'mænd ,ædvərtaɪzɪŋ/ *noun* advertising that stimulates demand for a specific product or brand

selective distribution /sɪ,lektɪv ,dɪstrɪ'bjuːʃ(ə)n/ *noun* use by a producer of a limited number of wholesalers and retailers in a particular area ○ *This specialized product will need selective distribution.* ○ *Selective distribution may not enable the goods to reach consumers in sufficient quantities.*

selective exposure /sɪ,lektɪv ɪk 'spəʊʒər/ *noun* the process by which consumers decide whether they will watch or listen to advertising information

selective mailing /sɪ,lektɪv 'meɪlɪŋ/ *noun* the mailing out of promotional material to a selected address list

selective retention /sɪ,lektɪv rɪ 'tenʃən/ *noun* the process by which people remember some information but not everything they hear

self- /self/ *prefix* referring to yourself

self-completion /self kəm'pliːʃ(ə)n/ *noun* a type of questionnaire that can be filled in without an interviewer being present ○ *These self-completion questionnaires can be sent out through the mail.* ○ *Self-completion is not a good idea if the respondents don't understand the questions.*

self-image /,self 'ɪmɪdʒ/ *noun* an idea that a person has about their own character and abilities

self-liquidating offer /self 'lɪkwɪdeɪtɪŋ ,ɒfər/ *noun* the offer of a free gift or the sale of another product at a discount, made when a product is bought, usually against proof of purchase. The intention is to encourage the customer to adopt the brand, and at the same time to cover the cost of the offer and reduce overall promotional costs for the product. ○ *Even with the self-liquidating offer our sales have not gone up very much.*

self-mailer /self 'meɪlər/ *noun* an item of promotional material sent through the mail, which includes a postage-paid reply section which can be sent back without an envelope and on which customers can make an order ○ *Only 10% of the self-mailers we sent out have elicited any response.*

self-reference criterion /self 'refrəns kraɪˌtɪriən/ *noun* the assumption that a product can successfully be sold abroad on the basis of its success in the home market

self-regulation /ˌself ˌregjə 'leɪʃ(ə)n/ *noun* the regulation of an industry by itself, through a committee which issues a rulebook and makes sure that members of the industry follow the rules

self-regulatory /self ˌregjʊ 'leɪt(ə)ri/ *adjective* referring to an organization which regulates itself

self-service petrol station /self ˌsɜrvɪs 'petrəl ˌsteɪʃ(ə)n/ *noun* a gas station where the customers put the gasoline in their cars themselves

self-service store /ˌself 'sɜrvɪs ˌstɔr/ *noun* a store where customers take goods from the shelves and pay for them at the checkout

self-sticking label /self ˌstɪkɪŋ 'leɪb(ə)l/ *noun* a label with glue on it, ready to stick on an item

sell *noun* an act of selling □ **to give a product the hard sell** to make great efforts to persuade customers to buy it ■ *verb* **1.** to exchange something for money ○ *to sell something on credit* ○ *The store sells washing machines and refrigerators.* ○ *They tried to sell their house for $100,000.* ○ *Their products are easy to sell.* **2.** to be bought ○ *These items sell well in the pre-Christmas period.* ○ *Those packs sell for $25 a dozen.* ◊ **hard sell** (NOTE: **selling – sold**)

　sell forward *phrasal verb* to sell foreign currency, commodities, etc. for delivery at a later date

　sell off *phrasal verb* to sell goods quickly to get rid of them

　sell out *phrasal verb* **1.** □ **to sell out of an item** to sell all the stock of an item ○ *to sell out of a product line* ○ *We have sold out of plastic bags.* ○ *This item has sold out.* **2.** to sell your business ○ *They sold out and retired to the seaside.*

sell-by date /'sel baɪ ˌdeɪt/ *noun* a date on a food packet which is the last date on which the food is guaranteed to be good

seller /'selər/ *noun* **1.** a person who sells ○ *There were few sellers in the market, so prices remained high.* **2.** something which sells ○ *This book is a steady seller.*

seller's market /ˌselərz 'mɑrkət/ *noun* a market where the seller can ask high prices because there is a large demand for the product. Opposite **buyer's market**

sell-in /'sel ɪn/ *noun* the amount of inventory of a product taken by retailers when it is launched

-selling /'selɪŋ/ *suffix* □ **best-selling car** a car which sells better than other models

selling agent /'selɪŋ ˌeɪdʒənt/ *noun* a person who sells for a business or another person and earns a commission

selling costs /'selɪŋ kɑsts/, **selling overhead** /ˌselɪŋ 'oʊvərhed/ *plural noun* the amount of money to be paid for the advertising, reps' commissions, and other expenses involved in selling something

selling price /'selɪŋ praɪs/ *noun* the price at which someone is willing to sell something

selling space /'selɪŋ speɪs/ *noun* the amount of space in a retail outlet which is used for displaying goods for sale

sellout /'selaʊt/ *noun* □ **this item has been a sellout** all the stock of the item has been sold

semantic differential /sɪˌmæntɪk dɪfə'renʃəl/ *noun* a scaling technique which provides a range of possible answers between two opposite descriptive words

semi- /'semi/ *prefix* half or part

semi-display advertisement /ˌsemi dɪˈspleɪ əd,vɜrtɪsmənt/ *noun* an advertisement that has some of the features of a display advertisement such as a border and its own typeface or illustrations, but which is printed on the classified advertisement page

semi-finished product /ˌsemi ˈfɪnɪʃt ,prɑdʌkt/ *noun* a product which is partly finished

semiotics /ˌsemiˈɑtɪks/ *noun* the use of such promotional tools as package design, logos, and slogans in marketing (NOTE: takes a singular verb)

semi-solus /ˌsemi ˈsoʊləs/ *noun* an advertisement that shares a page with other advertisements, but is not immediately next to any of them

semi-structured interview /ˌsemi ,strʌktʃəd ˈɪntərvju/ *noun* an interview using some pre-set questions but allowing some questions that have been chosen by the interviewer as well ○ *Part of a semi-structured interview consists in respondents describing their first reactions to the advertisement.*

semi-variable cost /ˌsemi ,veriəb(ə)l ˈkɔst/ *noun* the amount of money paid to produce a product, which increases, though less than proportionally, with the quantity of the product made ○ *Stepping up production will mean an increase in semi-variable costs.* Also called **semi-fixed cost**

send /send/ *verb*

   send away for *phrasal verb* to write asking for something to be sent to you ○ *We sent away for the new catalog.*

   send off for *phrasal verb* to write asking for something to be sent to you ○ *We sent off for the new catalog.*

sender /ˈsendər/ *noun* a person who sends □ **"return to sender"** words on an envelope or package to show that it is to be sent back to the person who sent it

sensitive /ˈsensətɪv/ *adjective* quick to respond to something ○ *The market is very sensitive to the result of the elections.* ◊ **price-sensitive**

sequential sampling /sɪ,kwenʃəl ˈsɑrmplɪŋ/ *noun* the process of carrying on the process of sampling until enough respondents have been interviewed to provide the necessary information

serial number /ˈsɪriəl ,nʌmbər/ *noun* a number in a series ○ *This batch of shoes has the serial number 25–02.*

service /ˈsɜrvɪs/ *noun* **1.** the fact of working for an employer, or the period of time during which an employee has worked for an employer ○ *retiring after twenty years service to the company* ○ *The amount of your pension depends partly on the number of your years of service.* **2.** the act of keeping a machine in good working order ○ *the routine service of equipment* ○ *The machine has been sent in for service.* ■ *verb* **1.** to keep a machine in good working order ○ *The car needs to be serviced every six months.* ○ *The computer has gone back to the manufacturer for servicing.* **2.** □ **to service a debt** to pay interest on a debt ○ *The company is having problems in servicing its debts.*

service bureau /ˈsɜrvɪs ,bjʊroʊ/ *noun* an office which specializes in helping other offices

service center /ˈsɜrvɪs ,sentər/ *noun* an office or workshop which specializes in keeping machines in good working order

service charge /ˈsɜrvɪs tʃɑrdʒ/ *noun* a charge which a bank or business makes for carrying out work for a customer (NOTE: The U.K. term is **bank charge.**)

service department /ˈsɜrvɪs dɪ ,pɑrtmənt/ *noun* the section of a company which keeps customers' machines in good working order

service engineer /ˈsɜrvɪs endʒɪ ,nɪr/ *noun* an engineer who specializes in keeping machines in good working order

service history /ˈsɜrvɪs ,hɪst(ə)ri/ *noun* a record of the times a machine has been serviced

service level /ˈsɜrvɪs ,lev(ə)l/ *noun* a measurement of how efficient a producer is in distributing goods, e.g., the minimum number of back orders at any one time or delivery frequency to an area ○ *Service levels must be improved to fight competition.* ○ *The product is competitive in itself, but sales are affected by a low service level.*

service level agreement /'sɜrvɪs ˌlev(ə)l əˌgrimənt/ *noun* an agreement between a supplier and a customer which stipulates the level of services to be rendered. Abbreviation **SLA**

services /'sɜrvɪsɪz/ *plural noun* benefits which are sold to customers or clients, e.g., transportation or education ○ *We give advice to companies on the marketing of services.* ○ *We must improve the exports of both goods and services.*

service station /'sɜrvɪs ˌsteɪʃ(ə)n/ *noun* a garage where you can buy gasoline and have small repairs done to a car

set /set/ *noun* a group of items which go together, which are used together, or which are sold together ○ *a set of tools* ■ *adjective* fixed, or which cannot be changed ○ *There is a set fee for all our consultants.* ■ *verb* to fix or to arrange something ○ *We have to set a price for the new computer.* ○ *The price of the calculator has been set low, so as to achieve maximum unit sales.* (NOTE: **setting – set**) □ **the auction set a record for high prices** the prices at the auction were the highest ever reached

set up *phrasal verb* to begin something, or to organize something new ○ *to set up a new department* □ **to set up a company** to start a company legally □ **to set up in business** to start a new business ○ *She set up in business as an insurance broker.* ○ *He set himself up as a freelance representative.*

set menu /set 'menju/ *noun* a cheaper menu in a restaurant where there are only a few choices

setting up costs /ˌsetɪŋ 'ʌp kɔsts/, **setup costs** /'setʌp kɔsts/ *plural noun* the costs of getting a machine or a factory ready to make a new product after finishing work on the previous one

settle /'set(ə)l/ *verb* **1.** □ **to settle an account** to pay what is owed **2.** to solve a problem or dispute

settlement /'set(ə)lmənt/ *noun* the payment of an account □ **we offer an extra 5% discount for rapid settlement** we take a further 5% off the price if the customer pays quickly □ **settlement in cash** *or* **cash settlement** payment of an invoice in cash, not by check

shadow economy /ˌʃædoʊ ɪ'kɑnəmi/ *noun* same as **black economy**

share /ʃer/ *noun* a part of something that has been divided up among several people or groups ■ *verb* to divide something up among several people or groups ○ *to share computer time* ○ *to share the profits among the senior executives* ○ *Three companies share the market.* □ **to share information** *or* **data** to give someone information which you have

share capital /'ʃer ˌkæpɪt(ə)l/ *noun* the value of the assets of a company held as shares

shared mailing /ʃerd 'meɪlɪŋ/ *noun* a mailing where two or more producers insert mailing pieces in the same envelope

shelf /ʃelf/ *noun* a horizontal flat surface attached to a wall or in a cupboard on which items for sale are displayed ○ *The shelves in the supermarket were full of items before the Christmas rush.*

shelf barker /'ʃelf ˌbɑrkə/, **shelf talker** /'ʃelf ˌtɔkər/, **shelf wobbler** /'ʃelf ˌwɑblər/ *noun* a card placed on or hung from a shelf to promote an item for sale

shelf filler /'ʃelf ˌfɪlər/ *noun* a person whose job is to make sure that the shelves in a store are kept full of items for sale

shelf life /'ʃelf laɪf/ *noun* the length of time during which a product can stay in the store and still be good to use

shelf space /'ʃelf speɪs/ *noun* the amount of space on shelves in a store

shift /ʃɪft/ *noun* a movement or change ○ *a shift in the company's marketing strategy* ○ *The company is taking ad-*

vantage of a shift in the market toward higher-priced goods.

ship /ʃɪp/ *noun* a large boat for carrying passengers and cargo on the sea □ **to drop ship** to deliver a large order direct to a customer's store or warehouse, without going through an agent ■ *verb* to send goods, but not always on a ship ○ *to ship goods to Kansas* ○ *We ship all our goods by rail.* ○ *The consignment of cars was shipped abroad last week.*

shipbroker /'ʃɪpˌbroʊkər/ *noun* a person who arranges shipping or transportation of goods for customers on behalf of ship owners

ship chandler /ˌʃɪp 'tʃændlər/ *noun* a person who supplies goods such as food to ships

shipment /'ʃɪpmənt/ *noun* **1.** goods which have been sent or are going to be sent ○ *Two shipments were lost in the fire.* ○ *A shipment of computers was damaged.* **2.** an act of sending goods ○ *We make two shipments a week to France.*

shipper /'ʃɪpər/ *noun* a person who sends goods or who organizes the sending of goods for other customers

shipping /'ʃɪpɪŋ/ *noun* the sending of goods ○ *shipping charges* ○ *shipping costs* (NOTE: **shipping** does not always mean using a ship.)

shipping agent /'ʃɪpɪŋ ˌeɪdʒənt/ *noun* a company which specializes in the sending of goods

shipping confirmation /'ʃɪpɪŋ kənfəˌmeɪʃ(ə)n/ *noun* an email message informing the purchaser that an order has been shipped

shipping instructions /'ʃɪpɪŋ ɪnˌstrʌkʃənz/ *plural noun* the details of how goods are to be shipped and delivered

shipping note /'ʃɪpɪŋ noʊt/ *noun* a note which gives details of goods being shipped

shop /ʃɒp/ *noun* U.K. **1.** a retail outlet where goods of a certain type are sold ○ *a computer shop* (NOTE: The usual U.S. term is **store**.) **2.** an advertising agency
  shop around *phrasal verb* to go to various shops or suppliers and com-pare prices before making a purchase or before placing an order ○ *You should shop around before getting your car serviced.* ○ *He's shopping around for a new computer.* ○ *It pays to shop around when you are planning to get a mortgage.*

shop audit /'ʃɒp ˌɔdɪt/ *noun* a market-research method by which a research company regularly checks a sample of retailers for unit sales and inventory levels of different brands ○ *Since subscribing to the store audit we have seen how much better we're doing than our competitors.*

shopbot /'ʃɒpbɒt/ *noun* an Internet search device that searches for particular products or services and allows the user to compare prices and specifications

shop floor /ˌʃɒp 'flɔr/ *noun* **1.** the space in a store given to the display of goods for sale **2.** □ **on the shop floor** in the factory or among the ordinary workers ○ *The feeling on the shop floor is that the manager does not know his job.*

shop front /'ʃɒp frʌnt/ *noun* a part of a store which faces the street, including the entrance and windows

shopkeeper /'ʃɒpkipər/ *noun* a person who owns or runs a store

shoplifter /'ʃɒplɪftər/ *noun* a person who steals goods from shops

shoplifting /'ʃɒplɪftɪŋ/ *noun* the practice of stealing goods from shops

shopper /'ʃɒpər/ *noun* a person who buys goods in a store ○ *The store stays open until midnight to cater to late-night shoppers.*

shoppers' charter /ˌʃɒpəz 'tʃɑrtər/ *noun* U.K. a law which protects the rights of shoppers against shopkeepers who are not honest or against manufacturers of defective goods

shopping /'ʃɒpɪŋ/ *noun* **1.** goods bought in a store ○ *a basket of shopping* **2.** the act of going to shops to buy things ○ *to do your shopping in the local supermarket*

shopping cart /'ʃɒpɪŋ kɑrt/ *noun* **1.** a software package that records the items that an online buyer selects for purchase together with associated data, e.g., the price of the item and the number of items required **2.** a metal basket on wheels, used by shoppers to put their purchases in as they go around a supermarket

shopping centre /ˈʃɑpɪŋ ˌsentər/ noun U.K. same as **shopping mall**

shopping experience /ˈʃɑpɪŋ ɪk ˌspɪriəns/ noun the virtual environment in which a customer visits an e-merchant's website, selects items, places them in an electronic shopping cart, and notifies the merchant of the order (NOTE: The shopping experience does not include a payment transaction, which is initiated by a message to a point-of-sale program when the customer signals that he or she has finished shopping and wishes to pay.)

shopping goods /ˈʃɑpɪŋ gʊdz/ plural noun high-priced goods whose purchase has to be considered carefully by customers, who compare the good points of competing brands

shopping mall /ˈʃɑpɪŋ mɔl/ noun an enclosed covered area for shopping, with stores, restaurants, banks, and other facilities

shopping precinct /ˈʃɑpɪŋ ˌprisɪŋkt/ noun a part of a town where the streets are closed to traffic so that people can walk about and shop

shopping trolley /ˈʃɑpɪŋ ˌtrɑli/ noun U.K. same as **shopping cart**

shop-soiled /ˈʃɑp sɔɪld/ adjective dirty because of having been on display in a store ○ These items are shop-soiled and cannot be sold at full price.

shopwalker /ˈʃɑpwɔkər/ noun an employee of a department store who advises the customers and supervises the store assistants in a department

shop window /ˌʃɑp ˈwɪndoʊ/ noun a large window in a store front, where customers can see goods displayed

shop window website /ʃɑp ˈwɪndoʊ ˌwebsaɪt/ noun a website that provides information about an organization and its products, but does not allow visitors to interact with it

shop-within-shop /ˌʃɑp ˌwɪðɪn ˈʃɑp/ noun an arrangement in large department stores, where space is given to smaller specialized retail outlets to trade

short /ʃɔrt/ adjective, adverb **1.** for a small period of time □ **in the short term** in the near future or very soon **2.** less than what is expected or desired ○ The shipment was three items short. ○ My change was $2 short. □ **when we cashed up we were $10 short** we had $10 less than we should have had □ **to give short weight** to sell something which is lighter than it should be □ **short of** lacking ○ We are short of staff or short of money. ○ The company is short of new ideas.

shortage /ˈʃɔrtɪdʒ/ noun a lack or low availability of something ○ a shortage of skilled staff ○ We employ part-timers to make up for staff shortages. ○ The import controls have resulted in the shortage of spare parts. □ **there is no shortage of investment advice** there are plenty of people who want to give advice on investments

short-change /ˌʃɔrt ˈtʃeɪndʒ/ verb to give a customer less change than is right, either by mistake or in the hope that it will not be noticed

short credit /ˌʃɔrt ˈkredɪt/ noun terms which allow the customer only a little time to pay

shorthanded /ˌʃɔrtˈhændɪd/ adjective without enough staff ○ We're rather shorthanded at the moment.

short lease /ˌʃɔrt ˈlis/ noun a lease which runs for up to two or three years ○ We have a short lease on our current premises.

short-range forecast /ˌʃɔrt reɪndʒ ˈfɔrkæst/ noun a forecast which covers a period of a few months

short-staffed /ˌʃɔrt ˈstæft/ adjective with not enough staff ○ We're rather short-staffed at the moment.

short-term /ˌʃɔrt ˈtɜrm/ adjective for a period of weeks or months ○ to place money on short-term deposit ○ She is employed on a short-term contract. □ **on a short-term basis** for a short period

short-term debt /ˌʃɔrt tɜrm 'det/ *noun* a debt which has to be repaid within a few weeks

short-term forecast /ˌʃɔrt tɜrm 'fɔrkæst/ *noun* a forecast which covers a period of a few months

short-term gain /ˌʃɔrt tɜrm 'geɪn/ *noun* an increase in price made over a short period

short-term planning /ˌʃɔrt tɜrm 'plænɪŋ/ *noun* planning for the immediate future

shout /ʃaʊt/ *noun* a bold statement promoting a book, either printed on the cover or on posters and leaflets ○ *The author disliked the shout on the cover suggested by the publisher's promotional manager.*

show /ʃoʊ/ *noun* an exhibition or display of goods or services for sale ○ *a motor show* ○ *a computer show*

showcard /'ʃoʊkard/ *noun* a piece of cardboard with advertising material, put near an item for sale

showcase /'ʃoʊkeɪs/ *noun* **1.** a cupboard with a glass front or top to display items **2.** the presentation of someone or something in a favorable setting ■ *verb* to present someone or something in a way that is designed to attract attention and admiration

showing /'ʃoʊɪŋ/ *noun* a measurement of an audience's exposure to outdoor advertising

showroom /'ʃoʊrum/ *noun* a room where goods are displayed for sale ○ *a car showroom*

shrink /ʃrɪŋk/ *verb* to get smaller ○ *The market has shrunk by 20%.* ○ *The company is having difficulty selling into a shrinking market.* (NOTE: **shrinking – shrank – has shrunk**)

shrinkage /'ʃrɪŋkɪdʒ/ *noun* **1.** the amount by which something gets smaller ○ *to allow for shrinkage* **2.** losses of inventory through theft, especially by the store's own staff (*informal*)

SIC *abbreviation* Standard Industrial Classification

sideline /'saɪdlaɪn/ *noun* a business which is extra to your normal work ○ *He* runs a profitable sideline selling postcards to tourists.

sight /saɪt/ *noun* the act of seeing □ **bill payable at sight** a bill which must be paid when it is presented □ **to buy something sight unseen** to buy something without having inspected it

sight draft /'saɪt dræft/ *noun* a bill of exchange which is payable when it is presented

sign /saɪn/ *noun* a board or notice which advertises something ○ *They have asked for planning permission to put up a large red store sign.* ○ *Advertising signs cover most of the buildings in the center of the town.*

signage /'saɪnɪdʒ/ *noun* all the signs and logos which identify an organization such as a retail group, chain of restaurants, or motorway service area

signature /'sɪgnətʃər/ *noun* a special authentication code, such as a password, which a user must enter to prove his or her identity

signature file /'sɪgnətʃər faɪl/ *noun* text at the end of an email message that identifies the sender and company name, address, etc. Abbreviation **sig file**

silver market /'sɪlvər ˌmarkət/ *noun* a market consisting of retired people (NOTE: also called **gray market**)

SINBAD *abbreviation* single income no boyfriend absolutely desperate

single column centimeter /ˌsɪŋg(ə)l ˌkaləm 'sentɪmitər/ *noun* a unit of measurement for newspaper and magazine advertisements, representing one column which is one centimeter in depth

single-currency /ˌsɪŋg(ə)l 'kʌrənsi/ *adjective* using or shown as an amount in only one currency

single European market /ˌsɪŋg(ə)l ˌjʊrəpiən 'markət/, **single market** /ˌsɪŋg(ə)l 'markət/ *noun* ♦ **European Union**

single sourcing /ˌsɪŋg(ə)l 'sɔrsɪŋ/ *noun* the practice of obtaining all of a company's supplies from one source or supplier ○ *The buying department believes that single sourcing will lead to* *higher raw-material costs.* ○ *Single sourcing has simplified our purchasing plans.*

site /saɪt/ *noun* the place where something is located ○ *We have chosen a site for the new factory.* ○ *The supermarket is to be built on a site near the station.*

situation /ˌsɪtʃuˈeɪʃ(ə)n/ *noun* a state of affairs ○ *the financial situation of a company* ○ *the general situation of the economy*

situation analysis /ˌsɪtʃuˈeɪʃ(ə)n ə ˌnæləsɪs/, **situation audit** /ˌsɪtʃu ˈeɪʃ(ə)n ˌɔdɪt/ *noun* the stage in marketing planning concerned with investigating an organization's strengths and weaknesses ○ *In the situation analysis particular attention was paid to existing production capacity.* ○ *It is clear from the situation analysis that distribution is our biggest problem.*

six-pack /ˈsɪks pæk/ *noun* a box containing six items, often bottles or cans

skim /skɪm/ *verb* to fix a high price on a new product in order to achieve high short-term profits. The high price reflects the customer's appreciation of the added value of the new product, and will be reduced in due course as the product becomes established on the market. ○ *We are skimming the market with a product that will soon be obsolete.*

skip scheduling /ˈskɪp ˌskedʒəlɪŋ/ *noun* the act of arranging for an advertisement to appear in every other issue of a publication

SKU /ˌes keɪ ˈju/ *noun* a unique code made up of numbers or letters and numbers which is assigned to a product by a retailer for identification and inventory control. Full form **stockkeeping unit**

SLA *abbreviation* service level agreement

slack season /ˈslæk ˌsiz(ə)n/ *noun* a period when a company is not very busy

slash /slæʃ/ *verb* to reduce something sharply ○ *We have been forced to slash credit terms.* ○ *Prices have been slashed in all departments.* ○ *The banks have slashed interest rates.*

sleeper /ˈslipər/ *noun* a product which does not sell well for some time, then suddenly becomes very popular

sleeper effect /ˈslipər ɪˌfekt/ *noun* an effect shown where a message becomes more persuasive over a period of time

slot /slɑt/ *noun* the period of time available for a TV or radio commercial ○ *They took six 30-second slots at peak viewing time.*

slot machine /ˈslɑt məˌʃin/ *noun* a machine which provides drinks or cigarettes, plays music, etc. when a coin is put in it

slow payer /ˌsloʊ ˈpeɪər/ *noun* a person or company that does not pay debts on time ○ *The company is well known as a slow payer.*

slump /slʌmp/ *noun* **1.** a rapid fall ○ *the slump in the value of the dollar* ○ *We experienced a slump in sales* or *a slump in profits.* **2.** a period of economic collapse with high unemployment and loss of trade ○ *We are experiencing slump conditions.* **3.** the world economic crisis of 1929–33 ■ *verb* to fall fast ○ *Profits have slumped.* ○ *The dollar slumped on the foreign exchange markets.*

small business /ˌsmɔl ˈbɪznɪs/ *noun* a little company with low turnover and few employees

small businessman /ˌsmɔl ˈbɪznɪsmæn/ *noun* a man who owns a small business

small print /ˈsmɔl prɪnt/ *noun* items printed at the end of an official document such as a contract in smaller letters than the rest of the text. People sometimes do not pay attention to the small print, but it can contain important information, and unscrupulous operators may deliberately try to hide things such as additional charges, unfavorable terms, or loopholes in it.

small-scale enterprise /ˌsmɔl skeɪl ˈentəpraɪz/ *noun* a small business

smart market /ˌsmart ˈmarkɪt/ *noun* a market where all business is conducted electronically using network communications

SMEs *abbreviation* small and medium-sized enterprises

smuggle /'smʌg(ə)l/ *verb* to take goods illegally into a country or without declaring them to customs ○ *They had to smuggle the spare parts into the country.*

smuggler /'smʌglər/ *noun* a person who smuggles

smuggling /'smʌglɪŋ/ *noun* the practice of taking goods illegally into a country or without declaring them to customs ○ *They made their money in arms smuggling.*

snap /snæp/ *verb*

  snap up *phrasal verb* to buy something quickly ○ *to snap up a bargain* ○ *She snapped up 15% of the company's shares.* (NOTE: **snapping – snapped**)

social /'souʃ(ə)l/ *adjective* referring to society in general

social audit /ˌsouʃ(ə)l 'ɔdɪt/ *noun* a systematic assessment of an organization's effects on society or on all those who can be seen as its stakeholders. A social audit covers such issues as internal codes of conduct, business ethics, human resource development, environmental impact, and the organization's sense of social responsibility. ○ *The social audit focused on the effects of pollution in the area.* ○ *The social audit showed that the factory could provide jobs for five percent of the unemployed in the small town nearby.*

social cost /'souʃ(ə)l kɔsts/ *noun* a negative effect of a type of production on society ○ *The report examines the social costs of building the factory in the middle of the town.* ○ *The industry's representative denied that any social cost was involved in the new development.*

social marketing /ˌsouʃ(ə)l 'mɑrkətɪŋ/ *noun* marketing with the purpose of contributing to society rather than just making a profit

social security /ˌsouʃ(ə)l sɪ'kjurəti/, **social insurance** /ˌsouʃ(ə)l ɪn'ʃurəns/ *noun* a government program where employers, employees, and the self-employed make regular contributions to a fund which provides unemployment pay, sickness pay, or retirement pensions ○ *He expects to receive $1,000 a month in social security payments.* ○ *She became disabled and subsequently lived on social security for years.*

social system /'souʃ(ə)l ˌsɪstəm/ *noun* the way society is organized

societal /sə'saɪət(ə)l/ *adjective* referring to society

societally conscious /səˌsaɪətəli 'kɑnʃəs/ *plural noun* people who are successful in life and want to work with groups of people

societal marketing /səˌsaɪət(ə)l 'mɑrkətɪŋ/ *noun* same as **social marketing**

society /sə'saɪəti/ *noun* **1.** the way in which the people in a country are organized **2.** a club for a group of people with the same interests ○ *We have joined a computer society.*

socio-cultural research /ˌsouʃiou ˌkʌltʃərəl rɪ'sɜrtʃ/ *noun* research into problems of society and culture, which gives insights into consumers and their needs

socio-economic /ˌsouʃiou ˌikə'nɑmɪk/ *adjective* referring to social and economic conditions, social classes and income groups ○ *We have commissioned a thorough socio-economic analysis of our potential market.*

socio-economic groups /ˌsouʃiou ikəˌnɑmɪk 'grups/ *plural noun* groups in society divided according to income and position

socio-economic segmentation /ˌsouʃiou ikəˌnɑmɪk ˌsegmən'teɪʃ(ə)n/ *noun* dividing the population into segments according to their incomes and social class

soft currency /ˌsɑft 'kʌrənsi/ *noun* the currency of a country with a weak economy, which is cheap to buy and difficult to exchange for other currencies. Opposite **hard currency**

soft sell /ˌsɔft 'sel/ *noun* the process of persuading people to buy, by encouraging and not forcing them to do so

software /'sɔftwer/ *noun* computer programs

sole /soʊl/ *adjective* only

sole agency /ˌsoʊl 'eɪdʒənsi/ *noun* an agreement to be the only person to represent a company or to sell a product in a particular area ○ *He has the sole agency for Ford cars.*

sole agent /ˌsoʊl 'eɪdʒənt/ *noun* a person who has the sole agency for a company in an area ○ *She is the sole agent for Ford cars in the locality.*

sole distributor /ˌsoʊl dɪ 'strɪbjətər/ *noun* a retailer who is the only one in an area who is allowed to sell a product

sole owner /ˌsoʊl 'oʊnər/ *noun* a person who owns a business on their own, with no partners, and has not formed a company

sole proprietor /ˌsoʊl prə'praɪətər/, **sole trader** /ˌsoʊl 'treɪdər/ *noun* a person who runs a business, usually by themselves, but has not registered it as a company

solicit /sə'lɪsɪt/ *verb* □ **to solicit orders** to ask for orders, to try to get people to order goods

solus /'soʊləs/ *adjective* alone

solus (advertisement) /'soʊləs əd ˌvɜrtɪsmənt/ *noun* an advertisement which does not appear near other advertisements for similar products

solus position /'soʊləs pəˌzɪʃ(ə)n/ *noun* a position for an advertisement which is alone on a page, or not near advertisements for similar products

solus site /'soʊləs saɪt/ *noun* a store which only carries products from one supplier

solution brand /sə'luʃ(ə)n brænd/ *noun* a combination of a product and related services, e.g., a computer system plus installation and maintenance, that meets a customer's needs more effectively than the product on its own

sorting /'sɔrtɪŋ/ *noun* the process of organizing a mailing list in a certain order (by name, by country, etc.)

source /sɔrs/ *noun* **1.** the place where something comes from ○ *What is the source of her income?* ○ *You must declare income from all sources to the IRS.* □ **income which is taxed at source** income where the tax is removed and paid to the government by the employer before the income is paid to the employee **2.** the person who sends a message ■ *verb* to get supplies from somewhere ○ *We source these spare parts in Germany.*

source credibility /'sɔrs kredə ˌbɪləti/ *noun* the image people have of someone which will determine that person's credibility

source power /'sɔrs ˌpaʊər/ *noun* the power derived by a source from being able to reward a customer

sourcing /'sɔrsɪŋ/ *noun* the process of finding suppliers of goods or services ○ *The sourcing of spare parts can be diversified to suppliers outside Europe.* ◊ **outsourcing**

space /speɪs/ *noun* an empty place or empty area □ **to take advertising space in a newspaper** to place a large advertisement in a newspaper

space buyer /'speɪs ˌbaɪər/ *noun* a person who buys advertising space in magazines and newspapers

spam /spæm/ *noun* articles that have been posted to more than one newsgroup, and so are likely to contain unsolicited commercial messages

spare parts /ˌsper 'pɑrts/ *plural noun* a stock of components for a machine that are kept in case the machine breaks down and needs to be repaired

spatial segmentation /ˌspeɪʃ(ə)l ˌsegmən'teɪʃ(ə)n/ *noun* the segmentation or division of a market according to areas or regions

spec /spek/ *noun* same as **specification** □ **to buy something on spec** to buy something without being sure of its value

special /'speʃ(ə)l/ *adjective* better than usual ○ *He offered us special terms.* ○ *The car is being offered at a special price.* ■ *noun* a product which a retailer buys for a special purpose, e.g., a premium offer

special drawing rights /ˌspeʃ(ə)l 'drɔɪŋ raɪts/ *plural noun* units of account used by the International Monetary Fund, allocated to each member country for use in loans and other international operations. Their value is calculated daily on the weighted values of a group of currencies shown in dollars. Abbreviation **SDRs**

specialist /'speʃəlɪst/ *noun* a person or company that deals with one particular type of product or one subject ○ *You should go to a specialist in computers or to a computer specialist for advice.*

specialization /ˌspeʃəlaɪ'zeɪʃ(ə)n/ *noun* the act of dealing with one specific type of product ○ *The company's area of specialization is accounts packages for small businesses.*

specialize /'speʃəlaɪz/ *verb* to deal with one particular type of skill, product, or service ○ *The company specializes in electronic components.* ○ *They have a specialized product line.* ○ *He sells very specialized equipment for the electronics industry.*

special offer /ˌspeʃ(ə)l 'ɔfər/ *noun* a situation where goods are put on sale at a specially low price ○ *We have a range of men's shirts on special offer.*

special position /ˌspeʃ(ə)l pə'zɪʃ(ə)n/ *noun* an especially good place in a publication for advertising ○ *If we are prepared to invest the money we could choose a special position for the advertisement.*

specialty /ˌspeʃi'æləti/ *noun* the specific business interest or specific type of product that a company has ○ *Their specialty is computer programs.*

specialty goods /'speʃ(ə)lti gʊdz/ *plural noun* a special type of product which sells to a limited market ○ *We only deal in specialty goods.* ○ *These specialty goods require expert personal selling.* ○ *There's a high profit margin on specialty goods.*

specialty store /'speʃ(ə)lti stɔr/ *noun* a store selling a limited range of items of good quality

specification /ˌspesɪfɪ'keɪʃ(ə)n/ *noun* detailed information about what or who is needed or about a product to be supplied ○ *to detail the specifications of*

a computer system □ **to work to standard specifications** to work to specifications which are acceptable anywhere in an industry □ **the work is not up to specification** *or* **does not meet our specifications** the product is not made in the way which was detailed

specify /'spesɪfaɪ/ *verb* to state clearly what is needed ○ *to specify full details of the goods ordered* ○ *Do not include sales tax on the invoice unless specified.* ○ *Candidates are asked to specify which of the three positions they are applying for.* (NOTE: **specifies – specifying – specified**)

specimen /'spesɪmɪn/ *noun* something which is given as a sample □ **to give specimen signatures on a bank mandate** to write the signatures of all the people who can sign checks for an account so that the bank can recognize them

spend /spend/ *verb* **1.** to pay money ○ *They spent all their savings on buying the store.* ○ *The company spends thousands of dollars on research.* **2.** to use time ○ *The company spends hundreds of person-hours on meetings.* ○ *The chairman spent yesterday afternoon with the auditors.* (NOTE: **spending – spent**) ■ *noun* an amount of money spent ○ *What's the annual spend on marketing?*

spending /'spendɪŋ/ *noun* the act of paying money for goods and services ○ *Both cash spending and credit card spending increase at Christmas.*

spending money /'spendɪŋ ˌmʌni/ *noun* money for ordinary personal expenses

spending power /'spendɪŋ ˌpaʊər/ *noun* **1.** the fact of having money to spend on goods ○ *the spending power of the student market* **2.** the amount of goods which can be bought for a sum of money ○ *The spending power of the dollar has fallen over the last ten years.*

sphere /sfɪr/ *noun* an area ○ *a sphere of activity* ○ *a sphere of influence*

spiff /spɪf/ *noun* special commission or special premium offers given to sales personnel or agents, based on sales over a specific period. Full form **special incentive for affiliates** ■ *verb* □ to spiff

up a product to enhance the sales of a product by offering special incentives to sales personnel

spinner /'spɪnər/ *noun* a revolving stand on which goods are displayed in a store ○ *There was a spinner with different types of confectionery at each checkout.*

spinoff /'spɪnɔf/ *noun* a useful product developed as a secondary product from a main item ○ *One of the spinoffs of the research program has been the development of the electric car.*

splash page /'splæʃ peɪdʒ/ *noun* a page, usually containing advertisements, that is displayed to visitors to a website before they reach the homepage

split run /splɪt 'rʌn/ *noun* the printing of the same issue of a publication in several production runs, so that different advertisements may be placed in different printings, allowing the effects of the advertising to be compared

sponsor /'spɒnsər/ *noun* **1.** a person who recommends another person for a job **2.** a company which pays part of the cost of making a TV program by taking advertising time on the program ■ *verb* to act as a sponsor for something ○ *a government-sponsored trade exhibition* ○ *The company has sponsored the soccer match.*

sponsorship /'spɒnsəʃɪp/ *noun* the act of sponsoring ○ *the sponsorship of a season of concerts* ○ *The training course could not be run without the sponsorship of several major companies.*

spot /spɒt/ *noun* **1.** a place □ **to be on the spot** to be at a place ○ *We have a man on the spot to deal with any problems which happen on the building site.* **2.** a place for an advertisement on a TV or radio show **3.** the buying of something for immediate delivery ■ *adjective* done immediately

spot cash /ˌspɒt 'kæʃ/ *noun* cash paid for something bought immediately

spot check /'spɒt tʃek/ *noun* a rapid and unannounced check to see if things are working properly

spot color /'spɒt ˌkʌlər/ *noun* one color, apart from black, used in an advertisement

spot market /'spɒt ˌmɑrkət/ *noun* a market that deals in commodities or foreign exchange for immediate rather than future delivery

spread /spred/ *noun* two facing pages in a magazine or newspaper used by an advertiser for a single advertisement running across the two pages

SRDS *abbreviation* Standard Rate & Data Service

SSL /ˌes es 'el/ *abbreviation* a method of providing a safe channel over the Internet to allow a user's credit card or personal details to be safely transmitted ○ *I only purchase goods from a web site that has SSL security installed.* ○ *The little key logo on my web browser appears when I am connected to a secure site with SSL.* Full form **secure sockets layer**

stability /stə'bɪləti/ *noun* the state of being steady or not moving up or down ○ *price stability* ○ *a period of economic stability* ○ *the stability of the currency markets*

stabilization /ˌsteɪbɪlaɪ'zeɪʃ(ə)n/ *noun* the process of making something stable, e.g., preventing sudden changes in prices □ **stabilisation of the economy** keeping the economy stable by preventing inflation from rising, cutting high interest rates and excess money supply

stabilize /'steɪbəlaɪz/ *verb* to become steady, or to make something steady □ **prices have stabilized** prices have stopped moving up or down □ **to have a stabilizing effect on the economy** to make the economy more stable

stable /'steɪb(ə)l/ *adjective* steady or not moving up or down ○ *stable prices* ○ *a stable exchange rate* ○ *a stable currency* ○ *a stable economy*

stable market /ˌsteɪb(ə)l 'mɑrkət/ *noun* a market where sales do not change much in response to changes in price and where demand is therefore steady

stage-gate model /ˈsteɪdʒ geɪt ˌmɑd(ə)l/ *noun* a business model for developing a new product from conception to its launch, where the development is divided into several stages at the end of which is a "gate" where the management has to take a decision as to how to proceed to the next stage

stagflation /stægˈfleɪʃ(ə)n/ *noun* inflation and stagnation happening at the same time in an economy

stagnation /stægˈneɪʃ(ə)n/ *noun* the state of not making any progress, especially in economic matters ○ *The country entered a period of stagnation.*

stake /steɪk/ *noun* an amount of money invested □ **to have a stake in a business** to have money invested in a business □ **to acquire a stake in a business** to buy shares in a business ○ *He acquired a 25% stake in the company.* ■ *verb* □ **to stake money on something** to risk money on something

stakeholder /ˈsteɪkhoʊldər/ *noun* **1.** a person such as a stockholder, employee, or supplier who has a stake in a business **2.** a person or body that is involved with a company or organization either personally or financially and has an interest in ensuring that it is successful (NOTE: A stakeholder may be an employee, customer, supplier, partner, or even the local community within which an organization operates.)

stakeholder theory /ˈsteɪkhoʊldər ˌθɪəri/ *noun* the theory that it is possible for an organization to promote the interests of its shareholders without harming the interests of its other stakeholders such as its employees, suppliers, and the wider community

stall /stɔl/ *noun* a small movable wooden booth, used for selling goods in a market

stallholder /ˈstɔlhoʊldər/ *noun* a person who has a stall in a market and pays rent for the site it occupies

stamp duty /ˈstæmp ˌdjuti/ *noun* a tax on legal documents such as those used, e.g., for the sale or purchase of shares or the conveyance of a property to a new owner

stamp trading /ˈstæmp ˌtreɪdɪŋ/ *noun* the giving out of stamps or vouchers to customers according to the value of their purchases, the stamps being exchangeable for more goods or for cash. Compare **trading stamp**

stand /stænd/ *noun* an arrangement of shelves or tables at an exhibition for showing a company's products

standard /ˈstændəd/ *noun* the usual quality or usual conditions which other things are judged against □ **up to standard** of acceptable quality ○ *This batch is not up to standard* or *does not meet our standards.* ■ *adjective* normal or usual ○ *a standard model car* ○ *We have a standard charge of $25 for a thirty-minute session.*

Standard & Poor's /ˌstændərd ən ˈpʊrz/ *noun* an American corporation which rates bonds according to the credit-worthiness of the organizations issuing them. Abbreviation **S&P**

standard costing /ˌstændəd ˈkɔstɪŋ/ *noun* the process of planning costs for the period ahead and, at the end of the period, comparing these figures with actual costs in order to make necessary adjustments in planning

standard costs /ˌstændəd ˈkɔsts/ *plural noun* planned costs for the period ahead

standard deviation /ˌstændərd ˌdiviˈeɪʃ(ə)n/ *noun* the way in which the results of a sample deviate from the mean or average

standard error /ˌstændərd ˈerər/ *noun* the extent to which chance affects the accuracy of a sample

Standard Industrial Classification /ˌstændəd ɪnˌdʌstriəl ˌklæsɪfɪˈkeɪʃ(ə)n/ *noun* the official listing and coding of industries and products. Abbreviation **SIC**

standardization /ˌstændədaɪˈzeɪʃ(ə)n/ *noun* the process of making sure that everything fits a standard or is produced in the same way ○ *standardization of measurements throughout the EU* ○ *Standardization of design is necessary if we want to have a uniform company style.* □ **standardization of**

products the process of reducing a large number of different products to a series which have the same measurements, design, packaging, etc.

standardize /'stændədaɪz/ *verb* to make sure that everything fits a standard or is produced in the same way

standard letter /ˌstændəd 'letər/ *noun* a letter which is sent without change to various correspondents

standard rate /'stændəd reɪt/ *noun* a basic rate of income tax which is paid by most taxpayers

Standard Rate & Data Service /ˌstændərd reɪt ən 'deɪtə ˌsɜrvɪs/ *noun* an American publication listing advertising rates, circulation, and other details of major American magazines, newspapers, and other advertising media. Abbreviation **SRDS** (NOTE: The comparable British publication is **British Rate and Data**.)

standing /'stændɪŋ/ *noun* a good reputation ○ *The financial standing of a company.* □ **company of good standing** very reputable company

standing order /ˌstændɪŋ 'ɔrdər/ *noun* an order written by a customer asking a bank to pay money regularly to an account ○ *I pay my subscription by standing order.*

standing room only /ˌstændɪŋ rum 'oʊnli/ *noun* a sales technique which suggests to the customer that the current offer will be available only for a very short time or may be changed in the near future

stand-out test /'stænd aʊt ˌtest/ *noun* a test designed to assess how well a package stands out or catches the eye on a shelf ○ *Stand-out tests were carried out to evaluate how effective the color of the new product packaging was.*

staple commodity /ˌsteɪp(ə)l kə 'mɑdəti/ *noun* a basic food or raw material

staple industry /ˌsteɪp(ə)l 'ɪndəstri/ *noun* the main industry in a country

staple product /ˌsteɪp(ə)l 'prɑdʌkt/ *noun* the main product

star /stɑr/ *noun* in the Boston matrix, a product which has a high market share and a high growth rate. It will need cash to finance its growth, but eventually should become a cash cow. ○ *We have only one star product but it's put our company on the map.* ○ *They're hoping that at least two of their new product range will turn out to be stars.*

starch ratings /'stɑrtʃ ˌreɪtɪŋz/ *plural noun* a method of assessing the effectiveness of an organization's advertising

start /stɑrt/ *noun* the beginning

starting point /'stɑrtɪŋ pɔɪnt/ *noun* the place where something starts

start-up /'stɑrt ʌp/ *noun* **1.** the beginning of a new company or new product ○ *We went into the red for the first time because of the costs for the start-up of our new subsidiary.* **2.** a new, usually small business that is just beginning its operations, especially a new business supported by venture capital and in a sector where new technologies are used

state enterprise /ˌsteɪt 'entərpraɪz/ *noun* a company run by the state

statement /'steɪtmənt/ *noun* □ **statement (of account)** a list of invoices and credits and debits sent by a supplier to a customer at the end of each month

state-of-the-art /ˌsteɪt əv ðɪ 'ɑrt/ *adjective* as technically advanced as possible

static market /ˌstætɪk 'mɑrkət/ *noun* a market which does not increase or decrease significantly over a period of time

statistical /stə'tɪstɪk(ə)l/ *adjective* based on statistics ○ *statistical information* ○ *They took two weeks to provide the statistical analysis of the opinion-poll data.*

statistical discrepancy /stə ˌtɪstɪk(ə)l dɪ'skrepənsi/ *noun* the amount by which sets of figures differ

statistical error /stəˌtɪstɪk(ə)l 'erər/ *noun* the difference between results achieved in a survey using a sample and what the results would be using the entire group of people surveyed. ◊ **law**

statistics /stə'tɪstɪks/ *plural noun* facts or information in the form of figures ○ *to examine the sales statistics for the previous six months* ○ *Government trade statistics show an increase in imports.* (NOTE: takes a plural verb)

steady demand /ˌstedi dɪ'mænd/ *noun* demand for a product which continues in a regular way

sticker /'stɪkər/ *noun* a small piece of gummed paper or plastic to be stuck on something as an advertisement or to indicate a price ■ *verb* to put a price sticker on an article for sale ○ *We had to sticker all the inventory.*

stickiness /'stɪkinəs/ *noun* a website's ability to retain the interest of visitors and to keep them coming back

sticky site /'stɪki saɪt/ *noun* a website that holds the interest of visitors for a substantial amount of time and is therefore effective as a marketing vehicle

stock /stɑk/ *noun* **1.** the available supply of raw materials ○ *large stocks of oil* or *coal* ○ *the country's stocks of butter* or *sugar* **2.** the quantity of goods for sale in a warehouse or retail outlet. Also called **inventory** □ **in stock** available in the warehouse or store ○ *to hold 2,000 lines in stock* □ **out of stock** not available in the warehouse or store ○ *The item went out of stock just before Christmas but came back into stock in the first week of January.* ○ *We are out of stock of this item.* □ **to take stock** to count the items in a warehouse **3.** shares in a company ■ *adjective* usually kept in stock ○ *Butter is a stock item for any good grocer.* ■ *verb* to hold goods for sale in a warehouse or store ○ *The average supermarket stocks more than 4500 lines.*

stock up *phrasal verb* to buy supplies of something which you will need in the future ○ *They stocked up with computer paper.*

stockbroker /'stɑkbroʊkər/ *noun* a person who buys or sells shares for clients

stock control /'stɑk kən,troʊl/ *noun* same as **inventory control**

stock controller /'stɑk kən,troʊlər/ *noun* a person who notes movements of stock

stock depreciation /'stɑk dɪpriʃi ,eɪʃ(ə)n/ *noun* a reduction in value of stock which is held in a warehouse for some time

stock figures /'stɑk ,fɪgəz/ *plural noun* details of how many goods are in the warehouse or store

stocking agent /'stɑkɪŋ ,eɪdʒənt/ *noun* a wholesaler who stocks goods for a producer, sells them, and earns a commission

stocking filler /'stɑkɪŋ ,fɪlər/ *noun* a small item which can be used to put into a Christmas stocking

stock-in-hand /ˌstɑk ɪn 'hænd/ *noun* stock held in a store or warehouse

stock-in-trade /ˌstɑk ɪn 'treɪd/ *noun* goods held by a business for sale

stockkeeping /'stɑk,kipɪŋ/ *noun* the process of making sure that the correct level of stock is maintained (to be able to meet demand while keeping the costs of holding stock to a minimum)

stockkeeping unit /'stɑkkipɪŋ ,junɪt/ *noun* full form of **SKU**

stock level /'stɑk ,lev(ə)l/ *noun* the quantity of goods kept in stock ○ *We try to keep stock levels low during the summer.*

stocklist /'stɑklɪst/ *noun* a list of items carried in stock

stockout /'stɑkaʊt/ *noun* a situation where an item is out of stock

stockpile /'stɑkpaɪl/ *noun* the supplies kept by a country or a company in case of need ○ *a stockpile of raw materials* ■ *verb* to buy items and keep them in case of need ○ *to stockpile canned food*

stockroom /'stɑkrum/ *noun* a room where stores are kept

stock size /'stɑk saɪz/ *noun* a normal size ○ *We only carry stock sizes of shoes.*

stocktaking /'stɑkteɪkɪŋ/, **stocktake** /'stɑkteɪk/ *noun* the counting of goods in stock at the end of an accounting period ○ *The warehouse is closed for the annual stocktaking.*

stocktaking sale /'stɑkteɪkɪŋ ˌseɪl/ *noun* a sale of goods cheaply to clear a warehouse before stocktaking

stock transfer form /ˌstɑk 'trænsfɜr fɔrm/ *noun* a form to be signed by the person transferring shares

stock turn /'stɑk tɜrn/, **stock turn-around** /ˌstɑk 'tɜrnəˌraʊnd/, **stock turnover** /ˌstɑk 'tɜrnoʊvər/ *noun* the total value of stock sold in a year divided by the average value of goods in stock

stock valuation /ˌstɑk ˌvælju'eɪʃ(ə)n/ *noun* an estimation of the value of stock at the end of an accounting period

stop /stɑp/ *noun* a situation where someone is not supplying or not paying something □ **account on stop** an account which is not supplied because it has not paid its latest invoices ○ *We put their account on stop and sued them for the money they owed.* □ **to put a stop on a cheque** to tell the bank not to pay a check which you have written ■ *verb* □ **to stop an account** not to supply an account anymore on credit because bills have not been paid □ **to stop payments** not to make any further payments

stoppage /'stɑpɪdʒ/ *noun* the act of stopping ○ *stoppage of payments* ○ *Bad weather was responsible for the stoppage of deliveries.* ○ *Deliveries will be late because of stoppages on the production line.*

stoppage in transit /ˌstɑpɪdʒ ɪn 'trænzɪt/ *noun* the legal right of sellers to stop delivery of goods that are in transit if they have reason to believe customers will not pay for them owing to insolvency

storage /'stɔrɪdʒ/ *noun* **1.** the act of keeping something in store or in a warehouse ○ *We rent our house and put the furniture into storage.* □ **to put a plan into cold storage** to postpone work on a plan, usually for a very long time **2.** the cost of keeping goods in store ○ *Storage rose to 10% of value, so we scrapped the stock.* **3.** the facility for storing data in a

computer ○ *a disc with a storage capacity of 100Mb*

storage capacity /'stɔrɪdʒ kə ˌpæsəti/ *noun* the space available for storage

storage company /'stɔrɪdʒ ˌkʌmp(ə)ni/ *noun* a company which keeps items for customers

storage facilities /'stɔrɪdʒ fə ˌsɪlətiz/ *plural noun* equipment and buildings suitable for storage

storage unit /'stɔrɪdʒ ˌjunɪt/ *noun* a device attached to a computer for storing information on disc or tape

store /stɔr/ *noun* **1.** a place where goods are kept **2.** a quantity of items or materials kept because they will be needed ○ *I always keep a store of envelopes ready in my desk.* **3.** a large shop ○ *a furniture store* ○ *a big clothing store* ■ *verb* **1.** to keep in a warehouse ○ *to store goods for six months* **2.** to keep for future use ○ *We store our pay records on computer.*

store audit /'stɔr ˌɔdɪt/ *noun* a market-research method by which a research company regularly checks a sample of stores for unit sales and stock levels of different brands

store brand /'stɔr brænd/ *noun* a brand owned by the retailer and not by the manufacturer

store card /'stɔr kɑrd/ *noun* a credit card issued by a large department store, which can only be used for purchases in that store

storekeeper /'stɔrkipər/, **storeman** /'stɔrmən/ *noun* a person in charge of a storeroom

storeroom /'stɔrum/ *noun* a room or small warehouse where stock can be kept

store traffic /'stɔr ˌtræfɪk/ *noun* the number of customers who enter a store

storyboard /'stɔribɔrd/ *noun* a series of drawings which give the outline of a movie or TV advertisement ○ *If the advertiser likes the storyboard, the agency will go ahead with the idea.*

straight line depreciation /ˌstreɪt laɪn dɪˌpriʃi'eɪʃ(ə)n/ *noun* depreciation calculated by dividing the cost of an asset, less its remaining value, by the number of years it is likely to be used

COMMENT: Various methods of depreciating assets are used; under the "straight line method", the asset is depreciated at a constant percentage of its cost each year, while with the "reducing balance method" the asset is depreciated at the same percentage rate each year, but calculated on the value after the previous year's depreciation has been deducted.

straight rebuy /streɪt ˈribaɪ/ *noun* a type of organizational buying decision where the same product is bought as before from the same supplier

strategic /strəˈtidʒɪk/ *adjective* based on a plan of action

strategic alliance /strəˌtidʒɪk əˈlaɪəns/ *noun* an agreement between two or more organizations to cooperate with each other and share their knowledge and expertise in a particular business activity, so that each benefits from the others' strengths and gains competitive advantage (NOTE: Strategic alliances can reduce the risk and costs involved in relationships with suppliers and the development of new products and technologies and have been seen as a response to globalization and the increasing uncertainty in the business environment.)

strategic business unit /strə ˌtidʒɪk ˈbɪznɪs ˌjunɪt/ *noun* a part or division of a large company which forms its own business strategy. Abbreviation **SBU**

strategic marketing /strəˌtidʒɪk ˈmɑrkətɪŋ/ *noun* marketing according to a set strategy, which is developed after analyzing the market, designing the advertising messages and launching the product

strategic partnering /strəˌtidʒɪk ˈpɑrtnərɪŋ/ *noun* collaboration between organizations in order to enable them to take advantage of market opportunities together, or to respond to customers more effectively than they could if each operated separately. Strategic partnering allows the partners to pool information, skills, and resources and to share risks.

strategic planning /strəˌtidʒɪk ˈplænɪŋ/ *noun* the process of planning the future work of a company

strategy /ˈstrætədʒi/ *noun* a course of action, including the specification of resources required, to achieve a specific objective ○ *a marketing strategy* ○ *a financial strategy* ○ *a sales strategy* ○ *a pricing strategy* ○ *What is the strategy of the HR department to deal with long-term manpower requirements?* ○ *Part of the company's strategy to meet its marketing objectives is a major recruitment and retraining program.* (NOTE: The plural is **strategies**.)

stratification /ˌstrætɪfɪˈkeɪʃ(ə)n/ *noun* **1.** the structure of a questionnaire which should help to ensure reliable answers and make it easy to evaluate results ○ *The results of the survey are hard to interpret owing to poor questionnaire stratification.* ○ *Good stratification will streamline the whole process.* **2.** a framework for the selection of a sample that ensures that it adequately represents the entire group of people surveyed

streaming /ˈstrimɪŋ/ *noun* technology that allows material to be downloaded from the Web and viewed at the same time. For example, a user can download enough of a multimedia file to start viewing or listening to it, while the rest of the file is downloaded in the background.

streamline /ˈstrimlaɪn/ *verb* to make something more efficient or more simple ○ *to streamline the accounting system* ○ *to streamline distribution services*

streamlined /ˈstrimlaɪnd/ *adjective* efficient or rapid ○ *We need a more streamlined payroll system.* ○ *The company introduced a streamlined system of distribution.*

streamlining /ˈstrimlaɪnɪŋ/ *noun* the process of making something efficient

street furniture /strit ˈfɜrnɪtʃər/ *noun* lamps, litter bins, bus shelters, etc., on which advertising can be placed

street vendor /ˈstrit ˌvendər/ *noun* a person who sells food or small items in the street

striver /'straɪvər/ *noun* in the VALS lifestyle classification, someone who likes spending money and wants to appear successful, rich, and fashionable

structure /'strʌktʃə/ *noun* the way in which something is organized ○ *the price structure in the small car market* ○ *the career structure within a corporation* ○ *The paper gives a diagram of the company's organizational structure.* ○ *The company is reorganizing its discount structure.* ■ *verb* to arrange in a specific way ○ *to structure a meeting*

structured interview /ˌstrʌktʃəd 'ɪntərvjuː/ *noun* an interview using preset questions and following a fixed pattern. Compare **unstructured interview**

stuff /stʌf/ *verb* to put papers into envelopes ○ *We pay casual workers by the hour for stuffing envelopes* or *for envelope stuffing.*

style /staɪl/ *noun* a way of doing or making something ○ *a new style of product* ○ *old-style management techniques*

style obsolescence /'staɪl ɒbsəˌles(ə)ns/ *noun* the redesign of a product in order to make previous models obsolete and therefore encourage buying of the latest one

suasionetics /sweɪʒə'netɪks/ *plural noun* the techniques used to persuade people to adopt ideas or behavior patterns (NOTE: takes a singular verb)

sub- /sʌb/ *prefix* under or less important

sub-agency /'sʌb ˌeɪdʒənsi/ *noun* a small agency which is part of a large agency

sub-agent /'sʌb ˌeɪdʒənt/ *noun* a person who is in charge of a sub-agency

subcontract *noun* /'sʌbˌkɒntrækt/ a contract between the main contractor for a whole project and another firm which will do part of the work ○ *They have been awarded the subcontract for all the electrical work in the new building.* ○ *We will put the electrical work out to subcontract.* ■ *verb* /ˌsʌbkən'trækt/ (*of a main contractor*) to agree with a company that they will do part of the work for a project ○ *The electrical work has been subcontracted to Smith Inc.*

subcontractor /'sʌbkənˌtræktər/ *noun* a company which has a contract to do work for a main contractor

subculture /'sʌbkʌltʃə/ *noun* a part or sector of society identifiable by factors such as lifestyle, religion, and race ○ *Studies were made of spending in the student subculture.* ○ *Different subcultures have different buying priorities.*

subhead /'sʌbhed/, **subheading** /'sʌbhedɪŋ/ *noun* a heading used to divide up text such as an email into separate sections

subject /'sʌbdʒɪkt/ *noun* the thing which you are talking about or writing about

subject line /'sʌbdʒɪkt laɪn/ *noun* the space at the top of an email template in which the sender types the title or subject of the email. It is the only part of the email, apart from the sender's name, that can be read immediately by the receiver.

sublease /'sʌbliːs/ *noun* a lease from a tenant to another tenant ○ *They signed a sublease for the property.*

subliminal advertising /sʌbˌlɪmɪn(ə)l 'ædvərtaɪzɪŋ/ *noun* advertising that attempts to leave impressions on the subconscious mind of the person who sees it or hears it without that person realizing that this is being done

subsample /'sʌbsæmpəl/ *noun* a subdivision of a sample

subscribe /səb'skraɪb/ *verb* □ **to subscribe to a magazine or website** to pay for a series of issues of a magazine or for information available on a website

subscribed circulation /səbˌskraɪbd ˌsɜːrkjə'leɪʃ(ə)n/ *noun* circulation of a publication that is paid for in advance

subscriber /səb'skraɪbər/ *noun* **1.** □ **subscriber to a magazine**, **magazine subscriber** a person who has paid in advance for a series of issues of a magazine or to have access to information on a website ○ *The extra issue is sent free to subscribers.* **2.** a user who chooses to receive information, content, or services regularly from a website

subscription /səb'skrɪpʃən/ *noun* money paid in advance for a series of issues of a magazine, for membership in a society, or for access to information on a website ○ *Did you remember to pay the subscription to the computer magazine?* ○ *She forgot to renew her club subscription.* □ **to take out a subscription to a magazine** to start paying for a series of issues of a magazine □ **to cancel a subscription to a magazine** to stop paying for a series of issues of a magazine

subscription-based publishing /səb,skrɪpʃən beɪst 'pʌblɪʃɪŋ/ *noun* a form of publishing in which content from a website, magazine, book, or other publication is delivered regularly by email or other means to a group of subscribers

subscription process /səb 'skrɪpʃən ,prɑsɛs/ *noun* the process by which users register and pay to receive information, content, or services from a website

subscription rate /səb'skrɪpʃən reɪt/ *noun* the amount of money to be paid for a series of issues of a magazine

subsidiary /səb'sɪdiəri/ *adjective* less important ○ *They agreed to most of the conditions in the contract but queried one or two subsidiary items.* ■ *noun* same as **subsidiary company** ○ *Most of the group profit was contributed by the subsidiaries in the Far East.*

subsidiary company /səb,sɪdiəri 'kʌmp(ə)ni/ *noun* a company which is more than 50% owned by a holding company, and where the holding company controls the board of directors

subsidize /'sʌbsɪdaɪz/ *verb* to help by giving money ○ *The government has refused to subsidize the car industry.*

subsidized accommodations /,sʌbsɪdaɪzd ə,kɑmə'deɪʃ(ə)nz/ *noun* cheap accommodations which are partly paid for by an employer or a local authority

subsidy /'sʌbsɪdi/ *noun* **1.** money given to help something which is not profitable ○ *The industry exists on gov-*

ernment subsidies. ○ *The government has increased its subsidy to the car industry.* **2.** money given by a government to make something cheaper ○ *the subsidy on rail transportation* (NOTE: The plural is **subsidies.**)

substitute /'sʌbstɪtut/ *noun* a person or thing that takes the place of someone or something else ■ *adjective* taking the place of another person or thing ■ *verb* to take the place of someone or something else

substitute product /'sʌbstɪtut ,prɑdʌkt/, **substitute good** /'sʌbstɪtut gʊd/ *noun* a product which may be bought instead of another when the price of the original product changes or if it becomes unavailable ○ *We must match our competitors since they produce substitute products to ours.* ○ *As the price of substitute products falls, they will be much in demand.*

substitution effect /,sʌbstɪ'tuʃ(ə)n ɪ,fɛkt/ *noun* the extent to which consumers will change from one product to another when the price of the product rises

suggestion /sə'dʒɛstʃən/ *noun* an idea which is put forward

suggestion box /sə'dʒɛstʃən bɑks/, **suggestions box** /sə'dʒɛstʃənz bɑks/ *noun* a place in a company where employees can put forward their ideas for making the company more efficient and profitable

suggestion selling /sə'dʒɛstʃən ,selɪŋ/ *noun* selling in such a way that the customer believes they really want the product ○ *Trainee salespeople learn the application of psychology to suggestion selling.*

sums chargeable to the reserve /sʌmz ,tʃɑrdʒəb(ə)l tə ðə rɪ'zɜrv/ *plural noun* sums which can be debited to a company's reserves

Sunday closing /,sʌndeɪ 'kloʊzɪŋ/ *noun* the practice of not opening a store on Sundays

Sunday supplement /,sʌndeɪ 'sʌplɪmənt/ *noun* a special extra section of a Sunday newspaper, usually on a special subject

supermarket /'supərmɑrkət/ *noun* a large store, usually selling food and housewares, where customers serve themselves and pay at a checkout ○ *Sales in supermarkets* or *Supermarket sales account for half the company's turnover.*

supermarket trolley /'supərmɑrkət ˌtrɑli/ *noun U.K.* same as **shopping cart**

supernormal profit /ˌsupərnɔrm(ə)l 'prɑfɪt/ *noun* profit earned by a business through having a monopoly ○ *This company has survived the recession owing to supernormal profits.*

supersite /'supərsaɪt/ *noun* a particularly large poster site ○ *If we cannot afford a supersite we will have to settle for a site in a subway station.* ○ *There are some key supersites at the side of the highway.*

superstore /'supərstɔr/ *noun* a very large self-service store (more than 25,000 square feet) which sells a wide range of goods ○ *We bought the laptop at a computer superstore.*

supplement *noun* a special addition to a magazine or newspaper which is given free to customers ○ *The color supplement is mostly full of advertising.* ○ *The supplement contains special articles on recent marketing strategies.* ○ *What are the advertising rates in that paper's supplement?*

supplier /sə'plaɪər/ *noun* a person or company that supplies or sells goods or services ○ *We use the same office equipment supplier for all our stationery purchases.* ○ *They are major suppliers of spare parts to the auto industry.* Also called **producer**

supplier development /sə'plaɪər dɪˌveləpmənt/ *noun* the development of close and long-term relationships between customers and suppliers that are intended to benefit both

supplier evaluation /sə'plaɪər ɪˈvæljuˌeɪʃ(ə)n/ *noun* the process of assessing potential suppliers of materials, goods, or services before placing an order, to find out which one of them will best satisfy the customer's requirements

(NOTE: When this process is undertaken after an order has been fulfilled, it is known as vendor rating.)

supplier rating /sə'plaɪər ˌreɪtɪŋ/ *noun* same as **vendor rating**

supply /sə'plaɪ/ *noun* **1.** the act of providing something which is needed **2.** □ **in short supply** not available in large enough quantities to meet the demand ○ *Spare parts are in short supply because of the strike.* **3.** stock of something which is needed ○ *Garages were running short of supplies of gasoline.* ○ *Supplies of coal to the factory have been hit by the rail strike.* ○ *Supplies of stationery have been reduced.* ■ *verb* to provide something which is needed ○ *to supply a factory with spare parts* ○ *The finance department supplied the committee with the figures.* ○ *Details of staff addresses and phone numbers can be supplied by the HR department.*

supply and demand /səˌplaɪ ən dɪ 'mænd/ *noun* the amount of a product which is available and the amount which is wanted by customers

supply chain /sə'plaɪ tʃeɪn/ *noun* the manufacturers, wholesalers, distributors, and retailers who produce goods and services from raw materials and deliver them to consumers, considered as a group or network

supply chain management /sə 'plaɪ tʃeɪn ˌmænɪdʒmənt/ *noun* the work of coordinating all the activities connected with supplying of finished goods (NOTE: Supply chain management covers the processes of materials management, logistics, physical distribution management, purchasing, and information management.)

supply price /sə'plaɪ praɪs/ *noun* the price at which something is provided

supply-side economics /sə'plaɪ saɪd ikəˌnɑmɪks/ *plural noun* an economic theory that governments should encourage producers and suppliers of goods by cutting taxes, rather than encourage demand by making more money available in the economy (NOTE: takes a singular verb)

support advertising /sə'pɔrt ˌædvərtaɪzɪŋ/ *noun* advertising which is designed to support other advertising in other media

support media /sə'pɔrt ˌmidiə/ *plural noun* non-traditional media which are used to reinforce messages sent to target markets through other more traditional media

surcharge /'sɜrtʃɑrdʒ/ *noun* an extra charge

surplus /'sɜrpləs/ *noun* more of something than is needed □ **these items are surplus to our requirements** we do not need these items ■ *adjective* more than is needed ○ *Profit figures are lower than planned because of surplus labor.* ○ *Some of the machines may have to be sold off as there is surplus production capacity.* ○ *We are proposing to put our surplus staff on short time.*

survivors /sə'vaɪvərz/ *plural noun* in the VALS lifestyle classification, elderly people who have no economic future

suspect /'sʌspekt/ *noun* any individual taken from a database of prospective customers

sustainers /sʌ'steɪnərz/ *plural noun* in the VALS lifestyle classification, people who are living at subsistence level and resent the fact that they have no money

swatch /swɑtʃ/ *noun* a small sample of a fabric ○ *The interior designer showed us swatches of the curtain fabric.*

sweep periods /'swip ˌpɪriədz/ *plural noun* times of the year when television audiences are measured

sweepstakes /'swipsteɪks/ *noun* a form of gambling promotion where customers put in their names for a draw and the lucky number wins a prize

switch /swɪtʃ/ *verb* to change from one thing to another ○ *to switch funds from one investment to another* ○ *The job was switched from our Tennessee factory to the Philippines.*

switch selling /'swɪtʃ ˌselɪŋ/ *noun* a selling technique which involves trying to persuade customers to buy something very different from what they wanted to buy in the first place ○ *Trainee sales staff are coached in switch selling.* ■

verb the practice of offering an apparently good bargain as bait in order to gain the attention of prospective customers then approaching them with a different offer which is more profitable to the seller

SWOT analysis /'swɑt əˌnæləsɪs/ *noun* a method of assessing a person, company, or product by considering their Strengths, Weaknesses, and external factors which may provide Opportunities or Threats to their development. Full form **Strengths, Weaknesses, Opportunities, Threats**

symbol /'sɪmbəl/ *noun* a sign, picture, or object which represents something ○ *They use a bear as their advertising symbol.*

symbol group /'sɪmbəl grup/ *noun* a group to which symbol retailers belong

symbol retailer /'sɪmbəl ˌriteɪlər/ *noun* a retailer that is a member of an independent group which secures favorable prices from suppliers through buying in bulk and has its own symbol or logo

synchro marketing /'sɪŋkroʊ ˌmɑrkətɪŋ/ *noun* the practice of finding ways to use spare resources during periods of low demand ○ *Synchro marketing will stop wastage of our production and storage capacity in the off-season.*

syndicate /'sɪndɪkeɪt/ *verb* to produce an article, a cartoon, etc., which is then published in several newspapers or magazines

syndicated program /ˌsɪndɪkeɪtɪd 'proʊgræm/ *noun* a program which is sold to a range of different stations across the country

syndicated research /ˌsɪndɪkeɪtɪd rɪ'sɜrtʃ/ *noun* market research carried out by agencies and sold to several different companies

syndication /ˌsɪndɪ'keɪʃ(ə)n/ *noun* an article, drawing, etc., which is published in several newspapers or magazines at the same time

synectics /sɪ'nektɪks/ *plural noun* group discussions designed to elicit creative solutions to problems ○ *We are be-*

ginning to apply synectics to our strategy formulation. ○ *Synectics is being encouraged as a method of approaching case-studies in business school.* (NOTE: takes a singular verb)

synergy /ˈsɪnərdʒi/ *noun* the process of producing greater effects by joining forces than by acting separately ○ *There is considerable synergy between the two companies.*

synthetic materials /sɪnˌθetɪk məˈtɪriəlz/ *plural noun* substances made as products of a chemical process

system /ˈsɪstəm/ *noun* an arrangement or organization of things which work together ○ *Our accounting system has worked well in spite of the large increase in orders.* □ **to operate a quota system** to regulate supplies by fixing quantities which are allowed ○ *We ar-*

range our distribution using a quota system – each agent is allowed only a specific number of units.

systems analysis /ˈsɪstəmz əˌnæləsɪs/ *noun* the process of using a computer to suggest how a company can work more efficiently by analyzing the way in which it works at present

systems analyst /ˈsɪstəmz ˌænəlɪst/ *noun* a person who specializes in systems analysis

systems management /ˈsɪstəmz ˌmænɪdʒmənt/ *noun* the directing and controlling of all the elements in an organization to achieve its basic objectives

systems selling /ˈsɪstəmz ˌselɪŋ/ *noun* the selling of an integrated system, not just separate products plus related services

T

table /'teɪb(ə)l/ *noun* **1.** a diagram or chart **2.** a list of figures or facts set out in columns □ **table of random numbers** a table of numbers in no particular order or pattern, which is used for selecting samples in market research

table of discounts /ˌteɪb(ə)l əv 'dɪskaʊnts/ *noun* a table showing discounts for various prices and quantities ○ *According to the table of discounts, there was no discount for purchases involving less than 100 items of each product.* Also called **discount table**

tabloid /'tæblɔɪd/ *noun* a small size of newspaper, as opposed to a broadsheet ○ *We're advertising in three tabloids concurrently.*

tachistoscope /tə'kɪstəskoʊp/, **T-scope** /'ti skoʊp/ *noun* a device used to measure the recognition level when a customer is exposed to a brand package or advertising material

tactic /'tæktɪk/ *noun* a way of doing things so as to be at an advantage ○ *Securing a key position at an exhibition is an old tactic which always produces good results* ○ *Concentrating our sales force in that area could be a good tactic.* ○ *The directors planned their tactics before going into the meeting.*

tactical /'tæktɪk(ə)l/ *adjective* referring to tactics

tactical campaign /ˌtæktɪk(ə)l kæm'peɪn/ *noun* a promotion that is planned according to a series of targets, in particular when attacking a competitor

tag /tæg/ *noun* a label ○ *a price tag* ○ *a nametag*

tailor /'teɪlər/ *verb* to design something for a specific purpose ○ *We mail out press releases tailored to the reader interests of each particular newspaper or periodical.*

tailor-made /ˌteɪlə 'meɪd/ *adjective* made to fit specific needs

tailor-made promotion /ˌteɪlər meɪd prə'moʊʃ(ə)n/ *noun* a promotion which is specifically made for an individual customer

take /teɪk/ *noun* the money received in a store ○ *Our weekly take is over $5,000.* ■ *verb* to receive or to get □ **the shop takes $2,000 a week** the store receives $5,000 a week in cash sales □ **she takes home $250 a week** her salary, after deductions for tax, etc. is $250 a week

takeaway /'teɪkəweɪ/ *noun U.K.* same as **takeout**

take-ones /'teɪk wʌnz/ *plural noun* advertising leaflets or promotional cards which are delivered to shops where they are displayed in racks

takeout /'teɪkaʊt/ *noun* **1.** a store which sells food to be eaten at some other place ○ *There is no sales tax on takeout meals.* ○ *There's a Chinese takeout on the corner of the street.* **2.** the food sold by a takeout

takeover /'teɪkoʊvər/ *noun* **1.** an act of buying a controlling interest in a business by buying more than 50% of its shares. Compare **acquisition 2.** the act of starting to do something in place of someone else

takeover bid /'teɪkoʊvər bɪd/ *noun* an offer to buy all or a majority of the shares in a company so as to control it ○ *They made a takeover bid for the company.* ○ *She had to withdraw her takeover bid when she failed to find any* *backers.* ○ *Share prices rose sharply on the disclosure of the takeover bid.*

taker /ˈteɪkər/ *noun* a person who wants to buy something ○ *There were very few takers for the special offer.*

takings /ˈteɪkɪŋz/ *plural noun* the money received in a store or a business ○ *The week's takings were stolen from the cash desk.*

target /ˈtɑːɡət/ *noun* something to aim for ○ *performance targets* □ **to set targets** to fix amounts or quantities which employees have to produce or reach □ **to meet a target** to produce the quantity of goods or sales which are expected □ **to miss a target** not to produce the amount of goods or sales which are expected ○ *They missed the target figure of $2m turnover.* ■ *verb* to aim to sell to somebody ○ *I'll follow up your idea of targeting our address list with a special mailing.* □ **to target a market** to plan to sell goods in a specific market

target audience /ˈtɑːɡət ˌɔːdiəns/ *noun* consumers at whom an advertisement is aimed ○ *TV advertising will fail unless we have a clear idea of who the target audience is for our product.* ○ *What is the best media to reach our target audience?*

target market /ˈtɑːɡət ˌmɑːkət/ *noun* the market in which a company is planning to sell its goods

target marketing /ˈtɑːɡət ˌmɑːkətɪŋ/ *noun* the aiming of advertising or selling at a specific group of consumers who all have similar characteristics

target population /ˈtɑːɡət pɒpjə ˌleɪʃ(ə)n/ *noun* a group of individuals or regions that are to be investigated in a statistical study

tariff /ˈtærɪf/ *noun* **1.** a tax to be paid on imported goods. Also called **customs tariff**. Compare **import levy 2.** a rate of charging for something such as electricity, hotel rooms, or train tickets

tariff barrier /ˈtærɪf ˌbæriər/ *noun* the customs duty intended to make imports more difficult ○ *to impose tariff barriers on* or *to lift tariff barriers from a product*

task /tæsk/ *noun* work which has to be done ○ *The job involves some tasks which are unpleasant and others which are more rewarding.* ○ *The candidates are given a series of tasks to complete within a time limit.* □ **to list task processes** to make a list of various parts of a job which have to be done ■ *verb* to give someone a task to do

task method /ˈtæsk ˌmeθəd/ *noun* the way of calculating an advertising appropriation by basing it on the actual amount needed to achieve the objectives

taste /teɪst/ *noun* a very small quantity of something taken to try it out

taste space /ˈteɪst speɪs/ *noun* different individuals or groups brought together into a database based on common interests

TAT *abbreviation* thematic apperception test

tax credit /ˈtæks ˌkredɪt/ *noun* **1.** a sum of money which can be offset against tax **2.** the part of a dividend on which the company has already paid tax, so that the stockholder is not taxed on it

tax-exempt /ˌtæks ɪɡˈzempt/ *adjective* **1.** referring to a person or organization not required to pay tax **2.** not subject to tax

tax-free /ˌtæks ˈfriː/ *adjective* with no tax having to be paid ○ *tax-free goods*

TC *abbreviation* till countermanded

team /tiːm/ *noun* a group of people who work together and cooperate to share work and responsibility

team approach /ˈtiːm əˌprəʊtʃ/ *noun* a method of measuring the effectiveness of an advertising campaign when the evaluators are actually involved in the campaign

team-building /ˈtiːm ˌbɪldɪŋ/ *noun* a set of training sessions designed to instill cooperation and solidarity in a group of employees who work together as a team

tear sheet /ˈter ʃiːt/ *noun* a page taken from a published magazine or newspaper, sent to an advertiser as proof that their advertisement has been run

teaser /'tizər/, **teaser ad** /'tizər æd/ *noun* an advertisement that gives a little information about a product in order to attract customers by making them curious to know more

technical /'teknɪk(ə)l/ *adjective* referring to a particular machine or process ○ *The document gives all the technical details on the new computer.*

technical press /'teknɪk(ə)l pres/ *noun* newspapers and magazines on scientific or technical subjects ○ *We need to advertise this product in the technical press.*

technique /tek'niːk/ *noun* a skilled way of doing a job ○ *The company has developed a new technique for processing steel.* ○ *We have a special technique for answering complaints from customers.*

technology adoption life cycle /tek,nalədʒi ə,dapʃən 'laɪf ,saɪk(ə)l/ *noun* a model that describes the stages in which various types of individuals and organizations start to use new technologies. The individual and organizations are usually classified as innovators, early adopters, early majority, late majority, or technology laggards.

technology laggard /tek'nalədʒi ,lægəd/ *noun* an individual or organization that is very slow or reluctant to adopt new technology

telcos /'telkouz/ *plural noun* telecommunications companies (*informal*)

telecommunications /,telikə ,mjuːnɪ'keɪʃ(ə)nz/ *plural noun* systems of passing messages over long distances (by cable, radio, etc.)

telecoms /'telikamz/ *noun* same as **telecommunications** (*informal*)

teleconferencing /'teli ,kanf(ə)rənsɪŋ/ *noun* the use of telephone or television channels to connect people in different locations in order to conduct group discussions, meetings, conferences, or courses

telemarketer /'teli,markɪtər/ *noun* a person who markets a product by telephone

telemarketing /'teli,markətɪŋ/ *noun* the selling of a product or service by telephone

telephone /'telifoun/ *noun* a machine used for speaking to someone over a long distance ○ *We had a new telephone system installed last week.*

telephone interview /'telifoun ,ɪntərvjuː/ *noun* same as **telephone survey**

telephone interview survey /,telifoun ɪntərvjuː 'sɜːveɪ/ *noun* a survey conducted by telephoning a selected group of people and asking them for their views on a particular subject

telephone order /'telifoun ,ɔːrdər/ *noun* an order received by telephone ○ *Since we mailed the catalog we have received a large number of telephone orders.*

telephone research /'telifoun rɪ ,sɜːrtʃ/ *noun* same as **telephone survey**

telephone sales representative /,telifoun 'seɪlz repri,zentətɪv/ *noun* someone who sells to customers over the phone. Abbreviation **TSR**

telephone selling /'telifoun ,selɪŋ/ *noun* the practice of making sales by phoning prospective customers and trying to persuade them to buy

telephone survey /'telifoun ,sɜːrveɪ/ *noun* an act of interviewing respondents by telephone for a survey ○ *How many people in the sample hung up before replying to the telephone survey?*

telesales /'teli,seɪlz/ *plural noun* sales made by telephone

teleshopping /'teli,ʃapɪŋ/ *noun* shopping from home by means of a television screen and a home computer

teletext /'telitekst/ *noun* a videotext broadcast by a TV company

television /,teli'vɪʒ(ə)n/ *noun* the broadcasting of moving images. Abbreviation **TV**

television consumer audit /,telivɪʒ(ə)n kən'suːmər ,ɔːdɪt/ *noun* an act of questioning a sample of television viewers on their viewing and impressions

television network /ˌtelɪvɪʒ(ə)n ˈnetwɜrk/ *noun* a system of linked television stations covering the whole country

television ratings /teli'vɪʒ(ə)n ˌreɪtɪŋz/ *plural noun* statistics showing the size and type of television audiences at different times of day for various channels and programs ○ *We will have to consult the television ratings before buying a spot.* Abbreviation **TVR**

tender /ˈtendər/ *noun* an offer to do something for a specific price ○ *a successful tender* ○ *an unsuccessful tender* □ **to put a project out to tender**, **to ask for** *or* **invite tenders for a project** to ask contractors to give written estimates for a job □ **to put in** *or* **submit a tender** to make an estimate for a job □ **to sell shares by tender** to ask people to offer in writing a price for shares ■ *verb* □ **to tender for a contract** to put forward an estimate of cost for work to be carried out under contract ○ *to tender for the construction of a hospital*

tenderer /ˈtendərər/ *noun* a person or company that tenders for work ○ *The company was the successful tenderer for the project.*

tendering /ˈtendərɪŋ/ *noun* the act of putting forward an estimate of cost ○ *To be successful, you must follow the tendering procedure as laid out in the documents.*

terminal /ˈtɜrmɪn(ə)l/ *noun* the building where you end a journey

terminal poster /ˈtɜrmɪn(ə)l ˌpoʊstə/ *noun* an advertising display in stations or airline terminals, etc.

termination clause /ˌtɜrmɪ ˈneɪʃ(ə)n klɔz/ *noun* a clause which explains how and when a contract can be terminated

terms /tɜrmz/ *plural noun* the conditions or duties which have to be carried out as part of a contract, or the arrangements which have to be agreed upon before a contract is valid ○ *to negotiate for better terms* ○ *She refused to agree to some of the terms of the contract.* ○ *By* or *Under the terms of the contract, the company is responsible for all damage to the property.* □ **"terms: cash with or-**

der" the terms of sale showing that payment has to be made in cash when the order is placed

terms of payment /ˌtɜrmz əv ˈpeɪmənt/ *plural noun* the conditions for paying something

terms of sale /ˌtɜrmz əv ˈseɪl/ *plural noun* the conditions attached to a sale

terms of trade /ˌtɜrmz əv ˈtreɪd/ *plural noun* the ratio of a country's import prices to export prices

territorial planning /ˌterɪtɔriəl ˈplænɪŋ/ *noun* the planning of a salesperson's calls, taking into account the best use of time in traveling and the priority of important customers ○ *The sales manager is giving the sales team some guidelines on territorial planning.* ○ *Bad territorial planning means time wasted in traveling.*

territorial rights /ˌterɪtɔriəl ˈraɪts/ *plural noun* the rights of a distributor, granted by the producer or supplier, to sell a product in a particular geographic area, often on condition that specific methods are used in the selling

territory /ˈterɪt(ə)ri/ *noun* an area visited by a salesperson ○ *We are adding two new reps and reducing all the reps' territories.* ○ *Her territory covers all of the Northeast.*

tertiary industry /ˌtɜrʃəri ˈɪndəstri/ *noun* an industry which does not produce raw materials or manufacture products but offers a service such as banking, retailing, or accountancy

tertiary readership /ˌtɜrʃəri ˈridərʃɪp/ *noun* the people who do not buy a newspaper or magazine but come across it as a result of another activity such as waiting for an appointment with the dentist ○ *Many glossy magazines have a relatively small circulation but a high tertiary readership.*

tertiary sector /ˈtɜrʃəri ˌsektər/ *noun* the section of the economy containing the service industries

test /test/ *noun* an examination to see if something works well or is possible ■ *verb* to examine something to see if it is working well ○ *We are still testing the new computer system.* □ **to test the**

market for a product to show samples of a product in a market to see if it will sell well ○ *We are testing the market for the toothpaste in New Jersey.*

test certificate /'test sə,tɪfɪkət/ *noun* a certificate to show that something has passed a test

test close /'test kloʊz/ *noun* an act of trying to obtain at least one immediate order from a buyer to see how promising a customer they are

test-drive /'test draɪv/ *verb* □ **to test-drive a car** to drive a car before buying it to see if it works well

testimonial /,testɪ'moʊniəl/ *noun* a written report about someone's character or ability ○ *She has asked me to write her a testimonial.*

testimonial advertising /,testɪ 'moʊniəl ,ædvərtaɪzɪŋ/ *noun* advertising which makes use of testimonials from famous or qualified people, or from satisfied customers, to endorse a product

testing /'testɪŋ/ *noun* the act of examining something to see if it works well ○ *During the testing of the system several defects were corrected.*

testing bias /'testɪŋ baɪəs/ *noun* bias that occurs when respondents to questionnaires know they are being tested and change their responses accordingly

test-market /'test ,mɔkət/ *verb* □ **to test-market a product** to show samples of a product in a market to see if it will sell well ○ *We are test-marketing the toothpaste in New Jersey.*

test marketing /'test ,mɔrkətɪŋ/ *noun* marketing a product in a specific area or to a specific audience to test the validity of the approach before launching a nationwide marketing campaign

test panel /'test ,pæn(ə)l/ *noun* a group of people used to test a product or service

test run /'test rʌn/ *noun* a trial made on a machine

text /tekst/ *verb* to send a text message on a cell phone or pager

text message /'tekst ,mesɪdʒ/ *noun* a message sent in text form, especially from one cellular phone or pager to another

T-group /'ti grup/ *noun* a group of trainees following a training method, often used in training sales staff, which uses group discussions and activities to develop social skills and general self-awareness

thematic apperception test /θɪ ,mætɪk ,æpər'seps(ə)n test/ *noun* a test used to find out attitudes or reactions to a brand, which consists of showing pictures to the subject who then constructs a story round them. Abbreviation **TAT**

thinker /'θɪŋkər/ *noun* in the VALS lifestyle classification system, a well-educated person with strong ideals who buys products that last a long time and are good value

threshold /'θreʃhoʊld/ *noun* the point at which something changes

ticket /'tɪkət/ *noun* a piece of paper or card which shows something

ticket counter /'tɪkət ,kaʊntər/ *noun* a place where tickets are sold

tie /taɪ/ *verb* to attach or to fasten with string, wire, or other material ○ *He tied the package with thick string.* ○ *She tied two labels on to the package.* (NOTE: **tying – tied**)

tie-in /'taɪ ɪn/ *noun* an advertisement linked to advertising in another media, e.g., a magazine ad linked to a TV commercial (NOTE: The plural is **tie-ins**.)

tie-up /'taɪ ʌp/ *noun* a link or connection ○ *The company has a tie-up with a German distributor.* (NOTE: The plural is **tie-ups**.)

tight money /,taɪt 'mʌni/ *noun* money which has to be borrowed at a high interest rate, and so restricts expenditure by companies

till /tɪl/ *noun* a drawer for keeping cash in a store

till countermanded /,tɪl 'kaʊntərmændɪd/ *noun* a clause in a contract which states that an advertisement will run until stopped by the advertiser. Abbreviation **TC**

time /taɪm/ *noun* **1.** a period during which something takes place, e.g., one hour, two days, or fifty minutes **2.** a period before something happens □ **to keep within the time limits** *or* **within the time schedule** to complete work by the time stated

time and duty study /ˌtaɪm ən ˈduti ˌstʌdi/ *noun* a study to see how effectively salespeople are using their time ○ *The time and duty study showed that 30% of time is wasted.* ○ *The aim of the time and duty study was to streamline our sales activities.*

time and motion expert /ˌtaɪm ən ˈmoʊʃ(ə)n ˌekspərt/ *noun* a person who analyzes time and motion studies and suggests changes in the way work is done

time buyer /ˈtaɪm ˌbaɪər/ *noun* a person who buys advertising time on radio or TV

timelength /ˈtaɪmleŋkθ/ *noun* the length of a cinema, television, or radio advertisement ○ *Find out the rates for the various timelengths before placing the commercial.*

time limit /ˈtaɪm ˌlɪmɪt/ *noun* the maximum time which can be taken to do something ○ *to set a time limit for acceptance of the offer* ○ *The work was finished within the time limit allowed.* ○ *The time limit on applications to the industrial tribunal is three months.*

time limitation /ˈtaɪm lɪmɪˌteɪʃ(ə)n/ *noun* the restriction of the amount of time available

time of peak demand /ˌtaɪm əv pik dɪˈmænd/ *noun* the time when something is being used most

time segment /ˈtaɪm ˌsegmənt/ *noun* a period set aside for advertisements on television

time series analysis /ˈtaɪm ˌsɪriz ə ˌnæləsɪs/ *noun* a method of assessing variations in data over regular periods of time such as sales per month or per quarter in order to try to identify the causes for the variations

time utility /ˈtaɪm juˌtɪləti/ *noun* the usefulness to a customer of receiving a product at a particular time ○ *Time utility has meant avoiding unreliable suppliers.* ○ *Some customers put time utility before place utility.*

tip *noun* **1.** money given to someone who has helped you ○ *The staff are not allowed to accept tips.* **2.** a piece of advice on buying or doing something which could be profitable ○ *The newspaper gave several stock market tips.* ○ *She gave me a tip about a share which was likely to rise because of a takeover bid.* ■ *verb* **1.** to give money to someone who has helped you ○ *He tipped the receptionist $5.* **2.** to say that something is likely to happen or that something might be profitable ○ *He is tipped to become the next chairman.* ○ *Two shares were tipped in the business section of the paper.* (NOTE: [all verb senses] **tipping – tipped**)

tip sheet /ˈtɪp ʃit/ *noun* a newspaper which gives information about shares which should be bought or sold

TIR *abbreviation* Transports Internationaux Routiers

tirekicker /ˈtaɪrˌkɪkər/ *noun* a prospective customer who wants to examine every option before making up his or her mind about a purchase (as opposed to a "first choice" who chooses the first option available)

token /ˈtoʊkən/ *noun* **1.** something which acts as a sign or symbol **2.** a device which involves the customer in an offer, e.g., a piece cut out of a newspaper which can be redeemed for a special premium offer **3.** a plastic or metal disc, similar to a coin, used in some slot machines

token charge /ˌtoʊkən ˈtʃɑrdʒ/ *noun* a small charge which does not cover the real costs ○ *A token charge is made for heating.*

token payment /ˈtoʊkən ˌpeɪmənt/ *noun* a small payment to show that a payment is being made

top-down information /ˌtɑp ˈdaʊn ɪnfərˌmeɪʃ(ə)n/ *noun* a system of passing information down from management to the work force

top-grade /'tɑp greɪd/ *adjective* of the best quality ○ *top-grade gasoline*

top management /ˌtɑp 'mænɪdʒmənt/ *noun* the main directors of a company

top-selling /ˌtɑp 'selɪŋ/ *adjective* which sells better than all other products ○ *top-selling brands of toothpaste*

tort /tɔrt/ *noun* harm done to a person or property which can be the basis of a civil lawsuit

torture testing /'tɔrtʃər ˌtestɪŋ/ *noun* the act of pushing products to their limits during product testing ○ *Torture testing will show up any product deficiencies while changes can still be made.*

total /'toʊt(ə)l/ *adjective* complete, or with everything added together ○ *The total amount owed is now $1000.* ○ *The company has total assets of over $1bn.* ○ *The total cost was much more than expected.* ○ *Total expenditure on publicity is twice that of last year.* ○ *Our total income from exports rose last year.*

total audience package /ˌtoʊt(ə)l 'ɔdiəns ˌpækɪdʒ/ *noun* a media owner's arrangement or scheduling of advertisements across time segments on television and radio

total cost of ownership /ˌtoʊt(ə)l kɔst əv 'oʊnəʃɪp/ *noun* a systematic method of calculating the total cost of buying and using a product or service. It takes into account not only the purchase price of an item but also related costs such as ordering, delivery, subsequent use and maintenance, supplier costs, and after-delivery costs.

total distribution system /ˌtoʊt(ə)l ˌdɪstrɪ'bjuʃ(ə)n ˌsɪstəm/ *noun* a system where all distribution decisions, including the purchasing of raw materials and parts, as well as the movement of finished products, are taken globally

total invoice value /ˌtoʊt(ə)l 'ɪnvɔɪs ˌvælju/ *noun* the total amount on an invoice, including transportation, VAT, etc.

total offer /ˌtoʊt(ə)l 'ɔfər/ *noun* a complete package offered to the customer including the product or service itself, its price, availability, and promotion

total quality management /ˌtoʊt(ə)l ˌkwɑləti 'mænɪdʒmənt/ *noun* a philosophy and style of management that gives everyone in an organization responsibility for delivering quality to the customer (NOTE: Total quality management views each production process as being in a customer/supplier relationship with the next, so that the aim at each stage is to define and meet the customer's requirements as precisely as possible.)

tracking /'trækɪŋ/ *noun* monitoring changes in the way the public sees a product or a firm, done over a period of years

trade /treɪd/ *noun* **1.** the business of buying and selling □ **to do a good trade in a range of products** to sell a large number of a range of products **2.** □ **to impose trade barriers on** to restrict the import of some goods by charging high duty **3.** a particular type of business, or people or companies dealing in the same type of product ○ *He's in the used car trade.* ○ *She's very well known in the clothing trade.*

trade in *phrasal verb* **1.** to buy and sell specific items ○ *The company trades in imported goods.* ○ *They trade in French wine.* **2.** to give in an old item as part of the payment for a new one ○ *The chairman traded in his old Mercedes for a new model.*

trade advertising /'treɪd ˌædvərtaɪzɪŋ/ *noun* advertising to trade customers and not to the general public

trade agreement /'treɪd əˌgrimənt/ *noun* an international agreement between countries over general terms of trade

trade association /'treɪd əsoʊsiˌeɪʃ(ə)n/ *noun* a group which links together companies in the same trade

trade barrier /'treɪd ˌbæriər/ *noun* a limitation imposed by a government on the free exchange of goods between countries. Also called **import restriction** (NOTE: NTBs, safety standards, and tariffs are typical trade barriers.)

trade counter /'treɪd ˌkaʊntər/ noun a store in a factory or warehouse where goods are sold to retailers

trade cycle /'treɪd ˌsaɪk(ə)l/ noun a period during which trade expands, then slows down, then expands again

trade debtor /'treɪd ˌdetər/ noun a debtor who owes money to a company in the normal course of that company's trading

trade delegation /'treɪd delə ˌgeɪʃ(ə)n/ noun a group of official delegates on a commercial visit

trade description /ˌtreɪd dɪ 'skrɪpʃən/ noun a description of a product to attract customers

trade directory /'treɪd daɪ ˌrekt(ə)ri/ noun a book which lists all the businesses and businesspeople in a town

trade down /ˌtreɪd 'daʊn/ verb to move to selling at lower prices to increase sales volume ○ We're trading down now because too many customers were put off by our high prices.

trade fair /'treɪd fer/ noun a large exhibition and meeting for advertising and selling a specific type of product ○ There are two trade fairs running in Atlanta at the same time – the carpet manufacturers' and the cell phone companies'.

trade-in /'treɪd ɪn/ noun an old item, e.g., a car or washing machine, given as part of the payment for a new one ○ She bought a new car and gave her old one as a trade-in.

trade-in price /'treɪd ɪn ˌpraɪs/, **trade-in allowance** /'treɪd ɪn ə ˌlaʊəns/ noun an amount allowed by the seller for an old item being traded in for a new one

trade magazine /'treɪd ˌmægəzin/ noun a magazine aimed at working people in a specific industry

trademark /'treɪdmɑrk/, **trade name** /'treɪd neɪm/ noun same as **registered trademark**

trade mission /'treɪd ˌmɪʃ(ə)n/ noun a visit by a group of businesspeople to discuss trade ○ He led a trade mission to China.

tradeoff /'treɪd ɔf/ noun an act of exchanging one thing for another as part of a business deal (NOTE: The plural is **tradeoffs**.)

trade-off analysis /'treɪd ɔf ə ˌnæləsɪs/ noun same as **conjoint analysis**

trade paper /ˌtreɪd 'peɪpər/ noun a newspaper aimed at people working in a specific industry

trade price /'treɪd praɪs/ noun a special wholesale price paid by a retailer to the manufacturer or wholesaler

trade promotion /'treɪd prə ˌmoʊʃ(ə)n/ noun the promotion of products to distributors ○ The new trade promotion campaign is designed to attract wholesalers in all our areas of distribution.

trader /'treɪdər/ noun a person who does business

trade route /'treɪd rut/ noun a route along which goods are transported for trade ○ The main trade routes were studied to see which areas of the country were most accessible. ○ When the Suez Canal was closed some vital trade routes were affected.

trade show /'treɪd ʃoʊ/ noun same as **trade fair**

tradesman /'treɪdzmən/ noun a storekeeper (NOTE: The plural is **tradesmen**.)

tradespeople /'treɪdzˌpip(ə)l/ plural noun storekeepers

trade terms /'treɪd tɜrmz/ plural noun a special discount for people in the same trade

trade up /ˌtreɪd 'ʌp/ verb to move to selling more expensive goods or to offering a more up-market service

trading /'treɪdɪŋ/ noun the business of buying and selling

trading account /'treɪdɪŋ əˌkaʊnt/ noun an account of a company's gross profit

trading area /'treɪdɪŋ ˌeriə/ *noun* a group of countries which trade with each other

trading channel /'treɪdɪŋ ˌtʃæn(ə)l/ *noun* a series of purchases and sales from company to company which are made until the finished product is purchased by the customer

trading company /'treɪdɪŋ ˌkʌmp(ə)ni/ *noun* a company which specializes in buying and selling goods

trading loss /ˌtreɪdɪŋ 'lɑs/ *noun* a situation where a company's receipts are less than its expenditure

trading partner /'treɪdɪŋ ˌpɑrtnər/ *noun* a company or country which trades with another

trading profit /'treɪdɪŋ ˌprɑfɪt/ *noun* a result where the company' receipts are higher than its expenditure

trading stamp /'treɪdɪŋ stæmp/ *noun* a special stamp given away by a store, which the customer can collect and exchange later for free goods

traffic /'træfɪk/ *noun* an illegal trade ○ *drugs traffic* or *traffic in drugs*

traffic builder /'træfɪk ˌbɪldər/ *noun* a software program which increases traffic to a website, by linking with search engines, etc.

tramp ship /'træmp ʃɪp/ *noun* a ship with no fixed schedule or itinerary that can be chartered by a company to transport goods

transaction /træn'zækʃən/ *noun* □ **fraudulent transaction** a transaction which aims to cheat someone

transaction e-commerce /træn ˌzækʃən 'i kɑmɜrs/ *noun* the electronic sale of goods and services, either business-to-business or business-to-customer

transfer /'trænsfɜr/ *noun* an act of moving an employee to another job in the same organization ○ *She applied for a transfer to our branch in British Columbia.* ■ *verb* to move someone or something to a different place, or to move someone to another job in the same organization ○ *The accountant was transferred to our Canadian*

branch. ○ *He transferred his shares to a family trust.* ○ *She transferred her money to a deposit account.*

transferable skill /træns,fɜrrəb(ə)l 'skɪl/ *noun* a skill that is not related to the performance of a particular job or task (NOTE: The skills that make people good at leadership, communication, critical thinking, analysis, or organization are among those thought of as transferable skills.)

transfer pricing /'trænsfɜr ˌpraɪsɪŋ/ *noun* prices used in a large organization for selling goods or services between departments in the same organization; also used in multinational corporations to transfer transactions from one country to another to avoid paying tax

transformational advertising /ˌtrænsfəmeɪʃ(ə)n(ə)l 'ædvərtaɪzɪŋ/ *noun* a form of emotional advertising that aims to relate emotional experiences to the product or service being advertised, and then tries to change these emotions into an active interest in purchasing

tranship /træn'ʃɪp/ *verb* another spelling of **transship**

transient advertisement /ˌtrænziənt əd'vɜrtɪsmənt/ *noun* an advertisement which the target audience cannot keep to look at again, e.g., a cinema advertisement, as opposed to an intransient one in a newspaper or magazine

transit /'trænsɪt/ *noun* the movement of passengers or goods on the way to a destination ○ *Some of the goods were damaged in transit.* □ **goods in transit** goods being transported from warehouse to customer

transit advertising /'trænsɪt ˌædvərtaɪzɪŋ/ *noun* advertisements on or inside buses, taxis, trains, etc.

transnational /trænz'næʃ(ə)nəl/ *noun* same as **multinational**

transnational corporation /ˌtrænz ˌnæʃ(ə)nəl ˌkɔrpə'reɪʃ(ə)n/ *noun* a large company which operates in various countries

transport /'trænspɔrt/ *noun U.K.* same as **transportation** ■ *verb* /træns 'pɔrt/ to move goods or people from one place to another in a vehicle ○ *The company transports millions of tons of goods by rail each year.* ○ *The visitors will be transported to the factory by air* or *by helicopter* or *by taxi.*

transport advertising /'trænspɔrt ˌædvərtaɪzɪŋ/ *noun* advertising appearing on or in forms of transportation such as buses or trains ○ *Transport advertising will reach too broad a public for our product.* ○ *Is your transport advertising on the sides of buses or in subway trains?*

transportation /ˌtrænspərˈteɪʃ(ə)n/ *noun* **1.** the moving of goods or people from one place to another ○ *air transportation* or *transportation by air* ○ *rail transportation* or *transportation by rail* ○ *road transportation* or *transportation by road* ○ *the public transportation services into Boston* ○ *What means of transportation will you use to get to the factory?* **2.** vehicles used to move goods or people from one place to another ○ *The company will provide transportation to the airport.*

transporter /trænsˈpɔrtər/ *noun* a company which transports goods

Transports Internationaux Routiers /ˌtrɔnspɔz ˌæntenæsjə 'noʊ ˌrutieɪ/ *noun* a system of international documents which allows dutiable goods to cross several European countries by road without paying duty until they reach their final destination. Abbreviation **TIR**

transship /trænsˈʃɪp/, **tranship** *verb* to move cargo from one ship to another. Another spelling of **tranship**

travel /'træv(ə)l/ *verb* to go from one place to another, showing a company's goods to buyers and taking orders from them ○ *She travels throughout the Midwest for an insurance company.* (NOTE: **traveling – traveled**)

traveler /'træv(ə)lər/ *noun* a person who travels (NOTE: The U.K. spelling is **traveller.**)

traveler's checks /'træv(ə)ləz tʃeks/ *plural noun* checks bought by a

traveler which can be cashed in a foreign country

traveling expenses /'træv(ə)lɪŋ ek ˌspensɪz/ *plural noun* money spent on traveling and hotels for business purposes

traveling salesman /ˌtræv(ə)lɪŋ 'seɪlzmən/ *noun* a salesman who travels around an area visiting customers on behalf of his company ○ *Traveling salesmen must make regular contact with company headquarters by phone.*

travel magazine /'træv(ə)l ˌmægəzin/ *noun* a magazine with articles on vacations and travel

travel organization /'træv(ə)l ˌɔrgənaɪzeɪʃ(ə)n/ *noun* a body representing companies in the travel business

treaty /'triti/ *noun* **1.** an agreement between countries ○ *The two countries signed a commercial treaty.* **2.** an agreement between individual persons □ **to sell a house by private treaty** to sell a home to another person not by auction

trend /trend/ *noun* a general way in which things are developing ○ *a downward trend in investment* ○ *There is a trend away from old-established food stores.* ○ *The report points to inflationary trends in the economy.* ○ *We notice a general trend toward selling to the student market.* ○ *We have noticed an upward trend in sales.*

trend analysis /'trend əˌnæləsɪs/ *noun* analysis of particular statistics over a period of time in order to identify trends ○ *Trend analysis has shown how soon major competitors begin to copy innovations.*

trial /'traɪəl/ *noun* a test to see if something is good □ **on trial** in the process of being tested ○ *The product is on trial in our laboratories.* ■ *verb U.K.* to test a product to see how good it is (NOTE: **trialling – trialled**)

trial balance /'traɪəl ˌbæləns/ *noun* the draft calculation of debits and credits to see if they balance

trial offer /'traɪəl ˌɔfər/ *noun* a promotion where free samples are given away

trial period /ˌtraɪəl ˈpɪəriəd/ *noun* the time when a customer can test a product before buying it

trial sample /ˈtraɪəl ˌsæmpəl/ *noun* a small piece of a product used for testing

triplicate /ˈtrɪplɪkət/ *noun* □ **invoicing in triplicate** the preparing of three copies of invoices

troll /trəʊl, trɑl/ *verb* to search websites for Internet addresses which are then added to an email address list for promotional purposes

trolley /ˈtrɑli/ *noun U.K.* same as **shopping cart**

truck /trʌk/ *noun* 1. a large motor vehicle for carrying goods 2. an open railroad wagon for carrying goods

truckage /ˈtrʌkɪdʒ/ *noun* the carriage of goods in trucks ○ *What will the truckage costs be for these goods?*

truck distributor /ˈtrʌk dɪˌstrɪbjətər/, **truck jobber** /ˈtrʌk ˌdʒɑbər/ *noun* a wholesaler who usually only delivers goods directly by truck to retailers

trucking /ˈtrʌkɪŋ/ *noun* the carrying of goods in trucks ○ *a trucking firm*

truckload /ˈtrʌkloʊd/ *noun* a quantity of goods that fills a truck

trust /trʌst/ *noun* a small group of companies which control the supply of a product

trustbusting /ˈtrʌstbʌstɪŋ/ *noun* the breaking up of trusts to encourage competition

T-scope /ˈti skoʊp/ *noun* same as **tachistoscope**

TSR *abbreviation* telephone sales representative

turn /tɜrn/ *verb*

   turn around *phrasal verb* to make a company change from making a loss to becoming profitable □ **they turned the company round in less than a year** they made the company profitable in less than a year

   turn over *phrasal verb* to have a specific amount of sales ○ *We turn over $2,000 a week.*

turnaround /ˈtɜrnəˌraʊnd/ *noun* 1. the value of goods sold during a year divided by the average value of goods held in stock 2. the action of emptying a ship, plane, etc., and getting it ready for another commercial journey 3. the act of making a company profitable again (NOTE: [all senses] The U.K. term is **turnround**.)

turnkey contract /ˈtɜrnki ˌkɑntrækt/ *noun* an agreement by which a contractor undertakes to design, construct, and manage something and only hand it over to the client when it is in a state where it is ready for immediate use

turnover /ˈtɜrnoʊvər/ *noun* 1. the amount of sales of goods or services by a company ○ *The company's turnover has increased by 235%.* ○ *We based our calculations on the forecast turnover.* 2. the number of times something is used or sold in a period, usually one year, expressed as a percentage of a total

TV /ˌti ˈvi/ *abbreviation* television

TVR *abbreviation* television ratings

TV spot /ˌti ˈvi ˌspɑt/ *noun* a short period on TV which is used for commercials ○ *We are running a series of TV spots over the next three weeks.*

24/7 /ˌtwenti fɔr ˈsev(ə)n/ *adverb* twenty-four hours a day, every day of the week (NOTE: Businesses often advertise themselves as being "open 24/7.")

24-hour service /ˌtwenti fɔr aʊr ˈsɜrvɪs/ *noun* help which is available for the whole day

twenty-four-hour trading /ˌtwenti fɔr aʊr ˈtreɪdɪŋ/ *noun* trading in bonds, currencies, or securities that can take place at any time of day or night (NOTE: Twenty-four-hour trading does not involve one trading floor being open all the time, but instead refers to the possibility of conducting operations at different locations in different time zones.)

twin-pack /ˈtwɪn pæk/ *noun* a banded pack of two items sold together

two-sided message /ˌtu saɪdɪd ˈmesɪdʒ/ *noun* a message which presents two arguments for purchasing a product or service

tying contract /'taɪɪŋ ˌkɑntrækt/ *noun* a contract under which a producer sells a product to a distributor on condition that the distributor also buys another product ○ *Tying contracts are used to get wholesalers acquainted with lesser-known products.*

typological analysis /taɪpə ˌlɑdʒɪk(ə)l ə'næləsɪs/ *noun* a categorization of households based on socio-economic factors and buying habits ○ *Typological analysis helped the company clarify what market segments the new product should be aimed at.*

U

ultimate /'ʌltɪmət/ *adjective* last or final

ultimate consumer /ˌʌltɪmət kən'sumər/ *noun* the person who actually uses the product

umbrella advertising /ʌm'brelə ˌædvərtaɪzɪŋ/ *noun* the advertising of an organization or an association of companies rather than a single product

umbrella organization /ʌm'brelə ˌɔrgənaɪzeɪʃ(ə)n/ *noun* a large organization which includes several smaller ones

unaided recall /ʌnˌeɪdɪd 'rikɔl/ *noun* same as **unprompted recall**

unavailability /ˌʌnəveɪlə'bɪləti/ *noun* the fact of not being available ○ *The unavailability of any reliable sales data makes forecasting difficult.*

unavailable /ˌʌnə'veɪləb(ə)l/ *adjective* not available ○ *The following items on your order are temporarily unavailable.*

uncontrollable /ˌʌnkən'trooləb(ə)l/ *adjective* not possible to control ○ *uncontrollable inflation*

uncontrollable variable /ʌnkən ˌtrooləb(ə)l 'veriəb(ə)l/ *noun* a variable or factor in marketing that cannot be controlled, e.g., legislation or the state of the country's economy ○ *There are too many uncontrollable variables for any real planning.* ○ *Changes in fashion constitute a dangerous uncontrollable variable for a clothes store.*

uncrossed check /ˌʌnkrɒst 'tʃek/ *noun* a check which does not have two lines across it, and can be cashed anywhere

under- /ʌndə/ *prefix* less important than or lower than

underbid /ˌʌndə'bɪd/ *verb* to bid less than someone (NOTE: **underbidding – underbid**)

underbidder /'ʌndəbɪdər/ *noun* a person who bids less than the person who buys at an auction

undercharge /ˌʌndər'tʃɑrdʒ/ *verb* to ask someone for too little money ○ *She undercharged us by $25.*

underclass /'ʌndərklæs/ *noun* a group of people who are underprivileged in a way that appears to exclude them from mainstream society

undercut /ˌʌndə'kʌt/ *verb* to offer something at a lower price than someone else ○ *They increased their market share by undercutting their competitors.* (NOTE: **undercutting – undercut**)

underdeveloped /ˌʌndədɪ'veləpt/ *adjective* which has not been developed ○ *Japan is an underdeveloped market for our products.*

underdeveloped countries /ˌʌndədɪveləpt 'kʌntriz/ *plural noun* countries which are not fully industrialized

underdeveloped market /ˌʌndərdɪveləpt 'mɑrkət/ *noun* a market which has not been fully exploited ○ *Japan is an underdeveloped market for our products.*

underlease /'ʌndərlis/ *noun* a lease from a tenant to another tenant

underline /'ʌndəlaɪn/ *noun* a short description printed underneath an illustration

underpayment /ˌʌndə'peɪmənt/ *noun* a payment of less than the correct invoiced amount

underpricing /ˌʌndəˈpraɪsɪŋ/ *noun* the charging of a lower price than is justified by demand ○ *The company's underpricing is due to ignorance of the growing market.* ○ *Underpricing can be used as a strategy to increase market share.*

undersell /ˌʌndəˈsel/ *verb* to sell more cheaply than someone ○ *to undersell a competitor* □ **the company is never undersold** no other company sells goods as cheaply as this one

under-the-counter sales /ˌʌndər ðə ˌkaʊntə ˈseɪlz/ *plural noun* black-market sales

undervaluation /ˌʌndəvæljʊˈeɪʃ(ə)n/ *noun* the state of being valued, or the act of valuing something, at less than the true worth

undervalued /ˌʌndərˈvæljud/ *adjective* not valued highly enough ○ *The dollar is undervalued on the foreign exchanges.* ○ *The properties are undervalued on the company's balance sheet.*

underweight /ˌʌndəˈweɪt/ *adjective* not heavy enough □ **the pack is twenty grams underweight** the pack weighs twenty grams less than it should

undifferentiated /ˌʌndɪfəˈrenʃieɪtɪd/ *adjective* which has no unique feature

undifferentiated marketing strategy /ˌʌndɪfəˌrenʃieɪtɪd ˈmɑːkɪtɪŋ ˌstrætədʒi/ *noun* a marketing strategy which seeks to present a product to the public without stressing any unique feature of the product, thus appealing to all segments of the market. ◊ **concentrated marketing, differentiated marketing strategy**

undifferentiated product /ˌʌndɪfəˌrenʃieɪtɪd ˈprɒdʌkt/ *noun* a product which has no unique feature to set it apart from others on the market ○ *Only an extra-low price will sell an undifferentiated product in a market where there is already a wide choice of brands.*

undue influence /ˌʌndu ˈɪnfluəns/ *noun* unfair pressure put on someone to sign a contract ○ *The sales force were discouraged from exerting undue influence on prospective buyers.*

unemployment rate /ˌʌnɪmˈplɔɪmənt reɪt/ *noun* the number of people out of work, shown as a percentage of the total number of people available for work. Also called **rate of unemployment**

uneven /ʌnˈiːv(ə)n/ *adjective* not smooth or flat

uneven playing field /ʌnˌiːv(ə)n ˈpleɪɪŋ fild/ *noun* a situation where the competing groups do not compete on the same terms and conditions. Opposite **level playing field**

unfair /ʌnˈfer/ *adjective* not just or reasonable

unfair competition /ˌʌnfer ˌkɒmpəˈtɪʃ(ə)n/ *noun* the practice of trying to do better than another company by using techniques such as importing foreign goods at very low prices or by wrongly criticizing a competitor's products

unfavorable /ʌnˈfeɪv(ə)rəb(ə)l/ *adjective* not favorable (NOTE: The U.K. spelling is **unfavourable.**) □ **unfavorable balance of trade** a situation where a country imports more than it exports □ **unfavorable exchange rate** an exchange rate which gives an amount of foreign currency for the home currency which is not good for trade ○ *The unfavorable exchange rate hit the country's exports.*

unfulfilled /ˌʌnfʊlˈfɪld/ *adjective* (*of an order*) which has not yet been supplied

unilateral /ˌjuːnɪˈlæt(ə)rəl/ *adjective* on one side only or done by one party only ○ *They took a unilateral decision to cancel the contract.*

unilaterally /ˌjuːnɪˈlæt(ə)rəli/ *adverb* by one party only ○ *The decision was taken to cancel the contract unilaterally.*

unique /juˈniːk/ *adjective* unlike anything else

unique selling point /juˌniːk ˈselɪŋ ˌpɔɪnt/, **unique selling proposition** /juˌniːk ˈselɪŋ ˌprɒpəzɪʃ(ə)n/ *noun* a special quality of a product which makes it different from other goods and is used as a key theme in advertising ○ *A five-year guarantee is a USP for this* *product.* ○ *What's this product's unique selling proposition?* Abbreviation **USP**

unit /'juːnɪt/ *noun* **1.** a single product for sale **2.** a separate piece of equipment or furniture **3.** a group of people set up for a special purpose

unit cost /'juːnɪt kɒst/ *noun* the cost of one item, i.e. the total product costs divided by the number of units produced

United Nations /juːˌnaɪtɪd 'neɪʃ(ə)nz/ *noun* an organization which links almost all the countries of the world to promote good relations between them

unit pack /'juːnɪt pæk/ *noun* a pack containing only one unit of a product ○ *Will the product be sold in unit packs, or in packs of ten or twenty units?*

unit price /'juːnɪt praɪs/ *noun* the price of one item

unit pricing /'juːnɪt ˌpraɪsɪŋ/ *noun* the pricing of items by showing how much each costs per unit of measurement, e.g., per foot or per pound

Universal Product Code /juːnɪˌvɜːs(ə)l 'prɒdʌkt ˌkəʊd/ *noun* the code which identifies an article for sale, usually printed as a bar code on the packet or item itself. Abbreviation **UPC**

universe /'juːnɪvɜːs/ *noun* the total population which is being studied in a survey and out of which a sample is selected ○ *Is this sample really representative of the universe?* ○ *In the survey, the universe is all American men between the ages of forty and fifty.* ○ *From a universe of two million, a sample of two thousand was chosen by random selection.*

unladen /ʌn'leɪd(ə)n/ *adjective* without a cargo ○ *The ship was unladen when she arrived in port.*

unlimited /ʌn'lɪmɪtɪd/ *adjective* with no limits ○ *The bank offered him unlimited credit.*

unlimited liability /ʌnˌlɪmɪtɪd ˌlaɪə'bɪləti/ *noun* a situation where a sole trader or each partner is responsible for all a firm's debts with no limit on the amount each may have to pay

unload /ʌn'ləʊd/ *verb* **1.** to take goods off a ship, truck etc. ○ *The ship is un-*loading at Hamburg. ○ *We need a forklift to unload the truck.* ○ *We unloaded the spare parts at New Orleans.* ○ *There are no unloading facilities for container ships.* **2.** to sell stock which is no longer needed at a lower price than usual ○ *They tried to unload some unsellable items onto the Far Eastern market.*

unloading /ʌn'ləʊdɪŋ/ *noun* the act of selling off goods at a lower price than usual, often when they are no longer being produced and the producers merely want to get rid of remaining stock ○ *Many customers are taking advantage of our unloading and are buying in bulk.*

unprofitable /ʌn'prɒfɪtəb(ə)l/ *adjective* not profitable

unprompted recall /ʌnˌprɒmptɪd ə 'wɜːnəs test/, **unprompted awareness test** /ʌnˌprɒmptɪd 'rɪkɔːl/ *noun* an advertising research test to see how well a respondent can remember an advertisement when he or she is given no help in remembering it ○ *A disappointing number of respondents did not remember the advertisement at all in an unprompted recall.* Compare **prompted recall**

unrealized profit /ʌnˌrɪəlaɪzd 'prɒfɪt/ *noun* same as **paper profit**

unseen /ʌn'siːn/ *adverb* not seen

unsold /ʌn'səʊld/ *adjective* not sold ○ *Unsold items will be scrapped.*

unsolicited /ʌnsə'lɪsɪtɪd/ *adjective* which has not been asked for ○ *an unsolicited gift*

unsolicited testimonial /ʌnsə ˌlɪsɪtɪd ˌtestɪ'məʊniəl/ *noun* a letter praising someone or a product, without the writer having been asked to write it

unstructured interview /ʌn ˌstrʌktʃəd 'ɪntəvjuː/ *noun* an interview which is not based on a series of fixed questions and which encourages open discussion ○ *Unstructured interviews are effective in eliciting original suggestions for product improvement.* ○ *Shy respondents often perform well in unstructured interviews where they have more freedom of expression.* Compare **structured interview**

unsubsidized /ˌʌn'sʌbsɪdaɪzd/ *adjective* with no subsidy

unused /ʌn'juzd/ *adjective* which has not been used ○ *We are trying to sell off six unused computers.*

UPC *abbreviation* Universal Product Code

update /'ʌpdeɪt/ *noun* information added to something to make it up to date ○ *Here is the latest update on sales.* ■ *verb* /ʌp'deɪt/ to revise something so that it is always up to date ○ *The figures are updated annually.*

up front /ˌʌp 'frʌnt/ *adverb* in advance

uplift /'ʌplɪft/ *noun* an increase ○ *The contract provides for an annual uplift of charges.*

upmarket /ˌʌp'mɑrkət/ *adverb, adjective* more expensive or appealing to a wealthy section of the population □ **the company has decided to move upmarket** the company has decided to start to produce more luxury items

upscale /'ʌpskeɪl/ *adjective* aimed at customers at the top end of the socioeconomic ladder, who are well-educated and have higher incomes

upselling /'ʌpselɪŋ/ *noun* selling extra products to go with the one the customer is planning to buy

upset price /'ʌpset praɪs/ *noun* the lowest price which the seller will accept at an auction

up-to-date /ˌʌp tə 'deɪt/ *adjective, adverb* current, recent, or modern ○ *an up-to-date computer system* □ **to bring something up to date** to add the latest information or equipment to something □ **to keep something up to date** to keep adding information to something so that it always has the latest information in it ○ *We spend a lot of time keeping our mailing list up to date.*

upturn /'ʌptɜrn/ *noun* a movement toward higher sales or profits ○ *an upturn in the economy* ○ *an upturn in the market*

usage /'jusɪdʒ/ *noun* the way in which something is used

usage pull /'jusɪdʒ pʊl/ *noun* the degree to which those who see or hear advertisements for a product buy more of it than those who do not ○ *We're only able to assess usage pull some time after the advertising campaign.*

usage segmentation /'jusɪdʒ segmenˌteɪʃ(ə)n/ *noun* the dividing of a market into segments according to the type of use which customers will make of the product

use-by date /'juz baɪ ˌdeɪt/ *noun* a date printed on a packet of food showing the last date on which the contents should be used. Compare **best-before date, sell-by date**

user /'juzər/ *noun* a person who uses something

user-friendly /ˌjuzər 'frendli/ *adjective* which a user finds easy to work ○ *These programs are really user-friendly.*

user's guide /'juzərz gaɪd/, **user's handbook** /'juzərz ˌhændbʊk/, **user's manual** /'juzərz ˌmænjʊəl/ *noun* a book showing someone how to use something

utility /ju'tɪləti/ *noun* the usefulness or satisfaction that a consumer gets from a product ○ *The price charged depends on the product's utility.*

utility goods /ju'tɪləti gʊdz/ *plural noun* basic goods that are necessary for everyday life ○ *Even some utility goods can be considered luxuries during a depression.* ○ *Consumers say that shopping for utility goods is routine and boring.*

V

valorem /və'lɔrəm/ *noun* ♦ **ad valorem duty**

VALS *noun* a system of dividing people into segments according to their way of living. Full form **Values and Lifestyles**

valuation /ˌvælju'eɪʃ(ə)n/ *noun* an estimate of how much something is worth ○ *to ask for a valuation of a property before making an offer for it* □ **to buy a shop with stock at valuation** when buying a store, to pay a price for the stock which is equal to the value as estimated by the valuer □ **to purchase stock at valuation** to pay the price for stock which it is valued at

value /'vælju/ *noun* the amount of money which something is worth ○ *the fall in the value of the dollar* ○ *She imported goods to the value of $2500.* ○ *The valuer put the value of the stock at $25,000.* □ **good value (for money)** a bargain, something which is worth the price paid for it ○ *That restaurant gives value for money.* ○ *Buy that computer now – it is very good value.* ○ *Vacations in Mexico are a good value because of the exchange rate.* □ **to rise** *or* **fall in value** to be worth more or less ■ *verb* to estimate how much money something is worth ○ *He valued the stock at $25,000.* ○ *We are having the jewelry valued for insurance.*

value added /ˌvælju 'ædɪd/ *noun* **1.** the difference between the cost of the materials purchased to produce a product and the final selling price of the finished product **2.** the amount added to the value of a product or service, being the difference between its cost and the amount received when it is sold. Also called **net output 3.** the features that make one product or service different from or better than another and so create value for the customer (NOTE: Value added in this sense is based on the customer's view of what makes a product or service more desirable than others and worth a higher price.)

value-added reseller /ˌvælju ædɪd 'riselər/ *noun* a merchant who buys products at retail prices and packages them with additional items for resale to customers

value-added services /ˌvælju ædɪd 'sɜrvɪsɪz/ *plural noun* services which add value to a service or product being sold

Value Added Tax /ˌvælju ædɪd 'tæks/ *noun* full form of **VAT**

value-adding intermediary /ˌvælju ˌædɪŋ ˌɪntə'midiəri/ *noun* a distributor who increases the value of a product before selling it to a customer, e.g., by installing software in a computer

value analysis /'vælju əˌnæləsɪs/ *noun* analysis by a producer of all aspects of a finished product to determine how it could be made at minimum cost ○ *Value analysis showed an excessive amount of rubber was used in manufacturing the product.*

value chain /'vælju tʃeɪn/ *noun* **1.** the sequence of activities a company carries out as it designs, produces, markets, delivers, and supports its product or service, each of which is thought of as adding value **2.** the pattern that people traditionally have in mind when considering their career prospects, which involves them identifying at each stage in their careers what the next, most obvious, upward move should be

valued impression per pound /ˌvæljud ɪmˌpreʃ(ə)n pər ˈpaʊnd/ *noun* a method of showing how many readers are reached by advertising for a given sum of money. Abbreviation **VIP**

value engineering /ˈvælju endʒɪˌnɪrɪŋ/ *noun* analysis by a producer of all aspects of a product at the design stage to determine how it could be made at minimum cost ○ *Value engineering allows very economical production and competitive prices at every stage in the distribution channel.*

value map /ˈvælju mæp/ *noun* an indication of the amount of value that the market considers a product or service to have, which helps to differentiate it from its competitors

value proposition /ˈvælju prɑpəˌzɪʃ(ə)n/ *noun* a statement by an organization of the way in which it can provide value for a customer

valuer /ˈvæljʊr/ *noun* a person who estimates how much money something is worth

Values and Lifestyles /ˌvælju ən ˈlaɪfstaɪlz/ *noun* full form of **VALS**

van /væn/ *noun* a small goods vehicle

van ship /ˈvæn ʃɪp/ *noun* a ship designed to carry goods in containers

VAR *abbreviation* value-added reseller

variable /ˈveriəb(ə)l/ *adjective* changeable

variable costs /ˌveriəb(ə)l ˈkɔsts/ *plural noun* production costs which increase with the quantity of the product made, e.g., wages or raw materials

variable pricing /ˌveriəb(ə)l ˈpraɪsɪŋ/ *noun* the practice of giving a product or service different prices in different places or at different times

variance /ˈveriəns/ *noun* the difference between what was expected and the actual results □ **at variance with** not in agreement with ○ *The actual sales are at variance with the sales reported by the reps.*

variation /ˌveriˈeɪʃ(ə)n/ *noun* the amount by which something changes □ **seasonal variations** variations which take place at different times of the year ○ *seasonal variations in buying patterns*

variety /vəˈraɪəti/ *noun* different types of things ○ *The store stocks a variety of goods.* ○ *We had a variety of visitors at the office today.*

variety chain store /vəˌraɪəti ˈtʃeɪn stɔr/ *noun* a chain store which sells a large range of goods ○ *The variety chain stores sell everything from jewelry to electrical products.*

variety store /vəˈraɪəti stɔr/ *noun* a store selling a wide range of usually cheap items

VAT /ˌvi eɪ ˈti, væt/ *noun U.K.* a tax on goods and services, added as a percentage to the invoiced sales price ○ *The invoice includes VAT at 17.5%.* ○ *The government is proposing to increase VAT to 22%.* ○ *Some items (such as books) are zero-rated for VAT.* ○ *He does not charge VAT because he asks for payment in cash.* Full form **Value Added Tax**

VAT declaration /ˈvæt dekləˌreɪʃ(ə)n/ *noun U.K.* a statement declaring VAT income to the VAT office

VAT inspector /ˈvæt ɪnˌspektər/ *noun U.K.* a government official who examines VAT returns and checks that VAT is being paid

VAT invoice /ˈvæt ˌɪnvɔɪs/ *noun* an invoice which includes VAT

VAT invoicing /ˈvæt ˌɪnvɔɪsɪŋ/ *noun U.K.* the sending of an invoice including VAT

VATman /ˈvætmæn/, **vatman** *noun U.K.* a VAT inspector (*informal*)

VAT office /ˈvæt ˌɔfɪs/ *noun U.K.* the government office dealing with the collection of VAT in an area

VDU *abbreviation* visual display unit

Veblenian model /veˈbleɪniən ˈmɑd(ə)l/ *noun* a theory of buying behavior proposed by Veblen, which explains consumption mainly in terms of social influences or pressures rather than economic ones ○ *A Veblenian model helps to illustrate the non-rational side of consumer behavior.*

vehicle /'viːɪk(ə)l/ *noun* a machine with wheels, used to carry goods or passengers on a road

vending /'vendɪŋ/ *noun* selling

vending machine /'vendɪŋ məˌʃiːn/ *noun* same as **automatic vending machine**

vendor /'vendər/ *noun* **1.** a person who sells something, especially a property ○ *the solicitor acting on behalf of the vendor* **2.** a person who sells goods

vendor rating /'vendər ˌreɪtɪŋ/ *noun* an assessment of a vendor by a buyer on the basis of the vendor's reliability and the quality and price of the goods on offer ○ *Vendor rating has already disqualified three suppliers on the grounds of price.* ○ *A good reputation for quick delivery is a key factor in the buying department's vendor ratings.*

venture /'ventʃə/ *noun* a commercial deal which involves a risk ○ *They lost money on several import ventures.* ○ *She's started a new venture – a computer store.* ■ *verb* to risk money

venture capital /ˌventʃə 'kæpɪt(ə)l/ *noun* capital for investment which may easily be lost in risky projects, but can also provide high returns. Also called **risk capital**

venture team /'ventʃər tiːm/ *noun* a group of people from different departments in a company who work together on a new product-development project ○ *The venture team met regularly to monitor progress in the product's development.*

version /'vɜːʒ(ə)n/ *verb* to adapt a website for different categories of customer by maintaining different versions of it

vertical /'vɜːtɪk(ə)l/ *adjective* upright, straight up or down

vertical communication /ˌvɜːtɪk(ə)l kəˌmjuːnɪ'keɪʃ(ə)n/ *noun* communication between senior managers via the middle management to the work force

vertical industrial market /ˌvɜːtɪk(ə)l ɪn'dʌstriəl ˌmɑːkət/ *noun* a market in which a product is used by only one industry

vertical integration /ˌvɜːtɪk(ə)l ˌɪntɪ'ɡreɪʃ(ə)n/ *noun* the extent to which supply-chain activities are controlled within an organisation. Same as **backward integration**

vertical marketing system /ˌvɜːtɪk(ə)l 'mɑːkətɪŋ ˌsɪstəm/ *noun* a distribution system that is a coordinated integrated unit involving the manufacturer, the wholesaler, and the retailer, where marketing decisions are taken globally

vertical publication /ˌvɜːtɪk(ə)l ˌpʌblɪ'keɪʃ(ə)n/ *noun* a publication for people working at different levels in the same industry. Compare **horizontal publication**

vessel /'ves(ə)l/ *noun* a ship

viable /'vaɪəb(ə)l/ *adjective* which can work in practice □ **not commercially viable** not likely to make a profit

videoconferencing /'vɪdiəʊˌkɒnf(ə)rənsɪŋ/ *noun* the use of live video links that enable people in different locations to see and hear one another and so to discuss matters and hold meetings without being physically present together in one place

videotape /'vɪdiəʊteɪp/ *noun* a magnetic tape for recording sound and vision, used for making original recordings or taping existing television material ○ *The advertiser studied the videotape of the advertisement and sent comments to the agency.* ■ *verb* to record something on videotape ○ *The reactions of respondents trying the product for the first time were videotaped.*

view /vjuː/ *verb* to watch a TV program

viewer /'vjuːər/ *noun* a person who watches television

viewing figures /'vjuːɪŋ ˌfɪɡəz/ *plural noun* figures showing the numbers of people watching a TV program

viral /'vaɪrəl/ *adjective* acting in the same way as a virus ■ *noun* a message spread by viral marketing

viral design /'vaɪrəl dɪˌzaɪn/ *noun* the design of a message that encourages recipients to forward the message on to others

viral effect /'vaɪrəl ɪˌfekt/ *noun* the number of recipients of a message who forward the message on to others

viral forwards /ˌvaɪrəl 'fɔrwərdz/ *plural noun* the number of messages forwarded

viral marketing /'vaɪrəl ˌmɑrkətɪŋ/ *noun* marketing by word of mouth or by spreading advertising messages on the Internet

virtual hosting /ˌvɜrtʃuəl 'houstɪŋ/ *noun* a hosting option, suitable for small and medium-sized businesses, in which the customer shares space on the hosting company's server that with other organizations (NOTE: In virtual hosting, the hosting company carries out basic maintenance on hardware, but the customer is responsible for managing the content and software.)

virtual office /ˌvɜrtʃuəl 'ɔfɪs/ *noun* a workplace that has no physical location but is created when a number of employees use information and communications technologies to do their work and collaborate with one another (NOTE: A virtual office is characterized by the use of teleworkers, telecenters, mobile workers, hot-desking and hoteling.)

virtual team /ˌvɜrtʃuəl 'tim/ *noun* a group of employees working in different locations who use communications technologies such as groupware, email, an intranet, or videoconferencing to collaborate with each other and work as a team

VISA /'vizə/ *trademark* a trademark for an international credit card system

visible /'vɪzɪb(ə)l/ *adjective* referring to real products which are imported or exported

visible exports /ˌvɪzəb(ə)l 'eksports/ *plural noun* real products which are exported, as opposed to services

vision statement /'vɪʒ(ə)n ˌsteɪtmənt/ *noun* a statement that sets out in general terms what an organization is aiming or hoping to achieve in the future (NOTE: Vision statements express corporate vision, and are related to mission statements.)

visual /'vɪʒuəl/ *adjective* which can be seen ■ *noun* a photograph, picture, chart, or graph used to display information or promotional material

visual display terminal /ˌvɪzjuəl dɪ'spleɪ ˌtɜrminəl/, **visual display unit** /ˌvɪzjuəl dɪ'spleɪ ˌjunɪt/ *noun* a screen attached to a computer which shows the information stored in the computer. Abbreviation **VDT, VDU**

visualizer /'vɪʒuəlaɪzər/ *noun* a person who produces visual ideas for advertisements or advertising campaigns

voicemail /'vɔɪsmeɪl/ *noun* an electronic communications system which stores digitized recordings of telephone messages for later playback

voiceover /'vɔɪsˌouvər/ *noun* the commentary for a TV or cinema advertisement, spoken by an actor who does not appear in the advertisement

volume /'vɑljum/ *noun* a quantity of items

volume discount /'vɑljum ˌdɪskaunt/ *noun* the discount given to a customer who buys a large quantity of goods

volume of output /ˌvɑljum əv 'autput/ *noun* the number of items produced

volume of sales /ˌvɑljum əv 'seɪlz/ *noun* the number of items sold □ **low** *or* **high volume of sales** a small or large number of items sold

volume segmentation /'vɑljum segmenˌteɪʃ(ə)n/ *noun* the segmentation or division of a market on the basis of the quantity of the product bought

volumetrics /ˌvɑljuˈmetrɪks/ *noun* analysis of the relative influence of various media by considering the number of people who are exposed to them, and their importance as buyers ○ *Volumetrics has been our most useful tool in media buying.* ○ *The marketing department consulted an expert in volumetrics to help plan the advertising campaign.* (NOTE: takes a singular verb)

voluntarily /ˌvɑlənˈterəli/ *adverb* without being forced or paid

voluntary /ˈvɒlənˌteri/ *adjective* **1.** done freely without anyone forcing you to act **2.** done without being paid

voluntary chain /ˈvɒlənt(ə)ri tʃeɪn/, **voluntary group** /ˈvɒlənt(ə)ri gruːp/ *noun* a group of distributors who join together to buy from suppliers so as to enjoy quantity discounts ○ *After joining the voluntary chain the store saved up to 20% in buying.*

voluntary control /ˌvɒlənt(ə)ri kən ˈtrəʊl/ *noun* a system adopted by the advertising industry for controlling possible abuses which involves following guidelines laid down for the industry as a whole ○ *If voluntary controls are not effective, the government will have to bring in legislation.*

voluntary organization /ˈvɒlənt(ə)ri ˌɔːɡənaɪzeɪʃ(ə)n/ *noun* an organization which does not receive funding from the government, but relies on contributions from the public

voucher /ˈvaʊtʃər/ *noun* **1.** a piece of paper which is given instead of money **2.** a written document from an auditor to show that the accounts are correct or that money has really been paid

W

waggon jobber /'wægən ˌdʒɑbər/
noun a limited function wholesaler, usually one who delivers goods by truck to
retailers

wagon /'wægən/ *noun* a goods truck
used on the railroad

walk-in /'wɔk ɪn/ *noun* a person who
approaches an organization for a job,
without knowing if any jobs are available (NOTE: The plural is **walk-ins**.)

want /wɑnt/ *noun* a need felt by a person, which is formed by that person's
education, culture, and character

WAP /wæp/ *noun* a technical language
and set of processing rules that enables
users of cell phones to access websites
(NOTE: WAP stands for Wireless Application Protocol and is the equivalent of
HTML for cell phones.)

warehouse /'werhaʊs/ *noun* a large
building where goods are stored □ **price
ex warehouse** the price for a product
which is to be collected from the manufacturer's or agent's warehouse and so
does not include delivery ■ *verb* to store
goods in a warehouse ○ *Our offices are
in St. Louis but our stock is warehoused
in Kansas.*

warehouse capacity /'werhaʊs kə
ˌpæsəti/ *noun* the space available in a
warehouse

warehouseman /'werhaʊsmən/
noun a person who works in a warehouse (NOTE: The plural is **warehouse-
men**.)

warehousing /'werhaʊzɪŋ/ *noun* the
act of storing goods in a warehouse ○
Warehousing costs are rising rapidly.

warranty /'wɑrənti/ *noun* a legal document which promises that a machine
will work properly or that an item is of

good quality ○ *The car is sold with a
twelve-month warranty.* ○ *The warranty
covers spare parts but not labor costs.*

waste /weɪst/ *noun* an unnecessary
use of time or money

waste coverage /'weɪst
ˌkʌv(ə)rɪdʒ/ *noun* media coverage
which goes beyond the target audience

waybill /'weɪbɪl/ *noun* a list of goods
being transported, made out by the carrier

wealth management /'welθ
ˌmænɪdʒmənt/ *noun* investment services offered by banks to people with
more than a specific amount of money
in liquid assets

web /web/ *noun* same as **World Wide
Web**

webcast /'webkæst/ *noun* a broadcast made over the web that enables an
event to be viewed by a large number of
people who are all connected to the
same website at the same time (NOTE:
Webcasts often use rich media technology.)

web commerce /'web ˌkɑmɜrs/
noun same as **e-commerce**

web form /'web fɔrm/ *noun* an electronic document similar to a printed
form, which can be used to collect information from a visitor to a website.
When the form has been filled in the
form, it is usually returned to the owner
of the website by e-mail.

web log /'web lɑg/ *noun* **1.** a record
of activity taking place on a website,
which can provide important marketing
information, e.g., on how many users
are visiting the site and what they are interested in, as well as highlighting any
technical problems. Also called **server**

log 2. a personal journal published on the Internet, which often encourages other users to make comments. Also called **blog**

web marketing /'web ˌmɑrkətɪŋ/ *noun* marketing that uses websites to advertise products and services and to reach potential customers

web marketplace /'web ˌmɑrkɪpleɪs/ *noun* a network of connections that enables business buyers and sellers to contact one another and do business on the web (NOTE: There are three types of web marketplace: online catalogs, auctions, and exchanges.)

webmaster /'webmæstər/ *noun* the person who looks after a website, changing and updating the information it contains and noting how many people visit it (NOTE: Several different people within an organization may share the job of webmaster.)

webpage /'webpeɪdʒ/ *noun* a single file of text and graphics, forming part of a website

website /'websaɪt/ *noun* a position on the web, which is created by a company, organization or individual, and which anyone can visit ○ *How many hits did we have on our website last week?*

weekly /'wikli/ *noun* a newspaper or magazine which is published each week ○ *The clothes were advertised in the fashion weeklies.* (NOTE: The plural is **weeklies**.)

weight /weɪt/ *noun* a measurement of how heavy something is □ **to sell fruit by weight** the price is per pound or per kilo of the fruit □ **to give short weight** to give less than you should

weighted average /ˌweɪtɪd 'æv(ə)rɪdʒ/ *noun* an average which is calculated taking several factors into account, giving some more value than others

weighted index /ˌweɪtɪd 'ɪndeks/ *noun* an index where some important items are given more value than less important ones

weighting /'weɪtɪŋ/ *noun* a statistical process which gives more importance to some figures or results than others in the process of reaching a final figure or result

weight limit /'weɪt ˌlɪmɪt/ *noun* the maximum weight ○ *The packet is over the weight limit for a letter, so it will have to go by parcel post.*

wet goods /'wet gʊdz/ *plural noun* goods that are sold in liquid form ○ *Special plastic containers have to be used for wet goods.* ○ *Inflammable wet goods are the most dangerous type of product to transport.*

wheel of retailing /ˌwil əv 'riteɪlɪŋ/ *noun* a model which explains changes in the evolution of the retailing trade

COMMENT: This model explains that retailers start as low-price downmarket stores and gradually trade up, and sometimes eventually go out of business, being replaced by new downmarket stores.

white coat rule /ˌwaɪt 'koʊt ˌrul/ *noun* a rule for advertising on TV stating that doctors or actors in white coats cannot promote medical products

white goods /'waɪt gʊdz/ *plural noun* 1. machines which are used in the kitchen, e.g., refrigerators, washing machines 2. household linen, e.g., sheets and towels

wholesale /'hoʊlseɪl/ *adjective, adverb* referring to the business of buying goods from manufacturers and selling them in large quantities to traders (retailers) who then sell in smaller quantities to the general public ○ *I persuaded him to give us a wholesale discount.* □ **he buys wholesale and sells retail** he buys goods in bulk at a wholesale discount and then sells in small quantities to the public

wholesale dealer /'hoʊlseɪl ˌdilər/ *noun* a person who buys in bulk from manufacturers and sells to retailers

wholesale price /'hoʊlseɪl praɪs/ *noun* the price charged to customers who buy goods in large quantities in order to resell them in smaller quantities to others

wholesale price index /ˌhoʊlseɪl 'praɪs ˌɪndeks/ *noun* an index showing the rises and falls of prices of manufactured goods as they leave the factory

wholesaler /'hoʊlseɪlər/ *noun* a person who buys goods in bulk from manufacturers and sells them to retailers

wholesale trade /'hoʊlseɪl treɪd/ *noun* trade that involves buying goods in large quantities at lower prices in order to resell them in smaller quantities and at higher prices to others

WIIFM *noun* the basic thoughts that affect the decision taken by a prospective customer. Full form **what's in it for me?**

wild cats /'waɪld kæts/ *plural noun* same as **problem children**

win /wɪn/ *verb* to be successful □ **to win a contract** to be successful in tendering for a contract ○ *The company announced that it had won a contract worth \$25m to supply buses and trucks.*

window /'wɪndoʊ/ *noun* an opening in a wall, with glass in it

window display /'wɪndoʊ dɪˌspleɪ/ *noun* the display of goods in a store window

window dressing /'wɪndoʊ ˌdresɪŋ/ *noun* the practice of putting goods on display in a store window, so that they attract customers

window shopping /'wɪndoʊ ˌʃɑpɪŋ/ *noun* the practice of looking at goods in store windows, without buying anything

windshield sticker /'wɪndshild ˌstɪkər/ *noun* an advertising sticker put onto the windshield of a car

win-win situation /ˌwɪn ˌwɪn ˌsɪtʃu 'eɪʃ(ə)n/ *noun* a situation in which, whatever happens or whatever choice is made, the people involved will benefit

wireless /'waɪələs/ *adjective* referring to communications systems and devices that use cell phone technology

women's magazine /'wɪmɪnz ˌmægəzin/ *noun* a magazine aimed at the women's market

word /wɜrd/ *noun* something spoken

word-of-mouth communications /ˌwɜrd əv maʊθ kəmˌjuni 'keɪʃ(ə)nz/ *plural noun* informal channels of communication such as friends and neighbors, colleagues, and members of the family

working capital /'wɜrkɪŋ ˌkæpɪt(ə)l/ *noun* capital in the form of cash, stocks, and debtors but not creditors, used by a company in its day-to-day operations. Also called **circulating capital, floating capital, net current assets**

work in process /ˌwɜrk ɪn 'prɑses/ *noun* the value of goods being manufactured which are not complete at the end of an accounting period ○ *Our current assets are made up of stock, goodwill, and work in progress.* Abbreviation **WIP** (NOTE: The U.K. term is **work in progress.**)

work-life balance /ˌwɜrk 'laɪf ˌbæləns/ *noun* the balance between the amount of time and effort someone devotes to work and the amount they devote to other aspects of life (NOTE: Work-life balance is the subject of widespread debate on how to allow employees more control over their working arrangements so that they have more time for their outside activities and responsibilities, but in a way that will still benefit the organisations they work for.)

works /wɜrks/ *noun* a factory ○ *There is a small engineering works in the same street as our office.* ○ *The steel works is expanding.* (NOTE: takes a singular or plural verb)

workshop /'wɜrkʃɑp/ *noun* a small factory

world /wɜrld/ *noun* **1.** the Earth □ **the world market for steel** the possible sales of steel throughout the world **2.** the people in a specific business or people with a special interest ○ *the world of big business* ○ *the world of lawyers* or *the legal world*

world enterprise /ˌwɜrld 'entəpraɪz/ *noun* an advanced form of international marketing

world rights /ˌwɜrld 'raɪts/ *plural noun* the right to sell the product anywhere in the world

worldwide /'wɜrldwaɪd/; /wɜrld 'waɪd/ *adjective, adverb* everywhere in the world ○ *The company has a world-wide network of distributors.* ○ *World-wide sales* or *Sales worldwide have topped two million units.* ○ *This make of computer is available worldwide.*

World Wide Web /ˌwɜrld ˌwaɪd ˈweb/ *noun* an information system on the Internet that allows documents to be linked to one another by hypertext links and accommodates websites and makes them accessible. Also called **web**

wrap /ˌræp ˈʌp/, **wrap up** *verb* to cover something all over in paper ○ *He wrapped (up) the package in green paper.* □ **to gift-wrap a present** to wrap a present in attractive paper

wrapper /ˈræpər/ *noun* a piece of material which wraps something ○ *The biscuits are packed in plastic wrappers.*

wrapping paper /ˈræpɪŋ ˌpeɪpər/ *noun* a special type of colored paper for wrapping presents

XYZ

xd *abbreviation* ex dividend

YAPPY /'jæpi/ *noun* a young affluent parent (*slang*)

yard /jɑrd/ *noun* a measure of length (= 0.91 meters) (NOTE: Can be written **yd.** or **yds** after numbers: **10 yd.**)

yearbook /'jɪrbʊk/ *noun* a reference book which is published each year with updated or new information

yellow goods /'jelou gʊdz/ *plural noun* high-priced goods which are kept in use for a relatively long time and so are not replaced very frequently. Compare **orange goods, red goods**

Yellow Pages /ˌjelou 'peɪdʒɪz/ *trademark* a section of a telephone directory printed on yellow paper which lists businesses under various headings such as computer shops or airlines

young old /ˌjʌŋ 'ould/ *noun* the market sector consisting of people aged between 60 and 75, that is with a median age of around 66

yuppies /'jʌpiz/ *plural noun* young professional people with relatively high incomes (NOTE: short for **young upwardly-mobile professionals**)

zero-rated /ˌzɪrou 'reɪtɪd/ *adjective* referring to an item which has a VAT rate of 0%

zero-rating /'zɪrou ˌreɪtɪŋ/ *noun* the rating of a product or service at 0% VAT

ZIP code /'zɪp koud/ *noun* a series of numbers and letters which forms part of an address, indicating the street and the town in a way which can be read by a scanner (NOTE: The U.K. term is **postcode.**)

zone /zoun/ *noun* an area of a town or country for administrative purposes ■ *verb* to divide a town into different areas for planning and development purposes □ **land zoned for light industrial use** land where planning permission has been given to build small factories for light industry

SUPPLEMENTS

VALS Lifestyle Segmentation

Social group	Description of members
Innovators	Successful, sophisticated people, often leaders in their profession, who are interested in new ideas and products and who buy a lot of expensive things
Thinkers	Well-educated and well-informed people, often idealistic, who buy things that last a long time and are good value for money
Achievers	Successful people with traditional tastes and values who buy expensive products that have a good reputation or that save them time
Experiencers	Young people who like new and unusual things and spend a lot of money on fashion and on their social life and hobbies
Believers	Conventional people with strong morals and ideals who like traditional, well-known products and are loyal customers
Strivers	People who want to appear successful, rich and fashionable, who enjoy shopping and would like to have more money to spend
Makers	Practical people who like to be independent and control their own lives and who buy goods that are good value for money but are not expensive or fashionable
Survivors	People without much money who cannot afford expensive things and buy only what they need, often at reduced prices

SWOT Analysis

Organization

Strengths
The services or products
or skills which the
organization is good at
doing or making

Weaknesses
The services or products
or skills which the
organization can't do or
doesn't do well

Market

Opportunities
Segments of the market
which are attractive, and
where changes in the
market might work in
favor of the organization

Threats
Segments of the market or
changes taking place in the
market which make it
difficult for the organization
to work there